Current Issues in Knowledge Management

Murray E. Jennex
San Diego State University, USA

INFORMATION SCIENCE REFERENCE

Hershey · New York

Acquisitions Editor: Kristin Klinger
Development Editor: Kristin Roth
Senior Managing Editor: Jennifer Neidig
Managing Editor: Sara Reed
Copy Editor: Ashley Fails
Typesetter: Larissa Vinci and Jamie Snavely
Cover Design: Lisa Tosheff
Printed at: Yurchak Printing Inc.

Published in the United States of America by
        Information Science Reference (an imprint of IGI Global)
        701 E. Chocolate Avenue, Suite 200
        Hershey PA 17033
        Tel: 717-533-8845
        Fax: 717-533-8661
        E-mail: cust@igi-global.com
        Web site: http://www.igi-global.com

and in the United Kingdom by
        Information Science Reference (an imprint of IGI Global)
        3 Henrietta Street
        Covent Garden
        London WC2E 8LU
        Tel: 44 20 7240 0856
        Fax: 44 20 7379 0609
        Web site: http://www.eurospanonline.com

Copyright © 2008 by IGI Global. All rights reserved. No part of this publication may be reproduced, stored or distributed in any form or by any means, electronic or mechanical, including photocopying, without written permission from the publisher.

Product or company names used in this set are for identification purposes only. Inclusion of the names of the products or companies does not indicate a claim of ownership by IGI Global of the trademark or registered trademark.

Library of Congress Cataloging-in-Publication Data

Current issues in knowledge management / Murray Jennex, editor.

    p. cm.

  Summary: "This book combines research on the cultural, technical, organizational, and human issues surrounding the creation, capture, transfer, and use of knowledge in today's organizations. Topics such as organizational memory, knowledge management in enterprises, enablers and inhibitors of knowledge sharing and transfer, and emerging technologies of knowledge management, offering information to practitioners and scholars in a variety of settings"--Provided by publisher.

  ISBN-13: 978-1-59904-916-8 (hbk.)

  ISBN-13: 978-1-59904-919-9 (e-book)

  1. Knowledge management. I. Jennex, Murray E., 1956-

  HD30.2.C868 2008

  658.4'038--dc22

                              2007046899

British Cataloguing in Publication Data
A Cataloguing in Publication record for this book is available from the British Library.

All work contributed to this book set is original material. The views expressed in this book are those of the authors, but not necessarily of the publisher.

If a library purchased a print copy of this publication, please go to http://www.igi-global.com/reference/assets/IGR-eAccess-agreement.
pdf for information on activating the library's complimentary electronic access to this publication.

Table of Contents

Detailed Table of Contents

Section I
Advances in Knowledge Management Foundations

This short chapter explores other motivations for organizations to implement knowledge management (KM). These motivations include obsolescence/innovation (these two go together as innovation leads to obsolescence), work process evolution, and persistence of knowledge. The goal of this discussion is to provide a basis for all organizations to justify KM initiative that is not just event-based.

Socialization, externalization, combination, and internalization: these four modes or processes show that the transfer of knowledge is dependent upon the transfer of a common understanding from the knower to the user of the knowledge. Common understanding consists of the context (the story behind the knowledge, the conditions and situations which make the knowledge understandable) and the experience (those activities which produce mental models of how the knowledge should be used) expressed in a culturally understood framework. Sherif and Sherif (2006) incorporate this common understanding into their definition of Social Capital. Social Capital or culture and context, either way, it is clear that these factors influence how knowledge is transferred and reused. This chapter discusses some of the issues associated with culture and context and how they impact the Nonaka and Takeuchi (1995) SECI knowledge transfer model.

Chapter III

Cultural diversity and wide disparities in the extent of up-to-date infrastructure make managing knowledge challenging in developing countries, even as the urgent human needs in these countries make knowledge management (KM) especially valuable as a tool in economic and human development. Cultural diversity and infrastructural gap issues are also related to a variety of government, educational, political, social and economic factors. These environmental factors interact with organizational variables and information technology to enable or constrain knowledge management processes in the creation and protection of knowledge resources. Case studies in India, The Gambia, and Nigeria are used to develop an empirically grounded contextual framework of knowledge management (KM). This guiding framework is intended to help organizations address contextual issues in knowledge management, leading to better preparation, implementation and assessment of KM projects.

Chapter IV

This chapter describes a knowledge management (KM) Success Model that is derived from observations generated through a longitudinal study of KM in an engineering organization, KM success factors found in the literature, and modified by the application of these observations and success factors in various projects. The DeLone and McLean (1992; 2003) IS Success Model was used as a framework for the model as it was found to fit the observed success criteria and it provided an accepted theoretical basis for the proposed model.

Section II
Advances in Knowledge Transfer, Sharing, and Flow

Chapter V

Knowledge transfer has been promoted as a critical and necessary condition for organizations to sustain competitive advantage. In this chapter, we argue that successful transfer of knowledge within organizations will depend on the accumulated social capital embedded within organizational social networks. We pose social capital as a critical factor for knowledge transfer and hypothesize that the structural, relational and cognitive dimensions of social capital must be developed within an organization for knowledge transfer to impact organizational performance. The study uses data collected from Egypt to test the model. Hofstede's Cultural Dimensions Model is used to explain how cultural attributes limit the accumulation of social capital and the effectiveness of knowledge transfer in developing countries.

Knowledge sharing is important for organizational success. Once IT-driven knowledge management (KM) approaches are proliferated, they sometimes fail to operate as expected. Social perspectives of KM, especially the human effect on knowledge sharing, are expected to be important because people can choose to share or conceal knowledge. Management of knowledge is not all about collection, but more about connection. This study investigates an individual's behavior type as a cooperator, reciprocator, and free rider with respect to knowledge contribution. We view shared knowledge in a community of practice as a public good and adopt a theory of reciprocity to explain how different cooperative types affect knowledge contribution. People are assumed to react in one of three ways; sharing knowledge without need for reciprocity (cooperators), feeling obligated to share their knowledge (reciprocators), or taking knowledge for granted (free riders). Results reveal that the fraction of cooperator is positively related to total knowledge contribution and to reciprocity level, while the reciprocity level positively affects knowledge contribution.

Managers and researchers alike have sought new ways to address the challenges of sharing dispersed knowledge in modern business environments. Careful consideration by sharers of receivers' knowledge needs and behaviors may improve the effectiveness of knowledge sharing. This research examines how sharers react to their perceptions of receivers' knowledge needs and behaviors when making choices relating to sharing knowledge. The focus of this chapter is to propose and explore a theoretical framework for a study of the role of the receiver in knowledge sharing—receiver-based theory. Data collected from two case studies highlight a key role played by perceived receiver knowledge needs and behaviors in shaping sharer choices when explicit knowledge is shared. A set of receiver influences on knowledge sharing is provided that highlights key receiver and sharer issues. The chapter concludes that companies should develop better ways to connect potential sharers with receivers' real knowledge needs. Further, the findings suggest that sharing on a need-to-know basis hinders change in organizational power structures, and prevents the integration of isolated pockets of knowledge that may yield new value.

This chapter raises issues concerning information and knowledge sharing in organizations and why such sharing is often difficult to achieve. In particular, it compares an organizational cultural analysis with an organizational political one. The authors believe that the issues raised are not only important but are often insufficiently attended to by practitioners who are attempting to build technological information and knowledge management systems. The driver for the chapter is the fact that despite impressive advances in technology, and its now almost ubiquitous presence in organizations, many of the benefits originally expected concerning improved information and knowledge sharing have not materialized as was once confidently expected. One of the authors argues a basic reason for this lies in the lack of attention to the cultural foundations of organizations, while the other contends it is more because matters relating to organizational power and political matters are often misunderstood, overlooked or ignored. These different perspectives are discussed and contrasted in order to tease out the important differences between them and assess the prospects for a synthesis. It is concluded that, while there are important commonalities between the two perspectives, there are also fundamental differences concerning what are causes and effects, and therefore, how to go about effecting change regarding information and knowledge sharing.

Chapter IX

Often, organizational members are separated not only geographically but also culturally. Information technology has inevitably become a facilitator of knowledge sharing. However, earlier studies have posited that culture can significantly facilitate or hinder knowledge sharing in culturally diverse teams. Greater enlightenment on the cultural effect is a useful contribution to understanding the most effective way of managing knowledge sharing in organizations. However, little effort has been put into dimensioning culture in such a way as to enable comparative and large scale study. This investigation tries to fill this gap by bringing together and examining the few attempts at dimensioning this concept. This review results in the proposing of cultural dimensions which are grouped into organizational and societal classes. The review also results in a proposal of a conceptual model that expresses knowledge sharing to be a function of organizational and societal cultural factors. We formulated two major hypotheses: H1 - There is a high positive relationship between organizational culture and knowledge sharing, and H2 - There is a high positive relationship between societal culture and knowledge sharing. The model requires further investigation as explained in the chapter.

Section III
Advances in Knowledge Management in Organizations

Chapter X

Knowledge reuse has long been an issue for organizations. The management, reuse and transfer of knowledge can improve project management capabilities (i.e., learning, memory, cycle time) resulting in continuous learning. Although knowledge management has been recognized as a critical success factor in program management, very little research has been conducted to date (Lycett, Rassau, & Danson, 2004; Soderlund, 2004). A framework is discussed that demonstrates how knowledge is created, transferred, captured and reused within project and program management, resulting in improved project management maturity. The framework utilizes a task- based approach to knowledge management and assumes that knowledge is created, transferred and reused as a result of an individual performing a specific task, which in this context is a project at the project level and a program at the program level.

Although it is widely accepted that alignment of knowledge with corporate strategy is necessary, to date, there have been few clear statements on what a knowledge strategy looks like and how it may be practically implemented. We argue that current methods and techniques to accomplish this alignment are severely limited, showing no clear description on how the alignment can be achieved. Core competencies, embodying an organization's practical know-how, are also rarely linked explicitly to actionable knowledge strategy. Viewing knowledge embedded in core competencies as a strategic asset, the chapter uses a case study to show how a company's core competencies were articulated and verified for either inclusion or exclusion in the strategy. The study is representative of similar studies carried out across a range of organizations using a novel and practically proven method. This method, StratAchieve, was used here in a client situation to show how the core competencies were identified and tested for incorporation or not in the strategy. The chapter concludes by considering the value of the approach for managing knowledge.

This chapter postulates that the problem-solving process in many domains involves identifying the class of problem on hand, identifying an appropriate solution, and recognizing opportunities for its reuse. A solution is suggested that builds up knowledge of a given domain by recording observations, diagnoses and actions in a '3Cs form' of cases, classifications and conclusions.

This solution allows knowledge workers in any domain where heuristics are relied on to form classifications, and then apply generalized conclusions on the basis of the given classification, to collaboratively refine and expand a topic by consistently asking users to confirm, add to, or refine the presented knowledge in the context of the current case being classified. The solution is presented in the context of the Corporate Call Centre and is a significant extension of the Multiple Classification Ripple Down Rules algorithm.

A 3Cs Logic Wiki is presented that takes the best features of current collaborative knowledge exchange mechanisms, and captures a logic structure on top of that which provides for rapid indexing of acquired knowledge.

This chapter is motivated by one simple question: Why do so many knowledge management systems (KMS) fail when implemented in organizational knowledge work practice? Indeed, imbalance between the desire for accurate content and the workload required to achieve this still appears to be a critical issue, resulting in KMS of little use for organizational members. Hence, KMS maintenance is an important research subject. With the objective to contribute recommendations for how to integrate KMS with everyday knowledge work, we apply general lessons learned from development of groupware applications as a theoretical lens to analyze empirical experiences of three implemented and evaluated KMS. Theorizing the relationship between the recommendations developed and extant KMS design theory, the chapter offers implications for IS research and practice.

In developing a conceptual framework of a Community of Practice's (CoP) role in organizational KM, this chapter summarizes preliminary findings of a long-term action research study. Interventions address CoP identification, group boundaries, trust-related issues, communication, knowledge work and resources. It is argued that these aspects equally need to be addressed as part of complex multilevel organizational KM strategy. The organizational challenge is to achieve strategic alignment between knowledge activities of informally operating CoPs and formalized organizational processes. The conceptual framework aims at providing a comprehensive approach to KM strategizing.

Section IV
Advances in Knowledge Management Development Methodologies

Since knowledge management (KM) is considered to be an important function of the successful business operation, many organizations are embracing KM. The success of a KM project is dependent upon its contents. This chapter presents a method for building an effective knowledge model which can help businesses analyze and specify knowledge contents. The method takes a decision-oriented view. For the modeling language of the method, Unified Modeling Language (UML) has been chosen. The method is applied to the vessel scheduling process in a maritime shipping company. The steps and rules are explained using an example, and the strengths and weaknesses of the method are discussed.

The Knowledge Modeling and Description Language (KMDL®) analyzes knowledge- intensive business processes which lead towards improvements. After modeling the business processes, knowledge and process potentials in daily business tasks in knowledge generation and handling can be unleashed. The following contribution presents the current state of specification of KMDL®. A real-life example in software engineering is used to explain the advantages of this approach.

Prior to the establishment of the Knowledge Management (KM) strategy, the British Council defined knowledge as 'objects'. Knowledge sharing was about sharing documents and information on the intranet or via global databases. Since December 2002, Dervin's Sense-Making Methodology has been applied to manage 'knowledge'. Knowledge is seen not as a product that can be transferred from one colleague to another, but as a communication practice. This means that shared knowledge has to be interpreted and made sense of by its recipients through genuine dialogue. During this phase of KM implementation, the focus shifted to linking up colleagues and providing space for dialogue through building global communities of practice and virtual teams. This chapter presents an example of how we have used the theory of Social Networking Analysis as a diagnostic tool to promote knowledge sharing amongst our newly formed thirty-people global leadership team. The three steps we have taken to carry out the exercise and its limitations are also discussed. Towards the end of the chapter, the author presents an alternative application of social networking analysis in a multinational consulting firm.

Section V
Advances in Knowledge Management Application

This chapter describes how the Center for Army Lessons Learned (CALL) has developed a unique, institutionalized knowledge reuse process. The chapter highlights several issues related to knowledge reuse, including the collection, distillation and dissemination of knowledge, the role of subject experts in the knowledge reuse process and how technology facilitates knowledge reuse.

The very fundamental mission of hospital management is to deliver quality healthcare services by utilizing highly specialized medical knowledge and solve other healthcare problems within various resource constraints. Similar to other knowledge-intensive industries which operate in highly challenging business environments, hospitals of all sizes must view the creation, organization, distribution, and application of knowledge as a critical aspect of their management activities. Knowledge management, therefore, represents a viable strategy as hospitals strive to simultaneously provide quality medical services, improve operational efficiency, and comply with governmental documentation and reporting regulations. This study examines the correlation as well as causal relationships between knowledge characteristics, knowledge acquisition strategy, implementation measures, and performance of knowledge management implementations in the context of hospital management. Using primary data collected in Taiwanese hospitals, our analyses showed that the characteristics of knowledge affect the ways in which knowledge management is implemented, and the implementation measure, in turn, has a significant impact on the results of knowledge management implementation.

Chapter XX

This chapter is about the design and implementation of an information system, using wiki technology to improve the emergency preparedness efforts of the Claremont University Consortium. For some organizations, as in this case, responding to a crisis situation is done within a consortia environment. Managing knowledge across the various entities involved in such efforts is critical. This includes having the right set of information that is timely, relevant, and is governed by an effective communication process. It is expected that issues such as training in use of system(s), a knowledge sharing culture between entities involved in emergency preparedness, and a fit between task and technology/system must be there to support emergency preparedness activities given such structures. This study explored the use of wiki technology to support knowledge management in the context of emergency preparedness within organizations. While initially found to be useful for supporting emergency preparedness, continuing experience with the system suggests that wikis might be more useful as a collaborative tool used to train people involved in emergency preparedness, rather than being used to support response activities during an actual emergency.

Chapter XXI

This chapter explores the use of knowledge management with emergency information systems. Two knowledge management systems that were utilized during Hurricane Katrina response are described and analyzed. The systems specified were developed by both federal agencies as well as grass root efforts without the support or mandate of government programs. These programs, although developed independently, were able to share data and interact in life-saving capacities, transcending traditional geopolitical boundaries. We conclude that emergency information systems are enhanced by incorporating knowledge management tools and concepts.

Preface

INTRODUCTION

Welcome to the second volume of Current Issues in Knowledge Management. This book series is dedicated to publishing top research in knowledge management (KM) on an annual basis. Each chapter has been published in Volume II of the International Journal of Knowledge Management with most being expanded to include additional data and discussion that could not be included in the journal version.

Knowledge management is an evolving discipline that is growing and becoming pervasive in many other disciplines. Initial KM research focused on the basics of KM: identifying the key goals of KM, specifying the knowledge artifact, and defining the components and characteristics of a KM system (KMS). This book documents how this initial research focus is changing. Researchers have pretty much established the foundations of KM and are moving towards new issues. Issues of interest include the impact of culture and context on knowledge representation, storage, and use; defining KM success; factors affecting knowledge transfer and flow; creating methodologies to assist researchers and practitioners in the design of KMS; and applying KM to new contexts such as health informatics, military science, and crisis response and management. This volume presents research on these issues with the chapters outlined in the following section.

BOOK ORGANIZATION

The book is designed for KM researchers, students, and practitioners to use to keep current on KM research. The book can also be used in a classroom setting, primarily as a reader rather than as a text. The book is organized into five major parts with a total of twenty-one chapters. These are summarized below:

Section 1: Advances in Knowledge Management Foundations, Chapters I–IV

This section discusses some of the basic issues affecting knowledge management. Chapter I, *The Need for Knowledge Management*, by Murray E. Jennex, explores the need for knowledge management on a basis other than worker transience and baby boomer retirements. Chapter II, *Culture, Context, and Knowledge Management*, by Murray E. Jennex, starts the discussion of issues affecting knowledge creation, capture, storage, and use by defining terms and exploring the impact of culture and context on knowledge users. Chapter III, *Addressing Contextual Issues in Knowledge Management: A Guiding Framework*, by Adekunle Okunoye and Nancy Bertaux, continues exploring the impact of culture and context on knowledge use and develops a framework for assessing context and culture impacts. Finally,

Chapter IV, *A Model of Knowledge Management Success*, by Murray E. Jennex and Lorne Olfman, provides a theoretically grounded model for assessing KM success and discusses what is necessary to create a successful KM initiative and KM system (KMS).

Section II: Advances in Knowledge Transfer, Sharing, and Flow, Chapters V–IX

This section focuses on research on issues that affect the flow of knowledge in an organization. Chapter V, *Think Social Capital before You Think Knowledge Transfer*, by Karma Sherif and Sherif Ahmed Sherif, applies social capital and network concepts to knowledge transfer using case research from Egypt. Chapter VI, *Human Effect of Knowledge Sharing: Cooperative Type and Reciprocity Level in Community of Practice*, by Jaekyung Kim, Sang M. Lee, and David L. Olson, uses quantitative research of a community of practice (CoP) to discover how participation levels of individuals contributing to KM affect knowledge flow. Chapter VII, *Toward a Receiver-Based Theory of Knowledge Sharing*, by Sharman Lichtenstein and Alexia Hunter, uses case studies to explore receiver motivations and behaviors in knowledge flow. Chapter VIII, *A Dialectic on the Cultural and Political Aspects of Information and Knowledge Sharing in Organizations*, by Dennis Hart and Leoni Warne, discusses why improvements in technology have not resulted in better knowledge transfer by applying organizational culture and power structure concepts to barriers to knowledge flow. Finally, Chapter IX, *Conceptualization of Cultural Dimensions as a Major Influence on Knowledge-Sharing*, by Abel Usoro and Matthew H. S. Kuofie, continues the exploration of the impact of culture on KM by proposing a conceptual model that incorporates cultural factors that influence knowledge transfer.

Section III: Advances in Knowledge Management in Organizations, Chapters X–XIV

This part focuses on how knowledge management has been used in organizations. Chapter X, *Integrating Knowledge Management with Program Management*, by Jill Owen, explores how KM can be used to improve project management process maturity. Chapter XI, *Developing and Analyzing Core Competencies for Alignment with Strategy*, by Keith Sawyer and John Gammack, explores how KM can be used to help organizations discover their core competencies. Chapter XII, *A Case-Classification-Conclusion 3Cs Approach to Knowledge Acquisition: Applying a Classification Logic Wiki to the Problem-Solving Process*, by Debbie Richards and Megan Vazey, explores how applying problem classification and KM collaborative technologies (wiki) improves problem-solving in organizations. Chapter XIII, *Knowledge Management Systems: Towards a Theory of Integrated Support*, by Dick Stenmark and Rikard Lindgren, explores how to integrate KMS into organizational work practices and processes. Finally, Chapter XIV, *Community of Practice: Aligning Knowledge Work with Organizational Knowledge Strategy*, by Gerlinde Koeglreiter and Luba Torlina, furthers the KM integration discussion by exploring how to link informal community of practice work processes into formal organizational work processes.

Section IV: Advances in Knowledge Management Development Methodologies, Chapters XV–XVII

This part proposes methodologies to assist KM designers and developers in designing and building KMS. Chapter XV, *A Method for Knowledge Modeling with Unified Modeling Language (UML): Building a Blueprint for Knowledge Management*, by Sung-kwan Kim, Seongbae Lim, and Robert B. Mitchell, applies UML to the analysis of KMS requirements. Chapter XVI, *Improvement of Software Engineering Processes by Analyzing Knowledge Intensive Activities*, by Jane Fröming, Norbert Gronau, and Simone Schmid, describes the use of the knowledge modeling and description language (KMDL®) for analyzing knowledge-intensive business processes. Finally, Chapter XVII, *Using Social Networking Analysis to Facilitate Knowledge Sharing Amongst Senior Managers in Multinational Organizations*, by Bonnie Wai-yi Cheuk, applies social networking analysis to identify critical knowledge flow paths and repositories.

Section V: Advances in Knowledge Management Application, Chapters XVIII–XXI

This part explores new applications of knowledge management to organizational needs. Chapter XVIII, *Leveraging Current Experiences for Future Actions: An Exemplar of Knowledge Reuse*, by Alton Chua and Wing Lam, describes how the United States Army uses knowledge management to improve reuse of lessons learned. Chapter XIX, *Knowledge Characteristics, Knowledge Acquisition Strategy and Results of Knowledge Management Implementations: An Empirical Study of Taiwanese Hospitals*, by Wen-Jang (Kenny) Jih, Cheng Hsui Chen, and Andy Chen, explores hospital application of KM. Chapter XX, *Emergency Preparedness and Information Systems—A Case Study Using Wiki Technology*, by Murali Raman, Terry Ryan, Lorne Olfman, and Murray E. Jennex, describes the use of collaborative KM technology (wiki) to improve the emergency planning process. Finally, Chapter XXI, *Knowledge Management and Hurricane Katrina Response*, by Tim Murphy and Murray E. Jennex, documents the use of knowledge and KM collaborative technology (wiki) to rapidly develop and deploy systems to aid Hurricane Katrina victims in finding survivors and shelter.

Section I
Advances in Knowledge Management Foundations

Chapter I
The Need for Knowledge Management

Murray E. Jennex
San Diego State University, USA

INTRODUCTION

Why do we need to do knowledge management (KM)? Much has been published about transient workforces taking knowledge with them when they walk out the door and about the baby boomers causing a retirement stampede that will drain organizations of their experience. I agree with these needs, but are there other reasons? I am concerned that focus on worker transience and aging workers may hurt KM in the long term because these are event-based motivations. What happens if workers stop changing jobs and organizations on a regular basis? Incentive programs and perhaps enlightened management may reduce transience to a much more manageable level. Also, the next couple of generations after the baby boomers will not have the same impact when they retire as they are not larger in proportion to the other generations in the workforce. I am concerned that organizations will view KM as less important after these two event-based motivations are managed.

This short chapter explores other motivations for organizations to implement KM. These mo-

tivations include obsolescence/innovation (these two go together as innovation leads to obsolescence), work process evolution, and persistence of knowledge. The goal of this discussion is to provide a basis for all organizations to justify KM initiatives that are not just event-based.

THE NEED FOR KNOWLEDGE MANAGEMENT

The Stories

The inspiration for this discussion comes from a road trip my eldest son and I took around the Western and Midwestern United States. During this trip, we stopped at the International Space Hall of Fame and Museum in Alamogordo, New Mexico. While there, we talked to a retiree from the space program. During this conversation, it came out that we were both engineers (he had served as a member of the capsule recovery team and a backup astronaut and my previous career before joining academia was as an engineer, manager, and project manager for a large nuclear utility).

Copyright © 2008, IGI Global, distributing in print or electronic forms without written permission of IGI Global is prohibited.

We got to talking engineering and he made the comment that it was too bad we could not get back to the moon. I, of course, agreed and expressed the desire for our government to allocate funds for it. He surprised me by saying it was not money that was the issue (although it would be if not for the following issue). What really prevents us from getting back to the moon is that we do not remember how to build Saturn V rockets, Apollo capsules, and Lunar Modules. It seems after the end of the Apollo program, management ordered all the plans put on microfiche and all but a few of the paper copies destroyed. This was done, however, when there was talk of going back to the moon and engineers went to retrieve the plans, the microfiche had decayed into unusable form, no usable paper copies could be found, and everyone who knew how to build the rockets, capsules, and modules were either dead or retired. Additionally, when the younger engineers began to reverse engineer these components, they were stymied because they did not understand the technology from that time; technology had advanced so much that the engineers had not been taught some of the fundamental issues faced by engineers of that time. In other words, we had forgotten the knowledge from the experience of solving the problems that prevented moon flights. (Note: the above is the opinion of the interviewee, but it does reflect what I have observed in the commercial nuclear industry.)

KM can be defined as the practice of selectively applying knowledge from previous experiences of decision-making to current and future decision-making activities with the express purpose of improving organizational effectiveness (Jennex, 2005). The above shows that the space program is an example of failed KM. They attempted to store relevant knowledge but when it came time to retrieve it, it could not be retrieved and applied to the current decision- making activity due to media volatility and a lack of capturing the relevant context that makes the critical knowledge usable.

We discussed this for awhile and it occurred to me that we are facing similar issues in other industries. The information technology industry is an example of where we have forgotten fundamental issues and their solutions. I was trained to program using the IBM PC and XT. Those who remember these machines recall that we were restricted to approximately 1 Megahertz CPU speeds, 56 Kilobytes of usable memory, and hard drive storage of 10 Megabytes. The techniques used at that time for memory management and performance optimization were invalidated by newer generations of computers that ran faster with more memory making it unnecessary to train current students in these techniques. Additionally, with today's larger fixed drives (60 Gigabytes or more) there is no pressure on users to save only that which is necessary; the drives can hold it all; and if you need to move a lot of files there are Gigabyte sized flash drives. This is probably okay, but what happens if we need to retrieve something critical? If we save everything it becomes difficult to find specific files, I know I am guilty of this; I save all iterations of my papers and presentations and it is becoming difficult to organize my storage due to the thousands of files I am keeping (and often times gets me asking myself if I really need all these files). Several years ago, I would have used risk management techniques to determine what file versions I truly could not afford to lose with the result that I would have had a fraction of the files to search through.

Additionally, what if we have to use an older machine or operating system or file management system to retrieve files? I recall my Windows operating system corrupted a couple of years ago. I called the manufacturer's help desk to see if there was a way to recover and was told to reformat using the recovery CD. This would cause me to lose my files and I asked about copying them. The help desk did not know how to do this, but while I was talking to them I was fiddling with the computer and started it in DOS. I remembered how to move files using DOS commands and asked if that was an option. The help desk said they did not know DOS commands. To make a long story short, I spent the next several minutes using basic DOS commands to backup my files on floppy disks while at the same time teaching the help desk how it could be done.

Another example is the commercial nuclear industry. The current generation of nuclear plants was designed and built by engineers who are now retiring or dead. This is a wealth of operational and design knowledge on using analog control and instrument systems, older material specifications, and older corrosion control systems that is no longer being taught to new engineers. Newer approaches rely on digital controls and displays, and newer materials with different corrosion control needs. Additionally, we have computerized processes that used to require manual calculations. As a young nuclear propulsion officer in the United States Navy, I was taught to manually calculate estimated critical rod positions and reactor restart times (to name a few). These calculations are now done automatically and require little operator knowledge or input. This progress is good and is resulting in safer nuclear power plants, but I wonder what could happen if terrorists were able to successfully attack these new digital systems requiring operators to return to the old manual processes and analog systems. Would our operators know how it used to be done? Would we have the requisite knowledge and data to do it the old way? As a Year 2000 (Y2K) project manager for contingency planning for a large utility, I learned that in many cases we no longer have the ability to backup our processes or systems using manual methods, and that if we lost these components or systems, we would not have the ability to maintain normal operations.

Storage Media

Is capturing knowledge enough? Hansen et al. (1999) discuss the importance of a representation and storage strategy. The above space program situation is an example of having a strategy that identifies critical knowledge and stores it, but failed to identify a successful storage strategy. I do not believe this case is unique. Over the last 20 years, I have seen a series of storage solutions, from microfiche to 8-inch floppies, 5 ¼-inch floppies, 3 ½-inch floppies, flash drives, storage networks, hard drive clusters, and so forth. Also, formats have changed from Wordstar in DOS to Word in Windows with a variety of software in-between (Word Perfect, various versions of Word, etc.). This also applies to database management systems (Dbase, Paradox, etc.) and spreadsheet systems (Visicalc, Lotus 123, etc.). What does this mean? Every time a standard changed, I saw the most commonly-used stored knowledge converted to the new standard, but the less-used knowledge was left as is with the expectation that it would be converted later. Did later ever come? In many cases, no, or at least, not yet. So what is the issue? Potentially critical knowledge is now stored in a variety of formats and standards that organizations may not be able to read or retrieve from. Is there concern? I think there is, but the concern is mild. Jennex (2005) found that use of knowledge had no correlation to its importance; in fact, it could almost be argued that knowledge that is seldom used is more valuable that that used frequently or even daily. Many do not understand what this means until they try to retrieve something from an old format and others possibly look at this as a good thing. After all, sales of music and videos tend to increase every time we change format and/or media. Video has gone from Beta to Laserdisc to VHS and now to DVD; where will it go next? Music has moved from 78s to 45s to 8 tracks to cassettes to CD to MP3, and is still changing. Books are moving from paper to audio to electronic books. Each of these changes ultimately causes owners to re-purchase their favorite titles when their old machines no longer work. I think content producers and distributors see this as a good thing. But is it? I do not think so; I think it only serves to keep us from facing the problem of lost data and knowledge.

Some Recommendations

Bergeron (2002) has a fascinating book exploring the issue of media volatility and discussing how society will cope when the digital knowledge fails. He is not very optimistic. Can anything be done? I propose a couple of actions. First, recognize consumer rights and require content producers and distributors when they change media and/or format to update products previously bought by consumers for the cost of the material. Consumers should not be forced to purchase new individual use copyrights when they already own them. I think this will force more organizations and individuals to consider the true costs of media and/or format changes and will raise awareness of how we are losing cultural treasures as after all, only those titles that are in consumer demand are re-mastered in the new media and/or format. As I get older, I find this frustrating as it gets harder and harder to find playable versions of the music, videos, and books I grew up with and want to enjoy again (as an example, my favorite band, the Ozark Mountain Daredevils, had to buy back the rights to their music and re-issue their albums on CD themselves just to get it out to their fans).

The second recommendation is that organizations and individuals use risk management techniques to select knowledge to be saved and continuously upgraded should media and/or formats change. As stated earlier, Jennex (2005) found that there is no correlation between the importance of knowledge and its importance. Organizations should not use frequency of use as a guide to what knowledge should be converted. Organizations should apply risk management to determine the impact to the organization should that knowledge be lost. Organizations should establish an acceptable risk threshold and monitor how much risk they are assuming by not updating knowledge storage media/formats. Additionally, organizations should include aggregation assessments as much knowledge, when looked at alone, may seem to have minimal impact to the organization should it be lost. However, this same knowledge, when assessed as an aggregated whole with other related knowledge or all knowledge stored on the same media/format, may now have an unacceptable impact on the organization should it be lost.

Finally, new technology and growing capacity is making it possible to capture everything. Is this a good thing? Again, I do not think so as we are overwhelming ourselves with data and knowledge of little value and making it harder for us to find those true golden nuggets of knowledge that provide innovative solutions to key problems. Shenk (1997) discusses this trend that he calls "Data Smog." His concern, and one I agree with, is that ultimately we will paralyze our decision-making ability with an over abundance of information and knowledge. Managers and knowledge workers are afraid to make decisions on what to capture and what not to. The result is we capture so much because we can, not because there is a need. The problem is it makes retrieving critical knowledge harder as we have to search through these massive amounts of knowledge to find that which we need. Can we do anything about this? Again, yes we can. I am a strong proponent of the use of risk management techniques to identify critical knowledge for capture and retention. I strongly dislike the idea of capturing everything. Will we miss something at some point? Probably, but again, if we do our jobs right, it w ill not be impossible to recover from this.

CONCLUSION

Why do we need knowledge management? We need KM because we need a formal process to help organizations identify, capture, store, and retrieve critical knowledge. We need KM processes to help organizations deal with changing storage strategies. We need KM to help us deal with the transience of knowledge workers. We need KM processes to help organizations manage a glut of knowledge. Ultimately, we need KM to help organizations make sense of what they know, to know what they know, and to effectively use what they know.

REFERENCES

Bergeron, B. (2002). *Dark Ages II: When the Digital data die*. Prentice Hall PTR.

Hansen M., Nohria, N., & Tierney, T. (1999). What's your strategy for managing knowledge?. *Harvard Business Review, March-April*, 106-116.

Jennex, M. (2005). The issue of system use in knowledge management systems. In *Proceedings of the 38th Hawaii International Conference on System Sciences, HICSS38*, IEEE Computer Society.

Jennex, M. (2005). What is knowledge management? *The International Journal of Knowledge Management, 1*(4), 1-4.

Shenk, D. (1997). *Data smog: Surviving the information glut*. HarperEdge Publishing.

Chapter II
The Impact of Culture and Context on Knowledge Management

Murray E. Jennex
San Diego State University, USA

INTRODUCTION

Jennex (2005) used an expert panel to generate the definition of knowledge management as the practice of selectively applying knowledge from previous experiences of decision-making to current and future decision-making activities with the express purpose of improving the organization's effectiveness. This was a consensus definition from the editorial review board that tells us what we are trying to do with knowledge management. However, knowledge management is being applied in multinational, multicultural organizations and we are seeing issues in effectively implementing knowledge management and transferring knowledge in global and/or multicultural environments. Chan and Chau (2005) discuss a failure of knowledge management that was in part caused by organizational culture differences between the home office (Hong Kong) and the main work location (Shanghai). Jennex (2006) discusses Year 2000, (Y2K) knowledge sharing projects that were

not as successful as expected due to cultural and context issues. These projects involved organizations that performed the same functions just in different nations, however, problems caused by culture and context were not expected. Other research in review with the International Journal of Knowledge Management explores issues of culture with respect to social capital and implementing knowledge management. None of these are far reaching studies that we can generalize issues from, but they do provide anecdotal and case study support that culture and context are issues we need to address.

Why consider culture and context? Davenport and Prusak (1998) view knowledge as an evolving mix of framed experience, values, contextual information and expert insight that provides a framework for evaluating and incorporating new experiences and information. They found that in organizations, knowledge often becomes embedded in artifacts such as documents, video, audio or repositories and in organizational routines,

Copyright © 2008, IGI Global, distributing in print or electronic forms without written permission of IGI Global is prohibited.

processes, practices, and norms. They also say that for knowledge to have value it must include the human additions of context, culture, experience, and interpretation. Nonaka (1994) expands this view by stating that knowledge is about meaning in the sense that it is context-specific. This implies that users of knowledge must understand and have experience with the context, or surrounding conditions and influences, in which the knowledge is generated and used for it to have meaning to them. This also implies that for a knowledge repository to be useful, it must also store the context in which the knowledge was generated. That knowledge is context-specific argues against the idea that knowledge can be applied universally, however, it does not argue against the concept of organizational knowledge. Organizational knowledge is considered to be an integral component of what organizational members remember and use meaning that knowledge is actionable.

First we need to define what we mean by the terms culture and context. The United Nations Educational, Scientific and Cultural Organization, UNESCO, states that culture is the "set of distinctive spiritual, material, intellectual and emotional features of society or a social group and that it encompasses, in addition to art and literature, lifestyles, ways of living together, value systems, traditions and beliefs" (UNESCO, 2002). The American Heritage Dictionary (2000) defines context as the part of a text or statement that surrounds a particular word or passage and determines its meaning and/or the circumstances in which an event occurs; a setting. Culture forms the basis for how we process and use knowledge by providing belief frameworks for understanding and using the knowledge, context provides the framing for the knowledge explaining how it is created and meant to be used. Both are critical to the transfer and reuse of knowledge, where we use the Nonaka and Takeuchi (1995) and Polyani (1967) view of knowledge as having tacit and explicit dimensions. Tacit knowledge is that which is understood within a knower's mind and which

cannot be directly expressed by data or knowledge representations. It is commonly referred to as unstructured knowledge. Explicit knowledge is that knowledge which can be directly expressed by knowledge representations. This is known as structured knowledge. We normally expect explicit knowledge to be easily transferred while we expect issues with transferring tacit knowledge. However, we are finding that transfer of either dimension of knowledge in a multicultural environment is not easy.

Next we need to discuss how knowledge is transferred. Knowledge transfer occurs when people, as members of the same and/or different organizations, exchange tacit and explicit knowledge. Nonaka and Takeuchi (1995) propose four modes (processes) for knowledge creation and transfer:

- **Socialization:** The process of sharing experiences, thereby creating tacit knowledge such as mental models and technical skills. Tacit knowledge can be obtained without the use of language, that is, through observation, imitation, and practice.
- **Externalization:** The process of articulating tacit knowledge in the form of explicit concepts such as metaphors, analogies, hypotheses and models.
- **Combination:** The process of systemizing concepts into a knowledge system by combining different bodies of explicit knowledge. Explicit knowledge is transferred through media such as documents, meetings, e-mail and phone conversations. Categorizing this knowledge can lead to the generation of new knowledge.
- **Internalization:** The process of converting explicit knowledge to tacit knowledge and is closely related to learning by doing.

These four modes or processes show that the transfer of knowledge is dependent upon the transfer of a common understanding from the knower to the user of the knowledge. Common understanding consists of the context (the story behind the knowledge, the conditions and situations which make the knowledge understandable) and the experience (those activities which produce mental models of how the knowledge should be used) expressed in a culturally understood framework. Sherif and Sherif (2006) incorporate this common understanding into their definition of social capital. Social capital or culture and context, either way, it is clear that these factors influence how knowledge is transferred and reused. The following paragraphs discuss some of the issues associated with culture and context and how they impact the Nonaka and Takeuchi (1995) SECI knowledge transfer model.

CULTURE

Why consider culture? Hofstede (1980, p. 25) refines the definition of culture as: "Culture consists in patterned ways of thinking, feeling and reacting, acquired and transmitted mainly by symbols, constituting the distinctive achievements of human groups, including their embodiments in artifacts; the essential core of culture consists of traditions (i.e. historically derived and selected) ideas and especially their attached values." His work focuses on identifying cultural differences between nations and illustrates that value systems are not the same the world over. The key to the impact of culture on knowledge transfer is in his expanded definition as cultures impact on artifacts and values influences how different social groups will externalize metaphors, analogies, hypotheses, and models; how groups will systemize concepts; how groups internalize concepts; and how groups understand experiences. Hofstede (1980; 2001) uses five dimensions to assess basic cultural values:

- **Power distance index:** Determines expectations regarding equity among group members.

- **Uncertainty avoidance index:** Determines typical reactions to situations considered different and/or dangerous.
- **Individualism index:** Determines the strength of the relationships between the individual and the society group.
- **Masculinity index:** Determines expectations regarding gender roles.
- **Long-term orientation index:** Determines the basic orientation of the society group to time.

Other authors look at culture and values and provide alternative frameworks for evaluating them. Schwartz (1992) identified ten distinct types of values: power, achievement, hedonism, stimulation, self-direction, universalism, benevolence, tradition, conformity, and security. How important the individual rates each of these values determines the individual's system of value priorities. The Schwartz Value Survey has been developed to help measure this. Additionally, Trompenaar (2004) identified value dimensions similar to Hofstede, but classifies them as: universalism, individualism, view of time, affectivity, how directed, and status.

Differences in culture, and Hofstede (1980; 2001) show that significant differences between nations can lead to differences between national groups within the same organization, causing those groups to either understand knowledge differently, or have significant barriers to participating in the sharing of knowledge. We must understand that culture is a unique component that is so deeply imbedded into people lives that our ignorance of it usually leads to failures. Knowledge management systems (KMS), as well as other systems created to improve organization's performance, should use all possible information about culture to escape systems' mistakes due to lack of cultural awareness and understanding. Probably no theory ever will be capable to capture all or even full knowledge about a specific culture, but there are enough theories (as discussed above) to establish a process and methodology for including cultural parameters in the design of KM initiatives and the system analysis and design activities.

Along with concerns about how national cultures affect the use and understanding of knowledge is the impact of organizational culture on knowledge use. Organizational culture impacts the flow of knowledge through the organization as well as the willingness of its members to share and reuse knowledge. Jennex and Olfman (2005) synthesized literature and research into a set of twelve critical success factors. Organizational culture was found to be a key critical success factor by several researchers (Davenport et al., 1998; Alavi & Leidner, 1999; Sage & Rouse, 1999; Jennex & Olfman, 2000; Bock & Kim, 2002; Forcadell & Guadamillas, 2002; Yu et al., 2004; Chan & Chau, 2005). Issues related to organizational culture include organizational reward, incentive, and personnel evaluation systems and management and leadership styles and support for KM.

CONTEXT

Why consider context? Davenport and Prusak (1998, p. 5) view knowledge as an evolving mix of framed experience, values, contextual information and expert insight that provides a framework for evaluating and incorporating new experiences and information. They found that in organizations, knowledge often becomes embedded in documents or repositories and in organizational routines, processes, practices and norms. They add that for knowledge to have value it must include the elements of human context, experience, and interpretation. Nonaka (1994) expands this view by stating that knowledge is about meaning in the sense that it is context-specific. This implies that users of knowledge must understand and have experience with the context (surrounding conditions and influences) in which the knowledge is generated and used for it to be meaningful. This suggests that for a knowledge repository to be useful it must also store the context in which the knowledge was generated. The suggestion that knowledge is context specific argues against the idea that knowledge can be applied universally.

Context is the collection of relevant conditions and surrounding influences that make a situation unique and comprehensible to the users of the knowledge (Degler & Battle, 2000). Context can be stored with knowledge and/or can be possessed by knowledge users. When a system's knowledge users are known, the knowledge that is captured is captured to support specific activities. KMS users are readily known when the KMS is built to support a specific team, project, or process and the users are those involved with that team, project, and/or process. These users tend to possess a high degree of shared context of understanding where context of understanding incorporates context and experience. Experience is what knowledge users use to generate mental models of how to use or apply the knowledge (Degler & Battle, 2000). Experience comes from the individual's own experience with the knowledge domain, other's shared experience with the knowledge domain, and/or a collective experience with the knowledge domain (Degler & Battle, 2000). Combined, this means that knowledge users in teams, projects, or even processes understand the organizational culture, the structure of organizational documents, organizational terminology and jargon, and how the organization works and are able to use posted knowledge, even if it does not include context, as they implicitly understand the context in which the knowledge was created and have experience in using this knowledge. On the other hand, when KMS users are not known, it is not possible to assume these users possess a common context of understanding or experience associated with the generation of the knowledge. This means the KMS will have to capture this context and experience for users to be able to utilize the captured knowledge effectively.

CONCLUSION

To summarize, culture and context are issues that affect how we represent knowledge, what we store for knowledge, and how we transfer and apply knowledge. It is not realistic to expect all users within the same multinational organization (and even less realistic if the users are in different organizations) to possess the same cultural and context attributes, so KM initiatives need to recognize these limitations and allow the differences. How we do this is something we need to address. It should also be anticipated that the initiators/designers/ developers of a KMS will not belong to the same culture of the expected users nor necessarily possess the context to understand how the expected users will transfer and use knowledge. Additionally, we need to realize that knowledge contributors/knowledge sources may be of a different culture than the knowledge users and that the knowledge users may not possess the same context knowledge as the knowledge contributors/sources. Not only traditions, but whole schemes of thinking as well as understanding and interpreting the order/classification of data/events/knowledge might be different. KMS are highly logical systems that only work properly when the logic of its user is captured properly. Therefore, we stress the importance of investigating the culture and understanding context before we can expect to design a successful KMS. Fortunately, there are frameworks we can use to assess culture and context (as discussed above) and we need research that applies these frameworks to KM situations. This issue of the International Journal of Knowledge Management hopefully starts this area of KM research and we hope to present more research dealing with these issues in the near future.

REFERENCES

Alavi, M., & Leidner, D. (1999). Knowledge management systems: Emerging views and practices from the field. In *Proceedings of the 32ⁿᵈ Hawaii International Conference on System Sciences*, IEEE Computer Society.

American Heritage Dictionary of the English Language, Fourth Edition. (2000). Houghton Mifflin Company. Updated in 2003.

Bock, G., & Kim, Y. (2002). Breaking the myths of rewards: An exploratory study of attitudes about knowledge sharing. *Information Resources Management Journal, 15*(2), 14-21.

Chan, I., & Chau, P. (2005). Getting knowledge management right: Lessons from failure. *International Journal of Knowledge Management, 1*(3), 40-54.

Davenport, T., DeLong, D., & Beers, M. (1998). Successful knowledge management projects. *Sloan Management Review, 39*(2), 43-57.

Davenport, T., & Prusak, L. (1998). *Working knowledge*. Harvard Business School Press.

Degler, D., & Battle, L. (2000). Knowledge management in pursuit of performance: The challenge of context. *Performance Improvement, ISPI, 39*(6). Retrieved October 7, 2002 from www.ipgems.com/writing/rolearticle.htm.

Forcadell, F., & Guadamillas, F. (2002). A case study on the implementation of a knowledge management strategy oriented to innovation. *Knowledge and Process Management, 9*(3), 162-171.

Hofstede, G. (1980). *Culture's consequences*. Thousand Oaks, CA: Sage Publications.

Hofstede, G. (2001). *Culture's consequences: Comparing values, behaviors, institutions, and organizations across nations*. Thousand Oaks, CA: Sage Publications.

Jennex, M. (2005). What is KM?. *International Journal of Knowledge Management, 1*(4), 1-4.

Jennex, M. (2006). Classifying knowledge management systems based on context content. *Hawaii International Conference on Systems Sciences,* IEEE Computer Society.

Jennex, M., & Olfman, L. (2000). Development recommendations for knowledge management/ organizational memory systems. In *Proceedings of the Information Systems Development Conference.*

Jennex, M., & Olfman, L. (2005). Assessing knowledge management success. *International Journal of Knowledge Management, 1*(2), 33-49.

Nonaka, I. (1994). A dynamic theory of organizational knowledge creation. *Organization Science, 5*(1), 14-37.

Nonaka, I., & Takeuchi, H. (1995). *The knowledge-creating company—How Japanese companies create the dynamics of innovation.* Oxford: Oxford University Press.

Polanyi, M. (1967). *The tacit dimension.* London: Routledge and Keoan Paul.

Sage, A., & Rouse, W. (1999). Information systems frontiers in knowledge management. *Information Systems Frontiers, 1*(3), 205-219.

Schwartz, S. (1992). Universals in the content and structure of values: Theoretical advances and empirical tests in 20 Countries. In: M. Zanna (Ed.), *Advances in experimental social psychology, 25,* 1-65. New York, NY: Academic Press.

Sherif, K., & Sherif, S. (2006). Think social capital before you think knowledge transfer. *International Journal of Knowledge Management, 2*(3), 21-32.

Trompenaar, A. (2004). *Managing people across cultures.* Capstone, Ltd.

UNESCO Universal Declaration on Cultural Diversity. (2002). *UNESCO Universal Declaration on Cultural Diversity.* Retrieved October 2, 2005 from http://www.unesco.org/education/ imld_2002/unversal_decla.shtml

Yu, S-H, Kim, Y-G, & Kim, M-Y, (2004). Linking organizational knowledge management drivers to knowledge management performance: An exploratory study. In *Proceedings of the 37th Hawaii International Conference on System Sciences,* IEEE Computer Society.

Chapter III
Addressing Contextual Issues in Knowledge Management:
A Guiding Framework

Adekunle Okunoye
Xavier University, USA

Nancy Bertaux
Xavier University, USA

ABSTRACT

Cultural diversity and wide disparities in the extent of up-to-date infrastructure make managing knowledge challenging in developing countries, even as the urgent human needs in these countries make knowledge management (KM) especially valuable as a tool in economic and human development. Cultural diversity and infrastructural gap issues are also related to a variety of government, educational, political, social, and economic factors. These environmental factors interact with organizational variables and information technology to enable or constrain knowledge management processes in the creation and protection of knowledge resources. Case studies in India, The Gambia, and Nigeria are used to develop an empirically grounded contextual framework of knowledge management (KM). This guiding framework is intended to help organizations address contextual issues in knowledge management, leading to better preparation, implementation, and assessment of KM projects.

INTRODUCTION

Cultural diversity and wide disparities in the extent of up-to-date infrastructure make managing knowledge challenging in developing countries, even as the urgent human needs in these countries make knowledge management (KM) especially valuable as a tool in economic and human development (Bertaux, Okunoye, & Abu-Rashed, 2005; Bertaux, Okunoye, & Oyelami, 2005). Cultural diversity and infrastructural gap issues are also related to a variety of government, educational, political, social and economic factors. These environmental factors interact with organizational

Copyright © 2008, IGI Global, distributing in print or electronic forms without written permission of IGI Global is prohibited.

variables and information technology to enable or constrain knowledge management processes in the creation and protection of knowledge resources. Case studies in India, The Gambia, and Nigeria are used to develop an empirically grounded contextual framework of knowledge management (KM). This guiding framework is intended to help organizations address contextual issues in knowledge management, leading to better preparation, implementation and assessment of KM projects.

How are knowledge management (KM) frameworks helpful to organizations? KM frameworks can assist us in establishing a focus for KM efforts (Earl, 2001; Shankar & Gupta, 2005). These frameworks can also help organizations to approach KM methodically and consciously. They can help to identify a specific approach to KM, to define goals and strategies, to understand the various knowledge management initiatives, and then to choose the best ones for the particular circumstances (Earl, 2001; Maier & Remus, 2001). There have been several proposed frameworks to guide KM efforts in organizations. However, these frameworks do not address KM across the full spectrum of organizational needs (Calaberese, 2000; Shankar & Gupta, 2005), but instead address certain KM elements. There is therefore a need for a comprehensive KM framework that considers the full range of organizational dimensions.

A number of reviews and models (Holsapple & Joshi, 1999; Lai & Chu, 2000; Rubestein-Montano et al., 2001; Shankar & Gupta, 2005; Bennet & Tomblin, 2006; Montequin et al., 2006) have discussed the components and assumptions of the frameworks proposed to date. There appears to be a consensus on the need for a more generalized framework, and, consequently, these authors also outline recommendations regarding such a framework. All agree that the basic components should be knowledge resources, KM processes and influences. Even though the existing and the suggested frameworks recognize varying organizational contexts, they have not considered differences in the operating environmental contexts. This is similar to the IS literature, where very few studies address global diversity (Walsham, 2001; Avgerou, 2002).

The importance of the local operating environmental context has already received some attention in e-commerce (Simon, 2001), ERP (Wassenar et al., 2002) and information systems development methodology research (INDEHELA Project, 1999). Also, King et al. (1994) comprehensively discuss institutional factors in information technology innovation. In knowledge management, however, there is a basic need for consideration of the diverse environmental context and how it could influence other issues involved. The framework described here is designed to address that need, by focusing on the local cultural and infrastructural factors that could interact with organizational factors and information technology and the resultant effect on knowledge processes and resources.

GLOBAL CULTURAL DIVERSITY MATTERS

Global cultural diversity has profound implications for the effective design and implementation of knowledge management (KM) projects. Thus, our view on global cultural diversity recognizes the existence of different organizational contexts and great care must be taken when making assumptions about patterns of organizational performance and innovations (Avgerou, 2002). For example, the wide gap in the availability and use of ICT across the world, and the influences ICT exerts on globalization, raise questions about the feasibility and desirability of efforts to implement the development of ICT through the transfer of best practices from Western industrialized countries to developing countries, and whether organizations can utilize such ICT in accordance with the socio-cultural requirements of the contexts (Avgerou, 1998; Morales-Gomez & Melesse, 1998; Walsham,

2001). Previous research (Bada, 2000; Walsham, 2001; Avgerou, 2002; Kridan & Goulding, 2006;) concludes that diversity and local context does matter, and that the global techniques employed in western industrialized countries should not be implemented mechanically in developing countries without consideration for the local context (Bada, 2000). Further, gender considerations have been shown to be of great importance in the successful adoption of ICT (Bertaux, Okunoye, & Abu-Rashed, 2006).

The concept of "de-scription" proposed by Akrich (2000) also expresses our understanding of global diversity and the significance of a context-aware framework. Akrich argues that when technologists define the characteristics of their object, they necessarily make hypotheses about the entities that make up the world into which the object is to be inserted. They also assume that the designers define actors with specific tastes, competences, motives, aspirations, political prejudices and the rest. They assume that morality, technology, society and the economy will evolve in particular ways. In a nutshell, they inscribe their vision, or prediction about the world, into the technical content of the new object. Karsten (2000, p. 21) also suggests that "the functions of these (technical) system are not predetermined, but only evolve within specific, socio-political contexts". Focusing on specific contexts will help to move away from unfruitful general claims and all-encompassing pictures, enabling us to see a technical change as embedded in a larger system of activity, as having consequences which depend on peoples' actual behavior, and as taking place in a social world in which the history of related changes may influence the new change.

We are aware of the force of globalization and its assumed homogeneity. However, globalization does not mean imposing homogenous solutions in a pluralistic world. It means giving a global vision and strategy, but it also means cultivating roots and individual identities. It means nourishing local insights, but it also means re-employing communicable ideas in new geographies around the world (Das, 1993). The adoption and usage of such a technology framework will vary according both to local socio-cultural and organizational contexts, and to the national context, including government, economic and political systems, educational systems and history, culture and infrastructure (Schneider & Barsoux, 1997).

A KM framework can be seen as an IS innovation (Avgerou, 2001), a technology (Walsham, 2001), or a technical object (Akrich, 2000). Considering the context in which they are designed and their designers, it can be argued that some basic assumptions (to be discussed later) about the KM processes and influences have been inscribed into these frameworks. An attempt to describe and apply the framework in another context might be problematic. Hence, a context-aware framework, with specific consideration for the operating environmental factors and for the organizational factors that are closely related to the environment, could help to move us toward a more universally applicable KM framework, as well as increasing our sensitivity to the importance of global diversity.

ADDRESSING CONTEXTUAL ISSUES IN KNOWLEDGE MANAGEMENT

Theoretical Background

In this chapter, we synthesize some the insights from our studies and well-known concepts and theories in organization studies to build a context-aware framework, including an explanation of its components. Leavitt (1965) calls for interdependence of organizational variables for effective organizational change and Scott (1998) asserts that environment and organization are inseparable. The institutionalist perspective of Powell and DiMaggio (1991) also supports the argument on the need to consider the operating environment in a KM framework. Following Pettigrew's contextualist approach (1987), for a study on change to contribute towards a robust theory or framework that can guide practice, it must examine change as a process and in a historical and contextual manner (Bada, 2000). Hofstede's (1997) cultural model and Galbraith's (1977) concept of organization design are also brought in to strengthen the arguments for the framework. Initially, the design of the study, data collection and analysis and subsequent theorizing and building of the framework was influenced by socio-technical systems (STS) theory. Thus, we next present a brief overview of the STS theory and knowledge management.

Socio-Technical Systems Theory and Knowledge Management

A socio-technical system is defined as a combination of a social and a technical subsystem (Trist, 1981). Rather than insisting that individual and social units must conform to technical requirements, the socio-technical systems theory emphasizes the needs of both (Scott, 1998). One of the guiding premises of this approach is that work involves a combination of social and technical requisites and that the object of design is to jointly optimize both components without sacrificing one to others. This approach provides a broad conceptual foundation as well as insights into the nature of routine and non-routine work design. STS has been applied both in systems development practice and in the analysis of ICT functionality and organizational

changes (Mumford & Weir, 1979; Lyytinen et al., 1998; Avgerou, 2002). There has also been application of socio-technical systems theory in KM (Pan & Scarbrough, 1998; Sena & Shani, 1999; Coakes et al., 2002).

In a similar manner, Leavitt (1965) recognized the complexity and diversity of organizations by identifying four socio-technical variables (structure, task, technology and people) that need to interact together in a balanced way to bring about organizational change. Scott (1998) added environment as another element, suggesting that organizations and environments are interdependent in terms of information systems and cognitive processes and in terms of environmental effects on organizational outcomes. They are also interdependent in more direct ways, since organizations attempt to directly influence environments and vice versa.

Leavitt's Diamond Organization Model

The Leavitt Diamond (Figure 1) gives a balanced view of the complexities that affect KM framework, by positioning technology in strong relationships to the tasks carried out, the people participating in these, and to the organization of the tasks and the people, that is, the structure. It has been widely adopted and cited (e.g., Schäfer et al., 1988; Mumford, 1993; Wiggins, 2000; El Sawy, 2001) as a basis for understanding organizational changes.

Leavitt's Diamond shows four sets of organizational variables, task, people (actors), technology,

Figure 1. Leavitt's diamond organization model (1965)

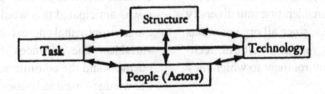

and structure. According to Leavitt (1965), these four groups of variables are highly interdependent, as indicated by the arrowheads, so that change in any one usually results in compensatory or retaliatory change in others. Technologies are considered to be tools that help organizations to get work done, and mechanisms for transforming inputs to outputs.

This view corresponds to ours: knowledge management is not only about managing knowledge-work processes or the people that carry out these processes, since technology and organizational structure are also affected. A position explored in the framework is that by studying the balance of all these variables, it is possible to bring out the value of the knowledge management efforts in an organization. Therefore, rather than trivializing any one of the variables, or neglecting one set (such as technology), the framework considers all equally and gives priority to all the variables so that knowledge management efforts can achieve maximal success.

Summary

The work of knowledge-based organizations is usually non-routine and needs to be supported by balancing all the variables mentioned above. Thus KM from the socio-technical perspective will require all activities that support the *social subsystems* (the nature of human capital, i.e., the people with knowledge, competencies, skills, experience, and attitudes), a *technical subsystem* (the production function, i.e., the inputs and the technology that convert inputs into outputs) and an *environmental subsystem* (including customers, competitors and a host of other outside forces) (Sena & Shani, 1999). Any framework to support KM should integrate these main variables and put proper emphasis and consideration into diversity in various environments, since all organizations exist in a specific geographical, cultural, technological, and social environment to which they must adapt.

To these general theoretical perspectives on the influence of local diversity in an organization's environment, we add our own insights concerning cultural and infrastructure diversity and their influences on KM based on findings from the multiple case study. The diversity in our study organizations—which include national and international organizations in different research fields—formed the basis for the evidence on contextual issues in organizational variables and information technology. We next present the methodology and approaches to data collection.

The Study

Most of the studies that form the basis of the existing frameworks have been carried out in organizations in western industrialized countries where there can be similar assumptions about the components of the framework. To add a new perspective, we conducted our study in developing countries. These countries afford us an opportunity to see the differences in culture (Hofstede, 1997) and infrastructure provision (The World Bank Group, 2004) at the local level. An empirical study was conducted on KM in six research organizations in Nigeria and The Gambia and two research organizations in India. Nigeria is representative of countries in sub-Saharan Africa due to its large population and huge natural resources. Oil exploration has particularly attracted many multinational companies that are characterized by western management styles. The Gambia presents a contrast to Nigeria as one of the smallest countries in sub-Saharan Africa but with a reliable infrastructure. India is representative of countries in South Asia, by population, culture and business environment. India is a major site for offshore software production (Lateef, 1997) and it was anticipated this would be evident in both the environmental context and the organizational variables. The advances of India in software business and the commitment of government in knowledge-based activities make it a strategic place to study KM. However, these industries are in the minority and could not be viewed completely as indigenous. The methodology used was a multiple case study with data analysis carried out on the organizational level (Korpela et al., 2001). Both quantitative and qualitative data were collected using questionnaires, interviews, non-participant observation, and reviews of historical documents.

Our discussion here summarizes relevant aspects of these studies. The results show differences in assumptions on the influence of KM, especially when the local operating environment context is considered. Our study shows how the availability and use of information and communication technologies could support KM processes and how the Internet especially appears to provide a gateway to the international research community. This would suggest raising IT to be a major component in a comprehensive KM model. These findings also indicated some issues about leadership, structure, and culture that are contextual to each organization and the environment in which they operate. A conclusion of our study is that a KM framework needs to have contextual relevance for organizations in diverse social-cultural environments. It should align information technology, people, structure, knowledge processes and socio-cultural and organizational influences to make knowledge management sustainable.

Research Methods

The contextual issues in a KM framework were studied through a multiple-case study and analysis of eight different research organizations. Yin (1994) observed that the triangulation of multiple sources of evidence permits convergence and corroboration of findings and building a stronger, more convincing basis for conclusions. While the conduct of a multiple-case study can require extensive resources and time, the evidence is often considered more compelling than from a single

case, and the study can be regarded as more robust. We carried out our study in two countries in sub-Saharan Africa, in Nigeria and The Gambia, and in two organizations in India. These countries have different levels of infrastructure and cultural differences. For example, in telecommunications, The Gambia has a significantly higher penetration (The World Bank Group, 2004). We assumed there would also be differences in organizational infrastructures across countries.

The Case Organizations

Of the six organizations in Nigeria, three are international: International Institute of Tropical Agriculture (IITA), Medical Research Council Laboratories (MRC), and International Trypanotolerance Center (ITC). Three are national: National Agricultural Research Institute (NARI), Nigeria Institute of Social Economic Research (NISER) and Nigerian Institute of Medical Research (NIMR). The national organizations are mainly dependent on the national government for their basic funding. Usually, the international organizations have a substantial number of expatriates working in them for the duration of their project. Three of the organizations are large, with more than 500 staff. The smaller three have 100-200 members of staff. All of the organizations carry out their research within several sites. Also, all of them have in-country and international collaboration with other institutions. Thus they all work in a wide network of sponsors, customers, and cooperating institutions. India's two organizations include International Crop Research Institute for the Semi Arid Tropics (ICRISAT), an international organization with a staff of more than 500, and National Institute of Mental Health and Neuroscience (NIMHANS), a national organization also with a staff of over 500.

The study used several methods of data gathering: the two main questionnaires were the KM diagnostic and the information technology infrastructure (ITI) services assessment instrument (see Okunoye & Karsten (2001) for more details). These were complemented with semi-structured interviews and short- time on-site observations of knowledge management enablers. Organizational documents and presentations by senior management about their KM-related initiatives were collected and analyzed. A similar approach in data gathering has been applied in a study on the relationship between IT infrastructure and Business Process Re-engineering (Broadbent et al., 1999). Between January and March 2001, we visited all the six organizations in Nigeria and during the summer of 2002, we visited the two organizations in India. The visits lasted for about two weeks each. Some of the research sites of each organization were visited and as many as possible of the relevant people were interviewed, especially the heads of sections, the IT managers and the librarians, to fill out the questionnaires and to provide the documents. Individual researchers provided valuable insight into the actual work processes. In the Nigeria study, a total of 48 people participated in the research: 29 were interviewed and did the questionnaire, 8 did the questionnaire only, and 11 were interviewed only. However, only 31 out of the 37 questionnaires were included in the final analysis, because six of them had to be eliminated due to low responses to the questions. In India, 26 people participated, 16 people were interviewed and completed the questionnaire, 6 did the questionnaire only, and 4 were interviewed only; 19 out of 22 questionnaires were included in the final analysis and three had to be eliminated due to low responses to the questions. The interviews were recorded on audiotape and in a field diary and later transcribed. As the visits were brief and as all instruments had to be filled out with the researcher present, the time was only sufficient for observation of some KM practices (see Okunoye & Karsten (2002a; 2002b; 2003); Okunoye et al. (2002) for detailed results).

ELEMENTS IN THE FRAMEWORK

Environmental Factors

Environmental factors include those factors outside the organization that directly influence its activities. Holsapple and Joshi (2000) include governmental, economic, political, social, and educational factors (GEPSE) here. There are also indirect factors such as *culture* and *national infrastructure*. The operating environment varies from organization to organization, between countries, and also from one site to another within a country. Yet many frameworks that guide organizational strategies and development simply assume a homogeneous environment and thus exclude it from their design. A common assumption is that organizations will consider the GEPSE factors that have a direct economic impact on their operation, but that indirect factors such as the culture and the infrastructure are irrelevant[1]. However, our empirical studies tell us that these indirect factors also significantly influence organizational variables. This is consistent with a growing literature in the U.S. that documents the importance of managing cultural diversity factors to improve organizational systems (Cox, 2001; Thomas et al., 2002).

Infrastructural Issues

The national infrastructure can be said to include education, banking, cooperatives, transportation and communication systems. Scholars have pointed out the influence that these systems have on the organizational IT infrastructure (Weill & Vitale, 2002). The infrastructural issues are derivatives of several other environmental factors and this discussion thus cuts across many other issues. The infrastructural capability of a country is likely to influence the kind of technology the organization can deploy. It could also determine the extent of the application and sustainability of this technology. The extent to which countries provide infrastructure at the national level clearly affects the infrastructure of organizations in these countries. Most of the technological problems associated with environmental factors are beyond the control of single organizations. There are considerable differences in the IT infrastructures globally between countries, for example, between western and developing countries (The World Bank Group, 2004). The differences within developing countries are also wide, as is illustrated in Table 1. Specifically, in our study and as evidenced in the literature (Odedra et al., 1993; Barata et al., 2001; Darley, 2001) and available statistics (The World Bank Group, 2004), the problem with the IT infrastructure is more pronounced in sub-Saharan Africa (SSA) than in India where the government has invested heavily in it. Most of the problems in SSA can be attributed to the government's lack of preparedness to commit sufficient resources to develop the national infrastructure, which could as a consequence improve the infrastructures available to organizations. The low availability and utilization of IT infrastructure in sub-Saharan Africa and the lack of expertise to support the physical infrastructure has been widely discussed (e.g., Odedra et al., 1993; Moyo, 1996). According to our study, while the availability of IT infrastructure has the expected significant effect on the knowledge management efforts,

its under-utilization and the lack of technical expertise to support its proper application to the knowledge management processes becomes an even bigger problem.

For example, in Nigeria, individuals were expected to bear the cost associated with Internet use in the national research organizations we studied:

...... if you understand, it [Internet] is not widely available for some reasons, cost, which implies that cost of access is high, even though your have opened it up to everybody, the cost is scaring them off and they are not using it. That is why I was a bit eh eh, but there is access. You have to pay N200 (about $2) for 15minutes of browsing, some of them use it when it is very important and critically... (Mr. B, NISER)

This was not the case in India and The Gambia. Also, the Indian government's long-term investment in educational and social infrastructures has provided a large pool of qualified IT practitioners (Lateef, 1997; Tessler & Barr, 1997). This has a high impact on the kinds of technology they are able to use in their organizations. They have been able to design the required KM applications and to provide adequate support, sometimes at a cheaper cost when compared to Nigeria and The Gambia. This was not the case in SSA, where getting qualified IT support and management

Table 1. Infrastructural differences between Nigeria, The Gambia, India and USA (The World Bank Group, 2004).

ICT infrastructure, computers and the Internet	Nigeria	The Gambia	India	USA
Fixed line and mobile phone subscribers (per 1,000 people)	79	-	85	1,223
Personal computers (per 1,000 people)	6.6	11.5	4.5	585.2
Internet users (per 1,000 people)	149	33	32	630
Internet speed and access [2]	2.5/7		3.6/7	6.6
Internet effect on business	3.3/7		3.2/7	5.0

personnel continue to be a major problem (Odedra et al., 1993).

These examples show the kind of influence the provision of infrastructure in a particular environmental context can exert on the information technology that can be deployed within an organization. It also shows the effect on usage; where individuals are responsible for the cost of using technology, it is likely to discourage the use of this technology. Thus, a framework that could be applicable in this context should provide for the assessment of infrastructural provision in the environment where the organization operates.

Cultural Issues

Several authors have demonstrated how national culture influences management practices. For example, Schneider and Barsoux (1997) relate culture to each of the organizational variables that have been identified as having a great influence on KM (APQC, 1996). Weisinger and Trauth (2002) have argued that cultural understanding is locally situated and negotiated by actors within a specific context. In information systems research, national culture has been noted to influence, among others, IT utilization (Deans at al., 1991), IT diffusion (Straub, 1994), and technology acceptance (Straub et al., 1997; Anandarajan et al., 2000). As noted above, earlier KM frameworks (Holsapple & Joshi, 1999; Lai & Chu, 2000; Rubestein-Montano et al., 2001) and recent frameworks and models (XXXX) recognize different organizational cultures but they are generally silent on the effect of different national cultures. However, Lucas and Ogilvie (2006) conclude that knowledge transfer and management is not a socially neutral process, instead knowledge transfer and management is social activities occurring within a social context and the success of knowledge management could be influenced by reputations, culture and incentives. According to Brookes et al. (2006) social processes, practices and patterns play significant roles in effective knowledge management.

The best-known and most widely used cultural model was developed by Hofstede based on a study conducted among IBM employees working in different countries in the late 1960s (Hofstede, 1997). Hofstede included four dimensions of national culture: power distance, uncertainty avoidance, individualism-collectivism, and masculinity-femininity. He later added a fifth dimension, long- versus short-term orientation, based on a study carried out in Asian countries. The model helps bring out issues related to cultural differences and it provides some universal measures with which to analyze them. According to Walsham (2001), however, such measures are too general and cannot be used to explain some cultural differences.

According to Hofstede, countries in West Africa differ culturally from the USA, especially in the power distance and individualism-collectivism dimensions. This study and our earlier experiences, however, report some differences within and between the countries in West Africa. In western Nigeria, where three of the study organizations are located, every village has a well-defined hierarchy and family structure. It is a societal norm to treat senior members with absolute respect and obedience. Their views and opinions are often accepted and their judgments are not to be publicly questioned.

... To certain extent, given that for any particular area, the programme leader is the expert in that area, It is a requirement for whoever is heading a particular programme to try during the course of his tenure as the programme leader and get the team under him involve in the day to day activities..., the people under you [the leaders] are really undergoing apprenticeship so to say... and they need to show respect. (Dr. SBO NARI)

There is thus a substantial gap between the leaders and their subordinates. Contrary behavior (even when not necessarily wrong) by any member of the community can be interpreted as

Figure 2. Organizational variables (adapted from concept of organization design, Galbraith, 1977)

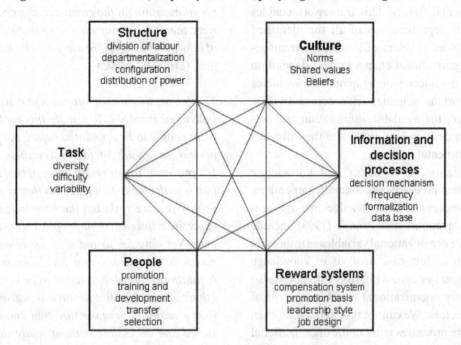

disloyalty and attract punishment. In the Nigerian national research organizations located in western Nigeria, it was very easy to recognize the leaders and people in position of power. Without careful attention to this, implementing a framework that assumes that everyone has freedom of expression and equal rights could yield undesirable outcomes in these settings. Our argument here is that each organization should be studied in its own cultural context and thorough knowledge of this should influence the application of the KM framework.

Organizational Variables

The organizational variables as a necessary concern are recognized in our study as well as several other studies and frameworks (APQC 1996; Holsapple & Joshi, 2000). To succinctly describe all organization issues that could influence KM, the conceptual framework (Figure 2) developed by Galbraith (1977) is adopted and modified by adding organizational culture which is another important component in organizational design

(Schein, 1985). Task, culture, structure, information and decision processes, reward systems, and people are the commonly included organizational variables. These need to be aligned for optimal results (Leavitt, 1965; Galbraith, 1977).

Organizational structure is the distribution of power and the shape of the organizational form. People have competence, nature and attitudes. Information and decision processes include especially the availability and accessibility of information. Reward systems tell how the organization compensates its members for effective performance (Nathanson et al., 1982). The task is the link between choices of strategy and organization structure, decision processes and individual personality vary systematically with the uncertainty of that task (Galbraith, 1977). The organizational culture includes the shared values, beliefs, norms, expectations and assumptions that bind people and systems. The organizational culture is particularly important in KM because it gives people a basis for stability, control and direction and helps them to adapt and integrate other variables and technology with the operating environmental factors. This framework enables a complete representation of all the identified organizational enablers of knowledge management. Organizational changes could depend on how well the interrelationship of these variables can support an organization's core activities, considering the available information technology (Markus & Robey, 1988) and the influence of environmental factors.

Organizational variables and knowledge management processes are mutually dependent. For the success of a knowledge management project, Davenport and Prusak (1998) include many of the organizational variables as important factors. In a multi-case analysis of knowledge management systems, Akhavan et al. (2006) also found many organizational variables as critical success factors. We cannot talk about KM even with all the processes without the organizational variables to support them (APQC, 1996). Due to several factors such as strategic alliance, internationalization of firms and services, technology transfer, globalization, and recent advances in ICT, western management styles and forms of organization have a great influence across the world. The success of multinational corporations and consulting firms add to the assumptions about the universality of management strategies, including knowledge management. Nevertheless, significant differences due to cultural diversity exist, as illustrated below.

The *people* dimension of KM enablers can be problematic in several respects, for example in our case, the international, expatriate staff members tended to come and go and take their knowledge with them. This had resulted in discontinuity: knowledge could not be assessed, sustained or divested in any systematic way, as illustrated by the quotes below:

When I came there was a tremendous knowledge gap... because there was no documentation at

all...there was no written information, there was no information on the computer, the people who were there, were only able to provide a little bit of information, but there was an awful knowledge gap. (Dr. SDL, MRC)

That's true, that sort of information rests with the individual involved. To handle this problem, we want people to be appointed before the previous person has already left to avoid creation of gap. It is a problem. You are right, most of that information is with people that left... Yes that is very true. I think you are right but the knowledge and the expertise is linked to some people. That is certainly true. Not only for us but also for other similar research institutions and local organizations. Institutional knowledge seems to be very fragile. I think that is right. But we have the infrastructure that is required to make sure that knowledge is stored and accessible without really depending on people...(Dr. SA, MRC)

The local staff members were often discouraged from ambitious projects as they were not seen able to perform beyond a certain level. They also often lacked the personal funds that the expatriates might have for supplementing the possibly meager resources at the institutes.

Surely there is a lot of obvious difference. For instance, the national research institutes and the universities which we called NARS, we put them under NARS. They are handicapped by funding. Their budgets are in Naira which keeps depreciating every time. And for them to procure materials and whatever, they have to purchase from abroad in dollar which is not available to them, they have to convert, and buy at very high rates and which may not be available. Apart from the facts that they are under-funded, the little they have, they can't convert it to dollars, secondly, most of them do not have the expertise we have, thirdly they lack IT systems ...Even they don't have up-

to-date books. Because they don't have enough funds to buy them, if you go to their library, they have outdated materials. So, that is why if you go to our library, you find many of them coming to use the library here. Many of their scientists and the lecturer of university come to use the library here.......... (Mr. YA, IITA)

The people working in an organization are directly influenced by their own identity (Walsham, 2001), which could be influenced by societal norms and values and controlled by social, economic, and educational factors. For example, while training and learning without any formal certification could be acceptable for employees in western industrialized countries, we found that employees in sub-Saharan Africa would normally like to have a certificate for their training. The reason is the importance attached to a certificate as evidence of knowledge, and the prospect of getting a well-paid job, based on the extent of certified training.

I think the financial incentive has mainly attracted people initially to do the on-the-job training (OJT) and it is also slightly more popular. But some of the main problems of OJT are still there. In the culture here, and I think in Africa in general, people don't see the same value in training unless there is a certificate or qualification attached to it. So that's one big part. Having a qualification attached to OJT is a big issue in giving OJT the credibility that it needs. (Dr. SA, MRC)

Similarly, knowledge as a source of power has a different meaning to western employees and their developing countries counterparts. In many developing countries, due to high unemployment rates, lack of social security and benefits, and the scarcity of well-paid jobs, employees may wish to protect their source of competitiveness and thus view sharing knowledge as giving away their power.

..........they should be jealous of their means of livelihood [their knowledge]......... (Prof. HOTA, NIMR)

The basic concept of knowledge varies from one culture to another. This could impact the effectiveness of organizational KM initiatives. In each of the countries in our study, there is a long tradition of recognizing some people as a repository of knowledge: for example, the griot in the Gambia, the babalawo in Yorubaland and the guru in India. Although it may not be formally recognized in research organizations, since it is basically overridden by the professional culture, attention needs to be paid to differences in people's notions of knowledge and the effect of this on organizations.

The Gurus are those with true knowledge and gives only to his beloved student, only one student. So since you ask about the knowledge and the India traditional culture, let us talk about "AMRITA" [Nectar of life], which if you drink you never die. The people who know the AMRITA never tell anybody. It automatically dies with them. Likewise the gurus committed, unknowingly, they committed..., I cannot say sin, they just did not see the importance of their knowledge and never share it widely. They never share their full knowledge, if they did, we would have the entire traditional medicinal things we had in the past. (Mr. Raju, ICRISAT)

One scientist in a national organization explained how ascription is being used to rate people's contributions instead of achievement, that is, people are judged by who they are and not necessarily by what they do.

There are some people who should be regarded as a source [of knowledge] and not a threat [to the leaders], but when you turn source to a threat, people become discouraged, ... People are not al-

ways evaluated and promoted by what they know but by who they know. (Prof. HOTA, NIMR)

As research organizations, our case organizations shared many similar cultural features and the scientists also shared a similar professional culture. Yet, there are notable differences in the organizational culture of national versus international organizations. While international organizations exhibit combinations of cultures (Weisinger & Trauth, 2002), which include corporate culture, industrial culture, professional culture and some national culture of the local environment, the national organizations are greatly influenced by the regional culture (e.g., western versus northern Nigeria). Also, the diversity in workforce of international organizations reduces the effect of the interaction of national or societal culture with organizational culture when compared to national organizations.

The people here are highly educated. The illiterate thinks the moment they share the information, the value is lost. But ours is a different organization. Ours is a multicultural organization and this culture is influenced by western culture and there is free flow of information. (Mr. V, ICRISAT)

The *task and structure* dimensions had to do with management—which was in some institutes better than in others—and with ability to carry out the tasks planned. Here, the external circumstances had their strongest impact: if there is no electricity, no working phone, and very slow mail, work in general is slowed down. Communication between people not working at the same site is greatly hampered. Visiting and sending messengers are the only possibilities, and they take time.

Of course, when we have electricity blackout and telecommunication breakdown, we can't reach anywhere and we can't physically travel, we just have to wait. (Dr. GE, MRC)

The organizational structure is closely related to the societal structure and the style of leadership could be influenced by the orientation of the people (Korpela, 1996). In the leadership pattern in western Nigeria, we also observe that superiors are often inaccessible and the power holders are entitled to privileges in the organization. The hierarchies in the community are also reflected in the organization. This is in contrast to organizations in The Gambia. This has implications for KM, as the organizational structure could affect knowledge sharing and communication (Davenport & Prusak, 1998).

Taken together, each of these has implications for KM efforts in organizations. In knowledge management research and practice, it has typically been suggested that particular attention be paid to organizational variables, (often called enablers or influences) without which the success of KM cannot be guaranteed. With evidence that the assumptions about these variables are contextual, we contend here that any framework to support KM needs to consider each variable in the context of each organization, with due consideration also for the interaction with the operating environment.

Information Technology

Information technology can support the processes for knowledge creation, sharing, application and storage (Alavi & Leidner, 2001). It can also enhance the interaction of individual, group, organizational, and inter-organizational knowledge (Hedlund, 1994; Nonaka & Takeuchi, 1995). Bennet and Tomblin (2006) also affirm that information and communication technology can provide support for knowledge management and organizational learning. Information technology availability and use varies between countries, but also within countries and between organizations. When there is little funding for an organization, there are fewer computers and software applications for use, with less access time to the Internet and other IT services.

The researchers are willing to learn but in a situation where resources are not available, research cannot be carried out without money. It is a money gulping thing, it takes a lot of money and you don't expect immediate results, particularly medical research. It is not something like industrial research where you have a very big breakthrough and you publicize that you have been able to invent these things. I think medical research is not like that. I think the past government was not too keen on that. They didn't make money available for our researchers to work with. They keep on searching for funding, except some of them that are ready to spend their own money. Somebody was just telling me that she needed a reagent for her research work, she had to take a cooperative loan to get it, the loan is not meant for that kind of thing, but she had no alternative for her research work, so that is a kind of problem we have. Maybe with this present government, things may improve.
(Mr. A, NIMR)

In contemporary organizations, information technology is not only considered to support other organizational processes, but as a source of competitive advantage and even organizational core capability. IT enables changes in the organizational structure and supports communication within and between organizations. IT can make the information and decision-making processes easier. There is hardly any aspect of organizations that IT has not affected, including the way people think and carry out their work processes (Lau et al., 2001).

According to Orlikowski and Barley (2001), the transformation in the nature of work and organizing cannot be understood without considering both the technological changes and the institutional (specifically environmental) context that are reshaping economic and organizational activities. They thus emphasize the interrelationship of the environment, organizational variable and technology. They argue that collaboration between organizational issues and information technology could increase the understanding of changes taking place in the organization. In our study, we found that organizations with high information technology capability were generally able to support knowledge processes better. The application of technology also depends on skills and abilities of individuals and the support of management, which are also organizational issues.

Many technologies can support KM processes. However, these technologies require a basic IT infrastructure, such as local area networking and Internet connectivity, to function optimally. There is also need for basic hardware and software. The provision of these IT infrastructures varies between organizations (Broadbent et al., 1999) and its use depends on the context of each organization. Apart from the statistic evidence, also in our study, we found differences in level of IT capability between national and international organizations, which we attribute to differences in level of funding, and other factors (discussed earlier),

An expatriate usually managed the IT units of the international organizations. The expatriate heads of the IT units were generally more experienced, and had knowledge of relevant modern technologies, due to their training in and access to the Western market. This usually had a positive influence on the performance of the IT unit and the adoption of technologies. The only international organization without a computer unit had an effective outsourcing strategy, which indirectly resulted in better services than national organizations with higher IT infrastructure services. The IT units of the international organizations were better staffed than the national organizations. Most of the staff had a university degree and had received some other special training. LAN and Intranet were only available in the international organizations.
(Okunoye & Karsten, 2003)

There were also differences in expertise to support these technologies. Although IT skill shortage is a global phenomenon, its extent varies between countries. Thus, it is important that a framework to support KM efforts in an organization recognizes these different levels of IT availability and use and that it supports the organization in making a right decision of which technology is most appropriate in their circumstances.

Knowledge Management Processes

Knowledge management processes are socially enacted activities that support individual and collective knowledge and interaction (Alavi & Leidner, 2001; Lucas & Ogilvie, 2006). These activities vary depending on which of the knowledge resources that the organization aims at improving. It is these activities that must be supported by the influences discussed earlier. Since each organization has a different focus, KM processes take place also in different contexts. These processes can be summarized as knowledge creation, knowledge storage/retrieval, knowledge transfer, and knowledge application. Thus the organization should consciously choose which of these activities they intend to support in order to choose appropriate organizational variables and technology to enable them.

For example, research organizations in sub-Saharan Africa are particularly interested in knowledge creation and transfer and they found the Internet to be an effective technology to support this process. One of our case organizations in India focuses on knowledge sharing among the scientists and the rural community and they also are using a global intranet (ICRISAT, 2001).

Knowledge Resources

The main targets of the knowledge management processes are the knowledge resources. Holsapple and Joshi (2001) present a comprehensive framework of organizational knowledge resources where they consider, including employee knowledge, knowledge embedded in physical systems (Leonard-Barton, 1995), human capital, organizational capital, customer capital (Petrash, 1998), external structures, internal structures, and employee competencies (Sveiby, 1996). Knowledge resources also include intellectual capital (Stewart, 1998), which according to Montequin et al. (2006) can include human capital, structural capital and relational capital. The main goal of knowledge management is the effective marshalling and use of these resources (Lai & Chu, 2000).

The benefit and strategic importance of knowledge management is in the ability of an organization to correctly identify which knowledge resources they can improve to gain sustainable competitive advantage. This is a reason for the popularity of KM as the process of identifying the resources and subsequent selection of processes are never the same. In addition, organizational variables and technology need to support these processes with varying complexity and with different levels of influence by the operating environment.

A CONTEXT-AWARE FRAMEWORK OF KM

In a context-aware KM framework, KM is seen as an effort to properly put all the organizational variables into best use, with the support of relevant information technology, in order to facilitate the knowledge processes. The main overall goals center on organizational productivity, responsiveness, innovation, and competency through the creation and protection of knowledge resources.

This framework (Figure 3) differs from those presented earlier in that it considers the relationships between and interdependency of all components with particular attention to the environmental context. This framework enables organizations to pay attention to the local context and how this affects the assumptions about

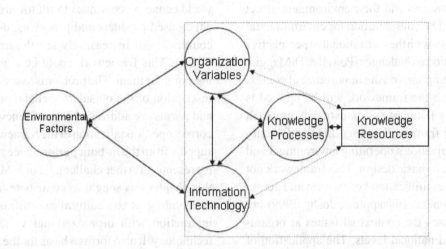

Figure 3. A context-based framework of knowledge management (Okunoye & Bertaux, 2006)

each component. The method and research approach used to arrive at the assumption about the components also ensure that the projected users are the actual users and the gap between the world inscribed in it and the world that will be described by its displacement can be expected to be narrowed.

As explained earlier, all the organization-related influences that could enable or constrain KM can be put together as *organizational variables*. *Information technology* is a separate component due to its strategic importance in supporting *the knowledge processes* of knowledge creation, storage, sharing and application. All these are directly affected by the *environmental factors* (e.g., Culture and infrastructure in our discussion) where the organization operates. The organizational variables and information technology can influence each another and they are both enablers of knowledge processes. On the other hand, the kind of knowledge to be created could determine which kind of information technology to be used and which variables in the organization need to be adjusted. Effective handling of knowledge processes yields the main aim of the KM, which is improving the *knowledge resources* in which the competitive advantage and all other benefits of KM lie. Also, knowledge resources could ef-

fectively affect knowledge processes. The double arrow that joins the organizational variables and the technology to the operating environment shows the interdependency between the organization and the environment, ensuring that KM processes are consistent with the external environment in which the organization operates and that those activities meant to improve knowledge resources are undertaken in a coordinated manner. Each component is linked to the others in a cyclic manner, which indicates the continuous dependency and influence between them. There is also a possibility of direct interaction between knowledge resources and organizational variables and also with information technology.

CONCLUSION

The guiding framework presented here is intended to help organizations address contextual issues in knowledge management, leading to better preparation, implementation and assessment of KM projects. We have emphasized a more universally applicable KM framework, one that increases our sensitivity to global diversity. The framework agrees with the recommendations of Leavitt (1965) that call for interdependence of the variables and with Scott (1998) in acknowledging that organizations and their environment affect each other. The consideration for environmental factors agrees with the institutionalist perspective of organizational challenges (Powell & DiMaggio, 1991). The emphasis on the importance of context within which the framework will be applied is informed by Pettigrew's contextualist approach (1987). Our framework recognizes the diversity in the organization's operating environment and utilizes it in its basic design. This framework not only achieves unification both within and across each component (Holsapple & Joshi, 1999) but also addresses the contextual issues at organizational and national levels. The application of this framework requires thorough understanding of the issues related to each component, that is, pre-knowledge of organizational variables and an ability to handle problematic areas are required. Knowledge of the technology and which knowledge processes it can support are also essential for the successful application of the framework. The organization also needs to identify the knowledge resources that are crucial to improving competitive advantage, and which knowledge processes could best support this. The framework also requires cultural sensitivity, including cultural knowledge of the environment and a realistic assessment of the available infrastructure. The GEPSE factors (governmental, economic, political, social, and educational factors) are often assessed with easily obtained statistics, but such statistics do not reveal many important qualitative details. Thus, input from local sources and local people are essential.

The framework could serve as a link between the organization and its environment, ensuring that KM is approached with consideration to the environment in which the organization operates. The framework also helps to ensure that the activities involved in KM are carried out in a well-guided manner. This framework shows the need for a multidisciplinary team when undertaking a KM project. In a multinational organization, a multicultural team is also required. As long as the world economy continues to tilt towards knowledge-based products and processes, developing countries will increasingly see the importance of KM. This framework could be a good starting point for them. The problems associated with inscription of the outsiders' beliefs, perception, and norms are addressed in the framework. The correct operationalization of the framework, with support from the in-built performance measures, represents a further challenge. For KM practice, this chapter has sought to contribute to our understanding of the cultural and infrastructural interaction with organizational variables and technology. It also forms a basis for the composition of a KM team as well as a means of control and balance. For researchers, it contributes to the conceptualization of a more universal framework, which allows for localized specific assumptions. The urgent human needs in developing countries increase the stakes in the effective implementation of KM projects, and greater attention to these contextual differences at the local level can potentially have a significant pay-off in the human and economic development efforts in these countries.

REFERENCES

Akhavan, P., Jafari, M., & Fathian, M. (2006). Critical success factors of knowledge management systems: A multi-case analysis. *European Business Review, 18*(2), 97-113.

Akrich, M. (2000). The description of technical objects. In: W. Bijker & J. Law (Eds.), *Shaping technology/building society: Studies in socio-technical change* (pp. 205-224). Cambridge, MA: The MIT Press.

Alavi, M., & Leidner, D. (2001). Knowledge management and knowledge management systems: Conceptual foundations and research issues. *MIS Quarterly, 25*(1), 107-136.

American Productivity and Quality Center (APQC). (1996). *Knowledge management: Consortium benchmarking study Final Report 1996.* Retrieved April 3, 2000 from http://www.store. apqc.org/reports/Summary/know-mng.pdf.

Anandarajan, M., Igbaria, M., & Anakwe, U. (2000). Technology acceptance in the banking industry: A perspective from a less developed country. *Information Technology and People, 13*(4), 298-312.

Avgerou, C. (1998). How can IT enable economic growth in developing countries? *Information Technology for Development, 8*(1), 15-29.

Avgerou, C. (2001). The significance of context in information systems and organizational change. *Information Systems Journal, 11*(1), 43-63.

Avgerou, C. (2002). *Information systems and global diversity.* Oxford: Oxford University Press.

Bada, A. (2000). *Global practices and local interests: Implementing technology-based change in a developing country context.* Doctoral dissertation, London School of Economics and Political Science, Department of Information Systems.

Barata, K., Kutzner, F., & Wamukoya, J. (2001). Records, computers, resources: A difficult equation for sub-Saharan Africa. *Information Management Journal, 35*(1), 34-42.

Bennet, A., & Tomblin, M. (2006). A learning network framework for modern organizations: Organizational learning, knowledge management and ICT support. *VINE: The Journal of Information and Knowledge Management Systems, 36*(1), 289-303.

Bertaux, N., Okunoye, A., & Abu-Rashed, J. (2006) Information technology education for women in developing countries: Benefits, barriers, and policies. *Global Business & Economics Review, 8*(1).

Bertaux, N., Okunoye, A., & Abu-Rashed, J. (2005). Knowledge management and economic development in developing countries: An examination of the main enablers. *Global Business and Economics Review, 7*(1), 85-99

Bertaux, N., Okunoye, A., & Oyelami, M. (2005). Rural community and human development through information technology education: Empirical evidence from western Nigeria. In *Proceedings of the IFIP WG 9.4 Working Conference* (pp. 169-179), *May 2005, Abuja, Nigeria.*

Broadbent, M., Weill, P., & St. Clair, D. (1999). The implications of information technology infrastructure for business process redesign. *MIS Quarterly, 23*(2), 159-182.

Brookes, N., Morton, S., Dainty, A., & Burns N. (2006). *International Journal of Project Management, 24,* 474-482

Calaberese, F. (2000). *A suggested framework of key elements defining effective enterprise knowledge management programs.* Doctoral dissertation, George Washington University, School of Engineering and Applied Science.

Calaberese, F. (2006). Knowledge organizations in the century: Knowledge-based organizations in context. *VINE: The Journal of Information and Knowledge Management Systems, 36*(1), 12-16.

Coakes, E., Willis, D., & Clarke, S. (Eds.). (2002). *Knowledge management in the socio-technical world: The graffiti continues.* London: Springer-Verlag

Cox, T. (2001). *Creating the multicultural organization: A strategy for capturing the power of diversity.* San Francisco, CA: Jossey-Bass.

Darley, W. (2001). The Internet and emerging e-Commerce: Challenges and implications for management in sub-Saharan Africa. *Journal of Global Information Technology Management, 4*(4), 4-18.

Das, G. (1993). Local memoir of a global manager. *Harvard Business Review, March-April,* 38-47.

Davenport, T., & Prusak, L. (1998). *Working knowledge: How organizations manage what they know.* Cambridge, MA: Harvard Business School Press.

Earl, M. (2001). Knowledge management strategies: Towards taxonomy. *Journal of Management Information Systems, 18*(1), 215-233.

El Sawy O. (2001). *Redesigning enterprise processes for e-business.* Boston, MA: Irwin/Mc-Graw-Hill.

Galbraith, J. (1977). *Organizational design.* Reading, MA: Addison Wesley.

Hedlund, G. (1994). A model of knowledge management and the N-form corporation. *Strategic Management Journal, 15,* 73-90.

Hofstede, G. (1997). *Cultures and organizations – Software of the mind.* New York, NY: McGraw Hill.

Holsapple, C., & Joshi, K. (1999). Description and analysis of existing knowledge management frameworks. In *Proceedings of the Thirty-second Hawaii International Conference on System Sciences,* January 3-6, Computer Society Press.

Holsapple, C., & Joshi, K. (2000). An investigation of factors that influence the management of knowledge in organizations. *Journal of Strategic Information System, 9*(2-3), 235-261.

Holsapple, C., & Joshi, K. (2001). Organizational knowledge resources. *Decision Support Systems, 31*(1), 39-54.

ICRISAT. (2001). Medium Term Plan 2002-2004, People First! International Crops Research Institute for Semi-Arid Tropics, Patancheru AP, India.

INDEHELA-Methods project. (1999). Retrieved March 2, 2003 from http://www.uku.fi/atkk/indehela/

Jafari, M., & Akhavan P. (2007). Essential changes for knowledge management establishment in a country: A macro perspective. *European Business Review, 19*(1), 89-110.

Karsten H. (2000). *Weaving tapesty: Collaborative information technology and organizational change.* Doctoral dissertation, Jyvaskyla Studies in Computing, No 3.

King, J., Gurbaxani, V., Kraemer, K., McFarlan, F., Raman, K., & Yap, C. (1994). Institutional factors in information technology innovation. *Information Systems Research, 5*(2), 139-169.

Korpela, M. (1996). Traditional culture or political economy? On the root causes of organizational obstacles of IT in developing countries. *Information Technology for Development, 7,* 29-42.

Korpela, M., Mursu, A., & Soriyan, H. (2001). Two times four integrative levels of analysis: A framework. In: N. Russo, B. Fitzgerald, & J. De-Gross (Eds.), *Realigning research and practice in information systems development. The social and organizational perspective* (pp. 367-377). Boston, MA: Kluwer Academic Publishers.

Kridan, A., & Goulding, J. (2006). A case study on knowledge management implementation in banking sector. *VINE: The Journal of Information and Knowledge Management Systems, 36*(2), 211-222

Lai, H., & Chu, T. (2000). Knowledge management: A theoretical frameworks and industrial cases. In *Proceedings of the Thirty-Third Annual Hawaii International Conference on System Sciences* (CD/ROM), January 4-7, Computer Society Press.

Lateef, A. (1997). *A case study of Indian software industry.* International Institute for Labor Studies, New Industrial Organization Programme, DP/96/1997.

Lau, T., Wong, Y., Chan, K., & Law, M. (2001). Information technology and the work environment–Does IT change the way people interact at work?. *Human Systems Management, 20*(3), 267-280.

Leavitt, H. (1965). Applied organizational change in industry: Structural, technological and humanistic approaches. In: J. March (Ed.), *Handbook of organizations* (pp. 1144-1170). Chicago, IL: Rand McNally & Co.

Leonard-Barton, D. (1995). *Wellsprings of knowledge: Building and sustaining the sources of innovation.* Cambridge, MA: Harvard Business School Press.

Lucas, L., & Ogilve D. (2006). Things are not always what they seem: How reputations, culture, and incentives influence knowledge transfer. *The Learning Organization, 13*(1), 7-24.

Lyytinen, K., Mathiassen, L., & Ropponen, J. (1998). Attention shaping and software risk - A categorical analysis of four classical risk management approaches. *Information Systems Research, 9*(3), 233-255.

Maier, R., & Remus, U. (2001). Toward a framework for knowledge management strategies: Process orientation as strategic starting point. In *Proceedings of the 34th Hawaii International Conference on Systems Sciences* (CD/ROM), January 3-6, Computer Society Press.

Markus, L., & Robey, D. (1998). Information technology and organizational change: Causal structure in theory and research. *Management Sciences, 34*(5), 583-598.

Montequin, V., Fernandez, F., Cabal, V., & Gutierrez, R. (2006). An integrated framework for intellectual capital measurement and knowledge management implementation in small and medium-sized enterprises. *Journal of Information Science, 32*(6), 525-538.

Morales-Gomez, D., & Melesse, M. (1998). Utilizing information and communication technologies for development: The social dimensions. *Information Technology for Development, 8*(1), 3-14.

Mumford, E. (1993). *Designing human systems for healthcare: The ETHICS method.* Cheshire: Eight Associates.

Mumford, E., & Weir, M. (1979). *Computer systems in work design—The ETHICS method: Effective technical and human implementation of computer systems.* Exeter: A. Wheaton & Co.

Nathanson, D., Kazanjian, R., & Galbraith, J. (1982). Effective strategic planning and the role of organization design. In: P. Lorange (Ed.), *Implementation of strategic planning* (pp. 91-113). Englewood Cliffs, NJ: Prentice Hall, Inc.

Nonaka, I., & Takeuchi, H. (1995). *The knowledge-creating company: How Japanese companies create the dynamics of innovation.* Oxford, UK: Oxford University Press.

Odedra, M., Lawrie, M., Bennett, M., & Goodman, S. (1993). International perspectives: Sub-Saharan Africa: A technological desert. *Communications of the ACM, 36*(2), 25-29.

Okunoye, A., & Karsten, H. (2001). Information technology infrastructure and knowledge management in sub-Saharan Africa: Research in progress. In *Proceedings of the Second Annual Global Information Technology Management (GITM) World Conference,* June 10-12, Dallas, TX.

Okunoye, A., & Karsten, H. (2002a). Where the global needs the local: Variation in enablers in the knowledge management process. *Journal of Global Information Technology Management, 5*(3), 12-31.

Okunoye, A., & Karsten, H. (2002b). ITI as enabler of KM: Empirical perspectives from research organisations in sub-Saharan Africa.

In *Proceedings of the 35th Hawaii International Conference on Systems Sciences,* January 7-10, Big Island, HI.

Okunoye, A., & Karsten, H. (2003). Global access to knowledge in research: Findings from organizations in sub-Saharan Africa. *Information Technology and People, 16*(3), 353-373.

Okunoye, A., Innola, E., & Karsten, H. (2002). Benchmarking knowledge management in developing countries: Case of research organizations in Nigeria, The Gambia, and India. In *Proceedings of the 3rd European Conference on Knowledge Management,* September 24-25, Dublin, Ireland.

Orlikowski, W., & Barley, S. (2001). Technology and institutions: What can research on information technology and research on organizations learn from each other. *MIS Quarterly, 25*(2), 145-165.

Pan, S., & Scarbrough, H. (1998). A socio-technical view of knowledge—Sharing at Buckman Laboratories. *Journal of Knowledge Management, 2*(1), 55-66.

Pettigrew, A. (1987). Context and action in the transformation of the firm. *Journal of management studies, 24*(6), 649-670.

Powell, W., & DiMaggio, P. (Eds.). (1991). *The new institutionalism in organizational analysis.* Chicago, IL: University of Chicago Press.

Rubenstein-Montano, B., Liebowitz, J., Buchwalter, J., McCaw, D., Newman, B., Rebeck, K., & The Knowledge Management Methodology Team. (2001). A systems thinking framework for knowledge management. *Decision Support Systems, 31*(1), 5-16

Schäfer, G., Hirschheim, R., Harper, M., Hansjee, R., Domke, M., & Bjorn-Andersen, N. (1988). *Functional analysis of office requirements: A multi-perspective approach.* Chichester: Wiley.

Schein, E. (1985). *Organizational culture and leadership.* San Francisco, CA: Jossey-Bass.

Schneider, S., & Barsoux, J.-L. (1997). *Managing across cultures.* London: Prentice Hall.

Scott, W. (1998). *Organizations: Rational, natural and open systems.* Upper Saddle River, NJ: Prentice-Hall, Inc.

Sena, J., & Shani, A. (1999). Intellectual capital and knowledge creation: Towards an alternative framework. In: J. Liebowitz (Ed.), *Knowledge management handbook.* Boca Raton, FL: CRC Press.

Shankar, R., & Gupta, A. (2005) Towards framework for knowledge management implementation. *Knowledge and Process Management, 12*(4), 259-277.

Simon, S. (2001). The impact of culture and gender on Web sites: An empirical study. *The DATA BASE for Advances in Information Systems, 32*(1), 18-37.

Stewart, T. (1997). *Intellectual capital: The new wealth of organization.* New York, NY: Double Day.

Straub, D., Keil, M., & Brenner, W. (1997). Testing the technology acceptance model across cultures: A three country study. *Information & Management, 31*(1), 1-11.

Straub, D. (1994). The effect of culture on IT diffusion: E-mail and fax in Japan and the U.S. *Information Systems Research, 5*(1), 23-47.

Sveiby, K. (1996). *What is knowledge management?.* Retrieved March 4, 2000 from http://www.sveiby.com.au/KnowledgeManagement.html

Tessler, S., & Barr, A. (1997). *Software R&D strategies of developing countries.* Stanford Computer Industry Project, Position Paper.

The World Bank Group, Data and Map. Retrieved December 27, 2004 from http://www.worldbank.org/data/countrydata/ictglance.htm

Thomas, R., Roosevelt, R., Thomas, D., Ely, R., & Meyerson D. (2002). *Harvard Business Review on Managing Diversity.* Boston, MA: Harvard Business Review Publishing.

Trist, E. (1981). The socio-technical perspective. The evolution of socio-technical systems as conceptual framework and as an action research program. In: A. Van de Ven & W. Jotce (Eds.), *Perspectives on organization design and behavior* (pp. 49-75). New York, NY: John Wiley and Son.

Walsham, G. (2001). *Making a world of difference: IT in a global context.* New York, NY: John Wiley and Sons.

Wassenar, A., Gregor, S., & Swagerman, D. (2002). ERP implementation management in different organizational and cultural settings. In *Proceedings of the European Accounting Information Systems Conference,* Copenhagen Business School, Copenhagen, Denmark.

Weill, P., & Vitale, M. (2002). What IT infrastructure capabilities are needed to implement e-Business models?. *MIS Quarterly Executive, 1*(1), 17-34.

Weisinger, J., & Trauth, E. (2002). Situating culture in the global information sector. *Information Technology and People, 15*(4), 306-320.

Wiggins, B. (2000). *Effective document management: Unlocking corporate knowledge.* Gower: Aldershot.

ENDNOTES

[1] Multinational organizations now selectively consider some infrastructure when considering location of new subsidiaries; nevertheless, they often have the capability and resources to come with their own infrastructure. Thus, they pay more attention to other factors beyond their control.

[2] Ratings from 1 to 7; 7 is highest/best

Chapter IV
A Model of Knowledge Management Success

Murray E. Jennex
San Diego State University, USA

Lorne Olfman
Claremont Graduate University, USA

ABSTRACT

This article describes a knowledge management (KM) success model that is derived from observations generated through a longitudinal study of KM in an engineering organization and KM success factors found in the literature, which were modified by the application of these observations and success factors in various projects. The DeLone and McLean (1992, 2003) IS Success Model was used as a framework for the model, since it was found to fit the observed success criteria and provided an accepted theoretical basis for the proposed model.

INTRODUCTION

Knowledge management (KM) and knowledge management system (KMS) success is an issue that needs to be explored. The Knowledge Management Foundations workshop held at the Hawaii International Conference on System Sciences in January 2006 discussed this issue and reached agreement that it is important for the credibility of the KM discipline that we be able to define KM success. Also, Turban and Aronson (2001) list three reasons for measuring the success of KM and KMS:

- To provide a basis for company valuation
- To stimulate management to focus on what is important
- To justify investments in KM activities.

Copyright © 2008, IGI Global, distributing in print or electronic forms without written permission of IGI Global is prohibited.

All are good reasons from an organizational perspective. Additionally, from the perspective of KM academics and practitioners, identifying the factors, constructs, and variables that define KM success is crucial to understanding how these initiatives and systems should be designed and implemented. It is the purpose of this article to present a model that specifies and describes the antecedents of KM and KMS success so that researchers and practitioners can predict if a specific KM and KMS initiative will be successful. The article assumes that KM and KMS success cannot be separated, which is based on a broad, Churchman view of what constitutes KMS and a definition of success that is not reliant solely on technical effectiveness. The other basic assumption for this article is that success and effectiveness, as used in the KM literature, are synonymous terms. The remainder of the article uses the term *KM* to refer to KM and KMS and the term *success* to refer to success and effectiveness. The reasoning for these assumptions is discussed later in the article.

The proposed KM Success Model is an explication of the widely accepted DeLone and McLean (1992, 2003) IS Success Model, which was used since it was able to be modified to fit the observations and data collected in a longitudinal study of Organizational Memory, OM, and KM. It fit success factors found in the KM literature, and the resulting KM Success Model was useful in predicting success when applied to the design and implementation of a KM initiative and/or a KMS. Additionally, the stated purpose of the DeLone and McLean (1992, 2003) IS Success Model is to be a generalized framework that describes success dimensions for which researchers can adapt and define specific contexts of success (DeLone & McLean, 2003). Before presenting the KM Success Model, we will discuss the concepts of knowledge, KM, KMS, and KM/KMS success. We then will discuss briefly the DeLone and McLean (1992, 2003) IS Success Model, present the KM Success Model, and discuss the

differences. We will conclude by summarizing studies that support the KM Success Model and will present operationalizations that can be used to evaluate the constructs used to define the KM Success Model dimensions.

KNOWLEDGE, OM, AND KM

Alavi and Leidner (2001) summarize and extend the significant literature relating to knowledge, knowledge management, and knowledge management systems. They view organizational knowledge and OM as synonymous labels, as do Jennex and Olfman (2002). This is useful, as it allows for the combination of research results from OM and KM. It is also born out in the literature. Huber, Davenport, and King (1998) summarize OM as the set of repositories of information and knowledge that the organization has acquired and retains. Stein and Zwass (1995) define OM as the means by which knowledge from the past is brought to bear on present activities, resulting in higher or lower levels of organizational effectiveness, and Walsh and Ungson (1991) define OM as stored information from an organization's history that can be brought to bear on present decisions.

Davenport and Prusak (1998) define knowledge as an evolving mix of framed experience, values, contextual information, and expert insight that provides a framework for evaluating and incorporating new experiences and information. Knowledge often becomes embedded in documents or repositories and in organizational routines, processes, practices, and norms. Knowledge is also about meaning in the sense that it is context-specific (Huber et al., 1998). Jennex (2006) extends the concepts of context also to include associated culture that provides frameworks for understanding and using knowledge. Ultimately, we conclude that knowledge contains information, but information is not necessarily knowledge. Also, we conclude that OM contains knowledge. However, for the sake of simplicity, we will use the term *knowledge* to refer to OM and knowledge throughout this article.

Various knowledge taxonomies exist. Alavi and Leidner (2001) and Jennex and Croasdell (2005) found that the most commonly used taxonomy is Polanyi's (1962, 1967) and Nonaka's (1994) dimensions of tacit and explicit knowledge. This article uses this taxonomy for knowledge. Tacit knowledge is that which is understood within a knower's mind. It consists of cognitive and technical components. Cognitive components are the mental models used by the knower, which cannot be expressed directly by data or knowledge representations. Technical components are concrete concepts that can be expressed readily. Explicit knowledge also consists of these technical components that can be directly expressed by knowledge representations. KM in an organization occurs when members of an organization pass tacit and explicit knowledge to each other. Information Technology (IT) assists KM by providing knowledge repositories and methods for capturing and retrieving knowledge. The extent of the dimension of the knowledge being captured limits the effectiveness of IT in assisting KM. IT works best with knowledge that is primarily in the explicit dimension. Knowledge that is primarily in the tacit dimension requires that more context be captured with the knowledge where context is the information used to explain what the knowledge means and how it is used. Managing tacit knowledge is more difficult to support using IT solutions.

Jennex (2005) looked at what KM is and found no consensus definition. However, using the review board of the *International Journal of Knowledge Management* as an expert panel and soliciting definitions of KM that were used by the board members, the following working definition is used to define KM for this article:

KM *is the practice of selectively applying knowledge from previous experiences of decision making to current and future decision making activities*
with the express purpose of improving the organization's effectiveness. (Jennex, 2005, p. iv)

KM is an action discipline; knowledge needs to be used and applied in order for KM to have an impact. We also need measurable impacts from knowledge reuse in order for KM to be successful. Decision making is something that can be measured and judged. Organizations can tell if they are making the same decisions over and over and if they are using past knowledge to make these decisions better and more quickly. Also, decision making is the ultimate application of knowledge. This working definition provides this direction for KM and leads to a description of success for KM as being able to provide the appropriate knowledge for decision making when it is needed to those who need it.

KNOWLEDGE MANAGEMENT SYSTEMS

Alavi and Leidner (2001) defined KMS as "IT (Information Technology)-based systems developed to support and enhance the organizational processes of knowledge creation, storage/retrieval, transfer, and application" (p. 114). They observed that not all KM initiatives will implement an IT solution, but they support IT as an enabler of KM. Maier (2002) expanded on the IT concept for the KMS by calling it an ICT (Information and Communication Technology) system that supported the functions of knowledge creation, construction, identification, capturing, acquisition, selection, valuation, organization, linking, structuring, formalization, visualization, distribution, retention, maintenance, refinement, evolution, accessing, search, and application. Stein and Zwass (1995) define an Organizational Memory Information System (OMS) as the processes and IT components as necessary to capture, store, and apply knowledge created in the past on decisions currently being made. Jennex and Olfman (2002) expanded this definition by incorporating the OMS into the KMS and by adding strategy and service components to the KMS. We expand the boundaries of a KMS by taking a Churchman view of a system. Churchman (1979) defines a system as "a set of parts coordinated to accomplish a set of goals" (p. 29) and that there are five basic considerations for determining the meaning of a system:

- System objectives, including performance measures
- System environment
- System resources
- System components, their activities, goals, and measures of performance
- System management

Churchman (1979) also noted that systems are always part of a larger system and that the environment surrounding the system is outside the system's control but influences how the system performs. The final view of a KMS is as a system that includes IT/ICT components, repositories, users, processes that use and/or generate knowledge, knowledge, knowledge use culture, and the KM initiative with its associated goals and measures. This final definition is important, as it makes the KMS an embodiment of the KM initiative and makes it possible to associate KM success with KMS success.

KM SUCCESS

The previous paragraphs define KM success as reusing knowledge to improve organizational effectiveness by providing the appropriate knowledge to those that need it when it is needed. KM is expected to have a positive impact on the organization that improves organizational effectiveness. DeLone and McLean (1992, 2003) use the terms *success* and *effectiveness* interchangeably. This article uses KM success and KM effectiveness interchangeably by implying that increasing decision-making effectiveness has a positive impact on the organization, resulting in successful KM. KM and KMS success also is used interchangeably. KMS success can be defined as making KMS components more effective by improving search speed, accuracy, and so forth. For example, a KMS that enhances search and retrieval functions enhances decision-making effectiveness by improving the ability of the decision maker to find and retrieve appropriate knowledge in a more timely manner. The implication is that by increasing KMS effectiveness, KMS success is enhanced, and decision-making capability is enhanced, which leads to positive impacts on the organization. This is how KM success is defined, and it is concluded that enhancing KMS effectiveness makes the KMS more successful as well as being a reflection of KM success.

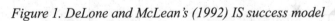

Figure 1. DeLone and McLean's (1992) IS success model

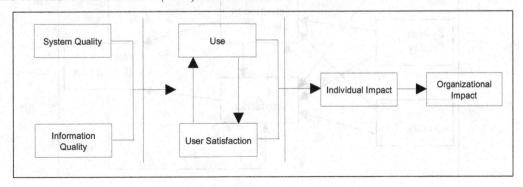

DeLone and McLean IS Success Model

In 1992 DeLone and McLean published their seminal work that proposed a taxonomy and an interactive model for conceptualizing and operationalizing IS success (DeLone & McLean, 1992). The DeLone and McLean (D&M) (1992) IS Success Model is based on a review and integration of 180 research studies that used some form of system success as a dependent variable. The model identifies six interrelated dimensions of success, as shown in Figure 1. Each dimension can have measures for determining their impact on success and on each other. Jennex, Olfman, Pituma, and Yong-Tae (1998) adopted the generic framework of the D&M IS Success Model and customized the dimensions to reflect the System Quality and Use constructs needed for an organizational memory information system (OMS). Jennex and Olfman (2002) expanded this OMS Success Model to include constructs for Information Quality.

DeLone and McLean (2003) revisited the D&M IS Success Model by incorporating subsequent IS success research and by addressing criticisms of the original model. One hundred forty-four articles from refereed journals and 15 papers from the International Conference on Information Systems (ICIS) that cited the D&M IS Success Model were reviewed, with 14 of these articles reporting on studies that attempted to empirically investigate the model. The result of the article is the modified D&M IS Success Model shown in Figure 2. Major changes include the additions of a Service Quality dimension for the service provided by the IS group, the modification of the Use dimension into a Intent to Use dimension, the combination of the Individual and Organizational Impact dimensions into an overall Net Benefits dimension, and the addition of a feedback loop from Net Benefits to Intent to Use and User Satisfaction. This article modifies the Jennex and Olfman (2002) OMS Success Model into a KM Success Model by applying KM research and the modified D&M IS Success Model.

KM SUCCESS MODEL

The model developed in this article was initially proposed by Jennex, et al. (1998) after an ethnographic case study of KM in an engineering organization. The model was modified by Jennex and Olfman (2002) following a five-year longitudinal

Figure 2. DeLone and McLean's (2003) revisited IS success model

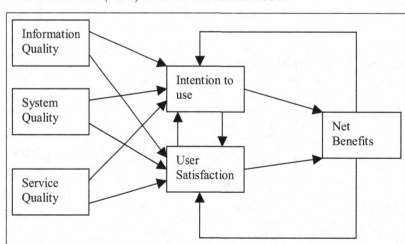

study of knowledge management in an engineering organization and is based on the DeLone and McLean (2003) revised IS Success Model. This final model was developed to incorporate experience in using the model to design KMS and for incorporating other KM/KMS success factor research from the literature. Figure 3 shows the KM Success Model. The KM Success Model is based on DeLone and McLean (2003). Since the KM Success Model is assessing the use of organizational knowledge, the Information Quality dimension is renamed the Knowledge Quality dimension. Also, because use of a KMS is usually voluntary, the KM Success Model expanded the Intention to Use dimension to include a Perceived Benefit dimension based on Thompson, Higgins, and Howell's (1991) Perceived Benefit model used

to predict system usage when usage is voluntary. Finally, since KM strategy/process is key to having the right knowledge, the feedback loop is extended back to this dimension. Dimension descriptions of the model follow.

SYSTEM QUALITY

Jennex and Olfman (2000, 2002) found infrastructure issues such as using a common network structure; adding KM skills to the technology support skill set; and using high-end personal computers, integrated databases; and standardizing hardware and software across the organization to be keys to building KM. The System Quality dimension incorporates these findings and defines system

Figure 3. KM success model

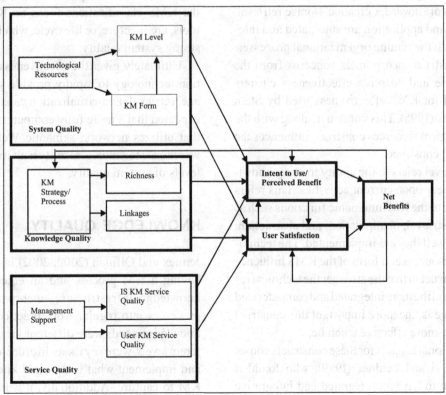

quality by how well KM performs the functions of knowledge creation, storage/retrieval, transfer, and application; how much of the knowledge is represented in the computerized portion of the OM; and the KM infrastructure. Three constructs—the technological resources of the organization, KM form, and KM level—are identified. Technological resources define the capability of an organization to develop, operate, and maintain KM. These include aspects such as amount of experience available for developing and maintaining KM; the type of hardware, networks, interfaces, and databases used to hold and manipulate knowledge, capacities, and speeds associated with KM infrastructure; and the competence of the users to use KM tools. Technical resources enable the KM form and KM level constructs.

KM form refers to the extent to which the knowledge and KM processes are computerized and integrated. This includes how much of the accessible knowledge is online and available through a single interface and how integrated the processes of knowledge creation, storage/retrieval, transfer, and application are automated and integrated into the routine organizational processes. This construct incorporates concerns from the integrative and adaptive effectiveness clusters proposed for KMS effectiveness used by Stein and Zwass (1995). This construct, along with the technological resources construct, influences the KM level construct.

KM level refers to the ability to bring knowledge to bear upon current activities. This refers explicitly to the KM mnemonic functions such as search, retrieval, manipulation, and abstraction, and how well they are implemented. The technological resources and form of the KMS influence this construct in that the stronger the technical resources and the more integrated and computerized knowledge is, the more important this construct is and the more effective it can be.

Additional support for these constructs comes from Alavi and Leidner (1999), who found it important to have an integrated and integrative

technology architecture that supports database, communication, and search and retrieval functions. Davenport, DeLong, and Beers (1998) found technical infrastructure to be crucial to effective KM. Ginsberg and Kambil (1999) found knowledge representation, storage, search, retrieval, visualization, and quality control to be key technical issues. Mandviwalla, Eulgem, Mould, and Rao (1998) described technical issues affecting KMS design to include knowledge storage/repository considerations; how information and knowledge is organized so that it can be searched and linked to appropriate events and use; and processes for integrating the various repositories and for reintegrating information and knowledge extracted from specific events and access locations, as users rarely access the KMS from a single location (leads to network needs and security concerns). Sage and Rouse (1999) identified infrastructure for capturing, searching, retrieving, and displaying knowledge and an understood enterprise knowledge structure as important. Finally, several of the KMS classifications focus on KM support tools, architecture, or life cycle, which all require strong system quality.

Ultimately, given the effectiveness of information technology to rapidly provide search, storage, retrieval, and visualization capabilities, it is expected that a more fully computerized system that utilizes network, semantic Web, and data warehouse technologies will result in the highest levels of system quality.

KNOWLEDGE QUALITY

Jennex and Olfman (2000, 2002) identified that having a KM process and an enterprise-wide knowledge infrastructure, incorporating KM processes into regular work practices, and that knowledge needs were different for users of different levels, were key issues in order to determine and implement what is the right knowledge for KM to capture. Additionally, it was found that

KM users have formal and/or informal drivers that guide them in selecting information and knowledge to be retained by KM and formal and informal processes for reviewing and modifying stored information and knowledge. The Knowledge Quality dimension incorporates this and ensures that the right knowledge with sufficient context is captured and available for the right users at the right time. Three constructs: the KM strategy/process, knowledge richness, and linkages among knowledge components are identified. The KM strategy/process construct looks at the organizational processes for identifying knowledge users and knowledge for capture and reuse, the formality of these processes including process planning, and the format and context of the knowledge to be stored. This construct determines the contents and effectiveness of the other two constructs. Richness reflects the accuracy and timeliness of the stored knowledge as well as having sufficient knowledge context and cultural context to make the knowledge useful. Linkages reflect the knowledge and topic maps and/or listings of expertise available to identify sources of knowledge to users in the organization.

Hansen, Nohria, and Tierney (1999) describe two types of knowledge strategy: personification and codification. They warn of trying to follow both strategies equally at the same time. These strategies refer to how knowledge is captured, represented, retrieved, and used. However, KM strategy/process also needs to reflect that the knowledge needs of the users change over time, as found by the longitudinal study (Jennex & Olfman, 2002) and that new users have a hard time understanding codified tacit knowledge (Koskinen, 2001). For example, new users will follow personification until they understand the context in which knowledge is captured and used, and then they are willing to switch to a codification strategy. Personification corresponds to linkages in the model shown in Figure 3 and refers to the situation in which new users initially feel more comfortable seeking knowledge contexts from recognized human experts on a particular subject. Following this phase, these users tend to switch to codified knowledge; thus, codification corresponds to richness in the model. Additionally, Brown, Dennis, and Gant (2006) found that as the procedural complexity and teachability of knowledge increased, the tendency of users to rely on linkages (person-to-person knowledge transfer) also increased. Jennex (2006) discusses the impact of context and culture on knowledge reuse, and the conclusion is that as knowledge complexity grows, the ability to capture the context and culture information needed to ensure the knowledge is usable and, used correctly, becomes more difficult, and the richness of the stored knowledge is less able to meet this need, which results in users shifting to using linkages and personification. This model disagrees with Hansen, et al.'s (1999) finding that organizations need to select a single strategy on which to concentrate, while using the other strategy in a support role by recognizing that both strategies will exist and that they may be equal in importance.

Additional support for these constructs comes from Barna (2003), who identified creating a standard knowledge submission process, methodologies, and processes for the codification, documentation, and storage of knowledge, processes for capturing and converting individual tacit knowledge into organizational knowledge as important. Cross and Baird (2000) found that in order for KM to improve business performance, it had to increase organizational learning by supporting personal relationships between experts and knowledge users, providing distributed databases to store knowledge and pointers to knowledge, providing work processes for users to convert personal experience into organizational learning, and providing direction to what knowledge the organization needs to capture and from which to learn. Davenport, et al. (1998) identified three key success factors for KM strategy/process: clearly communicated purpose/goals, multiple channels for knowledge transfer, and a standard, flexible knowledge structure. Mandviwalla, et al. (1998) described several strategy issues affecting KM design, which include the KM focus (who are the users); the quantity of knowledge to be captured and in what formats (who filters what is captured); what reliance and/or limitations are placed on the use of individual memories; how long the knowledge is useful; and the work activities and processes that utilize KM. Sage and Rouse (1999) identified modeling processes to identify knowledge needs and sources, KM strategy for the identification of knowledge to capture and use and who will use it, an understood enterprise knowledge structure, and clear KM goals as important.

SERVICE QUALITY

The Service Quality dimension ensures that KM has adequate support in order for users to utilize KM effectively. Three constructs—management support, user KM service quality, and IS KM service quality—are identified. Management support refers to the direction and support an organization needs to provide in order to ensure that adequate resources are allocated to the creation and maintenance of KM; a knowledge sharing and using organizational culture is developed; encouragement, incentives, and direction are provided to the work force to encourage KM use; knowledge reuse; and knowledge sharing; and that sufficient control structures are created in the organization in order to monitor knowledge and KM use. This construct enables the other two constructs. User KM service quality refers to the support provided by user organizations to help their personnel to utilize KM. This support consists of providing training to their users on how to use KM, how to query KM, and guidance and support for making knowledge capture, knowledge reuse, and KM use a part of routine business processes. IS KM service quality refers to the support provided by the IS organization to

KM users and to maintaining KM. This support consists of building and maintaining KM tools and infrastructure; maintaining the knowledge base; building and providing knowledge maps of the databases; and ensuring the reliability, security, and availability of KM.

Our previous KM success model versions included the previous constructs as part of the system quality and knowledge quality dimensions. These constructs were extracted from these dimensions in order to generate the constructs for the service quality dimension and to ensure that the final KM success model was consistent with DeLone and McLean (2003).

Additional support for these constructs comes from Alavi and Leidner (1999), who found organizational and cultural issues associated with user motivation to share and use knowledge to be the most significant. Barna (2003) identified the main managerial success factor as creating and promoting a culture of knowledge sharing within the organization by articulating a corporate KM vision, rewarding employees for knowledge sharing and creating communities of practice. Other managerial success factors include obtaining senior management support, creating a learning organization, providing KM training, precisely defining KM project objectives, and creating relevant and easily accessible knowledge-sharing databases and knowledge maps. Cross and Baird (2000) found that in order for KM to improve business performance, it had to increase organizational learning by supporting personal relationships between experts and knowledge users and by providing incentives to motivate users to learn from experience and to use KM. Davenport, et al. (1998) found senior management support, motivational incentives for KM users, and a knowledge-friendly culture to be critical issues. Ginsberg and Kambil (1999) found incentives to share and use knowledge to be the key organizational issues. Holsapple and Joshi (2000) found leadership and top management commitment/support to be crucial. Resource influences such as having sufficient financial support and skill level of employees were also important. Malhotra and Galletta (2003) identified the critical importance of user commitment and motivation but found that using incentives did not guarantee a successful KMS. Sage and Rouse (1999) identified incentives and motivation to use KM, clear KM goals, and measuring and evaluating the effectiveness of KM as important. Yu, Kim, and Kim (2004) determined that KM drivers such as a learning culture, knowledge-sharing intention, rewards, and KM team activity significantly affected KM performance

USER SATISFACTION

The User Satisfaction dimension is a construct that measures satisfaction with KM by users. It is considered a good complementary measure of KM use, as desire to use KM depends on users being satisfied with KM. User satisfaction is considered a better measure for this dimension than actual KM use, as KM may not be used constantly yet still may be considered effective. Jennex (2005) found that some KM repositories or knowledge processes such as e-mail may be used daily, while others may be used once a year or less. However, it also was found that the importance of the once-a-year use might be greater than that of daily use. This makes actual use a weak measure for this dimension, given that the amount of actual use may have little impact on KM success, as long as KM is used when appropriate and supports DeLone and McLean (2003) in dropping amount of use as a measurement of success.

INTENT TO USE/PERCEIVED BENEFIT

The Intent to Use/Perceived Benefit dimension is a construct that measures perceptions of the benefits of KM by users. It is good for predicting

continued KM use when KM use is voluntary, and amount and/or effectiveness of KM use depend on meeting current and future user needs. Jennex and Olfman (2002) used a perceived benefit instrument adapted from Thompson, et al. (1991) to measure user satisfaction and to predict continued intent to use KM when KM use was voluntary. Thompson, et al.'s (1991) perceived benefit model utilizes Triandis' (1980) theory that perceptions on future consequences predict future actions. This construct adapts the model to measure the relationships among social factors concerning knowledge use, perceived KM complexity, perceived near-term job fit and benefits of knowledge use, perceived long-term benefits of knowledge use, and fear of job loss with respect to willingness to contribute knowledge. Malhotra and Galletta (2003) created an instrument for measuring user commitment and motivation that is similar to Thompson, et al.'s (1991) perceived benefit model but is based on self-determination theory that uses the Perceived Locus of Causality that also may be useful for predicting intent to use. Additionally, Yu, et al. (2004) found that KM drivers such as knowledge-sharing intention significantly affected KM performance.

NET IMPACT

An individual's use of KM will produce an impact on that person's performance in the workplace. In addition, DeLone and McLean (1992) note that an individual impact also could be an indication that an information system has given the user a better understanding of the decision context, has improved his or her decision-making productivity, has produced a change in user activity, or has changed the decision maker's perception of the importance or usefulness of the information system. Each individual impact should have an effect on the performance of the whole organization. Organizational impacts usually are not the summation of individual impacts, so the association between individual and organizational impacts is often difficult to draw. DeLone and McLean (2003) recognized this difficulty and combined all impacts into a single dimension. Davenport, et al. (1998) overcame this by looking for the establishment of linkages to economic performance. Alavi and Leidner (1999) also found it important to measure the benefits of KM, as did Jennex and Olfman (2000).

We agree with combining all impacts into one dimension and the addition of the feedback loop to the User Satisfaction and Intent to Use/Perceived Benefit dimensions but take it a step further and extend the feedback loop to include the KM Strategy/Process construct. Jennex and Olfman (2002) showed this feedback in their model relating KM, OM, organizational learning, and effectiveness, as shown in Figure 4. This model recognizes that the use of knowledge may have good or bad benefits.

It is feedback from these benefits that drives the organization either to use more of the same type of knowledge or to forget the knowledge, which also provides users with feedback on the benefit of the KMS. Alavi and Leidner (2001) also agree that KM should allow for forgetting some knowledge when it has detrimental or no benefits. To ensure that this is done, feedback on the value of stored knowledge needs to be fed into the KM Strategy/Process construct.

OPERATIONALIZATION OF THE SUCCESS MODEL

Jennex and Olfman (2002) performed a longitudinal study of KM in an engineering organization that identified a link between knowledge use and improved organizational effectiveness. Although

Figure 4. The OM/KM model

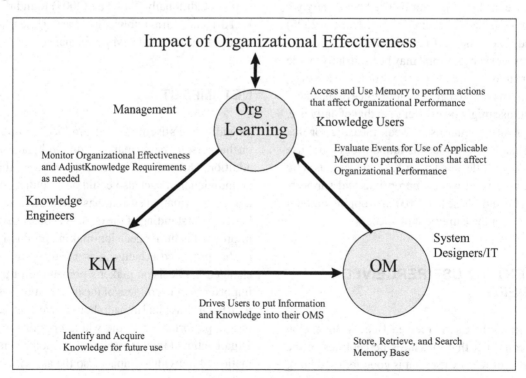

a great deal of quantitative data were taken, it was not possible to quantify productivity gains as a function of knowledge use. KM was found to be effective and to have improved in effectiveness over a five-year period. Additionally, the engineers were found to be more productive.

Jennex (2000) applied an early version of this model to the construction and implementation of a knowledge management Web site for assisting a virtual project team. It was found that applying the model to the design of the site resulted in the project going from lagging to a leading project in just a few months.

Hatami, Galliers, and Huang (2003) used the KM Success Model to analyze knowledge reuse and the effectiveness of decision making. They found the model useful in explaining the effects of culture and knowledge needs on the overall KM success.

Jennex, Olfman, and Addo (2003) investigated the need for having an organizational KM strategy to ensure that knowledge benefits gained from projects are captured for use in the organization. They found that benefits from Y2K projects were not being captured, because the parent organizations did not have a KM strategy/process. Their conclusion was that KM in projects can exist and can assist projects in utilizing knowledge during the project. However, it also led to the conclusion that the parent organization will not benefit from project-based KM unless the organization has an overall KM strategy/process.

The following discussion combines these studies to provide methods of operationalizing the constructs proposed previously. Table 1 summarizes the various measures applied in these studies.

SYSTEM QUALITY

Three constructs were proposed for the system quality dimension: technical resources, KM form, and KM level. Jennex and Olfman (2002)

Table 1. KMS success model data collection methods

Construct	Data Collection Method
Technical Resources	User competency survey, observation and document research of IS capabilities, interview with IS Manager on infrastructure
Form of KMS	Interviews and survey of knowledge sources and form
Level of KMS	Survey of satisfaction with retrieval times, usability testing on KMS functions
KM Strategy/Process	Survey on drivers for putting knowledge into the KMS and for satisfaction with the knowledge in the KMS, check on if a formal strategy/process exists
Richness	Usability test on adequacy of stored knowledge and associated context, interviews and satisfaction survey on adequacy of knowledge in KMS
Linkages	Usability test on adequacy of stored linkages, interviews and satisfaction surveys on satisfaction with linkages stored in KMS
Management Support	Interviews and Social Factors construct of Thompson, Higgins, and Howell's survey on perceived benefit
IS KM Service Quality	Interview with IS Manager on IS capabilities. Interviews with users on needs and capabilities. Suggest adding user satisfaction survey on service issues
User Organization KM Service Quality	Interview with user organization KM team on capabilities and responsibilities, and needs from IS. Interview with users on needs and capabilities. Suggest adding user satisfaction survey on service issues
User Satisfaction	Doll and. Torkzadeh (1988) End User Satisfaction Measure, any other user satisfaction measure
Intent to Use/ Perceived Benefit	Thompson, Higgins, and Howell's (1991) survey on perceived benefit
Net Impacts	Determine Individual and Organizational productivity models through interviews, observation, tend to be specific to organizations

found that the capabilities of the IS organization and the users can impact the success of KM. IS infrastructure and organizational capabilities that enhanced KM effectiveness included a fast, high-capacity infrastructure, strong application development skills, network skills, and awareness of the user organization's knowledge requirements. Users' capabilities that enhanced KM effectiveness included a high degree of computer literacy and high-end personal computers. Given the importance of these technical resources, operationalization of the technical resources construct can be accomplished by focusing on the overall experience of the development group in building and maintaining networked systems that support KM; the computer capabilities of KM end users; and the quality of hardware, network, application, and operating system capabilities of workstations supporting KM.

KM level was defined as the ability to bring past information to bear upon current activities. This can be measured in terms of Stein and Zwass' (1995) mnemonic functions, including knowledge acquisition, retention, maintenance, search, and retrieval. It is expected that more effective KM will include more sophisticated levels of these functions. For example, more sophisticated KM should contain the ability to do filtering, guided exploration, and to grow memory. Usability testing of these functions can serve as measures of how effective they are implemented.

KM form refers to the extent to which knowledge is computerized and integrated. In essence, the more computerized the memory (personification and codification approaches), the more integrated it can be. That is, if all knowledge sources are available in computer-based form, then it will be possible to search and retrieved knowledge more effectively. Integration also speaks to the external consistency of the various KM tools. Jennex and Olfman (2002) found that although much of the KM used by the engineering organization was computerized, there were many different KMS components, each with varying kinds of storage

mechanisms and interfaces. These components were poorly integrated, relying mainly on the copy-and-paste features of the Windows interface and, therefore, limited the ability of workers to utilize KM effectively. It was evident that more sophisticated technical resources could produce a more integrated set of components. Surveys of actual knowledge repositories that are used for KM can determine how much knowledge is stored in computerized forms. It is desired but not practical to have all knowledge in a computer. Assessment of this construct should focus on how much of the knowledge that is practical for computer storage is computerized.

KNOWLEDGE QUALITY

Knowledge quality has three constructs: KM strategy/process, richness, and linkages. Jennex and Olfman (2002) used surveys of users to determine drivers for putting knowledge into KM repositories and user satisfaction with the knowledge that was in these repositories. Jennex, et al. (2003) surveyed organizations to determine if they had a KM strategy and how formal it was. Jennex and Olfman (2002) used interviews of KM users to determine their satisfaction with the accuracy, timeliness, and adequacy of available knowledge. The need for linkages and personification of knowledge was found through interviews with users on where they went to retrieve knowledge. Additionally, it was found that users' KM needs vary, depending on their experience levels in the organization. Context of the knowledge is critical. New members did not have this context, and the knowledge repositories did not store sufficient context in order for a new member to understand and use the stored knowledge. It was found that new members need linkages to the human sources of knowledge. It is not expected that KM will ever be able to do an adequate job of storing context, so it is recommended that KM store linkages to knowledge.

SERVICE QUALITY

Service quality was defined previously as how well the organization supports KM. Three constructs are proposed: management support, IS KM service quality, and user KM service quality. Jennex and Olfman (2002) identified these constructs through interviews that found evidence to show that the service quality of the IS and user organizations can impact KM success and that service quality was determined by the organizations that possess certain capabilities. IS KM service consisted of IS being able to build and maintain KM components and to map the knowledge base. IS organizational capabilities that enhanced this service effectiveness included data integration skills, knowledge representation skills, and awareness of the user organization's knowledge requirements. User organization KM service consisted of incorporating knowledge capture into work processes and being able to identify key knowledge requirements. User organization KM capabilities that enhanced this service effectiveness included understanding and being able to implement KM techniques, such as knowledge taxonomies, ontologies, and knowledge maps, and to process analysis capabilities. Additionally, service was enhanced either by the IS or the user organization providing training on how to construct knowledge searches, where the knowledge was located, and how to use KM.

The key construct—management support—was measured by using interviews and the social factors measure of Thompson, Higgins, and Howell's (1991) survey on perceived benefit. The social factors measure uses a Likert scale survey to determine perceptions of support from peers, supervisors, and managers, and gives a good view of the ability of the organizational culture to support KM and management support for doing KM. Additionally, individual and organizational productivity models were generated by using interviews with managers that provide an assessment of the impact of knowledge use on individuals

and organizations and what incentives are being used to encourage KM participation.

IS organization KM support was measured by determining the overall experience of the development group in building and maintaining networked systems that support KM and the satisfaction of the KM end users with this support. User organization KM support was measured by determining what support was provided and how satisfied the users were with it. Measures assessing specific areas of capability can be used, should less-than-acceptable service satisfaction be found.

USER SATISFACTION

User satisfaction is a construct that measures perceptions of KM by users. This is one of the most frequently measured aspects of IS success, and it is also a construct with a multitude of measurement instruments. User satisfaction can relate to both product and service. As noted, product satisfaction often is used to measure knowledge quality. Product satisfaction can be measured by using the 12-item instrument developed by Doll and Tordzadeh (1988). This measure addresses satisfaction with content, accuracy, format, ease of use, and timeliness. Additionally, measures addressing satisfaction with interfaces should be used. Other user satisfaction measures can be used to assess the specific quality constructs, as discussed in previous paragraphs.

INTENT TO USE/PERCEIVED BENEFIT

Jennex, et al. (1998) used Thompson, Higgins, and Howell's (1991) Perceived Benefit Model to predict continued voluntary usage of KM by the engineering organization. The following four factors from the model plus one added by Jennex and Olfman were in the survey:

- Job fit of KM, near-term consequences of using KM
- Job fit of KM, long-term consequences of using KM
- Social factors in support of using KM
- Complexity of KM tools and processes
- Fear of job loss for contributing knowledge to KM

All five factors were found to support continued KM use during the initial measurements. Jennex and Olfman (2002) found continued KM use throughout the five years of observing KM usage and concluded that the Perceived Benefit model was useful for predicting continued use. Jennex (2000) used these factors to design the site, work processes, and management processes for a virtual project team, using Web-based KM to perform a utility Year 2000 project. Promoting the social factors and providing near-term job fit were critical in ensuring that the virtual project team utilized KM. KM use was considered highly successful, as the project went from performing in the bottom third of utility projects to performing in the top third of all utility projects.

NET BENEFITS

The net benefits dimension looks for any benefits attributed to use of the KMS. We attempted to measure benefits associated with individual and organizational use of KM through the generation of productivity models that identified where knowledge use impacted productivity. KM benefits for an individual are found in their work processes. Jennex and Olfman (2002) queried supervisors and managers in order to determine what they believed was the nature of individual productivity in the context of the station-engineering work process. The interviews revealed a complex set of factors. Those benefiting from KM include the following:

- Timeliness in completing assignments and doing them right the first time
- Number of assignments completed
- Identification and completion of high-priority assignments
- Completeness of solutions
- Quality of solutions (thoroughness and accuracy)
- Complexity of the work that can be assigned to an engineer
- Client satisfaction

While many of these factors are measured quantitatively, it was not possible to directly attribute changes in performance solely to KM use, although improvements in performance were qualitatively attributed to KM use. Additionally, Jennex and Olfman (2002) asked 20 engineers to indicate whether they were more productive now than they were five or 10 years ago, and all but one thought that they were. This improvement was attributed primarily to KM use but also was a qualitative assessment.

Organizational impacts relate to the effectiveness of the organization as a whole. For a nuclear power plant, specific measures of effectiveness were available. These measures relate to assessments performed by external organizations as well as those performed internally. External assessments were found to be the most influenced by KM use. Jennex and Olfman (2002) found measures such as the SALP (Systematic Assessment of Licensee Performance) Reports issued by the Nuclear Regulatory Commission and site evaluations performed by the Institute of Nuclear Power Operations (INPO). Review of SALP scores issued since 1988 showed an increase from a rating of 2 to a rating of 1 in 1996. This rating was maintained through the five years of the study. An INPO evaluation was conducted during the spring of 1996 and resulted in a 1 rating. This rating also was maintained throughout the five years of the study. These assessments identified several strengths directly related to engineer productivity using KM, including decision making, root cause analysis, problem resolution, timeliness, and Operability Assessment documentation. This demonstrates a direct link between engineer productivity and organization productivity. Also, since organization productivity is rated highly, it can be inferred that engineer productivity is high.

Two internal indicators were linked to KM use: unit capacity and unplanned automatic scrams. Unit capacity and unplanned scrams are influenced by how well the engineers evaluate and correct problems. Both indicators improved over time. These two indicators plus unplanned outages and duration of outages became the standard measure during the Jennex and Olfman (2002) study, and reporting and monitoring of these factors significantly improved during the study.

The conclusion is that net benefits should be measured by using measures that are specific to the organization and that are influenced by the use of KM. Suitable measures were found in all the studies used for this article, and it is believed that they can be found for any organization.

CONCLUSION

The DeLone and McLean IS Success Model is a generally accepted model for assessing success of IS. Adapting the model to KM is a viable approach to assessing KM success. The model presented in this article meets the spirit and intent of DeLone and McLean (1992, 2003). Additionally, Jennex (2000) used an earlier version of the KM Success Model to design, build, and implement intranet-based KM that was found to be very effective and successful. The conclusion of this article is that the KM Success Model is a useful model for predicting KM success. It is also useful for designing effective KM.

AREAS FOR FUTURE RESEARCH

DeLone and McLean (1992) stated, "Researchers should systematically combine individual measures from the IS success categories to create a comprehensive measurement instrument" (pp. 87–88). This is the major area for future KM success research. Jennex and Olfman (2002) provided a basis for exploring a quantitative analysis and test of the KM Success Model. To extend this work, it is suggested that a survey instrument to assess the effectiveness of KM within other nuclear power plant engineering organizations in the United States should be developed and administered. Since these organizations have similar characteristics and goals, they provide an opportunity to gain a homogeneous set of data to use for testing the model and, ultimately, to generate a generic set of KM success measures.

Additionally, other measures need to be assessed for applicability to the model. In particular, the Technology Acceptance Model, Perceived Usefulness (Davis, 1989) should be investigated as a possible measure for Intent to Use/Perceived Benefit.

REFERENCES

Alavi, M., & Leidner, D.E. (1999). Knowledge management systems: Emerging views and practices from the field. In *Proceedings of the 32nd Hawaii International Conference on System Sciences*, IEEE Computer Society.

Alavi, M. & Leidner, D.E. (2001). Review: Knowledge management and knowledge management systems: Conceptual foundations and research issues. *MIS Quarterly, 25*(1), 107–136.

Barna, Z. (2003). *Knowledge management: A critical e-business strategic factor*. Master's thesis, San Diego State University, San Diego, CA.

Brown, S.A., Dennis, A.R., & Gant, D.B. (2006). Understanding the factors influencing the value of person-to-person knowledge sharing. In *Proceedings of the 39th Hawaii International Conference on System Sciences.*

Churchman, C.W. (1979). *The systems approach.* New York: Dell Publishing.

Cross, R., Baird, L. (2000). Technology is not enough: Improving performance by building organizational memory. *Sloan Management Review, 41*(3), 41–54.

Davenport, T.H., DeLong, D.W., & Beers, M.C. (1998). Successful knowledge management projects. *Sloan Management Review, 39*(2), 43–57.

Davenport, T.H., & Prusak, L. (1998). *Working knowledge.* Boston: Harvard Business School Press.

Davis, F.D. (1989). Perceived usefulness, perceived ease of use, and user acceptance of information technology. *MIS Quarterly, 13*, 319–340.

DeLone, W.H., & McLean, E.R. (1992). Information systems success: The quest for the dependent variable. *Information Systems Research, 3*, 60–95.

DeLone, W.H., & McLean, E.R. (2003). The De-Lone and McLean model of information systems success: A ten-year update. *Journal of Management Information Systems, 19*(4), 9–30.

Doll, W.J., & Torkzadeh, G. (1988). The measurement of end-user computing satisfaction. *MIS Quarterly, 12*, 259–275.

Ginsberg, M., & Kambil, A. (1999). Annotate: A Web-based knowledge management support system for document collections. In *Proceedings of the 32nd Hawaii International Conference on System Sciences.*

Hansen, M.T., Nohria, N., & Tierney, T. (1999, March-April). What's your strategy for managing knowledge? *Harvard Business Review,* 106–116.

Hatami, A., Galliers, R.D., & Huang, J. (2003). Exploring the impacts of knowledge (re)use and organizational memory on the effectiveness of strategic decisions: A longitudinal case study. In *Proceedings of the 36th Hawaii International Conference on System Sciences.*

Holsapple, C.W., & Joshi, K.D. (2000). An investigation of factors that influence the management of knowledge in organizations. *Journal of Strategic Information Systems, 9*, 235–261.

Huber, G.P., Davenport, T.H., & King, D. (1998). Some perspectives on organizational memory (Working Paper for the Task Force on Organizational Memory). In *Proceedings of the 31st Annual Hawaii International Conference on System Sciences.*

Jennex, M.E. (2000). Using an intranet to manage knowledge for a virtual project team. In D.G. Schwartz, M. Divitini, & T. Brasethvik (Eds.), *Internet-based organizational memory and knowledge management* (pp. 241–259). Hershey, PA: Idea Group Publishing.

Jennex, M.E. (2005). What is knowledge management? *International Journal of Knowledge Management, 1*(4), i–iv.

Jennex, M.E. (2006). Culture, context, and knowledge management. *International Journal of Knowledge Management, 2*(2), i–iv.

Jennex, M.E., & Croasdell, D. (2005). Knowledge management: Are we a discipline? *International Journal of Knowledge Management, 1*(1), i–v.

Jennex, M.E., & Olfman, L. (2000). Development recommendations for knowledge management/organizational memory systems. In *Proceedings of the Information Systems Development Conference.*

Jennex, M.E., & Olfman, L. (2002). Organizational memory/knowledge effects on productivity: A longitudinal study. In *Proceedings of the 35th Annual Hawaii International Conference on System Sciences*.

Jennex, M.E., Olfman, L., & Addo, T.B.A. (2003). *T*he need for an organizational knowledge management strategy. In *Proceedings of the 36th Hawaii International Conference on System Sciences*.

Jennex, M.E., Olfman, L., Pituma, P., & Yong-Tae, P. (1998). An organizational memory information systems success model: An extension of DeLone and McLean's I/S success model. In *Proceedings of the 31st Annual Hawaii International Conference on System Sciences*.

Koskinen, K.U. (2001). Tacit knowledge as a promoter of success in technology firms. In *Proceedings of the 34th Hawaii International Conference on System Sciences*.

Maier, R. (2002). *Knowledge management systems: Information and communication technologies for knowledge management*. Berlin: Springer-Verlag.

Malhotra, Y., & Galletta, D. (2003). Role of commitment and motivation as antecedents of knowledge management systems implementation. In *Proceedings of the 36th Hawaii International Conference on System Sciences*.

Mandviwalla, M., Eulgem, S., Mould, C., & Rao, S.V. (1998). Organizational memory systems design [working paper for the Task Force on Organizational Memory]. In *Proceedings of the 31st Annual Hawaii International Conference on System Sciences*.

Nonaka, I. (1994). A dynamic theory of organizational knowledge creation. *Organization Science, 5*(1), 14–37.

Polanyi, M. (1962). *Personal knowledge: Toward a post-critical philosophy*. New York: Harper Torchbooks.

Polanyi, M. (1967). *The tacit dimension*. London: Routledge and Keoan Paul.

Sage, A.P., & Rouse, W.B. (1999). Information systems frontiers in knowledge management. *Information Systems Frontiers, 1*(3), 205–219.

Stein, E.W., & Zwass, V. (1995). Actualizing organizational memory with information systems. *Information Systems Research, 6*(2), 85–117.

Thompson, R.L., Higgins, C.A., & Howell, J.M. (1991). Personal computing: Toward a conceptual model of utilization. *MIS Quarterly, 15*(1), 125–143.

Triandis, H.C. (1980). *Beliefs, attitudes, and values*. Lincoln, NE: University of Nebraska Press.

Turban, E., & Aronson, J.E. (2001). *Decision support systems and intelligent systems* (6th ed.). Upper Saddle River, NJ: Pearson/Prentice Hall.

Walsh, J.P., & Ungson, G.R. (1991). Organizational memory. *Academy of Management Review, 16*(1), 57–91.

Yu, S.-H., Kim, Y.-G., & Kim, M.-Y. (2004). Linking organizational knowledge management drivers to knowledge management performance: An exploratory study. In *Proceedings of the 37th Hawaii International Conference on System Sciences*.

This work was previously published in International Journal of Knowledge Management, Vol. 2, Issue 3, edited by M.E. Jennex, pp. 51-68, copyright 2006 by IGI Publishing, formerly known as Idea Group Publishing (an imprint of IGI Global).

Section II
Advances in Knowledge Transfer, Sharing, and Flow

Chapter V
Think Social Capital Before You Think Knowledge Transfer

Karma Sherif
Texas Southern University, USA

Sherif Ahmed Sherif
The Egyptian Ministry of Foreign Trade and Industry, Egypt

ABSTRACT

Knowledge transfer has been promoted as a critical and necessary condition in order for organizations to sustain competitive advantage. In this article, we argue that successful transfer of knowledge within organizations will depend on the accumulated social capital embedded within organizational social networks. We pose social capital as a critical factor for knowledge transfer and hypothesize that the structural, relational, and cognitive dimensions of social capital must be developed within an organization in order for knowledge transfer to impact organizational performance. The study uses data collected from Egypt to test the model. Hofstede's Cultural Dimensions Model is used to explain how cultural attributes limit the accumulation of social capital and the effectiveness of knowledge transfer in developing countries.

INTRODUCTION

For the last decade, Knowledge Management (KM) (Davenport & Prusak, 1998) has been positioned as a business strategy that advances knowledge as a critical resource and the capacity to integrate pieces of it across the organization

as a distinguishing feature for success within the market (Grant, 1996). The strategy promotes the transfer of knowledge within organizations (Alavi & Leidner, 2001, Holsapple & Joshi, 2002), and focuses on the capture, articulation, and dissemination of knowledge in an effort to build dynamic capabilities and to respond quickly to

Copyright © 2008, IGI Global, distributing in print or electronic forms without written permission of IGI Global is prohibited.

environmental changes (Teece, Pisano & Shuen, 1997).

Research on knowledge transfer within and across organizations have focused on various factors, including individual attitudes toward knowledge sharing (Wasko & Faraj, 2005), knowledge processes (Markus et al., 2002), and technology (Alavi & Leidner, 2001) as means to enhance organizational capabilities in order to manage knowledge and to replicate successes across the organization. Despite relentless efforts to systematically define processes and market technology solutions, recent studies have pointed out that 70% of organizations implementing an organization-wide strategy for knowledge transfer fails to realize improvement in performance or to develop core competencies (Malhotra, 2005). Among the critical factors highlighted (Holsapple & Joshi, 2002; Massey, Montoya-Weiss, & O'Driscoll, 2002) are (1) failure to emphasize knowledge transfer as a business objective; (2) failure to embed knowledge transfer in daily processes; (3) failure to implement technology that facilitates the transfer of knowledge; and (4) failure to foster a knowledge-sharing culture.

In this study, we focus on social capital as another critical factor for the success of knowledge transfer. Social capital is defined as the resources inlaid in social networks that contribute to career success (Seibert, Kraimer & Liden, 2001) and the to development of intellectual capital (Nahapiet & Ghoshal, 1998). It includes the social relationships and the resources available through these relationships (Portes, 1998). Recent studies have empirically associated social capital with the transfer of knowledge (Tsai & Ghoshal, 1998; Inkpen & Tsang, 2005), focusing on the role of social relationships in facilitating the transfer of knowledge within and across organizations. The study is encouraged by the proposition that knowledge sharing develops better in social networks than within hierarchical organizational structures (Palmer & Richards, 1999). While it

is not the role of corporations to deliver *social* services, their abilities to enhance *social capital* by partnering with individual members can contribute both to development and to work to their own commercial advantage.

There has been movement within developing countries to adopt knowledge management programs in order to facilitate knowledge transfer. However, the focus largely has been on the use of Communication Technologies (CT) without the realization that CT's use depends, to a large extent, on the network structure (Ahuja, Galleta, & Carley, 2003) and to the accumulated social capital to which individuals have access (Powell, Koput & Smith-Doer, 1996). It is true that CT is capable of connecting people across space, time, and organizational boundaries. However, individual ties connected solely through CT likely are to be weak (Gargiulo & Benassi, 2000). Strong social ties, trust, and cooperation (Coleman, 1988; Walker, Kogut, & Shan, 1997) are critical in order for CT to facilitate knowledge transfer.

In this article, we argue that communities that are low in social capital will have limited capacity to transfer knowledge. A lack of connections, trust, and shared understanding will limit the accessibility to pools of knowledge and will throttle knowledge transfer. Building upon social capital (Coleman, 1988; Nahapiet & Ghoshal, 1998) and network structure (Burt, 1992; Putnam, 1995), we developed our conceptual model (see Figure 1). We validated our model using qualitative data collected from 13 organizations in Egypt. Hofstede's (1980) cultural dimensions model is used to analyze the data and to highlight the importance of *social capital* in moving toward a sustainable knowledge-sharing organizational culture.

The article is structured as follows: the conceptual model is developed in section 2; section 3 details the research methodology; and empirical results and their implications are discussed in section 4. The article concludes with a summary and implications for future research.

Conceptual Model

Prior research pointed out that some organizations appear to have the capability to effectively transfer knowledge better than other organizations. The underlying mechanisms that create this capability focus on formulating strategies that highlight the importance of knowledge transfer, embedding knowledge transfer within daily business processes and adopting technologies that facilitate knowledge sharing. This article proposes social capital as the underlying mechanism for transferring knowledge. We argue that the dimensions of social capital develop the right infrastructure on top of which initiatives to transfer knowledge across an organization can be capitalized and leveraged. The main thesis we develop is that social capital allows for relationships and exchanges to occur; both have been identified as preconditions for successful knowledge transfer (Davenport & Prusak, 1998). In order to explore this proposition, we examined how each of the three dimensions of social capital influences knowledge transfer.

Our model (Figure 1) connects social capital with knowledge transfer. It posits that in order for social relationships to have a positive impact on the transfer of knowledge, organizations need to accumulate social capital. We expect the structural element of social capital (connectivity) to establish and maintain a wide range of social relationships and to give access to diverse pools of knowledge

(Burt, 1992). As social ties become stronger through frequent communication and multiplex relationships, the relational element (trust) is likely to emerge, which, in turn, facilitates the transfer of complex knowledge and supports its recombination, extension, and application within organizations. Members of such a network are likely to share a common frame of reference (the cognitive dimension of social capital) that facilitates understanding and the ease the exchange of knowledge. This theoretical perspective has the potential to considerably enhance scholars' knowledge of the role of social processes in enabling the transfer of knowledge.

Social Capital

Social capital is a term that emerged from community studies in order to describe relational resources embedded within personal ties in a community. It is recognized as value embedded in social networks that facilitate the actions of individual members (Seibert et al., 2001) and contribute to the development of intellectual capital (Nahapiet & Ghoshal, 1998). Social capital constitutes the relationships and the resources available through these relationships (Portes, 1998). Three dimensions of social capital—structural, relational, and cognitive—combine to define ties that exist among members of the network (Tsai & Ghoshal, 1998). The dimensions individually and

Figure 1. A model of social capital and knowledge transfer

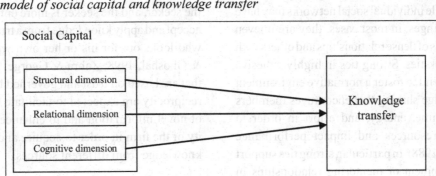

collectively confer several resources to members; among which are shared understanding, trust (Nahapiet & Ghoshal, 1998), knowledge sharing, and knowledge spillover (Ahuja, 2000).

The Structural Dimension

The structural dimension describes the connections established within the network. It is defined as "the arrangement of the differentiated elements that can be recognized as the patterned flows of information in a communication network" (Rogers & Kincaid, 1981, p. 82). Research on network structure has identified two main mechanisms that influence knowledge transfer: social cohesion and network range (Reagans & McEvily, 2003). Social cohesion measures the strength of ties among connected individuals in a network as well as the distance between the nodes. Strong ties are characterized by "sustained, focused, and relatively intense interaction" that involves frequent meetings with specific agendas in order to coordinate mutual dependencies (Ahuja, 2000, p. 430). The shorter the distance between individuals, the higher the possibility of overlapping ties among mutual third parties (Portes, 1998). Range measures the diversity of knowledge pools that are embedded within a network. Networks that span organizational units, organizational boundaries, and industries (Koka & Prescott, 2002; Tsai, 2000) are likely to be tied to different sources of knowledge, which enables members to combine, extend, and apply knowledge from different domains (Burt, 1992; Gargiulo & Benassi, 2000). While individual social networks may have different ranges, in most cases, they are uneven with regions of dense relationships and others with sparse weak ties. Strong ties in highly cohesive networks tend to foster a normative environment of knowledge sharing that encourages members to invest time, energy, and effort in order to exchange resources and impact performance (Coleman, 1988). In particular, strong ties support the development of mentoring relationships in

order to guide the knowledge creation activities of junior and less-experienced members (Seibert et al., 2001). In this article, we argue that a wide-range network with some strong ties is needed to facilitate knowledge transfer. As Tsai (2000) argues, "the sooner the actor can create a new relationship, the earlier it can obtain the required resources and support" (p. 927).

The Relational Dimension

The relational dimension of social capital refers to resources embedded in relationships that members develop as they interact with each other. The intense and repeated interaction among members of a network results in relationships characterized with trust and reciprocity. As members become comfortable with each other's competences and reliabilities, trust develops among members and increases the incentive to exchange knowledge (Nahapiet & Ghoshal, 1998).

Key elements of the relational dimension, reciprocity, and trust are believed to be a significant antecedent for the transfer of knowledge (Tsai & Ghoshal, 1998; Zahra & George, 2002). Without the norms of reciprocity, the social cost of sharing knowledge discourages knowledge transfer because of the fear of losing a comparative advantage without the collateral of getting credit or social benefits in return.

The development of trust reduces the need to monitor relationships and facilitates knowledge transfer, as the source becomes willing to invest time and intellectual resources in order to help the seeker, and the seeker is more enthusiastic to accept and apply knowledge from a trusted source who looks out for his or her own welfare (Tsai & Ghoshal, 1998; Zahra & George, 2002). Ties that are based on trust and governed by norms of reciprocity are expected to facilitate the transfer of novel information and to enhance the capacity of the firm in order to acquire and assimilate knowledge from different sources.

The Cognitive Dimension

The cognitive dimension of social capital refers to the common knowledge that develops among members of the network, as the frequency and depth of their social interactions intensify (Nahapiet & Ghoshal, 1998). Through interaction, members are able to recognize and comprehend specialized language and information exchanged in communication across the network. A frame of reference starts to surface, developing into shared goals and approaches to the achievement of tasks and outcomes (Inkpen & Tsang, 2005).

It is the shared context that explains the relevant conditions and surrounding influences that make knowledge comprehensible to the users (Jennex, 2006). Without a shared context, knowledge exchanges cannot be utilized readily. The development of common context is an important requisite for the transfer of knowledge (Nonaka, 1994), especially tacit knowledge (Seibert et al., 2001; Tsai & Ghoshal, 1998). The common understanding enhances the absorptive capacity of members and facilitates the assimilation of knowledge (Nonaka, 1994). Members are able to acquire the observable explicit knowledge as well as the deeper tacit knowledge embedded in insights and intuition. Without the cognitive dimension, it will be difficult to transfer knowledge among people with different cultures and different knowledge structures (Jennex, 2006; Kwan & Balasubramanian, 2003).

KNOWLEDGE TRANSFER

Knowledge transfer is the "process through which one network member is affected by the experience of another" (Inkpen & Tsang, 2005, p. 146). Through knowledge transfer, recipients increase their stock of knowledge and exploit it in ways that improve organizational processes. Thus, organizations that are able to transfer knowledge effectively among its members are better capable

to compete and respond to environmental changes (Argote, McEvily & Reagans, 2003).

Due to the limited ability of organizations to search and find new knowledge within its existing knowledge base, be it human or electronic, social networks play an important role in facilitating and speeding up the informal transfer of unstructured knowledge. As Powell states, "the most useful information is rarely that which flows down the formal chain of command in an organization. ... Rather, it is that which is obtained from someone you have dealt with in the past and found to be reliable" (Powell, 1990, p. 304).

The effectiveness of organizational knowledge transfer is facilitated by the strength of the tie, trust, and understanding that the recipient shares with the source. Strong ties create added opportunities for the transfer of knowledge and affect the flexibility and ease of knowledge exchange. Trust plays a key role in the willingness of organizational members to share valuable knowledge (Inkpen & Tsang, 2005). A lack of trust may lead to knowledge hoarding and competitive confusion, which limit organizational abilities to benefit from developed skills. As trust develops over time, members feel less pressured to protect their knowledge and skills and start to commit to the free exchange of knowledge. The shared understanding and the common language that evolve between members in the network ensure that knowledge is absorbed and exploited.

SOCIAL CAPITAL AND KNOWLEDGE TRANSFER

While each of the three dimensions of social capital forms a distinct and coherent construct, collectively they provide accumulated benefits to the organization in enabling knowledge transfer. The intensive and repeated communication among individuals within an organizational network helps to create strong ties that are based on trust and shared understanding. Trust increases the willingness of knowledge experts to share novel and tacit knowledge. Shared understanding, on the other hand, enables the seeker to absorb the knowledge shared and to exploit it in ways that are beneficial to the organization.

Failing to accumulate all three dimensions of social capital would limit the organization's capacity to transfer knowledge across its boundaries. First, the lack of repeated interaction may restrict knowledge sharing to just explicit knowledge. Members of the network will not be able to mobilize the knowledge fast enough in order for it to be integrated in a timely fashion to benefit the organization. The limited interaction likely will develop limited trust that becomes susceptible to the slightest behavior of opportunism. In such a network, there is no motivation for collaboration. The lack of persistent social ties leaves members preoccupied with promoting personal interests and less concerned with promoting the overall welfare of the community. A prisoner's dilemma is likely to occur with members trying to acquire knowledge from others without volunteering to share what they know. Over time, an environment of mistrust restricts the organization from locating or exploiting knowledge that it already has. Organizational members with authoritative power may be successful in coercing knowledge sources to externalize knowledge they have.

Based on this theory, we developed the following hypothesis:

Hypothesis 1: Companies experiencing difficulty in transferring knowledge across its boundaries will have low levels of social capital.

H1a: Companies experiencing difficulty in transferring knowledge will have low levels of the structural dimension of social capital.

H1b: Companies experiencing difficulty in transferring knowledge will have low levels of the relational dimension of social capital.

H1c: Companies experiencing difficulty in transferring knowledge will have low levels of the cognitive dimension of social capital.

KNOWLEDGE TRANSFER, SOCIAL CAPITAL, AND EGYPT

Given the recent interest of developing countries in managing knowledge and its focus on diffusing information and communication technologies to actualize knowledge management, we collected data from several organizations in Egypt in order to test whether the current level of social capital embedded within internal networks in Egyptian organizations will enable the success of the knowledge transfer initiatives.

It is our goal to study the appropriateness of applying our conceptual model in the context of developing economies. Toward this goal, we

Table 1. Organizations and participants

Type of organization	Number of organizations	Number of participants
Governmental agencies	2	13
Office for international Aid	1	1
Public Petroleum company	1	1
Telecommunication	1	1
Software development	5	1
Insurance	1	2
fitness center	1	1
Multinational office Equipment	1	1
Total	13	21

present the results of an empirical study in 13 organizations in Egypt. Table 1 shows the distribution for the participating organization and the participants in the study. The implications for a context-specific framework on knowledge transfer in organizations in developing countries then are presented.

Most of the knowledge related initiatives in Egypt have been at the country and community levels with limited emphasis at the organizational level. According to the World Development report for Africa, Egypt needs to work fast in order to increase its knowledge base, to invest in educating the people about knowledge management, and to take advantage of the new technologies for acquiring and disseminating knowledge (World Bank Group, 1998). The report emphasizes the importance of (1) instituting policies that enable them to narrow the knowledge gaps that separate poor countries from rich countries; (2) promoting collaborations among the organizations—governments, multilateral institutions, nongovernmental organizations, and the private sector—in order to work together; and (3) nurturing a knowledge-sharing culture.

In an attempt to test the model, we collected qualitative data from 21 individuals working in 13 organizations in Egypt. The questions focused on their beliefs regarding social capital and knowledge transfer in their organizations. Seven of the organizations came from the private sector, and six were governmental agencies. We limited the questions to social capital in closed networks, where all members of the network are connected.

We use Hofstede's (1980) cultural dimensions as a way of providing a context for our findings and a mean to generalize results in order to communities with similar cultural values. We found evidence for four of Hofstede's (1980) five dimensions[1]:

- **Power distance index (PDI):** Captures the degree of equality in power among members

of a society and opportunities for upward mobility.

- **Individualism (IDV):** Measures the degree to which the society values individual achievement over collective interpersonal relationships.
- **Uncertainty avoidance index (UAI):** Focuses on the degree of tolerance for uncertainty and ambiguity and readiness for change.
- **Long-term orientation (LTO):** Measures a country's long-term commitment to values and respect for tradition.
- **Power distance index (PDI):** The organizational culture in Egypt is different from that which is found in Western countries in that there is a default asymmetry of information between those who govern and those who serve. The overwhelming majority of organizations in Egypt follows a hierarchical structure, where the rules and policies allow the governing bodies the discretion to pursue policies that are aligned more with their interests than with the interests of the agents. The lack of transparency and accountability at the top of organizations has limited the positive effects of several economic development initiatives in Egypt. Thus, hopes for improving the dissemination of knowledge across organizations are tied to efforts to reduce the scope of power abuses within organizations and in the society as a whole (Stiglitz, 2002).
- **Individualism (IDV):** Despite the fact that the social setting is characterized as highly collective, where members of a community are linked closely and see themselves belonging to one or more collectives (e.g., family, religious affiliations, political group), the Egyptian industrial communities are highly individualistic with individuals motivated to pursue their own preferences and needs. Such an individualistic perspective has a tremendous effect on knowledge transfer

within organizations in Egypt. Knowledge and information are not exchanged freely within organizations. Being the main source of power for middle- and low-level managers, knowledge resources are guarded heavily. While agents have limited control over the upward movement of information and knowledge, the resources definitely are protected from being trickled down or disseminated laterally. The misuses of power within the system lead to a culture of mistrust where employees have doubts that they will get credit for voluntary information sharing with their superiors. They also fear that parting with information will diminish their bargaining power within the organization.

- **Uncertainty avoidance index (UAI):** Egypt's corporate world is guarded heavily with strict rules, regulations, and controls in order to reduce the amount of freedom that individuals at the lower level of the organization have at their discretion. The rules are defined by members of top management in order to reinforce their own leadership and control. Despite aspirations for change, efforts are made to maintain the status quo and to reduce risks.

- **Long-term orientation (LTO):** measures a country's long-term commitment to values and respect for tradition. At an aggregate level, it appears that Egypt experiences a high long-term orientation because it embraces traditions. Data collected in this study showed that at an individual level, there is a low long-term orientation. Individuals are skeptical that they will be rewarded in an instrumental way for following the rules. They understand that controls are set in place in order to prevent any usurpation practices for shaking the power structure in place. Their limited authority causes them to doubt the perceived benefits of process innovations like knowledge management.

Social Capital: The Structural Dimension in Egyptian Organizations

In agreement with the characterization that Egypt's social setting is highly collective, participants from private and public sectors alike believed that they enjoyed a central position on their closed network with frequent communication with members of the network. They believed communication is important for several reasons: to reach consensus on differences, to improve the flow of daily work activities, and to get work done. However, the network was not highly adaptable. Participants did not believe they could use the network for alternative objectives. The findings accord with earlier studies that reported the difficulty of managers to adapt relationships in closed networks. Closed networks are believed to restrict managers' abilities to adapt relationships in order to suit new task assignments (Gargiulo & Benassi, 2000).

The Relational Dimension in Egyptian Organizations

There were similar patterns in the beliefs regarding the relational dimension of social capital between participants in the public and the private sectors. The majority of participants believed that they cannot readily trust those with whom they frequently communicate. Several issues were raised, among which are culture, where one participant believes that "it is very hard to trust in the Egyptian environment." Credibility was also an issue, where participants believed that they have difficulty assessing the credibility of the information shared. Knowledge owners believed that they do not get credit for the information they share with others, reporting that "it is difficult to know if you get credit, especially if you get your instructions from somebody other than the boss," and "work is not reported to a higher level." Participants also believed that "it is not part of the spirit of the organization" to get credit for sharing knowledge. Participants added that organizations lack the right social norms in order to promote knowledge sharing. In only one case, a participant believed that members of his organization shared information (not knowledge) for reciprocity and to secure cooperation in future encounters. Their only obligation for knowledge sharing in Egyptian organizations is toward superiors in the organizational hierarchy, but members do not feel any social responsibility to promote the collective knowledge of the organization. The interesting observation is that participants share with their superiors but do not trust those above them to look out for their interests.

The Cognitive Dimension in Egyptian Organizations

Beliefs on the cognitive dimension among participants of the public and the private sectors again were similar. Participants believed that jargons in their field are common among members of the organization; however, technology-related vocabulary is not shared widely. There are some who are personally motivated to learn more about the technology and to know more than others. Shared narratives are common within Egyptian organizations, however, as one participant pointed out that "the narratives are frustrating" because "most of these stories are about frustrations we face in our work."

Knowledge Sharing in Egyptian Organizations

Participants in this study believed that knowledge sharing is important and needs to be fostered and promoted by top management. They believed that knowledge sharing only happens when accompanied by instructions but does not occur freely. Participants believed that members of the organization are not aware of where the knowledge

resides within the organization and are skeptical if others are willing to share.

Both the Power Distance Index and Individualism help to explain difficulty in knowledge transfers in corporate Egypt. The concentration of power at the top and lack of control at middle and low levels cause sources of knowledge at this level to protect their competitive positions and to constrain peer-to peer knowledge transfers. Individuals do not trust their superiors but continue to transfer knowledge upwards to keep their jobs. Since peers have little authority over promotions and job security, there is no incentive to share knowledge that may not be reciprocated.

DISCUSSION

Given the beliefs of participants in this study, we argue that actualizing knowledge transfer where it can affect performance and increase the joint value of organizations will be highly contingent on the social capital available for members of the organizations. The current study highlights the need for a change in network relationships and efforts to build the relational dimension of social capital. While the structural and cognitive dimensions are already in place, the insubstantiality of the relational dimension and the focus on individual achievement are curtailing members from sharing their expertise. It becomes apparent that establishing connections with significant others is not sufficient if trust is lacking. What we observed in the Egyptian organizations is an exchange of information related to frustrations with work rather than an exchange of knowledge related to work processes and outcomes. It is apparent that the lack of trust in getting credit for the information they share makes it hard for them to volunteer their expertise unless instructed to do so and unless they feel the risk of not obeying commands.

Organizations need to take a structured approach to build aspects of the different dimension of social capital to augment the newly born knowledge management spirit in Egypt. In particular, organizations need to take a systematic approach to build social norms that promote knowledge sharing. Given the individualistic orientation of corporate Egypt, it is unlikely that social capital can be accumulated without top management reform. The initiative has to start at the top in order for knowledge workers to have confidence in the system and to be able to cross the cultural gap between a knowledge-hoarding and a knowledge-sharing environment. The initiative must define several processes in order to enable the cultural transition. Among these are the following:

1. Launch initiatives to capture expertise and to ensure that they are regularly embedded within business processes. It is important to validate the knowledge in cultures with limited quality management capabilities.
2. Interject organizational structures that facilitate horizontal communication and sharing of knowledge. The creation of cross functional groups to discuss achievements and lessons learned on a regular basis will facilitate the sharing of information and make it a norm within the organization.
3. Create an incentive system that rewards members for knowledge sharing. The incentives will help to regain trust in the system by assigning credit where it belongs.
4. Stress the need for sharing at all levels of the organization. This will help to generate new ideas for improving business processes at the strategic and operational levels. It will also help to foster the collective spirit and to align individual goals with the overall organizational objectives.
5. While technology can help to capture and disseminate knowledge in these organizations, we stress the need for building the infrastructure before rushing into technological solutions. Results of technology implementation can favorably affect performance, if the technology is aligned with the business objectives and are tailored to daily business activities.

Although several researchers have promoted models for the facilitation of knowledge sharing in organizations (Davenport & Prusak, 1998; Holsapple & Joshi, 2002; Massey et al., 2002), they assumed that social capital already is accumulated. For example, Holsapple and Joshi (2002) synthesized factors affecting the management of knowledge to three main categories: economic, technological, and environmental. Massey, et al. (2002) posited that by focusing on business processes, roles, and technology, organizations can support the process of knowledge creation and knowledge transfer. Both of these models assumed that if organizations follow their prescriptive models, they will enable the transfer of knowledge. This article argues that the development of social capital as an infrastructure for knowledge transfer is a critical facilitator of knowledge transfer within organizations.

CONCLUSION

The purpose of this article is to examine the relationship between social capital and knowledge transfer. Theoretical work in the field of social networks was used as the foundation on which to examine this relationship. Our main theoretical premise is that social capital is a valuable resource that can lead to the creation of an abundance of other resources that lead to knowledge transfer. Previous studies have focused on the positive relationship between social capital and knowledge transfer. This study extends prior research by demonstrating the effect of a lack of social capital on knowledge transfer. The article emphasizes the need to develop trust in order to enable the formation of a knowledge-sharing culture in which knowledge is free to flow across the organization and in which all people have equal rights to it.

The study uses data collected from several organizations in Egypt. We used Hofstede's (1980) cultural dimensions in order to explain the lack of social capital in corporate Egypt. The analysis emphasized the need to overcome the challenges of political corruption in order for organizations to develop the capacity for knowledge transfer and for people to trust each other and to feel less protective of their knowledge. In order for members to be willing to share knowledge, they must recognize that cooperation and knowledge sharing can enhance their positions within their unit and within the organization as a whole. Combining members' knowledge resources can lead to collaborative knowledge creation that has the potential to limit the economic and knowledge gaps that exist within Egyptian organizations.

Social capital adds a whole new dimension to the understanding of knowledge transfer by accounting for the value of social relationships in organizations. The three dimensions of social capital have important implications for knowledge transfer. Each dimension facilitates one aspect of knowledge transfer within organizations. The structural dimension establishes connections among members of the organization and, thus, helps to identify the pockets of knowledge within the network. However, by itself, the structural dimension doesn't guarantee knowledge sharing, if members of the organization do not trust each other. Even when trust develops, a shared understanding also must exist among members in order to ensure that knowledge shared is actually absorbed and can be exploited across the organization.

One limitation of this study is the small size of our sample. In an effort to compare results across the public and private sectors, we had one participant in most of the sites we visited. Another limitation of the study is its scope: we only studied organizations in one developing country. We only can generalize our findings to communities with similar cultural values. Nonetheless, the findings have practical implications for managers of

businesses in general and, specifically, those in Egyptian organizations that are trying to enhance the organization capacity to transfer knowledge. Since resources within all businesses are relatively limited and particularly so in developing countries, the revelation that social capital can lead to more effective knowledge transfer makes the decision to support and nurture it much more credible. It is hoped that this study will serve as a point of reference for future research on the relationship between social capital and knowledge transfer. Additionally, it is hoped that this study will serve as a foundation for future studies looking at cross-cultural differences in the transfer of knowledge across organizations.

REFERENCES

Ahuja, G. (2000). Collaboration networks, structural holes, and innovation: A longitudinal study. *Administrative Science Quarterly, 45*(3), 425-457.

Ahuja, M.K., Galleta, D.F., & Carley, K.M. (2003). Individual centrality and performance in virtual R&D groups: An empirical study. *Management Science, 49*(1), 21-39.

Alavi, M., & Leidner, D. (2001). Review: Knowledge management and knowledge management systems: Conceptual foundations and research issues. *MIS Quarterly, 25*(1), 107-136.

Argote, L., McEvily, B., & Reagans, R. (2003). Managing knowledge in organizations: An integrative framework and review of emerging themes. *Management Science, 49*(4), 571-582.

Burt, R.S. (1992). *Structural holes: The social structure of competition*. Cambridge, MA: Harvard University Press.

Coleman, J.S. (1988). Social capital in the creation of human capital. *American Journal of Sociology, 94*, 95-120.

Davenport, T.H., & Prusak, L. (1998). *Working knowledge: How organizations manage what they know.* Boston: Harvard Business School Press.

Gargiulo, M., & Benassi, M. (2000). Trapped in your own net? Network cohesion, structural holes, and the adaptation of social capital. *Organization Science, 11*(2), 183-197.

Grant, R.M. (1996). Toward a knowledge-based theory of the firm. *Strategic Management Journal, 17*, 109-122.

Hofstede, G.H. (1980). *Culture's consequences.* Thousand Oaks, CA: Sage Publications.

Holsapple, C.W., & Joshi, K.D. (2002). Knowledge management: A threefold framework. *Information Society, 18*(1), 47-64.

Inkpen, A.C., & Tsang, E.W. (2005). Social capital, networks, and knowledge transfer. Academy of Management Review, 30(1), 146-165.

Jennex, M.E. (2006). Classifying knowledge management systems based on context content. *Hawaii International Conference on Systems Sciences.* IEEE.

Koka, B.R., & Prescott, J.E. (2002). Strategic alliances as social capital: A multidimensional view. *Strategic Management Journal, 23*, 795-816.

Kwan, M.M., & Balasubramanian, P. (2003). KnowledgeScope: Managing knowledge in context. *Decision Support Systems, 35*(4), 467-486.

Malhotra, Y. (2005). Integrating knowledge management technologies in organizational business processes: Getting real time enterprises to deliver real business performance. *Journal of Knowledge Management, 9*(1), 7-29.

Markus, M.L., Majchrzak, A., & Gasser, L. (2002). A design theory for systems that support emergent knowledge processes. *MIS Quarterly, 26*(3), 179–212.

Massey, A.P., Montoya-Weiss, M.M., & O'Driscoll, T.M. (2002). Knowledge management in pursuit of performance: Insights from Nortel networks. *MIS Quarterly, 26*(3), 269-289.

Nahapiet, J., & Ghoshal, S. (1998). Social capital, intellectual capital, and the organizational advantage. *Academy of Management Review, 23*(2), 242-266.

Nonaka, I. (1994). A dynamic theory of organizational knowledge creation. *Organization Science, 5*(1), 14-37.

Palmer, J., & Richards, I. (1999). Get knetted: Network behavior in the new economy. *Journal of Knowledge Management, 3*(3), 191-202.

Portes, A. (1998). Social capital: Its origins and applications in modern sociology. *Annual Review of Sociology, 24*, 1-24.

Powell, W. (1990). Neither market nor hierarchy: Network forms of organization. *Research in Organizational Behavior, 12*, 295–336. Retrieved from http://www.stanford.edu/~woodyp/paper_index.htm

Powell, W.W., Koput, K.W., & Smith-Doer, L. (1996). Interorganizational collaboration and the locus of innovation: Networks of learning in biotechnology. *Administrative Science Quarterly, 41*, 116-145.

Putnam, R.D. (1995). Bowling alone: America's declining social capital. *Journal of Democracy, 6*, 65-78.

Reagans, R., & McEvily, B. (2003). Network structure and knowledge transfer: The effects of cohesion and range. *Administrative Science Quarterly, 48*(2), 240-267.

Rogers, E.M., & Kincaid, D.L. (1981). *Communication networks: Toward a new paradigm for research.* New York: Free Press.

Seibert, S.E., Kraimer, M.L., & Liden. R.C. (2001). A social capital theory of career success. *Academy of Management Journal, 44*(2), 219-237.

Stiglitz, J. (2002). Transparency in government. In *The right to tell—The role of mass media in economic development* (pp. 27-44). Washington, DC: World Bank Institute, WBI Development Studies.

Teece, D.J., Pisano, G., & Shuen, A. (1997). Dynamic capabilities and strategic management. *Strategic Management Journal, 18*(7), 509-534.

The World Bank Group. (1998-1999). *Knowledge for development*. Retrieved April 3, 2004, from http://www.worldbank.org/ks/html/pubs_pres.html

Tsai, W. (2000). Social capital, strategic relatedness and the formation of intra-organizational linkages. *Strategic Management Journal, 21*, 925-939.

Tsai, W., & Ghosal, S. (1998). Social capital and value creation: the role of inter-firm networks. *Academy of Management Journal, 41*(4), 464-476.

Walker, G., Kogut, B., & Shan, W. (1997). Social capital, structural holes and the formation of an industry network. *Organization Science, 8*(2), 109-125.

Wasko, M.M., & Faraj, S. (2005). Why should I share? Examining social capital and knowledge contribution in electronic networks of practice. *MIS Quarterly, 29*(1), 35-57.

Zahra, S.A., & George, G. (2002). Absorptive capacity: A review, reconceptualization, and extension. *Academy of Management Review, 27*(2), 185-203.

ENDNOTE

[1] There were no comments with regard to gender equity or the Masculinity Index.

This work was previously published in International Journal of Knowledge Management, Vol. 2, Issue 3, edited by M.E. Jennex, pp. 21-32, copyright 2006 by IGI Publishing, formerly known as Idea Group Publishing (an imprint of IGI Global).

Chapter VI
Human Effect of Knowledge Sharing:
Cooperative Type and Reciprocity Level in Community of Practice

Jaekyung Kim
University of Nebraska, USA

Sang M. Lee
University of Nebraska, USA

David L. Olson
University of Nebraska, USA

ABSTRACT

Knowledge sharing is important for organizational success. Once IT-driven KM approaches are prolifer-ated, they sometimes fail to operate as expected. Social perspectives of KM, especially the human effect on knowledge sharing, are expected to be important because people can choose to share or conceal knowledge. Management of knowledge is not all about collection, but more about connection. This study investigates an individual's behavior type as a cooperator, reciprocator, and free rider with respect to knowledge contribution. We view shared knowledge in a community of practice as a public good and adopt a theory of reciprocity to explain how different cooperative types affect knowledge contribution. People are assumed to react in one of three ways; sharing knowledge without need for reciprocity (cooperators), feeling obligated to share their knowledge (reciprocators), or taking knowledge for granted (free riders). Results reveal that the fraction of cooperator is positively related to total knowledge contribution and to reciprocity level, while the reciprocity level positively affects knowledge contribution.

Copyright © 2008, IGI Global, distributing in print or electronic forms without written permission of IGI Global is prohibited.

INTRODUCTION

Knowledge is one of most important strategic resources of organizations in the postindustrial era, strengthening innovation capability, competitive advantage (Teece, 2000), and dynamic capabilities (Sher et al., 2004). Despite the enormous efforts and investments on knowledge management (KM), it is generally said that potential knowledge of organizations is not fully utilized through these KM initiatives (Desouza, 2003). The socio-technical view of information systems claims that optimal performance of systems is achieved through optimizing both the social and technical systems (Mumford, 2000). Knowledge management system also includes social and technical system perspectives. IT-driven knowledge management such as database management systems, data warehousing, data mining, and expert systems have proliferated. They are extremely efficient in storing, retrieving and distributing information. However, knowledge is not the same as information and the informational approach to the management of knowledge (storing, retrieving and distributing knowledge) is not as efficient as IT approaches toward information. In reaction to the struggle of IT-driven KM approaches, the role of people in KM success has recently received more attention under the consideration that people make the choice of sharing or concealing knowledge and management of knowledge is not all about collection, but more about connection (Dougherty, 1999).

In communities of practice (CoP), members share knowledge related to common interest. Members respond to the inquiries for knowledge despite weak or nonexistent personal ties (Hiltz et al., 1986; Walther, 1994; Constant et al., 1996; Wellman & Gulia, 1999). Rational choice and Nash equilibrium (Nash, 1950) assume that rational participants seek answers from the CoP without responding to questions from others because responding requires time and effort, and rational self-interest choice would get benefits without

incurring costs. If everyone in a CoP follows the behavior of a rational human being according to Nash equilibrium, all should seek information without contributing. However, in real-world settings interaction and information exchange are observed. This study asks why people contribute their insight and advice and provide recommendations for more cooperative CoP.

From the economic literature, three types of cooperative behaviors toward public goods have been identified: cooperators, reciprocators and free riders. The fraction of these types is consistently stable (Fischbacher et al., 2001; Kurzban & Houser, 2005). Shared knowledge in online communities has been viewed as a type of public good (Cabrera & Cabrera, 2002; Lu & Leung, 2004). The public good dilemma is that free riders will take advantage of publicly provided goods without contributing to the development of such goods. The dynamics from each type of sharing behaviors require the use of simulation to gather results on knowledge sharing estimation with varying possible situations in a CoP.

The chapter is organized as follows. First, we review the literature on public goods and theories on voluntary contributions. We also gathered previous studies on behaviors of cooperators, reciprocators, and free riders. Based on these empirical results of the cooperative type and reciprocity level, we develop analytic models and report simulation model results with various combinations of cooperative types to evaluate how these combinations actually affect the amount of shared knowledge in a certain amount of time. Finally, we discuss how our empirical findings improve our understanding on how knowledge is shared in a CoP based on the cooperative type and reciprocity level.

KNOWLEDGE SHARING

A great deal of research has been conducted to explain the knowledge sharing (contribution) behavior in weak relationships from varying perspectives including embeddedness (Uzzi & Lancaster, 2003), social exchange theory (Kankanhalli et al., 2005; Wasko & Faraj, 2005), and motivation theory (Bock et al., 2005). This study broadens the perspective on knowledge sharing behavior by investigating an individual's cooperative type as a cooperator, reciprocator, or free rider.

Communities of Practice

A community of practice is a conceptual gathering of people who are informally bound together in a shared expertise or practice. Wenger (1998) argued that strong interpersonal ties and norms of direct reciprocity are formed by joint sensemaking and problem-solving in a community of practice. While communities of practices reside inside of an organization through a relationship of complementary practices, one organization's communities of practice can be linked with those of other organizations through the common or shared practices. Brown and Duguid (2001) expanded the concept into the network version of community of practices, called networks of practice, which consist of a larger, loosely knit, geographically distributed group of individuals who may not know each other engaged in a shared practice. Building upon this general description of networks of practice, Wasko and Faraj (2005) defined an electronic network of practice as a special case of the broader concept of networks of practice where the sharing of practice-related knowledge occurs primarily through computer-based communication technologies. Here we use the term CoP to represent varying types of communities of practice, to include networks of practice and electronic networks of practice.

These previous studies suggest that a CoP provides a collective knowledge base to which varying members can access freely and contribute with or without expecting benefits. Stein (2005) found that organizational champions (e.g., cooperators) who bring sufficient knowledge and foster a rich intellectual environment are one of key success factors of CoP, especially in early growth and its survival. He observed that "Several core members …volunteered to make presentations until a network of 'topic providers' was created" (Stein, 2005, p. 17). Therefore, cooperators in CoP are important in terms of knowledge sharing and their effect should be investigated in detail.

Theories for Voluntary Contribution Types toward Public Goods

In voluntary contribution where goods and services are allocated among consumers, contributors of these goods and services do not have any entitlement or priority while users benefit from the contribution. These types of goods or service are called public goods (Komorita & Parks, 1994). Their defining feature is that they are both non-competitive and non-excludable (Croson, 1996). They are non-competitive because multiple people can consume the good simultaneously and non-excludable because it is not possible to exclude people who did not pay for the goods from consuming them. Three perspectives of public goods have been studied to explain the consequences or behavior of voluntary contribution. Becker's pure altruism (1974), Sugden's reciprocity (1984), and Andreoni's impure altruism (1989; 1990) provide unique models of voluntary contribution behavior.

Margolis' General Theory of Non-Selfish Behavior: Cooperator

Becker's pure altruism was the basis for Margolis (1982) concept of individual utility. As long as people maximize their own utility, no public goods exist. However, some people make contributions to CoP knowledge bases regardless of the contributions of others. Thus, there are people who do not free-ride and these people are not explained by utility maximization theory or by the theory of impure altruism. Margolis argued that each individual has two utility functions, S-utility representing one's self-interest and G-utility representing one's concern of the welfare of the group to which that individual feels he/she belongs. In his theory, group welfare levels appear positively in an individual's utility function. This is based on the theory of altruism (Becker, 1974), in which individuals act non-selfishly and are motivated by a concern for group members' welfare.

Andreoni's Impure Altruism: Free Rider

If some take the contributions of others as given, they will contribute less as others contribute more, and eventually will not contribute at all. These people are called free riders. Andreoni's impure altruism (1989; 1990) explains this negative correlation between an individual's contributions and the contributions of others. This definition is based on two assumptions. One is that people do not reduce consumption as their income increases. The other is that people behave in a manner that maximizes personal gain. From the perspective of free riders, there will not be any public good for anyone because everyone maximizes self-interest by consuming without contributing (Messick & Brewer, 1983; Dawes et al., 1997).

Sugden's Theory of Reciprocity: Reciprocator

Although Becker (1974) and Margolis (1982) provide possible explanations of voluntary contribution towards public goods through the theories of non-selfish behavior and impure altruism, there are still some unanswered questions which Sugden (1984) asked:

Suppose you have good reason to know that no one else in your group will contribute anything towards a certain public good, irrespective of what you do. The only beneficiaries of your contribution would be yourself and the other members of the group. Why are you obliged to help them, when they refuse to help you? (p. 774)

Sugden (1984) argued that the principle of unconditional commitment may not work because people are not morally obliged to contribute when no one else contributes and the existence of psychological barriers such as unfairness would repress contribution. He proposed a weaker version of the principle of unconditional commitment. One must not take a free ride when other people are contributing. This is opposed to the principle of unconditional commitment which says one must always contribute towards public goods.

Theory of reciprocity (Sugden, 1984; 2002) takes the position that individuals choose the level of effort that they would most prefer when all other group members are making an effort of at least a certain amount in the production of a public good. Theory of reciprocity holds that one is never required to contribute more than other people in the group, overcoming unfairness which arises from the principle of unconditional commitment. Sugden (1984) emphasized that the individual has obligations to any group of individuals from whose effort he drives benefits. Groups may not be formally constituted organizations, but may be occupational, racial, religious or political, local, national or international. In the CoP setting, when one felt that they had benefited from sharing knowledge with others, they may have a certain obligation to the group.

From these three theories on voluntary contribution to public goods, individuals can be categorized as free riders when they always maximize their own utility function by not contributing to other group members, cooperators if they always contribute towards public goods, and reciprocators if they always contribute no more than others contribute.

Shared Knowledge in CoP as a Public Good

Knowledge shared in a CoP can be regarded as a public good because people who do not pay or contribute to the CoP also can use the shared knowledge (non-excludable) and multiple people can access shared knowledge simultaneously (non-competitive). Cabrera and Cabrera (2002) conceptualized knowledge as a public good and analyzed knowledge sharing behaviors from the perspective of a public goods dilemma. In a CoP, one can choose to share or not to share one's knowledge with others, and others have the same options. If one avoids sharing, while others share their knowledge, free riders can take advantage of others. Conversely, if one chooses to share while others do not share their knowledge, one can be a cooperator or a reciprocator. Based on the literature on cooperative type and knowledge as public goods, we categorize CoP members into three types in terms of their knowledge sharing behavior.

Evolutionarily Stable Strategies: Cooperator, Reciprocator, and Free Rider

Some people prefer to be cooperators or free riders while others prefer to be reciprocators. In their public goods experiment, Fischbacher et al. (2001) focused on the subject's main task to identify the average contribution level of other group members by estimating how much each subject wanted to contribute to the public good. They found that 50% of the subjects conditionally contributed (reciprocator), and 33% of the subjects never contributed (free rider). Kurzban and Houser (2005) conducted a laboratory experiment and agent-based simulation that supported this result, arguing that individual strategies are not expected to be equally represented in the population and equilibrium levels exist where all strategies were equally advantageous (13% of average pay-offs) with certain proportions for each strategy (13% of cooperators, 63% of reciprocators, and 20% of free riders). This supports the literature consensus that reciprocators make up the majority of the population with respect to voluntary contribution of public goods, and the

other two types are found in relatively smaller fractions of the population.

Behavior of Reciprocator

Unlike cooperators and free riders, reciprocators contribute knowledge in reaction to other group members' knowledge sharing. In the context of knowledge sharing in a CoP, people may not know the exact amount of knowledge contribution made by others, but they may see that people share valuable knowledge in response to the inquiries of other members. As positive experience grows, reciprocators may feel some obligation to contribute to the group.

Laboratory experiments and simulations have shown how certain types of individuals behave differently in terms of their voluntary contribution tendency toward public goods (Fehr & Schmidt, 1999; Engle-Warnick & Slonim, 2005). Croson (1996) conducted an experiment studying the relationship between an individual's contribution and the contributions of the group for three types: free-riding (no correlation), cooperating (negative correlation), and reciprocating (positive correlation). In the experiment, an individual's contribution to a public good was compared with beliefs about the contribution of others in the group. Croson (1996) found a significant positive relationship between individual contributions and beliefs about those contributions. Engle-Warnick and Slonim (2005) conducted a repeated trust game and reviewed three extreme equilibrium strategies and found that relationship length was positively related to trust and reciprocity and the average reciprocity rate of twenty repeated games was about 77%. In online learning network and social network, Aviv and Ravid (2005) found that the average reciprocity was 0.43 with a standard deviation of 0.13 for online learning networks and 0.58 with a standard deviation of 0.14 for social networks. This implies that about half of the subjects reciprocated. Fehr and Gächter (2000) conducted ultimatum game experiments and found that the fraction of reciprocators was never below 40% and sometimes rose above 60%.

This literature shows that reciprocating as a voluntary contributing behavior on public goods does exist and has a positive relationship to the contributions of others. Therefore, we propose:

Proposition 1: There are three types of voluntary contribution behavior (cooperating, reciprocating, and free-riding).

Proposition 2: The three types of voluntary contribution behavior are stable with certain equilibrium ratios among populations.

Proposition 3: In free-riding and cooperating behavior, no correlation exists between an individual's contribution and other group members' contributions.

HYPOTHESES

Effect of Cooperator Policy

Given the nature of voluntary contribution behavior toward public goods, the amount of shared knowledge in a CoP depends on the proportions of cooperators, reciprocators, and free riders. Therefore, there should be a certain number of cooperators prior to reciprocator knowledge sharing. To improve the amount of shared knowledge in a CoP, a policy which guarantees a certain proportion of cooperators can be implemented. With the enforced initial cooperator fraction larger than natural (where no policy is implemented), the amount of shared knowledge is expected to increase faster in a given time period.

Hypothesis 1: The cooperator fraction is positively related to the amount of shared knowledge.

Although all reciprocators do not contribute knowledge, prospective contributors will share knowledge when they meet some conditions, for example, situation, factors, education, and experience (Croson, 1996; Fehr & Henrich, 2003). One of such factor may be other members' cooperative behaviors because reciprocators change their behavior based on the behavior of others. As a reciprocator experiences other member's voluntary contributions, the reciprocity level will increase.

Hypothesis 2: The fraction of cooperator will be positively related to the reciprocity level.

Effect of Reciprocity Level

Engle-Warnick and Slonim (2003) found that there are varying levels of reciprocating. The reciprocity level is the probability of reciprocating in response to cooperators or other reciprocators' contribution behaviors and a higher reciprocity level indicates a higher probability of reciprocating. The average reciprocity level found in their experiment was 77%. The reciprocity index (Zeggelink, 1993) is another measure of varying levels of reciprocity. Reciprocators with higher reciprocity levels will share more knowledge than reciprocators with lower reciprocity level. The arbitrary reciprocity level is greater than 0 (free rider) and less than or equal to 1 (if he receives one, he contributes one).

Hypothesis 3: The reciprocity level will be positively related to the total shared knowledge.

RECIPROCITY LEVEL

Among three cooperative types, contributors and reciprocators are contributing knowledge. Reciprocators are not only positively influenced by cooperators, but also by reciprocators who positively reciprocate. Therefore, we need to consider both the effect of cooperator policy and the increasing tendency of the reciprocity level reflected on the cooperator level simultaneously because both affect the reciprocity level.

As reciprocators have more contacts with other members, their reciprocity levels are adjusted and we assume that as reciprocators experience more of other members' sharing, their reciprocity level will increase. For this study, we label reciprocators as strong, median, and weak based on their initial reciprocity level of 70%, 50% and 30%. A demonstration of reciprocity levels as a function of cooperator fraction is provided in Table 1, which uses a membership ratio of 1-6-3 when initial reciprocity level is 0.7. A naïve reciprocator who never had negative experience from a CoP may believe that he or she will always get a response or answer from a CoP. So his or her initial reciprocity level is 0.7. However, as he or she experiences responses from a CoP with such combination, the probability the reciprocator gets a response is much less than his or her initial reciprocity level because of free riders and reciprocators. However, this reduction of overall response from the CoP converges at some point and adjusted reciprocity level is calculated based on the converged overall response shown in Table 1.

The fraction of cooperator in a group has positive effect on the reciprocity level (hypothesis 2). Under the consistency assumption, strong reciprocators are more encouraged to share knowledge as cooperator fraction increases. This means that reciprocators in 1-6-3 combination would be more discouraged and adjust their reciprocity level by lowering it, while reciprocators in 5-2-3 combination would be most encouraged and increase their reciprocity level. This verifies the hypothesis 2 that more cooperators in the CoP leads to higher adjusted reciprocity level of reciprocators. In the following section, this relationship between cooperative type and reciprocity level will be mathematically proven.

Reciprocity Function

In this section, we develop a reciprocity function based on the fraction of each cooperative type in the population. We analyze how these cooperative types interact and affect each other. Then, we develop these interactions into mathematical form. We use operational definitions of strong reciprocator, reciprocity level and overall response

Table 1. Change of response rate of strong reciprocators for 1-6-3 combination

Round	Contribution Fraction from			Overall Response (OR)	Adjusted Reciprocity Level (ARL)
	Cooperator (CFC)	Reciprocators (CFR)	Free Rider (CFF)		
0	100%	0%	0%	100%	70%
1	10%	42% $(=\frac{6}{10} \times 0.70 \times 1.0)$	0%	52%	36.40%
2	10%	21.84% $(=\frac{6}{10} \times 0.70 \times 0.52)$	0%	31.84%	22.29%
3	10%	13.37% $(=\frac{6}{10} \times 0.70 \times 0.3184)$	0%	23.37%	16.36%
4	10%	9.82% $(=\frac{6}{10} \times 0.70 \times 0.2337)$	0%	19.82%	13.87%
5	10%	8.32% $(=\frac{6}{10} \times 0.70 \times 0.1982)$	0%	18.32%	12.83%
6	10%	7.70% $(=\frac{6}{10} \times 0.70 \times 0.1832)$	0%	17.70%	12.39%
7	10%	7.43% $(=\frac{6}{10} \times 0.70 \times 0.1770)$	0%	17.43%	12.20%
8	10%	7.32% $(=\frac{6}{10} \times 0.70 \times 0.1743)$	0%	17.32%	12.13%

(probability of getting response) to develop the reciprocity function. The reciprocity function is formed as a first-order autoregressive time series model—AR (1) and adjusted reciprocity level is an increasing concave function of the cooperator fraction.

Strong Reciprocator

We define a strong reciprocator as anyone who reciprocates with 70% of what he received (chance of getting response). If all members of a CoP are contributors (10-0-0 combination), a reciprocator will have 100% chance of getting response (or overall response), and will reciprocate 70% of the time when asked to share knowledge. This means that if a strong reciprocator asks ten questions, the contributors will answer all the inquiries, and this strong reciprocator will respond to 7 questions out 10 inquiries received from other members. Therefore, the strong reciprocity level in 10-0-0 combination is 70%.

Adjusted reciprocity level = Overall response × Initial reciprocity level

This logic also applies to other combinations with varying cooperator fractions. As cooperator fraction increases, reciprocators will have more chance to meet cooperators, less chance to meet reciprocators, and same chance to meet free riders. Reciprocity level is changed or adjusted as cooperator fraction varies and we need to calculate the chance of getting response by considering cooperator fraction, reciprocator fraction, and free rider fraction.

Formation of Reciprocity Function

Overall response is the sum of contribution fraction from cooperators and reciprocators. Since free riders do not contribute to CoPs, we only consider contribution from cooperators and reciprocators.

Overall Response = Contribution from Cooperator + Contribution from Reciprocator

(1)

Cooperators always contribute their knowledge when they are asked. Therefore, they have a perfect response rate. Contribution from Cooperators is represented as below.

Contribution from Cooperator = Cooperator Fraction × 100% (or 1.0)   (2)

While cooperators always respond to inquires, reciprocators respond based on their previous experiences with other members. If a strong reciprocator has positive experiences with other members, he will behave positively by responding to inquiries from other members at a certain reciprocity level. If negative experience is obtained, no response will be given by the reciprocator. Therefore, he adjusts his reciprocity level based on the response experienced from the prior round (or step) and will adjust reciprocity level when responding to other inquiries in the next step.

Adjusted Reciprocity Level = Initial Reciprocity Level × Overall Response   (3)

The contribution from reciprocators can be calculated by multiplying (adjusted) reciprocity level with reciprocator fraction of the population.

Contribution from Reciprocator = Reciprocator Fraction × Adjusted Reciprocity Level

(4)

Finally, reciprocator fraction is calculated with following formula when the free rider fraction is 30%.

Reciprocator Fraction = 1 – Contributor Fraction – Free rider fraction (0.3)   or
0.7 – Contributor Fraction   (5)

Figure. 1. Summary of formulas for overall response

$$OR_t = CFC + CFR + CFF \qquad (1)$$

$$CFC = CF \times 100\% \qquad (2)$$

$$ARL = IRL \times OR_{t-1} \qquad (3)$$

$$CFR = RF \times ARL \qquad (4)$$

$$RF = (0.7 - CF) \qquad (5)$$

Where

OR_t = Overall Response at time t

CFC = Contribution Fraction from Cooperators

CFR = Contribution Fraction from Reciprocators

CFF = Contribution Fraction from Free riders and this value is always 0 since no contribution is made from free riders.

ARL = Adjusted Reciprocity Level

IRL = Initial Reciprocity Level; 0.7, 0.5, and 0.3 for strong, moderate, and weak reciprocator, respectively.

CF = Cooperator Fraction with range from 0 to 0.7

RF = Reciprocator Fraction with range of (0.7 − CF)

FF = Free Rider Fraction Set to 30% or 0.3

Figure 1 summarizes the formula with abbreviated notation.

To find the relationship between adjusted reciprocity level and cooperator fraction, we will show that the overall response is the function of cooperator fraction. First, let us insert Formula (2) into Formula (1). This leads to Formula (6).

$$OR_t = CF + CFR + CFF \qquad (6)$$

Inserting Formula (3) into Formula (4) leads to Formula (7).

$$CFR = RF \times IRL \times OR_{t-1} \qquad (7)$$

Inserting Formula (4) into Formula (1) and replacing CFF with the value of 0 leads to Formula (8).

$$OR_t = CF + (RF \times IRL \times OR_{t-1}) \qquad (8)$$

In Formula (8), RF is replaced with Formula (5) to make overall response (OR) as a function of cooperator factor (CF). This leads to Formula (9).

$$OR_t = CF + (0.7 - CF) \times IRL \times OR_{t-1} \qquad (9)$$

Now, Formula (9) is a first-order autoregressive time series model—AR(1). Let us replace *OR* as *y*, *CF* as *x* and $[(0.7 - CF) \times IRL]$ as *A* to make Formula (9) simple as shown in Formula (10).

$$y_t = x + A \cdot y_{t-1} \qquad (10)$$

Now we show how this first-order autoregressive time series model converges as interactions with other members are increased. As mentioned earlier, naïve reciprocators assume that the initial response rate is 100%, which means that $y_0 = 1$.

$$y_0 = 1$$
$$y_1 = x + A \cdot y_0 = x + A$$
$$y_2 = x + A \cdot y_1 = x + A \times (x + A) = x + A \cdot x + A^2$$
$$y_3 = x + A \cdot y_2 = x + A \times (x + A \cdot x + A^2) = x + A \cdot x + A^2 \cdot x + A^3$$
$$y_4 = x + A \cdot y_3 = x + A \times (x + A \cdot x + A^2 \cdot x + A^3) = x + A \cdot x + A^2 \cdot x + A^3 \cdot x + A^4$$
$$\vdots$$
$$y_n = x + A \cdot x + A^2 \cdot x + A^3 \cdot x + \ldots\ldots + A^{n-1} \cdot x + A^n$$
$$= x \cdot (1 + A + A^2 + A^3 + \ldots\ldots + A^{n-1}) + A^n$$

$$(11)$$

The portion of Formula (11), $x \cdot (1 + A + A^2 + A^3 + \ldots\ldots + A^{n-1})$ is in the form of geometric series which is simplified as $x \cdot \left(\dfrac{1 - A^n}{1 - A} \right)$. Then, we obtain Formula (12) as shown below.

$$y_n = x \cdot \left(\frac{1 - A^n}{1 - A} \right) + A^n \qquad (12)$$

In Formula (12), If $|A| < 1$, then $A^n \to 0$ as $n \to \infty$ and $y_n \to \dfrac{x}{1 - A}$. If $|A| > 1$, then $A^n \to \infty$ and y_n diverges. In Formula (12), $A = (0.7 - CF) \times IRL$, where CF is cooperator fraction and IRL is initial reciprocity level (either 0.7, 0.5, or 0.3). The range of CF is between 0 and 0.7, while IRL is 0.7, 0.5 or 0.3 and this makes $|A| < 1$. Since $|A| < 1$, y_n converges into $\dfrac{x}{1 - A}$ and Formula (13) is shown with replacing A with $(0.7 - x) \times IRL$.

$$y = \frac{x}{1 - (0.7 - x) \cdot IRL}, \quad where \quad 0 \le x \le .7$$
$$(13)$$

The range of x is the intersection between two ranges; range 1 between -1.3 and 2.7 (when IRL is .5, a moderate reciprocator) and range 2 between 0 (no cooperator) and 0.7 (70% cooperator). The graphical presentation of Formula (13) is shown in Figure 2.

Figure. 2. Cooperator fraction and overall response

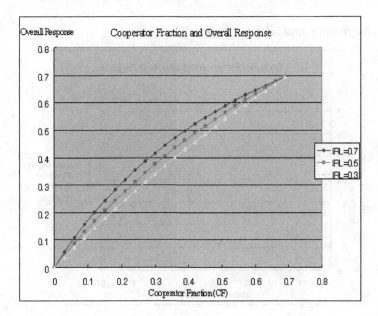

Adjusted Reciprocity Level

Formula (14) shows the adjusted reciprocity level, calculated by multiplying initial reciprocity level (0.7, 0.5 or 0.3) with overall response—Formula (3).

$$ARL = y \cdot IRL = \left(\frac{CF}{1 - (0.7 - CF) \cdot IRL} \right) \cdot IRL$$

(14)

A strong reciprocator's adjusted reciprocity level is calculated by multiplying overall response with initial reciprocity level as shown in Formula (3). Overall response is a function of cooperator fraction and cooperator fraction is positively related to the overall response as shown in Figure 2. Since adjusted reciprocity level is a function of overall response, cooperator fraction which is positively related to overall response is also positively related to adjusted reciprocity level.

Figure 3 depicts the relationship between cooperator fraction and adjusted reciprocity level, showing adjusted reciprocity level increase concavely as cooperator fraction increases. This is the proof of proposition 2 saying cooperator fraction has positive effect on reciprocity level.

SIMULATION

We adopt probability modeling (analytic models and simulation) to test the hypotheses of the study. Simulation is preferred to standard analytical modeling approaches because simulation can provide information about dynamic behaviors of various actors in a CoP. The assumption of a distribution of each cooperative type in the population also makes simulation the preferred method. This numerical approach also allows us to manipulate the model and to make some guesses on how quantitatively important the effect of fraction of cooperator and reciprocity level is in terms of knowledge sharing.

Assumptions

Based on the literature review in previous sections, the following conditions are assumed in conducting the simulation.

Figure 3. Cooperator fraction and adjusted reciprocity level

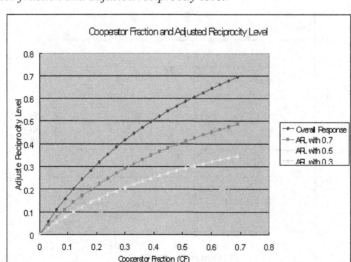

1. Knowledge is a type of public good.
2. Individuals fall into three types and the individual's type is stable.
3. A group's cooperative outcomes can be well predicted if one knows its type composition.
4. The amount of shared knowledge is determined by membership in the classes of cooperators, reciprocators, and free riders.

Algorithm for Classification of Cooperative Type

To represent the stable fraction of cooperators, reciprocators, and free riders in the population, we adopt a positive feedback process model which reinforces a given tendency of the system that can lead away from equilibrium states. Arthur (1990) built this model to explain why one technology would ultimately dominate over other technologies when multiple technologies are competing in the same market. In the positive feedback model, if one technology is slightly preferred against others in the initial stage, this initial small preference will attract more people to choose the technology instead of alternatives and more people will select the technology while less people will select alternative technologies eventually (Arthur, 1990).

In a CoP, some may prefer to be free riders who are not willing to share knowledge under any conditions, or cooperators willing to share anyway, while others act as reciprocators who sit back and watch what others are doing, and reciprocate based on others' behavior. Such preferences are initially set based on personal characteristics. As the positive feedback of each choice is processed or experienced, a certain portion of population will stick to certain cooperating types and the ratio of each type will be consistent (Kurzban & Houser, 2005). Using this cooperative type classification with the positive feedback process, the fraction of cooperators, reciprocators, and free riders will stabilize if we believe that there are fixed ratios

of behavior (Fischbacher et al., 2001; Kurzban & Houser, 2005).

Distribution of Reciprocity Level for Reciprocators

By studying the distribution of the reciprocity level of members from a social system such as a CoP, we can assume a positively skewed normal curve representing the distribution pattern of the reciprocity level in weak ties and a negatively skewed normal curve in strong ties. In a weak tie setting, people have difficulty identifying each other and reciprocators are less obligated to reciprocate by their positive experiences from cooperators. Thus, most reciprocators are gathered around the lower reciprocity level. In strong tie settings, people will contact each other physically and reciprocators are more obligated to reciprocate to their positive experiences from cooperators and other reciprocators. Consequently, most reciprocators are gathered around the higher reciprocity level. Since our setting of CoP is a weak tie, we assume most reciprocators are found at the weak reciprocity level.

To show the distribution of reciprocators with varying reciprocity level (theoretically, the reciprocity level is greater than 0 and less than 1), we use the Weibull probability distribution function with $\alpha=32$ and $\beta=2$ to represent positively skewed reciprocator distribution.

Simulation Results

Based upon the propositions, we developed a simulation model for varying combinations of cooperative types as shown in Table 2. We developed a system dynamics model for the reciprocity level and knowledge contribution based upon the positive feedback process (Hannon & Ruth, 1994). We set 5% of cooperators, 65% of reciprocators, and 30% free riders as the natural setting, since in an online environment where no physical contact

Table 2. Natural setting and cooperator policies

Combination	Cooperators	Reciprocator	Free rider
Natural Setting	5%	65%	30%
Policy1	10%	60%	30%
Policy2	15%	55%	30%
Policy3	20%	50%	30%
Policy4	25%	45%	30%
Policy5	30%	40%	30%

Figure 4. Simulation model

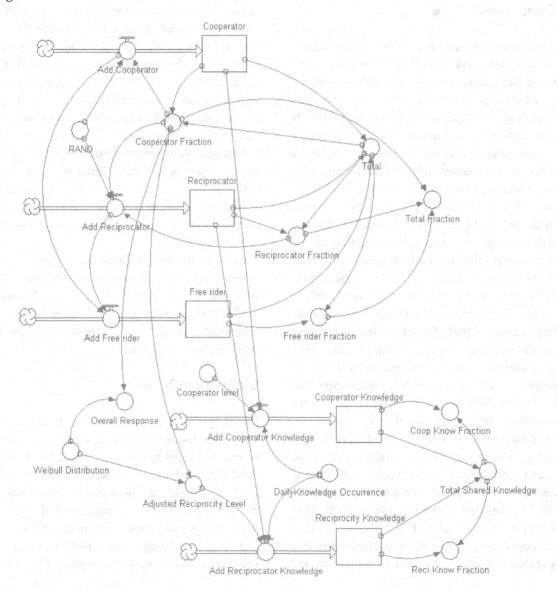

Table 3. Structure of data and statistical test

Interaction	Combination	Simulation Run	Knowledge from Cooperators	Knowledge form Reciprocators	Total Shared Knowledge	ANOVA
10th	0.5-6.5-3.0	1	3.8	2.1	5.9	Each combination is compared using the analysis of variance
		2	3.5	2.1	5.6	
		~	~	~	~	
		99	4.0	2.2	6.2	
		100	3.5	2.1	5.6	
	~	~	~	~	~	
	3.0-4.0-3.0	1	16	4.4	20	
		2	17	4.4	21	
		~	~	~	~	
		99	16	4.4	21	
		100	16	4.5	21	
20th						
~						
90th	~	~	~	~	~	
100th	0.5-6.5-3.0	1	39.25	13.55	52.8	Each combination is compared using the analysis of variance
		2	38.45	13.03	51.48	
		~	~	~	~	
		99	27.35	9.63	36.98	
		100	40.65	13.36	54.01	
	~	~	~	~	~	
	3.0-4.0-3.0	1	215.55	37.51	253.06	
		2	217.6	35.87	253.47	
		~	~	~	~	
		99	207.45	38.57	246.02	
		100	229.3	40.61	269.91	

exists, people have less tendency of contribution toward public goods and thus few cooperators are expected. We set five possible cooperator policies with varying fractions of cooperators and reciprocators. Then, we compared the amount of shared knowledge from the natural setting with other policies using variance analysis to check whether the difference in the amount of shared knowledge is statistically significant.

For each combination, we conducted 100 simulation runs. For each simulation, a reciprocator accesses the CoP for 100 interactions. In each interaction, each individual has a chance to share a piece of knowledge into a CoP; a cooperator contributes a piece of knowledge into a CoP, while a reciprocator shares partial knowledge based on the reciprocity level. The reciprocity level was calculated based on the overall response and various reciprocators' combinations followed the Weibull distribution. The cooperator level is calculated based on the positive feedback process. Each cooperative type was stable during the simulation although small fluctuation of each faction occurred due to the randomness. Free riders will never share their knowledge no matter how many interactions they have. Figure 4 depicts the simulation model for this study. To test hypotheses 1 and 3, we controlled the fraction of cooperators and measured the amount of

shared knowledge in the CoP simulation setting. Then, the amount of shared knowledge from each level of cooperators was compared and tested with one-way analysis of variance.

Data

For each simulation run, we recorded the amount of shared knowledge every 10 interactions in a total of 100 interactions. We tested the data from each tenth interaction using one-way analysis of variance to compare the results of each setting. Table 3 shows how we gathered data from simulation and how each combination was compared using the analysis of variance test.

Table 4. Result of ANOVA at the first 10 interactions

Dependent Variable	(I) Factor	(J) Factor	Mean Difference (I-J)	Sig.	Dependent Variable	(I) Factor	(J) Factor	Mean Difference (I-J)	Sig.
Knowledge Contribution from Cooperators	Natural Setting	Policy 1	-2.7085	0.041	Knowledge Contribution from Reciprocators	Natural Setting	Policy 1*	-0.8878	0.000
		Policy 2*	-5.4695	0.000			Policy 2*	-1.5489	0.000
		Policy 3*	-8.375	0.000			Policy 3*	-2.0272	0.000
		Policy 4*	-11.0025	0.000			Policy 4*	-2.2775	0.000
		Policy 5*	-13.871	0.000			Policy 5*	-2.5155	0.000
	Policy 1	Policy 2	-2.761	0.035		Policy 1	Policy 2*	-0.6611	0.001
		Policy 3*	-5.6665	0.000			Policy 3*	-1.1394	0.000
		Policy 4*	-8.294	0.000			Policy 4*	-1.3897	0.000
		Policy 5*	-11.1625	0.000			Policy 5*	-1.6277	0.000
	Policy 2	Policy 3	-2.9055	0.021		Policy 2	Policy 3	-0.4783	0.061
		Policy 4*	-5.533	0.000			Policy 4*	-0.7286	0.000
		Policy 5*	-8.4015	0.000			Policy 5*	-0.9666	0.000
	Policy 3	Policy 4	-2.6275	0.054		Policy 3	Policy 4	-0.2503	0.713
		Policy 5	-2.8685	0.024			Policy 5	-0.4883	0.051
	Policy 4	Policy 5	-2.8685	0.024		Policy 4	Policy 5	-0.238	0.756

* The mean difference is significant at the .01 level

RESULT

We start the analysis of variance test with data sets from tenth interactions. These data sets come from the result of the first 10 interactions in each combination. The mean differences between adjacent combination, which has 5% increase in cooperator fraction, were not statistically significant at $\alpha=0.01$ level for knowledge contribution from cooperators. However, if the cooperator fraction is increased to 10%, the mean difference of cooperators' knowledge contribution becomes statistically significant at $\alpha = 0.01$ level. Table 4 shows the details of the result of first 10 interactions.

Reciprocators' knowledge contribution is somewhat different from that of cooperators. As cooperator fraction increases from natural setting to policy 1 and from policy 1 to policy 2, this 5% increment significantly increase the reciprocators' shared knowledge. However, this is not the case for a 5% increase in cooperator fraction from policy 2 to policy 3, from policy 3 to policy 4, and policy 4 to policy 5. This is due to the nature of the reciprocity level. The reciprocity level shows an exponential distribution with a sharp increase in the reciprocity level during the early cooperator fraction increase and stagnant increase during the later cooperator fraction increase as shown in Figure 3.

Total shared knowledge in a CoP, a combined amount of shared knowledge from cooperators and reciprocators, is not increased significantly as cooperator fraction is initially increased in 5% at all comparisons, although the results are not included in Table 4.

After the second 10 interactions (from 11th to 20th) until the last 10 interactions (from 91st to 100th), all the mean differences between natural setting and five policies had statistically significant differences at $\alpha = 0.01$ level. The results are summarized in Table 5. The amount of shared knowledge significantly increased as the cooperator's fraction increased for 5%. All comparisons were found to be statistically significant. We thus accept hypothesis 1, positing that the cooperator fraction is positively related to the amount of shared knowledge. Knowledge from reciprocators also increased as the reciprocity level increased. We therefore accept hypothesis 3 which proposed that the reciprocity level would be positively related to total shared knowledge. We also accept hypothesis 2 in section 4.2 with graphical expression of the positive relationship between cooperator fraction and reciprocity level of reciprocators.

For the first 10 interactions, the knowledge did not increase. Reciprocators shared less amount of knowledge. After the first 10 interactions, increasing cooperators 5% shared enough knowledge to affect reciprocators who shared more knowledge,

Table 5. Result of analysis of variance

Interaction	Cooperator Fraction	Knowledge from Cooperators	Knowledge form Reciprocators	Total Shared Knowledge
10th	0.5 vs. 1.0	Accept H0	Accept H0	Accept H0
	0.5 vs. 1.5	Reject H0	Reject H0	Reject H0
	0.5 vs. 2.0	Reject H0	Reject H0	Reject H0
	0.5 vs. 2.5	Reject H0	Reject H0	Reject H0
	0.5 vs. 3.0	Reject H0	Reject H0	Reject H0
20th ~100th	All Comparisons	Reject H0	Reject H0	Reject H0

leading to statistically significant difference in the amount of shared knowledge. This implies that a cooperator policy which increases cooperators at least 5% will significantly increase shared knowledge not only from cooperators but also reciprocators after at least 20 interactions. As more interactions among CoP members occur, people will share knowledge more.

CONCLUSION

In this study, we found that raising cooperator fraction not only increase knowledge sharing but also encourage reciprocators to share more knowledge. Two possible ways to increase co-operator fraction are mentoring and utilizing retiree in an organization. Mentoring is one way of generating cooperators in CoP. Mentors can be experienced members in the organization who have more knowledge and willingness to share for other less experienced members (Kram, 1985). In the case study, Hunt (2005) argued that e-mentoring can be used as an effective develop-ment approach for organizations across distances. Bjørnsson and Dingsøyr (2005) found that the mentor program supports learning in a software consultancy company. Hiring retirees is another way to increase the cooperator fraction. Retirees are the most experienced employees in the field of their work and they have a vast amount of or-ganizational knowledge (Lesser & Prusak, 2001). Current employees may feel that they have fewer resources for contributing to a CoP as their cur-rent work takes all of their energy. Mentoring and hiring retirees may help both keep organizational knowledge and increase cooperators in a CoP.

This study has several limitations. First, we assume that free riders may not be affected by any condition. However, this may not be true. For our simulation settings, we controlled the free rider fraction at 30%. The average fraction of the contribution type may not be constant. For example, cooperators may migrate into recipro-

cators at a certain point while reciprocators may migrate into the free rider group. If the fraction of free riders changes and they are affected by other contributors, the shared knowledge amount would be greater than the simulation result of the study. Second, we arbitrarily selected the unit of shared knowledge and applied this to all cooperators and reciprocators. However, some cooperators may contribute more knowledge than other cooperators and this also might be the case for reciprocators. This varying unit of shared knowledge may inflate the result of the study. Lastly, the Weibull distribution with $\alpha=32$ and $\beta=2$ was also our arbitrary choice, motivated to match observed distributions. Varying share and scale parameters of the Weibull distribution may result in varying conclusions. Simulation is valuable as it allows changes in any of these assumptions.

We investigated the relationship between individual's contribution behavioral type and knowledge sharing in a CoP. We argued that the fraction of cooperators in a CoP not only affect the amount of shared knowledge, but also the sharing decision of reciprocators (reciprocity level) posi-tively, which increases the total shared knowledge in a CoP, and ran a simulation model adopting a positive feedback process to test the possible relationship between the fraction of cooperation and the amount of shared knowledge. Analysis of variance shows that raising the cooperator fraction by 5% will significantly increase total shared knowledge in a CoP, not only due to more cooperators, but also due to the higher reciprocity level of fewer reciprocators. Therefore, CoP can benefit by attracting more cooperators into the system where they positively influence reciproca-tors as well as share more knowledge.

One of the primary benefits of an online CoP is improving knowledge contribution since members share interest in relevant tasks and most organi-zational knowledge resides inside its members. We showed how cooperators increase knowledge contribution directly and indirectly through reciprocators. As information and communication technology (ICT) becomes ubiquitous and knowledge is a critical resource for most organizations' success, efforts to better utilize tacit knowledge resident among members should be a primary goal of organizations. We believe that findings of this study provide important insights to help scholars and practitioners for such endeavors.

REFERENCES

Andreoni, J. (1989). Giving with impure altruism: Applications to charity and Ricardian equivalence. *Journal of Political Economy, 97,* 1447-1458.

Andreoni, J. (1990). Impure altruism and donations to public goods: A theory of warm-glow giving. *Economic Journal, 100,* 464-477.

Arthur, B. (1990). Positive feedbacks in the economy. *Scientific American, 262,* 92-99.

Aviv, R., & Ravid, G. Reciprocity analysis of on-line learning networks. *Journal of Asynchronous Learning Networks* (In press).

Becker, G. (1974). A theory of social interaction. *Journal of Political Economy, 82,* 1063-1093.

Bjørnsson, F., & Dingsøyr, T. (2005). A study of a mentoring program for knowledge transfer in a small software consultancy company. *Proceedings of the PROFES 2005* (pp. 245-256).

Bock, G., Zmud, R., Kim, Y., & Lee, J. (2005). Behavioral intention formation in knowledge sharing: Examining the roles of extrinsic motivators, social-psychological forces, and organizational climate. *MIS Quarterly, 29,* 87-111.

Brown, J., & Duguid, P. (2001). Knowledge and organization: A social-practice perspective. *Organization Science, 12,* 198-213.

Cabrera, A., & Cabrera, E. (2002). Knowledge-sharing dilemmas. *Organization Studies, 23,* 687-710.

Constant, D., Sproull, L., & Kiesler, S. (1996). The kindness of strangers: The usefulness of electronic weak ties for technical advice. *Organization Science, 7,* 119-135.

Croson, R. (1996). *Contributions to public goods: Altruism or reciprocity?* Working paper.

Dawes, R., McTavish, J., & Shacklee, H. (1997). Behavior, communication and assumptions about other people's behavior in a commons dilemma situation. *Journal of Personality and Social Psychology, 35,* 1-11.

Desouza, K. (2003). Facilitating tacit knowledge exchange. *Communications of the ACM, 46*(6), 85-88.

Dougherty, V. (1999). Knowledge is about people, not databases. *Industrial & Commercial Training, 31*(7), 262-266.

Engle-Warnick, J., & Jim, S. (2003). *Inferring repeated game strategies from actions: Evidence from trust game experiments.* Working paper.

Engle-Warnick, J., & Slonim, R. Learning to trust in indefinitely repeated games. *Games and Economic Behavior* (In press).

Fehr, E., & Henrich, J. (2003). Is strong reciprocity a maladaptation? On the evolutionary foundations of human altruism. In: P. Hammerstein (Ed.), *Genetic and cultural evolution of cooperation* (pp. 55-82). Cambridge, MA: MIT Press.

Fehr, E., & Gächter, S. (2000). Fairness and retaliation: The economics of reciprocity. *Journal of Economic Perspectives, 14,* 159-181.

Fehr, E., & Schmidt, K. (1999). A theory of fairness, competition, and cooperation. *Quarterly Journal of Economics, 114,* 817-868.

Fischbacher, U., Gächter, S., & Fehr, E. (2001). Are people conditionally cooperative? Evidence from a public goods experiment. *Economics Letters, 71,* 397-404.

Hannon, B., & Ruth, M. (1994). *Dynamic modeling*. New York, NY: Springer-Verlag.

Hiltz, S., Johnson, K., & Turoff, M. (1986). Experiments in group decision-making: Communication process and outcome in face-to-face versus computerized conferences. *Human Communication Research, 13,* 225-252.

Hunt, K. (2005). E-mentoring: Solving the issue of mentoring across distances. *Development and Learning in Organizations, 19*(5) 7-10.

Kankanhalli, A., Tan, B., & Wei, K. (2005). Contributing knowledge to electronic knowledge repositories: An empirical investigation. *MIS Quarterly, 29,* 113-143.

Komorita, S., & Parks, C. (1994). *Social dilemmas*. Boulder, CO: Westview Press.

Kram, K. (1985). *Mentoring at work: Developmental relationships in organizational life*. Glenview, IL: Scott, Foreman and Company.

Kurzban, R., & Houser, D. (2005). Experiments investigating cooperative types in humans: A complement to evolutionary theory and simulations. In *Proceedings of the National Academy of Sciences of the United States of America, 102,* 1803-1807.

Lesser E., & Prusak L. (2001). Preserving knowledge in an uncertain world. *Sloan Management Review, 43*(1), 1010-1021

Lu, L., & Leung, K. (2004). *A public goods perspective on knowledge sharing: Effects of self-interest, self-efficacy, interpersonal climate, and organizational support*. Working paper.

Margolis, H. (1982). *Selfishness, altruism and rationality: A theory of social choice*. Cambridge, UK: Cambridge University Press.

Messick, D., Wilke, H., Brewer, M., Kramer, R., Zemke, P., & Lui, L. (1983). Individual adaptations and structural change as solutions to social

dilemmas. *Journal of Personality and Social Psychology, 44,* 294-309.

Mumford, E. (2000). Socio-technical design: An unfulfilled promise or a future opportunity. In: R. Baskerville, J. Stage, & J. DeGross (Eds.), *The social and organizational perspective on research and practice in information technology*. London: Champman-Hall.

Nash, J. (1950). Equilibrium points in n-person games. In *Proceedings of the National Academy of Sciences, 36,* 48-49.

Sher, P., Sher, P., & Lee, V. (2004). Information technology as a facilitator for enhancing dynamic capabilities through knowledge management. *Information & Management, 41*(8), 933-945.

Stein, E. (2005). A qualitative study of the characteristics of a community of practice for knowledge management and its success factors. *International Journal of Knowledge Management, 1*(3), 1-24.

Sugden, R. (1984). Reciprocity: The supply of public goods through voluntary contributions. *Economic Journal, 94,* 772-787.

Sugden, R. (2002). Altruistically inclined? The behavioral sciences, evolutionary theory, and the origins of reciprocity. *Journal of Economic Literature, 40,* 1242-1243.

Teece, D. (2000). *Managing intellectual capital*. Oxford: Oxford University Press.

Uzzi, B., & Lancaster, R. (2003). Relational embeddedness and learning: The case of bank loan managers and their clients. *Management Science, 49,* 383-399.

Walther, J. (1994). Anticipated ongoing interaction versus channel effects on relational communication in computer-mediated interaction. *Human Communication Research, 20,* 473-501.

Wasko, M., & Faraj, S. (2005). Why should I share? Examining social capital and knowledge contribution in electronic networks of practice. *MIS Quarterly, 29,* 35-57.

Wellman, B., & Gulia, M. (1999). Net surfers don't ride alone: Virtual communities as communities. In: P. Kollock & M. Smith (Eds.), *Communities and cyberspace.* New York, NY: Routledge.

Wenger, E. (1998). *Communities of practice.* Cambridge, UK: Cambridge University Press.

Zeggelink, E. (1993). *Strangers into friends. The evolution of friendship networks using an individual oriented modeling approach.* Amsterdam: Thesis Publishers.

Chapter VII
Toward a Receiver–Based Theory of Knowledge Sharing

Sharman Lichtenstein
Deakin University, Australia

Alexia Hunter
Deakin University, Australia

ABSTRACT

Managers and researchers alike have sought new ways to address the challenges of sharing dispersed knowledge in modern business environments. Careful consideration by sharers of receivers' knowledge needs and behaviours may improve the effectiveness of organisational knowledge sharing. This research examines how sharers react to their perceptions of receivers' knowledge needs and behaviours when making choices relating to sharing knowledge. The focus of this article is to propose and empirically explore a theoretical framework for a study of the role of the receiver in knowledge sharing — receiver-based theory. Data collected from two case studies highlight a key role played by perceived receiver knowledge needs and behaviours in shaping sharer choices when explicit knowledge is shared. A set of receiver influences on knowledge sharing is provided that highlights key receiver and sharer issues. The paper concludes that companies should develop better ways to connect potential sharers with receivers' real knowledge needs. Further, the findings suggest that sharing on a need-to-know basis hinders change in organisational power structures, and prevents the integration of isolated pockets of knowledge that may yield new value.

INTRODUCTION

Contemporary perspectives on organisational knowledge sharing have so far largely overlooked a consideration of the role of the receivers of knowledge in shaping sharer choices (Dixon 2002; Hendriks 2004). Yet, it is the sharers and receivers of knowledge whose beliefs, attitudes, intentions, and behaviours will have the greatest impact on the effectiveness of knowledge sharing strategies

Copyright © 2008, IGI Global, distributing in print or electronic forms without written permission of IGI Global is prohibited.

and, cumulatively, on organisational learning and capabilities (Andrews & Delahaye, 2000; Hinds & Pfeffer, 2003; Husted & Michailova, 2002). For receivers to access, retrieve, comprehend, and assimilate a sharer's knowledge, sharers must be aware and motivated, and share in skilled ways that meet receiver needs (Dixon, 2002). Hendriks has cautioned that "knowledge sharing is not seen as pushing packages of existing knowledge back and forth, but as a process that requires not only knowledge of the bringing party but also of the obtaining party" (Hendriks, 2004, p. 6). However, to date, there has not been sufficient exploration of knowledge sharing at the unit level of the individual in an organisational setting, where the sharer and receiver may individually consider one another, and how, in particular, feedback from receivers may influence individual sharer motivation and behaviour (Andrews & Delahaye, 2000; Dixon, 2002; Hinds & Pfeffer, 2003).

Current evidence suggests the existence of a relationship between receiver needs and behaviour, and sharer motivation and behaviour. First, a social relationship between sharer and receiver is widely believed to motivate sharing (Kilduff & Tsai, 2003). Second, the availability of receivers may influence sharer selection of communication channels (Straub & Karahanna, 1998). Third, when related knowledge is missing, receivers may experience learning difficulties (Dixon, 2002). Fourth, there may be conflicting sharer and receiver agendas that constrain knowledge sharing. On this point, Easterby-Smith, Crossan, and Nicolini (2000) wrote "... the time is ripe to start addressing learning and knowing in the light of inherent conflicts between shareholders' goals, economic pressure, institutionalised professional interest and political agendas" (p. 793).

In this chapter, we develop and explore a preliminary receiver-based theory of knowledge sharing. This theory proposes that an important aspect of understanding knowledge sharing lies in understanding the potential role played by receivers in shaping sharer choices. The theory

recasts the meaning of knowledge sharing as a need for understanding and supporting receiver knowledge needs based on accurate receiver feedback given throughout the different stages of knowledge sharing. The receiver-based theory of knowledge sharing developed in this chapter presents a micro-level dialogical theory of knowledge sharing where sharers are conscious of potential or present receivers, in their sharing choices. It aims to demonstrate how feedback from receivers at different stages of the knowledge sharing process can influence sharer perceptions of receiver needs and shape sharer attitudes and behaviours. In this chapter, we focus particularly on exploring the theory as it pertains to the sharing of explicit knowledge.

CONTEMPORARY PERSPECTIVES ON KNOWLEDGE SHARING

A popular transformational view of knowledge begins with codified observations from a marketplace of data which, when placed in a decision context, are transformed into information (Barabba & Zaltman, 1991). In the analysis of this information, intelligence is created. When high levels of confidence are developed in a body of intelligence, knowledge is created. Alavi and Leidner (1999) more broadly suggest that "information becomes knowledge once it is processed in the mind of an individual ('tacit' knowledge in the words of Polanyi [1962] and Nonaka [1994]). This knowledge then becomes information again (or what Nonaka refers to as 'explicit knowledge') once it is articulated or communicated to others in the form of text, computer output, spoken, or written words or other means" (p. 6). However, it is widely believed that not all tacit knowledge is easily explicated as explicit knowledge (e.g., Argote, 1999), and a process of socialisation has been suggested by Nonaka (1994) as one way to promulgate such tacit knowledge. According to Alavi and Leidner, explicit knowledge (information) can be cognitively processed by an individual receiver and internalised as tacit knowledge (Alavi & Leidner, 1999). The researchers note that a process of reflection, enlightenment and learning is required for explicit knowledge to become tacit in the mind of a receiver.

A strategy of knowledge sharing can enable an organisation to access and exploit its dispersed knowledge assets (Argote, 1999). An embracing conceptualisation of knowledge sharing describes it as a complex process involving the contribution of knowledge by the organisation or its people, and the collection, assimilation and application of knowledge by the organisation or its people (Hendriks, 2004; Huysman & de Wit, 2002). A useful definition of a *sharer* is any individual who possesses knowledge and is willing to share that knowledge with others, while a *receiver* is any individual who is willing to heed and interpret any knowledge provided by others (Dixon, 2002).

Hansen, Nohria, and Tierney (1999) discuss the two strategies of *codification* and *personalisation*. The codification strategy proposes that explicit knowledge is articulated and stored, and later retrieved, reconstructed and assimilated by receivers when needed for application (Hendriks, 1999). However, codification cannot represent valuable tacit knowledge (Tsoukas, 2003) or stimulate receivers to learn, create and innovate (Swan, Robertson, & Newell, 2002). Furthermore, receivers often cannot find the knowledge they seek (Kautz & Mahnke 2003) or signal their knowledge needs in the design (Markus, 2001). With personalisation, knowledge sharing takes place through personal communication. The dynamics of interaction support meaning negotiation and stimulate knowledge creation, knowledge integration and learning (Swan et al., 2002). We note however that current theories of codified and personalised knowledge sharing do not focus on sharer perceptions of receiver knowledge needs and behaviours.

A *community* perspective proposes that knowledge sharing is a situated social process in which knowledge exists only in terms of the community which produces, shares, and applies it (Wenger, McDermott, & Snyder, 2002). Knowledge is formative, socially constructed and comprises a shared understanding that can be translated into action and enhanced performance. However, while receivers can ask questions of potential sharers or provide other cues that indicate their knowledge needs, theoretical models for such communities do not explicitly include such feedback. A more complex theory is activity theory which revolves around distributed cognition systems and provides principles for analysing actions and interactions within a historical and cultural context (e.g., Boer, van Baalen, & Kumar, 2002). However, activity theory does not permit a study of the micro-processes in knowledge sharing and does not focus on individual receiver influences.

A fourth perspective conceives knowledge sharing in terms of the *power* thus transferred. While non-discriminatory sharing is an important goal (Freire, 1985), knowledge hoarding is frequently found in firms (cf. Hall, 2004; Husted & Michailova, 2002). We further note that current theories conceptualising the political perspective on knowledge sharing do not explicitly include receiver influences on the process.

RECEIVER-BASED PERSPECTIVE OF KNOWLEDGE SHARING

In seeking a theoretical framework for exploring individual, receiver-based influences on knowledge sharer choices, we investigated existing knowledge sharing and communication theories that explicitly include an individual sharer and individual receiver. We considered the communication model of Shannon and Weaver (1949) which includes a sharer, receiver, transmission and obstructing "noise" that interferes with the successful transfer of knowledge. However, this model does not include an explicit ongoing link from receiver to sharer. Although this and other individual transmission-based models of communication or knowledge sharing have been roundly criticised (e.g., Hislop, 2002), knowledge sharing experts investigating micro-influences in individual knowledge sharing have taken such a perspective in order to highlight the temporal, individual and mediated aspects of the process (e.g., Hendriks, 2004).

We therefore propose a process-oriented model of knowledge sharing that highlights individual sharer and receiver actions and interactions, and that presupposes feedback of knowledge-based needs and behaviours from receivers to sharers. We focus on how sharer perceptions of receiver knowledge needs and behaviours may shape sharer beliefs, attitudes and behaviours in knowledge sharing. We contend that sharers form beliefs and attitudes about receiver knowledge-based needs and behaviours, based on perceptions. Sharers are then likely to behave in accord with these attitudes (Fishbein & Ajzen, 1975). In several recent studies, the knowledge sharing behaviour of individuals was predicted from their beliefs and attitudes (e.g., Bock & Kim, 2002). By developing a process-oriented model that takes receiver feedback into account, we develop the

receiver-based theory further, enrich theory of the knowledge sharing process, and frame the later empirical analysis.

Several recognised theories of knowledge sharing deconstruct the sub-processes involved to better study important micro-influences (e.g., Hendriks, 2004; Huysman & De Wit, 2002). Hendriks (2004) offers a structured process-oriented model of knowledge sharing that enables us to examine the potential role of receivers in sharer choices. The model assumes a person who possesses knowledge (sharer), and includes five steps:

- Sharer becomes aware of the value of her knowledge to a potential receiver;
- Sharer brings knowledge to the attention of a potential receiver;
- Knowledge is transferred to a receiver through a channel;
- Receipt and assimilation of knowledge by receiver;
- Effective application of received knowledge in practice (Hendriks, 2004).

We recast and extend Hendrik's model by proposing an additional, sixth step:

Figure 1. A simplified receiver-based model of knowledge sharing

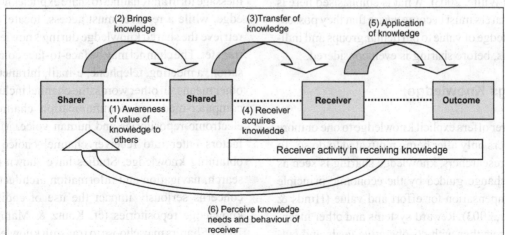

- Feedback from receiver to sharer about receiver knowledge needs and behaviours, including knowledge application.

This step transforms the model to represent a receiver-based perspective of knowledge sharing. We illustrate the six steps in a simplified model of receiver-based knowledge sharing (Figure 1) and discuss how, in each step, sharers may make choices based on perceptions of receiver needs and behaviour.

AWARENESS OF VALUE OF KNOWLEDGE TO OTHERS

How do knowledge carriers (potential sharers) become aware that they possess tacit knowledge of value to others? First, there may be position-oriented cues suggesting that their knowledge is relevant to others' work, an example being job roles (Schultz, 2003). Second, sharers may be alerted to their tacit knowledge by inquiry and other forms of dialogue where we try to understand what others know (Neve, 2003). By connecting through social networks, people may become aware of what others need or want to know (Kilduff & Tsai, 2003). Third, where codified knowledge repositories are involved, knowledge requirements can be provided to sharers through a knowledge audit (White, 2003). What is emphasised here is that sharers must become aware that they possess knowledge of value to particular groups and individuals, before sharing is even considered.

Brings Knowledge

A sharer offers explicit knowledge to one or more receivers only after being motivated to do so. To some researchers, knowledge sharing is seen as an exchange guided by the economic principle of compensation for effort and value (Hinds & Pfeffer, 2003). Reward systems and other incentives, together with co-operative goals and cul-

tures, may drive sharing (Hall 2001). However, a variety of receiver-based issues are also likely to be motivational. In firms, jobs are typically differentiated. Integration takes place through different integrative mechanisms such as routines and meetings (Grant, 1996). It is possible therefore that sharers look to job roles to ascertain the knowledge that is needed by the job incumbents. Sharers may seek some indication of the value of sharing their knowledge. The fact that receivers have previously applied a sharer's knowledge may thus encourage further sharing of the same type of knowledge (Hall, 2001). Social relationships are believed to play a role. When there are good relationships between sharers and receivers and a healthy level of trust, sharers are more inclined to share (Andrews & Delahaye, 2000). Compassion can also provoke a desire to alleviate suffering by contributing knowledge (Frost, Dutton, Worline, & Wilson, 2000). More directly, receiver questions can indicate a need or desire to know (Neve, 2003) while mutual exchanges of knowledge can increase sharing (Kilduff & Tsai, 2003). Perceived or formal receiver access privileges may also constrain the sharing of possibly confidential or otherwise sensitive knowledge (Hall, 2001).

Transfer of Knowledge

A sharer must select a communication strategy, message form and channel to share explicit knowledge, while a receiver must access, locate, and retrieve the shared knowledge during knowledge transfer. The channel may be face-to-face conversation, a meeting, telephone, e-mail, intranet, or other means. In other words, the channel includes computer-mediated communication channels, electronic repositories and human voice. Many factors enter into receiver channel choice for obtaining knowledge. Studies have shown that search, navigation and information architecture concerns seriously impact the use of codified knowledge repositories (cf. Kautz & Mahnke, 2003). Sharers may choose to transmit knowledge by channels known to be attended by receivers. Affecting this choice are emerging organisational environments of resource shortages, information overload, shrinking employee attention and self-managing teams. In such settings, employee commitments are increasingly negotiated rather than directed (Church & Burke, 1993). We argue that such changes influence the time available to share or receive, and the channels chosen by receivers and sharers for knowledge sharing. For example, e-mail was recently identified as the most popular organisational communication tool (Edwards & Shaw, 2004). Sharers may believe that they can reach their target receiver(s) by e-mail and so choose that channel.

Receiver Acquires Knowledge

A receiver assimilates shared knowledge by understanding, adapting, and re-creating knowledge for use in new local contexts. According to Freire's theory of dialogical communication, knowledge is the result of individual inquiry but requires the cooperation and skills of the sharer (Freire, 2000). Cross, Parker, Prusak, and Borgatti (2001) discovered in a study that "people who encourage true learning are those who think along with the seeker and participate in problem solving. Rather than simply loading information onto the seeker, these people first understand the problem as experienced by the seeker and then shape their knowledge to that problem". Also emphasising a cooperative approach, Bakhtin sees dialogue as a process where people anticipate one another's responses and learn from the differences revealed (Koschmann, 1999). Wells, after Vygotsky, defines dialogue as collaborative meaning making where individual and collective understandings are developed through successive contributions of individuals who continually anticipate one another's future responses in those contributions (Wells, 2000).

A receiver must be able to relate incoming knowledge to her existing knowledge (Dixon,

2002) however there may be a clash of different perspectives and cognition (Lane & Lubtkin, 1998). A common example is when sharer and receiver belong to different workgroups and experience difficulties relating to each other's specialised knowledge. While ideally, shared knowledge should be expressed as a good fit with receiver cognitive capacity (Hinds & Pfeffer, 2003; Neve, 2003), a dialogical process may be helpful to negotiate apparent gaps. This requires sharer understanding that the gap exists and an ability to co-structure the dialogue appropriately.

Clearly, such a level of consciousness and cooperation is most unlikely when codified repositories are employed to support knowledge sharing. Plato recognised the difficulties of learning without the sharer being present, with Quinn writing, "Texts only have value ... when their meaning can be explicated. They cannot stand alone as self-sufficient learning models. Their 'parent' or author must be present to teach their true meaning" (Quinn, 1998).

Application

Knowledge in organisations only gains value when it is applied usefully in a work context. When a sharer knows that previously shared knowledge has been usefully applied, sharers may share further (Hall, 2001). Sharers may also consider the purpose for which a receiver will apply the knowledge and choose whether and how to share, accordingly. For instance, a sharer may withhold knowledge that they suspect may be used by others to harm them (Husted & Michailova, 2002).

Perceive Receiver Knowledge Needs and Behaviours

Receiver knowledge needs and behaviours are perceived by sharers whose beliefs, attitudes, and behaviours are shaped accordingly. Many examples of different types of feedback have been provided in the discussions for the first five steps noted earlier. In practice, however, there is likely to be a range of ways that sharers form beliefs and attitudes about receiver knowledge needs and behaviours. We explored these ways empirically, however first we review the research design that was employed.

METHODOLOGY

Two interpretive case studies were conducted as the first stage of a large project investigating socio-technical aspects of intra-organisational knowledge sharing (Hunter, 2003; Lichtenstein, Hunter, & Mustard, 2004). As the topic is under-explored, it called for inductive exploratory studies where the findings are ground in proximate observation of the phenomena of study (Galliers, 1992). All case-related names that follow are fictitious. The research was carried out at a large Australian retail organisation, OzRetail, and at the Australian headquarters of a large multinational information technology corporation, GloTech. At the time of study, GloTech had an established global formal knowledge management initiative with many elements, while knowledge sharing ventures comprising intranets at OzRetail were recent, emergent and local. This difference provided an opportunity to account for issues such as the impact of formal management strategy. Units studied comprised the Web services and marketing teams at GloTech; the change control, production, development, and testing teams at OzRetail; and associated team leaders and managers. Thus, the views of people with a strong understanding of ICT and related issues were tapped, enabling us to focus on social and socio-technical issues.

The main data gathered comprised seventeen audio-taped, semi-structured, single interviews of an hour's duration conducted in July 2003 – October 2003. We also attended and observed several meetings, made written observations of knowledge sharing venues and knowledge technology use, and collected relevant documents. At the start of the interviews, key terms and definitions were provided to participants. Of particular interest, knowledge was defined as existing in the mind of an individual and created from information that had been processed in the mind of the individual and was believed (by that individual) to be authenticated and true. Interview questions were based on five key areas: knowledge sharing practices; ICT utilisation for knowledge sharing, motivators and inhibitors in knowledge sharing; knowledge sharing choices, and organisational culture. Key questions probed the decision to share knowledge with receivers (including codified and personalised strategies), individual rationale for the selection of channels for sharing knowledge, and issues that motivated or limited knowledge sharing. We discovered that more than seventy per cent of the responses that addressed motivational and behavioural factors in sharer choices involved receivers. This finding led to a more focused study of the receiver-based issues in the data, the results of which are reported in this chapter. An example of a question that revealed the impact of receivers on sharer choices was: "When do you share knowledge with others? What are the triggers?" Responses involving receivers enabled us to identify strong connections between sharer beliefs, attitudes, and behaviours; and perceived receiver knowledge needs and behaviours.

Coded categories and concepts discovered in the interview transcripts were inductively developed from a qualitative content analysis (Krippendorf, 1980) of the interview transcripts that focused on identifying receiver-based issues in knowledge sharing, as suggested by the key steps including feedback provided by receivers in the receiver-based model of knowledge sharing (Figure 1) and related theoretical concepts from the literature. Concepts evolved to conclusive states over iterative readings and were grouped into themes at the end of analysis. Additional insights gained from observations and documents were used for validation and enhancement of the themes.

KNOWLEDGE SHARING AT GLOTECH AND OZRETAIL

At GloTech's Australian head office, the knowledge sharing culture was team-based, with many teams having their own intranets on which they regularly stored and re-used business processes, applications, organisational directories, and corporate news. The Web services team developed internal and external Web sites for the Australian branch, while publishing and updating content for themselves and on behalf of other teams. The intranets were non-interactive. Personalised knowledge sharing mainly took place within teams or units, either face-to-face at desks, by e-mail, or in meetings. Given high employee mobility and significant contractor service provision, relationships were relatively undeveloped and in constant turmoil. There were no managerial incentives for sharing knowledge. Knowledge in the units, teams and intranets studied was slowly growing, but overall, the organisational culture was not favourable toward liberal and relaxed sharing of knowledge.

In contrast, OzRetail was relatively inexperienced with knowledge technologies, having deployed intranets for only two years at the time of study. Moreover, there were no formal knowledge management initiatives and most intranets had evolved from team motivation and were team-oriented. The four technical teams studied worked closely together to develop and maintain applications, yet maintained separate intranets for storing and re-using business processes and applications. Like GloTech, the intranets were non-interactive, with personalised knowledge sharing mainly taking place within teams or units, either face-to-face at desks, by e-mail, or in meetings. No incentives were offered for sharing knowledge. Many of the people in the teams studied had worked at OzRetail for five to twenty years, and held good working and social relationships with others both within and across teams. While most knowledge was shared within teams, there

was greater inter-team sharing than at GloTech due to some longstanding relationships. However, the organisational culture had been affected by a number of recent restructures over the previous decade, which had instilled some guardedness in sharing knowledge among the people lacking pre-established social relationships. Moreover, some participants expressed a lack of knowledge about what workers in other teams did.

RECEIVER INFLUENCES ON KNOWLEDGE SHARING

The findings reported in this section have emerged from an empirical study of the concepts represented by the receiver-based model of knowledge sharing (Figure 1). A number of known findings in the knowledge sharing literature were confirmed by this study—notably, the motivational and guiding roles of good social relationships and the exchange of value in the form of knowledge. The study has also broken new ground by suggesting the contribution to sharer behaviour of important receiver-based influences.

Not surprisingly, the influences identified were not limited to issues attributable to receiver needs; sharers also had needs relating to receivers and these needs drove some of their sharing behaviours. A group of issues attributable to *receiver* needs are summarised in Table 1. A second group of issues that can be attributed to *sharer* needs are summarised in Table 2. Attitudes are good predictors of intentions and behaviour, and sharers often reported their behaviour as well as their attitudes in interviews. We observed consistency between the reported behaviour and attitudes. To commence, the receiver-based influences on knowledge sharing, arising from receiver issues (Table 1), are discussed. We point out that, while participants were given a definition differentiating knowledge and information (as stated earlier), and were only asked questions about knowledge and knowledge sharing, they sometimes used the term "information" rather than "knowledge" within their responses. To ensure that we correctly interpreted such responses, the researcher checked with the participant to ascertain whether they were, in fact, discussing knowledge rather than information. We have marked all such corrected instances as "[knowledge]".

Need-to-Know

Dominating receiver-oriented reasons for motivating sharing was the sharer's perception of a receiver's (or a group of receivers') "need-to-know". Employing such a motivator was perceived as an efficient use of sharers' and receivers' time in that only apparently relevant knowledge was shared. Sharers had developed rules-of-thumb for assessing which individuals or groups might need their knowledge and precisely when they might need it.

Signal Need-to-Know

The default position for most sharers was that colleagues did not have a need for their knowledge unless there was a clear signal indicating a need-to-know:

If they don't need to know it, I don't think I would disclose it to them. (intranet contractor)

Sharers made assumptions about the knowledge that was needed by others. For example, in all cases where participants described only privately accessible work-related knowledge stored on their PCs, participants mentioned various tips, guidelines and solutions that may have been useful to other employees. However, sharers had no way of knowing whether their colleagues would find anything useful in such files as they had not disclosed them to anyone, nor had colleagues asked related questions that might suggest value in such disclosure. Moreover, sharers felt that the files would not be of value to others while in their current informal personalised form.

Importantly, sharers indicated that while they would share if directed to do so by management, other colleagues' needs provided a greater stimulus:

I share knowledge from my own initiative because I would rather share knowledge with people when there is a need for them to know, whereas if my

Table 1. Receiver issues influencing sharer beliefs and behaviours (case study findings)

Receiver Issue	Sub-issue	Description
Need to know	Signal need-to-know	- Receiver provides signal when knowledge is needed
	Specialised job role	- Receiver specialised job role indicates need-to-know
	Inquiry	- Receiver asks questions
Desire to know	Attitude	- Receiver shows interest in sharer's knowledge - Receiver shows interest in learning
	Prior relationship -	Good relationship between sharer and receiver
	Exchange -	Receiver shared knowledge previously - Previous recognition given by receiver to sharer
Accessibility	Cognitive capacity	- Receiver lacks relative absorptive capacity - Receiver cannot absorb unlimited knowledge
	Channel access -	Receiver channel attendance
	Resources	- Receiver lacks time to listen to or learn knowledge
Anticipated use	Performance	- Receiver / team performance needs improvement
	Altruism -	Receiver deserves compassion and help
	Power	- Receiver competes through knowledge acquisition

manager tells me to document things, I might not agree with what she perceives as being important. (Web developer)

This finding supports Bhatt's claim that "what kind of knowledge is shared and how knowledge will be shared are determined by the professionals, not by the management" (Bhatt, 2002, p.33).

Specialised Job Role

Sharer perceptions of receiver need-to-know were mainly founded on job role and perceived knowledge specialisation. This is not surprising considering that firms are grounded on such specialisation, with integration enabled through integrative mechanisms (Grant, 1996). As one participant stated:

This content should not be shared with any other team such as Marketing as it is not relevant to their work. (Web developer)

Such preconceptions about others and their needs reflect a limited understanding of how knowledge in different units and particular job roles may be inter-related, as well as revealing an insular tendency that does not promote a strong knowledge-sharing culture (Smith & McKeen,

2002). Instead, there was evidence of an occupational culture determined by specialised training and knowledge sets (Sackmann, 1991). Sackmann suggests such knowledge can define boundaries of affiliation and erect barriers, as was found for the teams studied at GloTech and OzRetail, although older established relationships at OzRetail that had survived various restructures enabled some level of inter-team sharing.

Inquiry

Another frequently mentioned signal to sharers that a receiver had a knowledge need was a direct inquiry:

It really does not make any sense for me to go and teach others. Unless there was a specific question, I would not normally share. (developer)

One problem with sharers relying on direct inquiry to ascertain receiver knowledge needs is that some receivers may be cognitively, linguistically or culturally ineffective at asking questions or may have related social difficulties (Neve, 2003). Moreover, inquiry requires proximity or an interactive medium, and unfettered access to sharers.

Table 2. Sharer issues influencing sharer beliefs and behaviours (case study findings)

Sharer Issue	Sub-issue	Description
Interruption	Interruptive receiver	- Sharer does not wish to be disturbed by a receiver who needs knowledge
Resources	Lack of resources	- Sharer lacks resources to accommodate demanding receivers
Altruism	Self-actualisation	- Sharer feels self-actualised when receiver is helped
Security	Confidentiality	- Receiver should not have certain knowledge as it is confidential
Power	Hierarchy	- Sharer hoards knowledge to retain position

Desire to Know

Sharers indicated that whether others appeared to desire their knowledge was relevant to choosing to share.

Attitude

Receiver attitudes of enjoyment, enthusiasm or interest affected sharer motivation:

A person's enthusiasm to learn affects how much knowledge I will share with them, because if they are not interested to know any more, then I will not tell them any more. (systems engineer)

This finding reflects the more social aspects of knowledge sharing (Kilduff & Tsai, 2003). About half the participants mentioned an interest in sharing with others who had a learning attitude in general and who therefore might provide a fruitful exchange:

If a person had previously shared knowledge with me, then that gives me a slight hint that he will be interested in the [knowledge] and that he is interested in learning new things. I would be more favourable towards sharing [knowledge] with him — not because he had previously shared [knowledge] with me, but rather that I think he might have something interesting to say. (Web developer)

While such sharing demonstrates a mature approach to knowledge sharing, its real value may rest in the wider application of such practices.

Prior Relationship

Many sharers spoke of sharing with people with whom they worked or with whom they had a relationship and of the impact of a lack of such a relationship:

I could not share my knowledge freely with people I did not know at all.

This supports current findings about social relationships (Andrews & Delahaye, 2000; Hall, 2001; Husted & Michailova, 2002).

Exchange

Some sharers indicated a willingness to view knowledge sharing as an exchange with receivers for something of value:

I would share my knowledge more if I did receive more recognition. I generally just receive an informal thank you from the person I am sharing or teaching my knowledge to. (developer)

Moreover, all sharers indicated that they would be more likely to share knowledge with someone who had first shared knowledge with them. Value exchange has been well reported in the knowledge sharing literature (e.g., Hinds & Pfeffer, 2003).

Accessibility

It mattered to sharers whether others could access their shared knowledge. Motivation, channel choice, and strategy used in knowledge transfer were decided accordingly.

Cognitive Capacity

Many participants believed that others' cognitive capacity to assimilate their knowledge was insufficient, a problem that has been discussed by Lane and Lubatkin (1998). Some participants mentioned the lack of prerequisite knowledge:

A person's prior knowledge limits how much knowledge I will share with them, because if they don't know the basics, then it is pointless for me to share my more advanced knowledge with them. (systems engineer)

Missing context was mentioned by a few participants as a reason why others would not be able to comprehend their knowledge:

Any [knowledge] that I keep for myself in my own notes, would probably only be interpretable by me because I wrote them down and I know the context in which they were written. (intranet developer)

Some participants appeared to recognise their vital role in others' learning (Freire, 2000; Koschmann, 1999):

I prefer that [chat] because on a personal level I retain more of that [knowledge] if somebody has actually spoken to me. (manager)

While none of the participants specifically mentioned taking an active role in receiver's learning as espoused by (Freire, 2000; Koschmann, 1999), a meeting concerning a planned Web service suggested considerable mutual consideration. In contrast, the static intranets did not exhibit any consideration of receiver learning needs and it was mentioned many times that intranets on their own were inadequate for providing deep receiver understanding of the business processes stored therein.

Channel Access

Sharers generally believed that they needed to capture receiver attention through the channel usually attended by receivers, in accord with Straub and Karahanna's (1998) findings:

If you send an email to a group with a new idea, most people seem to dismiss it as spam, so if you

put the knowledge on the intranet and provide a link in an email, that would be more effective. (Web developer)

Time sensitivity of knowledge to be shared by the sharer and the importance of that message reaching the target audience were also key influences in channel choices:

If there is something that is urgent that the group needs to know about, it's either sent through emails, or basically, we just turn around and talk to our team. (Web developer)

The size of the target audience that needed the knowledge also impacted sharer choice of channel, together with other factors. For example:

The intranet is really only for very high level [knowledge] or [knowledge] that is important to a lot of different people such as when you may have more than twenty people who need to know this [knowledge]. (marketing publisher)

However, e-mail had been appropriated by employees for other work purposes in addition to communication and knowledge transfer, including collective and individual memory, accountability and commitment:

I can go back and follow up, if nothing is done with the arrangements made in email. (marketing publisher)

Resources

Participants considered whether others were too busy to listen to them:

If everybody is really busy and there are too many projects being worked on, I will hold back my knowledge until the time is right. (team leader)

Anticipated Use

The fact that a receiver could use a sharer's knowledge to good effect was motivational, while any potentially harmful use of the knowledge had the opposite effect.

Performance

Team, individual (receiver), and company performance were often considered by sharers:

When you work in a team, for the team to be productive, all the members of the team should have a common knowledge base so that the team can progress faster and improve their skills. (intranet developer)

At times, performance considerations were combined with altruistic feelings:

I love seeing my team succeed and I don't think it is right not to share my knowledge with them. (team leader)

Altruism

Many sharers were compassionate and altruistic in their attitude towards receivers (Frost et al., 2000):

When people are doing things in an inefficient way and there are a lot of other alternatives out there, I feel sympathy for them and I just want them to see the light and I would like to make life easier for them. (developer)

Power

Some sharers thought that receivers may want to wrest control from them through application of shared knowledge. This belief led to knowledge being withheld during a period when receivers

could have a key impact on knowledge development:

I have found that if you keep people informed along the way they often try to get involved either positively or negatively, so I have found that it is usually better to wait until the end. (Web developer)

Table 2 presents the receiver-based issues that stem from sharer needs. We discuss these in subsequent paragraphs.

Interruption

A few sharers made comments indicating that they saw receiver needs for their knowledge as intruding on their scarce time, motivating them to share.

If I am constantly being asked the same [knowledge] regularly, I will publish it to the intranet to get people to leave me alone to complete my more pending daily tasks. (intranet developer)

Resources

While sharers thought about whether others were too busy to listen to them, receivers felt the same way with respect to sharer busy-ness:

If everyone is really busy and does not have the time to help me, then I will look up the instructions site. (developer)

Altruism

Sharers felt self-actualised when their knowledge was used by others as well as appreciated. For example:

I do feel a sense of intrinsic reward, I guess, when Joe is using Secure Copy and he does work a lot faster than when he was using FTP. People will generally thank you when they see the benefit of using it themselves. (developer)

Security

Sharers also mentioned the role of confidentiality in their decision to share knowledge with a receiver. Often this concept was mingled with the receiver's need-to-know:

Confidentiality is one thing (a reason not to share knowledge). If the knowledge is not necessary for them to perform their job, and if the [knowledge] I am telling them might infringe on GloTech's security or privacy policy, then I will not share that knowledge. (Web developer)

Power

Sharers often shared knowledge in line with job positions, thus demonstrating a desire to maintain their established positions and reinforce the status quo. As mentioned earlier, sharers were also aware of a power struggle that might ensue if knowledge was shared when projects or details were not yet finalised.

CONCLUSION

This chapter explored how and why sharers pay heed to perceived receiver knowledge needs and behaviours when making key choices in knowledge sharing. The chapter examined a number of theoretical perspectives of knowledge sharing and introduced a new theoretical approach — receiver-based theory of knowledge sharing — into research in organisational knowledge management, and demonstrated how this theory can be applied to study knowledge sharing. A model of receiver-based knowledge sharing (Figure 1) was developed from literature and we demonstrated its application to study knowledge sharing for

several teams in two large organisations. A set of key receiver-based influences on knowledge sharing emerged as a result of this research, highlighting both receiver issues and sharer issues that related to receivers and that impacted sharer choices (Table 1 and Table 2). The issues identified add new insights to existing theory in knowledge sharing theory and practice. The findings shed light on ways that intra-organisational knowledge sharing might be constrained or enhanced, and suggest that perceived receiver knowledge needs and behaviour are important motivators and inhibitors in intra-organisational knowledge sharing, complementing an emerging research stream that explores individual issues in knowledge sharing (Andrews & Delahaye, 2000; Neve, 2003).

We focus here on two key findings and their implications for companies aiming for more effective internal knowledge sharing. First, this study suggests that a sharer relies on her belief about whether a receiver needs her knowledge, before choosing to share. To form this belief, a sharer will rely to a significant extent on personal perceptions of job roles, specialisation, and specific receiver cues, such as asking questions. The default sharer belief is that receivers do not need her knowledge, and thus the default attitude and behaviour is to choose not to share. Related to this finding, power can be manifested through such beliefs and attitudes, as existing hierarchies and power structures tend to be preserved (as was happening in the two case studies), and those workers with integrated knowledge can keep those workers possessing only fragmented knowledge in positions where they are unable to progress. This finding suggests that for companies to achieve more effective knowledge sharing, they must move away from the paradigm of "need-to-know". Organisations must share more freely, so that valuable isolated knowledge can be integrated and synthesised, suggesting patterns that can reveal important issues and potential solutions, and developing more empowered employees. This will entail sharers proactively seeking out receivers with the capacity to integrate and apply the available knowledge, but who may currently be unaware of its existence.

In the second key finding, this study suggests that currently, a sharer develops a belief about whether a receiver is interested in her knowledge or is able to learn and apply it, prior to choosing to share it, using receiver cues such as enthusiasm and interest in learning. Moreover, many sharers are interested in actively participating in a receiver's learning processes. Thus, when a codified medium such as an intranet is present and applied in a static way, an important reason why it is under-utilised for knowledge sharing is the absence of a feedback loop. The implications from this finding are that new ways are needed to enable receivers and sharers to engage more effectively in dialogue and other collaborative learning processes in which the sharer catalyses receiver learning, using approaches such as communities of practice.

Clearly, the theory presented in this chapter is preliminary and requires further development:

- First, the findings from the case studies relate mainly to the sharing of explicit knowledge. The effort required for a sharer to share explicit knowledge is likely to be qualitatively different to the effort needed for sharing tacit knowledge that is difficult or impossible to articulate, and the risk of personal loss of power for the sharer will likely be less. Investigating receiver influences on the sharing of tacit knowledge that cannot be easily articulated would present a considerable challenge. In such circumstances it is likely that sharers would seek even greater receiver feedback to guide the process.
- Second, the model is individually based and there may be value therefore in considering the role of receiver influences in collective knowledge sharing theories such as those based on an activity theory approach (Boer

et al., 2002).

- Third, the set of receiver influences on knowledge sharing (Table 1 and Table 2) is also limited, having been developed from only two case studies set in a wider study of knowledge sharing. Thus, while excellent context was provided for this study, the data sets used were constrained. Richer data sets could be captured through more focused empirical studies of receiver influences on sharer choices, while the individual issues in Tables 1 and 2 can be separately explored.

In conclusion, our study suggests that sharers tend to share knowledge when they believe that a receiver *seems* ready — whether that is because of perceptions of job role, receiver cues, channels used, performance, or other indicators. Companies therefore need to develop better ways to connect potential sharers to *real* receiver knowledge needs at the key points that we have identified in the knowledge sharing process.

ACKNOWLEDGMENT

An earlier version of this chapter was presented at the 7th Australian Conference on Knowledge Management and Intelligent Decision Support (ACKMIDS 2004). The authors wish to thank Dr. Jamie Mustard and the anonymous reviewers for their helpful comments.

REFERENCES

Alavi, M. & Leidner, D. E. (1999). Knowledge management systems: Issues, challenges, and benefits. *Communications of AIS, 1*(Article 7), 1-37.

Andrews, K. M. & Delahaye, B. L. (2000). Influences on knowledge processes in organisational learning: The psychosocial filter. *The Journal of Management Studies, 37*(6), 797-810.

Argote, L. (1999) *Organizational learning, retaining and transferring knowledge*. Boston: Kluwer Academic.

Barabba, V. P. & Zaltman, G. (1991). *Hearing the voice of the market: Competitive advantage through creative use of market information*. Boston: Harvard Business School Press.

Bhatt, G. D. (2002) Management strategies for individual knowledge and organizational knowledge. *Journal of Knowledge Management, 6*(1), 31-39.

Bock, G. W. & Kim, Y. G. (2002). Breaking the myths of rewards: An exploratory study of attitudes about knowledge sharing. *Information Resources Management Journal, 15*(2), 14-22.

Boer, N., van Baalen, P. & Kumar, K. (2002). An activity theory approach for studying the situatedness of knowledge sharing. In *Proceedings of the 35th Hawaii International Conference on Systems Sciences*.

Cross, R., Parker, A., Prusak, L., & Borgatti, S. P. (2001). Knowing what we know: Supporting knowledge creation and sharing in social networks. *Organizational Dynamics, 30*(2), 100-120.

Dixon, N. (2002, March/April). The neglected receiver of knowledge sharing. *Ivey Business Journal*, 35-40.

Easterby-Smith, M., Crossan, M., & Nicolini, D. (2000). Organizational learning: Debates past, present and future. *Journal of Management Studies, 38*(6), 783-796.

Edwards, J. S. & Shaw, D. (2004). Supporting knowledge management with IT. In *Proceedings of DSS 2004*, Prato, Italy.

Fishbein, M. & Ajzen, I. (1975). *Belief, attitude, intention and behavior: An introduction to theory and research*. Addison-Wesley.

Freire, P. (1985). *The politics of education* (Trans.). London: Macmillan.

Freire, P. (2000). *Pedagogy of the oppressed* (M. Bergman Ramos, Trans.). New York: Continuum.

Frost, P., Dutton, J., Worline, M., & Wilson, M. (2000). Narratives of compassion in organizations. In S. Fineman, (Ed.), *Emotions in Organizations* (pp. 25-45). Thousand Oaks, CA: Sage.

Galliers, R. D. (1992). Choosing information systems research approaches. In R. D. Galliers (Ed.), *Information systems research: Issues, methods and practical guidelines* (pp. 144-162). Oxford: Blackwell Scientific Publications.

Grant, R. M. (1996, Winter). Towards a knowledge-based theory of the firm. *Strategic Management Journal, 17*, 109-122.

Hall, H. (2001). Input-friendliness: Motivating knowledge sharing across intranets. *Journal of Information Science, 27*(3), 139-146.

Hall, H. (2004). The intranet as actor: The role of the intranet in knowledge sharing. In *Proceedings of the International Workshop on Understanding Sociotechnical Action* (pp. 109-111), Edinburgh.

Hansen, M. T., Nohria, N., & Tierney, T. (1999, March 1). What's your strategy for managing knowledge? *Harvard Business Review*.

Hendriks, P. H. J. (1999). Why share knowledge? The influence of ICT on the motivation for knowledge sharing. *Knowledge and Process Management, 6*(2), 91-100.

Hendriks, P. H. J. (2004). Assessing the role of culture in knowledge sharing. In *Proceedings of Fifth European Conference in Organization, Knowledge, Learning and Capabilities (OKLC 2004)*, Innsbruk.

Hinds, P. J. & Pfeffer, J. (2003). Why organizations don't "know what they know": Cognitive and motivational factors affecting the transfer of expertise. In M. Ackerman, V. Pipek, & V. Wulf

(Eds.), *Sharing expertise: Beyond knowledge management.* Cambridge: MIT Press.

Hislop, D. (2002). Mission impossible? Communicating and sharing knowledge via information technology. *Journal of Information Technology, 17,* 165-177.

Hunter, A. (2003). *Utilisation of a corporate intranet for knowledge sharing and retention.* Unpublished honours thesis, School of Information Systems, Deakin University, Melbourne, Australia.

Husted, K. & Michailova, S. (2002). Diagnosing and fighting knowledge sharing hostility. *Organizational Dynamics, 31*(1), 60-73.

Huysman, M. & de Wit, D. (2002). *Knowledge sharing in practice.* Dordrecht: Kluwer Academics Publishers.

Kautz, K. & Mahnke, V. (2003). Value creation through IT-supported knowledge management? The utilisation of a knowledge management system in a global consulting company. *Informing Science, 6,* 75-88.

Kilduff, M. & Tsai, W. (2003). *Social networks and organizations.* Sage.

Koschmann, T. (1999). Toward a dialogic theory of learning: Bakhtin's contribution to learning in settings of collaboration. In *Proceedings of Computer Supported Collaborative Learning (CSCL '99)* (pp. 308-313). Retrieved January 21, 2005, from http://kn.cilt.org/cscl99/A38/A38.HTM

Krippendorf, K. (1980). *Content analysis: An introduction to its methodology.* Beverly Hills, CA: Sage Publications.

Lane, P. J. & Lubatkin, M. (1998). Relative absorptive capacity and interorganizational learning. *Strategic Management Journal, 19,* 461-477.

Lichtenstein, S., Hunter, A., & Mustard, J. (2004). Utilisation of intranets for knowledge sharing: A socio-technical study. In *Proceedings of Austral-asian Conference on Information Systems (ACIS 2004),* Tasmania, Hobart.

Markus, M. L. (2001). Toward a theory of knowledge reuse: Types of knowledge reuse situations and factors in reuse success. *Journal of Management Information Systems, 18*(1), 57-93.

Neve, T. O. (2003). Right questions to capture knowledge. *Electronic Journal of Knowledge Management, 1*(1), 47-54. Retrieved February 5, 2005 from http://www.ejkm.com/volume-1/volume1-issue1/issue1-art6-neve.pdf

Nonaka, I. (1994). A dynamic theory of organizational knowledge creation. *Organization Science, 5*(1), 14-37.

Polanyi, M. (1962). *Personal knowledge.* London: Routledge & Kegan Paul.

Quinn, P. (1998). Knowledge, power and control: Some issues in epistemology. In *Proceedings of Twentieth World Congress of Philosophy,* Boston. Retrieved January 23, 2005, from http://www.bu.edu/wcp/Papers/Poli/PoliQuin.htm

Sackmann, S. A. (1991). *Cultural knowledge in organizations: Exploring the collective mind.* Newbury Park, CA: Sage.

Schultz, R. (2003). Pathways of relevance: Exploring inflows of knowledge into subunits of multinational corporations. *Organization Science, 14*(4), 440-459.

Shannon, C. E. & Weaver, W. (1949). *The mathematical theory of communication.* Chicago: University of Illinois.

Smith, H. & McKeen, J. (2002). Instilling a knowledge sharing culture. In *Proceedings of Fifth European Conference in Organization, Knowledge, Learning and Capabilities (OKLC 2004),* Innsbruk.

Straub, D. & Karahanna, E. (1998). Knowledge worker communications and recipient availability:

Toward a task closure explanation of media choice. *Organization Science, 9*(2), 160-175.

Swan, J., Robertson, M. & Newell, S. (2002). Knowledge management: the human factor. In S. Barnes (Ed.), *Knowledge management systems: Theory and practice.* Thomson Learning.

Tsoukas, H. (2003). Do we really understand tacit knowledge? In M. Easterby-Smith, & M. Lyles (Eds.), *The Blackwell companion to organizational learning and knowledge management.* Oxford: Basil Blackwell.

Wells, G. (2000). Dialogic inquiry in education: Building on the legacy of Vygotsky. In C. D. Lee & P. Smagorinsky (Eds.), *Vygotskian perspectives on literacy research* (pp. 51-85). New York: Cambridge University Press.

Wenger, E., McDermott, R., & Snyder, W. M. (2002). *Cultivating communities of practice.* Boston: Harvard Business School Press.

White, M. (2003). *Creating an effective intranet.* Intranet Focus Ltd. Retrieved June 24, 2005, from http://www.intranetfocus.com/information/effectiveintranets.pdf

This work was previously published in International Journal of Knowledge Management, Vol. 2, Issue 1, edited by M.E. Jennex, pp. 24-40, copyright 2006 by IGI Publishing, formerly known as Idea Group Publishing (an imprint of IGI Global).

Chapter VIII
A Dialectic on the Cultural and Political Aspects of Information and Knowledge Sharing in Organizations[1]

Dennis Hart
Australian National University, Australia

Leoni Warne
Defence Science and Technology Organisation, Australia

ABSTRACT

This chapter raises issues concerning information and knowledge sharing in organizations and why such sharing is often difficult to achieve. In particular, it compares an organizational cultural analysis with an organizational political one. The authors believe that the issues raised are not only important but are often insufficiently attended to by practitioners who are attempting to build technological information and knowledge management systems. The driver for the chapter is the fact that despite impressive advances in technology, and its now almost ubiquitous presence in organizations, many of the benefits originally expected concerning improved information and knowledge sharing have not materialised as was once confidently expected. One of the authors argues a basic reason for this lies in the lack of attention to the cultural foundations of organizations, while the other contends it is more because matters relating to organizational power and political matters are often misunderstood, overlooked or ignored. These different perspectives are discussed and contrasted in order to tease out the important differences between them and assess the prospects for a synthesis. It is concluded that, while there are important commonalities between the two perspectives, there are also fundamental differences, including concerning what are causes and what are effects and, therefore, how to go about effecting change regarding information and knowledge sharing.

Copyright © 2008, IGI Global, distributing in print or electronic forms without written permission of IGI Global is prohibited.

INTRODUCTION

New organizational forms that are horizontally structured rather than functionally or vertically structured have been referred to, variously, as: modular, cluster, learning, network-centric, perpetual matrix organisations, spinout or virtual corporations (Miles & Snow, 1986; Bartlett & Ghoshal, 1989; Senge, 1990; Quinn, 1992). Regardless of the name, the defining characteristics of these new organizational forms are purported to be flatter hierarchies; decentralised decision-making; greater capacity for tolerance of ambiguity; permeable internal and external boundaries; capacity for renewal; self-organizing units, and self-integrating coordination mechanisms (Daft & Lewin, 1993; Warne et al., 2004). In such organizations, information and particularly knowledge is acknowledged to be the most strategically important resource, and organizational capabilities are viewed to be based on distinctive competencies in sharing and integrating this information and knowledge. The question then is why do so many efforts and systems that are targeted at enabling such sharing to take place fail as often as they do? If communication and sharing of information and knowledge are the keys to strategic organizational capabilities and there is little doubt that the technological capability exists to do it, then why is it rarely achieved, at least to the extent many think is worthwhile or even essential, (although see Hislop (2002) for a sceptical view regarding knowledge sharing via information technology)?

Knowledge management (KM), like information systems (IS) is derived from, and dependent on, a number of reference disciplines. The richness of both these newer disciplines could be said to be due, at least partially, to the multiple perspectives of the numerous branches of learning that are applied to the study of the effective use of information and knowledge in organizations. In information systems and knowledge management, many heated discussions haven taken place as researchers and practitioners argue their perspectives on everything from basic definitions to the intricacies of IS and KM systems. This is not necessarily a bad situation because often new understandings and innovative solutions are derived from wide-ranging but constructive argument and discussion. This chapter is intended to fit this mould—a wide-ranging but constructive argument, discussion and comparison of different views. More specifically, what the authors aim to achieve in this chapter is to first outline and compare an organizational culture perspective on information and knowledge sharing with an organizational political perspective (as represented by the views of the two authors). By doing so, the intention is to tease out the important differences between them, identify any irreconcilable aspects and assess the potential for a synthesis. Note, however, that while the two perspectives discussed are labelled "organizational culture" and "organizational politics", this is for brevity as well as convenience as two particular instances that may be fairly categorized thus, and are not intended as archetypes representative of all such views.

THEORETICAL BACKGROUND

For more than three decades, researchers and practitioners have been concerned about the high failure rate of information systems and, more recently, knowledge management projects (e.g., Lyytinen & Hirschheim, 1987; Ewusi-Mensah & Przasnyski, 1991; Sauer, 1993; Hart & Warne, 1997). As the industry has evolved, the search for factors influencing success and failure, however these are defined, has intensified. Although there may have been incremental improvements, this intensive activity seems not to have resulted in dramatic changes to the success rate for information systems and knowledge management projects. While definitions and rates of failures continue to be debated, information and the systems that provide it, have become an increasingly integral part of modern business life and knowledge generation, and no organization of any size can exist without them (Beynon-Davies, 2002; Applegate et al., 2003). A variety of factors have been identified by researchers as relevant to, or as contributing causes of, the problems that have been experienced and these are briefly surveyed before presenting and comparing the different perspectives below. First, however, a brief explanation is given as to why the authors do not discriminate in this chapter between information and knowledge—all widely acknowledged to be different although related concepts (e.g., Awad & Ghaziri, 2004).

Information and Knowledge

Of information and knowledge, the nature and definition of knowledge remains more controversial than does that of the other two. For example, Venzin et al. (1998) argue that knowledge has been conceived from three epistemologically distinct perspectives: the cognitivist (as exemplified by Simon, 1993), connectionist (as exemplified by Zander & Kogut, 1995) and autopoetic (as exemplified by Nonaka & Takeuchi, 1995). In addition, it has also been extensively argued that the tacit/explicit distinction represents an important difference of kind when it comes to types of knowledge (Polanyi, 1966). These distinctions, however, tend to impact largely on what counts as knowledge, or at least what type of knowledge it is, and how or through what mechanisms that knowledge might be shared, rather than *whether* and *why* knowledge—however it is conceived— will or will not be shared. Indeed, it has been argued that it is not possible to share knowledge at all, since knowledge inherently resides in the inaccessible mind of the knower; it is in fact only possible to share data (Boisot, 2002) and, arguably, information rather than knowledge itself. The authors believe, therefore, that the kinds of distinctions outlined above are of less importance

when it comes to the issues in which the authors are interested, namely assessing and comparing ideas about *whether* and *why*, rather than *what* and *how*, knowledge may or may not be shared. Indeed, for the purposes of the dialectic that is at the centre of this chapter, it is possible to put aside not only differences in conceptions of knowledge but also the clearer and more widely accepted differences between information and knowledge as well. That is, while the differences between the concepts of information and knowledge are acknowledged, they are treated as one in what follows as many and perhaps all of the issues addressed in this chapter affect them in similar if not identical ways.

Organizations and Information and Knowledge Sharing

The widespread application of information and communications technologies (ICT) has generally increased the complexity of the human workplace and has placed new demands on the thinking and communication of individuals. In such contexts, traditional rational systematic processes have limitations and greater demands are made on meta-cognition and intuitive thinking (Woodhouse, 2000; Crawford, 2003). Solving complex problems increasingly involves teams of people with effective communication and cooperation not only within the team itself but also with outsiders such as external stakeholders and those who will be affected by any emerging solution that may be developed. Typically, information gathering, knowledge generation and sharing of all these resources are involved. With the wider use of technologies to achieve routine or programmed tasks, the dynamic of human productivity in organizations has shifted into a 'meta-realm' of shared activity. Daneshar (2003) notes that, in such contexts, it is not only what a person knows that is important but also what they believe should be shared, when, how and with whom.

Despite the claimed benefits of sharing information and knowledge in organizations, and the undoubted and ever increasing capabilities of ICT to enable it, sharing evidently remains remarkably difficult. For example, over a decade ago, Davenport et al. (1992) said that "the rhetoric and technology of information management have far out-paced the ability of people to understand and agree on what information they need and then to share it [so] the information-based organization is largely a fantasy" and, arguably, the situation has not changed much since. Kendall and Kendall (2002), discussing the management of e-commerce projects, say "organizational politics can come into play, because often units feel protective of the data they generate and do not understand the need to share them across the organization". Evidently, motivations for sharing information and knowledge—and perhaps even more importantly, motivations for *not* sharing (e.g., Hart, 2002)—need to be better understood. But this understanding needs to be built on an appropriate underlying organizational theory or metaphor (e.g, Morgan, 1997) such as what is provided by the organizational culture or organizational politics-based views of organizational functioning. Moreover, the chosen theoretical base can be expected to influence the nature of the understanding developed, and it is this aspect on which our chapter is focussed.

Despite the impressive advances in both hardware and software information technology over several decades, and its now almost ubiquitous presence in organizations, the experience and research of both the authors, and others, shows that many of the benefits expected from improved information and knowledge sharing have not materialised. Moreover, the literature puts forward a range of factors as being of relevance to the issue, but it remains unclear as to which are primary and which are secondary or consequential factors in explaining why information and knowledge sharing in organizations are as difficult, while at the same time being as desirable, as they

evidently are. As mentioned earlier, the authors have somewhat different perspectives on these matters, one believing that the lack of attention to the cultural foundations of organizations are major factors, and the other thinking that issues relating to ownership, trust and organizational power and politics are more important. An outline of their different positions follows.

AN ORGANIZATIONAL CULTURE PERSPECTIVE

It is commonly argued that building information and knowledge management systems that people and organizations need and will use effectively is all about understanding how people work in the context of that organization's culture (e.g., Ahmed et al., 2002). However, it is first necessary to briefly review what is meant by "organizational culture" in this context.

Schein (1997) defines organizational culture or, as he more generally terms it, the "culture of a group" as:

A pattern of shared basic assumptions that the group learned as it solved its problems of external adaptation and internal integration that has worked well enough to be considered valid and, therefore, to be taught to new members as the correct way to perceive, think and feel in relation to those problems.

Other definitions differ in detail, but most include reference, in one form or another, to:

- Shared values, beliefs and foundational assumptions.
- Common norms of behaviour, customs, practices, rituals and symbols.
- Shared traditions, myths, meanings and cognitions of the group or organizational world that are inculcated into newcomers through a socialization process and, in what follows, this is the sense in which the term

"culture" is used, as it applies to organizations.

Individuals belonging to the same organization can be expected to have, to some degree, a common identity with other organizational members, to share an understanding of their organizational world and to subscribe, at least in general terms, to their organization's overall goals. If not, then they would not, or should not, be in that organization. A common identity gives everyone a similar way of describing and making sense of their world, of determining what is significant and important, and of how to use resources in the environment (Jordan, 1993). Having this common view of the workplace and one's role in it enables effective communication, the development of trust and shared understanding as well as acting to expedite sharing of information and knowledge, and improve learning and work processes. In turn, sharing information and knowledge acts in a positive feedback loop to enhance the common identity and shared understanding on which it is originally founded. Common identity is influenced by issues around goal alignment, cultural and social identity, language, morale, and workplace policies; in short—the organization's culture.

Common identity does not, however, imply that people in organizations have, or should have, robotic, identical points of view. Of course individual human beings are unique. But humans are social creatures, by and large, and like to band together under uniting banners, and in an effective organization, where employees feel valued and morale is high, these banners will be shared organizational objectives and a unifying degree of shared understanding. On the other hand, low morale brings about higher levels of alienation towards senior management (Ali et al., 2001; Warne et al., 2001) and this has obvious implications for the successful progression of organizations to an ideal standard from this common identity point of view.

Information and knowledge are strategically important resources because these many types of organizational capabilities are a direct result of sharing, integrating and applying them. The effective maintenance, communication, transfer and sharing of information and knowledge is the ubiquitous supportive framework that is needed for the creation and maintenance of strategic organizational outcomes and, if it is not already in place, requires a culture that encourages, supports and values the efforts of the members of the organization in achieving them.

Working collaboratively is essential to organizational success and for successful problem-solving. Very few people work alone or achieve results by themselves, so the people who interact together and yet have different tasks and responsibilities need to understand what each of them are trying to do, why they are doing it, how they are doing it, and what results to expect. This implies the need to specify and build information systems that give effect to this collaboration, enabling the sharing of information and knowledge so those who need it can find it, access it and use it when it is required. It is because many organizations now operate in a climate of uncertainty, dynamism and interdependence that they need to make better use of their information and knowledge-based systems and, among other things, it is this that implies the need for better user requirements analysis and an understanding of the organization's work culture for those systems. Improvements in this area, which the existence of an appropriate organizational culture enhances, would provide the ability to build adaptive systems people will use to share the information and knowledge they have or need. Such systems would support the way they want to work and collaborate rather than expecting workers to adapt to using whatever systems are built for them, as tends to be the case currently. Organizations, their work and the problems they face, are ever more dynamic, however, largely static systems are continuing to be built for them.

Clearly, adding information systems solutions is not always the way to fix problems. First, it is necessary to have a culture of collaboration and sharing and an incentive scheme that rewards teams rather than individuals, so it is clear the organization values teamwork and collaboration. (Warne et al., 2004)

Systems thinking is also tightly coupled with effective mobilisation of information and knowledge resources, and contributes to the development of common identity. Systems thinking, according to Senge (1992), requires a shift of mind—from seeing ourselves as separate to seeing ourselves as connected to, and part of, an organization or organizational sub-unit. The presence or absence of this type of thinking is closely linked to the nature of the organizational culture and, if present, supported and encouraged by that culture, and is accompanied by generally higher levels of interaction between staff and by higher levels of information and knowledge sharing. Because every individual in an organization needs information and other resources to solve problems, and since few, if any, ever solve a problem in complete isolation, an individual's network is one of their most important resources. Both personal and social networks are an important means of acquiring, propagating and sharing information and knowledge. Moreover, the individuals in the network can make their own knowledge, expertise and experience more readily available. In this way, the knowledge and other resources available to any one person, in their work and when problem-solving, are multiple, and there is no way it can be thought of as a solitary activity. Again, however, it is the existence of a supportive organizational culture that underpins, and in turn is itself enhanced by the creation and flourishing of such networks and the benefits they bring (Senge, 1992; Warne et al., 2003).

Apart from satisfying social needs, informal networks also play a pivotal role in knowledge propagation. New knowledge often begins with the individual making personal knowledge available to others as the central activity of knowledge creating organizations. Through conversations people discover what they know, what others know and in the process of sharing, new knowledge is created. Technology such as e-mails, faxes, and telephones are invaluable aids in the process of information and knowledge sharing, but they are only supporting tools. Sharing depends on the quality of conversations, formal or informal, that people have, and whether, and between whom, these conversations occur are dependent on the organizational culture that is in place (Warne et al., 2005). Webber (1993) aptly describes it as "Conversations—not rank, title, or the trappings of power—determine who is literally and figuratively 'in the loop' and who is not." Individual and shared perceptions of the organization, and how they operate, provide an essential backdrop to problem- solving within an organizational context. These perceptions may consist of deeply ingrained assumptions, generalisations, or even pictures or images that influence how people within an organization understand their organizational world and how they should act within it (Senge, 1992), and these, in turn, constitute the organizational culture.

The importance of these perceptions cannot be stressed enough, because they directly influence the construction of individuals' knowledge and understandings that they draw upon in their day-to-day-activities—their shared perceptions. One important example lies in appreciating the ways in which an organization's formal rules and processes can be bent to achieve a desired outcome. This class of knowledge can empower people to solve problems by expanding the range of solutions that may be available, and by giving them confidence to improvise or innovate. Conversely, a lack of knowledge or incorrect perceptions will constrain the types of solutions that can be found (Warne et al., 2005).

The role technology plays in all this is that of an enabler and aid in developing and supporting the right culture for information and knowledge sharing. An organizational culture that recognises the value of knowledge and its exchange is a crucial element in whether information and knowledge work is successfully carried out or not. Such a culture provides the opportunity for personal contact so that tacit knowledge, which cannot effectively be captured in procedures or represented in documents and databases, can be transferred. In a culture that values knowledge, managers recognise not just that knowledge generation is important for business success but also that it can be nurtured with time, and space (Davenport & Prusak, 1998). On the other hand, low morale, and its consequent effects on information and knowledge sharing, has frequently been coupled with comments about not understanding the motivation or agenda of more senior staff (Warne et al., 2005). Lack of understanding not only affects morale, but also has an impact on trust, organizational cohesiveness, goal alignment and common identity, and consequently, on opportunities and motivation for learning and innovation, and on general productivity.

Finally, while it has to be admitted that in most, if not all, organizations there are almost certainly going to be people who are motivated primarily by individual needs, power and politics, and who may even be corrupt or dishonest in their pursuit of their particular aims, this is not generally true. Most people, by contrast, enjoy the experience of working in teams towards shared goals and, provided with the right environment (organizational culture) and means (e.g., technological information or knowledge management systems) that are based on their *real* needs, through effective requirements analysis for example, will willingly engage in sharing their information and knowledge resources to solve organizational problems and give effect to their work (Warne et al., 2005).

AN ORGANIZATIONAL POLITICS PERSPECTIVE

The classical organizational theorists and, to a lesser extent, those belonging to the cultural school, subscribe to the view that organizations are normally characterized by a "philosophy of sharing trust and care for others" (Kakabadse & Parker, 1984). Those of which this is not true tend to be regarded as dysfunctional. However, the power and politics school of organizational thinkers reject this assumption, insisting instead that "power is part of all organizational behaviour" and the effective use of it, which is a political act, "secures both organizational and personal goals in most (if not all) organizational action" (Fairholm, 1993).

The power and political view pictures an organization as a collection of groups and individuals who are diverse in their aims, beliefs, interests, values, preferences and perceptions of their organizational world and, to this extent, is compatible with the cultural view. However, it also argues that differences of opinion are common, if not the norm, coalitions form and dissolve, and disagreements, conflict and political activity are a natural and inevitable part of organizational life. Nevertheless, as Ferris et al. (1989) say:

Organizational scientists have had different notions of what constitutes political behaviour. Some have defined organizational politics in terms of the behaviour of interest groups to use power to influence decision making [while] others have focused on the self-serving and organizationally non-sanctioned nature of individual behaviour in organization [and] still others have characterized organizational politics as a social influence process with potentially functional or dysfunctional organizational consequences ... or simply the management of influence (Ferris et al., 1989).

The authors see organizational politics in the same light as Checkland and Holwell (1998) and also Pfeffer (1981), the latter of whom says:

Organizational politics involves those activities taken within organizations to acquire, develop, and use power and other resources to obtain one's preferred outcomes in a situation in which there is uncertainty or dissens[ion] about choices (Pfeffer, 1981).

As Sauer (1993) says, "power accrues to those who control resources which are important to others" and, as seen above, politics entails the use of power to achieve desired ends in the face of dissension. Furthermore, the sources of a particular party's power will be significantly dependent on the pre-existing social and organizational structure, which will largely determine who has what degree of control over which resources. All organizational sections are generally custodians of some form of information and knowledge resources. And the power people have through their control of resources is not just a matter of formally assigned or de facto ownership, but of consciously and actually having arbitrary control over their availability and use. Indeed, there is not only the matter of what information and knowledge individuals and groups in the organization *actually* own or have control over (and, they think, rightly so), but also what they think or "know" they *should* own or have control over but which in fact they do not. As can be imagined, this may constitute a potent source of conflict and organizational politicking if different parties have significantly differing perceptions in this area. In fact, as roles in an organization become more defined by the information people and groups hold and control, they will increasingly view that information as a source of power and importance for them, being more protective of its ownership, and being less inclined to share it or devolve responsibility for it as a result (Davenport et al., 1992; Hart, 1999).

Arguably, the occurrence of power-based behaviour and organizational politicking when trying to succeed, or even just cope, in a dynamic, interlinked and mutually dependent environment is less likely when those who need to cooperate communicate effectively. But the effectiveness of communication is highly dependent on the level of trust between the involved parties too (Drucker, 1999). Research has demonstrated that the extent to which one individual (and, by extension, a group of individuals as well) trusts another has a significant effect on their willingness to exchange information and knowledge with the other (e.g., Erickson, 1979; Fine & Holyfield, 1996). It has been argued that this is especially true where there is uncertainty or ignorance as to the motives and actions of the other party, particularly with respect to possible actions and outcomes that may result from or be enabled by the act of sharing (Hart, 2004). If these could be predicted with absolute certainty, then trust would not be required, but when they cannot, as in most 'real world' circumstances, a degree of trust is necessary to make human action and interaction possible. Concerns over how others might use shared information or knowledge often restricts one's readiness to part with it (Erickson, 1979). Simply belonging to the same organization may not be enough to provide a basis for the kind of sharing that may, on overtly rational cost-benefit grounds, be both desirable and expected. Moreover, adding information systems to the mix complicates things further since once a piece of information or knowledge has been committed to such a system, direct control by its original owner over when, why and with whom it may then be shared will most likely be lost.

Common identity and shared understanding are often spoken of as enabling and in turn being supported by information and knowledge sharing. However, it may be argued against this view that, even if achievable, common identity and shared understanding are always provisional, incomplete and context-dependent since they are built upon communicative acts that are always subject to interpretation and, therefore, at least to some extent ambiguous (Marshall & Brady, 2001). Likewise, shared information and knowledge are subject to interpretation and the meanings derived from them are similarly dependent on context and other actor dependent factors. Therefore, no attempt at communication, whether person-to-person or through a technological information or knowledge management system, is ever completely unambiguous.

Indeed, it may be argued that it is never possible to truly achieve shared understanding because each of us, at least in certain important respects, constructs our own reality and individual understanding based on our own prior experience. According to this argument, shared understanding can only be achieved, at best, in a limited, provisional and incomplete sense since each individual interprets the same events or evidence in their own, and invariably unique way. Consider, for example, the different views people have of the motivations and meaning of the words and actions of their political leaders, even when these views are derived from exactly the same evidential base. Moreover, even if it could be achieved completely, shared understanding in no way would necessarily entail agreement about the implications of the mutually understood situation. The interests and motivations to action of the different parties who achieved this shared understanding could still diverge dramatically, potentially generating significant power struggles and political activity that could impede further information and knowledge sharing even despite the achieved mutual understanding.

According to the power and political view, organizations are best understood as sites where people and groups interact in pursuit of a range of interests (Dunford, 1992). Some of these interests may be compatible or complementary, in which case, limited collaboration may occur; other interests will differ and conflict. This political perspective highlights the complexity and multiplicity of objectives within organizations where outcomes are likely to revolve around the ability to get one's preferences accepted; to have the greatest influence on decisions made and directions taken; where actions can be analysed in terms of power interests; and the mobilisation

of support and negotiation, all of which are not always aligned with the organization's overall stated objectives. The impact of all this on information and knowledge sharing is, of course, that whether or not it occurs is heavily influenced by, and indivisible from, the political interests and assessments of the various parties involved.

All this is not to indict human beings or their motives either. In fact, it is quite possible for there to be extremely good and ethical reasons for not sharing information or knowledge. Organizations in the defence and security industries are good examples of where this could commonly be so. But even aside from these obvious cases, it may be argued (especially from an individual or group perspective) that it is in some situations better for overall organizational outcomes *not* to share some particular information or knowledge one owns or has in one's possession. This might occur, for instance, if the act of sharing is likely to lead, in the possessor's opinion and for whatever reason, to organizational indecision, less effective or possibly inappropriate action by others, misunderstandings, conflict or other deleterious effects. Of course, a decision not to share for these types of reasons would not be one to take lightly, but it is possible and perhaps even common that such decisions need to be taken anyway.

Instead, therefore, of trying to "overcome" resistance to sharing, it is important to recognise its sources and to accept that this sort of behaviour is not only endemic to but also more than likely inevitable in many if not all organizations, for the kinds of reasons outlined above. This means that it is vital to recognise the need of individuals and groups within the organization to manage their own information and knowledge resources—including deciding with whom, when, how and why to share them—in accordance with their understanding of their own, others and their organization's overall needs. Rather than fighting to defeat their control of these resources, they should be supported in their management of them, which includes *enabling* and making it easy for them to share with other people and groups in the organization as their understanding, discretion and willingness dictates, rather than attempting to *force* them to do so. The emergence of the Internet is perhaps both the classic and ultimate example, albeit a non-organizational one, of this kind of process at work. The author's experience indicates that anything more ambitious or directive is just not going to succeed as well as intended or desired.

A SUMMARY

Table 1 summarises and contrasts the main standpoints, by general topic area, put forward in the two perspectives outlined above.

COMPARING THE PERSPECTIVES

Having now outlined and characterized the two perspectives of interest, it should be possible to assess the major differences between them and to see what the prospects might be for some kind of synthesis.

Causality

Inspection and reflection on the contents of the Summary Table reveals that one important difference between the two views of information and knowledge sharing relates to causality. That is, which phenomena are causes and which are effects? In broad terms, and admittedly oversim-

Table 1.

Topic Area	The Organizational Culture- Based Perspective	The Organizational Politics- Based Perspective
Sharing and the coordination and integration of organizational work	Information and knowledge sharing are necessary for the effective coordination and integration of organizational work	Coordination and integration of organizational work are best effected by directed and selective information and knowledge sharing
Shared understanding and common identity	Information and knowledge sharing are both enabled by and improve shared understanding and common identity amongst organizational members	Context is all-important so, other than in a limited and local sense, shared understanding and common identity are unachievable ideals
Sharing and organizational alignment	Information and knowledge sharing lead to goal alignment and common purpose amongst organizational members	Information and knowledge sharing occur between organizational members who perceive their goals and purposes are already aligned
Sharing and organizational culture and politics	Information and knowledge sharing depend on the creation of an organizational culture that fosters and recognises the value of such sharing, thereby avoiding or reducing political problems	Changing culture is a long tedious and difficult process and, in any case, sharing (if it occurs) is more the outcome of normal organizational political motivations and assessments than it is of cultural characteristics.
Sharing and the communication of meaning (Sensemaking)	Information and knowledge sharing will enable the free flow of meaningful communication throughout the organization facilitating sensemaking	Meaning and sense-making is the result of a process of contextually mediated interpretation; and information does not, in itself carry any inherent meaning
Unwillingness to share	Information and knowledge sharing are inhibited by indefensible motives (such as self-interest, power and politics) inimical to proper organizational functioning	Unwillingness to share information or knowledge may be driven by genuine and valid concerns for better organizational functioning as well as by less defensible motivations
Approaches to sharing	Wider and more effective information and knowledge sharing can be achieved by better understanding organizational work and system requirements definition, as well as the fostering of a sharing internal culture	Supporting individuals and groups in the management of their own information and knowledge resources, but at the same time enabling and making it easy for them to share with whom and when they see fit, is the way to approach the sharing issue

plifying somewhat, the cultural perspective tends to regard information and knowledge sharing as recursive, as much a cause of other desirable organizational effects, as the reverse. For example, it is typically argued that sharing is necessary for and, by implication, leads to more effective coordination and integration of organizational activities; improves shared understanding and common identity as well as goal alignment and common purpose among organizational members; reduces political problems; and enhances the flow of meaningful communication. If, therefore, one could establish and embed information and knowledge sharing, then these effects could be expected to follow. By contrast, in at least one important respect, the political perspective sees things the other way around causally, and in other cases denies that the effect claimed by adherents to the cultural view is in fact achievable at all through attempts to share information and knowledge. In particular, according to the political perspective, information and knowledge sharing are more a *result* of goal and purpose alignment between organizational actors than they are a *cause* of it. Moreover, according to the cultural perspective, the assumption tends to be that it is necessary to create an organizational culture that would be conducive to and foster information and knowledge sharing in order to encourage and support the emergence of such sharing. That is, in simplified terms, the direction of the causal link is viewed as being essentially from the creation of the appropriate culture (the cause) to the occurrence of sharing (the effect). Of course, it is not that simple because of feedback effects, but nevertheless the emphasis does tend to be on the creation of an appropriate culture first, as a means of enabling information and knowledge sharing to occur. According to the political perspective, however, while it is usually acknowledged that culture has its effects, it is also viewed as much more resistant to intentional manipulation than is typically assumed by cultural theorists. Instead, information

and knowledge sharing are viewed as the outcome of a primarily political (i.e., power-based) process reflecting existing organizational stakeholders and their interests and relationships.

Levers of Change

Consequent upon the causal differences of the two perspectives are important differences regarding how change can be effected, or if indeed it can be effected by intentional action at all. In particular, because the cultural perspective tends to regard information and knowledge sharing as a cause of, or at least necessary precursor to, other desired effects, adherents of this view tend to focus primarily on means by which such sharing can be achieved. This accounts for arguments that propose, for example, that if the user requirements definition process in systems development could be improved to the point that the resulting systems actually served the real needs of the users, and supported the way they preferred to work, then information and knowledge sharing would follow naturally. Those of the political persuasion would tend to argue, however, that it matters not how "good" any technological system might be in enabling information and knowledge sharing—in the technical, design and usability sense—such sharing will not occur unless it is compatible with the existing political landscape in the organization. Accordingly, it is then urged, it is inappropriate and possibly even counter-productive to engage in systems development (no matter how good the user requirements definition process might be) if inadequate attention is paid to this political landscape and, if necessary, effort put into changing it before any systems to support information and knowledge sharing are constructed. Or, if it proves infeasible to significantly alter the political landscape of the relevant parts of the organization, then such systems should be explicitly designed to be compatible with that landscape. According to the political perspective, all else is pointless.

Impediments and Remedies

No matter whether one is of the cultural or political persuasion, it is evident and admitted that getting different parties to share organizational information and knowledge is often difficult to achieve. No disagreement there, but there is some disagreement when it comes to motivations. The culturally-oriented view characteristically admits few if any defensible reasons or motives against most information and knowledge sharing—which are essentially regarded as wholly beneficial to the organization. Any motive or reason standing in the way must therefore be an indication of some organizational dysfunction (e.g., an unwillingness to share may be a symptom of a conflict or a bid for more organizational power or influence). By contrast, the opposite view allows that refusal to share may not necessarily be nefarious, arising as it may through, for example, concerns about possible misinterpretations of significance or meaning by the receiving parties and potentially leading to mistakes or other organizationally deleterious actions. This difference means that cultural adherents draw the conclusion that refusal to share implies that the *people* who are refusing need to be encouraged or educated as to the benefits of sharing (or the organizational culture to which they belong needs changing) so their refusal can be *overcome*. On the other hand, political adherents accept that sharing will generally only occur between those who are already disposed to do so anyway, and attempts to encourage, educate or coerce wider or different patterns of sharing are likely not only to be unsuccessful but even counter-productive. It is instead better to make sharing *easier* without attempting to be more directive about what should be shared or with whom, and especially given that the motivations for not sharing may in fact be validly driven by concerns for the overall organizational functioning anyway.

Prospects for a Synthesis

Both the cultural and political views of organizations, among other metaphors, are well known and established (e.g., Morgan, 1997) and have been acknowledged as closely related and complementary (Ferris et al., 1989). Indeed, Ferris et al. (1989), who use the term "myth" to mean "a manifestation of the larger concept of organizational culture", say: "An integration of myths and politics seems to be a quite natural one [because] the content of many myths is often political in nature and myths are used to define the meaning of current political activities". However, while this may be so, according to our analysis there are still some important divergences between these perspectives when it comes to interpreting, understanding and explaining organizational information and knowledge sharing behaviour.

One potential approach to integrating the two perspectives may be via the concept of sub-cultures. Perhaps it is the case that politically contending parties in an organization, and more particularly, those that are reluctant or refuse to share information or knowledge with each other, can generally be identified with different sub-cultures within it? After all, by definition, different sub-cultures hold significantly different value sets, beliefs, assumptions, norms of behaviour and so on, and these could surely function as a source of power struggles, conflict and political activity concerning not only information and knowledge sharing but also other areas of organizational activity. Such an identification would, however, imply that political activity regarding information and knowledge sharing would occur much more often between individuals or groups belonging to different sub-cultures than within them and, as far as the authors are aware, this is a proposition that has yet to be empirically tested. But even if it should turn out to be so, this would most likely still leave some significant differences between what the authors have termed the cultural and political perspectives regarding organizational information and knowledge sharing, not least in their ascriptions of causality and therefore ideas on how to effect change.

CONCLUSION

Why is it that so many information systems and knowledge management initiatives do not reach their full potential or, at worst, result in failure? Technological tools of ever increasing sophistication are available for use in achieving the dissemination and sharing of information and knowledge across the organization. However, despite the existence and capability of these tools, information sharing and knowledge management initiatives in many organizations all too often do not deliver the benefits sought from them.

As the two perspectives outlined and contrasted above are intended to illustrate, the authors argue that the foundational assumptions from which matters of organizational information and knowledge sharing are viewed are an important issue that can materially affect the approaches taken to address these issues. Such foundational assumptions can significantly influence, for example, the ambition and scope of information-systems-based efforts to support organizational information and knowledge sharing and, if such efforts fail (for whatever overt reasons), they often fail both spectacularly and expensively for the organization concerned. It is critical, therefore, to better understand not only what *should* be attempted, but also what is *feasible* to attempt and *how* best to attempt it. Understanding the foundations from which one is approaching the problem is, therefore, far from simply an academic exercise since very practical implications attach to its outcome.

The authors and colleagues are pursuing ongoing research work, involving what are now called network-centric-organizations, intended to illuminate and clarify the kinds of fundamental issues raised in the debate presented in this chapter. The results and conclusions of this work will be reported in due course.

REFERENCES

Ahmed, P., Kok, L., & Loh, A. (2002). *Learning through knowledge management.* Butterworth Heinemann.

Ali, I., Warne, L., Agostino, K., Pascoe, C. (2001). Working and learning together: Social learning in the Australian Defence Organisation. *Informing Science Conference IS2001—Bridging Diverse Disciplines Proceedings* (CD-ROM), Krakow, Krakow University of Economics, Poland, June 19-22.

Applegate, L., Austin, R., McFarlan, F. (2003). *Corporate information strategy and management: Text and cases.* McGraw-Hill Irwin.

Awad, E., & Ghaziri, H. (2004). *Knowledge management.* Prentice-Hall.

Bartlett, C., & Ghosal, S. (1989). *Managing across borders: The transnational solution.* Boston, MA: Harvard Business School Press.

Beynon-Davies, P. (2002). *Information systems: An introduction to informatics in organizations.* Palgrave Publishing.

Boisot, M. (2002). The creation and sharing of knowledge. In: C. Choo & N. Bontis (Eds.), *The strategic management of intellectual capital and organizational knowledge.* Oxford University Press.

Checkland, P., & Howell, S. (1998). *Information, systems and information systems.* John Wiley & Sons.

Crawford, K. (2003). *Factors affecting learning and communication in organizations: A chapter commissioned by the Defence, Science and Tech-*

nology Organisation (DSTO). Creative Interactive Systems Pty Ltd.

Daft, R., & Lewin, A. (1993). Where are the theories for the "new" organizational forms? An editorial essay. *Organization Science, 4*(i-vi).

Daneshar, F. (2003). A methodology for sharing contextual knowledge in virtual communities. In *Proceedings of the 14th Annual IRMA International Conference,* Philadelphia, PA, May.

Davenport, T., Eccles, R., Prusak, L. (1992). Information politics. *Sloan Management Review, 34*(1), 53-65

Davenport, T., & Prusak, L. (1998). *Working knowledge: How organizations manage what they know.* Boston, MA: Harvard Business School Press.

Drucker, P. (1999). Beyond the information revolution. *The Atlantic Monthly,* Oct 1999.

Dunford, R. (1992). *Organisational behaviour: An organisational analysis perspective.* Sydney: Addison-Wesley.

Erickson, P. (1979). The role of secrecy in complex organizations: From norms of rationality to norms of distrust. *Cornell Journal of Social Relation, 14*(2), 121-138.

Ewusi-Mensah, K., & Przasnyski, Z. (1991). On information systems project abandonment: An exploratory study of organizational practices. *MIS Quarterly, 15*(1), 67-86.

Fairholm, G. (1993). *Organizational power politics.* Westpot, CT: Praeger.

Ferris, G., Fedor, D., Chachere, J., & Pondy, L. (1989). Myths and politics in organizational contexts. *Group and Organization Studies, 14*(1), 83-103.

Fine, G., & Holyfield, L. (1996). Secrecy, trust, and dangerous leisure: Generating group cohesion in voluntary organizations. *Social Psychology Quarterly, 59*(1), 22-38.

Hart, D., & Warne, L. (1997). *Information systems defining characteristics: A stakeholder centric view of success and failure.* Technical Chapter CS0197. University College UNSW, ADFA.

Hart, D. (2002). Ownership as an issue in data and information sharing: A philosophically based view. *Australian Journal of Information Systems,* (Special Issue), 23-29.

Hislop, D. (2002). Mission impossible? Communicating and sharing knowledge via information technology. *Journal of Information Technology, 17,* 165-177.

Jordan, B. (1993). Ethnographic workplace studies and computer-supported cooperative work. *Interdisciplinary Workshop on Informatics and Psychology.* Scharding, Austria.

Kakabadse, A., & Parker, C. (Eds.). (1984). *Power, politics, and organizations.* New York, NY: John Wiley & Sons.

Kendall, K., & Kendall, J. (2002). *Systems analysis and design* (p. 73). Upper Saddle River, NJ: Prentice-Hall.

Lyytinen, K., & Hirschheim, R. (1987). Information system failures: A survey and classification of the empirical literature. *Oxford Surveys in Information Technology,* (4), 257-309.

Marshall, N., & Brady, T. (2001). Knowledge management and the politics of knowledge: Illustrations from complex products and systems. *European Journal of Information Systems 10,* 99-112.

Miles, R., & Snow, C. (1986). Organizations: New concepts for new forms. *California Management Review, 28*(62-73).

Morgan, G. (1997). *Images of organization,* new ed. Sage Publications.

Nonaka, I., & Takeuchi, H. (1995). *The knowledge-creating company: How Japanese companies create the dynamics of innovation.* Oxford University Press.

Pfeffer, J. (1981). Understanding the role of power in decision making. In: J. Shafritz & J. Ott (Eds.), *Classics of organization theory.* Brooks/Cole.

Polanyi, M. (1966). *The tacit dimension.* Doubleday.

Quinn, J. (1992). *Intelligent enterprise.* New York, NY: New York Free Press.

Sauer, C. (1993). *Why information systems fail: A case study approach.* Alfred Waller, Henley-On-Thames, Oxfordshire: Alfred Waller.

Schein, E. (1997). *Organizational culture and leadership,* 2nd ed. Jossey-Bass.

Senge, P. (1992). *The fifth discipline: The art and practice of the learning organization.* Sydney: Random House.

Simon, H. (1993). Strategy and organizational evolution. *Strategic Management Journal, 14,* 131-142.

Venzin, M., von Krogh, G., & Roos, J. (1998). Future research into knowledge management. In: G. Von Krogh, J. Roos, & D. Kleine (Eds.), *Knowing in firms: Understanding, managing and measuring knowledge.* Sage Publications.

Warne, L., Ali, I., Pascoe C., Agostino, K. (2001). A holistic approach to knowledge management and social learning: Lessons learnt from military headquarters. *Australian Journal of Information Systems,* (Special Issue) on Knowledge Management, December: 127-142.

Warne, L., Ali, I., Bopping, D., Hart, D., & Pascoe, C. (2004). *The network centric warrior: The human dimension of network centric warfare (U.*

DSTO Report CR-0373, Defence Systems Analysis Division, ISL, Defence Science and Technology Organisation, Department of Defence, Edinburgh, S.A. (Approved for Public Release).

Warne, L., Ali, I., & Pasco, C. (2003). *Social learning and knowledge management – A journey through the Australian Defence Organisation: The final report of the Enterprise Social Learning Architectures Task.* DSTO Report, DSTO-RR-0257, Defence Systems Analysis Division, Information Sciences Laboratory, Department of Defence.

Warne, L., Hasan, H., & Ali, I. (2005). Transforming organizational culture to the ideal inquiring organization: Hopes and hurdles. In: J. Courtney, J. Haynes, & D. Paradice (Eds.), *Inquiring organizations: Moving from knowledge management to wisdom* (pp. 316-336). Hershey, PA: Idea Group.

Webber, A. (1993). What's so new about the new economy?. *Harvard Business Review, Jan-Feb,* 24-42.

Woodhouse, L. (2000). Personality and the use of intuition: Individual differences in strategy and performance on an implicit learning task. *European Journal of Personality, 4*(2), 157-169.

Zander, U., & Kogut, B. (1995). Knowledge and the speed of the transfer and imitation of organizational capabilities: An empirical test. *Organization Science, 6*(1), 76-92.

ENDNOTE

[1] This chapter is an updated version of the authors' 2006 paper "Comparing Cultural and Political Perspectives of Data, Information and Knowledge Sharing in Organizations", *International Journal of Knowledge Management, 2*(2), 1-15.

Chapter IX
A Conceptual Model for Knowledge Sharing as Dependent on Cultural Factors

Abel Usoro
University of the West of Scotland, UK

Matthew H. S. Kuofie
University of Michigan, USA

ABSTRACT

Often, organizational members are separated not only geographically but also culturally. Information technology has inevitably become a facilitator of knowledge sharing. However, earlier studies have posited that culture can significantly facilitate or hinder knowledge sharing in culturally diverse teams. Greater enlightenment on the cultural effect is therefore a useful contribution to understanding the most effective way of managing knowledge sharing in organizations. However, little effort has been put into dimensioning culture in such a way as to enable comparative and large scale study. This investigation tries to fill this gap by bringing together and examining the few attempts at dimensioning this concept. This review results in the proposing of cultural dimensions which are grouped into organizational and societal classes. The review also results in a proposal of a conceptual model that expresses knowledge sharing to be a function of organizational and societal cultural factors. We formulated two major hypotheses: H1—There is a high positive relationship between organizational culture and knowledge sharing, and H2—There is a high positive relationship between societal culture and knowledge sharing. The model requires further investigation as explained in the chapter.

INTRODUCTION

The current globalisation trend has promoted multi-cultural groups. Sometimes, a multi-cultural group is geographically spread and thus fit

Malhotra and Majchrzak's (2004) description of "far flung teams." Whether such a group is located in one building or are scattered around the world, information systems most likely constitute a central facilitator for knowledge sharing among

Copyright © 2008, IGI Global, distributing in print or electronic forms without written permission of IGI Global is prohibited.

the group members (Kuofie, 2005). Knowledge sharing requires more than information and communications technology per se. There is need for other crucial elements such as trust (Sharratt & Usoro, 2003; Zakaria et al., 2004) and shared understanding or "a collective way of organising relevant knowledge" (Hinds & Weisband, 2003, p. 21; Kuofie, 2005).

Knowledge sharing is generally conceived as an exchange (of knowledge) from a giver to a receiver. The receiver is not passively taking "knowledge." The receiver's perception of what is shared is influenced, inter alia, by his or her cultural background. According to Zakaria et al. (2004) "knowledge is filtered through cultural lenses, whether we are aware of such filters or not" (p. 16). Research in management recognizes organizational culture as affecting team performance and hence knowledge sharing (Kuofie, 2005). Culture has to be examined beyond the organizational to the national or societal level especially for global teams who are scattered in different cultural contexts in which they may belong. The use of the term "societal culture" is preferred because cultural boundaries do not often coincide with national boundaries (Kreittner & Kinicki, 2002, p. 88). The northern part of Nigeria, for instance, shares the same Arabic culture as the countries above Nigeria. There is current interest in researching the knowledge-sharing environment of global teams but little is done on the cultural element of the environment. The few studies (e.g., Ardichvili et al., 2006) are mainly qualitative and exploratory.

This chapter aims to identify the cultural elements that could influence knowledge sharing among multi-cultural groups whether or not they are globally located.

The rest of the chapter is organized into (a) culture, (b) organizational culture, (c) societal culture, (d) proposed conceptual model, (e) conclusion and areas for further investigations.

CULTURE

Culture is a concept that may be elusive to define[1], but because of its pervasive nature can undoubtedly be perceived among a group of people just as personality can be perceived in an individual. Geert Hofstede (2003) describes it as "the collective programming of the mind which distinguishes one group or category of people from another" (p. 89). Hofstede's mention of the mind indicates that culture has to do with the way we think and interpret information that comes to us. For example, a Nigerian in the UK would find it very unwelcoming if s/he is constantly asked how long s/he is staying in the UK though the enquirers are friendly and mean no harm. In Nigerian culture, it is a taboo to ask your visitor how long s/he is staying. The question is interpreted to mean you are asking the guest to leave immediately. To shake hands or not to, to say good morning to strangers or not to, to grow your hair or not to, and to express emotions or not may be determined by culture. "May" because culture makes a group of people tend to think and act in a particular way; culture is not deterministic, as suggested by Hofstede by the use of the word "programming", of the working of the mind of every member of a particular culture. As a free morale agent, an individual can decide to be different from his cultural group at least in some aspects of the group's culture. It is not impossible, for instance, to meet an African who is highly formal in his general communication with people, though African culture is broadly defined as informal in their communication.

Knowledge sharing, like communication, is carried out within a cultural context. The receiver interprets information s/he receives using his or her cultural perspective. In face-to-face communication, voice cues and body language is used to enhance the meaning of information shared. Except with video-conferencing, much of communication enhancements may be missing, therefore necessitating inevitably the use of the default context—culture—to assign meaning to communication. If not properly managed, cultural differences among team members can cause conflicts, misunderstandings and drain resources rather than improve efficiency (Shenkar & Zeira, 1992; Matveev & Milter, 2004). The cultural context that influences team members can be described as organizational and societal (Kreittner & Kinicki, 2002). One may tend to regard organizational culture as a subset or a mere reflection of societal culture with the argument that organizations get influenced by their societal environment (Steven, 1989). However, in the light of current global trend, organizations still, at the same time, tend to maintain some distinct internal culture that binds them irrespective of the societies they situate in (Oliver & Kandadi, 2006, pp. 7-8). South Africa, in some ways, can represent the world with multi-society. Finestone and Snyman (2005) found that South African companies they studied were determined to develop and maintain corporate culture and considered the societal (multi-)culture too sensitive to even acknowledge its existence in their organizations. Thus, especially for analysis purposes, this chapter will consider organizational and societal cultures separately.

ORGANIZATIONAL CULTURE

We cannot attempt to investigate organizational culture without attempting to define it. Studies of organizational culture are characterized by variations in definition and mainly qualitative rather than quantitative methods are used for investigation (Kreitner & Kinicki, 2002, p. 69). Ardichvili et al. (2006) is an example of a recent study of organizational culture from a qualitative approach. Schein (1999) views organizational culture as "the way we do things around here. In essence, corporate culture is the learned, shared, and tacit assumptions such as values, beliefs,

and assumptions" (p. 48). Similarly, Lemken et al. (2000) describe organizational culture as the totality of shared philosophies, assumptions, values, expectations, attitudes, and norms that glue together the organization. Core values or basic assumptions form the foundation of organizational culture. These values are exhibited in practices and individual behavior. They are also embedded in artifacts (e.g., space and buildings); stories, legends and myths; espoused philosophy and values; and structure and systems.

Studies that investigate failure of knowledge management initiatives have recognized organizational culture as a major barrier to success (Tuggle, 2000). Some studies have also recommended solutions. For instance, from a case study of five prominent organizations that practice knowledge sharing, McDermott and O'Dell (2001, pp. 76-85) concluded that cultural barriers can be overcome by (a) linking knowledge sharing to practical work, goals or results; (b) tying knowledge sharing to a pre-existing core value; (c) adapting knowledge sharing to the organizational style rather than the reverse; (d) using existing networks; and (e) using peer and superior pressure to encourage people to share knowledge. The problem, however, with these studies is that it is difficult to determine from them the aspects of organizational culture which, in the first place, would create a barrier[2] to knowledge sharing. This problem can only be addressed by first developing a sound dimensioning of culture as it affects knowledge sharing.

Researchers in organizational culture dimension the concept differently, but the dimensions can be broadly classified as (a) value-based and (b) work-practice-based. Reigle and Westbrook (2000) noted the inadequacy of measures for organizational culture. This is not surprising in view of the multilevel[3] nature of this concept. Park et al. (2004, p. 108) accept that the deep evaluation of an organization's culture requires more than a questionnaire since the inquirer would need to learn the history of the organization, visit the organization's site(s), talk to the organization's members and observe their behavior. Thus, most studies in literature are small scale and non-comparative because of the definition of organizational culture from values which are better investigated qualitatively rather than quantitatively (Van den Berg & Wilderom, 2004).

It is refreshing to realise that one is not bound to investigate organisational culture from only a qualitative approach. This is because several studies have demonstrated significant correlation between organizational culture and employee behavior and attitudes (Kreittner & Kinicki, 2002, p. 70). Edward Hall (1976b) indicated that the connection with behavior and work practices is of great research interest because it spares us the necessity to peel through the layers of culture to get embedded values which experts in culture, in any case, say lie beneath the threshold of our conscious awareness. In agreement with this view, Hofstede (2003) stated that culture is a construct and therefore is "not directly accessible to observation but inferable from behaviors and useful in predicting other behavior" (p. 69). Though Park

et al. (2004, p. 108) acknowledge the value-based approach to studying culture, they also argue that if the goal of a study is to obtain a global perception of an organization's culture, a questionnaire using a practice-based approach would be adequate. Thus, for their study, they dimensioned organizational culture into (a) trust, (b) sharing information freely, and (c) working closely with others or developing friends at work. This last item agrees with Goh's (2002) argument that the critical dimension that affects knowledge transfer is "co-operation and collaboration" with trust as one of its antecedents. The four items Park et al. (2004, p. 108) used were actually from 54 items developed by Block (1978) and later decreased to 44 items by Harper (2000). See Table 1.

Harper's cultural profile is a useful basket of attributes. However, the 44 attributes are not only too many as a basic dimension of a researchable concept, but they are also overlapping. For example "confront conflict directly" can overlap with "decisiveness." One approach to using the list is to handpick some attributes as done by Park

Table 1. Organizational culture profile attributes as modified by Harper (Park et al., 2004, p. 109)

Trust	Problem-solving	Demanding of employee
Flexibility	Being exact	Supportive of employees
Adaptability	Team oriented work	Having a good reputation
Stability	Decisiveness	Sharing information freely
Predictability	Being competitive	Socially responsible
Being innovative	Being aggressive	Being different from others
Compliance	Being result oriented	Security of employment
Experimentation	Fairness	Praised good performance
Risk taking	Informality	Fitting in at work
Being careful	Tolerant of failure	Confront conflict directly
Freedom of action	Taking initiative	Develop friends at work
Rule-oriented	Being thoughtful	Enthusiasm for the job
Attention to detail	Being easy going	Working closely with others
Take advantage of opportunity	Respect for individual's right	Being calm
High expectation for performance	Low level of conflict encouraged	

et al. (2004). Perhaps a better approach is to use cluster and factor analysis to endeavor to group and trim these attributes so that we can arrive at core organizational dimensions of organizational culture. Meanwhile, let us investigate how other recent researchers dimension organizational culture.

With the aim of enabling large-scale comparative studies so as to develop scientific knowledge, Van den Berg and Wilderom (2004) have defined organizational culture in terms of work practices (rather than values) based on Kostova's (1999) definition: "particular ways of conducting organizational functions that have evolved over time ... [These] practices reflect the shared knowledge and competence of the organization" (p. 309). While Van den Berg and Wilderom (2004) acknowledge values as an important element of organizational culture, they justify their adoption of work practices by Hofstede (2001, p. 394) research which demonstrated that organizations showed more differences in work practices than in values. From analyzing earlier dimensions of organizational culture (Hofstede et al., 1990; O'Reilly et al., 1991; Gordon & DiTomaso, 1992; Denison & Mishra, 1995; Van Muijen et al., 1999), Van den Berg and Wilderom (2004) have derived four dimensions to organizational culture, viz: (a) autonomy, (b) external orientation, (c) inter-departmental coordination, (d) human resource orientation, and (e) improvement orientation.

The first dimension, autonomy, is task-related and refers to the degree to which organization members are allowed discretion in their work. The second dimension, external orientation,

is included to reflect the fact that all organizations possess external environments. Both open system theory and literature on culture agree that external orientation is influenced by the internal workings of an organization (Hofstede, 2001). Similar to Van den Berg and Wilderom (2004), Denison and Mishra (1995) proposed the two-dimensional element of internal employees and external customers. So, internal orientation should be included as a dimension. The third dimension by Van den Berg and Wilderom (2004), interdepartmental coordination, is included since the perception of this organizational horizontal variable can increase or lesson the barrier to group effort. The fourth factor, human resource content, is found in many articles as an explicit component of organizational culture (Gordon, 1990; Gordon & DiTomaso, 1992; Marcoulides & Heck, 1993; Quinn, 1988). Finally, the fifth dimension, improvement orientation, is meant to capture the proactivity of the organization in improving its work practices. Denison and Mishra (1995) also added another dimensional-element of flexibility and stability or rigidity. The more flexible an organization is the less rigid would it be. So this element can be represented by a single entry of "flexibility."

The known most recent researchers[4] who have worked on dimensioning organizational culture from work-practice approach are Denison and Mishra (1995), Park et al. (2004) and Van den Berg and Wilderom (2004) whose studies have been presented. If we put their dimensions together, we have the ten dimensions shown in Table 2.

Table 2. Dimensions of organizational culture

Inter-departmental coordination	Human resource orientation
Trust	Autonomy
External orientation	Sharing information freely
Improvement orientation	Working closely with others
Internal orientation	Flexibility

SOCIETAL CULTURE

Some academics and researchers have argued that international communication is resulting in the formation of universal cultures especially among professionals such as commercial pilots, computer programmers, film directors, international bankers, media specialists, oil riggers and athletes (Barber, 1995). Also, the growth in information and communication technologies, tourism and globalization is creating some universalities in culture (Comeau-Kirschner, 1999). However, Huntington (1996) noticed little or no evidence that the emergence of pervasive global communication is producing significant convergence in attitudes and beliefs. Root's (1994) argument against a universal rather than a national culture agrees with Huntington's (1996) observation. It is safe to conclude therefore that while information, technology, globalization and professionalism is breaking cultural barriers, there still exist substantial differences in culture to create a significant impact on the work of organization members.

Writers in this area prefer to use national rather than societal culture. This chapter prefers to use the latter term because a particular culture can span more than one nation and in some cases too, a nation may be split into more than one culture. Edward Hall (1976a) proposed that the difference in communication among different societies lies in their context. 'High context' societies depend more on the external stimuli for behavioral cues. People in such societies value subtle and non-explicit details in communication whereas those in 'low context' cultures are more direct and explicit in their communication. The high-context societies would value less formal modes of communication while the low-context cultures would prefer formal approaches. Read the fine lines with high-context cultures and read between the lines with low-context cultures. The Chinese culture is given as an example of a high-context culture; and German culture as a low-context culture (Munter, 1993). With the Chinese culture, and

perhaps African as well, plenty of trust building precedes formal communication; whereas the German culture, like most western cultures, prefer to "cut the chase"[5] and launch directly into formal and explicit communication.

Another academic who has contributed to the dimension of societal culture is Hofstede (1980) with his four cultural dimension framework which is widely cited in literature. He classified cultures into (a) power distance; (b) uncertainty avoidance; (c) individualism vs. collectivism; and (d) career success vs. quality of life[6]. Hofstede's dimension appears to be the most widely cited and used in research.

Power distance refers to the socially accepted distribution of power among individuals and institutions within a particular culture. A society is ranked high on power distance if the unequal distribution is supported by the majority of individuals in it. Uncertainty avoidance refers to the extent to which society members can cope with uncertainty regarding the future. A society would rank high on this dimension if its members are easily threatened by risk and ambiguity and seek to avoid or reduce them. Uncertainty avoidance seems to match the low-context dimension[7] of Edward Hall (1976a). Members of low-context societies are supposed to prefer information to be explicit rather than implicit. However, it is not a perfect match because it is conceivable to have a low-context society that is ready to take risks (of the future), albeit calculated. A casino gambler may be described as belonging to a low-context culture as she would prefer the instructions on how to operate the casino machine to be explicit and straight forward whereas she is ready, at the same time, to take much future risks with her money and livelihood.

A culture practices collectivism when it operates close social networks and focuses on the good of the group to which individuals are supposed to be loyal. The reverse is the case with individualism whereby each individual considers herself as master of her destiny.

Career success places emphasis on assertiveness, acquisition of wealth without much regards to the quality of life and others, whereas the opposite is nurturing and people- oriented.

In 1991, Hofstede added a 5th dimension—long-term orientation to short-term orientation (to life). This addition emanated from the observation of the difference between "western" and "eastern" minds. Western organizations tend to focus on immediate problem-solving whereas eastern organizations, typified by Japan, aim for the survival of the company in the long run and do not mind too much the making of mistakes provided subsequent attempts bring improvements.

Trompenaars (1993) distributed questionnaires to over 15,000 managers from 28 countries over ten years. Using responses from 500 managers from 23 countries, he produced cultural dimensions, five of which Hoecklin (1995) has found relevant to business areas, viz:

a. Universalism vs. particularism: general rules vs. exceptions.
b. Individualism vs. communitarianism: personal vs. group goals.
c. Neutral vs. affective relationships: emotional orientation in relationships.
d. Specificity vs. diffuseness: degree of detail preferred.
e. Inner direction vs. outer direction: location of goodness and therefore direction.

As far as the context of this chapter is concerned, the fifth dimension appears to be eclipsed by the second. If a member of a culture considers

virtue to dwell outside himself or herself, s/he would be prone to submit to group goals, and vice versa.

The sixth dimension from Trompenaars' work is sequential timing vs. synchronous timing: degree to which time overlaps (Hampden-Turner & Trampenaars, 2000). To be useful in the context of the study that this chapter proposes, this dimension needs to be reframed to the *degree of time keeping*. Already, the different time-zone locations of global team members argue against synchronizing of communication and tasks. Timeliness can be worsened if some team members exhibit a *mayiana* (till tomorrow) approach which is common in some cultures.

Individualism vs. communitarianism coincides with Hofstede's (1980) individualism vs. collectivism.

Hampden-Turner and Trampenaars (2000) consider each dimension as a dilemma and argue that, except at the extremes, both parts of the dilemma are virtuous rather than vicious. It would be interesting to find out, from future studies, whether this is the case with knowledge sharing among multi-cultural workers.

An attempt to amalgamate the three major works on dimensioning societal culture, taking into consideration the arguments in this chapter, is shown in Table 3.

PROPOSED CONCEPTUAL MODEL

An attempt has been made to amalgamate the dimensions to form a set of organizational and

Table 3. Dimensions of societal culture

Uncertainty avoidance	Individualism vs. collectivism
Power distance	Universalism vs. particularism
High context	Career success vs. quality of life
Low context	Neutral vs. affective relationship
Degree of time keeping	Specificity vs. diffuseness

Figure 1. Theoretical model

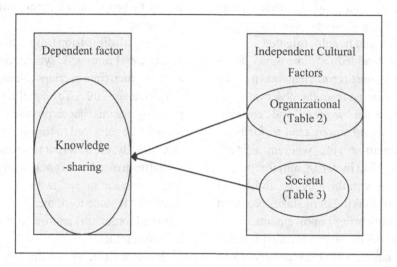

a set of social dimensions (see Tables 2 and 3). We can now propose a conceptual model that expresses knowledge sharing to be a function of organizational and societal cultural factors (see Figure 1). In this model two major hypotheses could be formulated, viz:

H₁: There is a high positive relationship between organizational culture and knowledge sharing.

H₂: There is a high positive relationship between societal culture and knowledge sharing.

Each of the sub-dimensions in Table 2 and Table 3 could be turned into a hypothesis that relates the sub-dimension with knowledge sharing. For instance, we could hypothesize that *high context* is negatively related to knowledge sharing. A supporting argument could be that most of the background information would be tacit which would call to question the success of persuading and enabling knowledge workers to express the information in their communication. The formation of hypotheses with supportive arguments is left for future work.

CONCLUSION

Culture is elusive but pervasive. Researchers have endeavored to dimension the concept from both organizational and societal points of view. Research on organizational culture is little and non-comparable because most of them take a value perspective. While these research efforts and techniques are worthwhile, this chapter has presented dimensions based on work-practice, with the argument that (a) this approach will enable wide-scale study, (b) research has established strong links between the value and the work-based perspectives, (c) it enables quantitative analysis, and (d) more recent studies are using this approach. This chapter has endeavored to identify these recent studies which have benefited from earlier studies which attempted to dimension culture. An attempt has been made to amalgamate the dimensions to form a set of organizational and a set of social dimensions (see Tables 2 and 3).

We then proposed propose a conceptual model that expresses knowledge sharing to be a function of organizational and societal cultural factors. We formulated two major hypotheses:

H₁: There is a high positive relationship between organizational culture and knowledge sharing.

H₂: There is a high positive relationship between societal culture and knowledge sharing.

For future work, we would operationalize the dimensions, conduct empirical study, and draw conclusions that establish the degree and direction of influence of these factors on knowledge sharing. The investigation of the sub-dimensions will enable the determination of their relative impact. Attempt can also be made to analyze and group Harper's basket of dimensions (see Table 1) for possible inclusion into the theoretical model presented by this chapter. This chapter has not answered all the questions but has proposed a conceptual model with pointers for future investigations. Such investigations should enlighten both research and practice on how best to manage multi-cultural knowledge workers. Meanwhile, practitioners can note that the various dimensions of culture discussed in this chapter could affect the performance of their knowledge workers.

REFERENCES

Al-Alawi, A., Al-Marzooqi, N., & Mohammed, Y. (2000). Organizational culture and knowledge sharing: Critical success factors. *Journal of Knowledge Management, 11*(2), 22-42.

Ardichvili, A., Maurer, M., Li, W., Wentling, T., & Stuedemann, R. (2006). Cultural influences on knowledge sharing through online communities of practice. *Journal of Knowledge Management, 10*(1), 94-107.

Barber, B. (1995). *Jihad vs. McWorld: How globalism and tribalism are reshaping the world.* New York, NY: Random House.

Blake, R., & Mouton, J. (1969). *Building a dynamic corporation through grid organizational development.* Reading, MA: Addison-Wesley.

Blake, R., & Mouton, J. (1985). *The managerial grid III.* TX: Gulf Publishing Company.

Block, J. (1978). *The Q-Sort method in personality assessment and psychiatric Research.* CA: Consulting Psychologists Press.

Comeau-Kirschner, C. (1999). It's a small world. *Management review, March,* 8.

Denison, D., & Mishra, A. (1995). Towards a theory of organizational culture and effectiveness. *Organization Science, 6,* 204-223.

Finestone, N., & Snyman, R. (2005). Corporate South Africa: Making multicultural knowledge sharing work. *Journal of Knowledge Management, 9*(3), 128-141.

Goh, S. (2002). Managing effective knowledge transfer: An integrative framework and some practice implications. *Journal of Knowledge Management, 6*(1), 23-30.

Gordon (1990). The relationship of corporate culture to industry sector and corporate performance. In: R. Kilmann, M. Saxton, & R. Serpa (Eds.), *Gaining control of the corporate culture* (pp. 103-125). San Francisco, CA: Jossey-Bass.

Gordon, G., & DiTomaso, N. (1992). Predicting corporate performance from organizational culture. *Journal of management studies, 9,* 783-798.

Gupta, A., & Govindarajan, V. (2000). Knowledge management social dimension: Lessons from Nucor Steel. *Sloan Management Review, 42*(1), 71-81.

Hall, E. (1976a). *Beyond culture.* NJ: Anchor Books.

Hall, E. (1976b). How cultures collide. *Psychology today, July,* 69.

Hampden-Turner, C., & Trompenaars, F. (2000). *Building cross-cultural competence: How to create wealth from conflicting values.* New York, NY: John Wiley & Sons.

Harper, G. (2000). *Assessing information technology success as a function of organizational culture.* Doctoral dissertation, University of Alabama, Huntsville, AL.

Hinds, P., & Weisband, S. (2003). Knowledge sharing and shared understanding in virtual team. In: C. Gibson & S. Cohen (Eds.), *Virtual teams that work: Creating conditions for virtual teams effectiveness* (pp. 21-36). San Francisco, CA: Jossey-Bass.

Hoecklin, L. (2003). Culture: What it is, what it is not and how it directs organizational behavior. In G. Redding & B. Stening (Eds.), *Cross-cultural management volume II* (pp. 75-104). Cheltenham: Edward Elgar Publishing Limited.

Hofstede, G. (1980). *Culture's consequences.* London: Sage.

Hofstede, G., Neuijen, B., Ohayv, D., & Sanders, G. (1990). Measuring organizational culture: A qualitative and quantitative study across twenty cases. *Administrative science quarterly, 35,* 286-316.

Hofstede, G. (2003). Cultural constraints in management theories. In G. Redding & B. Stening (Eds.), *Cross-cultural management volume II* (pp. 61-74). Cheltenham: Edward Elgar Publishing Limited.

Hofstede, G. (2001). *Culture's consequences: Comparing values, behaviours, institutions, and organizations across nations.* CA: Sage.

Huntington, S. (1996). *The clash of civilizations: Remaking of world order.* NY: Simon and Schuster.

Kroeber, A., & Luckhohn, C. (1952). *Culture: A critical review of concepts and definitions.* Cambridge, MA: Harvard University Press. Cited in Holden, N. (2002). *Cross-cultural management: A knowledge management perspective* (p. 26). London: Prentice Hall.

Kostova, T. (1999). Transnational transfer of strategic organizational practices: A contextual perspective. *Academy of Management Review, 24,* 308-324.

Kreitner, R., & Kinicki, A. (2002). *Organizational behavior.* London: McGraw Hill.

Kuofie, M. (2005). E-management: E-knowledge management for optimizing rural medical services. *International Journal of Management and Technology, 1,* September, 28-37.

Lemken, B., Kahler, H., & Rittenbruch, M. (2000). Sustained knowledge management by organizational culture. In *Proceedings of the 33rd Hawaii International Conference on System Sciences,* p. 64.

Malhotra, A., & Majchrzak (2004). Enabling knowledge creation in far-flung teams: Best practices for IT support and knowledge sharing. *Journal of Knowledge Management, 8*(4), 75-88.

Marcoulides, G., & Heck, R. (1993). Organizational culture and performance: Proposing and testing a model. *Organization Science, 4,* 209-225.

Matveev, A., & Milter, R. (2004). The value of intercultural competence of multicultural teams. *Team Performance Management, 10*(5-6), 104-111.

McDermott, R., & O'Dell, C. (2001). Overcoming cultural barriers to sharing knowledge. *Journal of Knowledge Management, 5*(1), 76-85.

Munter, M. (1993). Cross-cultural communication for managers. *Business Horizons,* May-June, 72.

O'Reilly, C., Al Chatman, J., & Caldwell, D. (1991). People and organizational culture: A profile comparison approach to assessing per-organization fit. *Academy of Management Journal, 34,* 487-516.

Oliver, S., & Kandadi, K. (2006). How to develop knowledge culture in organizations? A multiple case study of large distributed organizations. *Journal of Knowledge Management, 10*(4), 6-24.

Park, H., Ribière, V., & Schulte, Jr., W. (2004). Critical attributes of organizational culture that promote knowledge management technology implementation success. *Journal of Knowledge Management, 8*(3), 106-117.

Root, F. (1994). *Entry strategies for international markets.* NY: Lexington.

Quinn, R. (1988). *Beyond rational management: Mastering the paradoxes and competing demands of high performance.* San Francisco, CA: Jossey-Bass.

Reigle, R., & Westbrook, J. (2000). Organizational culture assessment. In *Proceedings of the National Conference of the American Society for Engineering Management,* Washington, D.C.

Schein, E. (1999). *The corporate culture survival guide: sense and nonsense about cultural change.* San Francisco, CA: Jossey-Bass.

Sharratt, M., & Usoro, A. (2003). Understanding knowledge-sharing in online communities of practice. *European Journal of Knowledge Management.* Retrieved from http://www.ejkm.com/volume-1/volume1-issue-2/issue2-art18-abstract.htm

Shenkar, O., & Zeira, Y. (1992). Role conflict and role ambiguity of chief manager officers in international joint ventures. *Journal of Applied Communication Research, 30*(3), 231-250.

Steven, C. (1989). *Postmodernist culture: An introduction to theories of the contemporary.* Oxford: Blackwell.

Trompenaars, F. (1993). *Riding the waves of culture.* London: The Economist Books.

Tuggle, F., & Shaw, N. (2000). The effect of organizational culture on the implementation of knowledge management. *Florida Artificial Intelligence Research Symposium (FLAIRS),* Orlando, FL.

Van den Berge, P., & Wilderom, C. (2004). Defining, measuring, and comparing organizational cultures. *Applied Psychology: An International Review, 53*(4), 570-582.

Van Muijen, J., Koopman, P., De Witte, K., De Cock, G., Susanj, Z., Lemoine, C., et al. (1999). Organizational culture: The focus questionnaire. *European Journal of Work and Organizational Psychology, 8,* 551-568.

Zakaria, N., Amelinckx, A., & Wilemon, D. (2004). Working together apart? Building a knowledge-sharing culture for global virtual teams. *Creativity and Innovation Management, 13*(1), 15-29.

ENDNOTES

[1] As far back as 1952, Kroeber and Luckhohn registered 164 definitions of culture.

[2] It has to be acknowledged though that organizational culture has the potential of acting not only as a barrier but also as motivation to high performance and initiative (Blake & Mouton, 1969; 1985).

[3] History is one of the levels.

[4] Al-Alawi et al. (2007) in their very impressive empirical study have used an organizational framework purported to originate from Gupta and Gowindarajan (2000). The framework categorizes organizational cultural into information systems, people, process, leadership, reward system and organizational structure. However, Gupta and Gowindarajan (2000) used those categories (*plus culture* as a category of its own) as determinants of social ecology. So rather than dimensioning culture, Gupta and Gowindarajan were apparently including culture in a list of predictors of social ecology.

5   Get to the point and avoid informal pre-
       ambles.

6   Hofstede initially labelled this masculinity
       vs. femininity.

7   And high-context dimension when we
       consider the low scale of uncertainty avoid-
       ance.

Section III
Advances in Knowledge Management in Organizations

Chapter X
Integrating Knowledge Management with Programme Management

Jill Owen
Monash University, Australia

ABSTRACT

Knowledge reuse has long been an issue for organisations. The management, reuse and transfer of knowledge can improve project management capabilities (i.e., learning, memory, cycle time) resulting in continuous learning. Although knowledge management has been recognised as a critical success factor in programme management very little research has been conducted to date (Lycett, Rassau, & Danson, 2004; Soderlund, 2004). A framework is discussed that demonstrates how knowledge is created, transferred, captured and reused within project and programme management, resulting in improved project management maturity. The framework utilises a task based approach to knowledge management and assumes that knowledge is created, transferred and reused as a result of an individual performing a specific task, which in this context is a project at the project level and a programme at the programme level.

INTRODUCTION

Organisations use projects to implement their strategy and change (Cleland, 1999). To achieve this, organisations need to utilise knowledge gained from earlier projects or project phases and not reinvent the wheel. One method of achieving this is for an organisation to develop a knowledge management strategy. A knowledge management strategy articulates how the organisation creates, values, preserves and transfers knowledge critical to its operations. As a way of ensuring that knowledge is effectively reused across projects they are often allocated to programmes. A pro-

Copyright © 2008, IGI Global, distributing in print or electronic forms without written permission of IGI Global is prohibited.

gramme is a group of projects managed together allowing added benefit and control that would not normally be achieved from managing projects individually (Project Management Institute, 2004; Turner, 1999).

Although knowledge management has been recognised as a critical success factor in programme management very little research has been conducted to date (Lycett et al., 2004; Soderlund, 2004). The focus of current research covers knowledge management in project management from intra- and inter-project learning (Kotnour, 1999) where it is important to capture knowledge as lessons learned where a full description of the project is captured allowing it to be used on other projects (Disterer, 2002). There has been a lack of formal knowledge exploitation in project management organisations.

A framework has been developed to demonstrate how knowledge is created, transferred, captured and reused within project and programme management. The framework utilises a task based approach to knowledge management and assumes that knowledge is situated within a specific context. Knowledge is created, transferred and reused as a result of an individual performing a specific task, in this context the task is a project at the project level and a programme at the programme level (Burstein & Linger, 2003). The framework shows how knowledge management can be integrated with project management.

The chapter is structured as follows, a background to knowledge management within project and programme management grounded in relevant literature is provided, including actor network theory (ANT). ANT describes the way that a project team can be viewed (Parkin, 1996) in terms of comprising both humans and nonhumans (machines, procedures, processes and documents) and how knowledge can be created, transferred and reused (Latour, 1987, 1999). The next section provides a framework for how knowledge is developed at the task level and is embedded into the project methodology of an organisation

allowing knowledge to be linked and reused in future projects and programmes. A description of a case study and a discussion of how knowledge management issues in the case study relate to the framework are then provided.

THE IMPORTANCE OF INTEGRATING KNOWLEDGE MANAGEMENT INTO PROJECT MANAGEMENT

The Project Management Institute (2000) defines a project as:

...a temporary endeavour undertaken to create a unique product or service. Temporary means that every project has a definite beginning and a definite end. Unique means that the product or services is different in some distinguishing way from all other products or services. (p. 4)

This definition offered by the Project Management Institute and widely used in both industry and academia focuses on project management as a tool rather than including project objectives, business performance (portfolio and programme management) that are fundamentally linked to project success (Morris, 2003). Morris (2003) offers an alternative definition:

Project management has to be about delivering business benefits through projects, and this necessarily involves managing the project definition as well as the downstream implementation. (p. 3)

Project success involves project management taking into account the traditional areas of project control and organisation, as well as the softer issues of stakeholder success, portfolio and programme management, project strategy, technology, and communication management (Morris, 2003). To achieve this, there needs to be a greater understanding of the integration of knowledge management into project management.

Different forms of knowledge exist in the project management environment — predominantly procedural (including tools) and contextual. While procedural knowledge is important, in larger or more complex projects contextual knowledge plays a key role both in learning and project success (Morris, 2003). Conversely if this procedural and contextual knowledge is not fully exploited the cost to an organisation could potentially be large in terms of time and dollars, reinventing the wheel and not reusing existing knowledge.

As project teams are temporary organisations need to ensure that knowledge from one project is available for use on future projects to reduce rework. Damm and Schindler (2002) argue that knowledge needs to be captured and indexed for future retrieval, however while it is important to capture explicit knowledge in a usable form it is also important to ensure that tacit knowledge can be tapped into (either personal knowledge or via a network)

Snowden (2002) argues that context is important in knowledge transfer because at one level people exchange knowledge personally based on trust and experience, while at the other level knowledge is coded for an unknown audience whose specific experience is unknown.

A knowledge management strategy is developed by organisations, including project organisations, for improving the way it develops, stores, and uses its corporate knowledge. Both tacit and explicit knowledge are important in the creation and reuse of knowledge. Organisational memory forms the basis of intellectual capital that is held in an organisation. Intellectual capital is the knowledge and capability to develop that knowledge in an organisation (Nahapiet & Ghoshal, 1998).

If an effective knowledge management strategy is not developed and managed by an organisation valuable intellectual capital can be lost, causing rework and lost opportunities. Better identification, transfer and management of knowledge allows intellectual capital to be effectively retained within the organisation, allowing it to be reused

on other projects, reducing the time staff spend recreating what has already been learned.

For a project management organisation to be competitive Project Managers need to build knowledge and improve project performance (Cooper, Lyneis, & Bryant, 2002). In a structured organisation the learning process is important as it helps Project Managers to build on their experience by delivering not just one but a succession of successful projects, and to develop the right sorts of capabilities, that is, the project management process, the product development process and the knowledge management process (Kotnour, 1999).

In a project management organisation learning is important as it helps project managers deliver not just one but a succession of successful projects, and to develop the right sorts of capabilities, that is, the project management process, the product development process, and the knowledge management process. Learning within (intra-project) and between (inter-project) projects is required for this (Kotnour, 1999). Knowledge needs to be developed within a project, where it is used and tested, before it can be transferred to other projects. The challenge within some projects, particularly long-term, is to look at the process for the capture and reuse of knowledge in future projects (or phases of the same project) and to ascertain how intra and inter project learning occur (McLoughlin, Alderman, Ivory, Thwaites, & Vaughan, 2000).

Four key factors are critical to a project organisations capacity to learn, and these in turn are influenced by:

- A culture that encourages learning,
- A strategy that allows learning,
- An organisational structure that promotes innovative development, and
- The environment (Fiol & Lyles, 1985).

These factors contribute to individuals creating, transferring and reusing knowledge leading to organisational learning (Argyris & Schon, 1978). For a project organisation to continually learn and develop organisational learning needs to occur. Organisational learning is the capacity or process within an organisation to maintain or improve performance based on experience (Nevis, DiBella, & Gould, 1995). Organisational learning is dependent on individuals improving mental models (representing a person's view of the world). To develop new mental models the existing models need to be captured allowing organisational learning to occur independently of any specific individual (Kim, 1993). Organisational learning occurs when:

... members of the organization act as learning agents for the organization, responding to changes in the internal and external environments of the organization by detecting and correcting errors in organizational theory in use and embedding the results of their inquiry in private images and shared maps of organization. (Argyris & Schon, 1978, p. 29)

A key component of this mapping process is the recording of organisational memory. Organisational memory comprises the sum of participating individual's knowledge (Argyris & Schon, 1978). Organisational memory is distributed across an organisation rather than in one central area. There are six repositories, five internal and one external: individuals, culture, transformations, structures, ecology, and external archives. Once this body of knowledge is created new people can use it and it survives people leaving the organisation (Walsh & Ungson, 1991). The sum of an organisation's knowledge exceeds the sum of the individuals (Nelson & Winter, 1982).

At a project level knowledge is created by individuals and groups building on existing knowledge and creating new knowledge (adapting McElroy's [2003] definition of knowledge production at an organisational level). This knowledge can either

be coded in project documentation or is stored with the project member.

PROGRAMME KNOWLEDGE

Knowledge Management is an important aspect of programme management. Programmes are the central point for the capture of knowledge such as project management policies, procedures and templates (Kerzner, 2003; Project Management Institute, 2004). Effective programme management allows for an enterprise or programme view of projects to be obtained via reporting and communication (Lycett et al., 2004) allowing for the more effective and efficient utilisation of schedules, resourcing, interface management, prioritisation, risk identification, mitigation, and management and forecasting (Lycett et al., 2004; Kerzner, 2003; Turner 1999).

At the programme level knowledge is shared, reused and created via training, mentoring, benchmarking, and capturing of lessons learned (Kerzner, 2003; Project Management Institute, 2004). In addition knowledge from previous projects can be stored and shared in a knowledge management system allowing for contextual searches for items such as lessons learned, financial data, processes, and procedures (Project Management Institute, 2004).

Project team members are often under pressure to move onto the next project rather than having time to reflect or transfer learning. Organisations need to develop a culture that allows knowledge to be captured and transferred (Lycett et al., 2004). It is suggested that it is a key role for programme management to foster this culture.

Knowledge management at the enterprise or programme level contributes to a learning organisation approach (Szymczak & Walker, 2003). Learning loops occur at regular review periods throughout a programme allowing benefits to be achieved (Thiry, 2002). These learning loops are a key point in knowledge creation, reuse, and transfer.

Successful organisations continually respond to change and reinvent themselves to maintain their competitiveness. Learning and knowledge management are key elements of the transformation and success (Thiry, 2002). Extending this it could be argued that learning and knowledge are embedded into the organisation (people, policies, and procedures).

ACTOR NETWORK THEORY

Project teams are temporary in nature with project team members moving back into operational roles, or onto another project, at the completion of a project or project phase (Cross, Nohria, & Parker, 2002; Blackburn 2002). Project management is associated with human and nonhuman (machines, tools, and artefacts) in temporary organisations, as in actor network theory (ANT) (Blackburn, 2002). ANT comprises heterogeneous actors comprising both humans and nonhumans, for example, machines, procedures, processes, and documents (Latour, 1987, 1999a). The creation of knowledge occurs within a network. Within a network, sucha as a project team, a situation is framed and structured according to the actors existing knowledge, skill sets and competencies, and the nonhuman actors present in the network. It is a dynamic situation and changes as actors come and go within the network (Callon, 1998). Knowledge is gained by interacting with actors within a network and in understanding how and why they have behaved in a particular way (Latour, 1993, 1999a). Programme and project teams are networks based on the concept of ANT. Knowledge within a project is unstable as knowledge is continuously built on and created as new situations emerge and project team members enter and leave the network (Callon, 1998).

An important element of a given network is the boundary of the network that is set and the links within the network. These links have properties via which actors can collaborate within the network (Law & Hassard, 1999). Both the actor and the network rely on the other (Callon & Latour, 1981). Networks are constantly redefined as situations change and actors enter and leave the network (Latour, 1999b).

Actors (both human and nonhuman) within ANT are linked to the external environment (including networks), which is constantly changing and existing knowledge is constantly being built on and created (Callon, 1998). Based on Callon's (1998) work it is argued that a programme or project has a network of connections with the outside world, usually with resources or actors (human and nonhuman) both within and outside the organisation. Overflows occur when an actor enters or leaves the network. Actors continually reconfigure their networks as they change and adapt.

The changing nature of the networks allows knowledge to be reused as the "black box" concept (Callon & Latour, 1981). Decisions that are made/adopted within networks utilise the concept of the "black box", allowing people to take known, accepted and established work of others as a resource and build on this work rather than reproducing and questioning it (Callon & Latour, 1981; Latour, 1987). Within a programme this is most likely artefacts such as processes, methodologies, and documentation.

THEORETICAL FRAMEWORK

Project Management

Projects typically have subject matter experts or application area specialists who are required to manage a project or input specialist knowledge into a project to ensure that it runs effectively and efficiently (Dinsmore, 1999; Project Management Institute, 2004). Activities are the specific tasks that must be performed to produce the various project deliverables (Project Management Institute, 2004). Deliverables are any measurable, tangible, verifiable outcome in a project that must be produced to complete a project or a phase of a project (Project Management Institute, 2004). These outputs (usually in explicit form) are organisational process assets that are embedded into the corporate knowledge base (Project Management Institute, 2004). As a number of different project team members may be involved in completing the same task tacit knowledge is created, transferred and reused at each deliverable (Owen et al., 2005).

As an individual conceptualizes the task and reuses and reapplies past knowledge and experiences it can be argued that organizational memory is accessed and built on at the work breakdown structure/activity level. Also, knowledge is created, transferred and reused as a result of performing a specific task (Burstein & Linger, 2003).

An output of a project, that is often required at regular review points throughout the project, is performance reporting. Performance reporting involves progress and status reporting and forecasting. This reporting provides details of actual performance/progress against projected progress. Measures cover scope, project schedule and quality. At these review points the method of reporting varies depending on the organisation (including industry and methodology used) and the type of project. Knowledge is captured and transferred at these performance reports at the explicit level through reporting and at the tacit level in the form of project review meetings (Project Management Institute, 2004).

Organisations have formal or informal methodologies in place (depending on the type of organisation and their level of project maturity) to allow a project to be managed on time and budget and develop appropriate risk mitigation strategies (Kerzner, 2001b; Project Management Institute, 2000). These methods are often linked to other processes within the organisation (Kerzner, 2001b). Knowledge is embedded and captured within the methodology (Project Management Institute, 2004). As identified earlier regular review points identified within the methodology allow knowledge to be captured and reused at the tacit and explicit level.

As a project moves into latter phases, past the initial scoping, the project can be planned in greater detail (including risks) it can be understood what resources in terms of manpower, facilities, proprietary knowledge, special expertise, and knowledge of the business and financials are required. People provide the knowledge, skills, capabilities, and talents of the firm's employees in terms of knowledge of the business, special expertise, and proprietary knowledge (Kerzner, 2001a). This progress inputs into an organisation's capability.

In order to sustain a competitive edge an organisation needs to continually develop capability, that is the ability to achieve a desired effect or outcome in a specific operating environment and be in a constant state of readiness (applying the military definition) (Hinge, 2000). Lessons learned need to be embedded into the way a firm does its work. Within the project environment improving capability is to deliver successful projects and develop a competitive edge. This could be extended to knowledge creation where knowledge is embedded and made available for reuse and sharing thereby developing capabilities. To be competitive or retain competitiveness an organisation needs to continually develop its capabilities. In order to be competitive, an organisation needs to improve its level of project management maturity (Kerzner, 2001a). As capability improves, the appropriate resources can be supplied improving project maturity (Kerzner, 2001a). Project Management capabilities can only improve if continuous learning occurs. Learning occurs via knowledge creation, transfer, and reuse. If knowledge is lost, an organisation's project management maturity can decline (Kerzner, 2001a).

Where issues cannot be resolved within the normal project environment and intervention is required, an escalation process is used identifying when, how and the issue will be resolved (Project Management Institute 2004). As well as resolving the issue in the short term a decision needs to be made if the project methodology should be improved. To develop and maintain a competitive advantage an organisation needs to embrace continuous improvement rather than becoming complacent allowing competitors to catch up or overtake (Kerzner 2001a).

Knowledge is embedded throughout the project lifecycle at both the tacit and explicit level. Tacit knowledge is captured and reused at the project level in the form of personal knowledge (utilisation of knowledge from earlier projects), networks (informal to obtain specialist knowledge), and informal lessons learned. At the performance reporting level tacit knowledge is captured via mentoring (formal mentoring at regular review points). At the capability level, tacit knowledge is transferred and reused via mentoring. Explicit knowledge is reused at the explicit level in terms of documentation, while at the performance reporting level it is captured in the form of action and issues (Owen et al., 2005). Project templates and the project methodology allow for consistent reporting and for lessons learned to be captured (Project Management Institute, 2004). Knowledge creation, capture, transfer, and reuse occur throughout different phases of the model, learning occurs at all of these points. Based on Beer's (1981) concept of sympathetic and parasympathetic flows where knowledge is created at the sympathetic flow, it is reused in the parasympathetic flow (Owen 2004).

Programme Management

Following Beer's (1981) concept of recursiveness this model can be linked to the programme level. Related projects are aligned to a programme to allow benefits to be gained that would not be achieved if the project was managed individually (Lycett et al., 2004).

Programmes of work focus on effectiveness and efficiency goals and business goals (Lycett et al., 2004). Key common areas for programme management are typically planning and resource management, monitoring and control, configuration management and change control, risk and issue management, benefits management, and stakeholder management. Programme management allows for consistent reporting and communication (Lycett et al., 2004). Knowledge is reused, created, and transferred via consistent reporting and communication.

Interfaces amongst projects are managed and aligned at the programme level. Alignment allows for a more efficient and effective use of resources, especially scarce and limited resources (Turner, 1999). In addition managing the interdependencies between projects can reduce the amount of rework between projects therefore reducing project delays and eliminating risks that arise between the interfaces of projects (Lycett et al., 2004).

Monitoring of the programme usually occurs within a project or programme management office (PMO). The PMO oversees the management of projects within a programme. Resources are shared and coordinated and a common set of tools and techniques are used allowing knowledge to be embedded within the PMO (Kerzner, 2003). As well as standardising processes, the PMO allows for an improvement in resource allocation and a more realistic prioritisation of work (Kerzner, 2003). The PMO is responsible for ensuring that knowledge is maintained and disseminated throughout the programme. Relevant tools and processes need to be available for the capturing of and dissemination of knowledge including: risk data, lessons learned, project plans, team meeting minutes, and subject matter experts (Kerzner, 2003). Organisational process assets allow knowledge to be embedded within the methodology. Organisational process assets can vary depending on the type of industry and application area but are often templates, processes, guidelines, standards, communication requirements, and change control procedures (Project Management Institute, 2004). A challenge is to ensure that the knowledge is distributed in a timely manner (Kerzner, 2003). In addition, knowledge can be transferred to Project Managers via programme management meetings.

One output of programme monitoring (and the PMO) is prioritised projects. Prioritisation of projects can be based around resource requirements, the length of the project, interdependencies of projects and the strategic and business initiatives (Turner, 1999). As a programme of work progresses and more knowledge about the programme (and projects within the programme) is gained, a greater level of project prioritisation can occur. The prioritisation of projects inputs into a programme's capability.

Within the programme environment improving programme capability is to deliver a successful programme of work. This could be extended to knowledge creation where knowledge is embedded and made available for reuse and sharing thereby developing capabilities. To be competitive or retain competitiveness, an organisation needs to continually develop its programme capabilities. In order to be competitive, an organisation needs to improve its level of project management maturity (Kerzner, 2001a). Capabilities must be improved over time allowing repeatable successes in programme management.

As capabilities are improved effective resource utilisation can occur (Lycett et al., 2004). There is an improvement in the effectiveness and efficiency of resources, including justification for allocating specialist and scarce resources to particular projects. Resources would be allocated based on project prioritisation (Lycett et al., 2004).

Improved monitoring of the programme leads to effective benefits realisation, including benefits associated with the delivery of key organisational capabilities and the associated outcomes over time (Thorp, 1998). Benefits can be the elimination of

risks arising from effective interface management, successful completion of projects and effective resource utilisation (Turner, 1999).

Effective capabilities of the programme lead to improved project and scope definition (Lycett et al., 2004). Where issues cannot be resolved within the normal programme environment a programme escalation is used identifying when, and how the issue will be resolved (Project Management Institute, 2004).

Framework

The theoretical framework provides a structure for linking programme management to knowledge management and mutually exploiting it (see Figure 1). The framework is a theoretical construct that represents the link between knowledge management and programme management.

As highlighted earlier, I choose to look at knowledge management using a bottom-up approach where knowledge is created, transferred, and reused as a result of a knowledge worker completing a task. Knowledge work is created, transferred and reused within a community of practice supported by a knowledge management system (Burstein & Linger, 2003).

A task is defined as:

...a substantially invariant activity with outcomes that include tangible output, central to the organization's viability and internal outcomes that are potential drivers of change. (Burstein & Linger, 2003, p. 290)

A project can be defined as a task where knowledge is created as the result of the activities that are carried out in a project by project teams and project team members (Owen et al., 2005).

Project team members create, transfer, and reuse knowledge in a community of practice (in this case it is most likely the project team) supported by a knowledge management system. This framework (Owen et al., 2005) caters for the

Figure 1. Knowledge management and project/programme management linked

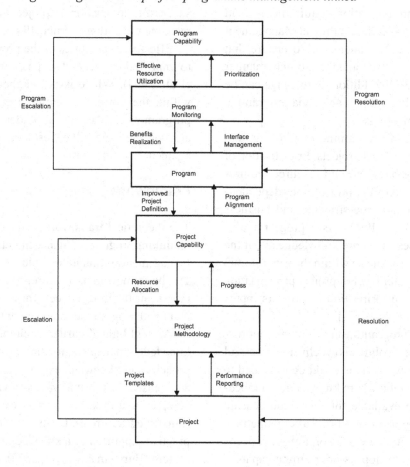

fact that when completing the task project team members will be able to conceptualise the task, reuse and apply past knowledge and experiences. Their knowledge work is supported via a knowledge management system (Burstein & Linger, 2003). The framework shows how knowledge is developed at the task level, is embedded into the project methodology, and improves the capability of an organisation.

This framework has alternative channels — sympathetic and parasympathetic flows. In order to maintain a stable environment where there is an input channel (sympathetic), there is an alternative channel (parasympathetic) which reports different information (Beer, 1981). The framework

utilises the concept of recursiveness and as such is extended from the project to the programme level (refer to Figure 1) (Beer, 1981).

CASE STUDY

Methodology

To initially test the project management component of the theoretical framework comprehensively within an organisation an exploratory case study, methodology was used allowing an insight to be gained into how knowledge was created, reused and transferred within and between projects

(Owen et al., 2005). Data was analysed to look at emerging patterns to the research questions. Two analytical techniques were used in the research: document analysis, and unstructured interviews, with project team members, from both projects were conducted; both providing different perspectives and enabling crosschecking (Sabherwal et al., 2001).

A framework was developed for recording and analysing the relevant project documentation. In addition an interview guide was developed for conducting in-depth interviews. Both instruments were mapped to the theoretical framework.

Relevant project documentation was studied, assessed, and analysed during the case study research. Nine in-depth interviews, each taking approximately one hour, were conducted from a random sample of project team members across both projects. Project team members were interviewed from all work streams, seniority levels, and permanent versus contract staff.

The theoretical framework provides a structure for showing how knowledge management can be applied to project management. This model identifies four main areas of research:

1. Intra-project/programme learning and knowledge creation;
2. Knowledge transfer and reuse across projects and programmes;
3. Whether project and programme knowledge becomes part of organisational memory or is retained as individual knowledge; and
4. Management of project and programme knowledge.

The Case Study Site

A case study was conducted in an engineering project management consulting organisation. Two linked projects from planning to implementation and closure were chosen in conjunction with the organisation and studied. The organisation treated the projects as two separate projects with separate deliverables and have been analysed as such. The projects were analysed at the completion of the projects with no intervention from the researcher.

The organisation studied for the project management component is a global consulting company and is recognised as a leader in the market place. The organisation is employee owned and has grown organically and via strategic mergers with organisations with similar cultures and values. Their mission is to focus on valued client relationships to achieve remarkable success for them. The firm has a commitment to service, quality, and high standards of safety and business ethics. Management of the organisation follows a global management structure. The management structure reflects the regional, business and functional unit structure. A wide range of knowledge workers including project managers, engineers and scientists are employed by the organisation.

The corporate vision is to deliver solutions to clients which create exceptional value. The strategy is a global approach through our local offices. The projects analysed for this research supported the strategy to deliver exceptional service for and create an ongoing relationship and reputation with key clients. A key strategy of the organisation is to invest in the future of the business; knowledge management has been recognised as a key contributor to the future of the business. To assist with this strategy there has been the appointment of a Knowledge Manager and the implementation of a knowledge management system. The knowledge management strategy is people centric rather than technology driven.

FINDINGS

Project

At the project level there is a reliance on both the existing network and actors in other networks (overflows). Documentation is usually in the form of a "black box", that is documentation that has been developed by others and is accepted as a resource, the documentation is built on rather than reinventing the wheel (Callon & Latour, 1981).

You use information that other people have worked on, particularly if you are running a project which is not like what you've done before. You ask around to find out who has the knowledge for that type of project and perhaps use their assistance.

Documents are stored on a server via job number, making it impossible to search contextually for documents (the organisation is in the process of implementing a knowledge management system) so explicit knowledge is often obtained from earlier projects that a person has worked on or obtaining the information from an expert. Documents are used as a starting point while more complex and detailed knowledge (such as financials and methodology) are obtained via tacit means, usually via human networks, that is, asking someone for the information.

It's a lot more efficient if you know who produced the file last time and you can go and ask them where it is...

Project Templates and Project Methodology

The organisation has a robust project management methodology with strong links to the methodology developed by the Project Management Institute (2000, 2004) Project Management Body of Knowledge (PMBOK). Each project follows a methodology based on: initiation, planning, execution, and closing phases. Business processes and project management systems also support the project and are aligned with the PMBOK methodology.

The project methodology has regular review points embedded into it allowing for performance to be reported against plan and allows for forecasting. The templates used cover scope, risk management and mitigation, project schedule, and quality. There is a reliance on existing templates and project methodology.

The critical steps in the process are signed off by the project manager and project director ... we register them with a budget ... and we monitor progress on a monthly basis we calculate earned value on the project online.

Performance Review and Reporting

Performance reporting occurs at regular review points of the project, using project templates; the performance of the project is measured against the project plan. Project templates that are used for performance reporting cover risk management, quality assurance, progress, performance against plan, and change management requests. The review points are identified by the project methodology.

As part of the reporting there is a review process (between the project director and project manager or an external reviewer and project manager/project team member), linked to the project methodology, where knowledge gained from one phase is incorporated into the next phase of the process. In this instance I would argue that the external reviewer, usually a quality assurance manager, is part of the external environment (including networks), which is constantly changing as they bring new knowledge into the project network during the review (Callon 1998).

Quality Assurance requirements are set up at the start of a project. Documents tend go through informal reviews to begin with, and then after changes are made, go back to the original reviewer for a formal review and sign off.

Capability

Mentoring is a key way of improving project capability, and is used within the existing network and via external networks (see Table 1). A Project director is appointed to mentor a project manager during the project. Mentoring occurs via regular review points.

The system of having a project director and project manager is one way that we reuse knowledge, because generally the director has more experience than the project manager. It's partly a mentoring system where the project director passes on knowledge to the project manager.

In addition more senior people (in terms of hierarchy and experience) external to the project mentor more junior project managers.

We've got a good mix of very senior guys and we try and get our junior guys to run projects and the senior guys feed the knowledge into the project...

Escalation/Resolution

Typically issues that cannot be resolved within the project are resolved by external networks. The project director and project manager meet with their alliance counterparts, and the client issues that cannot be resolved by the project team or the project manager/project director can be resolved.

There's an alliance leadership team (ALT) and an alliance management team (AMT). The ALT meeting is at a higher level than the AMT and takes a broad overview of issues. If the project team cannot resolve an issue, there is a process whereby the issue gets escalated for a decision up to the AMT or ALT. It's a case of using the experience of senior alliance members to resolve issues using a best for project approach.

Table 1. Knowledge use in project management

Phase of Model	Artefact	Actor
Project	• Informal Lessons Learned • Documentation • Informal networks	• Project team • 'Black box' documentation and experience • Specialists (informal and formal)
Performance Reporting	• Project Review Process • Mentoring • Review points	• Program Manager/ Project Director • Project Director • QA Manager
Project Templates	• Project Plans • Scope Documents • Review Documents	• 'Black box' documentation
Project Methodology	• Methodology/ Documentation	• Proj team utilize 'Black box' methodology
Progress	• Monitoring/ Mentoring	• Project Director/Project Manager monitoring and mentoring at regular review points
Project Capability	• Mentoring	• Project Director/Project Manager • Knowledge transfer from experienced employees to junior Project Managers
Resolution/ Escalation	• Alliance project meetings	• Project Director and Project Manager alliance meetings with their alliance counterparts

DISCUSSION

Knowledge is embedded and reused throughout the model. Knowledge creation, capture, transfer, and reuse, as stages of the implementation of a knowledge management strategy, occur throughout different phases of the model, learning occurs at all of these points. Based on Beer's (1981) concept of sympathetic and parasympathetic flows where knowledge was created at the sympathetic flow it was reused in the parasympathetic flow (see Table 2).

Networks

Networks, based on the concept of ANT, play a crucial role in the creation, capture, transfer and reuse of knowledge. The project manager and senior project team members initially relied on personal knowledge and then "overflowed" into their informal external networks throughout the project when external expertise was required (Callon, 1998). Formal networks (e.g., as established in the corporate e-mail system) were only tapped into if the relevant knowledge could not be obtained from the other sources. In most cases as well as utilising tacit knowledge people utilised informal networks when seeking explicit knowledge, that is, black box documentation that was accepted and established of others (Callon & Latour, 1981). People interviewed said it was quicker to ask the person who knew where the relevant documentation was rather than searching for it on the server or in folders.

Table 2. Project phases—How knowledge is managed and used

Knowledge Element	Type of Artefact	Existing Network /Overflow (Based on Callon 1998)	Phase of Project Component of Framework
Knowledge Creation	• Personal tacit knowledge • Collaborative tacit knowledge within project network • Tender/technical documentation • Tacit/explicit knowledge via external networks (informal/formal)	• Network • Network • Network • Overflow	• Project • Performance Reporting • Progress • Project Capability • Escalation • Resolution
Knowledge Capture	• Lessons Learned (formal/ informal) • Meeting minutes • Files • Project documentation	• Network/ Overflow • Network • Network • Network	• Project • Performance Reporting • Project Methodology • Progress • Project Capability • Escalation
Knowledge Transfer	• Collaborative tacit knowledge within project network • Project Documentation – Explicit • Tacit/explicit knowledge via external networks (informal/formal)	• Network • Network • Overflow	• Project • Project Templates • Project Methodology • Resource Allocation • Resolution
Knowledge Reuse	• Project Review documentation • Earlier project documentation/ methodology/ templates • Personal experience • Subject Matter Experts – Informal/ Formal	• Network – black box • Network – black box • Network/Overflow • Overflow	• Project • Project Templates • Resource Allocation • Project Capability • Resolution

Knowledge Creation

While there is a reliance on personal knowledge, explicit knowledge and collaboration within the projects external networks play a crucial role in terms of knowledge creation. These networks tend to be the informal networks of project team members and "overflow" (Callon, 1998) into the network when external knowledge or expertise is required.

Build up relationships with people over a period of time. You work with them and find out who the specialists are in areas of the company. You talk to a specialist call that person and ask questions on how they have approached something a relationship is established. As you build personal relationships you know who to call.

Knowledge Capture

Knowledge capture predominantly occurs within the project team, both formally and informally, usually at regular review points during the methodology. Formal lessons learned are stored by project (each project is allocated a project number) on the network server, or in individual paper-based files. While this network server can be accessed by more than one office it does not allow for contextual searches. As a result there has tended to be a reliance on informal knowledge capture and reuse.

Knowledge Reuse

Knowledge is embedded and reused throughout the model. Knowledge is informally reused or re-created from one project to another as the culture and system is not in place to formalise it. Several project team members have worked with the organisation for a number of years, and given the length of time that they have been with the organisation they have created informal networks

(usually people that they have worked with on previous projects).

The project team manager and senior project team members initially relied on personal knowledge and then their informal networks. Formal networks (e.g., as established in the corporate e-mail system) were only tapped into if the relevant knowledge could not be obtained from the other sources. In most cases, as well as utilising tacit knowledge people sought out explicit knowledge, that is, people interviewed said it was quicker to ask the person who knew where the relevant documentation was rather than searching for it on the server or in folders.

At the more senior levels of the organisation formal networks (across the distributed enterprise) also played a crucial role. In addition there was one exception where one team member relied predominantly on informal knowledge transfer but also documented everything so that if he was not in the organisation any longer another person could access the information, the only issue is that as everything (including all e-mails) were stored in hardcopy it would be difficult to find the most appropriate knowledge.

During project implementation a key reason that knowledge is reused, from documented lessons learned (explicit knowledge) and informal lessons learned (obtained from informal networks), is to deliver a solution where any potential pitfalls are known in advance allowing them to be overcome.

You remember the projects you've worked on the most, so you are more inclined towards them. But a lot of the time you pick up cost estimates and specifications and use information from projects other people have worked on, particularly if you are running a project which is not like what you've done before. You ask around to find out who has the knowledge for that type of project and perhaps use their assistance.

The knowledge derived from the formal lessons learned can form content for a knowledge-management system. An immature knowledge management system had been implemented within the case study site, however as project documentation was stored on a network server, a key question for the future is as the knowledge management system is utilised within the organisation will there still be the same reliance on informal lessons learned or will people start to rely on formal lessons learned that are stored in the system.

Knowledge Transfer

Knowledge is transferred from the project level to business unit and organisational levels contributing to the creation of organisational memory. Mentoring played a key role in knowledge transfer from the project director to the project manager at regular reviews/meetings throughout the project. In addition as part of the development of more junior project managers and in recognition that a lot of experience and knowledge was held by more senior people one business unit developed a system whereby a senior staff member of retirement age mentored and transferred knowledge to more junior project managers.

CONCLUSION

This chapter has established a theoretical framework for knowledge reuse based on a review of relevant literature. The literature is mainly concerned with how knowledge is integrated at both the programme and project level. Networks (both human and nonhuman) play a key role in knowledge creation, reuse, and transfer.

At both the project and programme level knowledge plays a crucial role in delivering successful projects and programmes of work. The chapter builds on Burstein and Linger's (2003) concept of task based management where the project is the task and knowledge is created as a result of project team members completing a task within the project team environment. The model shows that in order for an organisation to deliver successful projects, develop its project management maturity, and improve its capability continuous learning needs to occur.

This research is grounded by the principles of task based management where knowledge is created in a project by the project team member or project team completing the task. This article contributes to the overall body of knowledge by exploring the contribution of learning and knowledge to a project organisation's development in terms of capability. The framework will also make a substantial practical contribution in terms of developing guidelines for creating, sharing, and reusing knowledge in a project management environment.

ACKNOWLEDGMENT

This research is partly funded by Monash University, I am grateful to my supervisors Associate Professor Frada Burstein and Dr. Henry Linger for their support and constructive comments. I am also grateful to the support from the case study site. I acknowledge the reviewers and associate editors for the constructive comments that they made when reviewing this chapter.

REFERENCES

Argyris, C. & Schon, D. A. (1978). *Organizational learning: A theory of action perspective*. Addison Wesley Publishing Company.

Beer, S. (1981). *Brain of the firm*. Chichester, New York, Brisbane, Toronto: John Wiley & Sons.

Blackburn, S. (2002). The project manager and the project-network. *International Journal of Project Management, 20*(3), 199-204.

Burstein, F. & Linger, H. (2003). Supporting post-fordist work practices: A knowledge management framework for supporting knowledge work. *Information Technology and People, 16*(3).

Callon, M. (1998). An essay on framing and overflowing: Economic externalities revisited by sociology. In M. Callon (Ed.), *The laws of the markets.* Oxford and Keele, Blackwell and the Sociological Review.

Callon, M. & Latour, B. (1981). Unscrewing the big Leviathan: How actors macrostructure reality and how sociologists help them to do so. In K. D. Knorr-Cetina & A. V. Cicourel (Eds.), *Advances in social theory and methodology: Toward an integration of micro- and macro-sociologies.* Boston: Routledge.

Cleland, D. (1999). *Project management strategic design and implementation.* McGraw-Hill.

Cooper, K. G., Lyneis, J. M., & Bryant, B. J. (2002). Learning to learn from past to future. *International Journal of Project Management, 20*(3), 213-219.

Cross, R., Nohria, N., & Parker, A. (2002). Six myths about informal networks and how to overcome them. *Sloan Management Review, 43*(3), 67-75.

Damm, D. & Schindler, M. (2002). Security issues of a knowledge medium for distributed project work. *International Journal of Project Management, 20*(1), 37-47.

Dinsmore, P. C. (1999). *Winning in business with enterprise project management.* New York: AMA Publications.

Disterer, G.. (2002). Management of project knowledge and experiences. *Journal of Knowledge Management, 6*(5), 512-520.

Fiol, C. M. & Lyles, M. A. (1985). Organizational learning. *Academy of Management Review, 10*(4), 803-813

Hinge, A. (2000). *Australian defence preparedness: Principles, problems, and prospects.* Australian Defence Studies Centre Canberra ACT.

Kerzner, H. (2001a). *Strategic planning for project management using a project management maturity model.* New York: John Wiley and Sons.

Kerzner, H. (2001b). *Project management: A systems approach to planning, scheduling and controlling.* New York: John Wiley and Sons.

Kerzner, H. (2003). Strategic planning for a project office. *Project Management Journal, 34*(2), 13-25.

Kim, D. H. (1993). The link between individual and organizational learning. *MIT Sloan management Review, 35*(1).

Kotnour, T. (1999). A learning framework for project management. *Project Management Journal, 30*(2), 32-38.

Latour, B. (1987). *Science in action: How to follow scientists and engineers through society.* Cambridge, MA: Harvard University Press.

Latour B. (1993). *The pasteurisation of France.* Cambridge, MA: Harvard University Press.

Latour, B. (1999a). *Pandora's hope: Essays on the reality of science studies.* Cambridge, MA: Harvard University Press.

Latour B. (1999b). On recalling ANT. In J. Law & J. Hassard (Eds.), *Actor network theory and after* (pp. 15-25). Oxford: Blackwell.

Law, J. & Hassard, J. (Eds.). (1999). *Actor network theory and after.* Oxford and Keele: Blackwell and the Sociological Review.

Lycett, M., Rassau, A., & Danson, J. (2004). Programme management: A critical review. *International Journal of Project Management, 22,* 289-299

McElroy, M. (2003) *The new knowledge management.* Butterworth-Heinemann

McLoughlin, I. P., Alderman, N., Ivory, C. J., Thwaites, A., & Vaughan, R. (2000). Knowledge management in long term engineering projects. In *Proceedings of the Knowledge Management: Controversies and Causes Conference*. Retrieved May 19, 2003 from, http://bprc.warwick.ac.uk/km065.pdf

Marshall, C. & Rossman, G. B. (1995). *Designing qualitative research* (2nd ed.). London: Sage Publications.

Morris, P. W. G. (revised 2003). *The validity of knowledge in project management and the challenge of learning and competency development*. Retrieved May 23, 2005, from http://www.bartlett.ucl.ac.uk/research/management/Validityofknowledge.pdf

Nahapiet, J. & Ghosal, S. (1998) Social capital, intellectual capital, and the organizational advantage. *Academy of Management. The Academy of Management Review, 23*(2), 242-266.

Nelson, R. R. & Winter, S. G. (1982). *An evolutionary theory of economic change*. Cambridge, MA: Belknap Press of Harvard University Press.

Nevis, E. C., DiBella, A. J., & Gould, J. M. (1995). Understanding organizations as learning systems. *MIT Sloan Management Review, 36*(2).

Owen, J. (2004, November). *Developing program management capabilities: A knowledge management perspective*. Paper presented at the 7th Australian Conference on Knowledge Management and Intelligent Decision Support (ACKMIDS 2004).

Owen, J., Burstein, F., Linger, H., & Mitchell, S. (2005, January). *Managing project knowledge: The contribution of lessons learned*. Paper presented at IPSI-2005, Hawaii.

Owen, J., Burstein, F., & Mitchell, S. (2005). Knowledge reuse and transfer in a project management environment [Special issue]. *Journal of Information Technology Cases and Applications (JITCA), 6*(4).

Parkin, J. (1996). Organizational decision making and the project manager. *International Journal of Project Management, 14*(5).

Project Management Institute. (2000). *A guide to the project management body of knowledge*. Project Management Institute USA.

Project Management Institute. (2004). *A guide to the project management body of knowledge*. Project Management Institute USA

Sabherwal, R., Hirschheim, R., & Goles, T. (1998). The dynamics of alignment: A punctuated equilibrium model. *Organization Science, 12*(2), 17.

Scymczak, C. & Walker, D. H. T. (2003). Boeing — A case study example of enterprise management from a learning organisation perspective. *The Learning Organization, 10*(3), 125-137.

Snowden, D. (2002). Complex acts of knowing: Paradox and descriptive self awareness. *Journal of Knowledge Management, 6*(2), 100-111.

Thiry, M. (2002). Combining value and project management into an effective programme management model. *International Journal of Project Management, 20*, 221-227.

Thorp, J. (1998). *The information paradox, Realizing the business benefits of information technology*. Toronto: McGraw-Hill Ryeson.

Turner, J. R. (1999). *Handbook of project-based management: Improving the processes for achieving strategic objectives*. London: McGraw-Hill.

Walsh, J. P. & Ungson, J. R. (1991). Organizational memory. *Academy of Management Review, 16*(1), 57-91.

This work was previously published in International Journal of Knowledge Management, Vol. 2, Issue 1, edited by M.E. Jennex, pp. 41-57, copyright 2006 by IGI Publishing, formerly known as Idea Group Publishing (an imprint of IGI Global).

Chapter XI
Developing and Analysing Core Competencies for Alignment with Strategy

Keith Sawyer
Alpha Omega International, UK

John Gammack
Griffith University, Australia

ABSTRACT

Although it is widely accepted that alignment of knowledge with corporate strategy is necessary, to date there have been few clear statements on what a knowledge strategy looks like and how it may be practically implemented. We argue that current methods and techniques to accomplish this alignment are severely limited, showing no clear description on how the alignment can be achieved. Core competencies, embodying an organisation's practical know-how, are also rarely linked explicitly to actionable knowledge strategy. Viewing knowledge embedded in core competencies as a strategic asset, the chapter uses a case study to show how a company's core competencies were articulated and verified for either inclusion or exclusion in the strategy. The study is representative of similar studies carried out across a range of organisations using a novel and practically proven method. This method, StratAchieve, was used here in a client situation to show how the core competencies were identified and tested for incorporation or not in the strategy. The chapter concludes by considering the value of the approach for managing knowledge.

INTRODUCTION

Many companies have developed or adopted various knowledge management (KM) initiatives to try to surface and differentiate what they do know from what they need to know and also to identify the location of their knowledge gaps. Processes and tools that support efforts to capture knowledge

Copyright © 2008, IGI Global, distributing in print or electronic forms without written permission of IGI Global is prohibited.

are well known and widely used, such as expertise directories, intranets, communities of practice, knowledge audits, discussion forums, knowledge maps, building and documenting knowledge based and expert systems, storytelling, benchmarking, and the like. These efforts serve the strategy functions of organisations, aligning capability and know-how with strategic objectives.

Although the importance of strategic alignment is recognised, what is less understood is the practical means to determine what knowledge is strategically important and how this knowledge can be incorporated into the corporate strategy. Zack (1999) for example suggests that companies may have unique ways of doing this, (itself a competitive advantage) using techniques such as SWOT analysis. Zack's work, while providing a framework and some high-level questions, is light on actionable detail, and is silent on how the output of such efforts can be strategically assessed with sufficient reach to be implemented. The available literature on knowledge strategy alignment is generally very limited: although many documents refer to these issues, few go beyond noting the desirability of alignment, and even fewer provide any detailed methodological guidance. Few empirical studies appear to exist, and whilst academic comparison across unique cases is not always appropriate, the study reported in this chapter describes a generic method that has also been used in several other organisations. The approach described here addresses *what* organisations know, and how it aligns with their wider strategy.

All organisations need to "know what they know" (and know what they don't know) to make strategic decisions on (for example) sourcing, customer satisfaction, recruitment and training, investment, and in identifying areas for process re-engineering, market development, or innovation. The familiar saying, "If only we knew what we know" is, however, flawed because it presumes that what exists as knowledge in organisations is always useful and needs to be formalised and actioned. More appropriate is to say "If only we knew what we need to know". This means that organisations must also know what they no longer need to know because it no longer has a sufficient impact on the corporate objectives. Similarly, organisations must know what knowledge is most important and determine whether they already have this knowledge or need to acquire it. Apart from the rather limited SWOT analysis, or proprietary methods (e.g., AMERIN, n.d.) that may or may not include tools that help identify knowledge gaps, there are few clear statements on how, in practice, strategy may be structured in actionable alignment with organisational knowledge.

Organisations must structure their strategy so that strategic decisions and actions can be made on a variety of fronts, such as retaining and growing profitable customers, selling the right products to the right market, and recruiting and developing staff. To achieve this, organisations must manage their knowledge effectively to ensure it is directly translatable into strategic actions. Without knowing how to effectively manage their own stock of intellectual capital, such decisions cannot be actioned nor can the company be properly valued[1].

When turnover or loss of key staff is potentially a consequential threat, failure to manage the implicit knowledge assets underpinning this value may be seen as negligent. Intellectual capital is the main source of value creation (Edvinsson & Malone, 1997) and thus strategically linked directly to the organisation's future. In larger organisations especially, formalisation of this activity is required, not only for internal purposes, but also externally, such as shareholder value creation and outperformance of competitors. Identifying, securing and managing the various forms of intellectual capital (human and structural) within an organisation has thus become a central theme for knowledge management research as well as for knowledge valuing and reporting.

KM initiatives typically centre on the personnel who embody and can apply their knowledge in project or other business activity settings, and often entail recording or abstracting from the traces of their contextualised activities. Such KM initiatives implicitly recognise the centrality of the competencies of individuals and groups in transacting the strategic aims of the organisation at operational levels, and in potentially identifying the specific knowledge and abilities that give comparative advantages. Rarely, however, are such initiatives directly linked to corporate strategy and are (often inappropriately) typically designed and implemented through the organisation's IT support function (Berkman, 2001). A focus on the competencies related to strategic objectives and alignment with operational competencies is vital and is addressed in the following case study.

If organisations are centrally reliant on their knowledge for their survival, value and prosperity, their knowledge management strategies must be fully congruent with wider corporate strategy. Hackney, Burn, and Dhillon (2000) note, however, that comments on implementing such congruence have been few, and there remains a "prevalent disconnect between (business) and IT strategies". Their analysis of contemporary business strategy implies a reappraisal of the conventional and rational assumptions implicit in strategic IS planning (SISP) and where installing an IT "solution" is insufficient without coherent linkage to business strategy.

Hackney, Burn, and Dhillon (2000) cite research suggesting a necessary relationship between innovation and organisational *competence* and see assessing organisational competencies as a critically relevant challenge for SISP. The terms *competences* and *competencies* are both used in the literature to refer to such organisational abilities: we prefer to use *competencies* in this chapter. The knowledge embedded in organisational competencies can be a key strategic asset, and conversely, strategy emerging from inherent capabilities and competencies provides flexibility and responsiveness. Identifying such competencies is prerequisite to their assessment, valuation,

and incorporation into strategy. These competencies, which are typically knowledge based, can form the essence of a knowledge strategy embedded within a wider corporate strategy that is not simply cast in terms of KM technologies over some planning period.

A company's core competencies (Prahalad & Hamel, 1990) are the areas in which it has competitive strength and thus form a platform for its strategic thrusts. Not knowing or appreciating these means its strategies may fail and compromise proper valuation of a company's knowledge assets underlying the support, adaptation, and maintenance of its activities. Core competencies are the "cognitive characteristics of an organisation, its know-how…" (Hatten & Rosenthal, 2001, p. 50), that is, an organisation's collective (functional) expertise. Built on the skills and experience of individuals and teams, they are housed in characteristic business functions: examples Hatten and Rosenthal (2001) cite include McDonald's HR competency in recruiting, hiring, training, and retaining part time labour and Intel's technology competency in state of the art design of microprocessor chip families. Although such functions are not necessarily unique to an organisation, the know-how and processes involved in them may well be, thus conferring advantage.

Core competencies are necessarily part of a knowledge strategy which itself is part of the overall strategy. A focus on competencies (which implies active and generative abilities) rather than the knowledge traces itself is preferable, since in times of change, accumulated knowledge may be a hindrance to new thinking: what Leonard-Barton (1995) has called "core rigidities". To give a sustainable strategic advantage, competencies should be valuable, rare, hard to imitate or substitute, and ideally will confer a dominating ability in their area. Bollinger and Smith (2001) view the knowledge resource as a strategic asset, with the "collective organisational knowledge, (rather than that) of mobile individuals", that is the essential asset. This suggests a focal shift towards organisationally understood activity and process, not merely data and record storage requiring leverage by particular individuals for effectiveness.

In the knowledge based view, nicely contrasted with the conventional rational view of strategy by Carlisle (1999) the strategic focus is on value *creation* arising from uniquely effective internal capabilities and competencies, rather than value *appropriation*, which emphasises "optimisation" activity in imperfect markets. Although over time advantages may be eroded, organisations with developed "capabilities for managing knowledge creation and exploiting (its value) are better able to adapt by developing new sustainable core competencies for the future" (Carlisle, 1999, p. 24). Dawson (2000, p. 323) also notes "It is far more useful to think (about developing) dynamic knowledge capabilities than about knowledge as a static asset …to be managed".

The theoretical literature on core competencies does not however generally relate their development to concepts of knowledge management operation, nor to strategy implementation. Nor, although recognising that some competencies are more important than others, does it distinguish strategic from operational core competencies. Although the literature does not imply that strategic competencies arise from operational ones, we find it useful in practice to differentiate these since the only way strategy can be realised is at the operational level, by competent people performing activities that achieve strategic goals. For this to occur, an explicit linkage between strategic goals and operational activity, between strategic core competencies and their implementation (and reciprocally between operational competencies and strategic objectives) must be articulated. This theoretical claim is demonstrated in the present case study.

Since contemporary thinking on strategy emphasises ability to respond to environmental changes quickly at all levels rather than planning in a controlled environment, an embedded

knowledge strategy will act as the medium through which these levels can be brought into alignment and allow for emergent strategy to be developed across the organisation.

Klein (1998) asks the question "But how does a firm decide what set of operating-level initiatives would best meet its strategic goals?" and goes on to identify the "challenge of linking strategy with execution at the knowledge level" (p. 3) by a focus on various activities around intellectual capital. As an open research question however, specific implementation guidance is not offered, and associated literature (e.g., Graham & Pizzo, 1996) often notes only generic steps (identify strategic business drivers, determine business critical knowledge characteristics and locations, construct knowledge value chains, and find competency gaps).

Apart from private ownership tools, which may lack academic evaluation or an underlying original research base, there are few existing public domain management tools that offer help in modelling the different aspects a comprehensive knowledge-centric strategy development entails. These candidates include the "enterprise model" (Hatten & Rosenthal, 1999), later renamed the "action alignment (AA) model" and extended in Hatten and Rosenthal (2001); and more recently strategy maps (Kaplan & Norton, 2004). These generally provide broad areas for consideration, but give little or no guidance on strategy development or implementation beyond a flimsy structural outline. For knowledge strategy evaluation in financial terms, the KM valuation methodology of Clare and Detore (2000) applies, but this starts from a developed business strategy or KM project proposal.

The AA (Action Alignment) model is essentially a grid showing classical business functions (e.g., HRM, IT, and so on) crossed with business processes (e.g., order fulfilment) allowing visualisation of core junctures or problem (misaligned) areas, with supplementary tools to assess the fit or otherwise between customers and organisational capabilities and competencies. This appears to be essentially reactionary to the need for cross-functional alignment occasioned by new economy realities, but problematises the issue within an assumed industrial-era organisational structure of functionally defined silos, and without highlighting the knowledge activities required. The AA model has various other serious limitations in a knowledge-based view, in which traditional "Balkanised" organisational structures are considered obsolescent, and not conducive to the strategic planning and development of intangible assets and associated capabilities (Chatzkel, 2000).

The Balanced Scorecard (Kaplan & Norton, 1996) is a widely used performance measurement tool and has evolved since its origination in the early 1990s to more explicitly focus on strategy. Originally it aimed to address aspects of a company's performance not covered in simpler measures oriented primarily to financial performance. A customer perspective, an internal business perspective, an innovation and learning perspective, and a financial perspective provide a set of measures indicating aspects of performance relevant to various stakeholders. The strategy maps and supporting theory outlined in Kaplan and Norton (2004) are however very sketchy and conventional in relation to the knowledge based view — competency is effectively equated with job description (p. 225 et seq), and the references to the concepts of knowledge and KM are very shallowly treated. Furthermore, although the strategy maps show some linkages, the map's theoretical formulation is silent about the detailed linkages between these giving no guidance as to how the knowledge embodied in them can be identified, related to strategic competencies and leveraged with respect to achieving financially quantifiable targets such as market share, net profit or shareholder value, or other non-financial performance measures. Tools such as Kaplan and Norton's strategy map thus do not explicitly address knowledge-centric strategy development

and indeed a series of google searches in mid 2004 yielded few hits relevant to this aspect.

Yet an organisation's ability (or otherwise) to knowledgeably enact and leverage corporate processes and technologies is the essence of strategic competency. In a view of strategy that is not purely top down, but is essentially enacted dynamically by the knowledgeable activity of people in the "middle", it is crucial to reify these competencies in relation to strategy formulation. Current tools do not go far enough in guiding this, nor do they provide explicit methods for systematic engagement at this level.

THE CASE STUDY

Overview

We offer an approach addressing this by using a case study embodying action research techniques, beginning with a brief description of the organisation, its strategic position and the context of the fieldwork. A case study approach has been chosen since contemporary phenomena are being investigated in their real life context, with multiple variables of interest and converging sources of data; where the boundaries between the phenomena and the context are unclear and where the researcher has little control over behavioural events (Yin, 2002). The case study approach allows depth of understanding across many variables to occur. In this research an interpretivist position is adopted in which the organisation's own meanings and their negotiation are prioritised.

The case study reported here is of a UK accountancy company, and entailed the elicitation and reification of its hitherto poorly understood core competencies. The knowledge strategy was developed within a comprehensive corporate strategy overhaul and was built around the knowledge audit of its core competencies embodied in people and processes, supported by relevant technology.

The chapter proceeds as follows. Having identified the need to provide detailed guidance on reifying an organisation's core competencies and to relate those effectively to knowledge strategy, we outline processes that address this weakness and show how they can be implemented within more generic strategic planning processes.

We illustrate these in the case study context to show how the organisation systematically identified its core competencies, as well as determining the core competencies that are no longer of strategic importance. In the process, learning that the company not only did not have the strategic competencies it thought it had, but that it had knowledge assets which it had not realised, provided the capability to explicitly incorporate the competencies into the strategy.

The result was an articulation of what the company "knew" as well as what it did not know but needed to know, both strategically and operationally. This enabled the company to consciously leverage its strengths but also identify areas in which it was deficient and therefore strategically vulnerable. The case study concludes by showing how the company had achieved a strong competitive position from which to strategically value its knowledge and other intangible assets in an informed manner for forward planning and reporting to shareholders and others. The detailing of this valuation is part of our ongoing research.

The Organisation

The UK accountancy company featured in this case study is involved in a broad range of financial services to a wide variety of customers, both large and small. For purposes of this chapter, the company shall be called Target Accountancy. The company has 56 employees and has been in existence since 1987. Staff turnover is low as a result of high loyalty and good conditions of employment.

Target Accountancy had never produced a formal strategy plan but realised it could not achieve the success it wanted without one. The

saying "if you don't plan your company's future, it won't have one" was very pertinent in their case. The company possessed a rich abundance of talent but this was tacitly held in the minds of individuals; it wanted to be the formal owner of its capital knowledge. One of the aims of Target Accountancy was to verify whether the competencies it thought it possessed were being successfully engineered to generate the required competitive differentiators. There was thus a strong need to strategically specify and test the impact of its core competencies, to determine which were the most productive and identify gaps where new competencies were required.

The StratAchieve Method

One of us (Sawyer) was the external facilitator. The StratAchieve method[2] was chosen because of its proven capability in over 400 organisations to create and achieve strategies. Other tools currently on the market are geared either for helping to produce a strategy plan or to conduct project management, but not both. StratAchieve produces and combines the two, enabling iteration between the plan and implementation to take place.

The method is supported by software produced by Alpha Omega, which is used throughout the change programme. During a workshop session, a map is projected onto a screen and interactively developed through discussions, suggestions and learning from workshop delegates. An important aspect of the approach is its ability to integrate the various types of organisational strategies, such as customers, financial, HR, marketing, product, IS, and (crucially) knowledge, into a single, coherent corporate strategy.

The method enables organisations to determine, construct, legitimise, and achieve their strategy and conduct monitoring and controlling during implementation and provides the structure for all organisational strategic actions to be integrated. Thus, marketing, HR, finance, IT, and knowledge strategies are all holistically integrated into one coherent and comprehensive strategy. This will become apparent in the examples that follow.

The Strategy Tree provides the theoretical framework of the method (Sawyer, 1990) consisting of four or five layers of verb-fronted activities, logically related through *Why* and *How* connections. These Why and How relations provide a path that simultaneously justifies a given action at a higher level, whilst specifying an operational activity that achieves higher level aims. In discussions any given statement can be explored in either direction. For example rationale for the expressed operational competency *"Keep in regular contact with all clients"* was explored. The next higher-level activity was determined by asking, *"why should we Keep in regular contact with all clients"*? which elicited the response, because we want to *"Maintain excellent personal relationships with our clients"*. A further Why interrogation on this activity produced the parent, *"Retain our current clients"* and a further Why activity resulted in the parent *"Increase our revenues"*. A final

Why activity generated the high-level statement *"Increase our gross margin"* linked directly to strategic mission. In this example, a set of Why interrogations produced the higher-level activities which linked to the pre-set vision (increase our gross margin). Conversely, How statements can be elicited by starting with a high-level aim, and identifying child activities that follow from it, as reversing the previous example shows. Turning a competence into verb-fronted form emphasises a capability focus for knowledge, and leads eventually to activity based costing and specific required operational actions. The software tracking the map thus developed shows what must be done, when, how, why and by whom through specific supporting functions, and aids dynamic strategy construction.

Workshop Preparation

The process was initiated through a one-day workshop, attended by all senior members of Target

Figure 1. The Knowledge Positioning Matrix showing examples from the workshop

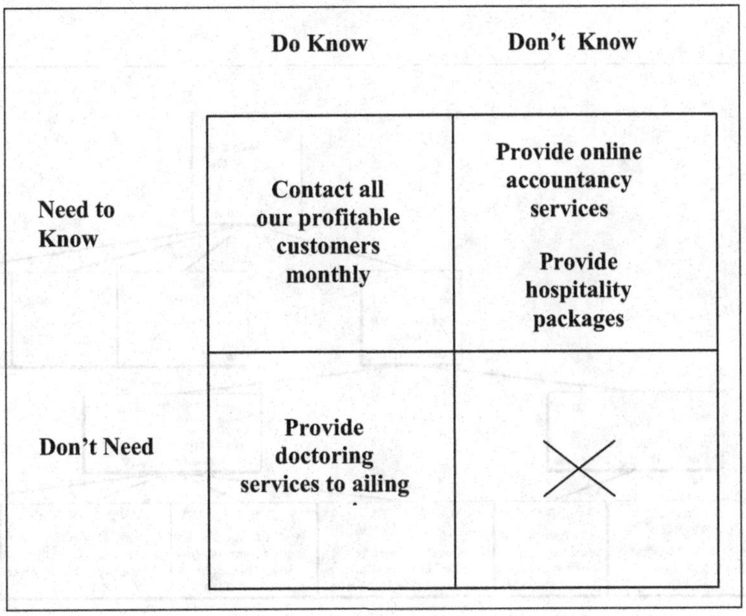

	Do Know	**Don't Know**
Need to Know	**Contact all our profitable customers monthly**	**Provide online accountancy services** **Provide hospitality packages**
Don't Need	**Provide doctoring services to ailing**	✕

Accountancy together with a range of staff from a variety of departments.

The Knowledge Positioning Matrix (KPM)

The KPM was developed to accommodate the core competency dimensions, as shown in Figure 1. The four quadrants provide a means for noting the knowledge that is strategically needed, and is already known; the knowledge that is required, but is not known; knowledge that is known, but not strategically required; and gaps in knowledge that do not bear on strategy anyway. Target Accountancy wanted to know whether its current set of core competencies were sufficiently robust to maximise their competitive performance. The company thus wanted to know what it *needed* to know (i.e., if only we knew what we needed to know) as opposed to the familiar saying "if only we knew what we know", to identify gaps in required knowledge, and to identify areas of knowledge that were no longer required. In other

words, the company wanted to know which core competencies should be modified, deleted and created.

The StratAchieve Structure

The method naturally provides the structure and operations for the Knowledge Positioning Matrix. Figure 2 shows a four-level map. The *vision* is the prime focus of the organisation's strategy. Each successive level below the vision provides increased detail about the vision—what it is, what it means and how it can be achieved. The mechanism that does this is through top-down *How* and bottom-up *Why* explorations and checking.

The top-most activity of the tree represents the vision in the case of a company-wide strategy or the key objective of a department, division, or sub-strategy such as a marketing or a finance strategy. The levels below the top-most activity increase in specificity so that the day-to-day actions can be specified and actioned. There is thus full alignment between the vision and the day-to-day operations.

Figure 2. A four-level StratAchieve Map showing all four company CSFs and two of the core competencies

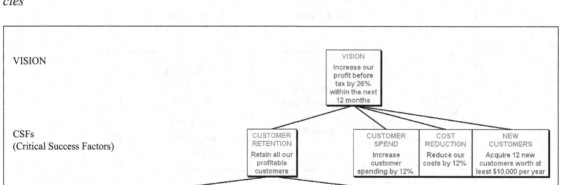

The second level of the StratAchieve Map is occupied by the Critical Success Factors (CSFs). CSFs are the vital factors that must be successfully actioned if the vision is to be fully achieved. The third level has the core competencies which in turn must successfully produce the CSFs. Traditionally, the number of organisational core competencies is suggested as five or six (Robson, 1994) at the maximum.

The top-down *How* and bottom-up *Why* structuring also provides the all-important alignment from the vision to the operational competencies on the lowest level of the StratAchieve Map. Only through this logical connectivity can alignment be achieved. This also provides a clear understanding to the fourth-level operational competencies. This also provides a clear understanding of what operational competencies must be actioned to achieve the core competencies, the CSFs and the vision. The process then provides for detailed operational specification of the requirement.

Knowing What We Need to Know

As mentioned, organisations need to "know what they need to know" (and know what they don't know) to make strategic decisions on various fronts. The first task in actioning the Knowledge Positioning Matrix is thus to establish "what needs to be known". From this capture, what is known and not known can then be determined.

To establish "what needs to be known", a set of core competencies was logically produced from the CSFs (top-down Hows) and verified through the operational competencies (bottom-up Whys). A fourth level of operational competencies were initially produced through logical How unpackings from the core competencies. Figure 2 shows two of the core competencies identified at the workshop, namely Customer Relationships and Requirements Satisfaction.

Although it would have been competitively desirable for Target Accountancy to action every

Figure 3. Product Quality shares child competencies fully with Value for Money which means Product Quality is a sub-competency

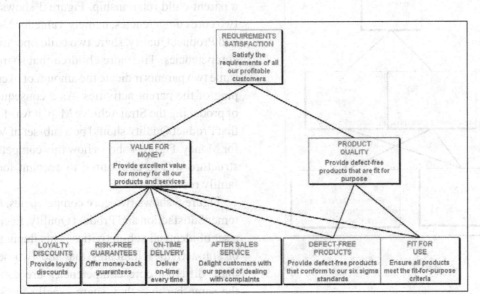

Figure 4. The revised structure showing Product Quality is a sub-set of Value for Money

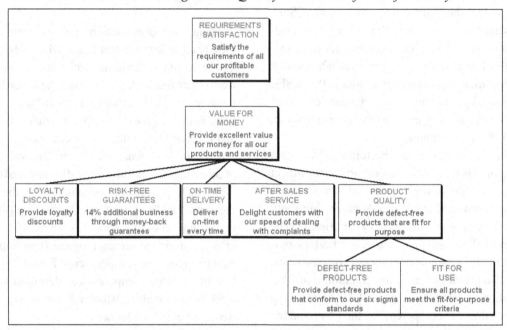

Figure 5. Product Quality and Customer Satisfaction are semantic duplications

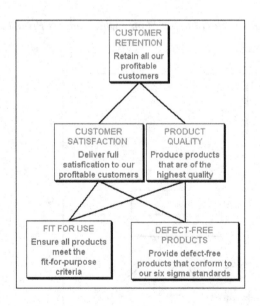

operational competency, in practice this was not feasible through resource and time constraints.

In the course of establishing "what we need to know", it was found that two of the competencies were not distinct but instead were linked in a parent-child relationship. Figure 3 shows that two core competencies, namely Value for Money and Product Quality, share two child operational competencies. The more children that share the same two parents indicate the amount of overlapping of the parent activities. As a consequence of producing the StratAchieve Map, it was found that Product Quality should be a sub-set of Value for Money. Figure 4 shows how this competency structure was re-configured to account for the family resemblance.

Figure 5 shows two core competencies, Customer Satisfaction and Product Quality. Each has a set of identical sub-activities. This duplication of sub-activities indicates that the two seemingly different core competencies are actually the same because they share exactly the same competency children. The degree of similarity between competencies is thus verifiable through the amount of shared sub-activities. Where there are no shared sub-activities, the core competencies are distinctly separate. The workshop delegates wanted to Product Quality to be featured on the StratAchieve Map and therefore showed it as a sub-activity. Alternatively, they could have eliminated the activity, and shown its two sub-activities under Customer Satisfaction.

Need to Know and Do Know

Once the set of core competencies were identified (need to know), the next stage was to identify which core competencies were known (available expertise) and those that were unknown (unavailable expertise). Figure 2 shows how the CSF, *Customer Retention* was unpacked, first into the respective core competencies, and then into operational competencies.

At the workshop, delegates were asked to produce a knowledge map showing their key actions. A comparison was then made between the logically derived core competencies using StratAchieve and those competencies actually held by the individuals. Several competencies were matched while others were unmatched. Examples are shown in Figure 1.

Need to Know and Don't Know

The StratAchieve Why and How creations and connections produced the activity "use the Internet to increase sales". It was agreed that this activity was important enough to be regarded as a potential core competency, where new skills would be needed. The exercise thus identified a knowledge gap, identifying what should be possessed as expertise and what was lacking.

The logical operational competency "operate hospitality packages" was created from the core competency "improve our customer relationship performance". The workshop delegates agreed that this activity (operate hospitality packages)

was an important competency that needed to be included in the strategy as part of the core competency "improve our customer relationship performance".

A further action the company took after the workshop was to determine which competencies they lacked and needed to purchase through recruitment and consultancy. The core competencies were also prioritised, based on agreed criteria such as contribution impact on the CSFs, resource demands (cost implications) and risk quantification. Through this process, it was possible to weight the core competencies and produce a ranked order of importance. Although supported within the method, this is not detailed further here.

Don't Need to Know and Know

The Knowledge Positioning Matrix shows "provide doctoring services to ailing companies" as a known competency, but one that does not have any impact on the current company-wide CSFs. Thus is because there is no logical Why connection into the newly formed CSFs. For example, there is no *Why* connect to Customer Retention since once the customer's company has been restored it will cease to be a customer. With no logical connection for this in the developed map, it was thus excluded.

Don't Need to Know and Don't Know

It follows that not knowing what we do not need to know is a null set and therefore is left blank in the Knowledge Positioning Matrix.

CONCLUSION

This chapter described the importance of core competencies and demonstrated the utility of the StratAchieve method for testing the validity of knowledge-laden core competencies for strategic goals. It has shown how to test core competencies for logical compatibility with the strategy plan as well as to identify core competencies that are essential for strategic success. The software support links these logically, and through separate functionality relates them to timescales, costing, human resources, and progress indicators for subsequent monitoring. In doing this, we needed to unpack the meaning of the word "know". For example, in the phrase *do we know what we need to know,* two uses of the term can be discerned, namely know-what and know-how respectively. Both relate to awareness, not necessarily the skills available.

The case study has demonstrated the formulation of a corporate strategy from a consideration of the core operational activities and associated knowledge competencies forming the organisation's intellectual capital resource. Meanings of the operational and other activities that produce the emergence of achieved strategic objectives have been systematically elicited, negotiated, and agreed within a multi-stakeholder framework, which explicitly links the strategic requirement to the necessary activities and identifies the knowledge requirements for each strategic objective.

Although simplified and indicative examples only have been shown here, linked and cohesive *Strategy Trees* for major business functions have been produced in a form that translates directly into actionable specifications, with a motivated logic chain of abstraction upwards towards, or implementation downwards from, strategic activities and competencies. Core strategic competencies, such as "contact all our profitable customers monthly" have been illustrated to show the alignment of activities, and how a competency at one level can provide an advantage at another. Equally less advantageous competencies, without strategic import, are highlighted by the method. An emphasis on the terminology and meanings understood within the company, and its reporting norms, helps strategy ownership and implementation. A sort of "mediated objectivity" applies, which explicitly links the strategic requirement to the necessary activities and identifies the knowledge requirements for each one.

By expressing the required activities in the structure the focus is shifted towards dynamic strategy achievement through knowledge capability, rather than merely managing the organisational resources and by-products of business activity. Evaluation of the strategy is provided for within the method, though beyond the scope of this chapter to describe. Monitoring, activity based costing, resource allocation, and progress and performance indicators are all linked explicitly to the strategy model developed. During the case study, each core competency was analysed to determine its value and hence impact contribution on the company's goals and vision. This core competency valuation and ranking method has been the subject of ongoing research.

The case study reported in this chapter is one of several conducted over a 15-year period with organisations large and small, public and private and whilst the case is unique, the methods involved are considered generic and stable. Individual studies such as this one lie within a "declared intellectual framework of systemic ideas, ultimately allowing general lessons to be extracted and discussed" as recommended by Checkland (1991, p. 401).

Although a case study does not aim at generalisation rich, contextual understanding and utility value are indicated. Apart from the direct pragmatic value to the organisation, the "story told" in reporting the notion of mediated objectivity may help convey insights that transfer to the understanding of similar situations. Results from action research studies can provide rich and useful descriptions, enhancing learning and understanding which may itself be abstractly transferable to other organisations, or provide an underpinning to future inductive theory development. This potentially allows further contextualisation of the work in the more nomothetic terms implicit in multiple case study research designs.

This case study has shown the development of strategy: further action research with the company will evaluate its impact and value. In general through work with this, and with other organisations we aim to develop a competency valuation method so that the value of operational competencies in relation to strategy may be assessed.

ACKNOWLEDGMENT

We thank the participants at Target Accountancy, three anonymous reviewers and the associate editors for constructive comments on earlier versions

REFERENCES

AMERIN Products. (n.d). *Creating value from intangible assets and human capital.* Retrieved July 12, 2005, from http://www.amerin.com.au/products.htm

Berkman, E. (2001). *When bad things happen to good ideas.* Retrieved July 20, 2004, from http://www.darwinmag.com/read/040101/badthingscontent.html

Bollinger, A. S. & Smith, R. D. (2001). Managing knowledge as a strategic asset. *Journal of Knowledge Management, 5*(1), 8-18.

Carlisle, Y. (1999). Strategic thinking and knowledge management. In *OU MBA Managing Knowledge Readings Part 1* (pp. 19-29). Milton Keynes: Open University Business School.

Chatzkel, J. (2000). A conversation with Hubert Saint-Onge. *Journal of Intellectual Capital, 1*(1), 101-115.

Checkland, P. B. (1991). From framework through experience to learning: the essential nature of action research. In H. E. Nissen, H. K. Klein, & R. Hirschheim (Eds.), *Information systems research: Contemporary approaches and emergent traditions.* Amsterdam: International Federation for Information Processing (IFIP).

Clare, M. & DeTore, A. W. (2000). *Knowledge assets.* San Diego: Harcourt.

Dawson, R. (2000). Knowledge capabilities as the focus of organisational development. *Journal of Knowledge Management, 4*(4), 320-327.

Edvinsson, L. & Malone, M. S. (1997). *Intellectual capital.* New York: Harper Collins.

Graham, A. B. & Pizzo V. G. (1996). A question of balance: Case studies in strategic knowledge management. *European Management Journal, 14*(4), 338-346. Reprinted in Klein DA (q.v.).

Hackney, R., Burn, J., & Dhillon, G. (2000). Challenging assumptions for strategic information systems planning. Theoretical perspectives. *Communications of the AIS, 3*(9).

Hatten, K. J. & Rosenthal, S. R. (1999). Managing the process centred enterprise. *Long Range Planning, 32*(3), 293-310.

Hatten, K. J. & Rosenthal, S. R. (2001). *Reaching for the knowledge edge.* New York: AMACOM.

Kaplan, R. S. & Norton, D. P. (1996). *The balanced scorecard.* Boston: Harvard Business School Press.

Kaplan, R. S. & Norton, D. P. (2004). *Strategy maps.* Boston: Harvard Business School Press.

Klein, D. A. (Ed.). (1998). *The strategic management of intellectual capital.* Boston: Butterworth-Heinemann.

Leonard-Barton, D. (1995). *Wellsprings of knowledge.* Boston: Harvard Business School Press.

Prahalad, C. K. & Hamel, G. (1990). The core competence of the corporation. *Harvard Business Review, 68*(3), 79-91.

Robson, R. (1994). *Strategic management and information systems.* London: Pitman.

Sawyer, K. (1990). *Dealing with complex organisational problems.* PhD Consortium, International Conference on Information Systems (ICIS), Copenhagen.

Sawyer, K. (1990). Goals, purposes and the strategy tree. *Systemist, 12*(4), 76-82.

Yin, R. K. (2002). *Case study research: Design and methods* (3rd ed.). Newbury Park: Sage.

Zack, M. H. (1999). Developing a knowledge strategy. *Californian Management Review, 41*(3), 125-145.

ENDNOTES

[1] The valuation of intellectual capital is significant: the most authoritative estimates typically suggest that around 75% of a company's value lies in its intangible assets (Handy [cited in Edvinsson & Malone, 1997; Kaplan & Norton, 2004, p. 4]).

[2] StratAchieve™ is a registered mark of Keith Sawyer.

This work was previously published in Knowledge Management and Business Strategies, Theoretical Frameworks and Empirical Research, edited by E. Abou-Zeid, pp. 282-295, copyright 2008 by Information Science Publishing (an imprint of IGI Global).

Chapter XII
A Case–Classification–Conclusion 3Cs Approach to Knowledge Acquisition:
Applying a Classification Logic Wiki to the Problem Solving Process

Debbie Richards
Macquarie University, Australia

Megan Vazey
Macquarie University, Australia

ABSTRACT

In this chapter, we postulate that the problem solving process in many domains involves identifying the class of problem on hand, identifying an appropriate solution, and recognising opportunities for its reuse. We suggest a solution that builds up knowledge of a given domain by recording observations, diagnoses and actions in a "3Cs form" of Cases, Classifications, and Conclusions. Our solution allows knowledge workers in any domain where heuristics are relied on to form classifications, and then apply generalised conclusions on the basis of the given classification, to collaboratively refine and expand a topic by consistently asking users to confirm, add to, or refine the presented knowledge in the context of the current case being classified. Our solution is presented in the context of the corporate call centre and is a significant extension of the Multiple Classification Ripple Down Rules algorithm. We present a 3Cs Logic Wiki that takes the best features of current collaborative knowledge exchange mechanisms, and captures a logic structure on top of that which provides for rapid indexing of acquired knowledge.

Copyright © 2008, IGI Global, distributing in print or electronic forms without written permission of IGI Global is prohibited.

INTRODUCTION

The move from product-based to service-based industries in developed countries is clearly seen in the central role now played by an organisation's support centre. In many cases the success of the organisation will depend not on the superiority of their product but on how well they handle support for that product. This is particularly true for the IT industry due to the complex nature of IT products.

We are presently involved in a project to improve the success of a sizeable multinational support-centre operating in the IT industry. In this context, success can be measured by the effectiveness and efficiency by which customer problems are handled, for example: reduced problem incidence, increased customer self-service, increased automation of problem diagnosis and solution matching, increased accuracy of solution matching as measured by reduced case revisits, increased solution re-use, reduced duplication of solutions, rapid fault and enquiry resolution times, increased customer satisfaction, increased in-line self-learning by support centre staff, increased staff satisfaction, and reduced staff turnover. As we can see, the solution is needed by all stakeholders, which includes customers, knowledge-workers, management and the organisation, and thus the solution must meet a wide range of goals including fitting in with the organisational culture and daily workflow.

This chapter is organised as follows: first we identify the problems that IT organisations face in their management of software and hardware products followed by a review of some of the solutions that have been offered. We then introduce the Multiple Classification Ripple Down Rules technology that we have adapted. Next, we describe our methodology and approach including the extensions needed to support the specifics of the support centre domain. In the final section we provide our conclusions and the current state of the project.

The Problem

Knowledge Management for Software and Hardware

The inherent difficulties in software, identified by Brooks (1987) as complexity, conformity, changeability, and invisibility, have ramifications not only for software engineering but for the management of knowledge related to that software. Since Brooks' landmark paper, the need to both change and conform to complex environments has increased beyond all expectations. For example, in earlier times, acceptance, integration and stress testing were performed with users, hardware, platforms, applications, inputs, and throughput that could be identified before the project started. For many systems that is no longer realistic. Old strategies such as user training to compensate for product shortcomings, designed to pass on the bridging knowledge, are no longer viable in cross-vendor and e-commerce applications.

Knowledge management is not just a problem for software. Managing knowledge about hardware has become more difficult since the (relatively) simple mainframe of the 1980s has been replaced in the 1990s with smaller, less expensive open system and windows servers that can be inexpensively clustered and failed-over as needed, along with dramatic improvements in disk drive capacity. Nowadays the most critical issue is usually data unavailability, data loss, or poor performance, rather than the loss of a single host or server. Discovering the cause of these can be both time consuming and difficult, in complex environments involving multiple vendors, machines, software products and topologies, in an infinite number of combinations. It is no longer possible to expect a single expert to quickly find and resolve such issues. A better approach is needed, to allow both the accumulation of knowledge with guided trouble shooting techniques, along with interfaces to all other relevant knowledge bases.

From Information to Knowledge

Information technology problems in the past have been primarily addressed via technological solutions. Database technology has provided us with the means to model and capture vast amounts of data. Transaction processing systems and decision support systems have assisted us in turning that data into useful information. Networking technology has allowed data and information to flow freely and enabled the rapid and pervasive uptake of the Internet and e-business applications.

It is widely recognised that the next key step is to go beyond data and information to knowledge management. But, unlike data that can be collected and information that can be summarised and sorted, knowledge is not easily codified and reused. In the expert systems of the 1980s and the more recent data mining approaches there is an implicit assumption that knowledge can be acquired like nuggets of gold. However, the contextual, evolving and socially situated nature of knowledge (Clancey, 1997) is becoming increasingly apparent. Additionally, the human element in storing, interpreting, defining, and applying the knowledge can not be underestimated. It could be said that "knowledge is in the eye of the beholder".

Examples of current approaches to knowledge sharing include: Internet discussion boards, Web forums, blog sites and chat rooms. However, the simple topic thread-to-post relational structure (typically 1:N) does not provide for efficient capture, refinement, and re-use of knowledge. Potential knowledge remains hidden by being unsearchable, disorganised, and disconnected. A system that helps a knowledge worker explicitly link only the relevant search hits to the search topic, and remember and learn from those links, can help to reduce the information bombardment that many users experience when searching for answers to their questions. We suggest a mix of explicit user linking, together with computer-driven inferencing.

An evolution of the Web forum is the Wiki. Wikipedia at http://wikipedia.org/ is a massive undertaking by the global Internet community to collaboratively build an online encyclopedia spanning every conceivable topic in every conceivable language. Wikipedia defines a Wiki as the collaborative software and resultant Web forum that allows users to add content to a Web site and in addition, to collaboratively edit it. The choice of what content to add is based on individual want, rather than time-proven community need. In this chapter, we propose a bottom-up Wiki, overlayed by a user-driven logical index. Rather than the knowledge being created with a top-down structured approach, the knowledge develops organically, and on an as-needed basis.

We adopt the philosophy that knowledge needs to be acquired in the context of specific cases. This view is in keeping with others in the knowledge management field such as Sternberg (1995) who uses work-place scenarios to measure tacit knowledge and Stenmark and Lindgren (2003) who suggest that knowledge be captured during normal work processes. We observe that humans are amazingly adept, and usually better equipped than computers, at recognising whether two cases belong to the same or different classifications, and whether a set of conclusions (i.e., a set of generalisations) fits a given classification.

The use of differences in human problem solving have been the basis of a number of theories and approaches including: ripple down rules (RDR) (Compton & Jansen, 1990), Personal Construct Psychology (PCP) (Kelly, 1955), repertory grids (Gaines & Shaw, 1993), Rough Set Theory (Pawlak, 1991), Formal Concept Analysis (Wille, 1992), some case based reasoning (CBR) techniques (e.g., PROTOS by Bareiss, 1989) and the psychology-based work of Markman and Gentner (1996) on structural alignment. Our work further contributes to this line of research that involves both cases and the identification of differences between cases to capture and modify knowledge. The end-result is a continuously learning expert system, able to evolve and adapt to *dynamic* knowledge, able to highlight areas where new knowledge is needed, and able to offer explicit knowledge in high-demand topic areas.

THE CALL CENTRE AND RELATED KNOWLEDGE MANAGEMENT RESEARCH

While our solution can be generalised to multiple domains, our research has been initially motivated by the problems facing high-volume support centres that support complex high-tech IT products. In this domain, support-centre personnel solve vast volumes of technical problems in a knowledge environment pressured by constant change: vendor divergence, technology convergence, and knowledge evolution over time results in endless possible problems, and a seemingly endless search space for solutions.

In this section we consider the types of knowledge found in this domain and various related solutions and concepts including those offered by vendors, KM researchers and organisational initiatives.

Islands of Knowledge

As discussed previously (Vazey & Richards, 2005), while studying our target Support Centre, we found that personnel were relying on at least four disparate sources of (explicit) knowledge when solving problems:

- **Engineering knowledge:** How does the product work?
- **Operational knowledge:** How do you use it?
- **Interoperability knowledge:** How does the product interact with third party products?

- **Problem solving knowledge:** How do you fix it?

As well, we found that the troubleshooting process required personnel to use a great deal of unspoken (tacit) knowledge, including:

- *Problem determination knowledge*, that is, what is the class of problem on-hand?
- *Search location knowledge*, that is, where should we search for a solution?
- And the *search criteria* to be applied, that is, what parameters should we use in our search for a solution?

Further, we found from studying the value networks that:

- Much of the knowledge was stored in people's heads (i.e., tacit) rather than documented in technical references (i.e., explicit).
- Existing documentation often missed the necessary detail or was ambiguous, and a significant amount of technical product information was cryptic at best, coming in the form of abbreviated slides, videos, or e-mails.
- Personal relationships were extensively and often exclusively relied upon to source basic product knowledge from pockets of information scattered throughout the company.

In the worst case, the impact of this fragmented framework of knowledge is a poor level of knowledge re-use that results in increased frustration levels amongst customers and staff, duplication of effort by support and engineering personnel, slower problem resolution, customer dissatisfaction, and overall organisational inefficiency. A high staff turnover rate is both an outcome and a contributing factor. Anecdotally, the staff retention period for Support Centres in the IT industry is 18-24 months.

Vendor Solutions

Historically at the support centre, vendors and corporations have focussed on *Defect Tracking* solutions that record case information such as: who raised the call, what is the product in question, what operating system is being used, which engineer the problem is assigned to, and so on. The purpose of such *Defect Tracking* solutions is to allow management and staff to track the progress of customer problems through the customer service organisation.

More recently, there has been a focus on *Solution* knowledge. Vendors provide *Solution Knowledge-bases* that record past solutions, together with indicative symptoms of the problem where this solution applies. Solutions can be searched for on the basis of their associated symptoms.

The separation between these two types of vendor offerings creates significant workflow inefficiency for the support centre. The insight here is that many of the problem attributes captured at the problem tracking stage, are exactly the attributes required to recognise that the user has a particular class of problem on hand, and consequently that a particular type of solution will apply. The double handling of these attributes on entry to the defect tracking software, and again in the solution knowledge base, leaves significant room for error, and can result in significant frustration for support centre personnel.

Perhaps more importantly, vendor solutions fail to capture and promote the re-use of the very problem solving knowledge that is central to the troubleshooting process, namely:

- **Problem determination knowledge:** The (classification) knowledge that allows an expert to determine the class of problem on hand.
- **Search knowledge:** The where-to-search and what-to-search-for knowledge that allows an expert to find an appropriate solution.

We have not found any vendor solutions at the call/support centre that actually guide staff progress through the problem-solving process and help a network of experts share their troubleshooting expertise. We have found that many products at most provide sophisticated problem/document/case management, but generally do not provide intelligence beyond limited inconsistency checking, assistance with template filling or Google-type searching for cases.

Our key motivation for seeking an alternative is that the knowledge, and the cases which provide the context for the knowledge, are changing. Additionally, we want to make extensive use of external sources of knowledge, such as a technical report from another vendor, where the source forms part of the solution.

Organisational Knowledge at the Support Centre

Based on Polyani's insight concerning the personal character of knowledge, and Wittgenstein's claim that all knowledge is, in a fundamental way, collective; Tsoukas and Vladimirou (2001) have constructed the following definition of organisational knowledge:

Organisational knowledge is the capability members of an organisation have developed to draw distinctions in the process of carrying out their work, in particular concrete contexts, by enacting sets of generalisations whose application depends on historically evolved collective understandings. (p. 983)

They concluded that knowledge management is the dynamic process of turning an unreflective practice into a reflective one by elucidating the rules guiding the activities of the practice, by helping give a particular shape to the collective understandings, and by facilitating the emergence of heuristic knowledge.

Our 3Cs approach is a practical application of such ideas as it compels members of a given community of practice to collaboratively articulate the rules underpinning their actions in the context of real cases that they deal with on a daily bases.

Tsoukas and Vladimirou (2001) reviewed the flow of organisational knowledge within a customer care call centre for Panafon, Greece's leading mobile phone operator in 2001. They observed that despite the Panafon call centre not being a knowledge-intensive environment, and despite the employee perception that answers to 95% of the questions asked were available "somewhere" in the computer system, several operators were observed constructing their own personal information systems, which contained photocopies of the relevant corporate manuals plus personal notes. In other words, alongside the formal organisational knowledge there existed an informal knowledge that was generated in action, and which represented the heuristic knowledge residing both in individual's minds and in the stories shared in their communities of practice.

They concluded that it was both feasible and desirable to capture this heuristic knowledge and through casting it into propositional statements, to turn it into organisational knowledge. While the abstract generalisations would be incomplete to capture the totality of organisational knowledge, they concluded that:

The more propositional statements and collective understandings become instrumentalised (in Polanyi's [1962] sense of the term); and the more new experiences are reflectively processed (both individually and collectively) and then gradually driven into subsidiary awareness, the more organisational members dwell in all of them, and the more able they become to concentrate on new experiences, on the operational plane. (Tsoukas & Vladimirou, 2001, p. 983)

In accordance with Polyani's observations that knowledge always contains a personal ele-

ment, they noted that an improvisational element would still be required for each interpretation of the collective organisational knowledge, and that it was the dialectic between the general and the particular, that gave organisational knowledge its dynamism. Finally, they concluded that:

The effective management of organisational knowledge requires that the relationship between propositional and heuristic knowledge be a two-way street: while propositional knowledge is fed into organisational members and is instrumentalised through application (thus becoming tacit), heuristic knowledge needs to be formalised (to the extent that this is possible) and made organisationally available. (Tsoukas & Vladimirou, 2001, p. 991)

Adria and Chowdhury (2002) believe that the ultimate purpose or effect of a call-centre implementation "is to streamline the pathway to information for the customer". They identified three dimensions of call centre employee skill: *responsibility*, *abstractness* and *interdependence*.

They defined *responsibility* as being both reputation, and organisational. *Reputation* since employees have a high impact on the customer's perception of quality during the customer interaction; and *organisational* since employees can be given responsibility to refine the processes and knowledge stored by the company to improve the customer interaction next time around.

They defined *abstractness* as the extent to which the employee must make a mental connection between the practical situation of the customer inquiry and the many possible approaches that might be taken to respond to that inquiry. Both Tsoukas and Vladimirou (2001) and Adria and Chowdhury (2002) used the example of customer disposition to highlight the contextual nature of responding to customers: the customer's disposition to communicate could be effected by their gender, culture, the time of day, geographical location, and/or their knowledge. Call-centre agents therefore need to assess the customer's disposition and mood, and then abstract and adapt in the course of providing the appropriate service to them.

They defined *interdependence* as the degree to which the effective completion of one task involves the sequential or simultaneous completion of another task.

They used these three dimensions to argue that call centres should allow decisions to be made as close as possible to the customer, including the employee decisions to add to, revise, and work with the corporation's knowledge base.

They identified the case of Sun Life, a group insurance company that took a team approach involving both front-line workers and technical experts to designing the service delivery operations so that the customer could experience a richer real-time interaction. They also highlighted the case of the Mayo Clinic in Rochester, Minnesota, where physicians post links on the clinic's intranet to Web sites that provide up-to-date and authoritative information about current medical treatments for use by clinic practitioners. For call centres to thrive, they argue that agents need an adequate amount of autonomy and responsibility, and that agents can have a role in updating and correcting the knowledge base. The RDR philosophy upon which our 3Cs approach is built takes the same view.

Using Geib, Reichold, Kolbe, and Brenner's (2005) architecture as a framework, our 3Cs approach can be viewed as a Knowledge Management system that supports the Customer Satisfaction Management objective of a CRM. In so doing, it is designed to support the CRM service delivery processes including the service management and complaint management processes. The CRM system we are implementing are operational and collaborative. Finally, we address all four categories of KM systems: content, competence, collaboration, and composition.

The Consortium for Service Innovation (CSI) is a non-profit alliance of customer service or-

ganisations, of which our host organisation is a member. Through a process of collective thinking and collective experience the Consortium members have developed principles and practices for Knowledge-Centred Support, Virtual Support Communities, incident and solution exchange standards, and a scenario-based framework for thinking about the future.

The CSI defines Knowledge-Centred Support as a "knowledge management strategy for service and support organisations. It defines a set of principles and practices that enable organisations to improve service levels to customers, gain operational efficiencies, and increase the organisation's value to their company" (see http://www.serviceinnovation.org/ourwork/kcs.php). With these principles to guide us, we provide an evolutionary team-based collaborative learning environment that is driven and organised by case context as described next.

MULTIPLE CLASSIFICATION RIPPLE DOWN RULES (MCRDR)

A Brief History

Ripple Down Rules (RDR) were developed in the late 1980s (Compton & Jansen, 1989) in response to the difficulties associated with acquiring and maintaining a rule-based system. It was observed that pathology experts had difficulty describing what they knew but that they were good at looking at a case and saying how they would handle it. When asked "why" they used attributes in the case to justify their conclusion. It was further noted that when a similar case was presented, the expert was quickly able to identify whether the same conclusion applied, or if a different conclusion was recommended then they would again pick a feature which distinguished the current case from the case that had prompted the original conclusion.

This process is mimicked by the multiple classification ripple down rules (MCRDR) knowledge acquisition technique. The use of cases to prompt and validate the acquisition of the knowledge and the use of (exception) rules to define and refine the knowledge has led to a knowledge based approach that is both case-based and rule-based.

The simplicity of the approach allows domain experts to be solely responsible for entering and maintaining the knowledge (Compton et al., 1990). A knowledge engineer is only needed in the initial phases to assist with structuring of cases and identification of features.

The approach is designed to allow incremental acquisition and validation of knowledge. The first deployed pathology system went into production with only 100 rules and grew to over 2000 rules in the following four years (Edwards, Compton, Malor, Srinivasan, & Lazarus, 1993). More recent pathology knowledge bases have been developed solely by pathologists and have grown up to 7000 rules, at a rate of one rule per minute (Lazarus, 2000). The knowledge base grows and evolves as more cases are seen.

MCRDR can be considered as a variant to the case-based reasoning (CBR) approach. CBR claims to solve new problems by adapting previously successful solutions to similar problems (Marir & Watson, 1994). In theory, it is a cyclical process comprising the four Rs of *retrieving* the most similar case, *reusing* the case to attempt to solve the problem on hand, *revising* the proposed solution if necessary, and *retaining* the new solution as a part of a new case (Aamodt & Plaza, 1994). CBR is appropriate where there is no formalised knowledge in the domain or where it is difficult for the expert to express their expertise in the format of rules.

Mansar and Marir (2003) have recently suggested the use of a case-based reasoning (CBR) technique for business process redesign (BPR). Their chapter highlights the limitations of the CBR approach — the manner in which cases are indexed is not well-defined for CBR systems. In their BPR example, users are manually required to order cases into a case hierarchy which can be a maintenance nightmare. As well, the manner in which cases are to be indexed, and similar cases identified is open and undefined.

Figure 1. MCRDR decision tree (case == hardware fault)

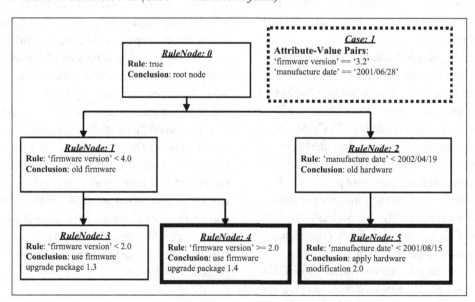

The MCRDR algorithm that we have adapted in our 3Cs solution addresses the indexing and maintenance problem of former CBR techniques by providing a mechanism for explicit and incremental indexing of cases. Heuristic rules are extracted that govern when a case applies to a given context from experts that are intimately knowledgeable of the case context.

The MCRDR algorithm is clearly and concisely explained its founding chapter (Kang, Compton, & Preston, 1995). The MCRDR algorithm can be summarised as follows:

- Start at the top of the rule tree.
- If a RuleNode evaluates to TRUE for a given case, evaluate the case for all the child RuleNodes immediately below it. Repeat until FALSE for all child and sibling RuleNodes.
- The classifications for the given case are given by the last TRUE RuleNode in each path through the rule tree.

For example, in Figure 1, when executing case 1 involving a hardware fault with the attributes (firmware version == 3.2) and (manufacture date == 2001/06/28), the last TRUE RuleNode in every path down the RuleNode tree gives the conclusions "use firmware upgrade package 1.4" and "apply hardware modification 2.0".

Next, for each classification:

- If you agree then say so:
- Confirm/register the classification.
- If you disagree then:
- Identify the distinguishing attributes of the case,
- Formulate a new rule based on these attributes, and
- Create a child RuleNode that offers a new alternate classification for the case.

To further clarify the process, if the user disagrees with the classification given:

- The new rule must be a valid Boolean expression which is able to be evaluated by the MCRDR engine.
- The rule for the new RuleNode would typically be different from the rules of its ancestor RuleNodes.
- The rule for the new RuleNode may optionally be restricted to a single test, for example, that (firmware version == 2), rather than a conjunction of tests.
- The new RuleNode must have either a different conclusion, or a different rule compared to its sibling RuleNodes.
- The new RuleNode must test for some feature of the Review Case and must evaluate to TRUE for the Review Case.
- The new RuleNode must distinguish between the Review Case and all of the Cornerstone Cases for the parent RuleNode.

New RuleNodes can be placed at one of two places in the tree (Kang et al., 1995):

- At the top of the rule tree to provide a new independent conclusion.
- Beneath the current RuleNode as a replacement conclusion or as a stopping conclusion.

MCRDR was first implemented on the Macintosh platform but the development of MCRDR for Windows for the PC was begun in 1995. Standard tools included in implementations of RDR are the ability to browse and visualise the tree, browse individual traces and examine rules and their status based on the current case. Various statistics are available such as a count of the number of times a conclusion is found in rules, the complexity of individual rules (the number of conditions in the antecedent), the frequency that whole conditions occur, the full complexity of a path, the number of rules in spine sub-trees, and a list of conclusions and which rules use them. Numerous other statistics can possibly be calculated.

METHODOLOGY AND APPROACH

Observations

This project has been concerned with determining the current problems faced by, and finding a solution for our host organisation: a regional support centre in the global support organisation of a large multi-national IT company. To better appreciate the issues facing knowledge-workers at the support centre, we met with experienced trouble-shooters and management and discussed the operational issues encountered by them. We spent time observing the day-to-day activities of support staff and interviewing them. We also undertook some of the training available to new hires. The outcome of the interviews, observations, training sessions and active participation was a "Health-Check" report to document the current situation. This report was reviewed by the organisation and formed the basis of our design goals.

Support Centre Survey

In order to better understand that nature of the troubleshooting process at our host organisation, we conducted a comprehensive survey to answer a number of support centre questions, including:

Q. What types of people are solving the problems, and how are they actually doing it?
Q. Is the troubleshooting process a team effort, or an individual effort?
Q. What types of resources are being used to solve problems?
Q. How successful is the team at solving customer problems?

The investigation was conducted with our host organisation's staff from two separate product groups (A and B), vertically across two separate support levels: level 1 (front-line support), and level 2 (technical support). Hence, four groups of approximately five participants were surveyed (20 staff). Survey Part A included 67 questions and took participants 50 minutes on average to complete.

Level 2 respondents had on average 12 years IT industry experience, 11 years of experience relevant to their role, and they had been working at the company for four years each.

Level 1 respondents had on average 7 years IT experience with 4 years of experience relevant to their role. Those working in the Product Group A had been with the company on average for 10 months while those working in Product Group B had been with the company on average for 2.5 years.

The survey had the following aims:

1. To determine the current tools and techniques for resolving customer problems,
2. To examine the pros and cons of the current work practice, and
3. To examine future opportunities for improving the troubleshooting process.

In support of our belief that knowledge re-use is worth pursing in the IT support centre, on average, survey respondents thought that:

• 64% of customer problems assigned to them had been previously seen by themselves or others, that is, they were repeat problems.
• 76% of customer problems assigned to them would be seen again by themselves or others within the organisation. (From the previous result, implying that 12% of incoming customer problems were new, but would be seen again.)
• 81% of solutions created and applied by Level 1 respondents are duplicate solutions where-as 44% of solutions created and applied by Level 2 respondents are duplicate solutions, that is, someone has conceived of this solution before.

- When a customer problem was assigned to them, in 67% of cases they would not know the solution straight away and would need to refer to other sources of information to solve the case.

In addition, respondents would involve their team-mates or others in 34% of the problem cases assigned to them.

Vendor Review

With an understanding of what a new system needed to achieve we reviewed current commercial solutions and investigated options with the current software in use. We reviewed various solutions to the help desk situation, including a number of RDR-based solutions, and found that none were able to meet all of our design goals. The design goals were thus used to motivate extensions to the current MCRDR approach and to design an architecture that could be integrated to existing databases, knowledge sources, workflows and practices. The design goals and architecture of the 3Cs approach that we have developed is described next. We have developed a prototype, known as FastFix, which we are in the process of evaluating.

Design Goals

The support centre domain has a number of features that necessitated extensions to the MCRDR technique. The extensions we made were based on a number of design goals: (1) reduce the complexity of the problem on hand through classification and generalisation, (2) facilitate collaboration to get the best from the available resources, (3) provide a feedback mechanism that allows the system to be continuously improved and refined, (4) provide a framework for capturing both explicit and tacit problem-solving knowledge, and (5) provide a design which is compelling—one that people will

contribute to and rely upon because it benefits them to do so.

In the next few sections we elaborate these design goals and in so-doing, we describe the paradigms that have led us to the solution described in the subsequent sections.

Reduce Complexity

Complexity can be better managed by decomposition. Given the situated nature of knowledge, one way to decompose knowledge is on a case-by-case basis. We may then view knowledge acquisition as a simple process of classification and generalisation of that case. What we mean by *classification* is the application of mental filters to identify the minimal set of attributes that uniquely defines a thing. What we mean by *generalisation* is the process by which we form conclusions and recognise the opportunity for reusing those conclusions amongst several different cases belonging to the same classification.

Our system relies on this process of assigning classifications and correlated generalisations (conclusions) to cases to develop an indexed knowledge base. The index simply records the links between cases, classifications and conclusions in a 3Cs structure as follows: Cases (N) to Classifications (N) to Conclusions (N).

In defining the attributes of a case, and therefore parameterising it, we ask the question: What is our *sense* of the case? That is, how does it look, sound, smell, taste, and feel? What are its properties? What are its symptoms? Cases and their attributes are *observation* oriented.

In our system, a classification is the result of a case evaluating to TRUE through a sequential set of RuleNodes, where each RuleNode has a Boolean test that examines the attributes of the case. The classifications in our system may or may not attract labels (sometimes known as intermediate classifications). Classifications are *diagnosis* oriented.

Conclusions[1] can be a single word, a lengthy passage of text, or even a directive to use a particular Internet search engine with a suggested set of search criteria to further navigate the solution space. A conclusion is the set of actions one should take as a result of arriving at a given classification. Conclusions are prescriptions. Conclusions are *action* oriented.

As a simple example, if we have the case of a Sydney Silky Terrier, it may have attributes recorded for it like breathes, moves, eats, barks and bites. Our rule tree might have a RuleNode that classifies cases (instances) that bark and bite as dogs, and another RuleNode that classifies cases that eat, breathe, and move as mammals. These dog and mammal classifications may in turn be linked to conclusions such as dog: keep on a leash and feed meat, and mammal: water, oxygenate, and provide space to move.

The underlying assumption behind our solution is that the domain in question can be parameterised and that the resultant attribute list is manageable in terms of its size and complexity.

In summary then, we build up our knowledge of a given domain by recording our observations, diagnoses and actions in the 3Cs form of Cases, Classifications, and Conclusions.

Facilitate Collaboration

Our design takes an open systems approach. Collaboration is needed to share knowledge, and part of the socialisation process identified by Nonaka, Takeuchi, and Umemoto (1996) as the first step in the tacit-explicit knowledge cycle. This process that is characteristic of experts showing novices "the ropes", turns into a gradual codification process. To encourage collaboration we need to minimise communication barriers and thus we allow participants to communicate, Wiki-style, with full create, insert, edit, and update privileges to the knowledge-base. This is a significant depar-

ture from current commercial implementations of MCRDR that expect one domain expert to be responsible for editing rules for a particular knowledge base. Along with this freedom, as described earlier, we provide structure in the form of attributes, cases, classifications, and conclusions. Additionally, we incorporate ontology to manage linguistic conflicts.

The process is as follows. Knowledge workers register themselves and supply their e-mail address. There is an audit trail on every modifiable element in the system via a change history, for example on cases, classifications, generalisations, and indices. While disincentives for misuse must be built into the system, for the most part, the system is built on trust, faith, and the open pursuit of common goals.

Closed Loop Feedback

We borrow an approach from the Engineering framework of Systems and Control: that the system must be *closed loop* in so far as it must solicit feedback from users. This will allow it to continuously adapt to changing knowledge, and continuously refine and improve its knowledge.

Typically a closed loop system will filter (parameterise and clean) the inputs, measure the output, and use the error between the desired (target) output and the actual output to feed back into the system as an input so that the system can adjust itself to achieve a more perfect output.

A stable closed loop system will find a neat compromise between the system tendency to react too quickly to new or conflicting knowledge, and the inertial system tendency to not react at all. We achieve this in our system by building confidence levels into solutions, based on the frequency that a solution has been viewed, applied, and confirmed as applicable to a given classification, and based on the time-proven experience of the user who authored it.

Explicit and Tacit Knowledge Capture

Most knowledge acquisition has focused on capturing explicit or codified knowledge. However, research has shown that decisions are arrived at through the combined use of almost *equal* amounts of tacit and explicit knowledge (Giunipero, Dawley, & Anthony, 1999). The approach that we offer captures knowledge-in-action via scenarios, which can be viewed as cases grounded in the real world and based on experience, thus spanning both codified (explicit) and practical (tacit) knowledge (Richards & Busch, 2002). The RDR approach does not attempt to distinguish between explicit and tacit knowledge but offers a mechanism for capturing the behaviour of experts; that is, to see a case and offer a response to it. The end result is that heuristic knowledge that might have been difficult to articulate without the context of a specific case becomes articulated and codified, a process that Nonaka et al. (1996) refer to as externalisation. Broadly speaking however, tacit knowledge is gained either through (a) personal experience over time and perhaps place

or (b) by serving in an apprenticeship fashion with someone who is senior and able to pass the knowledge on to the "trainee" (Goldman, 1990). While we agree that tacit knowledge cannot by its very nature be passed in written format, as at this stage the knowledge is no longer tacit, but explicit, our approach bridges the knowing-doing gap (Pfeffer & Sutton, 2000) through the capture of knowledge in action.

With regard to the capture of heuristic and tacit troubleshooting knowledge, we have the view that *when the question is ready, the (otherwise unstated) answer(s) will appear*. The focus of our 3Cs solution is therefore to formally prepare questions that challenge a team of experts to share with their team-mates the properties of each incoming unique class of problem that can be used to map out a path that will consistently lead subsequent trouble-shooters to the appropriate solution.

Make it Compelling

For a knowledge base to be of value it must be progressively populated and maintained. In the

Figure 2. Logic Wiki top level architecture

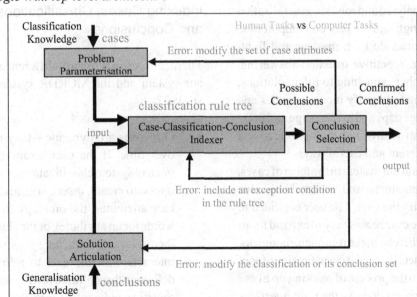

approach we offer we begin with an empty knowledge base that evolves over time as situations arise and knowledge comes to hand. Therefore, the system's usability and workflow integration will be critical in getting users to use it. The more users use it, the more knowledge it will contain, and the more useful it will become (Stenmark & Lindgren, 2003).

The most compelling features of the system that we envisage are as follows: the ability to eliminate mundane repetitive classification problems, the ability to increase the accuracy and efficiency of users arriving at classifications, the ability to instruct new participants on the classification process, the ability to identify knowledge holes and knowledge bottlenecks, the ability to restructure knowledge acquired in an ad-hoc bottom-up organic fashion to provide a top-down navigable hierarchy of knowledge, and the ability to constantly adapt to new knowledge in a dynamic knowledge environment.

Top Level Architecture

The top level architecture of our system is shown in Figure 2. In our system, we rely on humans to do what humans do best: problem classification (comparative analysis) and solution generalisation (decision making); and we rely on computers to do what computers do best: massive and light-speed indexing, repetitive question-answering, significant number crunching to infer solutions, and data mining to identify inconsistencies and reveal knowledge gaps and to rearrange and present knowledge structures with multiple views and in multiple different and useful ways.

Input arrives at our system in the form of cases. The cases are parameterised via attribute-value pairs that identify the case. The user is guided to interact with the case recursively to expand its attribute list and thereby make it explicit enough for our system to identify useful classifications for it. This is similar to the process of working up a case in the medical profession. As the right questions

are asked and more information comes to light the case develops to an extent that a decision regarding the best course of action can be made.

Our system identifies classifications for a case by evaluating its attributes against multiple paths of sequential rule nodes in a rule tree. The case will be found by the system to fit with one or more classifications according to the current rule tree. The system will offer the user one or more generalised conclusions for each classification that the case complies with. (This mechanism is described in more detail a little further on in the chapter).

The user will be asked to confirm or deny the presented conclusions. Where a given conclusion is rejected, the user is asked to either modify the set of attributes for the case so that it fetches a different conclusion, or update the system knowledge to include an exception condition, or update the system knowledge for the classification or its conclusions to reflect the new knowledge.

In Figure 2 the human's tasks include: problem parameterisation, solution articulation, conclusion and rule definition, and conclusion selection; and the computer's tasks include the indexation of cases, classifications, and conclusions.

Indexing Cases, Classifications, and Conclusions

There are several major differences between our system and the MCRDR system (Kang et al., 1995):

- Our cases are dynamic—they can change over time. If the user disagrees with the present system classifications, they have the option to create, insert, edit, and update the case attributes, the ontology (or substitute words for an attribute), or the classifications themselves. As well, our system recursively interacts with the user to refine the case definition through a narrowing set of context-sensitive and context-targeted questions.

- Our system is multi-user, allowing for the collaborative refinement of cases, attributes, the ontology, RuleNodes, classifications, and conclusions.

- The MCRDR structure uses an exception structure that overrides the conclusion from the previous RuleNodes on the pathway. However, there are times when a previous rule conclusion may be still valid, such as when one moves from a *superclass* to a *subclass*. For example, if a rule concludes that the case can be classified as a "bird" as well as a "swallow", currently it is necessary to add a new rule at the top of the tree to handle the additional classification and the relationship between the two conclusions is lost. However, if we allow users to specify that an exception rule can be treated as an augmenting conclusion rather than an overriding conclusion we can reduce the amount of knowledge acquisition, retain the relationship between the two conclusions and provide a mechanism for handling rules at multiple levels of abstraction.

- The MCRDR system has an entity relationship between cases and classifications of N to N. However, it considers a classification to be the same as a conclusion, that is, one to one. In our system, we recognise that one classification may result in multiple conclusions, and that those conclusions may be reused across many different classifications, so we manage an N to N relationship between classifications and conclusions.

Handling the Human Side

If critical mass of both content and users can not be achieved, then the system will be a failure (Stenmark & Lindgren, 2003). Achieving this critical mass relies not only on a technical solution but also a solution that addresses the human issues. These issues include the need to provide a strategy that supports easy maintenance that can be performed by multiple staff with domain expertise rather than a single knowledge engineer. The approach needs to be intuitive and easy to learn due to the high turnover of staff within support centres. As well, the system needs to provide enough incentive to ensure that staff will use it, benefit from it, enjoy it, and maintain it. In other words, the system needs to afford user participation (Stenmark & Lindgen, 2003).

Acceptance of the system will largely depend on successful workflow integration and possibly some workflow redesign where inefficiencies currently exist. Acceptance of knowledge-based systems also hinges on whether the knowledge they contain is deemed to be accessible, valuable and credible. Incoming problems are often solved via reference to a range of materials, including databases and documents from other vendors, and often involve a chain of people who may contribute to one or more (possible) solutions. Therefore, feedback and collaboration become important parts of the process.

Additionally, the system needs to be accessible, handle performance issues and be usable. Usability extends to system responsiveness, ergonomics, ease-of-use, and the intuitiveness of the interface. The key performance questions for trouble-shooters that we have observed are:

- How can the problem solver arrive at an appropriate solution with the minimum key presses, mouse clicks, and mental effort?

- What is the minimum set of information required to identify the problem, and find the solution; and what is the best way to capture and promote reuse of this information?

CONCLUSION AND FUTURE WORK

There are numerous commercial software applications to support knowledge management using a range of technologies such as case-based and rule-based reasoning systems, collaborative forum software, and knowledge structuring tools such as FAQ builders. Established and emergent technologies include clustering algorithms, neural networks, and genetic algorithms. However, we have found that much of what is offered as support centre/troubleshooting/case tracking systems are just sophisticated databases that are able to keep the current status of the case up-to-date and the customer informed. They don't help with problem determination or solution matching. Knowledge management research assists in improving our understanding of the situation, concepts and issues, which is essential for problem solving, but actual technological solutions offered are few.

The MCRDR expert system approach offers many attractive features including easy maintenance and intuitive knowledge acquisition performed by the user and grounded in real-world cases. Due to these strengths MCRDR has found commercial success in the pathology domain (Lazarus, 2000). We are however working within a support centre environment and corporate culture to develop a solution that works with existing case/databases and current work practices. The environment is complex and involves numerous knowledge workers and repositories. Complexity is exacerbated by the facts that knowledge in the form of problem cases and solutions are constantly evolving and tacit knowledge in the heads of workers keeps walking out the door. Such an environment requires a technique designed for maintenance of not only the knowledge (the rules) but also the cases that can be easily performed by support centre staff.

We conducted a series of presentations at our host organisation explaining and demonstrating the concepts of our approach and prototype, known as FastFIX. Initial feedback has been positive. Together with the survey data this interaction has given us a better picture of the day-to-day activities, problems and perceived solutions as well as suggestions regarding our approach and prototype.

We are currently undertaking a software trial and evaluation of the FastFIX prototype. The results will be fed into enhancements to the product. We anticipate that features such as the ability to search the knowledge, and separately navigate through it would be of high value. It may be that some of the case-based reasoning (nearest neighbour algorithm), formal concept analysis (concept lattice) (Wille, 1992) or data-mining techniques used by others will work well in concert with our 3Cs solution to provide useful knowledge paths that will enrich the user experience, particularly when the conclusions presented are insufficient for them to resolve the problem at hand. The use of natural language processing for the rule statements would doubtless improve the usability of the system. The simple solution suggested by Kang et al (1996) to display an explanation for each rule condition for the novice user is relatively easy to implement and may also be helpful.

The 3Cs Logic Wiki that we have presented takes the best features of current Internet-based collaborative knowledge exchange mechanisms, and captures a logic structure on top of that which provides for rapid indexing and retrieval of acquired knowledge in a manner that fits with the dynamic nature of the support centre and other domains in which it is necessary to match a problem space in the form of a case with a solution space in the form of a previously seen case or other knowledge source.

REFERENCES

Aamodt, A. & Plaza, E. (1994). Case-based reasoning: Foundational issues, methodological variations and system approaches. *AI Communications, 7*(1), S 35-39.

Adria & Chowdhury (2002). Making room for the call center. *Information Systems Management*, 1-80.

Bareiss, E. R. (1989). *Exemplar-based knowledge acquisition: A unified approach to concept representation, classification, and learning.* Boston: Academic Press.

Brooks, F. P. (1987). No silver bullet: Essence and accidents of software engineering. *IEEE Software, 4,* 10-19.

Clancey, W. (1997). The conceptual nature of knowledge, situations, and activity. In P. J. Feltovich, K. M. Ford, & R. R. Hoffman (Eds.), *Expertise in context: Human and machine* (pp. 247-291). Cambridge, MA: AAAI Press / MIT Press.

Compton, P. & Jansen, R. (1990). A philosophical basis for knowledge acquisition. *Knowledge Acquisition, 2,* 241-257.

Consortium for Service Innovation. (2005). *Knowledge-centered support brief, Version 3.0.* Retrieved from http://www.serviceinnovation.org/included/docs/library/programs/kcs_brief.doc

Giunipero, L., Dawley, D., & Anthony, W. (1999, Winter). The impact of tacit knowledge on purchasing decisions. *Journal of Supply Chain Management* [Electronic version].

Edwards, G., Compton, P., Malor, R., Srinivasan, A. & Lazarus, L. (1993). PEIRS: A pathologist maintained expert system for the interpretation of chemical pathology reports. *Pathology, 25,* 27-34.

Gaines, B. R. & Shaw, M. L. G. (1993). Knowledge acquisition tools based on personal construct psychology. *Knowledge Engineering Review, 8*(1), 49-85.

Geib, M., Reichold, A., Kolbe, L., & Brenner, W. (2005, March 1). Architecture for customer relationship management approaches in financial services. In *Proceedings of the 38th Hawaii International Conference on System Sciences 2005 (HICSS-38)*, Big Island, Hawaii. Los Alamitos, CA: IEEE Computer Society.

Goldman, G. (1990). The tacit dimension of clinical judgement. *The Yale Journal of Biology and Medicine, 63*(1), 47-61.

Kang, B., Compton, P., & Preston, P. (1995). Multiple classification ripple down rules: Evaluation and possibilities. In *Proceedings of the 9th AAAI-Sponsored Banff Knowledge Acquisition for Knowledge-Based Systems Workshop*, Banff, Canada, University of Calgary.

Kang, B., Yoshida, K., Motoda, H., Compton, P., & Iwayama, M. (1996). A help desk system with intelligent interface. In P. Compton, R. Mizoguchi, H. Motoda, & T. Menzies (Eds.), *PKAW'96: Pacific Rim Knowledge Acquisition Workshop* (pp. 313-332), Sydney, Dept. of Artificial Intelligence, School of Computer Science and Engineering, UNSW.

Kelly, G. A. (1955). *The psychology of personal constructs.* New York: Norton.

Kim, M. (2003). *Document management and retrieval for specialised domains: An evolutionary user-based approach.* Doctoral dissertation, UNSW, Sydney.

Lazarus, L. (2000). *Clinical decision support systems: Background and role in clinical support* (White Paper). Retrieved from http://www.pks.com.au/CDSS_White_Paper_doc.pdf

Mansar, S. L. & Marir, F. (2003). *Case-based reasoning as a technique for knowledge management in business process redesign.* Academic Conferences Limited.

Marir, F. & Watson, I. D. (1994). A categorised bibliography of case-based reasoning. *Knowledge Engineering Review, 9*(4), 355-381.

Markman, A. B. & Gentner, D. (1996). Commonalities and differences in similarity comparisons. *Memory and Cognition, 24*(2), 235-249.

Nonaka, I., Takeuchi, H., & Umemoto K. (1996). A theory of organisational knowledge creation. *International Journal of Technology Management, 11*(7/8), 833-845.

Pawlak, Z. (1991). *Rough sets: Theoretical aspects of reasoning about data.* Dordrecht: Kluwer Academic Publishers.

Pfeffer, J. & Sutton, R. (2000). *The knowing-doing gap: How smart companies turn knowledge into action.* Boston: Harvard Business School Press.

Polanyi, M. (1962). *Personal knowledge.* Chicago: University of Chicago Press.

Richards, D. & Busch, P. (2003, June). Acquiring and applying contextualised tacit knowledge. *Journal of Information and Knowledge Management, 2*(2), 179-190.

Stenmark & Lindgren (2003). Retrieved from http://w3.informatik.gu.se/~dixi/publ/dr-amcis.pdf

Sternberg, R. (1995). Theory and management of tacit knowledge as a part of practical intelligence. *Zeitschrift Für Psychologie, 203*(4), 319-334.

Tsoukas, H. & Vladimirou, E. (2001). What is organizational knowledge? *Journal of Management Studies, 38*(7), 973-993.

Vazey, M. & Richards, D. (2005, May 15-18). Intelligent management of call centre knowledge. In M. Khosrow-Pour (Ed.), *Managing Modern Organizations with Information Technology: Proceedings of the Information Resources Management Association International Conference (IRMA'05)* (pp. 877-879), San Diego, CA. Hershey, PA: Idea Group Publishing.

Wille, R. (1992). Concept lattices and conceptual knowledge. *Computers and Mathematics with Applications, 23*, 493-522.

ENDNOTE

[1] While rule conclusions in production (IF-THEN) rule systems may be a classification, such as mammal or igneous rock, or an action such as "don't spray" or "request blood test", we have distinguished between the type of conclusions depending on whether they return a class (classification) or an action (conclusion) as we believe this distinction is helpful in guiding knowledge acquisition.

This work was previously published in International Journal of Knowledge Management, Vol. 2, Issue 1, edited by M.E. Jennex, pp. 72-88, copyright 2006 by IGI Publishing, formerly known as Idea Group Publishing (an imprint of IGI Global).

Chapter XIII
Knowledge Management Systems:
Towards a Theory of Integrated Support

Dick Stenmark
IT University of Göteborg, Sweden

Rikard Lindgren
Viktoria Institute, Sweden

ABSTRACT

This chapter is motivated by one simple question: Why do so many knowledge management systems (KMS) fail when implemented in organizational knowledge work practice? Indeed, imbalance between the desire for accurate content and the workload required to achieve this still appears to be a critical issue, resulting in KMS of little use for organizational members. Hence, KMS maintenance is an important research subject. With the objective to contribute recommendations for how to integrate KMS with everyday knowledge work, we apply general lessons learned from development of groupware applications as a theoretical lens to analyze empirical experiences of three implemented and evaluated KMS. Theorizing the relationship between the recommendations developed and extant KMS design theory, the chapter offers implications for IS research and practice.

INTRODUCTION

Over the last decade or so there has been much debate in academic literature about concepts such as knowledge-based organizations, knowledge-creating companies, knowledge work, and organizational knowledge (Nonaka, 1994; Blackler, 1995; Spender, 1996; Schultze, 2000). Consistent with this debate, knowledge management has been promoted as an important approach for organizations trying to achieve competitive advantage (Hedlund, 1994). Knowledge management is often regarded as the generation, representation, storage, transfer, transformation, application,

Copyright © 2008, IGI Global, distributing in print or electronic forms without written permission of IGI Global is prohibited.

embedding, and protecting of organizational knowledge (Schultze & Leidner, 2002). While processes of knowledge generation, storage, and transfer do not necessarily result in improved organizational performance, effective knowledge application does (Alavi & Leidner, 2001).

According to the knowledge-based theory of the firm, the source of competitive advantage resides in the ability of an organization to turn knowledge into action and less on knowledge itself (Grant, 1996). Integration of knowledge, either explicitly or implicitly, of many different people to facilitate knowledge application, Grant argues, is the motivation for organizations comprising multiple individuals. Recognizing that integration of knowledge of organizational members is exceptionally difficult, Grant advocates that a key challenge for organizations to achieve effective knowledge application is to establish a mode of interaction facilitating that people's specialist knowledge is integrated.

As Davenport and Prusak (1998) note, there are several reasons for knowledge workers not to apply their knowledge. Chief amongst these are social factors such as distrusting the source of knowledge or lack of time or opportunity to apply knowledge (Alavi & Leidner, 2001). Observing that organizations tend to have a gap between what they know and what they do (Pfeffer & Sutton, 2000), many IS researchers suggest that information technology may have a positive influence on knowledge application (e.g., Alavi & Leidner, 2001; Nidimolu et al., 2001). For example, information systems can enhance knowledge application by facilitating the capture, updating, and accessibility of organizational information and knowledge (Mao & Benbasat, 1998). Also, information systems can increase the size of knowledge workers' internal social networks by allowing for organizational knowledge to be applied across time and space (Kock & McQueen, 1998).

However, while contemporary organizations typically expect knowledge management systems (KMS) to become major innovations in terms of the ways in which business can organize and be conducted (e.g., Gallivan et al., 2003; Scheepers et al., 2004), recent IS research indicates that such systems often fail when implemented in everyday knowledge work (Schultze & Boland, 2000). In response, several studies have explored the issue of how to support knowledge work with information systems (Hayes, 2001; Hayes & Walsham, 2001; Ellingsen & Monteiro, 2003; Levina & Vaast, 2005; Poston & Speier, 2005). However, despite the fact that KMS maintenance has been acknowledged as an important issue (Holtshouse, 1998; Hahn & Subramani, 2000), imbalance between the desire for accurate content and the workload required to achieve this still appears to be a critical problem, leading to systems of little use for organizations in their knowledge application processes (e.g., Lindgren & Stenmark, 2002; Lindgren et al., 2004). Following this, an important area of KMS research is the development of systems with the potential to bridge the knowledge application gap (Alavi & Leidner, 2001). In this context, a significant challenge is to develop design principles intended to keep KMS alive—updated, current, maintained—by encouraging use (Markus et al., 2002).

The problems KMS are facing today, that is, the fact that systems remain unused in day-to-day practice despite good theoretical reasons why they should work, show great resemblance to the difficulties experienced when introducing groupware applications in the 1980s. Being one of the first to study the challenges faced by groupware developers, Grudin observed that when groupware started to emerge as a new market, many of the early application developers were people who previously had focused exclusively on single-user applications. The maturing single-user application domain forced these developers to explore new territories and pushed them into areas of which they had little knowledge. The problems they ran into they had never experienced when supporting individuals and they were thus completely unprepared (Grudin, 1994). We believe that Grudin's observations are analogous to what we now witness on the knowledge management arena, where software vendors are being accused of re-labeling their old information systems to KMS (King, 1999), and that his influential work within the field of Computer Supported Cooperative Work (CSCW) (Grudin, 1987; 1988; 1994) can prove helpful to KMS developers.

Despite these similarities and although KMS as organizational-wide technologies have been discussed in terms of groupware (e.g., Alavi & Leidner, 2001; Hendriks, 2001; Robertson et al., 2001), Grudin's findings seem to be overlooked in the knowledge management literature. One of Grudin's chief findings is that situations where one party does the work and someone else receives the benefit often lead to failure. As activities on top of their ordinary responsibilities, organizational members cannot be expected to spend time and efforts feeding a "knowledge database" or maintaining a "knowledge system" for the benefit of the organization only (Stein & Zwass, 1995; Markus, 2001). Recognizing that contributions from all organizational members are an important prerequisite for successful KMS (Hahn & Subramani, 2000), there must be mechanisms to express or represent knowledge in ways that enable also the individual employee to make better use of his or her knowledge (Kankanhalli et al., 2005).

In this chapter, we draw upon empirical experiences from three implemented and evaluated KMS at Volvo Information Technology AB in Sweden. For the purpose of contributing recommendations for how to integrate KMS with everyday knowledge work, we shall here use Grudin's (1994) eight challenges for groupware developers as a theoretical lens to analyze why the systems studied failed. Theorizing the relationship between the recommendations developed and extant KMS design theory, the chapter offers implications for IS research and practice. First, our work extends earlier research addressing the KMS maintenance challenge. Second, our work

assists KMS developers in attempts to bridge the knowing-doing gap in organizations.

The structure of the chapter is as follows. In section two, a theoretical background covering characteristics of organizational knowledge application, related IS research on system support for knowledge work, and Grudin's challenges for groupware developers is outlined. Thereafter, we present the research site and describe the method used. This is followed by a presentation of the KMS included in our study. Then, we outline empirical experiences from three implemented and evaluated KMS. Using Grudin's groupware challenges for analyzing why the systems studied failed, section six develops our recommendations for how to integrate KMS with everyday knowledge work. In our discussion of the research findings, we theorize the relationship between the recommendations developed and extant KMS design theory and outline implications for IS research and practice.

THEORETICAL BACKGROUND

Formulated by researchers like Grant (1996), Nonaka and Takeuchi (1995), Spender (1996), and Tsoukas (1996), the knowledge-based theory of the firm postulates that services rendered by knowledge resources such as organization culture and identity, routines, policies, systems, documents, and individual employees form the basis for achieving competitive advantage.

Viewing the firm as an institution for knowledge application, however, Grant (1996) emphasizes that the competitiveness of an organization depends on its ability to effectively apply the existing knowledge and to take action rather than on the existing knowledge per se. Consistent with all theories of the firm acknowledging the efficiency gains of specialization, Grant suggests that the principal task of organization is to coordinate the efforts of many specialists. In this way, organizational capability can be seen as the outcome of integration of specialized knowledge of multiple individuals.

Discussing fundamental mechanisms for integrating knowledge to create organizational capability, Grant argues that reliance on high-interaction and non-standardized solutions increase as task complexity and uncertainty grows. In such situations, problem-solving relies less on organizational members following specifications and organizational routines and more on group efforts involving individuals with prerequisite knowledge and specialty. Distributed, unusual, and unstructured tasks and work processes requiring such personal and communication-intensive forms of integration can be described as characterized by variety rather than routine and problematic to describe in manuals, job descriptions, and charts (Brown & Duguid, 1991). Typically, this type of work is performed by professional with high level of skill and expertise, for example, researchers, product developers, advertisers, and consultants.

Unlike service work, knowledge work defies routinization and requires the use of creativity in order to produce idiosyncratic and esoteric knowledge (Blackler, 1995). Knowledge work is thus untidy in comparison with operational or administrative business processes, in which tangible inputs are acted on in some predictable, structured way and converted into outputs. The inputs and outputs of knowledge work, that is, ideas, interruptions, or inspirations, are often less tangible, and in knowledge work there are no predetermined task sequences that, if correctly executed, guarantee the desired outcome (Boland & Tenkasi, 1995; Davenport et al., 1996). Summarizing the characteristics of a knowledge work process, Markus et al. (2002, p. 184) define such a process as an "organizational activity pattern characterized by (1) an emergent process of deliberations with no best structure or sequence, (2) an actor set that is unpredictable in terms of job roles or prior knowledge, and (3) knowledge

requirements for general and specific distributed expertise."

Recognizing that knowledge work processes differ qualitatively from semi-structured decision-making processes, Markus et al. (2002) argue that existing types of systems and their associated design theories do not adequately serve the unique requirements of this class of design situations. More specifically, they assert that the development literature on decision support systems, executive information systems, expert systems, organizational communication systems, organizational knowledge repository systems, and organizational memory systems does not provide sufficient guidance for how to build systems that support knowledge work processes.

According to Markus et al., the poor fit between the requirements of such work processes and existing IS design theories stems from three disconnects. First, decision-making in knowledge work processes requires that expert knowledge is adapted or contextualized to specific local conditions. Intended to support semi-structured decision-making, decision support systems and executive information systems do not provide system features handling expert knowledge and contextualizing translation rules. Resulting from this, these types of systems inhibit creative problem finding and solution generation. While expert systems manage general expert knowledge, they fail to support contextual knowledge and the flexibility needed for process emergence. Second, decision support systems, executive information systems, expert systems, and organizational memory systems are all specifically designed for a known type of user. Being designed for a particular type of user community, however, these systems are not well adapted to emergent work processes characterized by shifting user types having varying knowledge requirements. Third, today knowledge workers have access to many different types of systems such as decision support systems, expert systems, executive information systems, organizational communication systems,

Table 1. Eight challenges for groupware developers (Grudin, 1994)

1. Disparity in work and benefit. A groupware application typically requires extra work from individuals who do no perceive a direct benefit from using the application.
2. Critical mass and prisoner's dilemma problem. A group support system may not attract the critical mass of users needed to be useful, or can fail because it is never to any one individual's advantage to use it.
3. Disruption of social processes. A groupware application can render activity that violates social norms, threatens political structures, or otherwise demotivates users critical to its success.
4. Exception handling. A group support system may fail to offer the wide range of exception handling and improvisation characterizing everyday group activity.
5. Unobtrusive accessibility. Support features for group processes are used rather infrequently, requiring unobtrusive accessibility and integration with more heavily used features.
6. Difficulty of evaluation. The problem of identifying and generalizing the factors underlying success or failure hampers learning from experience in the context of groupware development.
7. Failure of intuition. Intuition fails when the intricate demands on a groupware application are ignored, resulting in bad management and an error-prone design process.
8. The adoption process. Implementation of groupware in the workplace posits adoption challenges that go beyond past experiences of both product developers and large-scale information systems developers.

and organizational knowledge repositories. Since these systems often are isolated and not integrated into work practice, knowledge workers tend to manage their systems rather than getting the job done.

Arguing that a new IS design theory for systems supporting knowledge work processes is needed, Markus et al. develop a theory intended to assist systems developers in their efforts to design effective KMS. On the basis of characteristics of knowledge work processes and requirements for information technology support of such processes, this theory matches principles guiding the selection of system features and principles guiding the development process with the unique user requirements of knowledge work. Elaborating on the theory developed, they suggest a set of additional research challenges. One concern is about how to keep KMS alive—updated, current, maintained—by encouraging use.

Even though KMS differ in significant ways from CSCW or groupware systems, we believe there are analogies suggesting that there are lessons to be learned from importing Grudin's findings to the KMS realm. Grudin (1994) presents eight challenges for developers of groupware applications that we argue are productive for achieving updated, current, and maintained KMS (see Table 1). On a general level, Grudin's eight challenges call for better understanding of characteristics of work environments and for corresponding adjustments by systems developers. Whereas progress on the first five challenges requires better understanding of the requirements of the intended users' workplace, the final three require changes in the development process.

For the purpose of contributing recommendations for how to integrate KMS with everyday knowledge work, we shall here use Grudin's (1994) eight challenges for groupware developers as a theoretical lens to analyze our three case systems. Targeting the KMS maintenance challenge, our discussion of the relationship between the recommendations developed and the three disconnects as identified by Markus et al. (2002) extends existing IS research on the implementation and use of KMS.

METHOD

This work was carried out at Volvo Information Technology's (VIT) head office in Göteborg, Sweden, during August 1998 to December 2000. Employing some 4,300 people, and with offices in Sweden, Belgium, Brazil, Great Britain, Malaysia, and the USA, VIT is today a rather large IT consultant firm, and the Volvo Group's resource and expertise centre for IT systems. The main objective of VIT is to create global IT systems that generate value for their customers. Historically, VIT has achieved this by developing cost-effective systems where a significant percentage of the solutions were the same for the entire Volvo Group. A high degree of standardization was thus hailed as the optimal situation and VIT's centralized mainframe operation, which had received several international awards for high efficiency and cost-effectiveness, had always been one of the corner stones. By routinizing as much of the work as possible, VIT intended to ensure predictability, consistency, and quality in their services. However, VIT was not the exclusive provider of IT services since the companies within the Volvo Group could purchase IT services also from external providers if they so desired. But as long as mainframe processing was the core of the business, VIT was on top of the competition. The shift in the 1990s towards more Web-enabled solutions, however, opened the field for new, smaller, and quicker players. This situation put new demands on VIT's ability to change and adapt to new business solutions, and since then VIT has evolved from being a Volvo internal resource and expertise centre for IT solutions to become a global player serving customers also outside the Volvo Group.

The continuous development of knowledge, expertise, and skills needed for mobile services and IT in vehicles (telematics) is essential for VIT to continue to be a competitive partner in the future. The organization has therefore become, in part, more project-oriented and decentralized and in such a situation empowering the employees to act more quickly and autonomously is important. The more rapidly changing environment and the more frequent exposure to previously unknown problem areas has resulted in a learning-by-doing situation rather than an attend-a-course approach to competence development. Skills are thus acquired and disposed of at a more rapid pace than earlier and, like many large organizations, VIT has recognized the problem of knowing who within the organization knows what. In an attempt to tackle this problem, VIT has initiated a number of initiatives over the last years to reinforce its knowledge management process: creation of homepages for projects, groups, and departments, establishment of human networks related to particular competence and knowledge areas, evaluation of search engines and agent technology for the intranet, implementation of IT support for managing competencies, knowledge, and resources, and development of trainee and management programs. In this chapter, we report experiences from our involvement in VIT's efforts to implement and test support systems for knowledge work.

We think it is fair to describe this work as a case study. Yin (1994, p. 13) describes a case study as "an empirical inquiry that investigates a contemporary phenomenon within its real-life context, especially when the boundaries between phenomenon and context are not clearly evident." This definition captures eloquently the characteristics of our study of the role of support systems in knowledge work. Pointing to analytical differences and considerations, the literature distinguishes between multiple case studies and single case studies (Yin, 1994). However, in practical work the boundaries can become blurred. As asserted by Yin, reflecting the rationale behind multiple experiments, multiple case studies are typically carried out as to provide replication and thus be regarded more robust. Following this, the cases must be selected to produce either literal replication, that is, similar results are predicted, or theoretical replication, that is, different results but for predictable reasons (Yin, 1994).

The work described in this chapter has emerged out of three interrelated projects at VIT over a period of thirty months. Each of these projects has had its own research agenda, its own research questions, and has produced its own output (e.g., Stenmark, 2001; Lindgren & Stenmark, 2002; Lindgren et al., 2003; 2004). What we present in this chapter is a post hoc analysis of the entire process where we have revisited the original data and looked at it through a different theoretical lens. Although it is obvious that our work covers multiple cases, we do not claim it to be a multiple case study by Yin's definition because the objective has never been replication. Instead, we like to think of our research effort as a continuous study of a theme (system support for knowledge workers) that involves three interrelated cases, each providing distinct pieces to a collective puzzle. While Yin acknowledges that case studies can be used both qualitatively and quantitatively, it is evident from his text (the use of hypothesis to test, the concern for internal and external validity, and the issues of reliability) that he comes from a quantitative tradition. In comparison, we are more qualitatively oriented and our understanding of a case study is thus more in line with Walsham's (1995) description of the interpretive case study.

During the first project, referred to as the Watson case, the first author spent four months implementing an agent-based recommender system and studying its adoption and use. For this study, approximately 80 users were invited, of which 48 agreed to participate. The objective of the research, the concept of agent-based systems, the design rationale of the application, how to operate the system, how to register and login, and how to set up and run individual agents, were explained to all participants at a two-hour introduction meeting (in total, three such meetings were held). User experiences as well as hard

data were collected in several ways including interviews, questionnaires, and Web server log file analyses. First, all users were invited to a group interview/focus group session but only eight showed up. The remaining 40 users were then sent an e-mail questionnaire, which only 12 respondents answered. We thereafter conducted seven semi-structured and open-ended interviews each lasting between 28 and 66 minutes.

The second project, here called the TP/HR case, was a joint venture between the researchers and VIT practitioners. While VIT personnel did the actual coding, we as researchers were allowed to provide input to the implementation process. User viewpoints from the TP/HR system were collected through ten semi-structured interviews, which lasted between 45 and 60 minutes. The interviewees were selected to represent different organizational roles and positions, including management consultants, systems programmers, and personnel from the human resource (HR) department. Another important source of TP/HR data was archival records and project documentation (covering strategy plans for knowledge/competence management in VIT and written material about technical aspects). Being members of the TP/HR project team allowed us access to that kind of material.

The third project—the VIP case—was conducted on our initiative and again carried out as a collaborative effort involving researchers and VIT practitioners. However, the prototype was developed and implemented by our research team without active involvement of VIT members. Simply put, VIT had too many resources tied up in the TP/HR project to simultaneously engage in yet another development and implementation project. In order to gather empirical data, we conducted 16 semi-structured one-hour interviews with VIP users. The interviewees again occupied different positions within the organization, ranging from non-technicians such as HR staff members, project managers, department managers, and financial controllers to technology watchers and systems programmers (many of whom had also tested the TP/HR system).

As is evident from the above, this work stretches over several years and across multiple projects, resulting in that we have used a variety of research methods and techniques. Indeed, as noted by Mingers (2001), the combination of research methods can enable richer and more reliable research results. User experiences and hard data have been collected in several ways and from multiple sources, including interviews, focus groups, questionnaires, archival records, system documentation, intranet documents, and Web server log files. Two of the projects have included elements of action research where we have collaborated with the practitioner at the researched site. The first author was actually employed by the researched organization at the time of the three projects.

When we now reflect upon our research in retrospect, we are able to notice patterns that eluded us whilst being in the midst of things. Indeed, the three cases together allow us to draw conclusions not possible from the individual cases. Miles and Huberman (1984) describe the analytic phase as consisting of three concurrent flows of activity: data reduction, data display, and conclusion drawing. Data reduction refers to the process of selecting, simplifying, and abstracting the raw data that the researcher has in forms of field notes and transcribed interviews. Data reduction is part of the analysis because the researcher makes explicit choices of what categories to use, what sources to include, and what data to summarize. Data display is an organized spatial way of presenting the data systematically to the researcher in a form that helps the researcher see what is happening. Again, the process of data display is part of the analysis since deciding what data to present and in what form affects the result space. Conclusion drawing, finally, is to decide what things mean. This process is also part of the analysis. Conclusions first appear as vague hunches that subsequently are validated as the work proceeds. Qualitative data analysis is thus an iterative enterprise that also includes the data collection phase.

In our work, we have certainly made use of data reduction, data display, and conclusion drawing. However, since all data was collected as part of previous research projects, these activities have been separated from data collection. Ultimately, this means that we have been limited to data already collected (and to some extent also reduced and displayed). In terms of data analysis, this may have biased our understanding of the case. However, we have transcended the individual cases in retrospect by focusing on the learning process that has developed over the years and across the cases. In addition, we have also applied new theory to reinterpret the data.

The theoretical framework that has guided our analysis is based on Grudin's (1994) eight challenges for developers. During the analytic phases, the data has been read, categorized, conceptualized, and interpreted in an iterative fashion. Having data not only from one prototype but from three prototypes in sequence, we have been able to follow an over-time development for each of the themes suggested by Grudin. The three cases have been compared with and contrasted to each other and with Grudin's themes in an iterative fashion that has furthered our understanding of the phenomena under study.

SYSTEM DESCRIPTIONS

Our first case is the development and evaluation of the Watson (*What's on*) prototype. The Watson prototype project was initiated in August of 1998. VIT's intranet, which had been in place since 1995, was growing quickly both in terms of content, servers, and users and in 1998 it consisted of some 450 Web servers hosting little less than half a million documents. As a response to a rapidly growing intranet, our basic idea behind Watson was to examine how an agent-based recommender system could help knowledge workers to deal with information overload by providing awareness of relevant intranet information.

Watson was built on top of Autonomy's AgentWare software, which is a commercially available tool that uses neural networks and advanced pattern-matching techniques to find similarities between texts. Watson indexed VIT's intranet each night and synthesized each Web document to a 0.5K digital representation, that is, a "fingerprint". Once fingerprints had been created, the system's reasoning engine could perform concept matching, that is, finding documents with similar fingerprints. New users had to create a user profile in which they could describe their job role or work responsibilities in a free text fashion. If a user already had a CV stored elsewhere, it could be copied into this field. Once saved and stored, the user profile was then converted to a digital fingerprint. The user could thereafter set up and train an agent to look for information on a specified topic. This task corresponded to submitting a search engine query, but was expressed in natural language. Indeed, the best results were achieved when users pasted a large chunk of text from a known, relevant document and asked the agent to find more similar documents. The agent profile would then be converted to a fingerprint and compared to all other fingerprints in the system. The returned results could be inspected and the user could give the agent positive feedback when highly relevant documents had been found, thus further tuning the agent profile and enhancing the matching capabilities. The profiles used in the search could therefore be said to be implicit.

The rationale behind using software agents was to off-load VIT-members from having to search the intranet themselves, thus providing users with a direct and personal incentive to use the prototype. Since documents, user profiles, and agents were all represented as fingerprints, the system could be used to search for things other than pure information.

First, we implemented a *community feature* that was intended to enable knowledge workers to locate colleagues with similar assignments and organizational roles by matching their job profiles. Clicking the community button, the user's profile fingerprint would be compared to other users' profiles and a list of users with matching profiles was displayed. In this way, the user would get the name and contact information of all employees with similar job roles. The intention of this feature was to make users aware of each other's presence and thus facilitate the emergence of online communities. Second, the *similar agents feature* worked pretty much like the community feature, except for the fact that it was not the job profiles that were matched but the agent profiles. Initially, this was meant to allow users to find similar agents in order to have them cloned. In this way, new and inexperienced users would receive help to get their agents to a decent quality level more quickly. However, the cloning service was not implemented in time for the study. The only feature offered to the users during the test was the option to find other users with similar agents.

The Watson prototype was tested locally without top management support. Although user reactions were positive, the technology was considered too expensive (at the local level) and the prototype was not further developed.

The second case concerns our involvement in the implementation and evaluation of the Tieto Persona/Human Resource (TP/HR) system. Explicitly targeting management of core competence and skills, the TP/HR project had three key objectives: (1) to identify and construct a competence structure that could serve as a foundation for mapping the employees' expertise and knowledge, (2) to implement the competence structure in the TP/HR system, and (3) to develop and establish an accompanying maintenance control function for keeping the system structure updated and relevant.

TP/HR was a commercial off-the-shelf module-based client/server system that was implemented in February 2000 through a top down strategy where the competence structure was defined by management alone. In VIT's implementation of TP/HR, competence was divided into functional (i.e., tasks such as project management) and technical skills (e.g., java programming), which in turn had sub-levels ordered in a complex tree structure. This structure was the result of a multi-months process in which several of the companies in the Volvo Group had been involved. Despite the massive effort, the result was more complicated than originally anticipated and yet not perceived as optimal. Nonetheless, the employees were supposed to navigate the competence structure to find the individual competencies that applied to each user and then rate their competence level on a scale from 1 to 5. This data was then stored in the TP/HR system's database.

In order to preserve integrity, TP/HR did not allow knowledge workers to see each others' competence descriptions or search for particular expertise or skills. Such *finding competence* features were exclusively for managers who could search for and find employees holding a particular competence on a certain level, for example, a java programmer on level 3 or above. Managers could also invoke other fancy features such as *competence gap analyses* that would indicate any discrepancies between the aggregated competence level as recorded by the system and the estimated future need as calculated by management. VIT planned to use these competence analyses to support organizational activities such as resource and availability planning, internal and external recruiting, goal and personal development discussions, forming teams of employees, finding competence when manning assignments, and mission steering. In this way, TP/HR was intended to be a knowledge work support system for both short- and long-term objectives.

Not only was the TP/HR system heavily promoted by VIT management, but also from several other member companies in the Volvo Group. Despite the total cost of the system itself and the complicated process of constructing a competence system ready to implement, the system was endorsed and tested. However, as a result of negative test experiences associated with user commitment and system maintenance, VIT decided to put the TP/HR project temporarily on hold.

The third case concerns the implementation and evaluation of the Volvo Information Portal (VIP). In the winter of 2000 (January to April), this recommender system prototype was developed as an attempt to tackle an information overload situation that was even more articulated than during the Watson study. Resulting from a rapid growth, the intranet had increased to over 700 Web servers hosting close to 750,000 pages.

Similar to the Watson prototype, VIP was an agent-based recommender system built on Autonomy's AgentWare platform. VIP allowed knowledge workers in VIT to define information agents that searched an index database for intranet documents matching their interests. By defining one or more agents and providing each of these with an interest profile, VIP users were thus able to have the corporate intranet monitored for interesting items. From a user's point of view, the primary objective was to receive relevant and targeted information as effortlessly as possible. Therefore, it was in the users' own interests to define the interest areas as good as possible because a well-defined profile would reward the user with high precision search results. On a general level, the features offered by the Watson and VIP prototypes were pretty much the same. However, two major changes were implemented in the VIP prototype.

First, the user profiles, that is, the part were users explicitly stated their job descriptions, were abandoned since the Watson study had told us that the explicit profiles were not perceived as useful. Second, Watson's similar agent feature, which allowed users to locate other employees interested in the same areas, was, in contrast, heavily used and appreciated. Building on this learning outcome, we introduced a *find competence feature* that allowed employees to find a fellow colleague with an arbitrary interest (not just people with interests similar to their own but any interest). A user wanting to find someone dealing with XML could use this feature to type in a few XML-related keywords and receive a list presenting all employees with active XML agents. Since ordinary knowledge workers had been excluded from this kind of search for knowledge and skills in TP/HR, this specific feature was intended to provoke a reaction from the organization.

As was the case with Watson, VIP was a local initiative and there was virtually no top-management support to promote this type of solution. The prototype was not further developed, but some of the lessons learned were discussed in terms of implications for other KMS in VIT. In

particular, implications for systems supporting career management, recruitment and selection, and training were discussed.

Table 2 summarizes particularities of Watson, TP/HR, and VIP and design relationships between the three systems.

EMPIRICAL EXPERIENCES

Watson

When evaluating the Watson prototype, we soon realized that we had underestimated the difficulties involved in agent training. The users conceived setting up and training of agents as non-trivial and many users had experienced mainly negative results. A majority of the users reported "strange" or "unexpected" document matches. However, the

Table 2. Systems

	Watson	TP/HR	VIP
Duration	August-November 1998 (4 months)	July 1999-December 2000 (18 months)	January-August 2000 (8 months)
Technology	Agent software for information retrieval	Database for storage of competence data	Agent software for information retrieval
Motives for the organization	• Increased information awareness • Effective information management	• Systematic core competence mapping • Competence gap visualization capability	• Increased information awareness • Effective information management • Competence identification capability
Motives for individual knowledge workers	• More targeted information • Community building support	• Marketing of knowledge and skills	• More targeted information • Community building support • Expertise location support
System content	• Implicit profiles for information • Explicit profiles for community building	• Explicit competence descriptions	• Implicit profiles for both information and community building/expertise location
Level of support	Local	Central	Local
Outcome	The prototype was not further developed	VIT decided to put the TP/HR project temporarily on hold	The prototype was not further developed but some of the lessons learned were discussed in terms of implications for other KMS

most interesting results came from the community and similar agents features.

The community feature was intended to enable knowledge workers with similar job profiles to learn of each other's existence. Not many users exploited this feature, though. Those who actually did try this feature used it only once or, in one case, twice. The low interest was not due to bugs or technical malfunctions since most interviewees considered the community feature to be working, that is, it delivered what it was supposed to. Instead, the low interest was attributed to the fact that the result was just not very exciting in that the users already knew the people doing similar jobs. Many users with similar profiles worked at the same departments and were not too interested in finding like-minded colleagues. One of our respondents put it as follows:

What's the use of hooking up with people doing the same stuff I do? If I want to talk to these guys, I go talk to them. They sit over there. But take, eh... databases – SQL server or something – where I don't have a clue. I wouldn't know where to start. It would probably be better to team up with those who know stuff I don't know.

As a substitute, the respondents suggested that one should be able to search for people with profiles other than one self (because this was a design implication apparently shared by many users and one that seemed to be adding value, we implemented it in the VIP prototype). The low utilization of the community feature can be seen as an implicit critique of the underpinning principles of explicit profiles. One user actually explicitly complained about this specific feature, claiming to have been connected to people he did not know. This was not what he had expected and he concluded that "this was clearly a bug". While people are often viewed as performing their jobs in line with their formal job descriptions, the Watson evaluation provides evidence of the opposite. The community feature was built on static

profiles created by the users themselves to mirror the official responsibilities placed upon them by the organization. However, these profiles were not only already known to the members but also experienced as fictitious and depicting an espoused theory of work. A later inspection of the users' profiles suggested that they invested a minimum amount of time on these profiles. We found the profiles to be very short and sketchy, containing merely department name and job title.

Although the similar agents and the community features incorporated the same pattern-matching mechanisms and generated exactly the same output, the former was much more frequently used. Several respondents reported that they were surprised to find certain people sharing their interests. The interviewees were also intrigued by the fact that the similar agents feature returned users whom they had not expected to be interested in a particular topic. One of our respondents said:

Sometimes you think you're alone and then you find out you're not. And it's not... I mean, it's all kinds of different people. It's really interesting to see who else is searching for these sorts of things.

Users clearly appreciated this opportunity to see in what areas other organizational members applied their knowledge, considering these results to be useful new insights.

TP/HR

Many of the participants in the TP/HR pilot project were positive about the system, which, in their opinion, was a first step towards some structure and order in an otherwise rather chaotic situation. Even though they complained about the old-fashioned user interface, they thought that TP/HR would be a useful tool, particularly, in establishing a common terminology. An agreed common vocabulary helps make competence more tangible and thereby assists managers in both coaching dialogues with the employees and competence gap analyses. Updating of the competence description should be a responsibility shared jointly by the manager and the employee. Typically the employee performed the physical input closely assisted by, and in dialogue with, the manager. The competence description should be updated as often as possible to reflect developments since the last update. However, not only did the employees' knowledge and skills change frequently. The competence structure itself would not remain correct for long. While entirely new competencies made their appearance, existing knowledge and skills became obsolete much faster than the TP/HR system was designed to handle. A management consultant stated:

Earlier it was easier [to have an updated system] since there were few programming languages. Now the development is so fast. Yes, there are the fourth, fifth, and sixth generation.

To cope with this evolution, VIT established a maintenance organization. Keeping the system structure and the competence data up-to-date was a burdensome task, requiring a lot of administration, though. As the project proceeded negative aspects started to surface. It seemed that knowledge workers at the grass-roots level had no direct interest in providing information about their skills since they could not benefit from using the system. A management consultant pointed out:

TP/HR is hierarchically structured and closed. As an individual you can see nobody but yourself. If I search for a certain competence, the system should support me in identifying the appropriate person. Such features are missing in the system. Instead, I have to talk to someone who is familiar with the employees' knowledge and skills. In any case, I can't use the TP/HR system for doing it myself.

Despite the intended change towards a more project-oriented and decentralized organization, VIT's organizational structure can be described as hierarchical. This was reflected in TP/HR's closed system structure. While managers were authorized to see information about all their subordinates, employees in other positions could only access their own descriptions. However, during the initial phase of the TP/HR pilot project, the ability to search for and find a person with specific skills was considered an obvious feature. As the pilot project advanced this changed, resulting in the TP/HR system to be primarily a management vehicle including features for measuring the status of employees' competencies and gap analyses. The employees were presumed to regularly feed the system with competence information, but they did not get much in return. As highlighted by several respondents, this producer/consumer dilemma counteracted the employees' motivation to use TP/HR. During the evaluation, the interviewees discussed different motives as to why VIT had chosen to implement a system with a closed structure. One TP/HR project group member pointed out the following reason:

The more people involved in competence registration, the more regulations there must be. We don't want other managers to be able to conduct internal recruiting [by using TP/HR].

In line with this quotation, several project group members discussed TP/HR's closed system structure in terms of a means for avoiding internal recruiting in the organization. Many of these respondents argued that TP/HR could have been an important tool for employees to communicate their existing skills and ambitions for future development. A management consultant gave her opinion of the matter:

To use the system would be a way to market your self to get interesting assignments. The opponents to this argument are surely those ten percent who have come to a standstill in their competence development. Presumably, there are many mangers in this group.

However, the closed system structure conveyed that competence was primarily a personal thing of no interest to others. Furthermore, several respondents highlighted that TP/HR lacked features that handled information about employees' wanted skills and desired work tasks. Project management members did not seem to think that this was much of an issue, though. The TP/HR project manager claimed:

Interests are a long way down on the list. It's fundamentally a personal thing; interests have no strategic value according to my point of view. Interest is for your own sake and therefore it's not reasonable to assume that people should register this type of information in the system. [...] People won't invest their time in such work because they simply don't benefit from it.

However, some project members did not fully appreciate this standpoint since they saw interest as an important dimension of knowledge work. A project manager involved in the system implementation said this when discussing the rationale of TP/HR:

It's important that we're able to find and take care of people's interests. Definitely you perform better if you are interested in the work-task in question. And surely the employees' potential to learn increases when they find the actual area exciting.

In line with what this quote illustrates, there were people who had different perspectives as to what type of information that should be handled by the TP/HR system.

VIP

The system evaluation indicated that the interviewees viewed VIP and its content in different ways. Some users thought that VIP contained formal descriptions of skills and knowledge in a similar manner to TP/HR, while other respondents were uncertain as to what type of information VIP handled. This ambiguity is illustrated by the following quote from a software developer:

Well, the find competence feature; first I interpreted it as if you came to some kind of competence/skills database. There's one competence database that I subscribe to where you search for skills. For example, if someone knows C++ and COBOL and what have you; then you can search for it. So, it does not seem intuitive that this is called find competence, but maybe it's right. I guess it's something you have to get used to if you want to use it. But it does not seem intuitive [...]. I'm still puzzled when I look at it.

However, the majority of the interviewees were rather attracted to the fact that VIP managed a different type of information than TP/HR. VIP was based on people's everyday actions in the form of information seeking activities and several respondents saw the system's potential to present an updated picture of the organization's knowledge and skills. Pointing to its integrated character, one HR manager argued that VIP could indicate what people actually use their skills for:

TP/HR is a lot about order and being in control of the situation; to know what we have and the level of education of our employees... how many of these and how many of those. Then this prototype is something else. It is what people do on an everyday basis. It is what they used their skills for. It is sort of the next step.

According to many interviewees, VIP can provide VIT information about knowledge and skills that are applied in the organization. Also, VIP makes it possible to identify people searching for information outside their formal area of responsibility. As highlighted by the respondents, such actions typically indicate a natural driving force. The fact that VIP was a system with the ability to visualize people's commitment and interests attracted most of the participants in the system evaluation. Indeed, one of these was the manager of the TP/HR project:

It is interesting to be able to find colleagues who are interested in the same things. Because our main problem here is that there are people working with similar things everywhere and you don't really find them. For me it was natural to see the other users but also to signal my own presence and interests to them.

As people added, deleted, or retrained their agents, these unnamed communities would constantly change members to reflect the current situation and the actions of the users themselves. No organizationally appointed administrator had to define communities in advance according to some espoused theory and the organizational members were instead in control. A software developer, familiar with both information retrieval tools and the TP/HR system commented:

The advantage with this approach is who controls it, I guess. In a conventional system, the administrator measures the information and controls it, and builds the system himself. Here, as a user, I'm able to influence the result to a much higher degree. This system [VIP] is built on organizational needs. By using this system, I can affect my situation by expressing my wishes. I want to work with XML, for instance, although I don't do this in the present situation.

The VIP system was based on the intentions and actions of individuals. Discussing VIP in terms of a decentralized system where the users themselves to a large extent affected and decided upon the content, several interviewees associated the system with development, change, and learning.

RECOMMENDATIONS FOR KMS

Disparity in Work and Benefit

The fact that groupware applications expected to provide a collective benefit still means that some people will have to adjust more than others, which is probably something most groupware users have experienced. In other words, such applications often require additional work from individuals who do not directly benefit from using them (Grudin, 1994). As is evident from our Watson account, knowledge workers were expected to supply their own profile descriptions for enabling other users to find them when engaging the community feature. The profiles thus had to be created for someone else's benefit, resulting in predictable and uninteresting descriptions. The TP/HR system was based on a similar design rationale. Employees were supposed to create and maintain their own competence database entries without even being able to use the system. The expected benefit was on an organizational level only. To tackle this type of problem, Grudin suggests that making the additional work required someone's explicit job might be a workaround. Such a solution seems appropriate when large organizational KMS are involved and associated management incentives are present. Another approach perhaps more feasible is to design KMS with an accompanying process ensuring that usage creates tangible benefits for all key actors involved. Indeed, striking the right balance between cost/benefit for a multitude of actors is a challenge in itself.

Targeting situations where extra effort is needed from knowledge workers interacting with the KMS, our first recommendation is that support systems must result in perceived value to reinforce user commitment.

Critical Mass and Prisoner's Dilemma

A groupware application requires a high percentage of all group members to interact with it to be truly useful. Depending on individual role or status, one or two defections may be enough to thwart an otherwise successful deployment. The problem is often to induce early adopters to stay on and not abandon the tool until a critical mass of users is achieved and they all can start to benefit (Grudin, 1994). With only 50 or so users in the Watson case and approximately 30 in the VIP study, there were significant risks that individual users would create agents for which there were no matches. The community feature would in such cases result in zero hits, thus generating no additional value. Since the primary incentive for signing up with the applications was not to find community members but to receive targeted information as a result of them training an agent (the more accurate agents, the better results), the lack of community members may not have had a negative impact on the overall use. Grudin argues that management can force a critical mass by removing alternatives or mandate system usage until users experience benefits and thus voluntarily continue to use it. While this was the intended strategy in the TP/HR case, the benefits were never planned to occur on the individual level and reaching a critical mass did not help the system to survive. In contrast, the VIP system provided every individual user with targeted information. The incentive to participate was already there and a critical mass was not required to receive the primary benefits. Our second recommendation for developers of KMS is thus to lower system thresholds by minimizing the amount of additional work required and to build in incentives for use by making salient both individual and collective benefits.

Disruption of Social Processes

Group activities are highly dependant on implicit social, motivational, economic, and political factors that change over time. Developers of groupware applications ignoring such critical factors may inscribe behavior in their tools that is at odds with the subtle social dynamics of the organization. If the tools violate social taboos, upset existing power structures, or reduce financial motivation, organizational members are likely to put up resistance (Grudin, 1994). Since knowledge and skills are increasingly valuable resources in modern organizations, one can expect knowledge workers to be reluctant to make explicit their knowledge and allow it to be captured by some KMS for the good of the collective. Such a process may result in them losing not only power and money but ultimately their jobs. TP/HR was clearly a top-down system designed for managers, supporting a management perspective. Moreover, to avoid internal recruiting of experts and key individuals, the TP/HR system was closed to all but senior managers, thus effectively removing the possibility for individuals to market themselves. As our empirical experiences indicate, social factors with high influence on grass-root level were not considered. When discussing possible solutions, Grudin reminds us of the importance of avoiding the assumption that work is carried out in a "rational" fashion. Obviously, while some rationality is involved, everyday work has typically more to do with individual actors' hidden agendas than with some agreed-upon organizational goal. In the context of knowledge work practices, workers may be reluctant to make explicit their knowledge because they fear losing power and competitive advantage. In contrast, knowledge can also be seen as an infinite resource that is not reduced when shared. Indeed, which interpretation that prevails is highly situational. For KMS to be successful in organizations, our third recommendation is therefore that such systems must acknowledge and coexist alongside existing cultural and social processes.

Exception Handling

When groupware applications are designed and implemented based on official office work handbooks and other readily available work specifications, the resulting tools may end up supporting the way things are supposed to work (rather than the way they do work). Realizing that descriptions of standard procedure often are post hoc rationalizations, we may recognize that what makes possible efficient performance is the ad hoc problem-solving capacity of man (Grudin, 1994). For good reasons, the industrial organization has been preoccupied with structures and standards. However, the breakdown of bureaucracy occurs when exceptions start to outnumber the routine. When yesterday's knowledge is no longer a prerequisite for tomorrow's work, old knowledge does not only become obsolete, it may even be harmful to the organization. Obviously, knowledge must be renewed and find novel paths continuously to remain valuable. As we saw previously, TP/HR was implemented based on formal work manuals and corporate strategy policies. Resulting from this, many of the skills needed and work situations encountered during an ordinary office day were not covered by the system. Rather than supporting rational myths, Grudin argues, we must carefully study how work is actually done. Because exception handling and ad hoc problem-solving are the birthplaces of knowledge, KMS without the ability to facilitate these situations have less potential. Needless to say, KMS must be tailorable and provide flexibility, although these requirements present challenges in themselves. As knowledge workers apply their experiences and skills in innovative ways as to handle unstructured tasks, our fourth recommendation is thus that developers of

KMS should seek solutions with the capacity to leverage these everyday activities.

Unobtrusive Accessibility

Even in groupware applications, the bulk of the work is carried out as individual tasks performed by individual group members who mainly use groupware features to coordinate and communicate the result. As a consequence, groupware features are typically used less frequently than many of the features supporting individual activities (Grudin, 1994). Building on this observation, Grudin asserts that less frequently used features must be tightly integrated with features that most users engage to catch on. In addition, such integration must be unobtrusive not to obstruct the use of the more frequently used features. Except for once in a while, using the system for updating his or her profile to comply with corporate policy, the individual VIT employee had no reason to enter TP/HR. In contrast, VIP rewarded users by serving targeted information and monitoring the indicated fields of interest on their behalf. Assuming information handling to be something organizational members engage in on a day-to-day basis, information agents would probably be a welcomed and relatively often used resource. The profiles derived from agent usage would then be maintained both frequently and unobtrusively. Striking the right balance between being unobtrusive and yet accessible is otherwise indeed a challenge. Grudin suggests that infrequently used features should be added to and incorporated in existing and already successful applications rather than being launched as separate systems. With such an approach, Grudin argues, the system can over time educate the users and slowly make them aware of beneficial spin-offs. In terms of implications for KMS, such systems must not be introduced as explicit stand-alone applications that knowledge workers intentionally must interact with in addition to their other job responsibilities. Our fifth recommendation is, therefore, that KMS should instead be invoked when knowledge is applied in practice by exploiting spin-offs from activities that knowledge workers are already engaged in.

Difficulty of Evaluation

Whereas interaction with single-user applications can be sufficiently covered during an hour's observation, groupware interactions involve many different users and unfold over much longer periods of time. This makes evaluation of groupware applications more complex and less precise. While determining whether an application is a success or a failure may be easy, it is more difficult to identify the factor(s) responsible for the result (Grudin, 1994). We were able to evaluate the VIP prototype by studying single-users attending the primary objective of receiving relevant corporate information. However, we were less successful in evaluating the organizational impact of the system since such an evaluation would have required a much larger test population. The lack of historical data and ephemeral nature of the implicit profiles further added to the difficulties. However, TP/HR was even more difficult to correctly evaluate. Obviously, only three explicit competence profiles would have been a failure, but the existence of 30,000 profiles would not necessarily have indicated success. The question here is whether the organization or the individual should decide if a KMS is successful. As argued previously, there must be a benefit on the individual level before there can be a positive organizational effect. Yet, if return on investment is noticeable only at the individuals level, organizational sponsors may decide to abandon the system in lack of tangible proofs of success. Grudin's advice for how to deal with the problem of evaluation is to ensure the right mix of skills, that is, both technical, sociological, and organizational, is allocated for the development task and to disseminate the results actively to all stakeholders. His experience from the CSCW community is that too little accumulated learning

is taking place due to the inability to learn from experiences. An important note in the context of in situ KMS evaluations is that knowledge is an intangible resource typically affecting both individuals and the organization as a whole indirectly. Ultimately, this means that it is very difficult to isolate the single factor contributing to the result. It may in fact not be one single contributing factor but a chain of concurring factors. The inherent nature of knowledge itself thus makes evaluations of KMS even more complicated. Responding to this challenge, our sixth recommendation is that KMS evaluations must involve different knowledge worker groups and be designed as collaborative efforts targeting individual benefits as well as organizational effects.

Failure of Intuition

When software is constructed by the same people who are going to use it, intuition can be a reliable input to the design process—at least as far as single-user applications are concerned. Whereas most organizational members have informed ideas about what is required to get the job done, individual intuition is less likely to be able to predict the intricate demands on groupware tools that are to be used by a wide range of different users. In many cases, the unwelcome extra work required of other users to get the application to work is underestimated (Grudin, 1994). Developers typically rely on feedback from a few potential users (or sponsors), and it is often these actors who are expected to benefit the most. A parallel is the TP/HR system where mostly HR staff and managers (typical stakeholders) were involved in the evaluation. In contrast, Watson and VIP where designed by a knowledge worker for other knowledge workers. An interesting observation is that managers on average were less impressed with the VIP approach than were ordinary employees. According to Grudin, relying less on (stakeholders') intuition and more on user participation is the way forward. This may lead to fewer projects being run but hopefully also to more realistic design goals and higher success rate amongst those that are actually started. Reflecting this argument, systems designers capable of identifying managers' needs should be engaged when building KMS to support management, while entirely different developers should be brought in when designing for another user group. Our seventh recommendation therefore suggests that there should probably not be one large knowledge work support system solving everything but rather many small applications handling more specific aspects of knowledge management.

Adoption Processes

Due to the critical mass problem mentioned earlier, groupware applications require more careful introduction in the workplace than developers may appreciate. Hence, they must pay more attention to the adoption process than product developers have in the past. The lower visibility of groupware features, which in turn generates less management support, also means that groupware developers face more difficult acceptance problems than large-scale information systems developers (Grudin, 1994). In our field studies, we noticed how the number of volunteering test users decreased from Watson to VIP, which is something that typically happens when the group's curiosity wanes and people's attention returns to their ordinary work. Although our KMS prototypes were based on information seeking—a process most employees are familiar with—the tools themselves were new and unknown and obviously suffered from adoption problems. The small scale of our project, and consequently limited managerial attention, is likely to have contributed to the death of the prototypes. Grudin's solution to this problem is to sidestep the introduction problem as much as possible by adding features to existing applications, as discussed above. Building on the success of established systems and functions would, if not guarantee, at least substantially increase the

likelihood of survival. As people continue to use the system, they will eventually discover the benefits of the added features and system usage will be further reinforced. Our eighth and final recommendation is that in situations where KMS depend on input from and interaction with many knowledge workers in the organization, familiar applications used by many employees (e.g., e-mail applications, word processors, Web browsers or printer spooling systems) should be selected as hosts for the knowledge management features to be added.

DISCUSSION

The knowledge-based theory of the firm postulates that knowledge is a key to the continued vitality of organizations (Nonaka & Takeuchi, 1995; Grant, 1996; Spender, 1996; Tsoukas, 1996). However, whereas knowledge in organizations has the potential to be applied across time and space to yield increasing returns, managing knowledge as an organization-wide resource as to facilitate its application is not easy (Garud & Kumaraswamy, 2005; Tanriverdi, 2005). Seeking ways to reduce the knowledge gap, organizations are attempting to leverage their knowledge resources by employing various forms of KMS (Kankanhalli et al., 2005). For example, such support systems can enhance application of knowledge by facilitating the capture, updating, and accessibility of organizational information and knowledge (Mao & Benbasat, 1998). Needless to say, while technological capabilities are critical, having sophisticated support systems does not guarantee success in knowledge management initiatives (Kankanhalli et al., 2005). Indeed, although the rationale for investing in KMS supporting knowledge application may seem convincing in theory, such systems tend to fail when implemented in the everyday practice of contemporary organizations (Schultze & Boland, 2000). Following this, the development of systems with the capacity to bridge the knowing-doing gap in organizations has been recognized as a significant area of KMS research (Alavi & Leidner, 2001). In this context, as asserted by Markus et al. (2002), an important challenge concerns how to keep KMS alive—updated, current, maintained—by encouraging use.

This chapter reports empirical experiences from three implemented and evaluated KMS at VIT. Our evaluation of the three KMS revealed a number of insights that we believe have both theoretical and practical significance for the development of KMS. An important finding from our involvement in VIT's attempts to implement and test support systems for knowledge work is that knowledge applied in practice was what attracted organizational members. As an illustration, the Watson study clearly showed that profiles based on practice are considered more trustworthy than descriptions based on espoused theory. Indeed, several respondents highlighted that the prototype not only supported individual knowledge workers in their everyday actions but also the organization as a whole because valuable knowledge resources could be identified and used more effectively. This finding suggests that KMS need capabilities that cater for ongoing actions of organizational members as they sought to apply the knowledge necessary to perform their day-to-day tasks. As noted in the literature, however, to support what knowledge workers actually do by making authentic work activities the primary focus of KMS implementations, requires a thorough understanding of both the tasks and their performance of the tasks (Burstein & Linger, 2003).

Furthermore, when investigating the underlying reasons for the problematic introduction of TP/HR, we came to realize that the closed system structure in combination with the system's lack of future orientation negatively affected knowledge workers' willingness to use and contribute to it. Clearly, while TP/HR offered few use incentives on behalf of knowledge workers at the grass root level, however, the system added to the users'

workload and obliged them to do things in addition to what their tasks at hand required. This finding verifies earlier research suggesting that KMS must support various forms of employee incentives (such as enjoyment in helping others, better work assignments, and promotion) as to encourage usage and build a critical mass of users (Kankanhalli et al., 2005). Indeed, as recognized by Stein and Zwass (1995, p. 107) "a user's intrinsic motivation to contribute information to the system differs with the degree to which the contributed information is instrumental to the user's goals."

Building on the learning outcomes from Watson and TP/HR, the VIP prototype was specifically designed to test our idea that exploiting knowledge workers' everyday actions in an unobtrusively manner would actively afford user participation. According to our respondents, exploiting traces that knowledge workers' everyday activities leave behind in form of published documents and/or search queries is a promising way to reveal otherwise invisible patterns of knowledge application. In this way, they argued, the organization can begin to find expertise and skills as soon as knowledge workers start to apply their existing or emerging knowledge. In view of the fact that organizational routines for knowledge management often become so inflexible that they form the basis for stagnation (c.f. Garud & Kumaraswamy, 2005), this finding suggests that organizations should seek dynamic KMS capable of reducing the time and effort needed to capture, codify, and visualize knowledge. In this context, Kankanhalli et al. (2005) envision that future KMS will enjoy the capability to support the dynamism of knowledge work processes by allowing for more natural forms of knowledge contribution (e.g., audio or video) as opposed to purely text contributions.

Reflecting on these insights and the entire three year research project, we have used important observations from the CSCW field as a theoretical lens to pinpoint similarities between KMS failure and groupware failure. On the basis of our novel application of Grudin's work in the realm of KMS, the chapter contributes a set of recommendations for how to integrate KMS with everyday knowledge work. The eight recommendations identified and discussed are (1) KMS must render perceived value as to reinforce user commitment in situations where additional effort is required from knowledge workers interacting with the systems, (2) developers should try to lower systems thresholds by minimizing the amount of extra work required and to build in incentives for use by making salient both individual and collective benefits, (3) KMS must acknowledge and coexist alongside existing cultural and social processes, (4) developers of KMS should seek solutions with the capability to leverage knowledge workers' day-to-day activities, (5) KMS must not be introduced as stand-alone applications but rather as integrated systems exploiting spin-offs from activities knowledge workers are already engaged in, (6) evaluations of KMS need to include various knowledge worker groups and be designed as collaborative efforts seeking both individual benefits and organizational effects, (7) well-adapted system support for knowledge work is best achieved through many small applications that cater for specific aspects of knowledge workers' everyday practices, and (8) familiar applications used by a critical mass of employees should be selected as hosts for the knowledge management features to be added in situations where the support systems require input from and interaction with many knowledge workers.

Given our recommendations, we draw on Markus et al.'s (2002) discussion about the poor fit between specific requirements of knowledge work processes and existing IS design theories as to position our knowledge contribution. We are strong in our belief that our recommendations help developers as well as researchers to better understand and overcome the three disconnects as identified by Markus et al.

First, Markus et al. argue that today's support systems for knowledge work do not offer the flexibility needed for process emergence. Our recommendations #4 and #7 provide guidance for how to tackle this disconnect. As knowledge work defies routinization and requires the use of creativity in order to produce idiosyncratic and esoteric knowledge, such work practice is untidy compared to operational or administrative business processes. Hence, KMS must be able to go beyond written instructions and official task descriptions, thus appreciating exceptions not only as something inevitable but as a necessity. Indeed, the risk of support systems becoming too narrow and rigid can be decreased by exploiting the combined intuition of several different developers.

Second, Markus et al. assert that existing KMS are designed for a known user community, whereas emergent knowledge work practice is characterized by shifting user types having varying knowledge requirements. Our recommendations #3 and #6 provide guidance for how to tackle this disconnect. As different knowledge worker groups may have various social norms and values, support systems designed for one particular group can have built-in features conflicting with cultural structures of another group. Bearing this is mind, developers can facilitate adoption of systems across groups of knowledge workers by making salient norms and values that underpin their design and reflect upon what intended and unintended consequences these might render. An alternative way for KMS developers seeking to promote system adoption in new domains is to become aware of the different set of evaluation criteria for success that may exist in a given context and adjust to these conditions.

Third, analyzing the role of support systems in contemporary knowledge work practices, Markus et al. argue that knowledge workers either manage their tools instead of attending their work or ignore their tools altogether. Our recommendations #1,

#2, #5 and #8 provide guidance for how to tackle this disconnect. On a general level, our recommendations reflect the notion that KMS must not be isolated and should be integrated into work practice. For the purpose of avoiding situations where knowledge workers manage their systems rather than getting the job done, developers must recognize socio-technical issues associated with disparity in work and benefit. In this way, KMS capable of attracting a critical mass of users can be developed. In addition, paying attention to unobtrusive accessibility and the adoption process may deepen developers understanding of how support systems can be better integrated with both the day-to-day tasks of knowledge workers and their performance of the tasks.

CONCLUDING REMARKS

Related to our research is the growing interest in social media that we have witnessed during recent years. Coined by Tim O'Reilly, the term Web 2.0 is frequently used to describe the phenomenon of peer-to-peer services populating the Web. Although no clear definition exists, we shall here position our work vis-à-vis a few basic Web 2.0 tenets that can be observed on the Internet. What characterizes social media is the high level of integration. Essentially, social media seek to incorporate, exploit, and benefit from users' other online experiences and make them prominent. O'Reilly (2005) argues that the perceived quality of a [social media] feature increases with the number of people using it. What separates successful social media from mediocre ones is the use of the collective power of the many small sites that makes up the bulk of the Web's content (O'Reilly, 2005). Loosely referring to the power law distribution curve, Anderson (2004) labeled this phenomenon "the Long Tail".

Although only a small fraction of the users visiting a site is likely to add value explicitly due to the extra work it would require, their collective actions still add value if leveraged intelligently. Social media do this by benefiting from side-effects of ordinary use, thus avoiding adding to the workload of the individual. Given the potential of the long tail, applications that provide a natural incentive to contribute and as a spin-off offer additional benefits by "harnessing collective intelligence" are most likely to be the future winners (O'Reilly, 2005). Logging and tracking interest-driven activities on an intranet was a novel idea when we started this work in the late nineties (c.f., Stenmark, 1999; 2000; 2001; Lindgren & Stenmark, 2002; Lindgren et al., 2003)—and consequently met with some skepticism from both practitioners and reviewers—but we claim the current development with Web 2.0 shows the merits of our approach and proves its feasibility.

Rather than attempting to draft general laws that must be applied in every situation, in this chapter we suggest general recommendations for how to integrate KMS with everyday knowledge work. Clearly, these are more in line with Web 2.0 ideas about benefiting from the long tail than with traditional IS development practices. As we believe that the recommendations offer novel insights for how to overcome the three disconnects as identified by Markus et al. (2002), we suggest that developers of KMS should consider these recommendations in all projects aimed at bridging the knowing-doing gap. We conclude that additional studies focused on how to keep KMS alive—updated, current, maintained—by encouraging use are necessary if IS researchers are to provide useful advice to practitioners on the implementation and use of support systems with the potential to bridge the knowledge application gap in organizations. Indeed, our study offers a wealth of opportunities for further investigations of the many challenges surrounding deployment of support systems involving knowledge application.

REFERENCES

Alavi, M., & Leidner, D. (2001). Knowledge management and knowledge management systems: Conceptual foundations and research issues. *MIS Quarterly, 25*(1), 107-136.

Anderson, C. (2004). The long tail. *Wired Magazine, 12*(10), October.

Blackler, F. (1995). Knowledge, knowledge work and organisations: An overview and interpretation. *Organization Studies, 16*(6), 1021-1046.

Boland, R., & Tenkasi, R. (1995). Perspective making and perspective taking in communities of knowing. *Organization Science, 6*(4), 350-372.

Brown, J., & Duguid, P. (1991). Organisational learning and communities of practice: Toward a unified view of working, learning and innovation. *Organization Science, 2*(1), 40-57.

Burstein, F., & Linger, R. (2003). Supporting post-Fordist practices—A knowledge management framework for supporting knowledge work. *Information Technology and People, 16*(3), 289-305.

Davenport, T., Jarvenpaa, S., & Beers, M. (1996). Improving knowledge work processes. *Sloan Management Review, Summer,* 53-65.

Davenport, T., & Prusak, L. (1998). *Working knowledge.* Boston, MA: Harvard Business School Press.

Ellingsen, G., & Monteiro, E. (2003). Mechanisms for producing a working knowledge: Enacting, orchestrating, and organizing. *Information and Organization, 13,* 203-229.

Gallivan, M., Eynon, J., & Rai, A. (2003). The challenge of knowledge management systems—Analyzing the dynamic processes underlying performance improvement initiatives. *Information Technology and People, 16*(3), 326-352.

Garud, R., & Kumaraswamy, A. (2005). Vicious and virtuous circles in the management of knowledge: The case of infosys technologies. *MIS Quarterly, 29*(1), 9-33.

Grant, R. (1996). Towards a knowledge-based theory of the firm. *Strategic Management Journal, 17* (Winter Special Issue), 109-122.

Grudin, J. (1987). Social evaluation of the user interface: Who does the work and who gets the benefit?. In H. Bullinger & B. Shackel (Eds.), *Proceedings of INTERACT 1987* (pp. 805-811). Elsevier Science Publishers, Amsterdam.

Grudin, J. (1988). Why CSCW applications fail: Problems in the design and evaluation of oganisational interfaces. *Proceedings of CSCW 1988* (pp. 85-93). ACM Press.

Grudin, J. (1994). Groupware and social dynamics: Eight challenges for developers. *Communications of the ACM, 37*(1), 92-105.

Hahn, J., & Subramani, M. (2000). A framework of knowledge management systems: Issues and challenges for theory and practice. *Proceedings of the International Conference on Information Systems 2000* (pp. 302-312).

Hayes, N. (2001). Boundless and bounded interactions in the knowledge work process: The role of groupware technologies. *Information and Organization, 11,* 79-101.

Hayes, N., & Walsham, G. (2001). Participation in groupware-mediated communities of practice: A socio-political analysis of knowledge working. *Information and Organization, 11,* 263-288.

Hedlund, G. (1994). A model of knowledge management and the N-form corporation. *Strategic Management Journal, 15,* 73-90.

Hendriks, P. (2001). Many rivers to cross: From ICT to knowledge management systems. *Journal of Information Technology, 16,* 57-72.

Holtshouse, D. (1998). Knowledge research issues. *California Management Review, 40*(3), 277-280.

Kankanhalli, A., Tan, B., & Wei, K-K. Contributing knowledge to electronic knowledge repositories: An empirical investigation. *MIS Quarterly, 29*(1), 113-143.

King, W. (1999). Integrating knowledge management into IS strategy. *Information Systems Management, 16*(4), 70-72.

Kock, N., & McQueen, R. (1998). Groupware support as a moderator of interdepartmental knowledge communication in process improvement groups: An action research study. *Information Systems Journal, 8,* 183-198.

Levina, N., & Vaast, E. (2005). The emergence of boundary spanning competence in practice: Implications for implementation and use of information systems. *MIS Quarterly, 29*(2), 335-363.

Lindgren, R., Henfridsson, O., & Schultze, U. (2004). Design principles for competence management systems: A synthesis of an action research study. *MIS Quarterly, 28*(3), 435-472.

Lindgren, R., & Stenmark, D. (2002). Designing competence systems: Towards interest-activated technology. *Scandinavian Journal of Information Systems, 14,* 19-35.

Lindgren, R., Stenmark, D., & Ljungberg, J. (2003). Rethinking competence systems for knowledge-based organizations. *European Journal of Information Systems, 12*(1), 18-29.

Mao, J., & Benbasat, I. (1998). Contextualized access to knowledge: Theoretical perspectives and a process-tracing study. *Information Systems Journal, 8,* 217-239.

Markus, L. (2001). Towards a theory of knowledge reuse: Types of knowledge reuse situations and factors in reuse success. *Journal of Management Information Systems, 18*(1), 57-93.

Markus, L., Majchrzak, A., & Gasser, L. (2002). A design theory for systems that support emergent knowledge processes. *MIS Quarterly, 26,* 179-212.

Miles M., & Huberman, A. (1984). *Qualitative data analysis.* A sourcebook of new methods. London, England: Sage Publications.

Mingers, J. (2001). Combining IS research methods: Towards a pluralist methodology. *Information Systems Research, 12*(3), 240-259.

Nidimolu, S., Subramani, M., & Aldrich, A. (2001). Situated learning and the situated knowledge Web: Exploring the ground beneath knowledge management. *Journal of Management Information Systems, 18*(1), 115-150.

Nonaka, I. (1994). A dynamic theory of organisational knowledge creation. *Organization Science, 5,* 14-37.

Nonaka, I., & Takeuchi, H. (1995). *The knowledge creating company: How Japanese companies create the dynamics of innovation.* New York, NY: Oxford University Press.

O'Reilly, T. (2005). *What is Web 2.0? Design patterns and business models for the next generation of software.* The O'Reilly website. Retrieved December 19, 2007, from http://oreillynet.com/pub/a/oreilly/tim/news/2005/09/30/what-is-web-20.html.

Pfeffer, J., & Sutton, R. (2000). *The knowledge-doing gap: How smart companies turn knowledge into action.* Boston, MA: Harvard Business School Press.

Poston, R., & Speier, C. (2005). Effective use of knowledge management systems: A process model of content ratings and credibility indicators. *MIS Quarterly, 29*(2), 221-244.

Robertson, M., Sørensen, C., & Swan, J. (2001). Survival of the leanest: Intensive knowledge work and groupware adaptation. *Information Technology & People, 14*(4), 334-353.

Scheepers, R., Vencitachalam, K., & Gibbs, M. (2004). Knowledge strategy in organizations: Refining the model of Hansen, Nohria and Tierney. *Journal of Strategic Information Systems, 13,* 201-222.

Schultze, U. (2000). A confessional account of an ethnography about knowledge work. *MIS Quarterly, 24*(1), 3-41.

Schultze, U., & Boland, R. (2000). Knowledge management technology and the reproduction of knowledge work practices. *Journal of Strategic Information Systems, 9,* 193-212.

Schultze, U., & Leidner, D. (2002). Studying knowledge management in information systems research: Discourses and theoretical assumptions. *MIS Quarterly, 26*(3), 213-242.

Spender, J. (1996). Organisational knowledge, learning and memory: Three concepts in search for theory. *Journal of Organisational Change Management, 9*(1), 63-78.

Stein, E., & Zwass, V. (1995). Actualizing organizational memory with information systems. *Information Systems Research, 6*(2), 85-117.

Stenmark, D. (1999) Using intranet agents to capture tacit knowledge. *Proceedings of WebNet'99* (pp. 1000-1005), October 20-25, Honolulu, HI: AACE press.

Stenmark, D. (2000). Turning tacit knowledge tangible. In *Proceedings of HICSS-33,* January 4-7, Maui, HI: IEEE press.

Stenmark, D. (2001). Leveraging tacit organisational knowledge. *Journal of Management Information Systems, 17*(3), 9-24.

Tanriverdi, H. (2005). Information technology relatedness, knowledge management capability, and performance of multi-business firms. *MIS Quarterly, 29*(2), 311-334.

Tsoukas, H. (1996). The firm as a distributed knowledge system: A constructivist approach. *Strategic Management Journal, 17,* 11-25.

Walsham, G. (1995). Interpretive case studies in IS research: Nature and method. *European Journal of Information Systems, 4,* 74-81.

Yin, R. (1994). *Case study research. Design and methods,* (2nd ed). Thousands Oaks, CA: Sage Publications.

Chapter XIV
Community of Practice:
Aligning Knowledge Work with Organisational Knowledge Strategy

Gerlinde Koeglreiter
Deakin University, Australia

Luba Torlina
Deakin University, Australia

ABSTRACT

In developing a conceptual framework of a community of practice's (CoP) role in organisational KM, this chapter summarises preliminary findings of a long-term action research study. Interventions address CoP identification, group boundaries, trust-related issues, communication, knowledge work and resources. It is argued that these aspects equally need to be addressed as part of complex multilevel organisational KM strategy. The organisational challenge is to achieve strategic alignment between knowledge activities of informally operating CoPs and formalised organisational processes. The conceptual framework aims at providing a comprehensive approach to KM strategising.

INTRODUCTION

A shift from manual work towards knowledge work has not only opened the discussion on means and technologies to manage knowledge but more recently also the underlying social and informal aspects of work. The increase of knowledge work at lower hierarchical levels calls for corresponding strategic approaches to knowledge management.

This chapter explores a comprehensive model of knowledge management (KM) strategy with an

Copyright © 2008, IGI Global, distributing in print or electronic forms without written permission of IGI Global is prohibited.

emphasis on bottom-up initiatives by CoPs. The chapter is based on a long-term action research (AR) study on a small CoP of academic staff, with a domain focus of information technology (IT). CoP member teach technically-focused subjects, but also have substantial technical hands-on expertise in those areas. The chapter discusses three interventions following the recognition of the CoP, some of the problems it has been dealing with in its work and its role and position in strategy.

Conventionally, strategy development is the task of management in the higher ranks of an organisation. As a consequence, KM strategies have commonly been initiated at the top of organisations and have been propagated downwards. Top-down KM strategies frequently focus on the explicit part of organisational knowledge that can be documented, stored, retrieved and reused. This is often implemented by the use of computer-based information systems. Top-down approach faces a number of challenges. Firstly, strategy makers are often disconnected from the day-to-day work and the knowledge workers at the lower hierarchical levels of their organisations—the very workers that are instructed to follow the KM policies and use the KM systems that are specified by the strategy makers. Secondly, the big challenge to KM is the implicit or tacit part of organisational knowledge that resides within people's heads, is socially constructed and applied in doing.

As a consequence of the above, it can be argued that, in addition to top-down KM strategy, a forum of knowledge workers needs to be developed that is not only acquiring and using knowledge to perform knowledge work, but also involved in improving how things are done in an organisation by contributing to KM strategy from the bottom up. The concept of the CoP may be one such forum. Communities of practice (CoPs) have been attributed to a number of positive influences in organisations including collaborative learning and problem-solving, innovation and organisational improvement.

This chapter studies a CoP's involvement in bottom-up KM activities and its influence on top-down KM strategy. The role of the CoP in this project is seen as a vehicle for dealing with the complexities of multilevel organisational KM.

We explore two research questions:

- What is the role of a CoP's knowledge work in organisational KM?
- What are the interactions of a CoP with other functional units and how they impact on the organisational knowledge work and KM strategy?

The chapter is structured as follows. The Literature Review section provides an overview of the extant literature with regard to the major concepts used in this chapter: organisational knowledge, community of practice, knowledge work, KM strategy, and organisational boundaries. The research approach briefly outlines methodologies applied for data collection for each of the interventions as part of the action research (AR) framework. The Results section summarises the findings of the data collection process. The discussion section describes the conceptual framework that has been built and refined upon the findings of various AR interventions. The final section is a summary of the key insights obtained.

LITERATURE REVIEW

Organisational Knowledge

Starbuck (1992) defines knowledge-intensive firms as organisations that primarily use knowledge as input and might produce knowledge as output. A substantial fraction of the personnel in knowledge-intensive firms will be highly qualified experts in their fields. According to Starbuck (1992) knowledge-intensive firms demonstrate a high degree of individuality and distinctive competencies, generating high profits and competitive advantage.

Grant (1996) identifies the primary role of the firm to be knowledge integration. Characteristics of knowledge integration are efficiency of integration with regard to utilisation of knowledge by individuals in the organisation, scope of integration including the breadth of specialised knowledge, and flexibility of integration which is about the extent to which an organisation can induce additional knowledge or reconfiguration of existing knowledge or what Tsoukas (1996) terms continuous (re)constitution of organisational knowledge through the activities undertaken within a firm.

Tsoukas (1996) argues that a firm's knowledge as emergent, incomplete, indeterminate, distributed, and collective. The character of a firm, therefore, should be appreciated as a discursive practice which involves a "sense of community, where individuals share an unarticulated background of common understandings" (Tsoukas, 1996). To emphasise the importance of social relationships in relation of knowledge flows within organisations, Kogut and Zander (1996) define the firm "as a social community specialising in the speed and efficiency in the creation and transfer of knowledge."

Nahapiet and Ghoshal (1998) suggest that creation of intellectual capital is dependent on social capital and vice versa. Three dimensions are identified, which describe the role of social capital in the creation of intellectual capital. Firstly, the structural dimension which deals with the connections between actors with regard to who actors reach and how they reach each other. Secondly, the relational dimension which looks at relations people have, such as respect and friendship and the influence on their behaviour. Finally, the cognitive dimension includes resources providing shared representations, interpretations and systems of meaning among actors.

To encourage retention of knowledge in an organisation and create a common understanding of aspects related to collaboration, knowledge sharing has become an important facet of organisational life. Collective knowledge is highly context-dependent (Tsoukas, 1996) and embedded in organisational routines (Grant, 1996).

Grant (1996) introduces the notion of architectural knowledge which is the integration or sharing of knowledge across disciplinary and organisational boundaries within the firm. Either shared language and vocabulary, such as specialist jargon (Nahapiet & Ghoshal, 1998) or the capability to communicate by simplification of expert knowledge (Hinds & Pfeffer, 2003) are crucial in these kinds of situations.

To solve issues related to motivational limitations Hinds and Pfeffer (2003) suggest reduction of competition between groups and 'informalising' the organisation by supporting communities of practice and deemphasising status hierarchies. Spender (1996a) proposes a new view of the firm as a "dynamic evolving, quasi-autonomous system of knowledge production and application."

All organisations are knowledge-based to some extent and therefore developing an environment that is conducive to knowledge development, creation, sharing, reuse under the roof of knowledge management has become a crucial aspect of organisations' survival. Organisations have come to realise that while their main objective is to produce and sell products and services in a profitable manner, staff that constitute the organisational memory system need to be supported and nurtured for the organisation to be able to adjust to the ever changing business environment and maintain competitiveness. Rather than controlling staff and continuously measuring staff performance, managers need to become leaders that support their staff in their knowledge management efforts by motivating them and leaving them with sufficient time and space to develop and reflect on their work practice, interact meaningfully, and share knowledge with others across the organisation.

Community of Practice

The concept of CoP is defined as "groups of people who share a concern, a set of problems, or a passion about a topic, and who deepen their understanding and knowledge of this area by interacting on an ongoing basis (Wenger et al., 2002, p. 4). In a learning context a CoP has been identified as a group that shares knowledge, learns together, and creates common practices (McDermott, 1999).

Community is a Web of relationships, or a self-sustaining system exhibiting "systemic" behaviour. Community is viewed not as a place, but as "a process of becoming" (Stevenson & Hamilton, 2001). Nirenberg (1995) argues that community is an enabling form of organisation encouraging "fruitful participation." Participation is a matter of individual choice. Increases in productivity and employee satisfaction are seen to be the results of community participation.

Wenger (1998) lists the following dimensions of practice as the property of a community: Firstly, mutual engagement which might evolve through complementary contributions or overlapping forms of competence. Mutual relations in CoPs are complex and might include both positive and negative attributes of relationships including disagreements, tensions, and conflicts. This mutual engagement binds participants together into a social entity. Secondly, CoPs continually re-negotiate a joint enterprise, which is their negotiated response to their situation and thus belongs to them. Finally, the CoP produces and shares a repertoire which reflects a history of mutual engagement including words, artefacts, gestures, and routines.

From these definitions it becomes obvious that CoP have a higher calling than just doing their job. Their drive is to improve their practice through continuous learning by knowledge exchange and knowledge integration in their work. Nirenberg (1995) sees the main task of the community as knowledge-based including "sensing, gathering, interpretation, processing, and re-evaluation of information, concepts and ideas."

The concept of CoPs has been associated with social network theory. Social networks are fairly loose structures (Allee, 2002) including ad hoc interactions about work-related and non-work-related issues, involving a large number of actors. CoPs on the other hand demonstrate strong coherence driven by intense engagement in a particular practice. Sharing of expertise and learning requires self-exposure to the anxiety of facing the unknown and unfamiliar and having the guts to say "I don't know" (Kofman & Senge, 1993). This requires a high level of competence-based trust, focusing on ability, and benevolence-based trust, focusing on vulnerability (Cross & Parker, 2004, p. 99).

Formal structure is determined by three major elements: boundaries (organising units such as functions, products, and geography), decision rights (the authority to influence behaviour and the allocation of resources in an organising unit), and integrating mechanisms (methods for coordinating activities across units) (Cross & Parker, 2004, p. 116). Formal structures are defined by a task, while a CoP is defined by knowledge (Allee, 2002). Like informal networks, CoP evolve naturally rather than being created. Liedtka (1999) even suggests: "They exist in the minds of their members in the connection that they have with each other and with the larger institution in which they reside."

CoPs are highly innovative and adaptable due to continuous demands of practice that force the CoP to revise its relationship to its environment (Brown & Duguid, 1991). CoP's are self-managed, accepting informal leadership, as they tend to see themselves in the same role of just members (Orr, 1990). The CoP itself, however, might be seen as taking on a leadership position in a 'heroic' sense within an organisation (Kofman & Senge, 1993).

CoPs reject controlling managers, but welcome servant leaders (Kofman & Senge, 1993; Liedtka,

1999) who encourage a continuing dialogue and participative leadership, transform the private meaning of the CoP to a public meaning, and help them reconstruct their current meaning in a way that allows them to refocus and change (Liedtka, 1999). The result is "a shared sense of meaning and purpose that flows from the personal to the organisational, rather than one that is imposed from the top down" (Liedtka, 1999).

Knowledge Work

Early literature on knowledge work tended to take a Taylorist view, separating 'thinking' and 'doing' and comparing it with the fundamentally different but more familiar, type of manual work or blue collar work (Cuvillier, 1974; Drucker, 1999; Schultze, 2000).

Task performance within knowledge work cannot be compared with the sequential prescribed performance of manual work, by claiming that knowledge work is the exact opposite. Knowledge work not only involves "deep understanding" of the body of knowledge (Iivari & Linger, 1999), used and applied, it also enriches it by the use and creation of knowledge, extension of judgements, reasoning, theories, findings, conclusions, and expert advice (Cuvillier, 1974).

Contemporary concept of knowledge work integrates doing and thinking (Burstein & Linger, 2003; 2006) and involves continuous cycle of re-use and creation of knowledge, which can be compared to a process of learning by doing. It involves a large amount of tacit knowledge (Schultze, 2000).

Because of the evolving and ever changing nature of knowledge, which has been identified to be mediated, situated, provisional, and pragmatic (Blackler, 1995), knowledge work is often performed in an iterative manner where the actor continuously refines the output by injecting new knowledge until a judgement about completeness can be made. Scarbrough (1999) identifies knowledge work as unstructured and organisationally contingent.

Knowledge work can be considered as innovative and creative and may require not only the application but also the development or adaptation of tools or processes to suit the requirements of the task at hand. The task is defined and designed by the knowledge worker (Drucker, 1999) and knowledge workers are defined by the work they do (Scarbrough, 1999). This suggests that there is not only an interplay between task performance and knowledge (Burstein & Linger, 2003; 2006), but also a societal aspect in that knowledge work is used to categorise people.

In this context knowledge work is concerned with the highest level of complexity and therefore involves complex processes and structures that are continually adjusted. It contributes to organisational knowledge management with regard to (re)use, creation, interpretation, provision of knowledge both at an individual and organisational level.

A shared body of knowledge and enthusiasm about extension of this body of knowledge is a main characteristic of a CoP.

KM Strategy

In the past decade, consultants and researchers have determined that knowledge, being an increasingly important resource in organisations, needs to be managed in a structured way to sustain or achieve competitive advantage (Spender, 1996b). Strategic management literature has initially addressed this need by emphasising that organisations need to align KM strategy with organisational goals and objectives (Jennex et al., 2003).

Two philosophies for managing knowledge have evolved. Firstly, the codification or explicit-oriented approach, which aligns strategy with information management efforts, such as embedding knowledge in documents, which can be stored and reused. This approach is highly information-systems-dependent. Secondly, the personalisation strategy or tacit-oriented KM style emphasises the human and hence more complex part of tacit or implicit knowledge. Attempts to externalise and transfer this type of knowledge are based on communication strategies, both face-to-face and technology supported, by facilitating informal networks (Hansen et al., 1999; Choi & Lee, 2003).

Wilson et al. (2003) suggest that both strategies should be supported within the same firm to cater for the complex and dynamic nature of organisations. In their research, the codification strategy is identified as an explicit KM strategy that is heavily based on infrastructure and focuses on knowledge stocks, while the personalisation approach is perceived as an emergent KM strategy that is based on tacit knowledge and social relations and focuses on knowledge flows (Wilson et al., 2003).

From the above, it emerges that there are essentially two approaches to KM: one that focuses on the tangible part of knowledge that can be externalised, stored, transferred, and is often seen as an organisational asset (Teece, 1998). Secondly, a knowledge strategy that considers internalised, tacit, embrained, and encultured knowledge (Blackler, 1995), suggesting human-to-human interaction to facilitate the flow of knowledge across an organisation.

Traditionally, organisations tend to focus on the tangible part of knowledge, introducing information and communication systems to capture and document knowledge, even though these efforts might never have been explicitly termed a 'KM strategy' or aligned with organisational strategy. In recent years, however, KM researchers have realised that human KM is the challenge, which has revived the notion of social networks and in more specific terms CoPs.

Consistent with these two KM strategies, two philosophies have emerged: top-down KM, which is advocated and introduced by higher management levels in the organisation, and bottom-up KM which appears to happen on an individual

and group level lower in the hierarchy of an organisation, on a day-to-day basis.

Important questions discussed in the literature are: how these two types of knowledge strategies can be aligned; and how they can work together effectively in order to inform knowledge work on all organisational levels. Galliers' (2004) approach provides a framework for information systems strategising, where the emergent exploration strategy from bottom-up meets the deliberate exploitation strategy in a socio-technical environment based on the information infrastructure strategy, which in turn interacts with a collaborative business strategy. In his doughnut model of knowledge management, Wenger (2004) points out that "the development of Communities of Practice is a bottom-up process as well as a top-down one." While enthusiasm and initiative is built by members from the bottom-up, this should be supported by encouragement from the higher levels of the organisation. Researchers and consultants have termed this type of support nurturing, cultivating, or leveraging CoPs (Ward, 2000; Wenger et al., 2002; Saint-Onge & Wallace, 2003).

In practice these ideas often end up as simple recipes for creating and 'using' CoPs for competitive advantage. However, this approach frequently omits the subtleties of individuals having different work practice, social choices of employees when they decide who to interact with in the workplace for various reasons. This chapter emphasises social aspects of effective knowledge work at CoP level, showing that a CoP is not just a group of experts in a specific area that build a community, but individuals who have a history with each other, share a like-mindedness, trust each other and just get along really well (Wenger, 1998a; Koeglreiter et al., 2006). These attributes cannot be packed into recipes that top-managers can implement as a knowledge management strategy. Instead, managers need to be open to recognise an opportunity when it comes along.

While in previous sections the CoP, its characteristics and knowledge work were discussed, in this section and further we are looking into its interaction with the wider organisation. Essential for this is a requirement to understand the notion and characteristics of organisational 'boundaries'. Wenger (1998b, p. 103) identifies a number of aspects of organisational boundaries, including CoP identification through creating group boundaries, the need for spanning those boundaries, and the notion of creating CoP history through articulation with the rest of the world.

Boundaries

Organisational boundaries help to create group identities, focus on specific organisational activities, make procedures more effective and develop deeper knowledge. However, organisational boundaries may create barriers to information flows, limit decision-making capacity, and hinder innovation.

Boundaries within organisations may be categorised as social boundaries, information boundaries, structural boundaries, communication boundaries. *Social boundaries* are based on identification theory (Gefen & Ridings, 2003), which involves shared values and the perception of belonging. *Information boundaries* in organisations apply to information flows between hierarchical levels and organisational structures with regard to opportunities for creating new organisational knowledge (Brown, 1966). *Structural boundaries* refer to physical and geographic aspects, organisational design, and procedures (Brown, 1966) and their impact on information sharing, accessibility, and decision-making capacity. And finally *communication boundaries* relate to syntactic aspects (differences in language or jargon) and semantic aspects (differences in thought worlds) (Carlile, 2002).

Boundary spanning then looks at how these boundaries can be overcome and the building of knowledge interfaces. Knowledge interfaces determine how information flows and how the activities of different organisational entities are linked in organisational action, who can access knowledge, and how it is accessed, shared and acted upon. Organisational knowledge can, therefore, be viewed in terms of clusters of knowledge workers with their collective knowledge and group boundaries, and communication with other collective knowledge through boundary interfaces, boundary objects and boundary actors.

Boundary spanning activities facilitate this kind of communication and information flow and may occur on a formal level involving individuals on higher hierarchical levels (Aldrich & Herker, 1977) or informal communication and social networking (Tushman & Scanlan, 1981; Manev & Stevenson, 2001).

Boundary spanning roles are the link between the environment and the organisation. Individuals in boundary spanning roles must be strongly linked internally and externally to gather and disseminate information.

Boundary objects are objects that are shared and shareable across different problem-solving contexts. Categories of boundary objects include repositories, standardised forms and methods, objects or models (simple or complex representations), and maps of boundaries that represent the dependencies and boundaries that exist between different groups (Carlile, 2002).

The challenge of boundary spanning is to build a common understanding and language. To acquire practice-specific knowledge and learn from each other, the parties will need to be willing to alter their knowledge and capable to transform the knowledge of the other party (Carlile, 2002).

Because KM becomes more and more 'on-demand', KM activities require "the rapid deployment of relevant tools and systems for ad hoc, intensive and inter-organizational collaborations" (Tsui, 2005, p. 4). In turn, these call for more flexible and informal approaches, such as direct links to experts across organisational boundaries (Koeglreiter et al., 2008, forthcoming-a).

RESEARCH APPROACH

The research reported in this chapter is part of a larger action research (AR) project investigating the interaction between educational CoP and the wider organisation in a tertiary education environment. The study focuses on a group of tertiary educators who deliver undergraduate programs in the area of information systems implementation in business.

AR is considered as a framework aiming at a contribution to practical concerns resolving an immediate problem situation and the contribution to the goals of social science by joint collaboration within a mutually agreed ethical framework (Rapoport, 1970). AR is conducted in cycles of interventions, where outcomes examined in one cycle are the input to the next cycle. A cycle is structured into problem diagnosis, action planning, action taking, reflection, and specifying learning (Baskerville, 1999).

A number of interventions were conducted as part of the current AR project. These interventions and their outcomes will be discussed below.

Identification of the CoP

Informal conversations with the potential research subjects revealed that individuals were working on interesting technical teaching projects. A kick-off workshop was organised in order to declare the group intentions and to test self-awareness of a group as a CoP. The workshop activities included presentations made by a number of staff aiming at identifying group mutual interests and to evoke interaction with the rest of the staff. Follow-up interviews exploring questions of participation, goals of the CoP as well as extension of membership were conducted.

CoP Knowledge Work

In order to identify a priority project that would be of interest to all CoP members, an initiation

session was conducted. The methods utilised were brainstorming combined with a problem-solving process (Dwyer, 2005). The briefing document outlining areas of interest discussed in the CoP identification process was compiled. The participants discussed all items in the briefing document and other ideas that had emerged during the brainstorming session, and came to a consensus on concentrating on the university's strategic goal of modernising study material introducing electronic study guides.

The educational CD project became a centre point of the following intervention. A workshop on education technologies was conducted. A number of staff members who had implemented educational CDs or were known to have used other teaching technologies were asked to give a presentation. CoP members and invited experts from the other areas of the university shared their experience of using new technologies, as well as implementation and support issues. The presentations were followed by a question-and-answer session and brief discussion. A feedback session was conducted after the workshop to capture CoP immediate reaction. Individual semi-structured follow-up interviews with the participating CoP members were conducted shortly after the workshop. These interviews focussed on aspects of knowledge work and the role of the CoP in their department and wider organisation.

Boundary Spanning Intervention

Interviews held in a previous intervention had revealed that the university's central IT department (ITSD) was mentioned in a number of contexts impacting the CoP. The range of issues raised included lack of flexibility and poor communication, lack of response to urgent teaching needs and difficulties with receiving expert advice, and too rigid technical environment. To address this problem, the researchers decided to conduct a single intense intervention in the form of a face-to-face workshop involving members of the CoP and a representative of ITSD followed by one-on-one semi-structured interviews and discussions with the participants within several weeks of the workshop. At the workshop, each of these parties was given the opportunity to explain their role, and to refer to the challenges they encountered. Following these presentations, an open forum was conducted, where current and ongoing issues were discussed and a list of action points was constructed and distributed in a meeting summary. Approximately 18 months later, a series of follow-up interviews with the workshop participants took place to establish whether the situation had changed, in particular with reference to the major action points and issues recorded in the meeting summary that had been committed to as an outcome of the intervention. The interviews were focussing on issues and potential solutions of communication across organisational boundaries.

STUDY RESULTS

This section summarises the results of three interventions discussed in previous section. The findings include the characteristics of the informal group and the issues that impact, both positively and negatively, on the knowledge work of the CoP, as well as on the potential of this CoP to contribute to organisational knowledge management. Some of these issues have been discussed in more details in previous publications (Koeglreiter et al., 2005; 2006; 2008, forthcoming-a; 2008, forthcoming-b). They are summarised here in order to provide a context for new findings also reported in this section.

Identification of the CoP

An existing group was identified and its existence as a CoP was confirmed according to the characteristics by Wenger (1998b, p. 73) defining a CoP as,

a joint enterprise which is understood and continually renegotiated by its members. The group functions with mutual engagement that binds members together into a social entity, and the group produces a shared repertoire of communal resources (Wenger, 1998b).

Individuals identified themselves as belonging to a group interested in programming, Web technology, and systems implementation. The wider organisations were able to recognise this group with the above features. The *joint enterprise* was considered rather fluid and informal including knowledge sharing, ad hoc problem-solving and keeping abreast of new technology. *Renegotiation* was recognised when welcoming specific potential members with relevant expert knowledge to the group. Members rejected the concept of establishing certain roles and setting specific goals. The importance of equality and informality was emphasised. While individual CoP members might initiate certain activities, temporarily exhibiting thought leadership, all CoP members are considered on an equal level with no appointed leaders or other formal roles. *Social interaction* was maintained through frequent informal meetings as well as coffee and lunch rounds at which occasions, matters related to work were discussed. The shared understanding of what individuals' work and interests were as well as the shared experience of mutual projects can be seen as a *shared repertoire of communal resources*. Other potential resources identified include a meeting space, a technical library, a Web-based resources repository, and a technical "playroom."

Group Composition and Boundaries

Group boundaries were considered a sensitive matter and concerns with regard to impact on knowledge work had their origin in organisational politics and balance of power issues within the group.

Participants were able to identify specific organisational issues—reasons why "outsiders" might not be welcome. This includes a perception of as competition with other schools/departments and a subsequent conflict of interest may arise, if staff from those other schools/departments were to join the CoP. Further concerns were expressed with regard to relevance of the CoP's focus to other departments.

Where membership might go to people in positions of authority who might hold what is perceived as a position of political strength, the CoP members would feel constrained or inhibited to speak openly, so impacting on group dynamics. Myers and Young (1997) state that "everyone has an agenda" and what is emerging in the interviews is a concern that organisationally higher ranked members might pursue their own agendas within the CoP.

The emphasis on informality with regard to openness in communication, rejection of power and politics, equality, and relevance implies protective behaviour of individuals to ensure the preservation of the effectiveness of their support network. Independence of opinion and achieving consensus plays an important role in knowledge work of the CoP.

Bottom-up KM is manifested in a form of information quality assurance. Work-related information passed by group members to higher organisational management or other CoP-outsiders goes through a process of testing for usefulness, correctness and completeness with peers. As such, only what might be termed 'verified knowledge' passes to other areas of the organisation.

Boundary Spanning

Issues surrounding boundaries to other organisational areas go beyond the group's control and might require more effort to address. The detailed discussion of boundary issues can be found in (Koeglreiter et al., 2008, forthcoming-a; 2008, forthcoming-b).

The study found that boundary spanning between a CoP and the wider organisation is multidimensional, because of the formal structures that need to be considered. Boundary spanning and the inherent process of trust-building is an ongoing and time-consuming effort. Both CoP and other parties involved need to consciously appreciate and address issues of cultural difference as well as mutual understanding of the difficulties they may encounter. A difference in organisational culture and thought worlds accompanied by poor communication appeared to be the major issue.

This particular study looked at the boundaries between the CoP and central IT department. Even though both were sharing similar domain knowledge, significant differences in organisational culture were encountered. For example, predefined highly formalised procedures within the hierarchically organised IT department appeared to become a serious obstacle to establishing direct expert-to-expert links between CoP and ITSD specialists. On the other hand, the appointment of designated customer relationship managers was not effective in their boundary spanning roles because of poor communications. Difficulties in establishing informal expert networks have led to further communication problems, lack of access to specialist knowledge, distortion of information, and delays in delivering customised knowledge solutions.

While the appointment of designated boundary spanning staff is a first necessary step, a genuine effort also means the facilitation of social networks and direct links to experts as required. Finally, management could play a role to support the CoP in specific aspects in overcoming formal boundaries, particularly where the other party accepts a hierarchical management style.

The Role of Trust

The CoP provides a safe environment where like-minded individuals feel comfortable in sharing their expertise, ideas, and possibly some aspects of their personal lives. Lesser and Storck (2001) have linked this kind of social capital to business outcomes, and insist that trust relationships are essential for CoPs to function. This kind of trust is based on benevolence, where members of a CoP do not feel threatened or vulnerable when asking a question of their CoP colleagues, and so can learn and grow in the CoP environment (Cross & Parker, 2004).

Trust is a pre-requisite for a CoP to function well internally, as well as interacting with other areas of the organisation. While CoP members had initially rejected outsiders, specific organisation members were later identified, who might be accepted at least on a neutral level, because they had something useful and new to contribute (Koeglreiter et al., 2006). Extending membership is based on trustworthiness of the prospective member.

An absence of trust not only inhibits the growth of the group and its capacity to enter new knowledge terrain, but also stops knowledge flowing to the rest of the organisation on all hierarchical levels. This might result in duplicating efforts (different departments doing the same thing). The interviews confirmed that this CoP enacts many of the ten actions for building and maintaining trust in relationships as suggested by Cross and Parker (2004): They act with discretion; they match words and deeds and avoid hidden agenda; they communicate often and well; they have established and continually renegotiate a shared vision and language; they indicate knowledge domain boundaries and admit failures or what they don't know; and they have non-work-related commonalities—to name just a few.

Facilitating Communication

Electronic communication has emerged as an important factor in the operation of coherent CoPs in the contemporary organisation (Eales, 2003; Marshall et al., 2000; Sharp, 1997). Communities, which are focused upon shared technical expertise, can be supported by electronic means such as Internet newsgroups, digital libraries, and virtual forums (McLure Wasko & Faraj, 2000; Torlina & Lichtenstein, 2004) and video- or audio-conferencing and computer-supported communityware (CSCW) (van den Hooff et al., 2003).

While information technologies can be used successfully to overcome the problem of distance communication and save on travel costs, the importance and richness of face-to-face interaction should not be overlooked.

Face-to-face interaction is essential to this CoP. It is crucial for building and maintaining group coherence. The study revealed a number of issues which influence participation and impact on the CoP knowledge work. It was found that co-located CoP members were communicating more frequently, while the member located on a remote campus was consulted on more formal occasions, missing out on social interaction. This issue might be seen, in some sense, as a form of inequality of membership within the CoP, where modern communication technology is not able to overcome the social detachment of a remote CoP member. The other conditions limiting equal participation are travel costs, time constraints, and reduced opportunity for socialising due to formal meetings. On the positive side, it was noticed that a person that is "not around all the time," inject refreshing interactions and view points in the community (Koeglreiter et al., 2006).

Shared Resources

A number of issues emerged when CoP members were asked about communal resources (Koeglreiter et al., 2006). The notion of resources covered a number of things, including sources of knowledge, meeting rooms, hardware, and software to facilitate learning and experimentation. With regard to sources of knowledge, Teigland (2000) divides sources into organisation-internal and -external sources and tacit and codified sources.

The CoP under investigation used all aspects of internal and external sources. Consistent with classical top-down technology-driven approaches to KM, individuals had access to formal documentation, procedures and guidelines. Professional training offered by the organisation cannot cover the specialised knowledge needs of this CoP; therefore members would benefit from collaborative learning support. Those efforts might then be facilitated by electronic community memory support systems, such as collaborative tools for document management or tools to support emergent, dynamic, exploratory interpretation, as suggested by Marshall et al. (2000). When the idea of a central digital repository was rejected by school management, the CoP realised that a formal proposal might be the way to receive recognition and support.

The nature of academic work requires access to special technologies for conducting research and preparing teaching curricula. The CoP raised concerns about the centrally managed computer desktop and network infrastructure, which was perceived as rigid and restrictive. This lack of autonomy had resulted in frustration and prompted individuals to work around by setting up their own individual test environments. To enhance collaboration the idea of a technical 'playroom' managed by the CoP was brought up.

A further major communal resource is the discourse of the CoP sharing their knowledge, providing feedback to specific problems or validation of ideas as well as the provision of existing material for adaptation and reuse.

Strategic Alignment

Top-down KM implements and enforces the alignment of individual knowledge workers with strategic goals of the organisation. CoPs are often invisible to the strategy-making levels of the organisation due to the informal nature of the CoP. Imposing strategic alignment on a CoP would mean formalising the group. The formalised initiative might have been rejected by the group due to frequently expressed importance of informality. Therefore, like many other facets of the CoP's operation, strategic alignment would have to take place as a bottom-up initiative.

This study revealed that CoPs must be able to recognise a benefit for individuals and the group to align with business priorities. Several aspects of strategic alignment emerged in the interviews including recognition by management or the wider organisation, receiving support and resources for knowledge work, contribution to the shared practice, and increasing group visibility and relevance to the organisation.

Recognition

The CoP come to realise that group visibility and recognition of their activities by other staff and management might be critical for success. As outlined in the shared resources section above, the CoP was trying to receive funds to set up a technical system to support knowledge sharing within the group and possibly later across the School. The CoP had come to realise that a formal more structured proposal outlining costs and benefits might have assisted in convincing management of the importance of the system. A formal proposal might also include the involvement of staff of the wider School.

As mentioned earlier, management might be able to assist in regard to boundary conflicts in an escalation process.

Contribution to Shared Practice

Contribution to shared practice, aligned with one of the strategic directions, allowed the CoP to apply their skills and acquire new skills. When the desire of acquiring specific skills with regard to the creation of multimedia material for the educational CDs was expressed, management reacted quickly and made funds available for one of the CoP members to attend a training course.

This was followed by a knowledge sharing event involving the rest of the CoP and staff of the wider School. Not only had the group extended its shared knowledge and practice, but the CoP also became more visible and recognised to the wider organisation as experts in that particular area.

Relevance to the Organisation

For a CoP to contribute to current practice, relevance of the current undertakings has to be questioned and re-negotiated from time to time. At around the time when the information systems teaching profession in Australia started facing difficulties with many IS schools closing down,

management suggested a change of strategy to ensure the survival of the school. The priority was placed on high-volume subjects. Because of their understanding, commitment, and affection to the school, the CoP showed high flexibility in adjusting their practice and re-training. The strategic alignment of CoP with business objectives might be a joint decision of the group or individuals initiating the change with others following. Not all CoP members might be involved in this re-alignment process, which might trigger the emergence of sub-groups or a change of membership. Re-alignment might also change the focus of the group either temporarily or permanently.

Figure 1. The role of CoPs in organisational knowledge management (adapted from Koeglreiter et al., 2006)

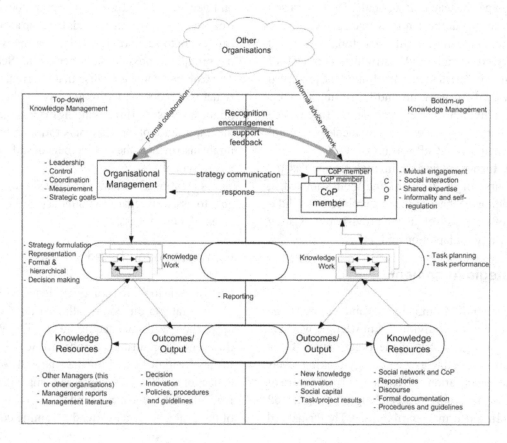

Further observations relevant to strategic alignment of CoPs emerged as follows:

- Strategic alignment combined with domain interest of the CoP attracts a high level of enthusiasm where CoP members are prepared to invest private time to follow through with the project.
- CoPs' strategic activities are not always recognised by management and sometimes formalisation is required to receive management attention and resources.

DISCUSSION

Conceptual Framework

The conceptual framework described in this section came about in a three-fold process. Firstly, initial work on the framework emerged in adapting an existing model of knowledge work in virtual groups (Torlina & Lichtenstein, 2004). In an initial step, the adaptation was linked to the concept of CoP, and based on further work with KM, and organisational science literature. Secondly, the analysis of collected data informed the further development of a framework (Koeglreiter et al., 2006). In subsequent interventions, some of the constructs have been tested further (Koeglreiter et al., 2008, forthcoming-a; 2008, forthcoming-b). Thirdly, additional work on the conceptual side has led to the refined framework depicted in Figure 1. Further work on testing the remaining constructs and links in the framework is in progress.

The conceptual framework aims at the alignment of informal (bottom-up) with formal (top-down) KM practices offering a comprehensive approach to organisational KM strategy. This section provides a description of the individual components of the framework as well as their interplay.

Other Organisations

Other organisations are formal entities that are not part of the top-down/bottom-up KM structure. This could be external companies or bodies or other departments of the same organisation. Organisational management maintains formal relationships with other organisations while the informal nature of the CoP seeks informal connections such as advice networks with the same or other organisations. A cloud shape was consciously chosen representing the 'other organisations' component, to indicate entities that are not controlled by the organisation.

Because of the CoP's preference to internally operate on an informal level, CoP members also seek direct informal connections to experts of their knowledge domain area in other functional units of the organisation in order to receive specialist advice. Organisational management formally representing functional units needs to maintain formal relationships and collaboration with other organisational units and entities external to the organisation. For both management maintaining formal links and CoPs maintaining informal links to external organisations, it can be a challenge to span boundaries and align different organisational cultures and jargons to achieve a collaborative environment.

Organisational Management

Organisational management is tasked with leadership, control, coordination, measurement (Holsapple & Joshi, 2000), and the formulation and implementation of strategic goals on all organisational levels. Management formally represents the organisation to the outside world and makes strategic and financial decisions.

Due to the high level of risk and responsibility involved, management's knowledge work is considered as high level. The researchers acknowledge that management might be part of a CoP inside or outside the organisation, but the intention of this framework is to visualise the formal role of management in the organisation, hence the separation of management representing top-down KM strategy and CoP representing bottom-up KM strategy.

The difference of knowledge work is not only determined by the formally assigned tasks and responsibilities and associated output, but also the resources utilised. Management has got the power to decide over financial and human resources, while resource decisions on CoP level are associated with decisions about task performance, such as the choice of methods and tools.

Top-down KM suggests a classic hierarchical structure with management determining and communicating knowledge strategy to individuals on lower levels of the organisation. The study found that in knowledge-intensive organisations, such as universities, individual knowledge workers and CoPs require a high level of autonomy to perform academic work. Therefore, this framework places management and the CoP on an equal level, even though hierarchical structures in the organisation might be different. The CoP under study responded well to a participative leadership style employed by some management staff.

Community of Practice

This model considers individual as well as group identity. Organisational members perform tasks individually and are part of formal teams. At the same time, they form a CoP engaging in the informal world of knowledge sharing, and problem-solving, re-interpreting the formal organisation to their needs. Group coherence is established through trust relationships and a strong focus on shared expertise with a goal of jointly improving their practice is exercised. This informal layer of knowledge work forms a bottom-up approach to KM.

The model signifies a formal relationship between individual CoP members and management through strategy implementation by management and response by the individuals. Formal responses include alignment, rejection, or passiveness.

The self-regulated CoP complements individual relationships by group responses such as feedback to management on usefulness of strategies or simply by adapting strategy to their needs. The double arrow in the model therefore depicts the informal relationship between management and the CoP. In an ideal organisation, management would recognise, encourage, and support the CoP's efforts allowing the CoP to actively contribute to top-down strategy by providing grass-roots feedback to management, so enabling continuous improvement of KM strategy and informed decision-making.

The study found that there can also be formal group responses, which were exhibited through a change of focus of the CoP when aligning with changed strategy. This response has to be initiated by the CoP rather than imposed from the top down. Furthermore, for a CoP to align with strategy, a benefit to the group must be recognisable as discussed in the Study Results section.

Knowledge Work

Knowledge work is the purpose of individuals in the organisation and it applies practice that is shared by the CoP.

This research adopts the task-based model of knowledge work (see Figure 2) by Burstein and Linger (2002). Knowledge work is divided into a pragmatic layer (doing) which is concerned with the work practice and the execution of the task, and a conceptual layer (thinking) which takes a more abstract perspective, focusing on two conceptual components associated with the task, that is structure and process.

In the context of knowledge work, task is defined as:

Figure 2. A task based model of work (Aarons et al., 2005; Aarons et al., 2006; Burstein & Linger, 2002, 2003, 2006)

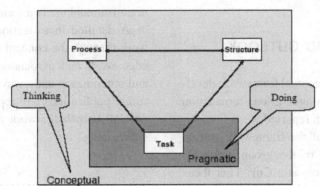

...a substantially invariant organisational activity with outcomes that include tangible outputs that are central to the organisation's viability and the internal outcomes that are potential drivers of organisational change (Burstein & Linger, 2006).

Structure is the understanding of what concepts are involved in performing the task. It is presented as a graph and refers to a model of the structure of the actor's knowledge about the task, interdependency, involvement of any other individuals or groups as well as organisational policies or politics to be taken into consideration (Burstein & Linger, 2006).

Process is the understanding *how* these concepts need to be applied. Process refers to a model of the actor's knowledge of the process required to perform the task, determination of which tools and methods are suitable to achieve the set objective (Burstein & Linger, 2006).

A detailed investigation of the CoP's task performance is in progress and a future publication is anticipated. The conceptual and pragmatic layers of CoP knowledge work will be examined. While task execution appears to happen on an individual level and in formal teams, the conceptual considerations of improving practice are to a large extent group-based.

Knowledge Resources, Output and Outcomes

Like any other type of work, knowledge work basically requires resources as input and creates outputs. A *knowledge resource* used by management might differ from the individual's knowledge resource because strategy-making requires knowledge of the wider organisation, financial situation, political tendencies and industry trends, while the individual bottom-level knowledge worker utilises knowledge resources supporting more specialised work.

Output is the defined result of the task and in most cases considered tangible and measurable.

Outcomes are intangible results that might not contribute directly to task performance, but benefit the worker either for future work or personally. This might include experience of performing the task and related knowledge acquired and created, social capital, a sense of self-fulfilment, and motivational factors.

Outputs and outcomes might feed back as resources for future work. Furthermore, outcomes and outputs of knowledge work performed by management and CoP members may lead to joint outputs or outcomes. On the other hand, joint tasks may produce different outcomes for the different parties. A detailed investigation into synergy of outcomes and outputs produced by the CoP and management is in progress.

CONCLUSION AND OUTLOOK

In this chapter, the conceptual framework developed in the course of an ongoing, long-term action research study has been reported.

The development of the framework started from internal aspects of the group revolving around the identification as a CoP. This focus then became extended to the wider organisation and associated matters such as organisational and group boundaries, the role of trust, communication, and resources.

Reflecting upon the reported results, a model of the role of a CoP in organisational knowledge management (KM) emerged, linking top-down and bottom-up KM strategies. Top-down KM reflects the formal organisational knowledge processes, while bottom-up KM is associated with informal facets of knowledge work performance by a CoP. Formalisation may be initiated by the CoP to receive management attention, encouragement and support, and to progress alignment of bottom-up and top-down KM initiatives.

Work towards resolution of boundary conflicts requires commitment and ongoing communication. Trust relationships are the basis of social coherence for this CoP internally and beyond the group and this is why the extension of membership and boundary spanning to other areas were cautiously approached.

The acquisition of resources and strategic alignment are strongly intertwined. Strategic alignment is initiated from the bottom-up and where management recognises benefits to the organisation the CoP would receive support. However, potential benefits to the CoP and to the wider organisation need to be made explicit to management.

The research completed has tested components of the conceptual framework, in the action research

mode, with particular focus of the operations of a CoP and its relation to other organisations and organisational management.

A detailed investigation of CoP knowledge work through the concept of task-based knowledge work and associated aspects of outputs and outcomes is underway. It is anticipated that future publications will report relevant research on CoP knowledge work and their role in KM strategising.

ACKNOWLEDGMENT

Helpful discussions with Associate Professor Frada Burstein (Monash University, Melbourne, Australia) and Professor Ross Smith (RMIT University, Melbourne, Australia), are gratefully acknowledged.

REFERENCES

Aarons, J., Burstein, F., & Linger, H. (2005). *What is the task?—Applying the task-based KM framework to weather forecasting.* Paper presented at the Australian Conference for Knowledge Management and Intelligent Decision Support (pp. 85-99), Novotel, Melbourne.

Aarons, J., Linger, H., & Burstein, F. (2006). *Supporting organisational knowledge work: Integrating thinking and doing in task-based support.* Paper presented at the International Conference on Organisational Learning, Knowledge and Capabilities, University of Warwick, UK.

Aldrich, H., & Herker, D. (1977). Boundary spanning roles and organization structure. *Academy of Management Review, 2*(2), 217-230.

Allee, V. (2002). Knowledge networks and communities of practice. *OD Practitioner, 32*(4).

Baskerville, R. (1999). Investigating information systems with action research. *Communications of the Association for Information Systems, 2,* 1-16.

Blackler, F. (1995). Knowledge, knowledge work and organizations: An overview and interpretation. *Organization Studies, 16*(6), 1020-1046.

Brown, J., & Duguid, P. (1991). Organizational learning and communities-of-practice: Toward a unified view of working, learning, and innovating. *Organization Science, 2*(1), 40-57.

Brown, W. (1966). Systems, boundaries, and information flow. *Academy of Management Journal, 9*(4), 318-327.

Burstein, F., & Linger, H. (2002). *A task-based framework for supporting knowledge work practices.* Paper presented at the 3rd European Conference on Knowledge Management (ECKM2002) (pp. 100-112), Trinity College Dublin, Ireland.

Burstein, F., & Linger, H. (2003). Supporting post-Fordist work practices: A knowledge management framework for supporting knowledge work. *Information Technology & People, 16*(3), 289-305.

Burstein, F., & Linger, H. (2006). Task-based knowledge management approach. In: D. Schwartz (Ed.), *Encyclopaedia of knowledge management.* Hershey, PA: Idea Publishing.

Carlile, P. (2002). A pragmatic view of knowledge and boundaries: Boundary objects in new product development. *Organization Science, 13*(4), 442-455.

Choi, B., & Lee, H. (2003). An empirical investigation of KM styles and their effect on corporate performance. *Information & Management, 40*(5), 403-417.

Cross, R., & Parker, A. (2004). *The hidden power of social networks: Understanding how work really gets done in organizations.* Boston, MA: Harvard Business School Press.

Cuvillier, R. (1974). Intellectual workers and their work in social theory and practice. *International Labour Review, 109*(4), 291-317.

Drucker, P. (1999). Knowledge-worker productivity: The biggest challenge. *California Management Review, 41*(2), 79-94.

Dwyer, J. (2005). *Communication in business: Strategies and skills,* 3rd ed. Prentice Hall.

Eales, J. (2003). Supporting informal communities of practice within organizations. In: M. Ackerman, V. Pipek, & V. Wulf (Eds.), *Sharing expertise - Beyond knowledge management* (pp. 275-297). Cambridge, MA: MIT Press.

Galliers, R. (2004). Reflections on information systems strategizing. In: Avgerou, C. Ciborra & Land (Eds.), *The social study of information and communication technology* (pp. 231-262). Oxford: Oxford University Press.

Gefen, D., & Ridings, C. (2003). IT acceptance: Managing user - IT group boundaries. *SIGMIS Database, 34*(3), 25-40.

Grant, R. (1996). Prospering in dynamically-competitive environments: Organizational capability as knowledge integration. *Organization Science, 7*(4), 375-387.

Hansen, M., Nohria, N., & Tierney, T. (1999). What's your strategy for managing knowledge?. *Harvard Business Review, 77*(2), 106.

Hinds, P., & Pfeffer, J. (2003). Why organizations don't "know what they know": Cognitive and motivational factors affecting the transfer of expertise. In: M. Ackerman, V. Pipek, & V. Wulf (Eds.), *Sharing expertis—Beyond knowledge management* (pp. 3-25). Cambridge, MA: MIT Press.

Holsapple, C., & Joshi, K. (2000). An investigation of factors that influence the management of knowledge in organizations. *The Journal of Strategic Information Systems, 9*(2-3), 235-261.

Iivari, J., & Linger, H. (1999). *Knowledge work as collaborative work: A situated activity theory view.* Paper presented at the 32nd Hawaii International Conference on System Sciences (HICSS) (pp. 1-9), Hawaii.

Jennex, M., Olfman, L., & Addo, T. (2003). *The Need for an Organizational Knowledge Management Strategy.* Paper presented at the 36th Hawaii International Conference on System Sciences (HICSS) (p. 9), Hawaii.

Koeglreiter, G., Smith, R., & Torlina, L. (2005). *Identification of an emerging community of practice in a knowledge workplace.* Paper presented at the Australian Conference for Knowledge Management and Intelligent Decision Support (pp. 197-208), Novotel, Melbourne.

Koeglreiter, G., Smith, R., & Torlina, L. (2006). The role of informal groups in organisational knowledge work: Understanding an emerging community of practice. *International Journal of Knowledge Management, 2*(1), 6-23.

Koeglreiter, G., Smith, R., & Torlina, L. (2008, forthcoming-a). *Knowledge interfaces: An informal CoP faced with formal boundaries.* Paper presented at the Australian Conference for Knowledge Management and Intelligent Decision Support, Monash University, Melbourne, Australia.

Koeglreiter, G., Smith, R., & Torlina, L. (2008, forthcoming-b). Reaching beyond the "boundaries": Communities of practice and boundaries in tertiary education. In C. Kimble & P. Hildreth (Eds.), *Communities of practice: Creating learning environments for educators.* Information Age Publishing.

Kofman, F., & Senge, P. (1993). Communities of commitment: The heart of learning organizations. *Organizational Dynamics, 22*(2), 4-23.

Kogut, B., & Zander, U. (1996). What firms do? Coordination, identity and learning. *Organization Science, 7,* 502-518.

Lesser, E., & Storck, J. (2001). Communities of practice and organizational performance. *IBM Systems Journal, 40*(4), 831-845.

Liedtka, J. (1999). Linking competitive advantage with communities of practice. *Journal of Management Inquiry, 8*(1), 5-16.

Manev, I., & Stevenson, W. (2001). Balancing ties: Boundary spanning and influence in the organization's extended network of communication. *Journal of Business Communication, 38*(2), 183-205.

Marshall, C., Shipman III, F., & McCall, R. (2000). Making large-scale information resources serve communities of practice. In E. Lesser, M. Fontaine, & J. Slusher (Eds.), *Knowledge and communities* (pp. 225-247). Boston, MA: Butterworth Heinemann.

McDermott, R. (1999). Learning across teams: How to build communities of practice in team organizations. *Knowledge Management Review, 2*(2), 32-36.

McLure Wasko, M., & Faraj, S. (2000). "It is what one does": Why people participate and help others in electronic communities of practice. *The Journal of Strategic Information Systems, 9*(2-3), 155-173.

Myers, M., & Young, L. (1997). Hidden agendas, power and managerial assumptions in information systems development—An ethnographic study. *Information, Technology, and People, 10,* 224-240.

Nahapiet, J., & Ghoshal, S. (1998). Social capital, intellectual capital, and the organizational advantage. *Academy of Management Review, 23*(2), 242.

Nirenberg, J. (1995). From team building to community building. *National Productivity Review,* 51-62.

Orr, J. (1990). Sharing knowledge, celebrating identity: Community memory in a service culture. In: D. Middleton & D. Edwards (Eds.), *Collective remembering* (pp. 168-189). London: Sage.

Rapoport, R. (1970). Three dilemmas in action research. *Human Relations, 23*(6), 499-513.

Saint-Onge, H., & Wallace, D. (2003). *Leveraging communities of practice for strategic advantage.* Boston, MA: Butterworth Heinemann.

Scarbrough, H. (1999). Knowledge as work: Conflicts in the management of knowledge workers. *Technology Analysis and Strategic Management, 11*(1), 5-16.

Schultze, U. (2000). A confessional account of an ethnography about knowledge work. *MIS Quarterly, 24*(1), 3-41.

Sharp, J. (1997). *Key hypotheses in supporting communities of practice.* Retrieved 14/10/04, 2003, from http://www.tfriend.com/hypothesis.html

Spender, J. (1996a). Making knowledge the basis of a dynamic theory of the firm. *Strategic Management Journal, 17*(Special Issue: Knowledge and the Firm), 45-62.

Spender, J. (1996b). Organizational knowledge, learning and memory: Three concepts in search of a theory. *Journal of Organizational Change Management, 9*(1), 63-78.

Starbuck, W. (1992). Learning by knowledge intensive firms. *Journal of Management Studies, 29*(6), 713-740.

Stevenson, B., & Hamilton, M. (2001). How does complexity inform community, how does community inform complexity. *Emergence, 3*(2), 57-77.

Teece, D. (1998). Capturing value from knowledge assets: The new Eeonomy, markets for know-how,

and intangible assets. *California Management Review, 40*(3), 55-79.

Torlina, L., & Lichtenstein, S. (2004). *Integration of knowledge management in virtual groups.* Paper presented at the IRMA International Conference, New Orleans, LA.

Tsoukas, H. (1996). The firm as a distributed knowledge system: A constructionist approach. *Strategic Management Journal, 17*(Special Issue: Knowledge and the Firm), 11-25.

Tsui, E. (2005). The role of IT in KM: Where are we now and where are we heading. *Journal of Knowledge Management, 9*(1), 3-6.

Tushman, M., & Scanlan, T. (1981). Characteristics and external orientations of boundary spanning individuals. *Academy of Management Journal, 24*(1), 83-98.

van den Hooff, B., Elving, W., Meeuwsen, J., & Dumoulin, C. (2003). Knowledge sharing in knowledge communities. In M. Huysman, E. Wenger, & V. Wulf (Eds.), *First International Conference on Communities and Technologies.* Amsterdam, Netherlands: Kluwer Academic Publishers, Dordrecht.

Ward, A. (2000). Getting strategic value from constellations of communities. *Strategy & Leadership, 28*(2), 4.

Wenger, E. (1998a). Communities of practice—Learning as a social system. *Systems Thinker.*

Wenger, E. (1998b). *Communities of practice—Learning, meaning, and identity.* Cambridge: Cambridge University Press.

Wenger, E. (2004). Knowledge management as a doughnut: Shaping your knowledge strategy through communities of practice. *Ivey Business Journal, 68*(3), 1-8.

Wenger, E., McDermott, R., & Snyder, W. (2002). *Cultivating communities of practice—A guide to managing knowledge.* Boston, MA: Harvard Business School Press.

Wilson, G., Jackson, P., & Smith, W. (2003). *Knowledge management strategies in a small and medium sized enterprise: A tale of two systems.* Paper presented at the 14th Australasian Conference on Information Systems (pp. 1-16), Perth, Western Australia.

Section IV
Advances in Knowledge Management Development Methodologies

Chapter XV
A Method for Knowledge Modeling with Unified Modeling Language (UML):
Building a Blueprint for Knowledge Management

Sung-kwan Kim
University of Arkansas at Little Rock, USA

Seongbae Lim
State University of New York at Geneseo, USA

Robert B. Mitchell
University of Arkansas at Little Rock, USA

ABSTRACT

Since knowledge management (KM) is considered to be an important function of the successful business operation, many organizations are embracing KM. The success of a KM project is dependent upon its contents. This chapter presents a method for building an effective knowledge model which can help businesses analyze and specify knowledge contents. The method takes a decision-oriented view. For the modeling language of the method, unified modeling language (UML) has been chosen. The method is applied to the vessel scheduling process in a maritime shipping company. The steps and rules are explained using an example, and the strengths and weaknesses of the method are discussed.

INTRODUCTION

Over the past years, interest in knowledge management (KM) has grown explosively. Today KM is considered to be an important function of the successful business operation, and many organizations are embracing KM. In general, KM activities include creating, structuring, organizing,

Copyright © 2008, IGI Global, distributing in print or electronic forms without written permission of IGI Global is prohibited.

retrieving, sharing, and evaluating an enterprise's knowledge assets. KM is a systematic approach to managing organizational knowledge. Numerous studies on KM have been conducted from general theories to specific KM systems. However, "the area occupied by methods and techniques that are neither too general nor specific" are not so well covered (Wiig, Hoog, & Spek, 1997, p. 15). Unlike in IT systems and architecture, research on the methods that help systematically analyze what organizations need to manage is less popular in KM sectors.

As pointed out by Cook (1996), most KM projects focus on the process rather than the knowledge contents that need to be managed. This approach assumes that organizations already understand what they need to know, though often not the case. Organizations must thoroughly analyze knowledge needs before they begin any KM projects. Knowing what one needs to know is the first and most important step in achieving success in KM. It is the knowledge contents that provide businesses with value. It is the contents that help corporations succeed in a global market. The success of a KM project is dependent upon its contents—contents to help understand the market, solve business problems, or support decision-making processes.

The key idea of KM is to provide a way whereby knowledge contents are created, shared, and utilized in an efficient and effective manner. Therefore, it is critical to analyze these knowledge requirements. Managers need a tool with which to analyze knowledge contents needed in business processes and decision-making. The knowledge model will help specify knowledge contents and show their flows into the business processes. This chapter presents the rationale for knowledge modeling as a foundation for successful KM projects. A method is proposed for building an effective knowledge model, taking a decision-oriented view. As a modeling language of the method, the unified modeling language (UML) has been

chosen. The method is then applied to the vessel scheduling process in a shipping company.

NEED FOR KNOWLEDGE MODELING

Modeling refers to creating a simplified representation of a complex reality. It is a means of creating abstraction. More rigorously, a model is a representation of a set of components of a process, system, or subject area, generally developed for the understanding, analysis, improvement, and/or replacement of the process. A model must specify the structures and formal relationships among components. Thus, a model helps in understanding a process or behavior, predicting an outcome, or analyzing a problem. Today, the role of modeling in specifying and documenting systems is gaining popularity (Eriksson & Penker, 2000).

A knowledge model is an abstraction of a KM system. What the knowledge model will do is to provide a simplified view of the knowledge needs, structures, and relationships among components of the KM system. It will act as the basis for communicating, improving, and defining knowledge requirements needed to support the business. The knowledge model functions as the plan for KM to support a business (Eriksson & Penker, 2000). It provides what is needed, not what is currently available, and it sets the environment for formulating strategy for obtaining knowledge not currently available. A knowledge model is stable and does not change frequently since it is built around business processes and the requisite knowledge at the conceptual level.

KNOWLEDGE MODELING METHODS IN PRACTICE

Conducting knowledge modeling effectively requires a collection of methods, techniques, and tools. Particularly, a method helps developers build effective knowledge models. There are various types of knowledge modeling methods used. The first group of methods focuses on the acquisition of knowledge. These methods have been widely used for knowledge elicitation and validation from domain experts for knowledge-based systems in the field of knowledge engineering (Tallis, Kim, & Gil, 1999). Popular methods include problem-solving methods (PSM) and knowledge acquisition and design structuring (KADS). In particular, KADS has been one of the most influential methods. It was one of the first approaches to distinguish modeling aspects of knowledge acquisitions from implementation aspects (Schreiber, Wielinga, & Breuker, 1993). CommonKADS is an enhanced version of KADS. CommonKADS is one of the major SW engineering standard for knowledge-based systems. It goes beyond mere knowledge acquisition method and is widely used as an enterprise-wide knowledge engineering methodology (Schreiber et al., 2000).

The second group of knowledge modeling methods involves the analysis and integration of knowledge processes. In these methods, the focus is on knowledge transfer, sharing, or capitalization. The methods emphasize investigating knowledge flow dynamics to enhance the flow of knowledge through the enterprise; the primary objective is to enable the transfer of knowledge from where it resides to where it is needed—across time, space and organizations as necessary (Caussanel & Chouraqui, 1999; Nissen, Kamel, & Sengupta, 2000; Nissen, 2002; Gronau, Kopecny, & Kratzke, 2006). For example, knowledge modeling and description language (KMDL) is one of the methods for building a process-oriented knowledge model. KMDL is used to model especially knowledge-intensive processes. It can effectively identify available knowledge existing in or necessary for processes (Fröming, Gronau, & Scmid, 2006). The third group involves knowledge mapping methods. Knowledge mapping creates high-level knowledge models in a graphical form (Speel et

al., 1999; Carnot et al., 2001; Briggs et al., 2004, Cañas et al., 2004). Knowledge mapping is the techniques and tools for visualizing knowledge and relationships in a clear form such as that business-relevant features are clearly highlighted (Vail III, 1999). Knowledge maps help managers get an overall picture of what knowledge is available and what is not in their organizations.

The next group includes ontology-based knowledge modeling methods. Ontology deals with the formal conceptualization of reality (Gruber, 1992). It attempts to explicitly specify the concepts in existence. Ontology can be used for building a knowledge model. For example, a framework for distributed organizational memories (FRODO) and corporate memory management through agents (CoMMA) are built on the ontology-based methods (Maedche et al., 2003).

Another group of methods are dedicated to building corporate memories. A corporate memory is an explicit, disembodied, persistent representation of an organizational knowledge (Van Heijst, Van der Spek, & Kruizinga, 1996). A corporate memory can be used to find, access, diffuse, and use the corporate knowledge in an effective and efficient manner. The examples include CYGMA (Cycle de vie et Gestion des Metiers et des Application), REX and MKSM (Method for Knowledge System Management) (Dieng, Corby, Giboin, & Ribière, 1999).

The last group of methods takes the life cycle approach. Life cycle methodologies provide systematic approach to building knowledge management system during the entire system development life cycle—that is, knowledge creating/capturing, organizing/storing, sharing/transferring, applying/reusing, and evolving (Davenport & Prusak, 1998; Nissen, 1999; Nissen et al., 2000).

In the following section, we propose our method for knowledge modeling. Unlike the methods introduced in this section, our method focuses on the analysis and identification of organizational knowledge contents and their structure. The emphasis is on the analysis of the input to decision-making processes, which determines the knowledge requirements.

A PROPOSED METHOD FOR KNOWLEDGE MODELING

A method is a way of doing something, especially a systematic and orderly approach, usually in steps. A method defines a set of activities that will achieve the goals of the project, including the purpose of each specific activity and what will result from that activity. Therefore, a method tells a modeler how to perform the activities and provides guidelines for using them. It includes the instructions for what to do, how to do it, when to do it, and why it is done. A method should be able to be used repeatedly, each time achieving similar results; a method can be taught to others within a reasonable timeframe and applied by others with a reasonable level of success, each time achieving significantly, and consistently, better results than other techniques of an ad hoc approach (Bernard, 2000).

A modeler requires a good method for developing and maintaining a successful knowledge model. The method introduced in this chapter is decision-oriented. Decision making is one of the fundamental processes for any business. A decision is a reasoned choice among alternatives (Mallach, 2000). Decision is a choice of the way to proceed in a given situation to achieve an intention. An intention expresses what the modeler wants to achieve. An intention can be strategic or operational and allow various levels of granularity in the decision-making process (Rolland, Nurcan, & Grosz, 1999).

Organizations are filled with decision making at various levels. Decision and decision making are the true essence of the organization and identify its boundaries, policies, procedures, customs, and theatre of operations (Marakas, 2003). Almost all managerial activities revolve around decision

making. A company has to make many decisions quickly and continuously. Decision making is where knowledge is needed. According to Simon (1960), the decision-making process consists of three phases: intelligence, design, and choice. In all three phases, knowledge is a critical input. Decision making is where one can analyze knowledge needs. An individual's decision making capability is limited by the knowledge available. Having knowledge available to decision makers is crucial to improving individual and organizational performance. Therefore, the decision-making oriented approach is a valid way of identifying knowledge requirements and, thereby, building a knowledge model (Kim, Lim, & Mitchell, 2004).

ELEMENTS OF THE PROPOSED METHOD

A model is composed of many elements: products, languages, and procedures (Henderson-Seller, 2003). Products are the goals that a method is trying to achieve. Our method produces two products: knowledge diagram and knowledge catalogue. A knowledge diagram is the static view of knowledge components of a knowledge model. A knowledge catalog is a detailed textual description of the internal structure of a knowledge component. These two products are explained in more detail in later sections.

A good method often includes a visual diagramming tool as a modeling language. A model is expressed in a modeling language. A modeling language is used to document work products and consists of notations—the symbols used in a model—and a set of rules directing how to use it (Gemino & Wand, 2003). The unified modeling language (UML) is used in this analysis.

Procedures are the rules and guidelines that define activities and how they are performed, including the products. Procedures, which are a collection of steps, should be concise and have a logical sequence. A step is a process with a series of related activities and conversations designed to gather input and convert it into a desired result. Each step defines the task that should be performed. Procedures of the proposed method are explained in more detail in later sections as the method is applied to the example of the vessel scheduling process in a shipping company.

UML AS A CHOICE OF MODELING LANGUAGE

One of the most important elements of a conceptual model is the modeling language. Since its standardization by Object Management Group (OMG) in 1997, the UML has had a large impact on how software systems are developed. Now UML is an industry standard mechanism for visualizing, specifying, constructing, and documenting software systems. The modeling language was originally intended for object-oriented (OO) system development. Although UML has been used mainly for modeling software systems, it can be used for many different types of analysis and design modeling. UML can be used without building OO applications; it can be used even outside of software modeling (Naiburg & Maksimchuk, 2001).

UML has proven to be effective for conceptual modeling; it has a very rich set of tools. As illustrated in this chapter, UML fits well with knowledge modeling. It has a very flexible extension mechanism to be adapted to the knowledge model. Especially in the proposed method, the mapping from one stage to another is very efficient. As will be explained in later sections, the mapping between steps is straightforward and easy (i.e., from activity diagram to knowledge diagram).

APPLICATION OF THE PROPOSED METHOD TO THE VESSEL SCHEDULING PROCESS

In applying the proposed method to build a knowledge model of the vessel scheduling process in a shipping company, this chapter first briefly describes the shipping company. The use of the method to produce the desired products is then explained.

The company (SYS) is located in Seoul, Korea. It is one of the subsidiaries of SYC. SYC is one of the largest cement producers in Korea. SYS was established to transport bulk cement produced by its sister company SYC. SYS operates 12 vessels to transport the bulk cement produced by SYC. The major production plant of SYC is located in DH, a port city located in the eastern part of Korea. From the port, 12 vessels transport the bulk cement to eight domestic ports. The 12 vessels are specialized cement tankers. The sizes of the vessels range from 5,500 to 15,000 Dead Weight Tonnage (DWT). (DWT is the term used for measuring the loading capacity of a vessel.) The intention of this analysis is not to accurately and completely represent the vessel scheduling process but to simplify the process to illustrate how the proposed method can be applied to actual business processes.

Step 1: Select the process for which to build a knowledge model

First, a business process for which to build a knowledge model is identified. The proposed method can be applied to a single business process, to multiple processes, or even to the entire firm. Identifying a major business process defines a conceptual framework for which to build a knowledge model. It also defines the scope of the project. The knowledge flows will be formed around the process. The major business processes of SYS include purchasing vessels, scheduling vessels, making long-term cargo contracts, and managing crews. One of the most important business activities is the vessel scheduling process. Vessel operation is the only source of revenues for SYS. Efficient vessel dispatching critically affects the profitability of the company. Many complex situations arise in the process of dispatching vessels.

Since a ship has very high fixed cost (insurance, crew cost, interest paid, etc.), inefficient vessel scheduling often incurs significant dollars of loss per day per vessel. Very sophisticated knowledge is required for decision making. The modeler chose the process and proceeded to build a knowledge model for the single process.

Figure 1. Activity diagram for the vessel scheduling process

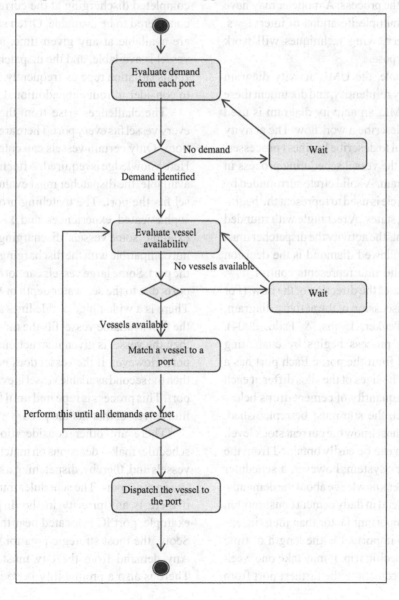

Step 2: Identify the key activities of the process selected

The second step is to identify the key activities of the process. This task is one of the most important steps of the method. The key activities are where knowledge requirements are analyzed. Each activity is filled with decisions to be made. While analyzing the task, one should be able to identify the knowledge needed for the activity. A modeler will conduct interviews with the domain expert and learn the scope, purpose, and key terminology of the process. A modeler may have to go through multiple iterations of interviews. Traditional interviewing techniques will work well for this purpose.

In this example, the UML activity diagram was used to analyze, identify, and document these activities. In UML, an activity diagram is used to analyze and describe a workflow. The activity diagram is useful to describe business processes. Figure 1 shows the vessel scheduling process in an activity diagram. A solid circle surrounded by a large empty circle is used to represent the beginning and ending states. A rectangle with rounded corners represents the activity the dispatcher must perform. The hollowed diamond is the decision symbol. The solid line represents control flow. The arrow indicates the direction of the flow. (For more detailed discussion of the activity diagram, see Eriksson, Penker, Lyons, & Fado, 2004). The scheduling process begins by evaluating cement demand from the ports. Each port has a silo of cement. The sizes of the silos differ at each port. Before the quantity of cement drops below the restock level, the silo must be replenished. The dispatcher must know the current stock level. The information can be easily obtained from the cement inventory system; however, a scheduler must have broader knowledge about the demands. For example, a trend in daily cement consumption rate is a more important factor than mere inventory level. Also important is the length of time required for a specific trip. It may take one week to transport the cement to the farthest port from the production site. The consumption rate depends on the construction business situation in the area covered by the port. An out-of-stock situation is critical in the construction industry; several construction projects may have to be delayed due to the shortage of cement. Often there are multiple ports that need cement supply at one time.

The second activity is to evaluate the availability of vessels. Many factors must be considered. It is easy to identify which vessel is free. Any vessel that has finished discharging or has nearly completed discharging at the current position is considered to be available. Often several vessels are available at any given time; sometimes no vessel is available, and the dispatcher must wait. If this situation repeats frequently, then it is time to consider introducing additional vessels.

The challenges arise from the fact that not every vessel fits every port. There are many restrictions. Only certain vessels can enter some ports. Here knowledge is required. After finding vessels available, the dispatcher must evaluate if the vessel fits the port. The matching process requires sophisticated experiences and knowledge. For example, some vessels' discharging equipment is not compatible with the discharging equipment of the port. Some large vessels cannot enter the same ports due to the sea water depth or berth lengths. There is a wide range of tide lines at the ports. If the first available vessel fits the most urgent port, then the vessel is given instructions to sail to the port. However, if the vessel does not fit the port, then the second available vessel is evaluated for the port. This process is repeated until the dispatcher finds a vessel that fits the port.

There are other considerations when the scheduler makes decisions on matching ports and vessels and, thereby, dispatching a specific vessel to a specific port. The scheduler must understand if there is any priority in the dispatching. For example, port IC is located near the capital city, Seoul, the most strategic area for the company. Any demand from the city must be first met. There is also a profitability issue involved. The freight rate is decided depending on the size of the vessels and travel distance. All these factors combined are very challenging. Knowledge about vessels, ports, voyage, profitability, and dispatching priorities is needed to mix and combine all these conditions.

Another factor to be considered is the voyage history. All vessels must visit the port PS in regular intervals, since PS is the main port, a hub for crew management. SYS recruits its crew in the port, and most of the crew has their homes in the city. When the vessel enters the port, the crew is released to visit and stay at home (except the crew on duty) until the vessel finishes discharging cement and is ready for the next voyage. The crews are free to go to their homes and spend time with their families. This policy plays a critical role in the vessels dispatching, since crews cannot sail for extended periods without visiting their homes.

Step 3: Analyze each activity in the activity diagram to identify the knowledge input to the activity

Next, the modeler analyzes each activity represented in the activity diagram to identify the knowledge input. The key is to ask what knowledge input a scheduler needs to make decisions in each activity. The first activity is to evaluate vessel demand. For example, to make a decision in the task, a scheduler must have knowledge about the port, such as silo information, restock level, daily consumption rate, and construction business situation in the area covered by cement supply from the port. The next activity is to evaluate vessel availability. To make a decision in the activity, the scheduler must have knowledge about each vessel: discharging equipment, length, depth, size, and speed. In the third activity, it is necessary for a scheduler to know cement supply

Figure 2. Knowledge input to the activity diagram

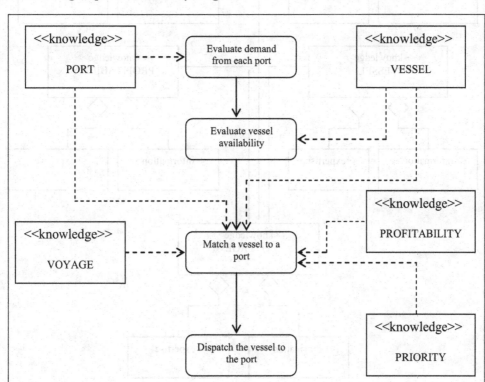

priority rules set by the company's policy and profitability factors (freight rate, port charges, fuel charge, fixed cost, and cement quantity to carry). Finally the scheduler must have knowledge about the each available vessel's voyage history, that is, how often did a vessel visit the port PS and what was the last voyage in which the crew visited their homes. This analysis is summarized in the Figure 2.

A UML stereotype was used to represent knowledge. UML has an extension mechanism that allows for creating a new type of concept. UML allows a modeler to define concepts, set notations for those concepts, and revise the related grammatical rules for constructing models. A stereotype is "a new kind of model element defined within a profile based on an existing kind of model element. It is essentially a new meta-class."

Figure 3. Knowledge diagram

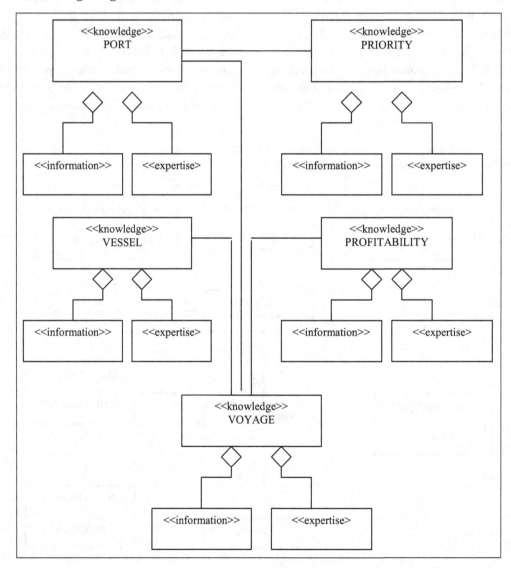

Figure 4. Example of the structure of knowledge component (PORT)

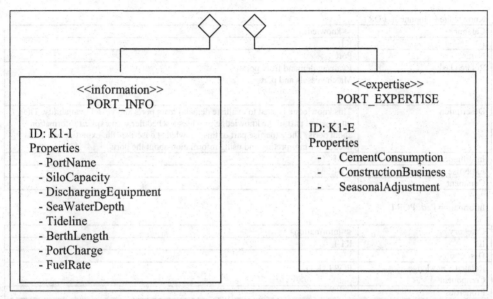

Stereotypes may extend the semantics but not the structure of pre-existing meta-model classes" (Rumbaugh, Jacobson, & Booch, 2005, p. 616). UML provides a modeler with flexibility so that he or she applies the language to all modeling tasks while providing consistency. In Figure 2, a solid line with an arrow represents the direction of the flow of the activity; a dotted line with an arrow represents knowledge input to the activity.

Step 4: Construct a Knowledge Diagram from the Activity Diagram

A knowledge diagram is actually a class diagram modified to incorporate knowledge. A class diagram illustrates a system's static structure and the relationships between different objects. Figure 3 is the knowledge diagram derived from the activity diagram. The diagrams can be related to each other in a number of ways: association, whole and parts, and generalization and specialization. The straight line between knowledge components represents an association. The diamond notation represents whole and parts relationships. It indicates that any knowledge is composed of an explicit information part and a tacit expertise part.

As shown in Figure 3, any knowledge contains a tacit dimension and explicit dimension. Knowledge is a combination of information and expertise. Information is the part of the knowledge you can easily identify and codify. Expertise is the part of the knowledge that represents the tacit dimension. It can be experience, interpretation capability, analyzing capability, and monitoring and synthesizing capabilities. Without expertise, the knowledge component is only data. Without the information part, the knowledge component may be mere intuition or guess. The result of the knowledge diagram is a broad and relatively high level overview of knowledge assets in an organization. The diagram permits a quick look at the crucial aspects of knowledge assets.

For the purpose of simplicity, the inside details of the knowledge components are not shown in Figure 3. For an illustration of the detailed description of knowledge components, PORT knowledge is used as an example, as shown in Figure 4.

Step 5: Document the Knowledge Diagram

The next part of the analysis is to construct the textual description. UML is a visually-oriented

Figure 5. Example of a knowledge catalog

Knowledge Component: PORT

Category	<<knowledge>>
ID	K1
Name	Port
Related task	Evaluate demand from ports Match vessels and ports
Description	This knowledge is used to evaluate demand from ports and vessel availability. The information part of the knowledge provides a scheduler with explicit information about ports. The expertise part of this knowledge describes the expertise and skills needed for interpreting and using information about the ports
Information component	K1-I
Expertise component	K1-E
Comment	

Information Part: PORT

Category	<<information>>
ID	K1-I
Description	
Related Knowledge Component	PORT (K1)
Properties	
	PortName: IN
	Silo Capacity: xxx ton
	Discharging Equipment: Type I
	Sea Water Depth: xx M
	Tide: High Water: xx M, Low water: xx M
	Berth Length: xx M:
	Port Charge: $ xxxx
	Fuel Charge: $ xxx
Owner	Cement Tanker Operation Department
Type	Explicit (Document)
Importance	Operational
Source	Internal source
Location	SYSVMS-1 (System module name)
Other comments	

Expertise Part: PORT

Category	<<Expertise>>
ID	K1-E
Description	
Related Knowledge Component	PORT (K1)
Properties	
	Interpret cement consumption rate
	Understand construction business situation
	Perform seasonal adjustment
Owner	Cement Tanker Operation Department
Type	Tacit
Importance	Tactical
Source	External
Location	
Other comments	To perform this job, at least three years experience is required.

language. It does not have a rich textual description tool. Even though use case analysis provides an excellent description tool, it is not designed for describing the structure of any item. Using the following knowledge catalog description template is suggested. A knowledge catalog is a detailed textual description of the internal structure of a knowledge component. The knowledge catalog works as a repository of knowledge components. Figure 5 is an example of the knowledge catalog for the knowledge component PORT.

Step 6: Evaluate and Maintain the Knowledge Model

Knowledge evolves and thus the model must be continuously updated. Regular audit and evaluation is necessary to maintain an effective knowledge model. Environmental changes should be incorporated into the model. The process of evaluation will highlight the addition of new knowledge and update/deletion of outdated knowledge. It is also important to plan and identify how the knowledge model can be utilized for decision support potential. The followings are a few examples of the key questions to be addressed (Dieng, Corby, Gibson, & Ribière, 1999, p. 592):

- "What will be the criteria for evaluation?"
- "When, how and by whom will such an evaluation be carried out?"
- "How will the evaluation results be taken into account?"

DISCUSSION

Using the proposed method, one can build a knowledge model as demonstrated through the example of the vessel purchase decision-making process. The products of the modeling method are the knowledge diagram and knowledge catalog. The method has several strengths. First, the focus

is on what to manage, not on how to manage it. One models what is required, not what is currently available. Therefore, future knowledge can be integrated and managed. If what is required today is not available, a way to acquire it is found. Building a knowledge model parallels performing high-level knowledge requirement analysis.

Second, the method is decision-oriented. The method highlights key decision-making points. Focusing on critical decision points avoids the distraction that can result with a detailed process. Decision making is the fundamental business task. By analyzing decision-making activity and input into the process, the decision maker can easily analyze knowledge requirements. As Curtice (1987) pointed out, "A method should encourage and promote a fresh examination of business. The method therefore must begin at a very fundamental level, providing the opportunity and encouragements to rethink the organization's basic concepts" (p. 6). A decision-making-oriented approach is a very effective way of identifying knowledge requirements and, thereby, building a knowledge model.

Third, the modeling language UML is easy to learn and use. It has proven to be an effective modeling tool. Users can easily analyze the major knowledge requirements of the business process: what the knowledge requirements are, how they are provided, how they are managed, and so forth. The mapping from one step to another can be easily implemented with UML.

The method, however, needs more empirical testing. A modeler needs to know if the method faithfully represents the domain with completeness and accuracy. "Otherwise, defects in the model might propagate to subsequent system implementation activities. If these defects are not discovered until late in the development process, they are often costly to correct" (Shanks, Tansley, & Weber, 2003, p. 85). A modeling method can be tested by reviews via focus group, questioning by stakeholders, or real problem-solving.

The proposed knowledge model is a structural model. It describes the static aspect of the knowledge model. It defines the structure of knowledge entities and their relationships. However, the dynamic aspect of the knowledge model has not been analyzed. The dynamic aspects such as knowledge flow and knowledge process are equally important parts of knowledge model. A further study is needed to analyze and highlight the dynamic aspects of the model.

In this chapter, we demonstrated using the proposed method for building a knowledge model for a single business process. However, in practice, even a small business organization consists of multiple processes. Using the proposed method, users may construct multiple knowledge models for multiple processes over time. For example, users may build a knowledge model for the process "A" at one time and a knowledge model for the process "B" in the different time frame. The knowledge models are likely to contain some knowledge items that are not consistent. There is a need for the enterprise-wide knowledge model. The lack of the enterprise-wide view results in the critical integrity problems in the knowledge model (e.g., knowledge duplication, knowledge inconsistency). The enterprise-wide knowledge model provides a complete view of knowledge components and their relationships in an holistic way. Even though the enterprise-wide integration issue of the knowledge model is beyond this chapter, we want to mention the three integration methods suggested by Maedche et al. (2003): inclusion, mapping, and combination. They are developed basically for multiple ontologies management. However, we think the methods can be well applied to the integration of multiple knowledge models. The combination method, where several data sources using a different concept are combined into a common, integrated concept, is very promising for the purpose.

CONCLUSION

As businesses move further into the intelligence age, knowledge continues to be a key competitive weapon. Thus knowledge management is a critical concern. Managers and organizations, however, need to focus on the knowledge requirements definition before implementing a system. This chapter proposes the decision-oriented knowledge modeling method. The method was applied to the vessel scheduling process in a shipping company. Overall, the method worked well. This architectural approach will help managers define their knowledge requirements. However, improvements in the method can occur as it is applied to more situations.

REFERENCES

Bernard, E. (2000). *What is a methodology?*. Retrieved May 1, 2004 from http://www.itmweb.com/essay553.htm.

Briggs, G., Shamma, D., Cañas, A., Carff, R., Scargle, J., & Novak, J. (2004). Concept maps applied to Mars exploration public Outreaches. In *Proceedings of the First International Conference on Concept Mapping*. Pamplona, Spain.

Carnot, M., Dunn, B., Cañas, A., Graham, P., & Muldoon, J. (2001). *Concept maps vs. Web pages for information searching and browsing*. Retrieved March 31, 2006 from http:www.ihmc.us/users/acanas/Publications/CMapsVSWebPagesExp1/CMapsVSWebPagesExp1.htm.

Cañas, A., Hill, G., Suri, N., Lott, J., Gómez, G., Eskridge, T., et al. (2004). CMAPTOOLS: A Knowledge modeling and sharing environment. In *Proceedings of the First International Conference on Concept Mapping*. Pamplona, Spain

Caussanel, J., & Chouraqui, E. (1999). Model and methodology of knowledge capitalization for small and medium enterprise. In *Proceedings of the Twelfth Workshop on Knowledge Acquisition, Modeling and Management.* Banff, Alberta, Canada.

Cook, M. (1996). *Building enterprise information architectures: Reengineering information systems.* Upper Saddle River, NJ: Prentice-Hall.

Curtice, R. (1987). *Strategic value analysis: A modern approach to systems and data planning.* Eaglewood Cliffs, NJ: Prentice-Hall.

Davenport, T., & Prusak, L. (1998). *Working knowledge: How organizations manage what they know.* Boston, MA: Harvard Business School Press.

Dieng, R., Corby, O., Giboin, A., & Ribière, M. (1999). Methods and tools for corporate knowledge management. *International Journal of Human-Computer Studies, 51.* Retrieved from http://ideallibrary.com.

Eriksson, H., & Penker, M. (2000). *Business modeling with UML: Business patterns at work.* New York, NY: John Wiley & Sons, Inc.

Eriksson, H., Penker, M., Lyons, B., & Fado, D. (2004). *UML 2 toolkit.* Indianapolis, IN: John Wiley & Sons, Inc.

Fröming, J., Gronau, N., & Schmid, S. (2006). Improvement of software engineering by modeling knowledge-intensive business process. *International Journal of Knowledge Management, 2*(4), 32-51.

Gemino, A., & Wand, Y. (2003). Evaluating modeling techniques based on models of learning. *Communications of the ACM, 46*(10), 79-84.

Gronau, N., Kopencny, A., & Kratzke, N. (2006). An interdisciplinary approach on operational knowledge process modeling and formal reasoning. *I-KNOW'06: Proceedings of the BPOKI'06 Conference Special Track.* Graz, Austria.

Gruber, T. (1992). Toward principles for the design of ontologies used for knowledge sharing. In *Proceedings of the International Workshop on Formal Ontology.* Padova, Italy.

Henderson-Seller, B. (2003). Method engineering for OO systems development. *Communications of the ACM, 46*(10), 73-78.

Kim, S., Lim, S., & Mitchell, R. (2004). Building a knowledge model: A decision-making approach. *Journal of Knowledge Management Practice, 5.* Retrieved from http://www.tlainc.com/articl68.htm.

Loucopoulos, L., & Kavakli, E. (1995). Enterprise modeling and the teleological approach to requirement engineering. *International Journal of Intelligent and Cooperative Information Systems, 4*(1), 45-79.

Maedche, A., Motik, B., Stojanovic, L., Studer, R., &Volz, R. (2003). Ontologies for enterprise knowledge management. *IEEE Intelligence System, 18*(2), 26-33.

Mallach, E. (2000). *Decision support and data warehouse system.* Boston, MA: McGraw Hill.

Marakas, G. (2003). *Decision support systems in the 21st century,* (2nd ed.) Upper Saddle River, NJ: Prentice Hall.

Naiburg, E., & Maksimchuk, R. (2001). *UML for database design.* Boston, MA: Addison Wesley.

Nissen, M. (2002). An extended model of knowledge flow dynamics. *Communications of the Association for Information Systems, 8,* 251-266

Nissen, M. (1999). Knowledge-based knowledge management in the Re-engineering domain. *Decision Support Systems, 27,* 47-65.

Nissen, M., Kamel, M., & Sengupta, K. (2000). Integrated analysis and design of knowledge systems and processes. *Information Resources Management Journal, 13*(1), 24-43.

Rolland, C., Nurcan, S., & Grosz, G. (1999). Enterprise knowledge development: The process view. *Information & Management, 36*(3), 121-184.

Rumbaugh, J., Jacobson, I., & Booch, G. (2005). *The unified modeling language reference manual,* (2nd ed). Boston, MA: Addison Wesley.

Schreiber, A., Akkermans, J., Anjewierden, A., De Hoog, R., Shadbolt, N., Van de Velde, W., & Wielinga, B. (2000). *Knowledge engineering and management: The CommonKADS methodology.* Cambridge, MA: MIT Press.

Schreiber, G., Wielinga, B., & Breuker, J. (1993). *KADS: A principled approach to knowledge-based system development.* London, UK: Academic Press.

Shanks, G., Tansley, E., & Weber, R. (2003). Using ontology to validate conceptual models. *Communications of the ACM, 46*(10), 85-89.

Simon, H. (1960). *The new success of decision making.* New York, NY: Harper & Row.

Speel, P., Shadbolt, N., De Vries, W., Van Dam, P., &O'Hara, K. (1999). Knowledge mapping for industrial purposes. In *Proceedings of the Twelfth Workshop on Knowledge Acquisition, Modeling and Management.* Banff, Alberta, Canada.

Tallis, M., Kim, J., & Gil, Y. (1999). User studies of knowledge acquisition tools: Methodology and lessons learned. In *Proceedings of the Twelfth Banff Knowledge Acquisition for Knowledge-Based Systems Workshop.* Banff, Alberta, Canada.

Vail III, E. (1999). Mapping organizational knowledge. *Knowledge Management Review, 8*(May/June), 10-15.

Van Heijst, G., Van Der SPek, R., & Kruzinga, E. (1996). Organizing corporate memories. In *Proceedings of the Twelfth Banff Knowledge Acquisition for Knowledge-Based Systems Workshop.* Banff, Alberta, Canada.

Whitman, L., Ramachandran, K., & Ketkar, V. (2001). A taxonomy of a living model of the enterprise. In *Proceedings of the Winter Simulation Conference.* Arlington, VA.

Wiig, K., Hoog, R., & Spek, R. (1997). Supporting knowledge management: A selection of methods and techniques. *Expert Systems with Applications, 13*(1), 15-27.

Chapter XVI
Improvement of Software Engineering Processes by Analyzing Knowledge Intensive Activities

Jane Fröeming
University of Potsdam, Germany

Norbert Gronau
University of Potsdam, Germany

Simone Schmid
University of Potsdam, Germany

ABSTRACT

The knowledge modeling and description language (KMDL®) analyzes knowledge-intensive business processes which lead towards improvements. After modeling the business processes, knowledge and process potentials in daily business tasks in knowledge generation and handling can be unleashed. The following contribution presents the current state of specification of KMDL®. A real-life example in software engineering is used to explain the advantages of this approach.

INTRODUCTION

Software development is a knowledge-intensive business process. Until now, no adequate methods were available to improve knowledge management in software engineering by appropriate models, analyses and concepts. It seems useful to base on more than ten years of experience in the modeling and analysis of information processing tasks applying methods like event-driven process chains and to establish a new modeling paradigm focused on knowledge creation, flow and usage. Its application in the area of software engineering is described in the following contribution.

Copyright © 2008, IGI Global, distributing in print or electronic forms without written permission of IGI Global is prohibited.

The main focus of the contribution refers to two principal objects: First, knowledge-intensive business processes in software engineering can be identified and improved using an adequate modeling language. Second, the specification of the knowledge modeling and description language (KMDL®) is used to model an exemplary software engineering processes. The modeling language is used to describe knowledge-intensive business processes, tacit and explicit knowledge, knowledge and information flows.

QUESTIONS AND PROBLEMS OF KNOWLEDGE MANAGEMENT IN SOFTWARE ENGINEERING

The dynamic behavior of the actual business environment will gain speed and complexity. The market for software products will transform very quickly and the pressure due to competition is expected to increase massively. Specially small and medium-sized enterprises have to cope with the high pressure in the software engineering sector consisting in the rivalry between themselves and major players (Groff & Jones, 2003). Therefore, methods and applications are needed to identify potentials in daily business processes (Hamel & Prahalad, 1990). The knowledge and use of these potentials can be a decisive competitive advantage. The management and processing of organizational knowledge are increasingly being viewed as critical to organizational success (Inkpen & Dinur, 1998).

The contribution is based on the central thesis:

The productivity of software engineering will be increased using appropriate knowledge management applications. This can strengthen the competitiveness of software developing companies especially regarding future turbulences.

Software engineering processes have to be improved in a way that relevant information and knowledge has to reach the appropriate employee at the right time. If so, employees reduce unnecessary search time for information and knowledge, therefore tasks can be completed faster. Another way to increase the productivity of software engineering is a constant documentation and optimization of recurring sub-processes and to reuse these as patterns in other projects. Knowledge management activities in software engineering can only be effective if they are implemented and applied consequently throughout the company. Even the greatest strategies will be unsuccessful without the support of employees. Staff members have to deal with knowledge management and its advantages have to be made clear.

In the following sections, the central thesis will be discussed, applying it to a real-life example of software engineering in small and medium-sized enterprises. German software engineering firms were analyzed within the research projects M-WISE[1] and IOSE-W[2] within the German federal government software engineering research initiative. The interdisciplinary organized projects aim to promote knowledge management in software engineering. Existing methods and applications to model knowledge-intensive business processes were improved and a new specification of a modeling language in software engineering was developed and tested in multiple real-life environments.

Modeling of Software Engineering Processes with the Knowledge Modeling and Description Language (KMDL®)

In the following section, the knowledge modeling and description language (KMDL®) is introduced. KMDL® is currently under development at the University of Potsdam in Germany. The theoretical framework of KMDL® as well as a general procedural model for its implementation is described. Finally, this chapter will point out the use of KMDL®. Further references towards the modeling method are available in Gronau and Weber (2004) and Gronau and Weber (2004a).

Knowledge-Intensive Business Processes in Software Engineering

Within process-oriented knowledge management, the knowledge-intensive business process is the primary perspective (Remus, 2002). Several attempts have been made in the literature to define knowledge-intensive business processes. Heisig points out the opportunity to schedule the knowledge demand and evaluates knowledge-intensity according to the existence of variability and exceptions (Mertins et al., 2000; Heisig, 2002). Other sources define a processes knowledge-intensive if an improvement with conventional methods of business reengineering is not or only partially possible (Remus, 2002). Davenport recognizes the knowledge-intensity by the diversity and uncertainty of process input and output (Davenport & Prusak, 2000). A process is knowledge-intensive if its value can only be created through the fulfillment of the knowledge requirements by the process participants. Several properties which are typical for knowledge-intensive business processes are introduced in the following list (Gronau et al., 2005):

- In knowledge–intensive processes, knowledge contributes significantly to the values added within the process. Innovation and creativity plays a major role in such processes (Eppler et al., 1999). People within the process have a large scope in the freedom of decision, meaning that they can decide autonomously.
- The event flow of knowledge-intensive business processes is not clear in advance, as it

can evolve during the process (Davenport & Prusak, 2000).
- The participants in the process have different experiences and bring in knowledge from different domains with a varying level of expertise (Heisig, 2002).
- The life-time of knowledge involved in the process is often very short (Eppler et al., 1999), It quickly becomes obsolete. It is usually very time-intensive to build up this knowledge.
- Usually knowledge-intensive business processes do not follow structured working rules and often lack metrics to evaluate the success of the process (Davenport & Prusak, 2000).
- IT-tools for knowledge-intensive business processes are generally not very sophisticated because the knowledge is usually transferred through socialization and informal exchange of knowledge.
- Often the costs of knowledge-intensive processes are very high.

Software engineering consists of different knowledge fields like for example requirements analysis, software design, software testing and software configuration management (Abran et al., 2004). These fields can be analyzed and evaluated in terms of their knowledge-intensive characteristics. Except for the software configuration management, all mentioned fields of applications are affected by a high degree of innovation and autonomy. They do not follow structured working rules and various individuals with different expertise are involved in the process. All the knowledge fields have in common that there is great variety of sources and media, a high demand for communication, a short half-life period of knowledge and high process costs, and therefore can be defined as knowledge-intensive processes.

In order to successfully create knowledge-intensive business processes in software engineering, a method to reflect knowledge flows is necessary. This dimension cannot be brought out adequately by methods like event-driven process chains (Van der Aalst, 1998), because the ability to display the essential elements of knowledge flows are missing—especially the description of tacit knowledge. The process-based approach can provide an efficient way to capture and navigate knowledge (Kim et al., 2003).

Theoretical Foundation of KMDL®

The motivation for the development or the KMDL® was the lack of appropriate methods to model knowledge-intensive business processes. At the University of Potsdam, KMDL® was continuously improved by the Knowledge Management Research Group. A procedural model was developed as well as a mechanism for the process analysis. KMDL® is a semiformal description language that has the ability to identify available knowledge that exists in or is necessary for the process including its origin and application. The following section introduces the theoretical concepts that are used to define the Knowledge Modeling and Description Language. The first paragraph outlines the tacit and explicit knowledge defined by Nonaka and Takeuchi. In the second paragraph, the concept of knowledge conversion will be introduced.

Tacit and Explicit Knowledge

KMDL® uses the understanding of tacit knowledge according to Nonaka and Takeuchi (1995). They follow the thoughts of Polanyi who has introduced the terms of tacit knowledge and explicit knowledge. Polanyi defines tacit knowledge as personal knowledge bound to humans (Polanyi, 1958). This type consists of mental models, beliefs and perspectives (Nonaka & Takeuchi, 1995). It is partially unconscious and therefore difficult to be communicated and explained by the persons who possess it.

Explicit knowledge on the other hand can easily be expressed in handbooks, papers, patents or software (Gronau & Weber, 2004). It is formal, codified, systematic, easy to communicate, shared and can be articulated in writing and numbers (Schmidt et al., 1996). This also means that it can be transmitted and stored for reuse by other people.

Numerous life cycle models adopt a similar staged view of knowledge flow (Nissen, 2002; Nissen & Levitt, 2004). Nonaka goes further still, as he introduces a model describing a "spiral" of five dynamic interactions between tacit and explicit knowledge along an epistemological dimension, and he characterizes four processes (socialization, externalization, combination, internalization) that enable individual knowledge to be "amplified" and effect organizational knowledge "crystallization" along the ontological dimension (Nonaka & Takeuchi, 1995).

KMDL® DESCRIPTION LANGUAGE

The basis for an informal specification of KMDL® is version 2.1 (Figure 1) in which two views can be distinguished. Tasks represent the frame of the KMDL® process view. They describe the logical sequence of the business process and are executed by roles. If knowledge-intensive tasks can be identified, it is possible to analyze them closer in the activity view. The activity view focuses on knowledge and information flows and decomposes every task in different activities. An activity uses information and knowledge objects as input and generates output as information and knowledge objects. Knowledge objects which are seen as tacit knowledge (see section 3.2.1) are attached to persons. The attribute level describes the qualification of each knowledge object and task requirement. At present, the attribute level contains four degrees: 0 means no knowledge, 1 means basic knowledge, 2 means intermediate knowledge and 3 means expert knowledge.

Figure 1. Associations and objects of KMDL® v2.1

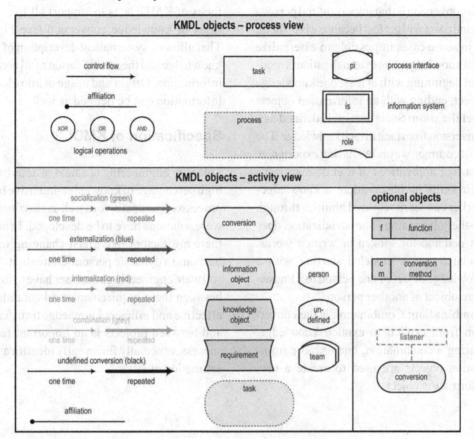

Attributes are used for a more detailed description of objects. For instance, the attribute "knowledge domain" is provided for each knowledge and information object, assigning it to a specific topic. This enables a hierarchical assignment of knowledge and information objects and hence the description of used explicit and tacit knowledge within the considered process.

The activity view enables the visualization of knowledge flows (see Figure 1). From the business process perspective, the flows of knowledge as well as the conversions of knowledge into other knowledge types are of significant importance. New objects of knowledge or information are created by the transformation of objects existing in the process. This transformation is performed by an interaction of knowledge and information objects. As an analogy to Nonaka and Takeuchi, KMDL® distinguishes between four types of knowledge conversion (Gronau & Weber, 2004):

- **Internalization:** Internalization means the conversion of explicit into tacit knowledge. It is very closely related to learning-by-doing. Experiences made through socialization, externalization or combination are internalized and integrated into the individual's knowledge framework. The internalization is started by an information object and ends with a knowledge object.

- **Externalization:** Externalization is defined as the transformation of tacit into explicit knowledge. The problematical aspect within this conversion is that important and person-bound parts will get lost because it is difficult or in some cases impossible to externalize tacit knowledge. The externalization is modeled beginning with at least one knowledge object, ending with an information object.

- **Socialization:** Socialization is defined as a conversion from tacit to tacit knowledge. The most common way is by sharing experience: Just like apprentices of a craftsman learn their skills by observation, a knowledge-worker can learn required abilities through on-the-job training. The socialization does not demand for spoken or written words. Socialization is modeled starting with a knowledge object of one person to a knowledge object of another person.
- **Combination:** Combination is the conversion from explicit to explicit knowledge. During a combination, one or more information objects are used to create a new information object.

Unlike other process modeling tools, the main focus of KMDL® is to support all four expressions of knowledge conversion (see Figure 2). That allows a systematical description of process knowledge and the identification of all containing information. Origin and usage of knowledge and information can be defined as well.

Specification of KMDL®

Software engineering is a field of activity with a high percentage of knowledge-intensive business processes. Competitive as well as sustainable software solutions have to be developed. In addition, there are factors like a fast-changing technical basis and a dynamic personnel situation. Modern software engineering processes have to find a way between these requirements and conditions. An effective and efficient knowledge transfer within and between projects is an important factor for success, especially for an early identification and estimation of risks.

Figure 2. Model of the dynamics of knowledge creation

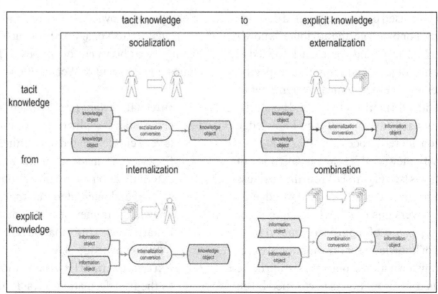

Besides the description of classical business processes, KMDL® provides the systematical identification and analysis of knowledge flows and transformations. This allows the identification of knowledge monopolies, unused competencies or unsatisfied demands. Thereby actions to enhance knowledge-intensive processes can be taken. Starting points of the KMDL® development were the complex and to a high degree knowledge-intensive software engineering processes of several business partners that accompanied the project. The project partners gave a significant input to determine requirements and evaluate the KMDL® methodology (Rombach et al., 1993). Simultaneously, the K-Modeler tool that supports the modeling of knowledge-intensive SE-processes, was developed and a prototype implemented.

Analysis of Potentials with KMDL®

The K-Modeler automatically identifies and evaluates various design patterns in the modeled processes, hence, helps to analyze the process. These process patterns are derived from known disadvantageous process elements and structures found in knowledge-intensive processes (Brown et al., 1998). The concept of patterns was coined originally by the architect and mathematician Christopher Alexander. Patterns can be used to find solutions for recurring problems, reusing existing knowledge (Greenfield, 2004; Kirchner & Jain, 2004). During the nineties the concept of patterns and best-practice solutions was transferred in sub-areas of software engineering (Gamma et al., 1995). The principle of patterns is used in KMDL® to analyze knowledge-intensive business processes (KMDL, 2006). Thereby a single process pattern describes a specific situation which repeatedly occurs during these processes. It is an indicator for hidden process potentials and points out opportunities for an alternative process design.

Process Pattern:

- **Multi-step pattern:** The multi step pattern category describes a combination of two conversions, whereby transitions from tacit to the explicit process level and vice versa will be analyzed. There is also an examination of conversion doubling on the same level. Twelve different combinations of knowledge conversions are imaginable, but only some of the combinations can be used to improve the process design. The multi-step socialization pattern is one example of a multi-step pattern, where knowledge gets lost during a double socialization ("Chinese Whisper").

Besides the pattern concept, KMDL® process models can be analyzed with various reports and special process views:

Process Reports (Static Analysis):

- **Occurrence report:** The occurrence report shows where specific objects appear with exceptionally high frequency in the activity view. The occurrence report can show that one person holds knowledge of high relevance for the process. This can indicate a knowledge monopoly and problems can surge when the person resigns. A better responsibility assignment can be a valid improvement. The occurrence report can also be used to determine the occurrence of other objects, for example, information objects.
- **Externalization report:** The externalization report describes which information results of a conversion and on which knowledge objects this is based. Information objects which were created on the basis of many knowledge objects can be business critical documents. Knowledge objects which are used several times during the creation of information can be business-specific knowledge.

- **Relevance report:** The relevance report shows the proportion between the four conversion types in the activity view. This points up which conversion types are used frequently and which are disregarded.
- **Competency report:** Knowledge profiles can be created within this report. This shows how often specific knowledge is available and where this knowledge is required.

Process Views:
- **Communication view:** Besides the process and activity view, also, a communication view is available. The view visualizes the communication structure in the processes. This can be used to revise the enterprise organization. Therefore, informal communication can be identified and integrated into the formal process structure.

Usually, the mentioned process patterns, reports and views cannot be identified without modeling the business process. Therefore, modeling knowledge-intensive business processes with KMDL® is an important step to detect strength and weaknesses and a basis for process improvements.

Real-Life Application of KMDL®

In this section, the application of KMDL® in a software developing company will be described. First, the company will be introduced and then the main objectives of the real-life example will be explained. This will provide a better understanding of usage of KMDL® in software engineering.

The real-life application was carried out in a small software developing company with 30 employees located in Munich, Germany. The company has been developing complex and custom-made products and integrating future-orientated IT solutions.

PRINCIPAL OBJECTS OF THE PRACTICAL EXAMPLE

For a reasonable design and analysis of software engineering processes, an adequate modeling is fundamental. Thereby it is of great importance to consider the knowledge-intensive processes that occur during the development of new software products and even build the main part of it. Based on the already existing Knowledge Modeling and Description Language (KMDL®), the investigation in the company had two intentions:

- Analysis of the existing software engineering processes.

The complete analysis of the existing software engineering processes is the first step for a company to reorganize and therefore to improve these processes. Furthermore, the existent knowledge in the company should be identified, which could be useful for future developments. In this real-life example, the main focus was directed on the analysis of software engineering projects.

Further Development of the Knowledge Modeling and Description Language (KMDL®)

The existing version of KMDL® had to be adapted towards the theoretical and practical requirements of the software engineering processes. The implementation in practice identified problems which led to extensions and revisions of KMDL®. Putting KMDL® to practice allowed discovery of critical points and insufficiencies in general. A further intention was to point out opportunities for improvement and to check the KMDL® approach for its relevance in software engineering.

KMDL® Procedural Model

The procedural model ensures the correct collection of data and information (see Figure 3). It is the basis for KMDL® process models and it was used in the following real-life example:

After project acquisition and preparation, it is necessary to put up an agreement on objectives and to identify a relevant business process. Then a process view can be generated. For the selection of a knowledge-intensive task, a criteria catalogue can be used. It consists of more than thirty qualities which are typical for a high knowledge-intensity. In the next phase, the activity process model is developed which can be analyzed in the K-Modeler tool. Then possible process improvements can be generated. In the first step, the recommendations were implemented and evaluated.

RESULTS

The following section will describe the results of the KMDL® real-life application. Within an iterative procedure, a KMDL® process model was developed. Especially, the areas of research and development as well as service support could be identified as highly knowledge-intensive and

were improved within the activity view (Figure 4). This was the basis for further analysis like patterns, reports and views.

Figure 5 shows the KMDL® person occurrence process report. It could be recognized that the software developers have great influence over the future ES module development. Apart from the developers, it could be shown that a multitude of further roles are involved in the process because strategic elements as well as distributional aspects and customer requirements were also considered. This is different to the service support process where the implementation of support inquiries is solely realized by software developers.

The enterprise system development process is characterized by a multitude of socialisations (Figure 6). In contrast, there are only few externalizations. This is a typical phenomenon for small- and medium-sized companies. Developers' documentation is often neglected which could be verified in the externalization report. The proportion between externalization and socialization is more balanced in the MES module where differentiated information objects are generated in the development process.

Figure 3. KMDL® procedural model

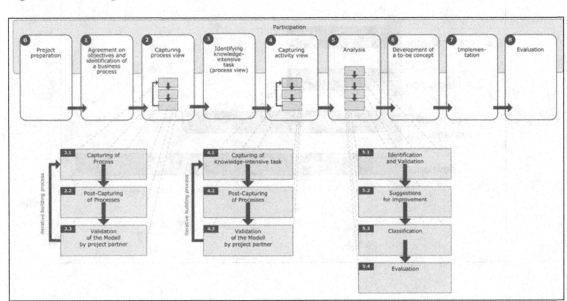

Figure 4. Example for KMDL® activity process model

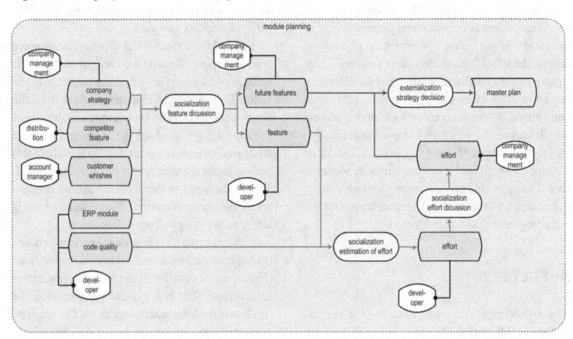

Figure 5. Person occurrence process report

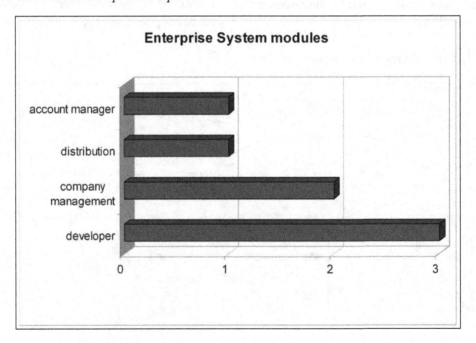

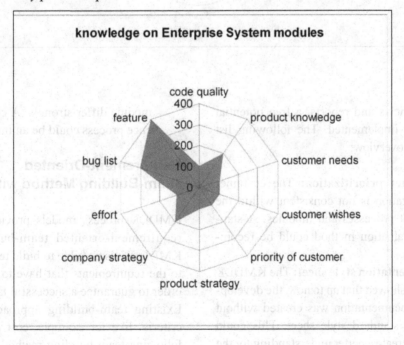

Figure 6. Relevancy process report

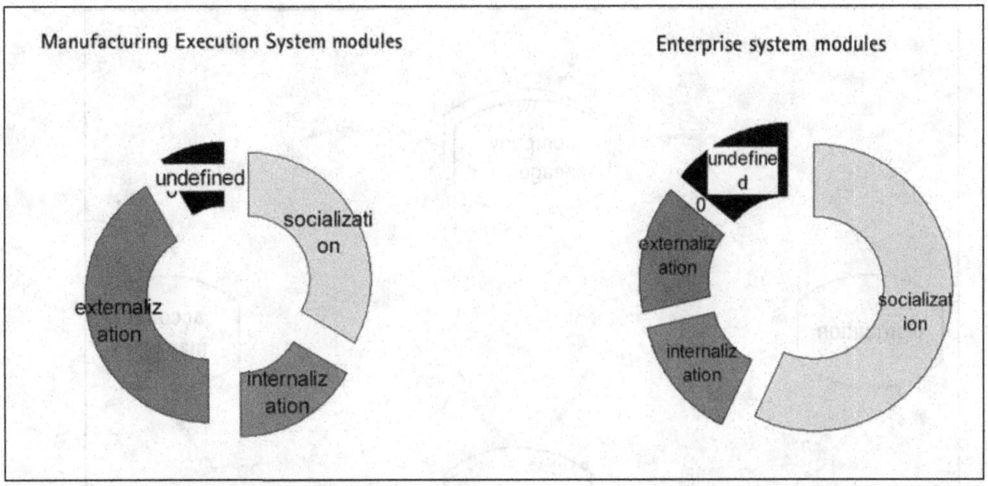

Figure 7. Competency process report

Furthermore, a knowledge profile for the ES module could be developed (Figure 7). Knowledge about features, bug lists, products and the corporate strategy are obviously the most important knowledge objects.

Generally, the enterprise system module is promoted by one developer (Figure 8) who is therefore the central person in the support process as well. Limited communicational exchange is realized with the distribution department, the account manager and the company management.

Figure 8. Communication process view

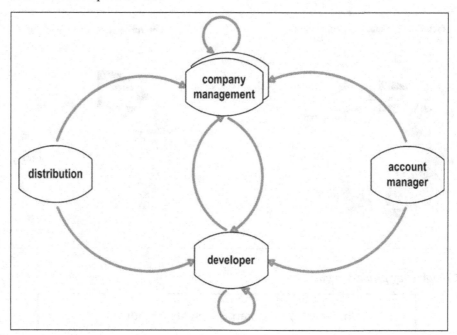

Besides views and reports, a free potential analysis was implemented. The following list gives a short overview:

- **Customer prioritization:** The customer prioritization is not consistent within the different processes and modules. A standard evaluation method could be recommended.
- **Documentation style sheet:** The KMDL® reports showed that up to now, the development documentation was created without using a standard style sheet. This could help to create a better understanding for the traceability of new functions and changes.
- **Software checklist:** During the project, the employees asked for checklists in the area of software extensions. This could include criteria like customer priority, budget information and reusability.
- **Research and development:** Up to now, research and development processes for each

module differ strongly. A consistent reference process could be an improvement.

Requirement-Oriented Team-Building Method with KMDL®

KMDL® process models provide a basis for requirement-oriented team-building. Using KMDL®, it is possible to build teams according to the requirements that have to be fulfilled in order to guarantee a successful task realization. Existing team-building approaches focus on criteria, like for example, cost and time. The following team-building method will present a way to cope with the specific requirements and the knowledge scope. Therefore the following preconditions have to be fulfilled:

- KMDL® process models, including tasks and requirements
- A semantic net that has the ability to connect all the concepts (knowledge and require-

ment objects) occurring within the process model.

- A knowledge object repository which contains all knowledge objects of a specific person.

Figure 9 describes the procedural model of the team-building component. In order to identify similar knowledge objects and to compute the knowledge scope, a semantic net is created. The semantic net is a dynamic structure that can be adapted, for example, whenever new concepts (for knowledge or requirement objects) are introduced. With help of the KMDL® business process models, it is possible to improve and optimize the semantic net. There are four possible specifications for semantic nets: taxonomy, thesaurus, topic map or ontology. In this contribution, the semantic net is an extended taxonomy, but also an ontology can be used. There are two possible procedures to create the taxonomy. First of all, the taxonomy can be created top-down. If this seems

to be difficult, concepts from already-considered process instances can be adapted. Therefore, the taxonomy has to be created by using the bottom-up technique. At first, all relevant concepts that are used in the company have to be identified and structured hierarchically. The relations generalization/specialization, aggregation, composition and synonym have to be integrated and therefore build the extended taxonomy (see Figure 10). After comparison with the mentioned requirements, a new team composition can be generated. One or more tasks that should be solved within a team have to be chosen. Requirements refer to the knowledge which has to be available in order to fulfill a task successfully, considering specific time and quality restrictions. To save time and costs, it is of high importance to find a team which is able to fulfill the task efficiently and effectively according to the requirements. The team-building method consists of three steps. At first, a matrix consisting of available persons and requirements has to be generated. The requirements as well as

Figure 9. Team building procedure model

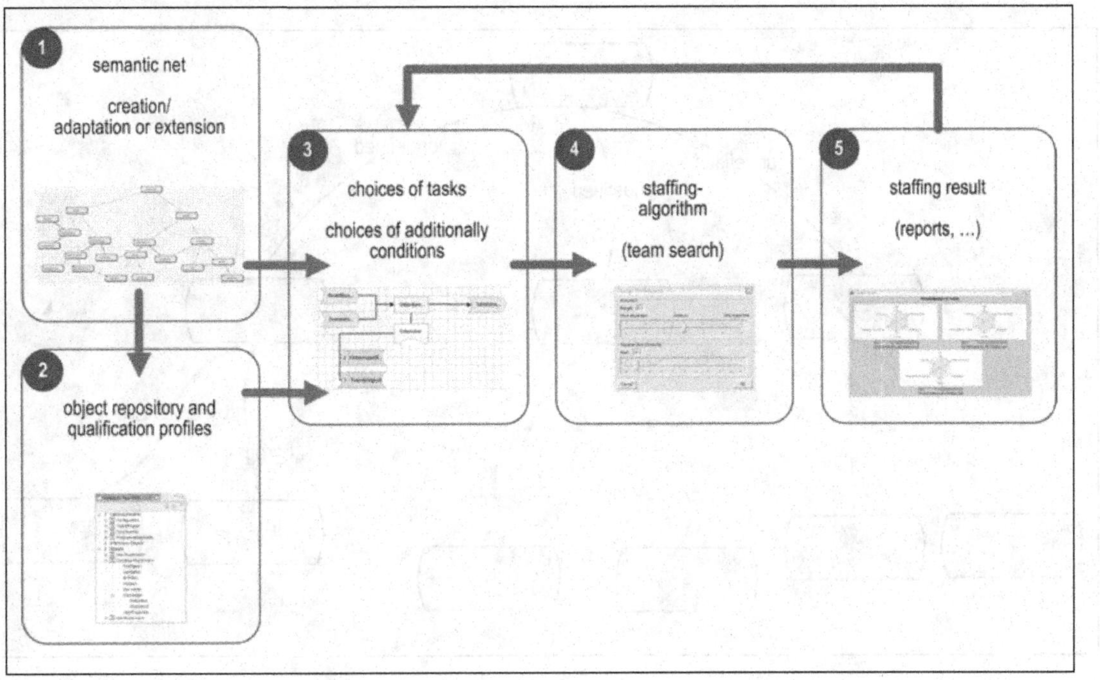

the personal knowledge objects are based on the business process model and structured within the extended taxonomy.

The types of relations used in the extended taxonomy are shown below (see Figure 10):

- **Synonym:** Concept 6 equals concept 8.
- **Aggregation:** Concept 7 consists of concept 8 and concept 9. If a person holds concept 7, he either holds concept 8, concept 9 or both.
- **Composition:** Concept 1 consists of concept 2 and concept 3. If anybody holds concept 1 as knowledge object, the person also holds concept 2 and 3.
- **Generalization/specialization:** Concept 4 is more generic than concept 5 or 6. The opposite happens with concept 5 and 6 (and synonym 8), which are more specialized than concept 4.
- **Undefined:** There are no relations between concept 0 and concepts 1, 4 or 7. If anybody

holds concept 0 as knowledge object, the team-building algorithm cannot make associations with concept 1, 4 or 7 and vice versa.

The team-building algorithm is structured as follows: The algorithm calculates "0", if the knowledge object and the requirement refer to the same object in the extended taxonomy (no graphical distance between the offered and the required knowledge object). For all other relations, the algorithm calculates values depending on distance within the taxonomy. If a person does not hold the requested concept, but can offer a more specific concept (specialized knowledge in a specific area which is part of the whole concept), the resulting value is low. If a person does not hold the requested concept, but can offer a more general concept, the resulting value depends on the distance within the taxonomy. The knowledge scope has to be defined by the user before the team-building algorithm starts (see Figure 11).

Figure 10. Possible types of relations in the extended taxonomy

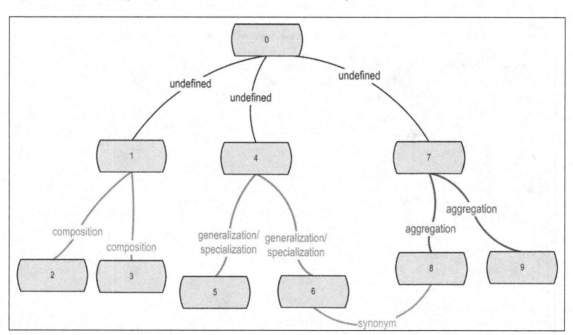

Regarding the requirement scope, similar personal knowledge concepts can be found.

The closer the distance between the requirements and the personal knowledge concepts is, the better a person is able to fulfill the task. On the left side in Figure 11, the task requirements are illustrated, on the right side three persons and their individual knowledge scope. Person A holds all required knowledge objects. Person B holds some of the required knowledge objects inside the knowledge scope. Hence, the team-building algorithm would suggest person A. But in most cases, each person contributes only some of the required objects and through combined knowledge of the individuals the task can be fulfilled within a group. The team-building algorithm determines which persons are skilled in at least one of the task requirements. Therefore, it is possible to define minimum requirements that have to be held by every single team member. Furthermore, it is possible to use weighting factors for the requirements, enabling further differentiation. If no weighting factors are assigned, all requirements are considered equally.

Depending on the value of the knowledge scope, different teams can be found and evaluated. For the determination of the measured value, the entire team and its knowledge will be considered. Furthermore, the efficiency of the team will be evaluated due to the fact that smaller teams are less expensive than bigger teams. The team-building component supplies suggestions for the management. Nevertheless, the final choice about a team composition has to be extended, considering further criteria, for example, corporate culture. The following section explains the team building component based on an example in the software engineering area.

Figure 11. Knowledge scopes of person A, person B and person C

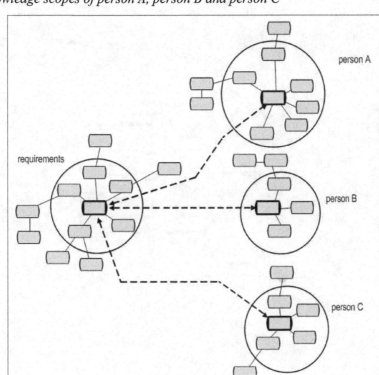

REQUIREMENT-ORIENTED TEAM-BUILDING

The team-building component is based on the taxonomy as shown in Figure 12. To explain the team-building algorithm, Table 2 shows the object repository including all the involved persons and their knowledge objects. These objects are also included in the taxonomy. Only black-marked concepts are important for the following example; the remaining concepts are only relevant to understand the full software engineering context.

A basic precondition for the team-building component is a task. A task just means a couple of requirements which have to be fulfilled by a number of persons. In the practical example, a Linux server was purchased and a java-based application for Lotus Notes/Domino has to be developed. This task should be fulfilled by a new team, whose composition is determined by the algorithm. Therefore, the following requirements (see Table 1) were defined.

Let us assume the maximum distance between the individual knowledge concepts and the requirements is "2." At first, a matrix has to be created consisting of task requirements and available knowledge objects (see Table 3). Skills which are essential for all of the team members

Figure 12. Extended concept taxonomy (extract)

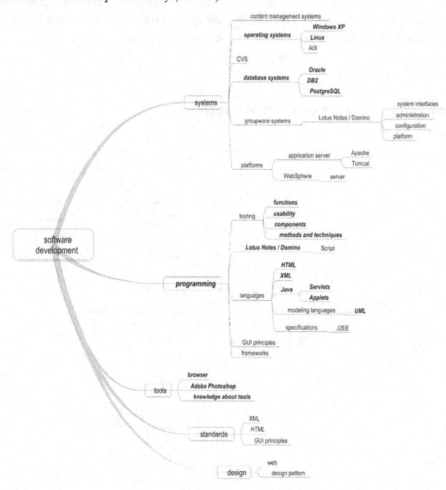

Table 1. Requirements

	necessary knowledge (amount of persons)	weight 7/7
operating systems	at least one person	1/7
Linux	at least one person	1/7
database systems	at least one person	1/7
PostgreSQL	at least one person	1/7
Lotus Notes/Domino	at least one person	2/7
XML	at least one person	1/7
Java	every team member	1/7

Table 2. Object repository

Steve	Peter	George	Jane	Mary
operating systems, Windows XP, Linux, Lotus Notes/Domino, Java	database systems, Oracle, DB2	HTML, XML, Java, DB2	programming, Lotus Notes/Domino, Java, Windows XP	Linux, database- systems, PostgreSQL, Java, programming

Table 3. Team-building matrix with knowledge scope

	operating systems	Linux	database systems	Postgre SQL	Lotus Notes / Domino **	XML	Java *
Steve	yes + Linux, Windows XP, Lotus Notes/ Domino	yes + operating systems, Windows XP	no, but operation systems, Linux, Windows XP, Lotus Notes/ Domino	no	yes	no, but Java	yes
Peter	no	no	yes	no	no	no	no
George	no, but DB2	no	no, but DB2	no, but DB2	no	yes + HTML, Java	yes + HTML, XML
Jane	no, but Lotus Notes/Domino, Windows XP	no, but Window XP	no, but Lotus Notes/Domino, Windows XP	no	yes	no, but programming, Java	yes + programming, XML
Mary	no, but Linux, database systems, PostgreSQL	yes	yes + Linux, PostgreSQL	yes + database systems	no	no, but programming, Java	yes + programming

Table 4. Staffing algorithm results

Team Search	Team Based Knowledge Benchmark
Steve, Mary	230
Jane, Mary	215
Steve, Mary, George	204
Jane, Mary, George	167
Jane, Steve, Mary	165
Steve, Mary, George, Jane	120

Figure 13. Knowledge gap of teams

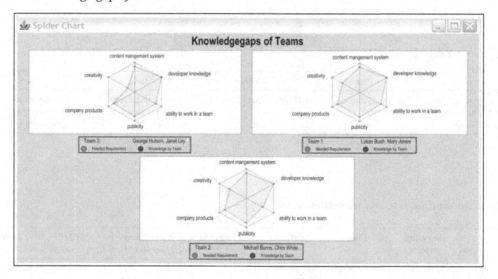

are marked with (*) and requirements of particular importance and a high weighting will be indicated with (**).

It is obvious that "Peter" will no longer be considered for the team, because the knowledge object "java" is required for every member. Table 4 shows the output of the team-building algorithm.

Within the assessment and the team efficiency, two teams would be proposed to accomplish the task:

1. Steve and Mary
2. Jane and Mary

The suggested teams do not match completely with the requirements. More specialized or more general knowledge is available to close the gap. For the proposed team, it is possible to visualize the knowledge gaps (see Figure 13).

GENERAL CONCLUSION AND FUTURE PROSPECTS

Applied to knowledge-intensive software engineering processes, KMDL® has proven to be a working concept. Current research focuses on the analysis of KMDL® process models in order to identify possible process improvements. The real-life example showed that the application of knowledge management can increase productivity in software engineering. By pointing out process patterns, reports and views, potential improvements were identified. Therefore, long-winded coordination processes could be accelerated and optimized. But it has to be considered that knowledge management activities will only be accepted by employees if the advantages are clearly shown and the required effort is kept within a limit.

Based on the research results as well as the successful commercial implementation of KMDL® v1.1, KMDL® v2.0 now builds the backbone for the current development of KMDL® v2.1. The focus on knowledge conversions and the extension of the theory of Nonaka et al. leads towards a more powerful method that represents the actual conducted knowledge transfer, application and creation. By introducing methods for the knowledge conversions, it is easy to distinguish the different knowledge conversions and classify them. Therefore, they contribute to the expressiveness of the language. On the other hand, this can be used to identify best practice methods in the analysis of knowledge-intensive processes.

Actual research in the field of KMDL® cope with skill management and staffing, simulation of knowledge intensive business processes, process-model-based configuration of knowledge management tools, inter- organisational knowledge management, and semantic annotation of process models.

REFERENCES

Abran, A., Moore, J.W., Bourque, P., Dupuis, R. & Tripp, L.L. (2004). Guide to the software engineering body of knowledge. Swebok®: A project of the software engineering coordination committee. *IEEE Computer Society Press*. 1.

Brown, W.J., Malveau, R.C., McCormick, H.W., & Mowbray, T.J. (1998). *AntiPatterns: Refactoring software, architectures, and projects in crisis.* John Wiley & Sons.

Davenport, T.H., and Prusak, L. (2000). *Working knowledge.* Harvard Business School Press.

Eppler, M., Seifried, P., & Röpnack, A. (1999). Improving knowledge intensive processes through an rnterprise knowledge medium. In: Prasad, J. (Eds.), *Proceedings of the 1999 Conference on Managing Organizational Knowledge for Strategic Advantage: The Key Role of Information Technology and Personnel.* New Orleans.

Gamma, E., Helm, R., Johnson R., & Vlissides, J. (1995). *Design patterns.* Addison-Wesley Pub Co.

Groff, T.R., & Jones, T.P. (2003). *Introduction to knowledge management: KM in business.* Butterworth-Heinemann.

Greenfield, J., Short, K., Cook, S., Kent, S., & Crupi, J. (2004). *Software factories: Assembling application with patterns, frameworks, and tools,* (1st ed.). Wiley.

Gronau, N., & Weber, E. (2004). Modeling of knowledge intensive business processes with the declaration language (KMDL®). In M. Khosrow-Pour (Eds.), *Innovations through information technology.* Idea Group Inc. 2004 Information Resources Management Association International Conference.

Gronau, N., & Weber, E. (2004a). Management of knowledge intensive business processes. In J. Desel, B. Pernici, & M. Weske, (Eds.), *Business process management.* Springer: Heidelberg.

Gronau, N., Müller, C., & Uslar, M. (2004). The KMDL® knowledge management approach: Integrating knowledge conversions and business process modeling. In D. Karagiannis, & U. Reimer, (Eds.), *Practical aspects of knowledge management.* Springer-Verlag: Berlin, Heidelberg.

Gronau, N., Müller, C., & Korf, R. (2005). KMDL®—Capturing, analysing and improving knowledge-intensive Business Processes. *Journal of Computer Science. 4*, 452-472.

Hamel, G., & Prahalad, C.K. (1990). The core competence of the corporation. *Harvard Business Review.*

Heisig, P. (2002). GPW-WM: Methoden und Werkzeuge zum geschäftsprozessorientierten Wissensmanagement. In A. Abecker, K. Hinkelmann, & M.Heiko, (Eds.), *Geschäftsprozessorientiertes Wissensmanagement.* Berlin. Springer.

Inkpen, A.C., & Dinur. A. (1998). Knowledge management processes and international joint ventures. *Organization Science, 9*(4), 454-468.

Kim, S., Hwang, H., & Suh, E. (2003). A process-based approach to knowledge-flow analysis: A case study of a manufacturing firm. *Knowledge and Process Management, 10*(4), 260-276.

Kirchner, M., & Jain, P. (2004). *Pattern-oriented software architecture.* Pattern for resource management (Wiley Software Pattern Series). John Wiley & Sons.

KMDL. (2006). *Knowledge modeling and description language.* Retrieved March 30, 2006: http://www.kmdl.de

Mertins, K., Heisig, P., Vorbeck, J., & Mertens, K. (Eds.) (2000). *Knowledge management: Best practices in Europe.* Springer.

Nissen, M.E. (2002). An extended model of knowledge-flow dynamics. *Communications of the Association for Information Systems, 8*, 251-266.

Nissen, M.E., & Levitt, R.E. (2004). Agent-based modeling of knowledge dynamics. *Knowledge Management Research & Practice, 2*(3), 169-183.

Nonaka, I., & Takeuchi, H. (1995). *The knowledge-creating company.* How Japanese companies create the dynamics of innovation. Oxford University Press: New York.

Polanyi, M. (1958). *Personal knowledge—Towards a post-critical philosophy.* The University of Chicago Press, Chicago.

Remus, U. (2002). *Process oriented knowledge management, concepts and modeling.* PhD thesis. University of Regensburg. Germany. Regensburg.

Rombach, H.D., Basil, V.R., & Selbey, R.W. (1993). *Experimental software engineering issues: Critical assessment and future directions.* International Workshop, Dagstuhl Castle. Germany. September 14 (Lecture Notes in Computer Science). Springer.

Schmidt, S.R., Kiemele, M.J., & Berdine, R.J. (1996). *Knowledge based management: Unleashing the power of quality improvement.* Air Academy Press.

Van der Aalst, W.M.P (1998). *Formalization and verification of event-driven process chains.* Computer Science Reports. Eindhoven.

ENDNOTES

[1] http://www.m-wise.de
[2] http://www.iose-w.de

Chapter XVII
Using Social Networking Analysis to Facilitate Knowledge Sharing Amongst Senior Managers in Multinational Organisations

Bonnie Wai-yi Cheuk
Global Head of Knowledge & Information, Environmental Resources Management (ERM), UK

ABSTRACT

Prior to the establishment of the knowledge management (KM) strategy, the British Council defined knowledge as 'objects'. Knowledge sharing was about sharing documents and information on the intranet or via global databases. Since December 2002, Dervin's sense-making methodology has been applied to manage 'knowledge'. Knowledge is seen not as a product that can be transferred from one colleague to another, but as a communication practice. This means that shared knowledge has to be interpreted and made sense of by its recipients through genuine dialogue. During this phase of KM implementation, the focus shifted to linking up colleagues and providing space for dialogue through building global communities of practice and virtual teams. This chapter presents an example of how we have used the theory of social networking analysis as a diagnostic tool to promote knowledge sharing amongst our newly formed thirty-people global leadership team. The three steps we have taken to carry out the exercise and its limitations are also discussed. Towards the end of the chapter, the author presents an alternative application of social networking analysis in a multinational consulting firm.

BACKGROUND

The purpose of the British Council is to build mutually beneficial relationships between people in the UK and other countries, and to increase appreciation of the UK's creative ideas and achievements. Much focus has been on sharing knowledge and experience with customers. To

Copyright © 2008, IGI Global, distributing in print or electronic forms without written permission of IGI Global is prohibited.

take the organisation to another level, the British Council promotes knowledge sharing among its 7,000 employees, who are located in 109 different countries. The ultimate aim is to empower staff to get the knowledge they need to serve their customers to the highest standard possible.

The knowledge management (KM) program was officially launched in December 2002 with the appointment of the new director of knowledge management. Following a comprehensive six-month knowledge audit exercise, the global knowledge management strategy was approved by the senior management team in December 2003. The knowledge management vision is to enable the British Council to develop and deliver world class products and services to its customers by effectively sharing and utilising collective knowledge. This will be achieved by finding the best ways to connect its employees with each other and by providing them with easy access to relevant documents and resources.

Over the last two years, we have launched a number of projects to increase awareness of knowledge management, and to get the buy-in of senior management for the program to invest in the tools and approaches needed to improve global knowledge sharing. Specific KM projects which are beginning to embed into the organisation include:

a. Knowledge audit conducted using Dervin's sense-making methodology (Dervin, 1992)
b. Development of knowledge management strategies for business units
c. Building communities of practices using seven-phase methodology (Cheuk, 2004)
d. Enhancement of the intranet, collaboration tools and global databases
e. Applying social networking analysis to support collaborative working (Anklam, 2003; Cross & Parker, 2004)
f. Applying narrative techniques to conduct project debriefs

In 2005, knowledge management was widely recognised as an enabler to deliver the British Council's overall business strategy. Over 100 knowledge champions worldwide have attended training on knowledge management and over 70 global communities of practice have been developed[1].

BUSINESS CONTEXT

During 2004-2005, the overseas operations of the British Council were significantly re-structured. Thirteen regions have been introduced to replace the existing 109 country operations which were each managed as individual entities. Each new region is made up of a number of existing country operations.

Thirteen regional directors were appointed. They have to work closely with the seventeen senior management team members based in the UK to set strategic direction for the organisation. This thirty-person team is referred to as Global Leadership Team (GLT).

The restructuring provides an excellent opportunity to promote knowledge sharing beyond country operations, as well as to promote knowledge sharing between overseas operations and the UK headquarters. However, it also presents a challenge. Any organisational re-structure leads to the creation of new teams, which can be to the detriment of any existing knowledge sharing culture. This presents a challenge to the knowledge management team.

What is the Nature of Knowledge?

A review into the knowledge management literature largely defines knowledge using Nonaka and Takeuchi's (1991) definition of 'tacit' knowledge (i.e., knowledge in a person's head which has a personal quality and is hard to formalise and communicate) and 'explicit' knowledge (i.e., knowledge that is transmittable in formal, systematic language). Sutton (2001) defines the latter as 'codified knowledge' (i.e., knowledge which can be written down) and uses it interchangeably with 'information'. Taken this view, KM systems were created to 'capture' the knowledge of experts. The 'capture' approach continued with an emphasis on 'capturing knowledge' in databases, manuals, books and reports, and then sharing it in a hard form. (Hildreth & Kimble, 2002).

Wilson (2002) argues that one should not use the term 'information' and 'knowledge' interchangeably. He proposes that everything outside the mind that can be manipulated in any way is defined as 'data' or 'information'. They take the form of papers in a journal, e-mail messages, manuscript letters in an archive, and so forth. However, knowledge (i.e., what we know) can never be managed, except by the individual knower and, even then, only imperfectly. Wilson defines knowledge as 'what we know'. He elaborates that 'knowledge involves the mental processes of comprehension, understanding and learning that go on in the mind and only in the mind, however much they involve interaction with the world outside the mind, and interaction with others. Whenever we wish to express what we know, we can only do so by uttering messages of one kind or another—oral, written, graphic, gestural or even through 'body language'. Such messages do not carry 'knowledge', they constitute 'information', which a knowing mind may assimilate, understand, comprehend and incorporate into its own knowledge structures. These structures are not identical for the person uttering the message and the receiver, because each person's knowledge structures are, as Schutz (1967) puts it, 'biographically determined'. Therefore, the knowledge built from the messages can never be exactly the same as the knowledge base from which the messages were uttered. He argues that 'knowledge' cannot be managed, and knowledge management is a 'nonsense' concept.

Dervin takes on an alternative view that it is not important to distinguish information and knowledge from a communication perspective, because 'knowledge' is not an object but rather a communication process or flow. 'Knowledge' (regardless of what label you give it) is anything that makes sense to the users through a dialogic communication process. 'Knowledge' can only be defined from the users' perspectives (Dervin, 2003).

Prior to the establishment of the knowledge management strategy in December 2003, the British Council took the traditional view and defined 'knowledge' as information and documents that can be managed as objects. Knowledge management was seen as sharing documents and information on the intranet or via global databases.

The launch of the knowledge management strategy in December 2003 employed Dervin's sense-making theory to provide the organisation with an alternative perspective in knowledge sharing. Knowledge is no longer seen as a product that can be transferred from one colleague to another, but as a two-way communication practice. In addition to connecting employees to 'information' using KM systems, we begin to focus on linking up employees with employees, and in particular, to facilitate genuine dialogue between employees. Instead of asking the question 'what information should we manage?', we begin to ask the question 'who should be linked up?' in order to maximise business outcomes.

During this phase of KM implementation, the focus was on providing space for dialogue through building global communities of practice and virtual teams to deliver strategic programmes. At the British Council, we put in facilitators to manage these communities and supported them with Web-based collaboration tools. Social networking analysis was also introduced as a diagnostic tool to support team-building, as well as to evaluate the performance of the communities.

Theory Behind Social Networking Analysis

Social network analysis has emerged as a set of methods for the analysis of social structures; methods which are specifically geared towards an investigation of the relational aspects of these structures. The use of these methods, therefore, depends on the availability of relational rather than attribute data (Scott, 1992).

Social networking analysis can be used to address various organisational issues such as supporting partnership and alliances; assessing strategy execution; improving strategic decision-making in top leaderships networks; integrating networks across core processes; promoting innovation; ensuring integration post-merger or large scale change; developing communities of practices; personal networks and leadership development (Cross, 2004).

The importance of social networks is highlighted by Cross et al. (2001) who found that despite easy access to a world class knowledge management system, 85% of managers got information (that had an impact on the success of a project) from their personal network.

Snowden (2002) emphasises that knowledge is not only stored in documents. He argues that 'we always know more than we can say, and we can always say more than we can write down'. He suggests that we must pay attention to managing social networks—this is how knowledge in people's heads is transferred naturally and rapidly across an organisation.

Informed by these theories and associated research findings, the British Council has introduced social networking analysis as a diagnostic tool to improve strategic decision- making in the newly-formed global leadership team.

What Have we Done to Promote Knowledge Sharing?

We started with the thirteen newly-appointed regional directors in charge of setting strategic direction for the British Council and the delivery of products and services overseas. They are geographically dispersed, they have to work closely with the seventeen senior management team members in the UK headquarters, and this global leadership team will meet only twice a year in the UK.

The knowledge management team wanted to help them to understand what knowledge sharing across countries and regions is really like. They needed to understand what knowledge has to be shared to help them and their staff to get their work done, and what needs to be in place to make knowledge transfer effective. The KM team wanted to give them practical experience before they went on to introduce new knowledge sharing approaches to the teams within their region.

A series of activities were designed to promote knowledge sharing amongst the thirteen global leaders, as well as between them and the seventeen senior management team members in the UK. They included:

1. An initial community building meeting to help them to get to know one another
2. An audit exercise to find out what knowledge, resources, expertise and help they need to get work done
3. The establishment of a Web-based collaboration site
4. The appointment of a community facilitator
5. The establishment of an events calendar
6. Carrying out a social networking analysis exercise to identify opportunities and gaps

How did we Conduct the Social Networking Exercise?

The knowledge management team conducted a social network analysis exercise for the thirty global leaders as part of a global leadership development event. The aim was to help the team to visualise their existing relationships, and allow the group to reflect on how they network with one another.

There are three steps to complete this exercise:

- **Step 1:** A data collection template was developed and circulated to the thirteen regional directors (as well as the seventeen senior management team members in the UK). They were asked to complete the form prior to the event (Appendix 1).
- **Step 2:** The findings were analysed and presented to the group during the 60-minute knowledge management session.
- **Step 3:** The participants were given the opportunity to discuss the findings and come up with interventions to focus on during the next three months (Appendix 2).

The knowledge management team emphasized that social networking analysis is best employed as a diagnostic tool to generate discussion relating to team-building and communications. It is not meant to evaluate the performance of the group or that of individual members. A step-by-step guide to the process is presented below:

Step 1: Data Collection

The following template was circulated to the thirteen leaders (and the seventeen senior management team members in the UK) before and during the event. Altogether, thirty colleagues were given the form. The template was designed to be simple and self-explanatory. Only two questions were asked in this case:

Table 1.

Reflect on your interaction with the following global leaders since Sept. 2004 and answer the following questions					
Scoring:	0 = Never	1 = Once in two months	2 = Once a month	3 = Weekly	4 = Daily
Name:					
Ref No	Names - Alphabetically sorted	Q1: To whom, and from whom did you send and receive information, documents, plans and other resources?	Q2: With whom do you have informal discussions about your work and/or new ideas?		
1	Alan				
2	Andrew				
3	James				
4	Martin				
5	Michael				
6	Morna				
8	Philip				
9	Rob				
10	Rod				
11	Rosemary				
12	Sarah				
13	Stephan				
…	…				
30	…				

Figure 1.

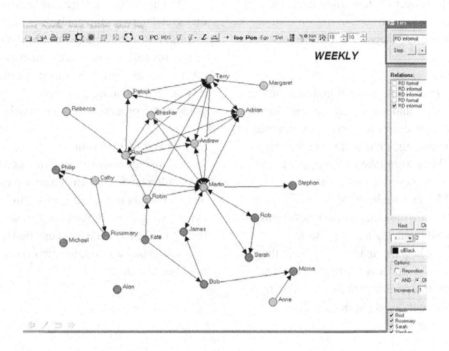

Q1: Who did you send information to and receive it from? (Documents, plans and other resources)

Q2: With whom did you have *informal* discussions about your work and/or new ideas?

Step 2: Data Analysis and Visualisation

Only twenty-three colleagues out of thirty global leaders completed the data collection template. The knowledge management team used UCINET software to visualise the data using social networking analysis (SNA) maps. During the event, the global leaders were first given an introduction to social network analysis (SNA), and then presented with the findings in terms of three anonymous daily, weekly and monthly SNA maps. Each map demonstrated the frequency of colleagues' contact with one another for formal information exchange. The nodes representing colleagues based in the UK and overseas are coloured green and red, respectively. Figure 1 shows one of the SNA maps.

Step 3: Discussion

The leaders were invited to discuss the following questions:

1. What patterns do you see?
2. Where do you think you sit in the SNA map?
3. What do you see as the key strength of this network?
4. What do you see as the potential weakness of this network?

We respected the privacy of the data, as it disclosed the relationship between colleagues. At first, we showed a diagram which did not provide names of individual nodes. To our surprise, all the participants asked for the results to be disclosed during the event and immediately gave consent for their names to appear in the SNA map.

As a result, we presented the map above. They were given time to reflect on the above questions again and then discuss these questions:

1. As a group, what needs to be changed in three months' time in order to achieve the global leadership team's objectives?
2. As an individual, what would you like to change in three months' time?

What did the Group Learn?

The newly-appointed global leaders agreed that the SNA map represents a reasonably accurate reflection of the situation at that time, given that the majority of global leaders were newly in post. In addition, they highlighted the following issues regarding knowledge flow:

- There were strong relationships between UK-based staff
- There was relatively little overseas/UK interface
- Only a few overseas leaders were talking to one another
- There was little difference in terms of formal and informal networking patterns

They also reflected on the strength and weakness of their network. The strength was that the monthly SNA map showed the volume of communication that was already taking place. The weaknesses were:

- The preponderance of nodes in the headquarters. This might hinder widespread communication of messages.
- More networking was needed between the global leaders.
- There was a need to set clear, defined tasks to ensure that communication takes place.

As a result of the discussion, they identified some actions to improve networking.

- Several leaders agreed to form a "mini-group" to work on issues together.

- A monthly Web meeting was arranged to allow the group to discuss issues.
- The need to nurture existing sub-groups, for example, several regional leaders were already discussing issues informally with one another. They wanted to make an effort to keep that going.

What Impact has Resulted?

As a result of the interventions that the global leaders identified to improve networking amongst themselves, on top of their busy schedule, they make a conscious effort to touch base with one another through online knowledge sharing sessions. Over time, they have built up a better understanding of one another, and share the challenges they face and how they overcome them in their region. Improved networking amongst the global leadership team members has also led to unexpected outcomes, whereby knowledge exchange is not limited to topics on the set agenda, but takes place on a more informal basis covering a range of other topics.

In summary, through improved social networking, the global leaders have led by example and contributed to improve knowledge sharing in a number of ways:

1. It has increased the number of documents shared on the collaborative Web site (as a result of the need to exchange documents to prepare for or as a follow up to a networking event).
2. The global leaders share important projects they are implementing in their regions and who the employees are leading on them. This information is in turn shared by the regional director with their regional team, and has resulted in increasing networking between managers in different regions.
3. It has open up the eyes of global leaders of the power of social network through good

Diagram 1. The SNA map on John's scorecard

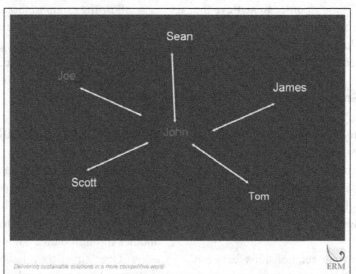

Diagram 2. The SNA map on Joe's scorecard

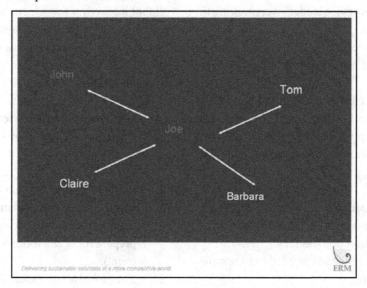

facilitation. Many regional directors have expressed an interest in conducting a similar social networking exercise with their own regional management team.

An Alternative SNA Application

The author has subsequently moved on to head up a global knowledge management program for Environmental Resources Management (ERM), a multinational environmental consulting firm.

There, she experienced an alternative approach to use social networking analysis to facilitate collaboration amongst over forty senior partners.

As part of the annual strategic planning exercise, every senior partner has to define targets and objectives for the next financial year. Once the objectives are set, each partner is asked to draw a social networking map by specifying any other senior partners with whom they have to build relationship with in order to deliver the business targets. These draft social networking maps are all posted on the wall of a big hall.

The partners then spent time going around the hall and studying each others social networking map. They can add their names (or suggest other names) to be added to any SNA maps. If they have highlighted a senior partners' name on his/her own SNA map, he/she has to ensure that this is a reciprocal relationship (See Diagram 1 and 2).

This process includes a lot of negotiation between the senior leaders before the 'required' relationship to grow the business can be agreed on and subsequently included in each senior partner's scorecard.

The discussion itself is a fruitful exercise as it forces them to critically review the formal and informal relationship amongst themselves, and increase their consciously of how other strategic decisions can impact on the effectiveness of these networks. In addition, by building the SNA map into senior partners' scorecards, they are held accountable to build and nurture the relationship.

In this example, no SNA software tool has been used. The methodology is simpler than the British Council example and yet the result is as powerful.

LIMITATIONS

In the case of the British Council, a number of participants pointed out the limitations of the social networking map. These included:

- A successful SNA map requires a 100% response rate—all participants must fill in the data collection sheets. This is difficult to achieve. At the British Council, we achieved this through distributing the form at a compulsory event. However, only twenty-three out of thirty global leadership team members have completed the data collection template.
- There were many nodes on the network (especially in the UK). This can lead to the false conclusion that the more nodes, the stronger the network.
- A number of leaders mentioned that the SNA map only reported the situation at that time. The maps should be used with care as they can only provide a snapshot at any one point in time. The group thought it would be useful to go through the same exercise again at a later date to see the shifts in type and strength of relationship.

The other limitation is that in this social networking exercise, only twenty-three people participated. When applied to a larger number of staff (e.g., beyond 1,000), the resulting SNA map can be more complex, and the discussion as to what a person can do as an 'individual' to change and improve networking can be more difficult. Additional applied research has to be done to understand the value of SNA to the business.

CONCLUSION

This chapter presents an example of how the British Council has used the theory of social networking analysis as a practical tool to support our knowledge management program. It proves that SNA exercises are simple to carry out and the results can provide a focal point for discussion in improving knowledge flow.

The global leaders who attended the session agreed that it was worth completing the exercise, and that the SNA maps provided them with alternative perspectives on their own knowledge flow and networking habits. They begin to recognise the need to balance the sharing of knowledge through documents against people-to-people networking. It helps them to improve understanding that knowledge management as a subject encompasses more than document exchange. They recommended that SNA exercises be adopted for supporting team-building at a regional level.

The example of how SNA is applied in the multinational environmental consulting firm provides additional insight on how simple SNA maps can help senior leaders to focus on relationship building to deliver strategic objectives.

REFERENCES

Anklam, P. (2003). KM and the social network. *Knowledge Management Magazine*, May 2003.

Cheuk, B. (2004). Applying sense-making methodology to establish communities of practice: Examples from the British Council. In: Bruno et al. (Eds.), *People, knowledge and technology: What have we learnt so far?* (pp. 55-65).

Cheuk, B. (2004). A seven stage guide to community implementation. In S. Lelic (Ed.), *Communities of practice: Lessons from collaborative leading enterprises* (pp. 83-91). London: Ark Group Limited.

Cheuk, B., & Dervin, B. (1999). A qualitative sense-making study of the information seeking situations faced by professionals in three workplace contexts. *The Electronic Journal of Communication, 9*(2-4), (Online).

Cross, R. http://www.robcross.org/sna.htm

Cross, R., & Parker, A. (2004). *The hidden power of social networks.* Harvard Business School Press.

Cross, R., Parker, A., Prusak, L., & Borgatti, S. (2001). Knowing what we know: Supporting knowledge creation and sharing in social networks. *Organizational Dynamics, 30*(2), 100-120.

Dervin, B. (1992). From the mind's eye of the user: The sense-making qualitative quantitative methodology. In J. Glazier & R. Powell (Eds.), *Qualitative research in information management* (pp. 61-84). Englewood, CO: Libraries Unlimited.

Dervin, B., Foreman-Wernet, L., Lauterbach, E. (2003). *Sense-making methodology reader: Selected writings of Brenda Dervin.* New Jersey: Hampton Press.

Hildreth, P., & Kimble, C. (2002). The duality of knowledge. *Information Research*, *8*(1), (online) http://informationr.net/ir/8-1/paper142.html.

Nonaka, I., & Takeuchi, H. (1995). *The knowledge-creating company.* New York, NY: Oxford University Press.

Schutz, Alfred. (1967). *The phenomenology of the social world.* Evanston, IL: Northwestern University Press.

Scott, J. (1992). *Social network analysis.* Newbury Park, CA: Sage.

Snowden, D. (2002). Complex acts of knowing: Paradox and descriptive self-awareness. *Journal of knowledge management, 6*(2), 100-111.

Sutton, D. (2001). What is knowledge and can it be managed?. *European Journal of Information Systems, 10*(2), 80-88.

Wilson, T. (2002). The nonsense of 'knowledge management'. *Information Research*, *8*(1), (online) http://informationr.net/ir/8-1/paper144.html#sch67

ENDNOTE

[1] One community of practice qualified as a finalist in the KM category of the Information Management 2004 Award. Another community of practice received a commendable award in the KM category in the Information Management 2005 Award.

Section V
Advances in Knowledge Management Application

Chapter XVIII
Leveraging Current Experiences for Future Actions:
An Exemplar of Knowledge Reuse

Alton Y.K. Chua
Nanyang Technological University, Singapore

Wing Lam
Universitas 21 Global

ABSTRACT

This chapter describes how the Center for Army Lessons Learned (CALL) has developed a unique, institutionalized knowledge reuse process. The chapter highlights several issues related to knowledge reuse, including the collection, distillation and dissemination of knowledge, the role of subject experts in the knowledge reuse process and how technology facilitates knowledge reuse.

INTRODUCTION

Motivations for Knowledge Management

Corporate spending on knowledge management (KM) has increased substantially over the years (Ithia, 2003). Fuelled by the notion that knowledge is a key resource upon which an organization's competitiveness depends (Kogut & Zander, 1992), organizations are implementing various KM initiatives to identify, share and exploit their knowledge assets. Several highly-publicized KM

success stories include Buckman Laboratories' Knowledge Network (Zack, 1999), Xerox's Eureka database (Brown & Duguid, 2000), Tech Clubs in DaimlerChrysler, the communities of practice among quantitative biologists in Eli Lilly (Wenger et al., 2002), and various KM initiatives in BP Amoco (Hansen, 2001).

The potential benefits of KM are numerous—improved decision-making, increased productivity, sharing of best practices, less need to reinvent, and improved staff development. In some cases, the reported benefits from KM have been nothing short of spectacular. Xerox, for ex-

Copyright © 2008, IGI Global, distributing in print or electronic forms without written permission of IGI Global is prohibited.

ample, estimates to have saved $100 million from its Eureka database (Brown & Duguid, 2000). It is therefore understandable why organizations are drawn to KM.

Knowledge Reuse

Central to KM in organizations are the overlapping processes of knowledge creation (Nonaka & Takeuchi, 1995; von Krogh, 1998), knowledge transfer (Dixon, 2000; McDermott & O'Dell, 2001) and knowledge reuse (Grant, 1996). Knowledge is created through two generic mechanisms, namely combination and exchange (Nahapiet & Ghoshal, 1998). Combination involves the confluence of elements previous unconnected or developing new ways of putting together elements previously associated. Exchange involves the transfer of tacit and knowledge among individuals and groups. Knowledge transfer refers to the flow of knowledge from one part to other parts of the organization. The idea is to minimize performance variations particularly among similar functional units (Szulanski, 2003). Intricately related to the processes of knowledge creation and transfer, knowledge reuse refers to the acquisition and capture of knowledge from one part of the organization and the subsequent reuse of the knowledge by itself or by other parts of the organization. In Xerox, for example, the goal of the Eureka project was to facilitate knowledge reuse among its technical reps (Brown & Duguid, 2000). Whenever a rep has discovered ways to solve a problem, he or she submits an entry to a panel of reviewers who are also reps. Through an internal process of vetting, rejection and refinement, entries deemed valuable are stored in the Eureka database. In this way, tried-and-tested tips and insights culled from the day-to-day experience of individual reps are retained, disseminated and eventually become entrenched commonly-accepted practices organization-wide.

Knowledge reuse has been labeled differently by different scholars even though the essence of the notion remains largely consistent. For example, Markus (2001) describes knowledge reuse as a process which involves sharing best practices or helping others to solve common technical problems. Kuwada (1998) and Thomas et al. (2001) conceive knowledge reuse as "strategic knowledge distillation", a process through which experiential knowledge at the business level becomes infused into the modus operandi at the corporate level. New knowledge acquired within a specific organizational locale is effectively leveraged by the entire organization, enabling strategic learning to take place within.

Through the grid of expectancy theory (Vroom, 1964), Watson and Hewett (2006) argue that knowledge reuse can be facilitated by (1) the belief that the effort to reuse existing knowledge will result in solving the problem at hand successfully (expectancy), (2) the belief that reusable knowledge can be obtained (instrumentality) and that (3) the knowledge accessed and reused is valuable (valence).

Other scholars (e.g., Szulanski, 2003; NCDDR, 2003) investigate the constituents along the knowledge reuse process and identify four major elements, namely, the source, the content, the context and the recipient. The source, sometimes called the knowledge producer, refers to the organization, workgroup or individual who creates the knowledge. The content refers to the knowledge intended to be applied. Context refers to the environment in which knowledge is transferred from the source to the recipient. The recipient, sometimes called the knowledge consumer, refers to the organization, workgroup or individual who apply the knowledge. In studying the transfer and adoption of best practices across homogeneous workgroups, Szulanski (2003) elucidates nine factors that could impede the knowledge reuse process. These factors are lack of motivation of the source to share knowledge, lack of credibility of the source, unproven content, causal ambiguity which is the incomplete understanding of why the use of the knowledge could lead to an intended

Table 1. Summary of the literature related to knowledge reuse

Main Thoughts	Explanation	References
What is knowledge reuse?	A process that involves sharing best practices or helping others to solve common technical problems.	(Markus, 2001)
	A way through which strategic learning takes place in an organization	(Kuwada, 1998; Thomas et al., 2001)
What elements are involved in knowledge reuse?	They are the source (knowledge producer), the content (knowledge to be applied), the context, the recipient (knowledge consumer) and the knowledge intermediary	(Markus, 2001; NCDDR, 2003; Szulanski, 2003)
How will knowledge reuse be facilitated?	Three factors drawn from Expectancy Theory have been identified.	(Watson &Hewett, 2006)
How will knowledge reuse be impeded?	Nine factors related to the source, content, context and the recipient have been identified.	(Szulanski, 2003)
What are the knowledge reuse situations?	Knowledge reuse by shared work producers, knowledge reuse by shared work practitioners, knowledge reuse by expert-seeking novices and knowledge reuse by secondary knowledge miners	(Markus, 2001)

outcome, arduous relationship between the source and the recipient, unfavorable organizational context for knowledge reuse, lack of motivation of the recipient to apply the knowledge, lack of absorptive capacity of the recipient to recognize the value of the new knowledge, and lack of retentive capacity of the recipient to institutionalize the use of the new knowledge.

Apart from the source (knowledge producers) and the recipient (knowledge consumers), Markus (2001) highlights another role in the knowledge reuse process, namely, that of the knowledge intermediary. This is one who facilitates knowledge reuse by eliciting, indexing, summarizing, sanitizing, packaging and distributing knowledge to the recipient.

Additionally, Markus (2001) proposes four distinct situations under which knowledge reuse occurs. Each type is characterized by who the recipients are and what purposes the applied knowledge serves. The first situation is knowledge reuse by shared work producers. Shared work producers are people working together on a team who produce knowledge for their own

use. An example of shared work producers are members of a software development team. The purposes of knowledge reuse are to keep track of current status in the team, recall reasons for decisions which have been made and learn how the team can perform better in the next project. The second situation is knowledge reuse by shared work practitioners. Shared work practitioners are people doing similar work in different work units or organization who produce knowledge for each other's use. An example of shared work practitioners are human resource management professionals in various industries. The purposes of knowledge reuse are to acquire new knowledge that others have created, and obtain advice on how a particularly challenging situation should be handled. The third situation is knowledge reuse by expertise-seeking novices. Expertise-seeking novices are those who have an occasional need for expert knowledge that they do not possess. However, they do not need to acquire themselves because they need it rarely. The purposes are to answer a question or solve an ad hoc problem and to approximate the performance of the experts. The final situation is knowledge reuse by secondary knowledge miners. Secondary knowledge miners are people who seek to answer new questions or develop new knowledge through analyzing the records produced by other people for different purposes. They have general analytic expertise but are completely divorced from the sources of the knowledge they try to apply.

On the basis of the foregoing discussion, a summary of the literature related to knowledge reuse is illustrated in the Table 1.

The remainder of this chapter describes a unique knowledge reuse process instituted by the Center for Army Lessons Learned (CALL), an intelligence unit within the U.S. Army. Materials related to CALL were developed by searching through a variety of credible sources such as academic journals, military databases and in-house publications. To ensure the authenticity of the case, quotations cited have been faithfully reproduced from their original sources and the context carefully preserved. Compared to many KM cases published hitherto, CALL offers an interesting context for examining knowledge reuse. For one, CALL is situated within a not-for-profit environment where the deliberate management of the process of knowledge reuse is imperative. It also exemplifies a working model of a 'top-down', strategic approach to managing knowledge reuse. Furthermore, CALL represents an organization where the process of knowledge reuse is not an ad hoc activity but an institutionalized mechanism.

The Background of Center for Army Lessons Learned (CALL)

The Center for Army Lessons Learned (CALL) was established by the U.S. Army in 1985 as a unit for collecting new lessons as they emerged from Army operations either in a live situation, such as the Iraq war, or during simulations such as training exercises. CALL's mission statement is as follows:

The Center for Army Lessons Learned (CALL) collects and analyzes data from a variety of current and historical sources, including Army operations and training events, and produces lessons for military commanders, staff, and students. CALL disseminates these lessons and other related research materials through a variety of print and electronic media, including this web site (http://call.army.mil/).

Previously, the army had no means for gathering such lessons, so valuable knowledge about military operations was never captured and was therefore lost. CALL operates as a small unit of 60 staff located in Fort Leavenworth, Kansas. Since its inception, CALL has developed a reputation within the Army for offering practical support to leaders, trainers and soldiers.

Overview of the Knowledge Reuse Process

CALL has access to a pool of subject matter experts tapped from the Army. These experts are assembled, trained and sent into the field to observe missions firsthand. Insights obtained from the field are interpreted from multiple sources and disseminated as lessons learned in various forms such as written reports, videos or training simulations. A concise example of a lesson learned, taken from CALL's December 2004 newsletter, is given in Table 2.

The overall goal is to provide users with knowledge that enables them to rapidly learn from ongoing practices and, in turn, create new knowledge to meet the challenges of future events.

Over the years, CALL has developed a process that transforms raw data into knowledge that can be acted upon, distributes knowledge out to the whole organization and produces rapid behavioral change based on the knowledge. The process is based on the following four-step model:

Table 2.

Topic N: Use of Local Nationals on the Battlefield (OP 1.2.3.1 Coordinate DOD Civilian and Contractor Support)
Observation: Many local nationals are not coming to work because of threats they, or their family, receive because they work for U.S. Forces.
Discussion: Many in the local workforce, employed by U.S. Forces, received threats and many did not return to work because of these threats. The Army employs local nationals as truckers, on and off forward operating bases (FOB), mechanics, plumbers, material handling equipment (MHE) with operators, and electricians. The local national employees are vital to the success of the mission especially in quality of life issues. The electricians and plumbers are familiar with the local infrastructure in which much of the living and workspace of the Forces are located.
Insights/Lessons Learned: • To combat the loss of skilled workers, many units are teaching force protection classes on how to avoid the ones who are threatening them and their families. • The locals are told that if they report those who threaten, the Army will do what they can to protect them. • Not many of the locals report the threats because they do not trust the U.S. Forces to protect them.
DOTMLPF Implication/Recommendation: • The force protection classes need to be continued and expanded to the local population where possible to enhance the trust in U.S. Forces. Trust is the key in getting the locals to report those who are working counter to U.S./Iraqi interests (Leadership and Education).

Source: http://www.globalsecurity.org/military/library/report/call/iir-mosul-ops_stryker-bde_21dec2004.pdf

1. Identifying learning opportunities
2. Observing and collecting knowledge
3. Creating knowledge product
4. Deploying expertise

Command Sgt. Maj. Cynthia Pritchett of the Combined Arms Center and Fort Leavenworth, Kansas, revealed:

This is all about sharing knowledge so soldiers can do their jobs better. Soldiers want to know what's going on. They don't want to reinvent the wheel to address problems that someone else has already solved (Agency Group 09, 2002).

To facilitate knowledge transfer throughout the Army, CALL has consistently published materials that are related to specific operations, exercises or subjects. These materials provide information on general topics such as military leadership and tactics, techniques and procedures and emerging doctrine, as well as more specific topics such as a country's history in relation to current events, cultural do's and don'ts, language, and environmental cautions.

CALL is also well-stocked with comprehensive training resources for the Army. It has a collection of "how to" videos on direct fire planning, attack helicopter employment and situation awareness. For the Haiti operation, CALL developed more than one hundred vignettes and prepared a video briefing for commanders to use and create training simulations for the replacement troop entering Haiti. It also produced documents to help clarify how the Army should work with non-Army organizations such as the local government, Haitian police and multinational forces. More recently, CALL has produced a report called "On Point" that discusses a host of logistics-related challenges encountered by the military during the assault on Baghdad in 2003. For example, the report offered insights into why stocks of food and petroleum products barely kept up with frontline demand (Cooke, 2006).

After Action Reviews (AAR)

In the Army, much work is performed during crisis. Withholding information can sometimes cost lives. Soldiers are therefore taught to freely share information. Being a part of the Army, personnel in CALL are encouraged to view information as a communal property rather than a source of individual power.

The Army has institutionalized a process called after action reviews (AAR) which is akin to debriefing sessions after each mission or training exercise. Facilitators ask four questions, namely:

1. What was intended?
2. What happened?
3. What was learned?
4. What implications are there for the future?

Examples of after action reports, the documented output from AARs, can be found at http://www.globalsecurity.org/military/ops/oif-lessonslearned.htm. Many CALL staff members were once AAR facilitators.

Central to the benefit of the AAR is the idea of immediately applying the lesson learned the next time the same task occurs. Hence, the institutionalization of AAR has created a climate in which actions are repeatedly reflected over time.

On the Army's mission to Haiti in 1994, one unit was assigned the task of clearing caches of weapons from towns thought to be in the hands of rebels. In the unit's first attempt, the townspeople were completely uncooperative. During the AAR, someone observed that the military police's large German shepherd dogs frightened the Haitians. Another person suggested showing off the dogs during weapons sweeps to impress the townspeople. The unit tried this tactic in the next town to be cleared of weapons and had better success. In the ensuing AAR, someone commented that the unit was always confronting belligerent men and not women. If a woman commanded the unit, the townspeople's cultural expectations would be shaken and the unit might get better cooperation. So in the next town to be cleared, a female lieutenant took command, with the men visibly saluting her and bolstering her appearance of authority. At the same time, the unit continued to showcase the dogs. This combination produced even better success. In the AAR following this second attempt, someone mentioned that townspeople accosted by soldiers in the streets were more hostile and less cooperative than those approached in their homes. In the third town to be cleared, the unit continued to show off the dogs, continued to openly support the command of a woman, and added the step of going to people's homes. The effect was an overwhelming success; the unit thoroughly cleared the town of guns and ammunition (Baird et. al., 1997).

Lieutenant Colonel Joe Moore, a seasoned army practitioner who has managed and trained using the AAR explains:

In a complex situation, most of what you learn from a single experience is the wrong answer. So you go out and choose a different answer to the problem, and it's wrong too, but maybe it's less wrong.... You've got to learn in small bites, lots of them, over time, and they'll work, eventually, into a complete solution to the problem. This cannot be accomplished in a onetime reflection event that happens only after a project is complete (Darling & Parry, 2001, p. 64).

Event Selection

In the past, data collection for organization learning had not been focused on specific learning objectives. This approach resulted in an avalanche of raw data that overloaded the Army's capacity to turn it into useful lessons for future engagements. CALL recognized this pitfall and has since developed a framework to select an event for observation which has high potential for generating knowledge with future strategic value.

These events are selected on the basis of the insights they offer, the impact they exert and the setting they afford that test strategic beliefs, theories and practices. These events are characteristically occasions where is it possible to learn from experience, what the Army calls the "ground truth". Events which CALL has selected in the past include combat operations such as Operation Just Cause at Panama (1989), Operation Desert Storm at Kuwait (1991) and Operation Enduring Freedom in Afghanistan (2002) as well as non-combat operations such as disaster relief in the wake of Hurricane Andrew (1992) and peacemaking missions in Somalia (1992) and Bosnia (1996).

For each selected event, CALL staff work with senior officers in the Army to identify a set of specific learning objectives. Some examples of learning objectives include building a bridge in a particular type of terrain, achieving seamless transition to the replacement troop, launching the arrival troops from an aircraft carrier and how command can be transferred to a non-U.S. military body.

Data Collection in the Field

To observe a targeted event, teams of data collectors comprising between 8 to 50 subject experts are drawn from various units across the Army and assemble at CALL. The size of the data collection team is dependent on the mission. Collectors external to the context of the event rather than ground staff are deployed primarily because they have not been too entrenched in the processes of the event. Thus, the likelihood of introducing bias to the data collected is reduced.

Marine Maj. Gen. Gordon Nash, commander of the Joint War-fighting Cente, explained the roles of the collection team in Operation Iraqi Freedom:

The collection team's mission was to gather observations and data, conduct analyses and develop recommendations focused on improving joint warfighting capabilities and ensure victory in future conflicts. The value of collecting information for lessons learned is to save lives, money and improve the military's capability (Agency Group 09, 2003).

Each collection team comprises collectors from different fields of expertise. The cross-disciplinary nature of each team enables deep knowledge to be collected for each event. For example, for Operation Iraqi Freedom, CALL produced analysis of tactical operations at all military levels, ground operations in terms of movement, mobilization processes of units at their home-stations, aviation operations, communications in terms of command and control and digitization of the battlefield. Furthermore, events can be analyzed from different perspectives, enhancing the reliability and validity of learning. For example, the team assembled for Haiti comprised specialists in areas such as logistics, ground combat and communications. The logisticians were required to liaise with the Navy deliveries. The team even included a pastor and a linguist to address cultural issues that were important to that event (Thomas et al., 2001).

Collectors are recruited based on their interpersonal skills in addition to their area of specialization. They must be able to build their credibility and rapport quickly, but remain emotionally unbiased from the people and situation in which they would be deployed. Furthermore, they must have large networks of colleagues from whom they can tap for information and support. An added advantage of having these collectors who are temporarily attached to CALL is that they facilitate the dissemination of the new knowledge developed from the field when they return to their respective units after their secondment is over.

Prior to deployment, the collectors go to CALL headquarters at Fort Leavenworth for up to eight weeks to learn the skills of data collection. CALL develops a customized collection plan with each collector. The collection plan comprises hierarchical levels of questions in increasing degree of detail concerning events that collectors are expected to observe in the field. It helps to keep each collector focused on critical information requirements and provides a structure to organize the myriad of details collected during actual observation. At this stage, an initial report will be prepared from archival knowledge that provides contextual information such as the local weather, disease threats, topography and politics. After the training is completed, collectors are sent off together with ground troops.

For example, in Operation Iraqi Freedom, teams were deployed and embedded throughout the U.S. Central Command theatre of operations at ten or more sites, including, Qatar, Kuwait, Bahrain, Saudi Arabia and Iraq. Once on site, collectors are provided unrestricted access, where possible, throughout the operation. They observe events in real time rather than retrospectively. Army Brig. Gen. Robert Cone, director of the Operation Iraqi Freedom Joint Lessons Learned Collection Team, summarized that the tasks of the collection teams are to examine "what happened, why it happened and then determine what should be done about it." Gen. Cone added:

Watching key decisions being made, problems being solved and generally being provided unrestricted access to the business and conduct of the war absolutely essential to having a good understanding of what went down. This was not a secret inspection, and there were no hidden agendas. We were there to basically assist as observers, collect data and be helpful to the extent that we could (Agency Group 09, 2003).

Colonel Mike Heimstra, the director of CALL, concurred that the collectors are not sent with ground troops in the field to deliberately look for failures and mistakes. Rather, they are there to understand current events and enable the Army to be better prepared for the future. Col. Heimstra noted:

They take the simple statements of 'this happened' to 'this happened and this is what it means for the future' or 'this is what it means for current or future doctrine.' Often times what we're looking for are tactics, techniques and procedures that units have applied in the field

that have worked for them. If something has not gone well, we look for why it didn't go well and what can be done to make it better the next time. We don't dwell on 'this didn't work.' We're not an Inspector General. We're not there to critique or evaluate their performance. We're there to learn from what they're doing to be a part of a unit's team (Russell, 2003).

Collectors capture the reality of the situation using various media to depict the original account as fully as possible. Typically, digital video and photographs, rich descriptions as well as diagrams that show possible causes and consequences are used to reconstruct the firsthand experience. For example, in Haiti, the vignettes, videos and descriptions effectively conveyed the scenario of belligerent crowds, barking dogs and rotting garbage. Users are able to witness the events in great visual detail and re-live the experience of the actual participants.

In Operation Iraqi Freedom, collectors performed more than 400 focus interviews with key leaders and staff officers during the war. They were able to obtain nearly 4,000 data files of key activities and briefings conducted during the war. Gen. Cone commented:

This has proven to be very useful to us getting at the key points and underlying issues to this conflict (Agency Group 09, 2003).

Collectors also gather feedback and interpretations from various relevant personnel to collect multiple perspectives on a given event. In this way, besides being able to obtain a rich, in-depth account of the event, they are able to arrive at a consensus of why it occurred and what course of action can be taken in the future. For example, an observed event is that companies and platoons are not achieving fire superiority. After culling interpretations from a variety of sources, collectors are able to make specific recommendations. First is the 33% rule, which states that if the enemy is believed to be 100 meters wide, units should assault at least 33 meters to the left and right of the known objective, and be prepared to fight beyond that. Second, before assaulting the enemy, units must use direct and indirect fire to fix the enemy. This allows them to exploit a weakness before the enemy can reinforce or reorganize. Third, units must not expose themselves to the assault until the conditions are set. Fourth, units should maintain a base of fire to fix the enemy in place rather than wasting ammunition.

Collectors try to focus on identifying systemic problems rather than those due to temporary anomalies. On the basis of their subject matter expertise and prior experience, they seek to trace the path of the problem back to its source to gain a rich understanding of what happened and why, collecting evidence along the way. Attention is also paid to "workaround" solutions and exemplary ways to solving problems. Gen. Cone explained:

Sometimes we may want to document something that went extremely well, and certainly we had many cases of that. Other times we want to try an address a problem or help institutionalize a solution to a problem so that we can take our experience and spread it across the Department of Defense. Perhaps the most exciting case is when we see something that works, but we begin to think about better ways to have done it. In many cases this is thinking about the case of what might be if we made certain changes. That is really the exciting part of being in the lessons learned process (Agency Group 09, 2003).

On a mission in Haiti, collectors took thousands of hours of observations and notes while attending AAR meetings, planning sessions and command updates with key decision-makers. They talked with people at all levels and recorded the details of issues related to their domain of expertise as defined in their customized collection plans. Immediately following the mission, collectors

discuss and verify their observations with the commander of the mission, eliciting the leadership perspective. Later on the same evening, they also discuss the raw data further among themselves to bring multiple perspectives to bear on the narratives they have generated. This also serves as a reality check.

Knowledge Distillation

The collection team collaborates online on a daily basis to discuss emerging "insights" into the war and to share feedback. In Haiti, collectors sent observations of events to CALL at a rate of 5 to 10 per day in the form of thick descriptions. The diagrams or videos that supported these observations were sent later by mail ship or personal carrier.

New information generated daily from multiple collectors from different sites is sent back to another group of experts, known as the analysts, at CALL. The analysts serve as an information conduit and help gather input and insights from other Army experts. They are responsible for constructing new knowledge from these disparate sources through the process of "sense-making".

Awareness of the potential for interpretation bias is promoted throughout CALL. Hence, similar to the collection process, the interpretation process also applies multiple perspectives to ensure objectivity. Raw data of observations undergo an expanded interpretation process that includes feedback from around the Army before they are turned into lessons. The roles of the collectors and the analysts are kept separate as a mechanism to minimize the risk of bias in developing lessons.

The analysts index and format the observations before releasing them electronically to solicit simultaneous review from other knowledgeable professionals around the Army. Observations posted to the electronic bulletin board are aimed at a wide audience while those posted to distribution lists are targeted at networks of appropriate specialists with a specific interest. For example, experts in logistics subscribe to a logistic distribution list to receive postings from CALL. With such technologies, geographically dispersed experts are brought together to share and refine ideas and perspectives.

The role of the analysts is to keep the interpretative discussion open and redirect issues to other participants. This ensures that that an issue does not prematurely converge or close. Thus, before a final lesson was concluded, knowledge from the field had already been moved around the Army.

Analysts use the feedback that emerge from the active dialogue among experts to ascertain relationships between new knowledge and existing organizational knowledge and expand the circle of interest on new observations. New issues and questions are then identified and communicated back down to the ground team for additional data collection.

The process of transforming data collected from the field to knowledge that can be acted upon can be summarized by the following cycle:

- Collectors observe, collect data, and report to the analysts.
- The analysts post the data for experts to read.
- Experts give feedback to the analysts.
- Based on the feedback, the analysts redirect the collectors.

The processes of collection, interpretation and dissemination, are intertwined and multi-step rather than sequential. Observations are interpreted, codified and eventually become known as lessons. After having generated a critical mass of lessons, collectors return to Fort Leavenworth and spend a few days ploughing through and discussing all the lessons compiled. The aim is to deliberate on lessons which are important enough to be distributed. This final step, known as a "murder board", represents a collective effort among the collectors and analysts to decide which lessons should be put on hold and which should be released.

In Haiti, CALL used this method to deliver validated lessons to ground troops within five days of the original observations. In addition, CALL produced 26 scenarios, including video footage, simulations, and scripts, of situations faced by the troops in Haiti. These scenarios became the training materials for the 25th Infantry Division troops, who were scheduled to replace the 10th Mountain Division. When the 25th Infantry arrived, they felt as though they were on familiar territory. They actually encountered 23 of the 26 situations they had studied, and due to their training, the transition was seamless (Baird et al., 1997).

Knowledge Dissemination

CALL's effectiveness is established on its credibility and the quality of its published content. Even though CALL has no authority to mandate the implementation of the lessons it compiles, many of its lessons have been integrated into the military's organizational routines. For example, the lesson drawn from the Iraqi ambush in 2003 that resulted in the capture of Pvt. Jessica Lynch has led to changes in the way the Army conducted and armored its supply convoys (Mathis, 2006). Likewise, a CALL's report on the deficiencies of the Stryker, a combat armored vehicle, drew quick response from the U.S. army and set in motion a series of refinements such as an upgrade to the remote weapons station and the production of a new ballistic shield (Troshinsky, 2005). Hence, by focusing on how to add value to Army operation and delivering high quality content, CALL seeks to create both a "pull" and "push" effect for its lessons.

Lessons are delivered by offering multiple perspectives and accounts of the original events. In addition, a combination of different media including rich textual accounts, digital videos and photographs are used to facilitate the dissemination of tacit knowledge. The purpose is to allow users to experience the nuances of the original events such as the emotional reactions and leadership tactics.

To make its lessons available to U.S. military users worldwide, CALL is using the World Wide Web and other wide-area networks as global dissemination engines. CALL's homepage features its own publications as well as Army and joint operational records and lessons learned. In addition, it not only directs Army, joint, Department of Defence and other service users to other Web-based sources of information, it assembles best-of-class search-engines capabilities that allow users to navigate through the vastness of networked knowledge resources. CALL's Web site attracts weekly hits averaging in the order of hundreds of thousands.

The CALL database (call.army.mil/calldb. htm), an information archive representing nearly three million pages of information, is supported by a team that comprises people from various information and military disciplines military analysts, management analysts, library scientists, historians, archivists, archives specialists, records and information managers, lexicographers, search engineers, and information technology specialists. The database includes both a restricted database for Army personnel and public database that is available to anyone with Web access.

The restricted database includes records of Army operations, including after-action reports and other records of Army operations and training events. About 5,000 Army personnel regularly access the restricted CALL database, which can be accessed from any Internet connection. Users of the restricted CALL database typically search for techniques, procedures and research materials while preparing for or while engaged in operations or training. In a bid to provide Army personnel with fast, accurate search results, CALL has invested in RetrievalWare, an enterprise search and categorization solution which allows users to sort the result list. For example, if a user searched the term "bomb truck" and wanted to know the geographic location of each of the 200 results, that data could be sorted with one click.

To ease searching, the CALL database uses two indexing schemes. The first is a structural indexing based on keywords, attributes of the learning events such as time, place and date, as well as army-wide coding scheme of conditions, tasks and standards. The second is a process-based indexing scheme based on the organizational processes and functions mapped in the "Blueprint of the Battlefield" used in the Army. Dale Steinhauer, a historian and archivist at CALL, disclosed information about the response rate of the database:

The electronic system enables requests to be filled anywhere from 15 minutes to a maximum of about three days for the largest and most complex requests. If the data is stored in one of CALL's internal databases, an average request is usually completed in minutes. If outside sources are necessary, the job takes about an hour (Caterinicchia, 2003).

The public database contains some 25 gigabytes of public information about the Army that has been approved for unlimited dissemination, including academic papers completed by Army personnel, and back issues of Military Review, a journal published at Fort Leavenworth, Kansas.

In general, lessons are delivered via three channels, namely, self-service, customized and mass market. Self-service learning occurs when users remotely login to CALL's knowledge base to do their own research. This channel is currently the least used, although CALL is working to promote its use.

Customized lessons are developed in response to specific requests. For example, lessons can be immediately returned to the field as answers to questions, developed into reports for specialized units, or used as custom-designed responses to critical questions asked by senior leaders. In Bosnia, Gen. Nash, the U.S. commander, ordered that lessons learned be pulled together and disseminated to all units instead of letting each unit develop its own operational lore. As a result, CALL received several lessons from the field and the best ones were quickly e-mailed to all units. One early lesson warned convoys to be careful of snow-covered roads that have no tracks because they may be mined. Another lesson cautioned convoys who are caught in a minefield not to turn around but back out. Every 72 hours, a new list of lessons was distributed. Army officials credit the rapid dissemination of such guidelines with helping minimize U.S. casualties in a region riddled with mines and booby traps (Ricks, 1997).

Lessons delivered via mass market are intended for a wide audience and are published in the form of handbook, newsletters, and training materials or incorporated into the Army doctrine. For example, a handbook on stability and support operations has been compiled. It contains lessons derived from Bosnia, combat operations in Enduring Freedom and Iraqi Freedom, and it provides a quick-reference guide to leaders and soldiers with tactics, techniques and procedures on how to conduct stability operations and support operations on site, at a roadblock or checkpoint, or prior to conducting an arrest of a suspect. Newsletters are regular publications that address a specific subject, such as civil disturbance, urban operations or synchronization of fires.

In recognition of its pioneering effort, CALL's database won both Vice President Al Gore's Hammer Award and an honorable mention in the Computer World Smithsonian Award in 1996. The Hammer Award recognizes systems that support ex-president Bill Clinton's National Performance Review principles of customer support, elimination of red-tape and empowerment of employees, while the Computer World Smithsonian Award acknowledges the visionary use of information technology.

Retired Gen. Gordon Sullivan, a former Army chief of staff commended CALL's effort:

You are applying knowledge management to real tasks completed by real people. You are using knowledge to develop a common base of understanding. This allows you to move knowledge around so you can share lessons learned through the Army. This ultimately allows you to successfully fight and win our nation's wars (Agency Group 09, 2002).

The knowledge developed by CALL is not stored in a static or stable form but held in a way that allows it to be continually reconfigured and reanalyzed as new needs arise. To maintain the quality of its lessons, CALL assesses them periodically for accuracy through informal customer evaluation and solicits suggestions for improvements.

It must be noted that CALL's analysis does not always provide new insight. Sometimes it simply reinforces current policies or doctrine. Col. Heimstra said that one of the most significant conclusions reached through CALL's analyses of Operations Enduring Freedom and Iraqi Freedom is that the training provided at the Army's four combat training centers—the National Training Center, the Joint Readiness Training Center, the Combat Maneuver Training Center and Battle Command Training Program—played a huge role in the Army's success in those two conflicts. Col. Heimstra continued:

Several years ago, the Training and Doctrine Command began to change the training, or at least the environment, that was provided at the combat training centers into the contemporary operational environment. We migrated what the units were facing in terms of the OPFOR (opposing force) and the environment to better reflect what we thought we would encounter in real world situations. More and more now, we are understanding that the things that we anticipated about the contemporary operational environment were true, and they were replicated in Iraq, and they were replicated in Afghanistan. So we think that we've done a good job of portraying the right kind of environment at the combat training centers to prepare people to do what they have to do (Russell, 2003).

CONCLUSION

This chapter describes how the Center for Army Lessons Learned (CALL) has developed a unique, institutionalized knowledge reuse process. Through a series of routinized procedures including event selection, data collection, knowledge distillation and knowledge dissemination, CALL seeks to cull lessons systematically from past experiences and presents them in formats suitable for subsequent reuse.

Researchers interested in the knowledge reuse process may wish to consider the following areas for further research. One is to examine the facilitation and impediments to knowledge reuse process driven largely by a top-down approach. In an ad hoc or voluntary setting, the dynamics that exist between the source and the recipient are particularly linear and salient. Factors such as the source's motivation, the source's reputation and the recipient's motivation have been commonly identified (Szulanski, 2003). However, in an institutionalized setting such as CALL's, the dynamics among multiple sources (e.g., the data collectors and analysts), and multiple recipients (e.g., military generals, trainers and ordinary soldiers) become much more complex. In lieu of a singular identified recipient, a source (e.g., a data collector) who has been tasked to furnish data may need to consider the interests and agenda of the immediate superior, and those above. He or she may also need to contend with fellow data collectors and other analysts in order to be perceived in a favorable light. Hence, politics, for example, could have a profound impact on the knowledge reuse process in a top-down approach, and could be studied in greater depths.

Another area for further research is the extent to which CALL's approach can be applied to commercial organizations. Apart from its ability to tap into extensive expert networks throughout the U.S. Army, CALL possesses abundant resources to deploy independent teams of data collectors, analysts and technical personnel. However, commercial organizations are often subject to a fiercely competitive environment and are usually driven by the twin goal of cost reduction and revenue maximization. Thus, the downward-scalability of CALL's model could be examined in a commercial context, thus providing guidance to commercial organizations with limited resources intending to adopt an approach similar to CALL's.

REFERENCES

Agency Group 09. (2002). Knowledge warriors' amass at symposium. *FDCH, Regulatory Intelligence Database.*

Agency Group 09. (2003). Lessons learned process on Iraq War explained. *FDCH, Regulatory Intelligence Database.*

Baird, L., Henderson, J., & Watts, S. (1997). Learning from action: An analysis of the Center for Army Lessons Learned (CALL). *Human Resource Management, 36*(4), 385-395.

Brown, J., & Duguid, P. (2000). Balancing act: How to capture knowledge without killing it. *Harvard Business Review, 78*(3), 73-78.

Caterinicchia, D. (2003). Search system answers CALL. *Federal Computer Week dated,* Jan. 20.

Cooke, J. (2006). The supply chain lesson of the "Iron Hills". *Logistics Management, 46*(2), 72.

Darling, M., & Parry, C (2001). After-action reviews: Linking reflection and planning in a learning practice. *Reflections, 3*(2), 64-72.

Dixon, N. (2000). *Common knowledge.* Boston, MA: Harvard Business School Press.

Grant, R. (1996). Towards a knowledge-based theory of the firm. *Strategic Management Journal, 17,* 109-122.

Hansen, M. (2001). Introducing t-shaped managers. *Harvard Business Review, 79*(3), 106-116.

Ithia, A. (2003). UK lawyers spend more on KM. *KM Review, 5*(6), 11.

Kogut, B., & Zander, U. (1992). Knowledge of the firm, combative capability and the replication of technology. *Organization Science, 3,* 383-397.

Kuwada, K. (1998). Strategic learning: The continuous side of discontinuous strategic change. *Organization. Science, 2*(6), 719-736.

Markus, M. (2001). Toward a theory of knowledge reuse: Types of knowledge reuse situations and factors in reuse success. *Journal of Management Information Systems, 18*(1), 57-93.

Mathis, J. (2006). *Teaching soldiers to think creatively.* Associated Press Newswires.

McDermott, R., & O'Dell, C. (2001). Overcoming cultural barriers to sharing knowledge. *Journal of Knowledge Management, 5*(1), 76-85.

NCDDR. (2003). *National Center for the Dissemination of Disability Research.* Retrieved September 12, 2005 from http://www.ncddr.org/du/products/review/review6.html.

Nahapiet, J., & Ghosal, S. (1998). Social capital, intellectual capital, and the organizational advantage. *The Academy of Management Review, 23*(2), 242-266

Nonaka, I., & Takeuchi, H. (1995). *The knowledge-creating company.* Oxford: Oxford University Press.

Ricks, T. (1997). Lessons learned: Army devises system to decide what does, and does not work. *Wall Street Journal, A1,* 10.

Russell, R. (2003). *Center gathers lessons learned in Iraq.* Retrieved July 1, 2005 from http://www-wtradoc.army.mil/pao/TNSarchives/May03/CALL.htm

Szulanski, G. (2003). *Sticky knowledge: Barriers to knowing in the firm.* Sage Publications.

Thomas, J., Sussman, S., & Henderson, J. (2001). Understanding "strategic learning": Linking organizational learning, knowledge management and sense-making. *Organizational Science, 12*(3), 331-345.

Troshinsky, L. (2005). Stryker fixes in progress, Army official says. *Aerospace Daily & Defense Report, 214*(2), 4.

Vroom, V. (1964). *Work and motivation.* New York, NY: Wiley.

von Krogh, G. (1998). Care in knowledge creation. *California Management Review, 40*(3), 133-153.

Theoretical model of knowledge transfer in organizations: Determinants of knowledge contribution and knowledge reuse. *Journal of Management Studies, 43*(2), 141-173.

Wenger, E., McDermott, R., & Snyder, W. (2002). *Cultivating communities of practice.* Boston, MA: Harvard Business School Press.

Zack, M. (1999). Managing codified knowledge. *Sloan Management Review, 40*(4), 45-58.

Chapter XIX
Knowledge Characteristics, Knowledge Acquisition Strategy and Results of Knowledge Management Implementations:
An Empirical Study of Taiwanese Hospitals

Wen-Jang (Kenny) Jih
Middle Tennessee State University, USA

Cheng Hsui Chen
National Yun-Lin University of Science and Technology, Taiwan, ROC

Andy Chen
National Cheng-Kung University, Taiwan, ROC

ABSTRACT

The very fundamental mission of hospital management is to deliver quality healthcare services by utilizing highly specialized medical knowledge and solve other healthcare problems within various resource constraints. Similar to other knowledge-intensive industries which operate in highly challenging business environments, hospitals of all sizes must view the creation, organization, distribution, and application of knowledge as a critical aspect of their management activities. Knowledge management, therefore, represents a viable strategy as hospitals strive to simultaneously provide quality medical services, improve operational efficiency, and comply with governmental documentation and reporting regulations. This study examines the correlation as well as causal relationships between knowledge characteristics, knowledge acquisition strategy, implementation measures, and performance of knowledge management implementations in the context of hospital management. Using primary data collected in Taiwanese hospitals, our analyses showed that the characteristics of knowledge affect the ways in which knowledge management is implemented, and the implementation measure, in turn, has a significant impact on the results of knowledge management implementation.

Copyright © 2008, IGI Global, distributing in print or electronic forms without written permission of IGI Global is prohibited.

INTRODUCTION

Hospitals of all sizes are currently faced with a multitude of management pressures, including industry competition, customer satisfaction, shortage of specialized personnel, compliance with government regulation, cost reduction, and the ever-increasing demand for more effective cures (Camilleri & O'Callaghan, 1998; Porter & Teisberg, 2004). In coping with these challenges, hospitals have actively experimented with various management initiatives and programs, such as total quality management and knowledge management, with varying performance results. Emerging as a new multidisciplinary management field, knowledge management (KM) promises to enhance competitive advantage in the highly dynamic knowledge economy by treating valuable and scarce knowledge as a critical organizational asset and managing it in a systematic manner (Sharkie, 2003; Ulrich & Smallwood, 2004). From the knowledge management point of view, many hospital services involve knowledge-intensive processes that are carried out to solve patient health-related problems (Wickramasinghe et al., 2005). Because of the knowledge-intensive nature of healthcare services, much of a hospital's success depends on effective and efficient creation, organization, validation, dissemination, and application of its highly specialized, medical knowledge and hospital management expertise.

Traditional knowledge management mechanisms in most hospitals typically include morning meetings, apprenticeships, internships, professional seminars, research partnerships with outside research institutions, and other forms of human interaction. Sophisticated information technologies are also being deployed in some hospitals to manage medical images and to capture scarce expertise (e.g., medical expert systems and data mining technologies) (Davenport & Glaser, 2002; Wickramasinghe et al., 2005). The addition of Internet technologies to the portfolio of information processing and management systems

further offers a new set of powerful tools for communications and collaboration as hospitals seek to enhance the implementation of their knowledge management initiatives.

In light of the strategic value of highly specialized, professional knowledge, hospitals increasingly recognize a need to more actively manage their intellectual capital. The field of knowledge management provides the frameworks and techniques that are deployed to transform an organization into an adaptive learning system (Leonard-Barton, 1995; Hansen, 1999; Gupta & Govindarajan, 2000; Adams & Lamont, 2003; Awad & Ghaziri, 2004; Becera-Fernandes et al., 2004). These frameworks and techniques emerge from the inquiries conducted and experiences acquired in a variety of contexts; including manufacturing (Kim, Hwang, & Suh, 2003), customer relationship management (Gebert, Geib, Kolbe, & Brenner, 2003), consulting (Sarvary, 1999), retail chain (Tsai, Yu, & Lee, 2005), and healthcare (Daqvenport & Glaser, 2002; Wickramasinghe & Davison, 2004; Ford & Angermeier, 2004; Powers, 2004). Much of the literature, however, has been either case studies or conceptual discussions in nature. Empirical studies based on the primary data collected in the field, however, are important for advancing the field of knowledge management toward maturity.

Motivated by the dearth of empirical inquiries in knowledge management that address issues in hospital management, we conduct this study to identify the relationship between some factors that play a significant role in successful knowledge management implementations in the healthcare environment. Our purpose is to understand how knowledge management is practiced and the result of implementation in this knowledge-intensive sector. We also seek to contribute to hospital management by offering empirical evidence for the value of knowledge management in coping with the multi-faceted management challenges faced by today's hospitals.

The remainder of the chapter is structured as follows. The next section describes an interview process conducted with hospital executives and medical doctors for the purpose of selecting the constructs for our research model. We review some of the existing knowledge management literature relating to our research constructs. We also discuss our research hypotheses that are formulated as a result of field interviews and literature review. The section on research methodology describes the research framework, data collection approaches, and data analysis techniques. This is followed by the results of data analysis. The last section discusses some implications of the research findings for hospital knowledge management in particular and knowledge management in general. Suggestions for future research in knowledge management are also presented.

Identification of Research Constructs

Knowledge management has increasingly received attention as an important multidisciplinary field in both the academic and the corporate arena over the past years (Davenport et al., 1998; Adams & Lamont, 2003; Gloet & Berrell, 2003; Sharkie, 2003; Becera-Fernandez et al., 2004). A common denominator among knowledge management researchers is the belief that, in the knowledge economy that is characterized by rapid change and fierce competition, knowledge should be viewed as a strategic and manageable resource, just like traditional assets such as capital, raw material, energy, technology, and factory facility (Leonard-Barton, 1995; Liebowitz & Wilcox, 1997; Davenport & Prusak, 2000; Soo et al., 2002). Various conceptual frameworks for effective implementations of knowledge management programs or projects have been proposed to facilitate knowledge sharing and stimulate continuous innovation both within and across organizational boundaries (Wiig, 1994; Tiwana, 2000; Davenport & Glaser, 2002; Lee & Hong, 2002; Soo et al.,

2002; Wang, 2002; Awad & Ghaziri, 2004). Due to the knowledge-intensive nature of healthcare delivery processes, there has been an urgent call for implementation of knowledge management in the context of hospital management in their pursuit of sustainable competitive advantage (Davenport & Glaser, 2002; Van Beveren, 2003; Powers, 2004; Wickramasinghe et al., 2005).

In order to better understand the unique characteristics of hospital management from the perspective of knowledge management, we conducted hour-long interviews with two hospital executives and three medical doctors in a regional medical center. A structured questionnaire was used in the interviews, supplemented by open-ended questions. The specific purpose of the interviews was to identify the relevant research constructs for our inquiry. Several points stood out to provide directions for the study. First of all, medical services (esp. clinical care) are very context-sensitive. A specific clinical care problem may be attributed to the patient's personal condition, disease specifics, disease history, family background, treatment history, medication history, and so forth. Effective treatment must collectively consider a wide variety of factors. The complexity of clinical care knowledge, in other words, often comes from a great number of factors and the subtle relationships between these factors that need to be considered in the treatment decision. The ability to distinguish between the relevant and irrelevant factors, and the insight to understand the relationships between these factors often constitute a core competency of true experts. Although theoretical knowledge distributed by such published avenues as books and articles is valuable in developing medical expertise, learning through reading is not enough. Ultimately, it is the practical experience in dealing with specific cases that truly builds up a medical doctor's professional expertise and collectively represents the most valuable aspect of the hospital's knowledge stock. In other words, most medical knowledge accumulated over years is practical knowledge that is not preserved in any printed media. These findings lead to the selection of knowledge characteristics as an important research construct.

We also found from the field interviews that specific implementation measures such as the availability of information infrastructure that facilitate KM activities, incentive programs, and other people-related factors, play a key role in the success (or failure) of the KM implementation program. Information technologies are used to digitize and store knowledge content. Once kept in the systems, valuable knowledge content can be easily disseminated, integrated, and deployed. Each specialization unit in a hospital usually represents an organizational silo, separated from other specialization units. A well-designed information system enables the sharing of related information and knowledge by "baking" the system capabilities in the daily business processes (Davenport & Glaser, 2002). Furthermore, the interviews identified two preferred indicators for assessing the performance of the KM implementation: improvement of internal process and overall organizational performance. Two research constructs, KM implementation measures and KM performance, are identified as the result. Finally, the research construct, knowledge acquisition strategy, is included in the research model in order to evaluate the strategic role played by the source of knowledge for effective hospital management. Based on the findings of these interviews, the scope of this study is limited to four research constructs: the characteristics of medical knowledge, the strategy used to acquire valuable knowledge, how KM concepts are implemented, and the result of KM implementations. The following section reviews the literature relating to these four constructs.

Knowledge Characteristics

As a service-oriented and knowledge-intensive organization, a hospital typically deals with specialized knowledge in a variety of categories: customer (patient) knowledge, service (treatment) knowledge, medication knowledge, process knowledge, and account management, to name just a few. In generic terms, knowledge can be characterized in many ways: shallow vs. deep, procedural vs. declarative, explicit vs. tacit, domain-independent vs. domain-specific, common-sense knowledge vs. professional knowledge, static vs. dynamic, proprietary vs. nonproprietary, and so forth. (Nonaka & Takeuchi, 1995; Howells, 1996; Polanyi, 1996; Gupta & Govindarajan, 2000; Davenport & Glaser, 2002; Gloet & Berrell, 2003; Awad & Ghaziri, 2004; Ulrich & Smallwood, 2004). A recent list of knowledge attributes proposed by Holsapple (2003) consists of twenty-three items. According to the healthcare practitioners that we interviewed, for the medical and healthcare service industry, four knowledge characteristics are deemed most relevant: knowledge mode (explicit vs. implicit), knowledge complexity, strength knowledge appropriability (difficulty of replication and transferring), and knowledge volatility (dynamic vs. static). These four characteristics were identified using a rating questions list, augmented by open-ended elaborative discussions.

Explicit knowledge is represented in the form of recorded products such as printed documents, formulas, software, database, system manuals, and hardware equipments, while implicit knowledge primarily is undocumented and resides in human memory (Nonaka & Takeuchi, 1995; Howells, 1996; Polani, 1996; Zack, 1999). Hospitals vary in their perception of and relative emphasis on the explicitness—implicitness continuum of their valuable healthcare knowledge. Different perceptions and preferences may lead to different strategies being adopted for knowledge acquisition and other important aspects of knowledge management implementation. Explicit knowledge is more amenable to technologically-oriented solutions such as a document base and a knowledge map, whereas implicit knowledge is primarily handled through social networks.

Complex knowledge is difficult for individuals and organizations to acquire. Once acquired, however, it can become a valuable source of competitive advantage (Teece, 1998; Holsapple, 2003). Knowledge complexity is determined by the abstract nature of knowledge, the number of knowledge components, and the interaction of these components (Soo, Devinney, Midgley, & Deering, 2002). In the healthcare domain, both the great amount and the intricately interactive effect of professional medical knowledge pose a substantial challenge for the hospitals in striving to provide quality healthcare services.

Knowledge that is nonproprietary in nature can be easily transferred across organizational boundaries. The proprietary nature of knowledge usually is often determined by the extent to which the knowledge is tightly tied to the specific organization (Soo, Devinney, Midgley, & Deering, 2002; Teece, 2003). From the system development point of view, proprietary knowledge usually is highly domain-specific. Both domain-specific and domain-independent knowledge are important in solving complex problems. However, past successes of expert system technology applications demonstrate that domain-specific knowledge usually contributes more than what domain-independent knowledge does in solving difficult problems. This notion of organizational specificity associated with knowledge management is well illustrated by Gupta and Govindarajan (2000) in a case study of the Nucor Steel Corporation. The consistently superior performance of Nucor Steel demonstrates that once knowledge creation and sharing are embedded in the management practice and the daily operational routines, the resultant proprietary knowledge can establish a solid foundation for a truly sustainable competitive advantage (Adams & Lamont, 2003). The value of proprietary knowledge is obvious in hospital management, especially in dealing with challenging healthcare problems.

Currency of knowledge can be an important issue at times where new knowledge renders old knowledge useless. In these cases, knowledge must be subject to frequent updating in order to stay valuable. The optimal updating frequency is determined by the dynamic (or static) nature of the knowledge. The issue of knowledge updating has been addressed in expert systems development (Liebowitz & Wilcox, 1997). In fact, one of the criteria in the selection of knowledge-based expert system application domains is that the domain knowledge must be relatively static. The complexity involved in knowledge updating and validation poses a significant challenge for keeping a knowledge base current and having the system accessible at the same time. In the broader context of medical care service delivery, updating of the knowledge repository may affect the strategy for knowledge acquisition as well as the knowledge management implementation measures.

Knowledge Strategy

A knowledge strategy, as defined by Zack (1999, p. 135), "describes the overall approach an organization intends to take to align its knowledge resources and capabilities to the intellectual requirements of its strategy." Zack's knowledge strategy framework consists of two dimensions: exploitation vs. exploration, and internal vs. external. While the exploitation vs. exploration dimension distinguishes a creator from a user of knowledge, the internal vs. external dimension describes the organization's primary sources of knowledge. Internal knowledge is characterized as being "resident within people's heads; embedded in behaviors, procedures, software and equipment; recorded in various documents; or stored in databases and online repositories" (Zack, 1999, p. 138). External sources of knowledge include: publications, university alliances, government agencies, professional associations, personal relations, consultants, vendors, knowledge brokers, and inter-organizational alliances. Illustrating with Nucor Steel's experience, Gupta and Govindarajan (2000) argued that internally-created knowledge tended to contribute more to an organization's competitive advantage than external approaches.

Another useful KM strategy framework is represented by a codification vs. personalization dichotomy. According to Hansen et al. (1999), the codification-oriented KM strategy is suitable for explicit, recordable, formal, and replicable knowledge, and the personalization-oriented strategy works better for implicit knowledge. Whereas information technology plays a central role within the codification strategy, it primarily provides tool support for the personalization strategy. The choice of primary knowledge acquisition strategy usually is determined by a variety of factors, among which is the characteristics of knowledge (Wiig, 1994; Davenport & Prusak, 2000; Tiwana, 2000; Awad, 2004).

Knowledge Management Implementation Measures

Knowledge management is generally viewed as a collection of management practices consisting of knowledge accumulation, knowledge organization, knowledge dissemination, and knowledge application (Davenport & Prusak, 2000; Awad & Ghaziri, 2004). The implementation of organizational KM projects typically involves technical as well as non-technical measures. A flexible and efficient information technology infrastructure is an essential requirement. The subsequent distribution and application of the organizational knowledge depends on digital representation, computerized storage, dissemination of the knowledge content and the application context. Additionally, properly designed incentive programs must be in place to discourage knowledge hoarding and promote knowledge sharing (Davenport & Prusak, 2000; Soo et al., 2002). Sufficient resources must be committed to encourage active learning and perpetual updating of the professional staff's knowledge base.

Knowledge Management Performance Measurement Issues

Measuring the results of KM projects is a challenging task. The subjective nature of the benefit measurement and the lengthy lead time required for the benefit to become quantitatively measurable are usually cited as the main sources of difficulty (Abeysekera, 2003; Stone & Warsono, 2003). Although the organizational benefit resulting from KM project implementation must eventually be expressible in financial terms, a significant portion of the benefit is qualitative and can only be measured subjectively. Most literature, therefore, suggests a portfolio approach to measuring the result of KM implementation such as innovative capability, which would include both financial and non-financial data (Chourides et al., 2002; Soo et al., 2002; Darroch, 2003). Furthermore, it is increasingly recognized that in order for KM to achieve its greatest success, KM functions must be tightly integrated with major business processes. For example, Davenport and Glaser (2002) indicate that based on their experience at a major medical center in Boston, medication knowledge must be embedded into the doctors' prescription writing process in order to make knowledge application a natural part of daily work practice. The tight integration of knowledge management process and other business processes contributes at least partially to a straightforward measurement of the result of KM implementation (Darroch, 2003).

The input from the practitioners also suggests the relationships to be examined in the study as listed below:

1. The primary knowledge acquisition strategy is significantly affected by knowledge characteristics (knowledge characteristics → knowledge acquisition strategy).

Rationale: Knowledge is either created from within the organization or collected from external sources. Each knowledge acquisition strategy has its pros and cons, depending on the nature of business, the available resource, and other factors. Knowledge that is created internally tends to better fit the organizational needs and contributes more to the competitiveness, for example. Although both internal and external sources can be used, an organization usually has a primary knowledge acquisition strategy regarding how to build up its knowledge stock. Everything else being equal, the perceived knowledge characteristics may determine the primary knowledge acquisition strategy that is adopted by the organization.

2. Knowledge management implementation measures are significantly affected by knowledge characteristics (knowledge characteristics → KM implementation measures).

Rationale: When the valuable knowledge is perceived to be primarily tacit, it is less likely that a significant amount of resource would be invested in building sophisticated information systems to support knowledge management activities. Rather, most of the KM implementation measures would be people-oriented. Further, in an effort to cope with knowledge complexity, volatility, and to encourage the development of proprietary knowledge, an organization may pay more attention to its incentive program, expertise development, and human resource planning. Therefore, it is reasonable to assume that the way a hospital chooses to implement KM programs is significantly influenced by its perception of knowledge characteristics.

3. Knowledge implementation measures are significantly affected by the primary knowledge acquisition strategy (primary knowledge acquisition strategy → KM implementation measures).

Rationale: Creating knowledge internally often requires knowledge workers to share knowledge with the rest of the organization. Knowledge sharing usually is not a natural component of organizational culture in most Taiwanese hospitals, where high work pressure and departmental silos tend to encourage knowledge hoarding. In order to encourage internal creation of knowledge through knowledge sharing, hospitals must implement a portfolio of facilitating measures such as incentive programs, expertise development, human resource planning, and technological infrastructure. We, therefore, postulate that KM implementation measures are affected by the primary knowledge acquisition strategy.

4. KM performance is significantly affected by the primary knowledge acquisition strategy (primary knowledge acquisition strategy → KM implementation performance).

5. KM performance is significantly affected by KM implementation measures (KM implementation measures → KM performance).

Rationale: O'Dell et al. (2003) identified three general categories of value propositions for KM program implementation—customer intimacy, product-to-market excellence, and operational excellence—as a result of APQC's first benchmarking study on best practices in KM. Operational excellence is the most relevant to the context of hospital management. The value proposition defines the goal for KM implementation. Since the degree to which the goal is achieved can be significantly affected by the approach (strategy) and the specific actions (implementation measures) taken to pursue the goal, we set up these two hypotheses to validate our presumptions.

RESEARCH DESIGN

Research Framework, Variables, and Hypotheses

For the purpose of this research, KM was defined as a management function responsible for the acquisition, organization, evaluation, sharing, distribution, and application of both tacit and explicit knowledge for an organization. In order to gather data to analyze how KM was practiced in Taiwanese hospitals, we postulated that the hospital management professionals' perception of knowledge characteristics would affect the primary strategy adopted to acquire knowledge and would also affect the hospitals' KM implementation measures. We further assumed that these latter two sets of variables in turn would affect the result of KM implementation. These hypothesized relationships between the research variables were derived from the result of literature and our field interviews with healthcare professionals in Taiwanese hospitals. The diagrammatic depiction of our research model is shown in Figure 1. The five research hypotheses established to validate our presumption are also indicated in the diagram.

Operational Definition of Research Variables

The characteristics of knowledge were represented by four important dimensions of medical and hospital management knowledge that we identified in our preliminary interview with medical professionals: knowledge mode (explicit vs. tacit nature

of knowledge), complexity, strength of knowledge appropriability, and knowledge volatility.

The primary strategy adopted to acquire knowledge in this study was dichotomized into internally-oriented acquisition and externally-oriented acquisition. Internal sources included apprenticeships, intranet, internal documentation, morning meetings, internal medical databases, and department meetings. External sources included collaboration with universities, external consultants, internships in other hospitals, seminars, and professional conferences.

The knowledge management implementation measures were represented by activities in four areas: information infrastructure, incentive programs for knowledge-sharing, expertise development, and human resource planning. The first three items corresponded to three basic entities involved in knowledge management programs: people (incentive programs), knowledge (expertise development), technological tools (information infrastructure). The fourth item (human resource planning) corresponded to both people and knowledge.

Two categories of variables were used to represent the performance measure of knowledge management implementation in hospitals: internal

Figure 1. Research framework

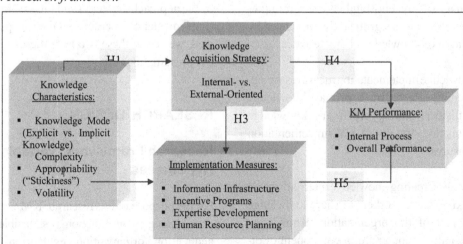

process improvement and overall organizational performance enhancement. Internal process improvements consisted of communications and efficiency improvement measures, such as problem-solving time, employee participation, decision-making cycle time, and employee interaction. Overall, organizational performance measures covered such items as service quality, customer focus, absenteeism, and customer (patient) satisfaction. With these definitions of the research variables, the research hypotheses were formulated as follows:

Hypothesis 1 (H1): The primary knowledge acquisition strategy is significantly affected by knowledge characteristics.

Hypothesis 2 (H2): KM implementation measures are significantly affected by knowledge characteristics.

Hypothesis 3 (H3): KM implementation measures are significantly affected by the primary strategy adopted for knowledge acquisition.

Hypothesis 4 (H4): KM implementation performance is significantly affected by the primary knowledge acquisition strategy.

Hypothesis 5 (H5): KM implementation measures significantly affected KM performance.

Questionnaire Design and Data Collection

All research variables, except knowledge acquisition strategy, were represented by multiple questions using five-point Likert scales, with 1 indicating very poor or highly disagree and 5 indicating very good or highly agree. A check list was devised for knowledge acquisition strategies. Twenty head physicians in four medical centers were sent a questionnaire. This first version of the questionnaire was tested using results from the 12 respondents. Based on feedback from the pilot test, the questionnaire was revised by removing the questions with low reliability coefficients and modifying the ones lacking semantic clarity. The revised version consisted of a total of 44 Likert scale questions. There were 15 questions for knowledge characteristics, 18 questions for KM implementation measures, and 11 questions for the performance measures. A copy of the questionnaire was mailed to the president of each of the 126 hospitals on the list compiled by the Department of Health of Taiwan. Hospital presidents were targeted on the assumption that they were familiar with the issues under study.

Due to the exploratory and empirical nature of the study, the questionnaire was limited in the criterion validity and the construct validity. Both the content validity and the discriminant validity were assumed to be proper since the questions were based on the literature and the input from the practicing professionals. The reliability measures, as represented by Cronbach's α, of all research variables are above 0.70, an indication of acceptable reliability (Nunnally, 1978). Table 1 summaries the reliability measures of all research variables. Note that two questions were removed from the original set of 46 questions as a result of this analysis.

Data Analysis Method

In order to test the hypotheses listed above, several statistical analysis techniques were employed to analyze the data. In particular, t-test was conducted to evaluate the effect of knowledge characteristics on the primary acquisition strategy and the effect of the knowledge acquisition strategy on the KM implementation measures. Canonical correlation analysis was conducted to determine the correlation relationship between knowledge characteristics and implementation measures, both of which are multiple variables. Finally, step-

Table 1. Reliability of research variables

Variables	Sub-dimensions	Question Items	Cronbach α
Knowledge Characteristics	Explicitness	1, 2, 3, 4	0.8239
	Complexity	5, 6, 7, 8	0.7605
	Appropriability	9, 10, 11, 12*	0.7187
	Volatility	13, 14, 15, 16	0.7905
Implementation Measures	Information Infrastructure	17, 18,19, 20, 21	0.8827
	Incentive Program	22, 23, 24, 25	0.8191
	Expertise Development	26, 27, 28, 29, 30*, 31	0.8063
	Human Resource Planning	32, 33, 34, 35	0.7674
Performance Measures	Internal Process	36, 37, 38, 39, 40, 41	0.9115
	Overall Performance	42, 43, 44, 45, 46	0.8374

Questions are subsequently removed due to insufficient reliability measures.

wise regression analysis was used to determine the impact of the KM implementation measures on both of the performance measures.

RESEARCH FINDINGS

The questionnaire was mailed to 126 hospitals in Taiwan, from which 50 questionnaires were returned. The questionnaire was addressed to the person who was most familiar with knowledge management practices in the hospital. Three questionnaires were removed due to incomplete answers. The remaining 47 accounted for an effective response rate of 37.3%: 10 questionnaires were filled out by hospital presidents, 7 by vice presidents, 1 by a physician, and 29 by hospital management staff. The Kolmogorov-Smirnov statistics for knowledge characteristics, implementation measures, and performance measures all exhibited normal distribution at the 0.001 significance level.

Hypothesis 1 stated that the primary knowledge acquisition strategy is significantly affected by knowledge characteristics. The frequency distribution of knowledge acquisition strategies summarized in Table 2 showed that the most common internal source of knowledge was morning meetings, and the most widely used external knowledge source was outside meetings. Table 3 showed the means and standard deviations of each of the four dimensions of knowledge characteristics. The measures of knowledge characteristics were dichotomized, using averages as the thresholds, into two distinct levels: high and low. A t-test was performed to determine the correlation relationship between knowledge acquisition strategy and knowledge characteristics. Table 4 showed that the adoption of internal-oriented strategy was significantly affected by the level of knowledge explicitness (t = 1.152, p-value = 0.012), and the use of external-oriented knowledge was significantly affected by knowledge complexity (t = 1.224, p-value = 0.000). In other words, the internal-oriented strategy was used more to acquire knowledge with high explicit levels, whereas the external-oriented strategy was used more for knowledge with high complexity levels. These were indications that, in general, hospitals in Taiwan tended to rely on external sources to update and upgrade their knowledge base. The lack of resource and the competitive pressure from the environment were keeping most of them from actively investing in internal research and

Table 2. Distribution of primary knowledge acquisition strategy

Types of KA Strategy		Freq.	%	Freq. Total	%
Internal-Oriented	Manual and Instruction Management	1	2.1	20	42.6
	Morning Meeting	12	25.5		
	Group Discussion within Department	6	12.8		
	Hospital-wide Medical Database	1	2.1		
External-Oriented	Collaboration with University	3	6.4	27	57.4
	Consultant	2	4.3		
	Internship with other Hospitals	2	4.3		
	Outside Meeting	20	42.6		

Table 3. Relationship between knowledge characteristics and KA strategy

Knowledge Characteristics	Knowledge Acquisition Strategy			
	Internal-Oriented	External-Oriented	t-value	p-value
Explicitness	3.8241	3.4825	1.152	0.012*
Complexity	3.2167	2.7621	1.224	0.000**
Appropriability	3.5667	3.4074	0.998	0.328
Volatility	3.1375	3.0185	0.610	0.545

Table 4. Means (μ) and standard deviations (σ) of knowledge characteristics

Knowledge Characteristics	μ	σ
Knowledge Mode	3.7872	0.5874
Complexity	2.9043	0.4056
Appropriability	3.4752	0.5462
Volatility	3.0691	0.6567

Table 5. Canonical correlation analysis between knowledge characteristics and implementation measures

Knowledge Characteristics	Canonical Variate $\chi 1$	Implementation Measures	Canonical Variate $\eta 1$
Knowledge Explicitness	0.688*	Information Infrastructure	0.71*
Complexity	-0.005	Incentive Program	0.708*
Appropriability	0.854*	Expertise Development	-0.128
Volatility	0.918*	Human Resource Planning	0.921*
Extracted Variance	51.16%	Extracted Variance	46.76%
Wilks Λ	0.465	Redundancy	0.174
F-value	2.13	Canonical Correlation (ρ)	0.61
p-value	0.011	ρ2	0.37

*Absolute value of canonical loading > 0.6

Figure 2. Path diagram of canonical correlation analysis between knowledge characteristics and implementation measures

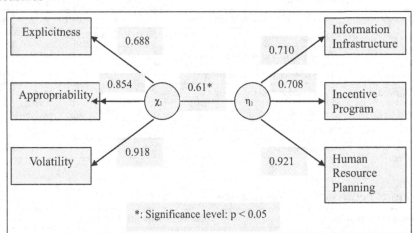

Table 6. Effect of knowledge acquisition strategy on knowledge management performance

KM Performance	KA Strategy (μ)		t-value	p-value
	Internal-Oriented	External-Oriented		
Internal Process	3.2583	3.5123	-1.028	0.310
Overall Organizational Performance	3.4500	3.5852	-0.645	0.522

development to create valuable knowledge from within the organization. With a few exceptions (e.g., Chang-Hua Christian Hospital), only the medical centers that are affiliated with research universities had the capability and resource to carry out knowledge creation activities in a systematic manner.

Hypothesis 2 stated that KM implementation measures are significantly affected by knowledge characteristics. Since both knowledge characteristics and implementation measures consist of four variables, canonical correlation analysis was employed to determine the correlation relationship. As summarized in Table 5 and graphically presented in Figure 2, the result of canonical analysis identified that the linear composition of three knowledge characteristics (knowledge explicitness, appropriability, and volatility) were significantly correlated with the linear composition of three implementation measures (informa-

tion infrastructure, incentive program, and human resource planning). The correlation coefficient (ρ) was 0.61 at the significance level 0.05.

Hypothesis 3 stated that KM implementation measures are significantly affected by the primary strategy adopted for knowledge acquisition. The result of the t-test indicated that two implementation measures were significantly affected by the knowledge acquisition strategies. Internal-oriented strategy adopters scored higher in information infrastructure than external-oriented strategy adopters, whereas external-oriented adopters scored higher in incentive measures.

Hypothesis 4 stated that the performance of KM implementation is significantly affected by the primary knowledge acquisition strategy. The result of the t-test (Table 6) showed that different knowledge acquisition strategies did not cause significant difference in either dimension (internal process and overall organizational performance) of the performance of KM implementation. Hypothesis 4 was rejected. Since internally-created knowledge usually is considered more likely to contribute to an organization's competitive advantage (Gupta & Govindarajan, 2000), this finding indicated that the hospitals in Taiwan still lacked a proper understanding of the strategic value of the locally created knowledge.

Hypothesis 5 stated that knowledge management performance is significantly affected by implementation measures. Three stepwise regression analyses were conducted to test this hypothesis. The first test was a simple regression analysis, in which both the performance measures and the implementation measures were treated as single, composite variables. The second test treated the performance measures as one variable and the four dimensions of the implementation measures as four variables. The third test treated each of the two dimensions of the performance measures as a dependent variable. The first test resulted in a regression equation:

KM Performance = 1.086 + 0.684 * KM Implementation Measures
F-value = 15.517, (p < 0.1 for the intercept and p < 0.001 for the regression coefficient), Adjusted R2 = 0.24

This result showed that the implementation measures did exhibit significant influence on the performance measures. The second and the third regression analyses were conducted to further investigate this relationship.

In the second regression analysis, each of the four dimensions of the KM implementation measures was treated as an independent variable, with the performance measures as a single composite variable. The third regression analysis related the four dimensions of the KM implementation measures with the two dimensions of the performance measures. Table 7 showed that only human resource planning and the incentive measures significantly affected the performance of KM efforts. Between the two dimensions of the performance measures, human resource planning and incentive measures contributed significantly to both the internal process and the overall performance, as shown in Table 8. The second and the third regression analysis essentially confirmed the result of the first regression analysis, and also provided a greater understanding of the importance of people factors in effective KM.

CONCLUSION AND DISCUSSION

This study investigated the practice and the effect of KM in hospital management. It examined the effect of knowledge characteristics on knowledge acquisition strategy and KM implementation measures, the effect of knowledge acquisition strategy on implementation approaches and performance measures, and the effect of implementation approaches on KM performance. Using primary data gathered in Taiwanese hospitals, the study found that knowledge characteristics significantly

Table 7. Impact of implementation measures on KM performance (stepwise regression analysis)

Implementation Measures	Standardized Regression Coefficient	Correlation Coefficient (R)	R^2	F-value	p-value
Human Resource Planning	0.506	0.638	0.407	30.851	0.000*
Incentive Program	0.305	0.695	0.482	20.510	0.000*
Standardize Regression Equation: KM Performance = 0.506 x Human Resource Planning + 0.305 x Incentive Program					

Level of significance p < 0.001

Table 8. Impact of implementation measures on KM performance

	Internal Process		Overall Organizational Performance	
	Regression Coefficient	p-value	Regression Coefficient	p-value
Intercept	-0.225	0.731	0.615	0.333
Information Infrastructure	-0.231	0.170	0.083	0.602
Incentive Program	0.380	0.019*	0.260	0.016*
Expertise Development	0.046	0.530	0.051	0.469
Human Resource Planning	0.850	0.000**	0.437	0.015*
F-value	11.487		6.258	
p-value	0.000		0.000	
Adjusted R^2	0.522		0.373	

$*p < 0.05; **: p < 0.001$

affected implementation measures, and implementation measures, in turn, had a significant effect on the result of KM implementation. More specifically, the level of explicitness of knowledge (knowledge mode) was found to have a significant effect on the adoption of the internal-oriented knowledge acquisition strategy. The complexity of knowledge was significantly related to the external-oriented knowledge acquisition strategy. In general, people factors, such as incentive programs and human resource planning, appeared to have more impact on the result of KM than technology factors, confirming a popular belief regarding the importance of non-technological factors in KM, as reported in the existing literature.

The correlation relationship between knowledge characteristics and implementation measures is worth noting. In addition to incentive programs and human resource planning, information infrastructure was found to be significantly affected by three knowledge characteristics: explicitness, proprietary nature, and variation. The enabling capability of information technology for knowledge storage, dissemination, and application allows for integration of specialized knowledge with routine business processes, such as disease diagnosis and medicine prescription in the healthcare domain (Davenport & Glaser, 2002).

Increasingly, hospitals are relying on technological measures as a strategic vehicle in coping with both professional and managerial challenges. The emphasis of information technology applications can be attributed to the collaboration between major hospitals and universities. Information technology development and applications have been a major thrust in Taiwan. Many universities set up research centers to function as an interface between information system researchers and the regional hospitals. Some technologies resulting from these collaborations are either adopted by or shared with smaller hospitals. The maximal benefit of information technology deployment has yet to be realized, however. The value of technological tools is maximized when they become integral parts of truly integrated business processes.

This study contributed to the field of KM in several ways. For practicing KM professionals and business functional managers, the study demonstrated the importance of matching KM implementation measures with knowledge characteristics. Understanding characteristics of valuable knowledge in an organization is a prerequisite to effective management of its organizational knowledge. Similarly, knowledge-driven organizations must consciously evaluate and adopt their implementation measures. When properly implemented, KM programs may produce visible benefits, including those associated with operationally-oriented goals and those associated with long-term financial outcomes.

For KM research, this study empirically revealed the correlation between knowledge characteristics and KM implementation measures. The performance impact of implementation measures, especially those associated with people element, was also confirmed. The lack of the knowledge acquisition strategy's influence on performance measures suggested that hospitals may have acknowledged the value of both internal and external sources of knowledge and indiscriminately adopted both strategies to enrich their knowledge repositories.

Because of several limitations of the study, however, due caution must be exercised in interpreting and applying the results of this study. For example, since the data was gathered in the hospitals in Taiwan, cultural and other environmental differences may limit ones ability to generalize the research findings. Similar researches must be conducted in a variety of cultural and societal settings to establish the external validity in a more general fashion.

Another research limitation was that some questionnaires were filled out by the targeted respondents' delegates, including medical doctors and information technology managers. Although the delegates possessed proper understanding of knowledge characteristics or implementation measures, they might not be the best people to answer the questions about overall organizational performance resulting from KM implementation. Additionally, the subjective nature of the questionnaire responses based on the Likert scale constituted a limitation that might discount the validity of the research results.

Healthcare organizations in the United States use information technology extensively to automate important processes and support other aspects of operations. An industry expert estimated that spending in healthcare information technology will increase around 9% per year for the next three years and would reach $30 million in 2006 (Powers, 2004). In light of the important role played by healthcare organizations in our daily life, more research is needed to provide knowledge about how to improve the quality of hospital management. Based on the findings of this research, three directions may be suggested for future research in this particular domain. Firstly, in-depth case studies may be conducted to verify the validity of our research findings in specific contexts and to assess how contextual factors impact the linkages between knowledge characteristics, KM implementation measures, knowledge acquisition strategy, and KM performance measures. Secondly, our research model may be replicated in different societies to allow for cross-cultural comparison. Such comparison is necessary in order for the research model to become better established in the KM literature. Thirdly, in light of the importance of collaboration in medical works, recent developments in the area of Web 2.0 (or enterprise 2.0) technologies must be aggressively experimented to determine their role in supporting hospital knowledge management. Web 2.0 tools allow the professional to more conveniently participate in experience sharing and problem-solving (McAfree, 2006). Medical doctors must constantly update their knowledge base. However, medical doctors are also in one of the busiest professions. The asynchronous nature of Internet-based communications and the rich content of Web 2.0 applications may provide a powerful solution to coping with this dilemma.

REFERENCES

Abeysekera, I. (2003). Intellectual accounting scorecard—Measuring and reporting intellectual capital. *Journal of American Academy of Business, 3*(1-2), 422-440.

Adams, G., & Lamont, B. (2003). Knowledge management systems and developing sustainable competitive advantage. *Journal of Knowledge Management, 7*(2), 142-154.

Awad, E., & Ghaziri, H. (2004). *Knowledge management*. Upper Saddle River, NJ: Pearson Prentice Hall.

Becera-Fernandez, I., Gonzales, A., & Sabherwal, R. (2004). *Knowledge management: Challenges, solutions, and technologies*. Upper Saddle River, NJ: Pearson Prentice Hall.

Camilleri, D., & O'Callaghan, M. (1998). Comparing public and private hospital care service quality. *International Journal of Healthcare Quality Assurance, 11*(4), 127.

Chourides, P., Longbottom D., & Murphy, W. (2002). Excellence in knowledge management: An empirical study to identify critical factors and performance measures. *Measuring Business Excellence, 7*(2), 29-46.

Davenport, T., & Glaser, J. (2002). Just-in-time delivery comes to knowledge management. *Harvard Business Review, 80*(7), 107-111.

Davernport, T., & Prusak, L. (2000). *Working knowledge: How organizations know what they know*. Boston, MA: Harvard Business School Press.

Davenport, T., De long, D., & Beers, M. (1998). Successful knowledge management projects. *Sloan Management Review*, 443-457.

Darroch, J. (2003). Developing a measure of knowledge management behaviors and practices. *Journal of Knowledge Management, 7*(5), 41-54.

Forcadell, F., & Guadamillas, F. (2002). A case study on the implementation of a knowledge management strategy oriented to innovation. *Knowledge and Process Management, 9*(3), 162-171.

Ford, R., & Angermeier, I. (2004). Managing the knowledge environment: A case of study from healthcare. *Knowledge Management Research & Practice, 2,* 137-146.

Gebert, H., Geib, M., Kolbe, L., & Brenner, W. (2003). Knowledge-enabled customer relationship management: Integrating customer relationship management and knowledge management concepts. *Journal of Knowledge Management, 7*(5), 107-123.

Gloet, M., & Berrell, M. (2003). The dual paradigm nature of knowledge management: Implications for achieving quality outcomes in human resource management. *Journal of Knowledge Management, 7*(1), 78-89.

Gupta, A., & Govindarajan, V. (2000). Knowledge management's social dimension: Lessons from Nucor Steel. *Sloan Management Review, 42*(1), 71-80.

Hair, J., Anderson, R., Tatham, R., & Black, W. (1995). *Multivariate Data Analysis,* 4th Edition. New Jersey: Prentice-Hall.

Hansen, M., et al. (1999). What's your strategy for managing knowledge?. *Harvard Business Review, 77*(2), 106-116.

Holsapple, C. (2003). Knowledge and its attributes. In: C. Holsapple (Ed.), *Handbook on knowledge management (vol. 1)* (pp. 166-188). Springer.

Howells, J. (1996). Tacit knowledge, innovation and technology transfer. *Technology Analysis & Strategic Management, 8*(2), 106-116.

Kim, S., Hwang, H., & Suh, E. (2003). A process-based approach to knowledge flow analysis: A case study of a manufacturing firm. *Knowledge and Process Management, 10*(4), 260-276.

Lee, S., & Hong, S. (2002). An enterprise-wide knowledge management system infrastructure. *Industrial Management + Data Systems, 102*(1-2), 17-25.

Leonard-Barton, D. (1995). Wellsprings of knowledge. *Harvard Business Review, 71*(2), 75-84.

Liebowitz, J., & Wilcox, L. (1997). *Knowledge management*. Ft. Lauderdale, FL: CRC Press.

McAfee, A. (2006). Enterprise 2.0: The dawn of emergent collaboration. *MIT Sloan Management Review, 47*(3), 21-28.

Nonaka, I., & Takeuchi, H. (1995). *The knowledge-creating company: How Japanese companies create the dynamics of innovation*. London, New York, NY: Oxford University Press.

Nunnally, J. (1978). *Psychometric theory,* 2nd Edition. McGraw-Hill.

O'Dell, C., Elliott, S., & Hubert C. (2003). Achieving knowledge management outcomes. In: C. Holsapple (Ed.), *Handbook on knowledge management* (pp. 253-287).

Polanyi, M. (1996). *The tacit dimension*. London: Routledge & Kegan Paul.

Porter, M., & Teisberg, E. (2004). Redefining competition in healthcare. *Harvard Business Review, 82*(6), 65-72.

Powers, V. (2004). Improving IT wellness—Healthcare organizations adopt knowledge-enabled technology. *KM World,* 10, 11, & 26.

Sarvary, M. (1999). Knowledge management and competition in the consulting industry. *California Management Review,* 41(2), 95-107.

Sharkie, R. (2003). Knowledge creation and its place in the development of sustainable competitive advantage. *Journal of Knowledge Management, 7*(1), 20-31.

Stone, D., & Warsono, S. (2003). Does accounting account for knowledge?. In: C. Hosapple (Ed.), *Handbook on knowledge management* (vol. 1). Springer.

Soo, C., Devinney, T., Midgley, D., & Deering, A. (2002). KM: Philosophy, process, and pitfall. *California Management Review, 44*(4), 129-150.

Teece, D. (1998). Research directions for knowledge management. *California Management Review, 40*(3), 289-292.

Teece, D. (2003). Knowledge and competence as strategic assets. In C. Holsapple (Ed.), *Handbook on knowledge management* (vol. 1, pp. 129-188).

Tiwana, A. (2000). *The knowledge management toolkit*. Upper Saddle River, NJ: Prentice-Hall.

Tsai, M.-T., Yu, M.-C., & Lee, K.-W. (2005). Developing e-business systems based on KM process perspective —A case study of Seven-Eleven Japan. *Journal of American academy of business, 6*(1), 285-289.

Ulrich, D., & Smallwood, N. (2004). Capitalizing on capabilities. *Harvard Business Review, 82*(6), 119-128.

Van Beveren, J. (2003). Does healthcare for knowledge management?. *Journal of Knowledge Management, 7*(1), 90-95.

Wang, S. (2002). Knowledge maps for managing Web-based business. *Industrial Management + Data Systems, 102*(7), 357-364.

Wickramasinghe, N., & Davison, G. (2004). Making explicit the implicit knowledge assets in healthcare: The case of multidisciplinary teams in care and cure environments. *Healthcare Management Science, 7,* 185-195.

Wickramasinghe, N., Gupta, J., & Sharma, S. (2005). *Creating knowledge-based healthcare organizations*. Hershey, PA: Ideas Group Publishing.

Wiig, K. (1994). *Knowledge management: The central management focus for intelligent-acting organizations*. Arlington, TX: Schema Press.

Zack, H. (1999). Developing a knowledge strategy. *California Management Review, 41*(3), 125-145.

APPENDIX 1: SUMMARY OF HYPOTHESIS TESTING RESULTS

H1	The primary knowledge acquisition strategy is significantly affected by knowledge characteristics.	Partially Accepted
H1.1	The primary knowledge acquisition strategy is significantly affected by knowledge mode.	Accepted
H1.2	The primary knowledge acquisition strategy is significantly affected by knowledge complexity.	Accepted
H1.3	The primary knowledge acquisition strategy is significantly affected by the proprietary nature of knowledge.	Rejected
H1.4	The primary knowledge acquisition strategy is significantly affected by knowledge volatility.	Rejected
H2	Knowledge management implementation measures are significantly affected by knowledge characteristics.	Accepted
H3	Knowledge management implementation measures in the hospitals are significantly affected by the primary strategy adopted for knowledge acquisition.	Partially Accepted
H4	Knowledge management performance is significantly affected by the primary knowledge acquisition strategy.	Rejected
H5	Knowledge management performance is significantly affected by knowledge management implementation measures.	Accepted
H5.1	Internal processes are significantly improved by information infrastructure	Rejected
H5.2	Internal processes are significantly improved by incentive measures for KM implementations.	Accepted
H5.3	Internal processes are significantly improved by expertise development measures.	Rejected
H5.4	Internal processes are significantly improved by human resource planning.	Accepted
H5.5	Overall performance is significantly improved by information infrastructure.	Rejected
H5.6	Overall performance is significantly affected by incentive measures for KM implementations.	Accepted
H5.7	Overall performance is significantly affected by expertise development.	Rejected
H5.8	Overall performance is significantly affected by human resource planning.	Accepted

APPENDIX 2: SURVEY QUESTIONNAIRE

(Measurement Scale: 1 means highly disagree, 5 means highly agree.)

Questions about Knowledge Characteristics:

1. Documentation has been created for all medical expertise.
2. Medical service delivery processes have formal specifications.
3. Doctors' practice experience may be documented in writing.
4. Doctors can share their professional expertise without any obstacles.
5. Major surgical operations are all accomplished by taskforce teams.
6. Significant differences of expertise exist between the doctors in the same specialty.
7. Outside experts are often called upon to assist with major surgery operations.
8. Mutual support between the doctors within the same specialty usually is difficult to come by.
9. Medical expertise is tightly integrated with hospital management and organizational culture.
10. Outsourcing is often used due to inadequacy of medical expertise.
11. Innovations of medical practices are difficult to be obtained by competition.

12. Doctors are expected to remain up to date with data in their expertise.
13. The frequency of rare case treatment experience is higher than competition.
14. New and innovative medical knowledge and technology are adopted faster than competition.
15. Knowledge used around here advances fast.

Knowledge Management Implementation Measures:

16. Information systems are aggressively developed to enable organization, dissemination, and application of knowledge.
17. Doctors are strongly encouraged to access document bases and systematically construct medical databases.
18. Operation automations through information technology are actively pursued to support doctors' work.
19. Substantial amounts of financial resources are invested in information technology.
20. Doctors are encouraged to use the Internet to enhance medical expertise exchange and diffusion.
21. Knowledge sharing is an important criterion in performance evaluation.
22. Proposals for creative idea are rewarded, even when the ideas prove to be wrong.
23. Knowledge creation and sharing are often rewarded with salary increase and bonus.
24. Knowledge creation and sharing are rewarded with promotion.
25. Doctors are always willing to accept trainings and work assignments that are tougher than competition.
26. The hospital is not hesitant in increasing headcounts of supporting technical specialists.
27. Doctors are willing to accept the challenges to enhance their professional expertise.
28. Doctors often explicitly reject the idea of being evaluated by personnel from other fields.
29. Competition among the doctors in the same field often hinders knowledge sharing.
30. Doctors are strongly encouraged to learn and to innovate.
31. Open and smooth channels of communication exist in the hospital.
32. Doctors are frequently encouraged to engage themselves in experience and expertise exchange
33. One-on-one mentor and apprentice style training of resident doctors is common here.

Knowledge Management
Performance (5 for Much Better, 3 for About the Same, and 1 for Much Worse):

34. Doctors' expertise and experience exchange
35. Handling of doctors' suggestions with regard to medical operations
36. Doctors' sense of participation
37. Decision-making speed
38. Proposal preparation cycle time
39. Overall efficiency improvement
40. Overall quality of service
41. Patient satisfaction
42. Decrease of number of administrative personnel

43. Reduction of impact caused by turnover
44. Handling of medical service improvement projects

Primary Strategy for Knowledge Acquisition (Check only one of the following):

___ University   ___ Mentor and apprentice system   ___ Consultant
___ Internship with other hospitals   ___ Morning meetings   ___ Intranet
___ Departmental meetings
___ Outside seminars and conferences   ___ Medical databases in the hospital
___ Documentation management (including operational manuals and instructions)
___ Others _____

Chapter XX
Emergency Preparedness and Information Systems:
A Case Study Using Wiki Technology

Murali Raman
Monash University, Malaysia

Terry Ryan
Claremont Graduate University, USA

Lorne Olfman
Claremont Graduate University, USA

Murray Jennex
San Diego State University, USA

ABSTRACT

This chapter is about the design and implementation of an information system, using wiki technology to improve the emergency preparedness efforts of the Claremont University Consortium. For some organizations, as in this case, responding to a crisis situation is done within a consortia environment. Managing knowledge across the various entities involved in such efforts is critical. This includes having the right set of information that is timely, relevant, and is governed by an effective communication process. It is expected that issues such as training in use of system(s), a knowledge sharing culture between entities involved in emergency preparedness, and a fit between task and technology/system must be there to support emergency preparedness activities given such structures. This study explored the use of wiki technology to support knowledge management in the context of emergency preparedness within organizations. While initially found to be useful for supporting emergency preparedness, continuing experience with the system suggests that wikis might be more useful as a collaborative tool used to train people involved in emergency preparedness, rather than being used to support response activities during an actual emergency.

Copyright © 2008, IGI Global, distributing in print or electronic forms without written permission of IGI Global is prohibited.

INTRODUCTION

Research about emergency management information systems has accelerated since the 9/11 events (Campbell et al., 2004). However, researchers do not use a common terminology to describe emergency management information systems. Jennex (2004; 2004a) for instance, calls these systems, emergency information systems (EIS). Campbell et al. (2004) use the term emergency response systems. Turoff (2002) uses the term emergency response management information systems (ermis), and extends this idea to the notion of a dynamic emergency response management information system (DERMIS) (Turoff et al., 2004). Nevertheless, the majority of the researchers in this area seem to agree that despite different naming conventions, emergency management information systems should be designed to support emergency preparedness, and guide effective response during an actual crisis situation. In addition, although researchers do not explicitly link the idea of emergency management information systems to knowledge management, the influence of the latter on emergency management systems is evident in the literature.

This chapter presents a case study about the implementation of a Web-based knowledge management system to support the Claremont University Consortium (CUC) and the Claremont Colleges in general, in emergency preparedness. The academic nature of this study centers on how an information system (specifically, a knowledge management system) can improve emergency preparedness within a consortium environment. The practical nature of the research concerns how CUC was made more ready to respond to and recover from emergencies that it might experience.

This study suggests that wiki technology might be useful to support knowledge management in the context of emergency preparedness within organizations. However, issues such as training in use of system(s), a knowledge sharing culture between entities involved in emergency preparedness, and a fit between task and technology/system

must be there to support emergency preparedness activities given such structures.

Turoff et al. (2004) take a design stance in discussing emergency management systems. We suggest that design of any emergency management system be tied to knowledge management principles. In addition, our findings suggest that in addition to design, issues such as training with technology, fit between tasks and technology, and the existence of a knowledge sharing culture are crucial when an organization intends to implement a knowledge management system to support emergency preparedness efforts.

RELEVANT LITERATURE

Davenport and Prusak (1998) define knowledge as an evolving mix of framed experience, values, contextual information and expert insight that provides a framework for evaluating and incorporating new experiences and information. Knowledge often becomes embedded in documents or repositories, and in organizational routines, processes, practices, and norms. Knowledge is also about meaning in the sense that it is context-specific (Huber, Davenport, & King, 1998). Jennex (2006) extends the concepts of context to also include associated culture that provides frameworks for understanding and using knowledge. A simpler definition of knowledge is that it is the how and why of something. Gaining knowledge is gaining insight into how and why things happen. To be useful, this knowledge must be framed in context and culture, the information and data that explain how the knowledge was generated, what it means, and how it should be used.

Alavi and Leidner (2001) define a KMS as "IT-based systems developed to support and enhance the organizational processes of knowledge creation, storage/retrieval, transfer, and application" (p. 114). They observe that not all KM initiatives will implement an IT solution, but they support IT as an enabler of KM. Additionally, they discuss various perspectives on knowledge that help determine how a KMS should be designed and used to support KM. Gupta and Sharma (2004) divide knowledge management systems into several major categories as follows: Groupware—including e-mail, e-logs and wikis; decision support systems; expert systems; document management systems; semantic networks; relational and object-oriented databases; simulation tools; and artificial intelligence.

Maier (2002) expands on the IT concept for the KMS by calling it an information and communication technology (ICT) system that supports the functions of knowledge creation, construction, identification, capturing, acquisition, selection, valuation, organization, linking, structuring, formalization, visualization, distribution, retention, maintenance, refinement, evolution, accessing, search, and application.

Stein and Zwass (1995) define an organizational memory information system (OMS) as the processes and IT components necessary to capture, store, and apply knowledge created in the past on decisions currently being made. Jennex and Olfman (2005) expand this definition by incorporating the OMS into the KMS and adding strategy and service components to the KMS.

Emergency response systems (ERS) are used by organizations to assist in responding to an emergency situation. These systems support communications, data gathering and analysis, and decision-making. ERS are rarely used but when needed, must function well and without fail. Designing and building these systems requires designers to anticipate what will be needed, what resources will be available, and how conditions will differ from normal. An early model for an ERS is from Bellardo, Karwan and Wallace (1984) and identifies the components as including a database, data analysis capability, normative models, and an interface. This model is only somewhat useful as it fails to address issues such as how the ERS fits into the overall emergency response plan, emergency response infrastructure, business structures consisting of multiple organiza-

tions, knowledge and lessons learned from past emergencies, and integration of work process and enterprise information systems.

Jennex (2004) defines an emergency information system (EIS) as any system that is used "by organizations to assist in responding to a crisis or disaster situation" (p. 2148). He further adds that an EIS should be designed to: (1) support communication during emergency response, (2) enable data gathering and analysis, and (3) assist emergency responders in making decisions.

Lee and Bui (2000) document vital observations about the use of EIS during the massive earthquake that hit the city of Kobe in Japan several years ago. Key lessons for emergency management systems designers based on Lee and Bui's work are as follows:

- Relevant information should be included in the emergency response system prior to the actual disaster situation. This is to ensure that emergency responders have sufficient information to guide decision-making processes in responding to an emergency. The authors imply that the task of gathering relevant information to support emergency response should be incorporated as part of the emergency preparedness strategic initiative.

- Information from prior experiences should become part of the emergency management system. The system should somehow be able to capture both tacit and explicit knowledge about how prior crisis situations were handled. Lessons learned can be used to guide future action. The authors in this regard imply that the design of any emergency preparedness system should support some form of organizational memory component.

In addition to designing relevant systems features to support emergency planning and response, researchers suggest that successful implementation of any emergency management system is contingent on how well people are trained to use such systems (Turoff, 1972; Patton & Flin, 1999; Lee & Bui, 2000). Turoff et al. (2004) state that emergency management systems that are not normally used will not be used when an actual emergency situation occurs.

Churchman also notes that systems are always part of a larger system and that the environment surrounding the system is outside the system's control, but influences how the system performs. The final view of a KMS is as a system that includes IT/ICT components, repositories, users, processes that use and/or generate knowledge, knowledge, knowledge use culture, and the KM initiative with its associated goals and measures.

In summary, researchers indicate that emergency management information systems should support the following features inherent in any knowledge management system: (1) enable individuals and groups to create, share, disseminate and store knowledge (Turoff, 1992; Turoff et al., 2004); (2) offer the ability to document experiences and lessons, which have been learned to form the overall organizational memory for dealing with crisis situations (Lee & Bui, 2000); (3) support asynchronous and collaborative work (Campbell et al., 2004); (4) provide emergency-response-related information that is relevant, accurate and presented in a timely manner (Turoff, 1992; Turoff et al., 2004; Jennex, 2004); and (5) enhance the overall communication process between people involved in emergency preparedness and response by inserting more structure into the manner in which information is organized and documented (Turoff, 1992; Turoff et al., 2004).

METHODOLOGY

This chapter uses canonical action research to conduct this study (Suman & Evered, 1978; Davidson et al., 2004; Lindgren et al., 2004). Both qualitative and quantitative data were collected and analyzed throughout the research process. One of the authors worked for CUC as the emergency management assistant for three years. The research process in canonical action research starts with the involvement of the researcher with an identified organization. This is followed by the problem diagnosis by the researcher to determine issues and challenges faced by the organization.

The diagnosis leads to action planning, that is, a formal proposal is made to the client/organization in terms of a proposed solution/system. Upon approval by the client, the proposed solution is implemented. Action or intervention then occurs. Evaluation and reflection of the solution/system that is implemented is then conducted.

THE CASE SETTING

The Claremont University Consortium (CUC) provides services to the seven members of the Claremont Colleges[1] by operating programs and central facilities on their behalf. Each college maintains its own emergency preparedness plan. Every plan calls for the activation of a college-level emergency operations center (EOC) in the event of an emergency. The Multi Agency Coordination Center (MACC) exists to coordinate responses among the seven colleges and CUC. MACC's action plan is guided by the Claremont Colleges Emergency Preparedness Plan. This plan defines an emergency as preparing for and responding to any situation "associated with, but not limited to, disasters such as earthquakes, life threatening incidents, terrorist attacks, bio-terrorism threats and other incidents of a similar capacity" (p. 1).

The MACC is a group that becomes active whenever emergencies occur at any of the Colleges and CUC that could impact any one or more of the consortium members. It is intended to: (1) coordinate among the colleges and external agencies; (2) prioritize and fill requests for assistance from central resources; and (3) assist the colleges in returning to normalcy as soon as possible.

The Problem

Prior to embarking on the systems design and implementation initiatives, interviews were conducted with nine representatives from five colleges and CUC involved in emergency preparedness. Through these interviews, it was found that the top three issues pertaining to emergency preparedness at CUC (and within the Claremont Colleges at large) are: (1) communication between college level EOCs and the MACC, both before and during an emergency can be improved; (2) coordination between CUC and college level EOCs, in terms of activities and overall efforts in preparing for an emergency can be enhanced, and (3) emergency-related information/knowledge could be shared seamlessly. This includes access to information about drills, policy documentation, emergency notification protocols, access to college level emergency plans, status and availability of emergency resources such as debris removal equipment, housing, and medical expertise. The following statements offer several examples:

Communication issues across the colleges in terms of who knows what, when they know it is vital, but I don't think that we are there yet. For example, in a recent incident I was informed after five hours only. So communication is an issue. My struggle with that was, if we are indeed mobilized, we need to know and be contacted earlier. The communication of when there is an incident, when a contact is made, this is a concern for all of us.

Communication between colleges can be improved. We need a load of practice in this area to ensure better informational flow. Mutual aid agreement, sharing of resources to handle localized incidents needs to be shared and communicated. Training, and this would include training conducted in a jointly organized fashion. Use of technology during drills that are simulated can help the above.

We rely on written plans and rely on documentation when we need information. This can take time and cost. When we need to update some document we need to make sure that everyone has updated their respective documents. Again, time and cost is involved. The documents that we have are easy to read, but knowing exactly what to do when something happens, remains a challenge.

We at this college do have some of the information available online, on the Web [PDFs] which is used by the building managers. These are secured and restricted to those involved in emergency preparedness. Again, the information may not be easy to retrieve, even in Web format. We need more quick links, shortcuts, and need to know what is new when it comes to emergency preparedness.

Extended Problem Diagnosis

In Stage two of the problem diagnosis, interviews were conducted with an additional twenty-five CUC personnel involved in emergency preparedness. The objective was to focus on the knowledge management issues in the context of emergency preparedness within the Claremont Colleges. A fifteen-question questionnaire was developed to ascertain the critical success factors for implementing a knowledge management system for CUC. These questions were based on the KMS success model (Jennex & Olfman, 2005). The KMS Success Model is based on three main constructs: system quality, knowledge/information quality, and service quality (Jennex & Olfman, 2006). The respondents were asked to rank the extent to which they either agreed or disagreed with the statements on a five-point Likert scale. Table 1 lists the statements, and how these map to the KMS success model constructs. Table 1 also provides a summary of the data analyzed using SPSS.[2]

The average scores for the statements ranged between 3.12 and 4.56. The high average scores for most of the statements that relate to the key success

Table 1. Linking the KMS success model to emergency preparedness at the claremont colleges

	Concept (From the KMS Success Model)	Constructs (From the KMS Success Model)	Min	Max	Mean	Std. Dev.
CUC has the necessary resources to develop a KMS to support emergency planning/preparedness.	System Quality	Technological resources				
	1.00	5.00	3.16	1.07		
CUC has the necessary resources to update a KMS to support emergency planning/preparedness.	System Quality	Technological resources				
	1.00	5.00	3.16	1.03		
CUC has the necessary resources to maintain a KMS to support emergency planning/preparedness.	System Quality	Technological resources				
	1.00	5.00	3.12	1.01		
More information about emergency preparedness at CUC can be converted to Web format.	System Quality	KMS form	2.00	5.00	4.04	0.79
Knowledge about emergency preparedness from individuals can be made available online.	System Quality	Level of KMS	2.00	5.00	4.12	0.83
Knowledge about emergency preparedness from relevant groups can be made available online.	System Quality	Level of KMS	2.00	5.00	4.24	0.72
Information about emergency preparedness could be automated, shared and retrieved from a single Web interface.	Knowledge/Information Quality					
	Richness	2.00	5.00	4.16	0 .90	
A KMS for emergency preparedness should simplify searching and retrieving of information.	Knowledge/Information Quality					
	Richness	2.00	5.00	4.24	0.72	
A KMS can enhance the strategic planning process for teams involved in emergency preparedness.	Knowledge/Information Quality					
	Knowledge Strategy/ Process					
	3.00	5.00	4.32	0.69		
A KMS should provide timely information for staff involved in emergency preparedness to support emergency planning.	Knowledge/Information Quality					
	Richness	3.00	5.00	4.32	0.69	
A KMS should provide accurate/up-to-date information for staff involved in emergency preparedness to support emergency planning.	Knowledge/Information Quality					
	Richness	3.00	5.00	4.40	0.58	
A KMS should provide relevant information for staff involved in emergency preparedness to support emergency planning.	Knowledge/Information Quality					
	Richness	3.00	5.00	4.36	0.57	
A KMS to support emergency planning should provide linkages to external and internal information sources.	Knowledge/Information Quality					
	Linkages	3.00	5.00	4.56	0.58	
Top management support is needed in implementation of a KMS to support emergency preparedness.	Service Quality	Management Support	3.00	5.00	4.40	0.71
I welcome the idea of being trained in using a KMS to support emergency preparedness activities at CUC.	Service Quality	Management Support	1.00	5.00	4.28	1.02

factors of implementing a Web-based knowledge management system suggest the following:

- The system should provide key features of managing emergency-related knowledge, such as being able to provide timely and relevant information.
- The system should provide links to both internal and external sources of knowledge about emergency preparedness.
- The top management within CUC must support the system implementation.
- The system must support committees involved in emergency preparedness to make strategic decisions.

The first three statements relate to post-implementation resource issues. The average scores for these statements (between 3.12 and 3.16) are relatively lower than the other statements. The majority of the respondents feel that CUC may not have the necessary resources to develop, update, and maintain a knowledge management system to support emergency preparedness. This is due to the fact that involvement in emergency preparedness activities, for the majority of the staff, is not part of their main job function. In addition, CUC has a limited budget for emergency preparedness activities.

Proposed System

The potential use of wiki technology as an instantiation of a knowledge management system to support emergency preparedness within the Claremont Colleges was discussed with the CEO and key IT personnel. Three criteria guided the selection of a suitable Web-based knowledge management system to support CUC's emergency preparedness efforts.

- **Cost:** During the initial discussion with the CEO, she made it clear that for the time being, any system developed to support CUC's

emergency-related activities had to rely on open source solutions. This is due to the fact that CUC does not have a sufficient budget to implement any commercially available knowledge management system.

- **Our experience:** We were allowed to develop any system that we were familiar with, as long as it was in the best interest of the organization in the context of its emergency preparedness initiatives.
- **Issues faced:** The system that is developed has to address the key emergency preparedness issues/concerns faced by the Claremont Colleges, as described earlier.

These criteria were then used to examine the list of options available to CUC. Gupta and Sharma's (2004) categorization of knowledge management systems was used to examine if a particular category met the three-system selection criteria discussed above. It was decided to implement an instantiation of a knowledge management system using wiki technology given budgetary and resource constraints, with regards to emergency preparedness, faced by CUC. The technology was also selected given our familiarity with using wikis for teaching and learning (Raman & Ryan, 2004).

Why Wikis?

Wiki is a Hawaiian word that refers to "being quick". Leuf and Cunningham (2001) define a wiki as "a freely expandable collection of interlinked Web pages, a hypertext system for storing and modifying information—a database where each page is easily editable by any user with a forms-capable Web browser client" (p. 14).

Leuf and Cunningham (2001) suggest that wiki technology can support knowledge management initiatives for organizations. The authors state that three collaborative models are available over the network today: e-mail exchanges, shared folders/file access, and interactive content update and access. They suggest that use of e-mail systems solely may not enable effective management of knowledge for an organization based on the following reasons: (1) e-mail postings cannot be edited easily; (2) a central archiving system might be necessary to support effective documentation of information. This implies that using some form of database that hosts various postings directly might be a more effective manner of managing information flow for the organization; and (3) e-mail systems may not necessarily support shared access to a particular information base.

The second model to support collaborative work and knowledge sharing is the shared access system (Leuf & Cunningham, 2001). The main difference between a shared file system and an e-mail system is that the former enables users to access a common information base. In this regard, different users could be allowed to edit/update "based on varying degrees of freedom" (p. 6) a particular information base. Nevertheless, this system is still similar to an e-mail system in that discussions and knowledge sharing is contingent upon threaded postings, or in a worst case, governed as a regular e-mail system (Leuf & Cunningham, 2001).

Wiki technology is an example of the interactive server model that offers users a newer avenue to share knowledge and participate in online collaborative work (Leuf & Cunningham, 2001). The main components of an interactive server model are the database, the Web server, and user access to a common front end. The authors suggest that the main benefits of using collaborative server models include among others: (1) allowing more effective organization of information by individuals and groups, and (2) enabling ad hoc groups to collaborate on specific projects.

Wagner (2004) examines the use of different knowledge management systems that can be categorized based on two dimensions: (1) how knowledge is distributed in organizations, and (2) the nature of the task involved. He asserts that in an organizational context, the source of knowledge

is either centralized or distributed. The nature of the task is either ad hoc or repetitive. Based on these two dimensions, he proposes a particular form of knowledge management system to support a particular organizational need to manage knowledge. Table 2 summarizes the "knowledge management system fit based on knowledge distribution and task repetitiveness" (p. 267) in an organizational context.

Wagner's framework suggests that an organization's need for a knowledge management system is contingent upon the nature of the task involved, and where knowledge resides in the organization. Use of FAQs, for instance, is suitable when knowledge is centralized, and when tasks are repetitive in nature. Conversational knowledge management systems, in contrast, are more suitable when the source of knowledge is distributed. Wagner's classification of knowledge management systems implies that conversational technologies might be relevant to support emergency preparedness activities at CUC. This is because emergency preparedness at CUC involves tasks that are ad hoc and dependant upon knowledge that is distributed across the different EOCs and between the MACC members. Wiki technology can support numerous knowledge management requirements for organizations. These include filtering knowledge from noise, ensuring knowledge quality, providing search functions, tracing the source of knowledge, building/enhancing knowledge continuously, and supporting the need for dynamically changing information content in a given system (Wagner, 2004). The system selection criteria, our prior experience with wikis, and support from relevant literature led us to choose wiki technology.

TikiWiki—Emergency Management System for the Claremont Colleges

The first step during the intervention stage of the project was to install and test a prototype wiki clone. In December 2004, TikiWiki version 1.7.4 was installed onto a test server. TikiWiki is

Table 2. Knowledge management system tasks and sources of knowledge[3]

Knowledge management system type	Knowledge source	Task
Conversational technologies	Distributed	Ad hoc
FAQ	Centralized	Repetitive
Search engine	Distributed	Repetitive
Portals	Distributed-Centralized	Ad hoc-Repetitive

only one instance of wiki technology. TikiWiki bundles together the requirements for a Web server (Apache), a database server (mySQL) and the front end Web pages (written using Python).

Components of the TikiWiki that were viewed as relevant to the requirements specified by the users were then selected for activation. Only two features have been enabled in the current prototype of the system. These are the TikiWiki module and linking features. The module feature (administered by the system administrator) was used to create particular groupings of quick links to information about emergency preparedness. For the purpose of the prototype, the following modules were created:

- **CUC links:** Provides links to key information sources about emergency preparedness for CUC. This module is based on CUC EOC's organization structure. It has links to the information requirements for each of the EOC members, based on her/his respective job functions. The planning and intelligence coordinator, for instance, has access to weather information, notification protocols, phone trees, hazardous material information, lessons learned from tabletop sessions, and online maps of the Claremont Colleges.
- **MACC information:** A quick link and reference to emergency resources/supplies

available thorough CUC's Central Services/Physical Plant. The MACC module is now extended to include other key elements relevant to the MACC.

- **Calendar of events:** Information about meetings, meeting summaries, drills, training events, and other related activities. The objective of this module is to assist all EOCs and the MACC to coordinate their respective activities.
- **Knowledge base:** This module has links to local weather conditions, transcripts from tabletop (drill) sessions, and links to federal and local emergency response agencies.
- **Maps:** Online maps for the Claremont Colleges and CUC.

The other feature that was implemented in the TikiWiki was the linking function. TikiWiki permits users to create multiple links within the system itself. This can be done through the use of the back link function. For example, through a back link, the CUC overview page is linked to the system's homepage. TikiWiki also permits users to create links to external sources.

The focus of systems design and implementation in stage 2 was to improve the communication issues related to emergency planning at CUC. When a crisis of a particular magnitude occurs within the Claremont Colleges, the MACC is activated. The MACC consists of members from

CUC and a representative from all the Claremont Colleges. The MACC members provide inputs to the MACC Chair and Operations Co-coordinator, based on information received from the respective College EOCs. Based on the current protocol, the information flow between MACC and the colleges is facilitated through the use of telephones and information that is documented on a 6 x 8 foot white board located inside the MACC room.

The CUC was aware that during a crisis the flow of information between the MACC and the college EOCs was subject to 'noise' and inaccuracy. The CUC was also aware based on participation in drills that the MACC does not have sufficient information about actual crisis situations within the respective colleges. This makes response efforts rather difficult during certain incidents. To overcome the communicational issues, an additional module in the system called the MACC Situation Board was developed. This module consists of four main elements:

- **Situation:** This section enables the MACC representatives to document real-time information about a particular situation at their respective college.
- **Action:** This section is used to document specific actions that a college/CUC has taken to address a particular emergency situation.
- **Need:** Links to another page that consolidates the emergency resources (such as debris removal equipment, temporary housing, search and rescue teams, food, and first-aid supplies) needed by all colleges and CUC to respond to an emergency. The MACC chair and operations coordinator were given access to the consolidated resource needs page. This can be used to guide the decision on resource allocation between CUC and the colleges. The consolidated information about resources needed is expected to improve the communication between MACC and the respective college EOCs.

- **Sharing:** Links to another page that consolidates all information about resources that each college and CUC is willing to share to support a particular emergency response initiative. The type/category, quantity, and status of emergency-related resources within the Claremont Colleges will be made known to all MACC members through the system in the near future.

The purpose of this module is twofold. Firstly, as mentioned, it is designed to facilitate documentation of resources required by respective colleges during an emergency. Through this module, member institutions can record a particular type of resource that they need and are willing to share with other colleges when a particular emergency situation occurs. This information, unlike before, is now available via the Web, easily accessible to every EOC and MACC member. Secondly, the information can be used by the MACC operations coordinator to facilitate resource allocation between the colleges when an emergency occurs.

Evaluation

Effectiveness of the system was evaluated through a series of one-on-one interviews with the MACC members who had participated in two separate training sessions (in February 2005) where the system was used. Thirteen individuals were interviewed. The instrument used to facilitate the process had ten open-ended questions, divided into two categories: (1) general feedback/overall impression of the system, and (2) extent of goal achievement — ability of the system to facilitate the knowledge management requirements within the context of emergency preparedness.

Findings

The following subsections list several of the responses for the open-ended questions by the respondents. These responses are organized based on the two categories mentioned earlier. Given the action-oriented nature of this study, we acknowledge the potential bias of our involvement in the project, and the findings, particularly with reference to the use of wiki technology.

Category 1: General Feedback/Impression

Overall, the respondents were pleased with the system. The feedback received was largely positive. The majority of the respondents felt that the system was simple to use. One of them said the following:

My immediate reaction was very good. I thought that the ease of use of the system was there and that the visual layout was very clear. That's not how I often feel when I am exposed to new systems. It was logical too. Visually it made sense to me. I don't always react very positively to new systems. My immediate reaction was very positive. In prior cases I have had the experience of feeling 'Oh My God', what do we have here? This was not the case this time.

However, not everyone was totally comfortable in using the system. One respondent mentioned the following:

It is a key step but it is a little daunting in some ways. One must be a computer savvy person to really play with the system. I look at it from an end user standpoint, particularly how it can be used better. But it sure seems like we are moving in the right direction especially after the last drill at the MACC when there was chaos in there – that was really wild. This is a good start, but there are issues that we need to address.

Another respondent suggested that the system could improve the overall communication process. Specifically she said:

It seemed like it would be a very useful tool and could eliminate many of the previous problems with communication. I was excited to hear there would be a standard protocol for us to transfer information from our campus EOCs to the MACC.

Assisting Emergency Preparedness Efforts

On balance, the majority of the respondents felt that the system could assist CUC and the colleges in emergency preparedness efforts. However, this is contingent upon continuous training, access control, and willingness of emergency planners to update the system with relevant information. The following statements offer evidence:

I do think that the system can assist emergency preparedness. Specifically the system can provide better and quicker access to information. However, before this works, people need to populate the system and be diligent in updating the information base in the system. I am not sure about controlled access though with the wiki technology. Anyone can update or delete the information. People can go in and mess around even though we can assume that they would not.

The system provides for an additional method of communication between all entities involved in emergency preparedness. The system facilitates a more effective written communication process. This can reduce any misunderstanding between the emergency responders. After all, visual aids are better to process and faster to comprehend as well. By providing a place where various human and material resources can be listed prior to being needed, enables more common space, and a means of documenting what happens during a response.

Aspect of Emergency Preparedness Supported

The general consensus from the respondents was that the system might support the following aspects within emergency preparedness: (1) coordinating planning efforts; (2) offering a better mechanism to document processes; (3) assisting in communication efforts; and (4) sharing of emergency-related information. The following statements offer evidence:

I am tempted to say that the system helps emergency planning but I don't think the system supports planning solely. If used well, the system can save us all a lot of time in terms of communication. It provides us with an overview of what is happening across the colleges when an emergency occurs, through the MACC Situation Board Module. The campus status for every college is right there. This is why I say that it will help us in all future emergency planning efforts.

I think the system supports both information storing and the emergency response communication process. In terms of communication, the information that is available readily to the users can help them communicate more effectively. The right word might be information that is immediately viewable or accessible can support the communication process. Also, the system provides a quick way of getting information. The system surely helps to capture knowledge as well. As I mentioned, you have everyone from the respective colleges who report to MACC there and they post their knowledge and information into the system. This seems like a very organized way of capturing information.

Category 2—Goal Achievement

Improving Communications

The majority of the users felt that the system can enhance emergency-related communication both before and during an actual emergency. One respondent even suggested that the system might benefit recovery communication with external agencies such as FEMA. However, before

this happens, issues such as training, willing to share information, and trust between one another, must be resolved. The following statements offer examples:

The system can improve the overall communication process. This is due to the fact that all the schools have access to the system and all the schools should be posting information relevant to emergency response. And one can access the system from anywhere. It does not matter which part of the world you are from, you can get to it as it is Web-based.

The system helps us to communicate better even after an emergency has ended, as the information will be at everyone's fingertips, which could later be served as data for any report or justification in an inquiry, such as FEMA and other agencies that may need that information.

The system can facilitate communication during an emergency. However, before this works, we need to make sure that people are willing to trust each other. For example, under the resources to share and resources needed pages, people need to be aware that just resources available as they have been posted pre-crisis, may not necessarily be available when an actual crisis occurs.

Emergency Preparedness Knowledge Capture

The users also generally felt that the system can facilitate some aspects of knowledge management. Specifically, benefits such as being able to archive information, capture knowledge and information about emergency preparedness and offer a more structured way to manage information were noted. The following statements offer evidence:

I think that it will help us create an archive of every drill, actual emergency, and also any other related activities that we conduct. This tells me that the system might serve as a useful knowledge book or 'book of knowledge' so to speak. People must be willing to contribute to this book though.

The system can help us capture information/knowledge about emergency planning and response. The scribe could copy and paste information into any Microsoft program such as Excel or Microsoft Word for later usage.

The system allows us to better manage emergency related information because now we have a written record of everything that is done and by whom. This is useful for future references too. The system also provides a common platform/space, structuring of information

Knowledge Sharing

The users were also optimistic about the ability of the system to facilitate knowledge and information sharing between individuals and entities involved in emergency preparedness. However, this is contingent upon the willingness of people to share information and trust the source of information/knowledge that resides in the system. Some of the responses to this issue are as follows:

Frankly, I don't think all the members from the various colleges have a knowledge sharing culture. Based on my experience here, my guess is that people need to share more information about emergency planning with each other. It seems easier to share with some relative to others. I guess we are comfortable with speaking directly with people and may not be willing to share information in an open platform. This needs to change though. People must be willing to share information with each other.

As mentioned, easy access to the system and a fairly direct way to input ideas will allow people to share knowledge about emergency preparedness with each other. It will —it will allow them

to populate the database or to fill in the blanks. But people must be willing to do this.

The system has useful refreshing abilities and allows to share information and knowledge with each other instantaneously. It provides timely information and therefore can help better communication between the EOCs and the MACC.

General Concerns

Several issues must be addressed before the value of the system to support emergency preparedness within CUC and the Claremont Colleges is maximized. The respondents mentioned the following general concerns:

I think for the system to work, training is key. People at MACC need to be trained to use the system. But, as you know, the people that report to MACC either don't show up for training sessions or keep changing. Then, there is this issue of the information sharing culture that I spoke to you about. This must change for the system to be used effectively. People should put personality differences aside and be willing to share and communicate with each other. The technology itself seems powerful and is a great idea. It can handle different and very dynamic sets of information when an actual crisis occurs. But at the heart of all of this is the willingness to be trained and share information. For this to happen, emergency preparedness must become part of peoples' job function. With the exception of a few people on MACC, for the majority of us, emergency preparedness is not of a primary concern. We prepare only when we think about drills, otherwise, it seems to be lost in our daily primary functions.

I would be concerned if we don't have Internet connectivity. I think we need a paper-based system as a backup. This is really my only concern. And I saw during our drill, some people are not too Web savvy. There might be issues with training;

people who are not familiar with a web-based system need to be trained. Also the colleges keep sending new people to the MACC. If we have new people who don't know how to use the system or have not been trained to do so, this could cause some problems as well. In the event of an emergency there might not be any IT staff to support the use of the system. This again could become an issue. Ongoing training for staff involved in emergency preparedness is necessary.

I think the challenge is keeping everyone constantly abreast of the system. I think the idea of playing with the system every month when the MACC meets is welcomed. Your re-learning time or start-up time will become longer if this is not done. We need to make sure that people know where to fill information and not do this inaccurately. Also, people should not edit other people's information.

I think people need to be trained continuously. In addition, it only makes sense if the EOCs for all colleges use this system too; after all they need to provide MACC representatives with the information needed.

If it is used properly, updated and maintained, then this will work. However, this is subject to some budget being approved for a system-resource or admin staff that helps in this task. Also we need to make sure that people do not mess up due to poor access control.

DISCUSSION AND LESSONS LEARNED

Feedback from the evaluation phase suggests that the system that has been implemented can impact emergency preparedness activities for CUC and the Claremont Colleges in two ways: (1) improve communication, and (2) assist in emergency preparedness knowledge/information sharing.

Communication

Key staffs involved in emergency preparedness now realize that, through the project, the Web-based system can assist the overall emergency preparedness communication process by:

- Providing a centralized information base about emergency situations, campus action, resource status, and MACC action, which are now accessible to all relevant groups and individuals involved in emergency planning.
- Minimizing the overflow of information within MACC, and thereby reducing the possibility of 'communication chaos'.
- Empowering staffs involved in emergency preparedness to update information as and when it is received, without the need for relying on the MACC scribe to do so.
- Providing a structured way of documenting emergency-related information, which can support external communication and recovery efforts, for example, claiming for reimbursement from FEMA and other federal agencies. Wiki technology has a function called history, which documents exactly what was entered into the wiki, by whom, and when.

Knowledge Sharing

Anyone can contribute to a wiki page, in a given wiki community (Leuf & Cunningham, 2001; Wagner, 2004; 2006; Raman, 2006). Wiki technology thrives on the principle of being open (Wagner, 2004). Emergency preparedness and response within the Claremont Colleges involves both knowledge and experience from a diverse set of individuals. Within CUC alone, there are staffs that have been trained in particular emergency preparedness areas. Examples are people who are trained in search and rescue, earthquake evacuation procedures, hazardous material handling, CPR, and first aid response.

Critical Success Factors

Our findings suggest that the positive outcomes of the system can fully materialize only if the following factors are taken into consideration by the CUC's top management involved in emergency preparedness:

• People involved in emergency preparedness are willing to share information with one another. The MACC Situation Board module, for instance, can support the operations coordinator to plan for and allocate resources during an actual crisis, only if the 'resource available' template is filled a priori, by the respective college EOCs. As one respondent mentioned:

I am not sure if people will be willing to share information with one another particularly about the status of their resources.

• The technology is designed to support a knowledge sharing culture. However, we are uncertain if this culture exists between every EOC and individuals involved in emergency preparedness in this case.

• The system must play a vital role in every emergency response drill and training session. Unless the system is used during drills and such events, it will not be used during an actual emergency.

• The technology must support and not hinder the existing emergency response protocol. In this context, the CEO indicated the concern that:

Everyone [with reference to the EOCs] can act prematurely and go talk directly to one another, without going thorough the central body (MACC) to coordinate efforts. The system should support existing protocols that we have. People should be trained to use it to ensure that the technology supports MACC's role. This can be done.

Figure 1. Theoretical framework

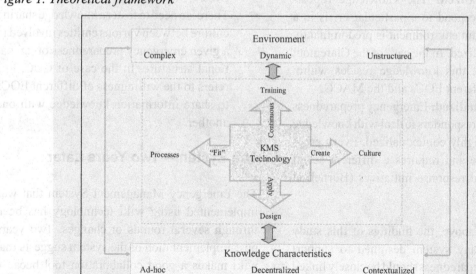

THEORETICAL IMPLICATIONS

Figure 1 illustrates how the project findings might further inform theory about emergency management information systems. This study suggests that the environment faced by emergency responders is complex, dynamic, and unstructured (e.g., Burnell et al., 2004; Kostman, 2004; Van Kirk, 2004). The majority of literature about emergency management information systems does not clearly state that systems designed to support emergency preparedness are associated with knowledge management. This study suggests that the environment faced by emergency responders forces them to deal with the following characteristics of knowledge:

- **Ad hoc:** Knowledge within emergency responders at the Claremont Colleges is largely tacit and utilized as and when an emergency occurs. Individuals and groups involved in emergency preparedness may not necessarily think about responding to a particular situation beforehand. This implies that the knowledge that they need to respond to an emergency is ad hoc in that it is required as and when a crisis occurs.
- **Decentralized:** The knowledge repository to respond to a particular crisis in a consortium environment is predominantly decentralized. In the case of the Claremont Colleges, this knowledge resides within eight different EOCs and the MACC.
- **Contextualized:** Emergency preparedness requires responders to deal with knowledge that is highly contextualized. Every crisis is unique and requires a different set of ideas and response initiatives (Burnell et al., 2004).

Given the above, the findings of this study suggest that any system designed to support emergency preparedness should be closely linked to ideas inherent within the domain of knowledge

management. A particular technology selected to support emergency preparedness should cater to knowledge that might be decentralized, ad hoc, and highly contextualized.

We suggest that wiki technology might be a simple yet cost effective option for organizations that intend to use/design any information system to manage information/knowledge-related to emergency preparedness. Wiki technology is appropriate for knowledge that is dynamic and decentralized (Wagner, 2004). Nevertheless, technology alone is not sufficient to foster effective emergency preparedness initiatives. The system should be designed to cater to the requirements of emergency responders and must be used in every drill and emergency training activities (Turoff et al., 2004). Figure 1 also suggests that in addition to effective design and training considerations, two additional factors are required when thinking about emergency information management systems:

- A fit between the knowledge management system and the existing emergency preparedness policies must be sought. Stated differently, the technology should support and not hinder emergency response initiatives.
- There is a need to foster a knowledge sharing culture between various entities involved in a given emergency preparedness organizational structure. In the case of CUC, this refers to the willingness of different EOCs to share information/knowledge with one another.

The System—Two Years Later

The Emergency Management System that was implemented using wiki technology has been through several rounds of changes. Two years post-implementation of the system suggests that wiki makes a good collaboration tool because of its communicative ability and resulting in better recommendations during emergency response. However, the individuals and teams involved in emergency response at the Claremont Colleges have a hard time separating a system into emergency preparation and emergency response. Similar responses were found during the Katrina disaster. The operations coordinator for MACC, for instance, suggested that the technology is more appropriate as a tool that is used to train people on emergency response. However, its use during an actual emergency was doubtful.

There have been changes to the CUC EMS. The lead author is no longer working with CUC. He was recently informed by the CUC Emergency Preparedness consultant that the wiki was not comfortable for several users during the various training and drill sessions. The system now has a more blog-and-chat style feature. Apart from providing read-only access to several core pages on the site, a college-specific blog space has been created. The changes to the original system were made based on the request and feedback from the users.

This blog- and chat-driven system, continues to be used to facilitate meetings, drills and other emergency training sessions. This implies, as suggested earlier, collaborative systems seem to play a more vital role in preparation for emergencies, rather than being used during an actual one.

CONCLUSION

An organization's emergency preparedness activities might involve collaborative efforts between various entities. A vital activity is responding to an actual crisis situation that hits one or more of the member organizations/entities. For some organizations, as in this case, responding to a crisis situation in done within a consortium environment. Managing knowledge across the various entities involved in such efforts is critical. This includes having the right set of infor-

mation that is timely, relevant, and is governed by an effective communication process. Given such organizational structures, and the need to manage knowledge in these environments, IT, which manifests itself in the form of knowledge management systems, might play a crucial role. However, before this occurs, the following issues must be considered. Sufficient training in use of system(s) must take place, a knowledge sharing culture between entities involved in emergency preparedness should exist, and a 'fit' between task and technology/system must be guaranteed.

REFERENCES

Alavi, M., & Leidner, D. (2001). Review: Knowledge management and knowledge management systems: Conceptual foundations and research issue. *MIS Quarterly, 25*(1), 107-136.

Bellardo, S., Karwan, K., & Wallace, W. (1984). Managing the response to disasters using microcomputers. *Interfaces, 14*(2), 29-39.

Burnell, L., Priest, J., & Durrett, J. (2004). Developing and maintaining knowledge management system for dynamic, complex domains. In J. Gupta & S. Sharma (Eds.), *Creating knowledge-based organizations.* London: IGP.

Campbell, C., DeWalle, B., Turoff, M., & Deek, F. (2004). *A research design for asynchronous negotiation of software requirements for an emergency response information system.* Paper presented at the Americas Conference on Information Systems, New York, NY.

Davenport, T., & Prusak, L. (1998). *Working knowledge.* Boston, MA: Harvard Business School Press.

Davidson, R.M., Martinsons, M.G., & Kock, N. (2004). Principles of canonical action research. *Information Systems Journal, 14,* 65-86.

Gupta, J., & Sharma, S. (2004). *Creating knowledge-based organizations.* Hershey, PA: IDEA Group Publishing.

Huber, G., Davenport, T., & King, D. (1998). Some perspectives on organizational memory. In: F. Burstein, G. Huber, M. Mandviwalla, J. Morrison, & L. Olfman, (Eds.), *Unpublished Working Paper for the Task Force on Organizational Memory, Presented at the 31st Annual Hawaii International Conference on System Sciences.* Hawaii.

Jennex, M. (2004). *Emergency response systems: Lessons from utilities and Y2K.* Paper presented at the Americas Conference on Information Systems, New York, NY.

Jennex, M. (2004a). Emergency response systems: The utility Y2K experience. *Journal of Information Technology Theory and Application, 6*(3), 85-102.

Jennex, M. (2006). Culture, context, and knowledge management. *International Journal of Knowledge Management, 2*(2), i-iv.

Jennex, M., & Olfman, L. (2005). Assessing knowledge management success. *International Journal of Knowledge Management, 1*(2), 33-49.

Jennex, M., & Olfman, L. (2006). A model of knowledge management success. International Journal of Knowledge Management, 2(3), 51-68.

Kostman, J. (2004). 20 rules for effective communication in a crisis. *Disaster Recovery Journal, 17*(2), 20.

Lee, J., & Bui, T. (2000). *A template-based methodology for disaster management information systems.* Paper presented at the Hawaii International Conference on Systems Science, Hawaii.

Leuf, B., & Cunningham, W. (2001). *The WIKI WAY. Quick collaboration of the Web.* Addison-Wesley.

Lindgren, R., Henfridsson, O., & Shultze, U. (2004). Design principles for competence management systems: A synthesis of an action research study. *MIS Quarterly, 28*(3), 435-472.

Maier, R. (2002). *Knowledge management systems: Information and communication technologies for knowledge management.* Berlin: Springer-Verlag.

Patton, D., & Flin, R. (1999). Disaster stress: An emergency management perspective. *Disaster Prevention and Management, 8*(4), 261-267.

Raman, M., & Ryan. T. (2004). *Designing online discussion support systems for academic setting-"The Wiki Way".* Paper presented at the Americas Conferences on Information Systems (AMCIS). New York, NY.

Stein, E., & Zwass, V. (1995). Actualizing organizational memory with information systems. *Information Systems Research, 6*(2).

Susman, G., & Evered, R. (1978). An assessment of the scientific merits of action research. *Administrative Science Quarterly, 23,* 583-603.

Turoff, M. (1972). Delphi conferencing: Computer-based conferencing with anonymity. *Journal of Technological Forecasting and Social Change, 3*(2), 159-204.

Turoff, M. (2002). Past and future emergency response information systems. *Communications of the ACM, 45*(4), 38-43.

Turoff, M., Chumer, M., Van de Walle, B., & Yao, X. (2004). The design of a dynamic emergency response management information systems (DERMIS). *Journal of Information Technology Theory and Application, 5*(4), 1-35.

Van Kirk, M. (2004). Collaboration in BCP skill development. *Disaster Recovery Journal, 17*(2), 40.

Wagner, C. (2004). WIKI: A technology for conversational knowledge management and group collaboration. *Communications of the Association for Information Systems, 13,* 265-289.

ENDNOTES

[1] There are seven colleges within the Claremont Colleges: Claremont Graduate University, Harvey Mudd College, Scripps College, Pomona College, Keck Graduate Institute, Pitzer College and Claremont McKenna College (http://www.claremont.edu/).

[2] N=25.

[3] Adapted from Wagner (2004) – Figure 1 (p. 267).

Chapter XXI
Knowledge Management and Hurricane Katrina Response

Tim Murphy
Autonomechs, LLC, USA

Murray E. Jennex
San Diego State University, USA

ABSTRACT

This chapter explores the use of knowledge management with emergency information systems. Two knowledge management systems that were utilized during Hurricane Katrina response are described and analyzed. The systems specified were developed by both federal agencies as well as grass root efforts without the support or mandate of government programs. These programs, although developed independently, were able to share data and interact in life-saving capacities, transcending traditional geo-political boundaries. We conclude that emergency information systems are enhanced by incorporating knowledge management tools and concepts.

INTRODUCTION

Emergency response in the U.S. is evolving from something that was locally handled to something that is standardized under federal control. The U.S. implemented the National Incident Management System (NIMS) in 2004 to accomplish this. NIMS established standardized incident management protocols and procedures that all responders are to use to conduct and coordinate response actions (Townsend, 2006).

It was expected that on August 27th, 2005, when President George W. Bush declared a state

of emergency for three coastal states days before the August 29th landfall of Hurricane Katrina that this approach would be sufficient to handle necessary emergency response. However, Mississippi, Alabama, and Louisiana would be the site of the worst natural disaster in U.S. history, stretching government resources far beyond their ability to respond to the instantaneous and growing number of casualties. Running out of shelter and supplies for the growing number of victims, the government became logistically overwhelmed and under-equipped. Private citizens and companies (all non-government offices) responded immediately.

Copyright © 2008, IGI Global, distributing in print or electronic forms without written permission of IGI Global is prohibited.

Multiple independent, yet collaborative by design, knowledge management systems (KMS) were developed and implemented for immediate use to help victims find housing, medical supplies, post requests for immediate evacuation, as well as help find those separated in the storm. Via the Internet, people as far north as Michigan were able to help find housing in Washington State for people in southern New Orleans. This chapter proceeds to describe how theses systems were developed, implemented, and used. We will describe the situation that led to the need of these systems, how these systems were created, the resources required for each, which category of knowledge management system each falls within, use of the systems by the end users, and finally describe the end result of these systems.

This chapter discusses two of these systems developed to respond to Hurricane Katrina. The purpose of this discussion is to illustrate the use of knowledge management (KM) and KMS in emergency response. The chapter will discuss how KM was implemented and how effective the resulting systems were.

BACKGROUND

Before discussing these systems it is important that we establish what we mean by knowledge, KM, and a KMS as well as provide a framework for how KM fits into disaster and/or emergency response.

Knowledge

Davenport and Prusak (1998) define knowledge as an evolving mix of framed experience, values, contextual information and expert insight that provides a framework for evaluating and incorporating new experiences and information. Knowledge often becomes embedded in documents or repositories and in organizational routines, processes, practices, and norms. Knowledge is also about

meaning in the sense that it is context-specific (Huber, Davenport, & King, 1998). Jennex (2006) extends the concepts of context to also include associated culture that provides frameworks for understanding and using knowledge. A simpler definition of knowledge is that it is the *how* and *why* of something. It is the insight into why something happens that creates knowledge. To be useful though, this knowledge needs to be framed in context and culture, the information and data that explain how the knowledge was generated, what it means, and how it should be used.

Knowledge Management

Jennex (2005) defines knowledge management (KM) as the practice of selectively applying knowledge from previous experiences of decision making to current and future decision-making activities with the express purpose of improving the organization's effectiveness. KM is an action discipline; knowledge needs to be used and applied for KM to have an impact. Inherent in KM is communication between knowledge creators and/or possessors and knowledge users. A knowledge management system (KMS) is the system developed to aid knowledge users in identifying, sharing, retrieving, and using knowledge they need. The following section further defines a KMS.

Knowledge Management Systems

Alavi and Leidner (2001) defined a KMS as "IT (Information Technology)-based systems developed to support and enhance the organizational processes of knowledge creation, storage/retrieval, transfer, and application" (p. 114). They observed that not all KM initiatives will implement an IT solution, but they support IT as an enabler of KM. Maier (2002) expanded on the IT concept for the KMS by calling it an ICT (Information and Communication Technology) system that supported the functions of knowledge creation, construction, identification, capturing, acquisition, selection, valuation, organization, linking, structuring, formalization, visualization, distribution, retention, maintenance, refinement, evolution, accessing, search, and application. Stein and Zwass (1995) define an Organizational Memory Information System (OMS) as the processes and IT components necessary to capture, store, and apply knowledge created in the past on decisions currently being made. Jennex and Olfman (2002) expanded this definition by incorporating the OMS into the KMS and adding strategy and service components to the KMS. We expand the boundaries of a KMS by taking a Churchman view of a system. Churchman (1979) defines a system as "a set of parts coordinated to accomplish a set of goals" (p. 29); and that there are five basic considerations for determining the meaning of a system:

- System objectives, including performance measures
- System environment
- System resources
- System components, their activities, goals and measures of performance
- System management

Churchman (1979) also noted that systems are always part of a larger system and that the environment surrounding the system is outside the system's control, but influences how the system performs. The final view of a KMS is as a system that includes IT/ICT components, repositories, users, processes that use and/or generate knowledge, knowledge, knowledge use culture, and the KM initiative with its associated goals and measures.

Key to the KMS is a strategy that determines what knowledge is captured, how well the KMS performs the mnemonic functions of search, retrieve, manipulate, extract, and visualize, and knowledge repositories. There are three types of knowledge repositories: paper documents,

computer-based documents/databases, and self memories:

- Paper documents incorporate all hard copy documents and are organization-wide and group-wide references that reside in central repositories such as a corporate library. Examples include reports, procedures, pictures, video tapes, audio cassettes, and technical standards. An important part of this knowledge is in the chronological histories of changes and revisions to these paper documents as they reflect the evolution of the organization's culture and decision-making processes. However, most organizations do not keep a separate history of changes, but do keep versions of these documents.
- Computer-based documents/databases include all computer-based information that is maintained at the work group level or beyond. These may be made available through downloads to individual workstations, or may reside in central databases or file systems. Additionally, computer documents include the processes and protocols built into the information systems. These are reflected in the interface between the system and the user, by who has access to the data, and by the formats of structured system inputs and outputs. New aspects of this type of repository are digital images and audio recordings. These forms of knowledge provide rich detail but require expanded storage and transmission capacities.
- Self-memory includes all paper and computer documents that are maintained by an individual as well as the individual's memories and experiences. Typical artifacts include files, notebooks, written and un-written recollections, and other archives. These typically do not have an official basis or format. Self-memory is determined by what is important to each person and reflects his or her experience with the organization.

Repositories can overlap each other, as an example, the computer repository stores the specific knowledge but the context and culture needed to use the knowledge is captured in paper procedure documents used to guide the knowledge use and in the mind of the knowledge user as a result of training in how to use the knowledge. Other examples include paper documents being indexed or copied into computer databases or files, self memory using paper and computer-based documents/databases, and computer databases or files being printed and filed. Typically it is desired to capture as much knowledge as possible in computer- and paper-based memories so that the knowledge is less transient. It would be expected that organizations that are highly automated and/or computerized would be expected to have a greater dependence on computer-based repositories while less automated organizations may rely more on paper- or self-memory-based repositories.

A recent development in KMS technology is the use of the wiki. A wiki is a web site or similar online resource which allows users to add and edit content collectively and/or collaboratively (Parlament of Victoria, 2005; Wikipedia, 2006). The wiki originated in 1994/1995 (Cunningham, 2005), but has only recently come become popular as a content management system (Mattison, 2003). Very recent research has found that wikis are useful for KM as they provide content management combined with knowledge exchange/communication and collaboration capabilities. Vazey and Richards (2006) found improved decision making and knowledge acquisition while (Raman et al., 2006) applying a wiki as a tool for improving emergency response.

Knowledge Management Systems and Emergency Response

Jennex (2004) identified an expanded model of an emergency information system (EIS). This model considers an EIS as more than the basic components of database, data analysis, norma-

tive models, and interface outlined by Belardo (1984); adding trained users, methods to communicate between users and between users and data sources, protocols to facilitate communication, and processes and procedures used to guide the response to and improve decision making during the emergency. The goals of the EIS are to facilitate clear communications, improve the efficiency and effectiveness of decision making, and manage data to prevent or at least mitigate information overload. EIS designers use technology and work flow analysis to improve EIS performance in achieving these goals. Turoff et al. (2004) expanded the expanded EIS model by introducing the concept of a dynamic EIS and identifying design requirements that expanded EIS capabilities in group communication and data/information/knowledge management. The result is that the focus of an EIS is on communication and facilitating decision making; both are also key attributes of a KMS.

Additionally, in recent years, disaster managers have realized the potential of KMS for faster and more organized response to natural disasters. The large number of groups that respond to a disaster all need access to a wide range of real-time information, requiring coordination. Groups have proposed and created KMS that allow for more efficient use of data and faster response. One example that has been proposed is the Information Management System for Hurricane disasters (IMASH) (Iakovou & Douligeris, 2001). IMASH is an information management system based on an object-oriented database design, able to provide data for response to hurricanes. IMASH was designed with the premise that the World Wide Web is the medium of choice for presenting textual and graphical information to a distributed community of users. This design is much more effective in the fast-changing environment of a natural disaster than the historical use of static tools which, out of necessity, have been the tools used in disaster response. Kitamato (2005) describes the design of an information management system, Digital

Typhoon, designed to provide a hub of information on the Internet during a typhoon disaster. The Digital Typhoon provides access to information from official sources (news, satellite imagery) as well as a forum for individuals to provide information (local, personal). It effectively became a hub of information, but created questions about organization, filtering, and editing. Systems used for Hurricane Katrina response realized the benefits and difficulties of these systems. Like IMASH, the systems described below use the Internet to distribute data to a community of users, and like the Digital Typhoon, the knowledge management systems described for Hurricane Katrina response became hubs of information that required data management to reduce repetition and allow for editing.

In summary, there is a fusion of EIS with KM and KMS. This is because decision makers, when under stress, need systems that do more than just provide data, they need systems that can quickly find and display knowledge relevant to the situation in a format that facilitates the decision maker in making decisions. It is expected that EIS evolution will continue to utilize KM concepts and approaches as experience in responding to disasters is showing that these systems are more effective than traditional EIS. Examples of how KM aids emergency response includes using knowledge of past disasters to design communication and data/information capture protocols and templates, capturing emergency response knowledge in procedures and protocols; incorporating lessons learned into response team training, interface and display design, and the generation of heuristics guiding decision making; and using knowledge to guide the creation of experience knowledge bases that responders can use to generate emergency response actions. The rest of this chapter illustrates how KM can help disaster response by looking at two systems used in response to Hurricane Katrina.

PEOPLEFINDER

Problem Emerges and Information Overload Occurs

During the first days after Hurricane Katrina hit the Gulf Coast, the Gulf Coast News Web site (http://www.gulfcoastnews.com) had setup a

Table 1. Web sites and the number of survivor records each held (PeopleFinderTech, 2005)

Web site	Number of Entries
http://www.msnbc.msn.com/id/9159961/	143,000
http://www.familylinks.icrc.org/katrina/people	135,222
http://wx.gulfcoastnews.com/katrina/status.aspx	42,477
http://www.publicpeoplelocator.com/	37,259
http://www.katrina-survivor.com/	9,071
http://www.lnha.org/katrina/default.asp	4,500
http://connect.castpost.com/fulllist.php	2,871
http://www.findkatrina.com	2,474
http://www.katrinasurvivor.net	2,400
http://theinfozone.net	1,300
http://www.cnn.com/SPECIALS/2005/hurricanes	1,120
http://www.wecaretexas.com/	200,000
http://www.scribedesigns.com/tulane/	1,933

Web page for people to talk about their hurricane stories. Obviously geared for stories talking about how New Orleans spent a few days without power, the site quickly became an online repository for people to look for victims and post requests for help. Posts on the Web site ranged from asking for directions out of town, to people from other states asking if someone can check on or save their family members at flooded addresses. This trend grew, and quickly 23 different Web sites had people posting that they survived, as well as people looking for information on victims that had not been found. Anyone looking for loved ones would have to check each Web site as there was, at that time, no central repository for information. There also lacked a way to leave contact information should your search query be matched. As Table 1 indicates, many Web sites hit upon the same idea at the same time to host servers for survivors to post their status to. Although this was a terrific response from mostly civilian Internet companies, it created confusion on which sites to post to and search at, which created the need for a site like PeopleFinder (PeopleFinderTech, 2005).

Table 2. The note schema (Lal, Plax & Yee, 2005) Note_record_id is the primary key

NOTE Table	
string	note_record_id
string	person_record_id
string	linked_person_id
date	entry_date
string	author_name
string	author_email
string	author_phone
bool	found
string	email_of_found_person
string	phone_of_found_person
string	last_known_location
text	text

Proposed Knowledge Management Solution

David Geihufe of the Social Software Foundation had been working on an open source customer relationship management (CRM) system called CiviCRM (Geihufe, 2005). During the intelligence phase (Kersten, Mikolajuk *and* Yeh, 1999), David envisioned using his CRM system to create a Web-based, data-driven decision support system (DSS) (Power & Kaparthi, 2002) form of KMS that would be a central repository for victims and people looking for them. The Web site would accept data in an open standard from other Web sites, as well as allow people to post information directly to the server. Not having the resources necessary to use this system, David received corporate support from the Salesforce Foundation. In 24 hours, the Salesforce servers were accepting PFIF (PeopleFinder Interchange Format). Twenty-four hours after that, 60,000 records had been inputted by global volunteers to the PeopleFinder knowledge management system. Some inputs were parsed ('scraped') from sites such as Craigslist, and the Gulf Coast News. Ultimately, over 620,000 records were searchable and over 500,000 searches processed. Tables 2 and 3 show the database schema.

The note table is necessary as it is a lesson learned from the September 11th World Trade Center attacks (Lal et al., 2005). Entries may be updated multiple times, and syncing data between servers can become very difficult. The notes table solves this problem by keeping a log of who has made what change, and what changes were made. The timestamp on each file can be used as a quantitative metric on which entry is the most recent.

Integrity of data, a key component of a successful database management system (DBMS), while syncing between multiple servers was non-trivial. Multiple approaches were considered, and the decision was made to keep all data sets as read-only throughout the entire transaction

Table 3. The person schema (Lal et al., 2005) Person_record_id is the primary key

PERSON table	
string	person_record_id
date	entry_date
string	author_name
string	author_email
string	author_phone
string	source_name
string	source_date
string	source_url
string	first_name
string	last_name
string	home_city
string	home_state
string	home_neighborhood
string	home_street
int	home_zip
string	photo_url
text	other

process, except for the field entry_date, which would indicate when that entry had been posted to the server (Lal et al., 2005).

Figure 1 shows the data flow diagram depicting how the data transverses the system. Table 4 details the decision table providing a rule set for when to manually enter the data into the PFIF repository, and when to request to have a parser written.

Leaderless Development

A wiki was used to coordinate tasks and development for the PeopleFinder system. Anyone wanting to make changes to the wiki had to register on it. Similar to public bulletin board Web sites, registration was automated and required no formal approval (Aronsson, 2002). When a developer found bugs or noticed new features that needed to be added to the system, they could post a task that needed to be completed. One of the other developers could assign themselves to the task to complete it, give status on its development, and clear the task upon completion. Sites to be scraped were handled like this as well. Sites that had information to share could be listed on the wiki, and people could either manually transfer the information record by record, or coders could write parsers to grab the information and repost it into the Salesforce server in PFIF. The determination on whether to manually parse the site, or write a parser for it was determined by the number of entries on the site, the number of entries expected on the site, and whether or not the author of the original site had made safeguards to prevent scripts from parsing the site (People-FinderTech, 2005).

With any Web site that can be modified by the general public, vandalism is an immediate and valid concern. For example, there was nothing to keep political protestors from registering and defacing the Web site with a political message

Table 4. Decision table for assessing how to proceed with new Web sites discovered.

Potential Conditions	Actions to be performed		
	Manual entry	Task a parser for later development	Task a parser for immediate development
If (postings) <25	X		
If (postings) <25 but anticipate growth	X	X	
If (postings) > 25		X	
If (postings) > 100			X

Figure 1. Data flow diagram (based on Lal et al., 2005)

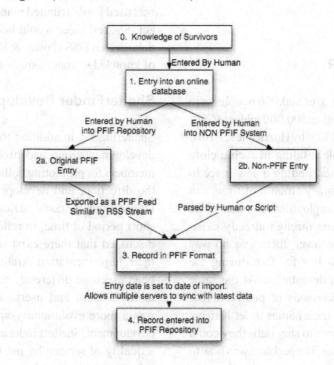

that has nothing to do with the purpose of the Web site. Fortunately, editors on the web site kept vandalism suppressed by monitoring the Recent Changes page (Tanaka, 2005).

PeopleFinder Analysis

PeopleFinder went from an idea to operationally functioning within a 72-hour window. Due to the nature of the Web site, few users would be inclined to leave feedback to make the site more helpful. Therefore, features may have been incorrectly prioritized based on what the developers thought would be helpful, rather than what the user base needed. Future concerns about this type of project will most likely include privacy rights. When someone wants their online entry removed from the database, perhaps to avoid any risk of identity theft, there is currently no feature that allows them to be removed. In fact, the data

network is setup to maintain the entries at all cost. It is also difficult to have an easy-to-use Web site that allows distraught people to find their family and friends, while making sure that those with criminal intentions are filtered out. Regardless of the security downfalls, PeopleFinder was a success as soon as the first person was able to quickly ascertain the status of a loved one.

KM use in PeopleFinder is reflected in its construction. The system itself reflects the capture of lessons learned and is itself a repository of knowledge. Knowledge capture and use is also reflected in the capture of notes and the history of notes for each person. KMS features implemented in the system include knowledge repositories and the implementation of good mnemonic functions (search, retrieve, visualize). As stated, it was not expected that feedback would be left by users; this needs to be compensated by researchers who need to collect some system satisfaction data so that future systems can learn from mistakes in this system.

SHELTERFINDER

FEMA estimated that over 500,000 people were left homeless, and another 500,000 jobless (California Political Desk, 2005) by Hurricane Katrina. With that many people residing in such a close proximity to each other, finding a new place to live, even for a temporary amount of time, can be near impossible. Employment in other cities could be located online through already existing jobs databases; however, there was no way to find somewhere to live for free during the victims' rebuild from devastation. At the same time, hundreds of thousands of people across the nation offered up their homes to let Katrina victims have somewhere to stay until they could find permanent housing. The problem was how to coordinate information so that people who were in the affected areas could find housing across the nation. Like PeopleFinder, multiple Web sites began to popup to offer housing, but there was no organized meta-search, allowing users to check one centralized location.

Collecting Shelter Data for Hosting

ShelterFinder (2005) was set to solve the same problem as PeopleFinder. Continuing with open standards for the systems data formats, Shelter-Finder maintained a means for a single server to stream new data feeds to multiple servers, while simultaneously being ready to respond to requests for data from other servers. Rather than PFIF that was designed for victims, ShelterFinder used standard formats such as CSV (Comma Separated Values) and XML (Extensible Markup Language) (Walsh, 2003). These formats allowed an independent team of developers to write database search systems as well as another independent team to build the GIS front end for more efficient use of the database system. Like PeopleFinder, a wiki was used for distributed management of the project. ShelterFinder would become a Web-based, data-driven DSS (Power & Kaparthi, 2002) form of knowledge management system.

ShelterFinder Development

ShelterFinder, in addition to being a distributed development group, had three constant managing members for promoting collaboration, managing the direction, and development of the system. Despite the fantastic strides made in such a short period of time, in reflection, the team has discussed that there exist some key aspects of their implementation strategy that could have been executed differently to get more attention to the system and users. While PeopleFinder was a more evolutionary approach to software development, ShelterFinder attempted to maintain a quality of service by not releasing code until it had been thoroughly tested by the users, and implemented by the lead developer. Keeping the system off-line until specific milestones were met kept ShelterFinder unavailable during potentially critical periods of time. A different software development methodology could have helped garner more resources, and get more users while attention was still focused on the amazing open source efforts emerging.

ShelterFinder Analysis

ShelterFinder gained huge acceptance due to two major components. First, it was a combined search engine that hosted records for more homes or shelters than most housing search engines. Letting the victims choose a specific city, even if it is on the opposite side of the United States, allowed victims to try to find temporary housing near family or in areas they might be able to get jobs. This helped the families find shelter near helpful social resources, while decreasing the stress that the increased number of people could inadvertently cause on the resources of an area. When large amounts of people have been displaced, any opportunity to place them in different geographic areas helps the relief effort.

Second, the GUI was uniquely easy to use and made finding homes or shelters near specific addresses incredibly easy and intuitive. The GUI was a result of the recent introduction of Google Maps (http://maps.google.com/). Using built-in Google Maps XML parsing engine, it provided a graphical front end allowing users to see where in America homes were available, as well as an intuitive graphical representation on the map of how many spaces were free at each shelter based on icon color. At a community level, Google Maps has developed a means for conventional GIS developers to become Web-based GIS developers and create Web-based applications, quickly and cheaply.

KM use in ShelterFinder is also reflected in its construction. The system itself reflects the capture of lessons learned and is itself a repository of knowledge. However, this system is actually a reflection of a failure to capture and use knowledge. The system should have been designed to capture and use knowledge of survivor preferences and housing and service characteristics to obtain better fits of survivors to available housing other than fits based on location. Allowing searchers to pick locations that they thought best is convenient, but not ideal as reflected in reported dissatisfaction with survivors in a number of communities that took in and housed survivors. A key issue was the widespread dispersion of current or former criminals to locations who did not know what they were getting. Knowledge use could have mitigated these issues. KMS features implemented in the system include knowledge repositories (although they were weak repositories based on location knowledge) and the implementation of good mnemonic functions (search, retrieve, visualize).

LEADERLESS DEVELOPMENT APPROACHES

The alternative software development approach taken by ShelterFinder shows that leaderless development systems can still explore the same variety of software development approaches, as well as share the same need for system requirements as their traditionally managed counterparts. The non-traditional leaderless system does have the hindrance of not necessarily being able to replace the traditional roles that a managed software development project would identify at the start of the project. In a leaderless system, this role is replaced by a group of personnel who claim and execute the publicly obtainable tasks, which would typically be reserved for a specific role. This type of open-task claiming, allows willing members of the development team to attempt and execute tasks that they would not normally be aware of, if the task is not normally assigned to the traditional role they would play. When a task is overburdened and risks holding back the other parts of the project, team members that would not normally characterize themselves within a specialty, can claim tasks that they are capable of accomplishing.

CRITICAL MASS REQUIREMENT

Distributed, by definition, requires capability to be stretched across large redundant numbers. Leaderless development worked especially well for the PeopleFinder project, given the varying expertise available to the project by the massive number of constantly changing contributors. PeopleFinder was fortunate to have some early members that specifically spent their time advertising PeopleFinder, which in turn helped attract more development personnel, feeding the leaderless system. ShelterFinder, relying on a lesser quantity of members to oversee these tasks, were partially overwhelmed with the amount of work and the pressing timeline, and was unable to advertise the site in the same way as People-Finder. This identifies a weakness in the leaderless system that if sufficient numbers of personnel are lacking, necessary functions can go without execution. Without other team personnel able to identify underperforming tasks within the project, the lacking tasks will continue until noticeable system degradation occurs, if noticed at all. For example, without team members persistently advertising the systems capability, users will not know about the site and the site will not be used to it's maximum capacity. Non-marketing groups, perhaps isolated from usage statistics, might not know that the site is not being used or factors that might be keeping the site from being used. In a rapid application development with a critical timeline such as disaster response, this can be a fatal system flaw.

CONCLUSION

Even as recently as the Sumatra-Andaman earthquake of 2004, disaster management response required printed maps, and specially trained disaster management personnel to coordinate the deployment of resources. Military groups such as the U.S. Army's Civil Affairs branch and NGOs such as the American Red Cross, have specially trained personnel to sort through the overwhelming amounts of information that arrives and interact directly with victims. The incoming information arrives in a variety of formats, inconsistent for the operations center, but usually in a consistent format from each source. This type of work usually requires specialized operations centers, a specialty staff to manage the data, and requires significant time to sort through the paper records submitted from the disaster area. Everyday, citizens that would like to contribute are unable to, not only because they

are not inside the physical operations center but also because there was no way for responders to reach out to the community to look for resources. Knowledge management systems, such as IMASH and the Digital Typhoon, have been researched and developed to help coordinate response to disasters. However, only by assessing how these types of systems actually worked in a disaster can improvements be made and resources like these used most efficiently in the future.

The technologies discussed here are changing the traditional approach to disaster response. Conventional, expensive, and isolated operations centers are morphing into a series of scalable, cheap, distributed, and highly networked information portals that can be used wherever a computer and Internet access are available. The more wireless options that become available to people in disaster-Fstruck areas, from WiMax to satellite, the more options this new breed of distributed systems will have for helping people in real-time wherever tragedies strike.

The social approach of these two projects is fairly unconventional in comparison to both commercial America as well as traditional disaster response. Leaderless cells performing specific actions are historically more comparable to terrorist networks than they are humanitarian operations. The concept of groups self-determining their order of operations is counter-traditional management approaches. However, the unsuccessful initial Hurricane Katrina response by the government (CNN, 2005) has shown that a rigid management can become overwhelmed when emergencies are too geographically widespread, or too many people have been affected. Distributed teams that can utilize knowledge management systems and can dynamically call upon the continually growing user base of the Internet for expert resources and manpower have a better chance to respond to the myriad of future emergencies.

Finally, the use of KM and KMS functions is shown to improve the speed and quality of response actions. This is expected and it is our conclusion that future EIS should incorporate KM considerations.

REFERENCES

Alavi, M., & Leidner, D. (2001). Review: Knowledge management and knowledge management systems: Conceptual foundations and research issues. *MIS Quarterly, 25*(1), 107-136.

Aronsson, L. (2002). Operation of a large scale, general purpose wiki Web site. In: J. Carvalho, A. Hübler, & A. Baptista (Eds.), *Proceedings of the 6th International ICCC/IFIP Conference on Electronic Publishing* (pp. 27-37). Berlin, Verlag für Wissenschaft und Forschung.

Bellardo, S., Karwan, K., &Wallace, W. (1984). Managing the response to disasters using microcomputers. *Interfaces, 14*(2), 29-39.

California Political Desk. (2005). Kennedy, colleagues urge the administration to rebuild gulf coast in a way that is fair to workers. *American Chronicle*. Retrieved October 29, 2005 from http://www.americanchronicle.com/articles/view-Article.asp?articleID=3229

Churchman, C. (1979). *The systems approach* (revised and updated). New York, NY: Dell Publishing.

CNN. (2005). People making decisions hesitated: More officials' jobs may fall to Katrina response criticism. Retrieved October 31, 2005 from http://www.cnn.com/2005/US/09/13/katrina.response/index.html.

Cunningham, W. (2005). *Wiki history*. Retrieved October 29, 2005 from http://c2.com/cgi/wiki?WikiHistory

Davenport, T., & Prusak, L. (1998). *Working knowledge*. Boston, MA: Harvard Business School Press.

Geilhufe, D. (2005). *CRM project one pager - Confluence*. Retrieved October 29, 2005 from http://objectledge.org/confluence/display/CRM/CRM+Project+One+Pager.

Huber, G., Davenport, T., & King, D. (1998). Some perspectives on organizational memory. Unpublished Working Paper for the Task Force on Organizational Memory. Presented at the *31st Annual Hawaii International Conference on System Sciences.*

Iakovou, E., & Douligeris, C. (2001). An information management system for the emergency management of hurricane disasters. *International Journal of Risk Assessment and Management, 2*(3-4), 243-262.

Jennex, M. (2004). Emergency response systems: The utility Y2K experience. *Journal of IT Theory and Application, 6*(3), 85-102.

Jennex, M. (2005). What is knowledge management?. *International Journal of Knowledge Management, 1*(4), i-iv.

Jennex, M. (2006). Culture, context, and knowledge management. *International Journal of Knowledge Management, 2*(2), i-iv.

Jennex, M., & Olfman, L. (2002). Organizational memory/knowledge effects on productivity- A longitudinal study. In *Proceedings of the 35th Annual Hawaii International Conference on System Sciences*. IEEE Computer Society, Kona, HI.

Kersten, G., Mikolajuk, Z., & Yeh, A. (Eds.). (1999). *Decision support systems for sustainable development in developing countries* (pp. 293-296). Boston, MA: Kluwer Academic.

Kitamato, A. (2005). Digital typhoon: Near real-time aggregation, recombination and delivery of typhoon-related information. In *Proceeding of the 4th International Symposium on Digital Earth*. Tokyo, Japan. Retrieved October 26, 2005 from http://www.cse.iitb.ac.in/~neela/MTP/Stage1-Report.pdf.

Lal, K., Plax, J., & Yee, K. (2005). *People Finder Interchange Format 1.1*. Retrieved October 29, 2005 from from http://zesty.ca/pfif/1.1

Maier, R. (2002). *Knowledge management systems: Information and communication technologies for knowledge management*. Berlin: Springer-Verlag.

Mattison, D. (2003). Quickwiki, Swiki, Twiki, Zwiki and the Plone wars – Wiki as PIM and collaborative content tool. *Searcher: The Magazine for Database Professionals, 11*(4), 32.

Parlament of Victoria. (2005). *Victorian electronic democracy—Final Report*. Retrieved October 29, 2005 from http://www.parliament.vic.gov.au/sarc/E-Democracy/Final_Report/Glossary.htm.

PeopleFinderTech. (2005). Retrieved October 29, 2005 from http://www.katrinahelp.info/wiki/index.php/PeopleFinderTech.

Power, D., & Kaparthi, S. (2002). Building Web-based decision support systems. *Studies in Informatics and Control, 11*(4), 291-302. Retrieved October 29, 2005 from http://www.ici.ro/ici/revista/sic2002_4/art1.pdf.

Raman, M., Ryan, T., & Olfman, L. (2006). Knowledge management systems for emergency preparedness: The Claremont University Consortium Experience. *The International Journal of Knowledge Management, 2*(3), 33-50.

ShelterFinder. (2005). Retrieved October 29, 2005 from http://katrinahelp.info/wiki/index.php/ShelterFinder.

Stein, E., & Zwass, V. (1995). Actualizing organizational memory with information systems. *Information Systems Research, 6*(2), 85-117.

Tanaka, B. (2005). The oddmuse wiki engine. *Linux Journal*. Retrieved October 29, 2005 from http://www.linuxjournal.com/article/7583.

Townsend, F. (2006). *The federal response to Hurricane Katrina, lessons learned*. Department of Homeland Security, United States of America.

Turoff, M., Chumer, M., Van de Walle, B., & Yao, X., (2004). The design of a dynamic emergency response management information system (DERMIS). *The Journal of Information Technology Theory and Application, 5*(4), 1-35.

Vazey, M., & Richards, D. (2006). A case-classification-conclusion 3Cs approach to knowledge acquisition: Applying a classification logic wiki to the problem-solving process. *The International Journal of Knowledge Management, 2*(1), 72-88.

Walsh, N. (2003). *A technical introduction to XML*. Retrieved October 29, 2005 from http://www.dsi.unive.it/~xml/docs/introduction.pdf

Wikipedia. (2006). *Wiki*. Retrieved March 30, 2006 from http://en.wikipedia.org/wiki/Wiki.

This work was previously published in International Journal of Knowledge Management, Vol. 2, Issue 4, edited by M.E. Jennex, pp. 52-66, copyright 2006 by IGI Publishing, formerly known as Idea Group Publishing (an imprint of IGI Global).

Compilation of References

Aamodt, A. & Plaza, E. (1994). Case-based reasoning: Foundational issues, methodological variations and system approaches. *AI Communications, 7*(1), S 35-39.

Aarons, J., Burstein, F., & Linger, H. (2005). *What is the task?—Applying the task-based KM framework to weather forecasting.* Paper presented at the Australian Conference for Knowledge Management and Intelligent Decision Support (pp. 85-99), Novotel, Melbourne.

Aarons, J., Linger, H., & Burstein, F. (2006). *Supporting organisational knowledge work: Integrating thinking and doing in task-based support.* Paper presented at the International Conference on Organisational Learning, Knowledge and Capabilities, University of Warwick, UK.

Abeysekera, I. (2003). Intellectual accounting score-card—Measuring and reporting intellectual capital. *Journal of American Academy of Business, 3*(1-2), 422-440.

Abran, A., Moore, J.W., Bourque, P., Dupuis, R. & Tripp, L.L. (2004). Guide to the software engineering body of knowledge. Swebok®: A project of the software engineering coordination committee. *IEEE Computer Society Press.* 1.

Adams, G., & Lamont, B. (2003). Knowledge management systems and developing sustainable competitive advantage. *Journal of Knowledge Management, 7*(2), 142-154.

Adria & Chowdhury (2002). Making room for the call center. *Information Systems Management*, 1-80.

Agency Group 09. (2002). Knowledge warriors' amass at symposium. *FDCH, Regulatory Intelligence Database.*

Agency Group 09. (2003). Lessons learned process on Iraq War explained. *FDCH, Regulatory Intelligence Database.*

Ahmed, P., Kok, L., & Loh, A. (2002). *Learning through knowledge management.* Butterworth Heinemann.

Ahuja, G. (2000). Collaboration networks, structural holes, and innovation: A longitudinal study. *Administrative Science Quarterly, 45*(3), 425-457.

Ahuja, M.K., Galleta, D.F., & Carley, K.M. (2003). Individual centrality and performance in virtual R&D groups: An empirical study. *Management Science, 49*(1), 21-39.

Akhavan, P., Jafari, M., & Fathian, M. (2006). Critical success factors of knowledge management systems: A multi-case analysis. *European Business Review, 18*(2), 97-113.

Akrich, M. (2000). The description of technical objects. In: W. Bijker & J. Law (Eds.), *Shaping technology/building society: Studies in socio-technical change* (pp. 205-224). Cambridge, MA: The MIT Press.

Al-Alawi, A., Al-Marzooqi, N., & Mohammed, Y. (2000). Organizational culture and knowledge sharing: Critical success factors. *Journal of Knowledge Management, 11*(2), 22-42.

Copyright © 2008, IGI Global, distributing in print or electronic forms without written permission of IGI Global is prohibited.

Alavi, M. & Leidner, D. E. (1999). Knowledge management systems: Issues, challenges, and benefits. *Communications of AIS, 1*(Article 7), 1-37.

Alavi, M. & Leidner, D.E. (2001). Review: Knowledge management and knowledge management systems: Conceptual foundations and research issues. *MIS Quarterly, 25*(1), 107–136.

Alavi, M., & Leidner, D. (1999). Knowledge management systems: Emerging views and practices from the field. In *Proceedings of the 32nd Hawaii International Conference on System Sciences,* IEEE Computer Society.

Alavi, M., & Leidner, D. (2001). Knowledge management and knowledge management systems: Conceptual foundations and research issues. *MIS Quarterly, 25*(1), 107-136.

Alavi, M., & Leidner, D.E. (1999). Knowledge management systems: Emerging views and practices from the field. In *Proceedings of the 32nd Hawaii International Conference on System Sciences*, IEEE Computer Society.

Aldrich, H., & Herker, D. (1977). Boundary spanning roles and organization structure. *Academy of Management Review, 2*(2), 217-230.

Ali, I., Warne, L., Agostino, K., Pascoe, C. (2001). Working and learning together: Social learning in the Australian Defence Organisation. *Informing Science Conference IS2001—Bridging Diverse Disciplines Proceedings* (CD-ROM), Krakow, Krakow University of Economics, Poland, June 19-22.

Allee, V. (2002). Knowledge networks and communities of practice. *OD Practitioner, 32*(4).

American Heritage Dictionary of the English Language, Fourth Edition. (2000). Houghton Mifflin Company. Updated in 2003.

American Productivity and Quality Center (APQC). (1996). *Knowledge management: Consortium benchmarking study Final Report 1996.* Retrieved April 3, 2000 from http://www.store.apqc.org/reports/Summary/know-mng.pdf.

AMERIN Products. (n.d). *Creating value from intangible assets and human capital.* Retrieved July 12, 2005, from http://www.amerin.com.au/products.htm

Anandarajan, M., Igbaria, M., & Anakwe, U. (2000). Technology acceptance in the banking industry: A perspective from a less developed country. *Information Technology and People, 13*(4), 298-312.

Anderson, C. (2004). The long tail. *Wired Magazine, 12*(10), October.

Andreoni, J. (1989). Giving with impure altruism: Applications to charity and Ricardian equivalence. *Journal of Political Economy, 97,* 1447-1458.

Andreoni, J. (1990). Impure altruism and donations to public goods: A theory of warm-glow giving. *Economic Journal, 100,* 464-477.

Andrews, K. M. & Delahaye, B. L. (2000). Influences on knowledge processes in organisational learning: The psychosocial filter. *The Journal of Management Studies, 37*(6), 797-810.

Anklam, P. (2003). KM and the social network. *Knowledge Management Magazine,* May 2003.

Applegate, L., Austin, R., McFarlan, F. (2003). *Corporate information strategy and management: Text and cases.* McGraw-Hill Irwin.

Ardichvili, A., Maurer, M., Li, W., Wentling, T., & Stuedemann, R. (2006). Cultural influences on knowledge sharing through online communities of practice. *Journal of Knowledge Management, 10*(1), 94-107.

Argote, L. (1999) *Organizational learning, retaining and transferring knowledge.* Boston: Kluwer Academic.

Argote, L., McEvily, B., & Reagans, R. (2003). Managing knowledge in organizations: An integrative framework and review of emerging themes. *Management Science, 49*(4), 571-582.

Argyris, C. & Schon, D. A. (1978). *Organizational learning: A theory of action perspective.* Addison Wesley Publishing Company.

Aronsson, L. (2002). Operation of a large scale, general purpose wiki Web site. In: J. Carvalho, A. Hübler, & A. Baptista (Eds.), *Proceedings of the 6th International ICCC/IFIP Conference on Electronic Publishing* (pp. 27-37). Berlin, Verlag für Wissenschaft und Forschung.

Arthur, B. (1990). Positive feedbacks in the economy. *Scientific American, 262,* 92-99.

Avgerou, C. (1998). How can IT enable economic growth in developing countries? *Information Technology for Development, 8*(1), 15-29.

Avgerou, C. (2001). The significance of context in information systems and organizational change. *Information Systems Journal, 11*(1), 43-63.

Avgerou, C. (2002). *Information systems and global diversity.* Oxford: Oxford University Press.

Aviv, R., & Ravid, G. Reciprocity analysis of online learning networks. *Journal of Asynchronous Learning Networks* (In press).

Awad, E., & Ghaziri, H. (2004). *Knowledge management.* Upper Saddle River, NJ: Pearson Prentice Hall.

Bada, A. (2000). *Global practices and local interests: Implementing technology-based change in a developing country context.* Doctoral dissertation, London School of Economics and Political Science, Department of Information Systems.

Baird, L., Henderson, J., & Watts, S. (1997). Learning from action: An analysis of the Center for Army Lessons Learned (CALL). *Human Resource Management, 36*(4), 385-395.

Barabba, V. P. & Zaltman, G. (1991). *Hearing the voice of the market: Competitive advantage through creative use of market information.* Boston: Harvard Business School Press.

Barata, K., Kutzner, F., & Wamukoya, J. (2001). Records, computers, resources: A difficult equation for sub-Saharan Africa. *Information Management Journal, 35*(1), 34-42.

Barber, B. (1995). *Jihad vs. McWorld: How globalism and tribalism are reshaping the world.* New York, NY: Random House.

Bareiss, E. R. (1989). *Exemplar-based knowledge acquisition: A unified approach to concept representation, classification, and learning.* Boston: Academic Press.

Barna, Z. (2003). *Knowledge management: A critical e-business strategic factor.* Master's thesis, San Diego State University, San Diego, CA.

Bartlett, C., & Ghosal, S. (1989). *Managing across borders: The transnational solution.* Boston, MA: Harvard Business School Press.

Baskerville, R. (1999). Investigating information systems with action research. *Communications of the Association for Information Systems, 2,* 1-16.

Becera-Fernandez, I., Gonzales, A., & Sabherwal, R. (2004). *Knowledge management: Challenges, solutions, and technologies.* Upper Saddle River, NJ: Pearson Prentice Hall.

Becker, G. (1974). A theory of social interaction. *Journal of Political Economy, 82,* 1063-1093.

Beer, S. (1981). *Brain of the firm.* Chichester, New York, Brisbane, Toronto: John Wiley & Sons.

Bellardo, S., Karwan, K., & Wallace, W. (1984). Managing the response to disasters using microcomputers. *Interfaces, 14*(2), 29-39.

Bennet, A., & Tomblin, M. (2006). A learning network framework for modern organizations: Organizational learning, knowledge management and ICT support. *VINE: The Journal of Information and Knowledge Management Systems, 36*(1), 289-303.

Bergeron, B. (2002). *Dark Ages II: When the Digital data die.* Prentice Hall PTR.

Berkman, E. (2001). *When bad things happen to good ideas.* Retrieved July 20, 2004, from http://www.darwin-mag.com/read/040101/badthingscontent.html

Bernard, E. (2000). *What is a methodology?*. Retrieved May 1, 2004 from http://www.itmweb.com/essay553.htm.

Bertaux, N., Okunoye, A., & Abu-Rashed, J. (2005). Knowledge management and economic development in developing countries: An examination of the main enablers. *Global Business and Economics Review, 7*(1), 85-99

Bertaux, N., Okunoye, A., & Abu-Rashed, J. (2006) Information technology education for women in developing countries: Benefits, barriers, and policies. *Global Business & Economics Review, 8*(1).

Bertaux, N., Okunoye, A., & Oyelami, M. (2005). Rural community and human development through information technology education: Empirical evidence from western Nigeria. In *Proceedings of the IFIP WG 9.4 Working Conference* (pp. 169-179), *May 2005, Abuja, Nigeria*.

Beynon-Davies, P. (2002). *Information systems: An introduction to informatics in organizations*. Palgrave Publishing.

Bhatt, G. D. (2002) Management strategies for individual knowledge and organizational knowledge. *Journal of Knowledge Management, 6*(1), 31-39.

Bjørnsson, F., & Dingsøyr, T. (2005). A study of a mentoring program for knowledge transfer in a small software consultancy company. *Proceedings of the PROFES 2005* (pp. 245-256).

Blackburn, S. (2002). The project manager and the project-network. *International Journal of Project Management, 20*(3), 199-204.

Blackler, F. (1995). Knowledge, knowledge work and organisations: An overview and interpretation. *Organization Studies, 16*(6), 1021-1046.

Blake, R., & Mouton, J. (1969). *Building a dynamic corporation through grid organizational development*. Reading, MA: Addison-Wesley.

Blake, R., & Mouton, J. (1985). *The managerial grid III*. TX: Gulf Publishing Company.

Block, J. (1978). *The Q-Sort method in personality assessment and psychiatric Research*. CA: Consulting Psychologists Press.

Bock, G. W. & Kim, Y. G. (2002). Breaking the myths of rewards: An exploratory study of attitudes about knowledge sharing. *Information Resources Management Journal, 15*(2), 14-22.

Bock, G., & Kim, Y. (2002). Breaking the myths of rewards: An exploratory study of attitudes about knowledge sharing. *Information Resources Management Journal, 15*(2), 14-21.

Bock, G., Zmud, R., Kim, Y., & Lee, J. (2005). Behavioral intention formation in knowledge sharing: Examining the roles of extrinsic motivators, social-psychological forces, and organizational climate. *MIS Quarterly, 29*, 87-111.

Boer, N., van Baalen, P. & Kumar, K. (2002). An activity theory approach for studying the situatedness of knowledge sharing. In *Proceedings of the 35th Hawaii International Conference on Systems Sciences*.

Boisot, M. (2002). The creation and sharing of knowledge. In: C. Choo & N. Bontis (Eds.), *The strategic management of intellectual capital and organizational knowledge*. Oxford University Press.

Boland, R., & Tenkasi, R. (1995). Perspective making and perspective taking in communities of knowing. *Organization Science, 6*(4), 350-372.

Bollinger, A. S. & Smith, R. D. (2001). Managing knowledge as a strategic asset. *Journal of Knowledge Management, 5*(1), 8-18.

Briggs, G., Shamma, D., Cañas, A., Carff, R., Scargle, J., & Novak, J. (2004). Concept maps applied to Mars exploration public Outreaches. In *Proceedings of the First International Conference on Concept Mapping*. Pamplona, Spain.

Broadbent, M., Weill, P., & St. Clair, D. (1999). The implications of information technology infrastructure for business process redesign. *MIS Quarterly, 23*(2), 159-182.

Brookes, N., Morton, S., Dainty, A., & Burns N. (2006). *International Journal of Project Management, 24,* 474-482

Brooks, F. P. (1987). No silver bullet: Essence and accidents of software engineering. *IEEE Software, 4,* 10-19.

Brown, J., & Duguid, P. (1991). Organizational learning and communities-of-practice: Toward a unified view of working, learning, and innovating. *Organization Science, 2*(1), 40-57.

Brown, J., & Duguid, P. (2000). Balancing act: How to capture knowledge without killing it. *Harvard Business Review, 78*(3), 73-78.

Brown, J., & Duguid, P. (2001). Knowledge and organization: A social-practice perspective. *Organization Science, 12,* 198-213.

Brown, S.A., Dennis, A.R., & Gant, D.B. (2006). Understanding the factors influencing the value of person-to-person knowledge sharing. In *Proceedings of the 39th Hawaii International Conference on System Sciences.*

Brown, W. (1966). Systems, boundaries, and information flow. *Academy of Management Journal, 9*(4), 318-327.

Brown, W.J., Malveau, R.C., McCormick, H.W., & Mowbray, T.J. (1998). *AntiPatterns: Refactoring software, architectures, and projects in crisis.* John Wiley & Sons.

Burnell, L., Priest, J., & Durrett, J. (2004). Developing and maintaining knowledge management system for dynamic, complex domains. In J. Gupta & S. Sharma (Eds.), *Creating knowledge-based organizations.* London: IGP.

Burstein, F. & Linger, H. (2003). Supporting post-fordist work practices: A knowledge management framework for supporting knowledge work. *Information Technology and People, 16*(3).

Burstein, F., & Linger, H. (2002). *A task-based framework for supporting knowledge work practices.* Paper presented at the 3rd European Conference on Knowledge Management (ECKM2002) (pp. 100-112), Trinity College Dublin, Ireland.

Burstein, F., & Linger, H. (2003). Supporting post-Fordist work practices: A knowledge management framework for supporting knowledge work. *Information Technology & People, 16*(3), 289-305.

Burstein, F., & Linger, H. (2006). Task-based knowledge management approach. In: D. Schwartz (Ed.), *Encyclopaedia of knowledge management.* Hershey, PA: Idea Publishing.

Burt, R.S. (1992). *Structural holes: The social structure of competition.* Cambridge, MA: Harvard University Press.

Cabrera, A., & Cabrera, E. (2002). Knowledge-sharing dilemmas. *Organization Studies, 23,* 687-710.

Calaberese, F. (2000). *A suggested framework of key elements defining effective enterprise knowledge management programs.* Doctoral dissertation, George Washington University, School of Engineering and Applied Science.

Calaberese, F. (2006). Knowledge organizations in the century: Knowledge-based organizations in context. *VINE: The Journal of Information and Knowledge Management Systems, 36*(1), 12-16.

California Political Desk. (2005). Kennedy, colleagues urge the administration to rebuild gulf coast in a way that is fair to workers. *American Chronicle.* Retrieved October 29, 2005 from http://www.americanchronicle.com/articles/viewArticle.asp?articleID=3229

Callon, M. & Latour, B. (1981). Unscrewing the big Leviathan: How actors macrostructure reality and how sociologists help them to do so. In K. D. Knorr-Cetina & A. V. Cicourel (Eds.), *Advances in social theory and methodology: Toward an integration of micro- and macro-sociologies.* Boston: Routledge.

Callon, M. (1998). An essay on framing and overflowing: Economic externalities revisited by sociology. In M. Callon (Ed.), *The laws of the markets.* Oxford and Keele, Blackwell and the Sociological Review.

Camilleri, D., & O'Callaghan, M. (1998). Comparing public and private hospital care service quality. *International Journal of Healthcare Quality Assurance, 11*(4), 127.

Campbell, C., DeWalle, B., Turoff, M., & Deek, F. (2004). *A research design for asynchronous negotiation of software requirements for an emergency response information system.* Paper presented at the Americas Conference on Information Systems, New York, NY.

Cañas, A., Hill, G., Suri, N., Lott, J., Gómez, G., Eskridge, T., et al. (2004). CMAPTOOLS: A Knowledge modeling and sharing environment. In *Proceedings of the First International Conference on Concept Mapping.* Pamplona, Spain

Carlile, P. (2002). A pragmatic view of knowledge and boundaries: Boundary objects in new product development. *Organization Science, 13*(4), 442-455.

Carlisle, Y. (1999). Strategic thinking and knowledge management. In *OU MBA Managing Knowledge Readings Part 1* (pp. 19-29). Milton Keynes: Open University Business School.

Carnot, M., Dunn, B., Cañas, A., Graham, P., & Muldoon, J. (2001). *Concept maps vs. Web pages for information searching and browsing.* Retrieved March 31, 2006 from http:www.ihmc.us/users/acanas/Publications/CMapsVSWebPagesExp1/CMapsVSWebPagesExp1.htm.

Caterinicchia, D. (2003). Search system answers CALL. *Federal Computer Week dated,* Jan. 20.

Caussanel, J., & Chouraqui, E. (1999). Model and methodology of knowledge capitalization for small and medium enterprise. In *Proceedings of the Twelfth Workshop on Knowledge Acquisition, Modeling and Management.* Banff, Alberta, Canada.

Chan, I., & Chau, P. (2005). Getting knowledge management right: Lessons from failure. *International Journal of Knowledge Management, 1*(3), 40-54.

Chatzkel, J. (2000). A conversation with Hubert Saint-Onge. *Journal of Intellectual Capital, 1*(1), 101-115.

Checkland, P. B. (1991). From framework through experience to learning: the essential nature of action research.

In H. E. Nissen, H. K. Klein, & R. Hirschheim (Eds.), *Information systems research: Contemporary approaches and emergent traditions.* Amsterdam: International Federation for Information Processing (IFIP).

Checkland, P., & Howell, S. (1998). *Information, systems and information systems.* John Wiley & Sons.

Cheuk, B. (2004). A seven stage guide to community implementation. In S. Lelic (Ed.), *Communities of practice: Lessons from collaborative leading enterprises* (pp. 83-91). London: Ark Group Limited.

Cheuk, B. (2004). Applying sense-making methodology to establish communities of practice: Examples from the British Council. In: Bruno et al. (Eds.), *People, knowledge and technology: What have we learnt so far?* (pp. 55-65).

Cheuk, B., & Dervin, B. (1999). A qualitative sense-making study of the information seeking situations faced by professionals in three workplace contexts. The Electronic Journal of Communication, 9(2-4), (Online).

Choi, B., & Lee, H. (2003). An empirical investigation of KM styles and their effect on corporate performance. *Information & Management, 40*(5), 403-417.

Chourides, P., Longbottom D., & Murphy, W. (2002). Excellence in knowledge management: An empirical study to identify critical factors and performance measures. *Measuring Business Excellence, 7*(2), 29-46.

Churchman, C. (1979). *The systems approach* (revised and updated). New York, NY: Dell Publishing.

Clancey, W. (1997). The conceptual nature of knowledge, situations, and activity. In P. J. Feltovich, K. M. Ford, & R. R. Hoffman (Eds.), *Expertise in context: Human and machine* (pp. 247-291). Cambridge, MA: AAAI Press / MIT Press.

Clare, M. & DeTore, A. W. (2000). *Knowledge assets.* San Diego: Harcourt.

Cleland, D. (1999). *Project management strategic design and implementation.* McGraw-Hill.

CNN. (2005). People making decisions hesitated: More officials' jobs may fall to Katrina response criticism. Retrieved October 31, 2005 from http://www.cnn.com/2005/US/09/13/katrina.response/index.html.

Coakes, E., Willis, D., & Clarke, S. (Eds.). (2002). *Knowledge management in the socio-technical world: The graffiti continues.* London: Springer-Verlag

Coleman, J.S. (1988). Social capital in the creation of human capital. *American Journal of Sociology, 94,* 95-120.

Comeau-Kirschner, C. (1999). It's a small world. *Management review, March,* 8.

Compton, P. & Jansen, R. (1990). A philosophical basis for knowledge acquisition. *Knowledge Acquisition, 2,* 241-257.

Consortium for Service Innovation. (2005). *Knowledge-centered support brief, Version 3.0.* Retrieved from http://www.serviceinnovation.org/included/docs/library/programs/kcs_brief.doc

Constant, D., Sproull, L., & Kiesler, S. (1996). The kindness of strangers: The usefulness of electronic weak ties for technical advice. *Organization Science, 7,* 119-135.

Cook, M. (1996). *Building enterprise information architectures: Reengineering information systems.* Upper Saddle River, NJ: Prentice-Hall.

Cooke, J. (2006). The supply chain lesson of the "Iron Hills". *Logistics Management, 46*(2), 72.

Cooper, K. G., Lyneis, J. M., & Bryant, B. J. (2002). Learning to learn from past to future. *International Journal of Project Management, 20*(3), 213-219.

Cox, T. (2001). *Creating the multicultural organization: A strategy for capturing the power of diversity.* San Francisco, CA: Jossey-Bass.

Crawford, K. (2003). *Factors affecting learning and communication in organizations: A chapter commissioned by the Defence, Science and Technology Organisation (DSTO).* Creative Interactive Systems Pty Ltd.

Croson, R. (1996). *Contributions to public goods: Altruism or reciprocity?* Working paper.

Cross, R. http://www.robcross.org/sna.htm

Cross, R., Baird, L. (2000). Technology is not enough: Improving performance by building organizational memory. *Sloan Management Review, 41*(3), 41–54.

Cross, R., & Parker, A. (2004). *The hidden power of social networks: Understanding how work really gets done in organizations.* Boston, MA: Harvard Business School Press.

Cross, R., Nohria, N., & Parker, A. (2002). Six myths about informal networks and how to overcome them. *Sloan Management Review, 43*(3), 67-75.

Cross, R., Parker, A., Prusak, L., & Borgatti, S. (2001). Knowing what we know: Supporting knowledge creation and sharing in social networks. *Organizational Dynamics, 30*(2), 100-120.

Cunningham, W. (2005). *Wiki history.* Retrieved October 29, 2005 from http://c2.com/cgi/wiki?WikiHistory

Curtice, R. (1987). *Strategic value analysis: A modern approach to systems and data planning.* Eaglewood Cliffs, NJ: Prentice-Hall.

Cuvillier, R. (1974). Intellectual workers and their work in social theory and practice. *International Labour Review, 109*(4), 291-317.

Daft, R., & Lewin, A. (1993). Where are the theories for the "new" organizational forms? An editorial essay. *Organization Science, 4*(i-vi).

Damm, D. & Schindler, M. (2002). Security issues of a knowledge medium for distributed project work. *International Journal of Project Management, 20*(1), 37-47.

Daneshar, F. (2003). A methodology for sharing contextual knowledge in virtual communities. In *Proceedings of the 14ᵗʰ Annual IRMA International Conference,* Philadelphia, PA, May.

Darley, W. (2001). The Internet and emerging e-Commerce: Challenges and implications for management in sub-Saharan Africa. *Journal of Global Information Technology Management, 4*(4), 4-18.

Darling, M., & Parry, C (2001). After-action reviews: Linking reflection and planning in a learning practice. *Reflections, 3*(2), 64-72.

Darroch, J. (2003). Developing a measure of knowledge management behaviors and practices. *Journal of Knowledge Management, 7*(5), 41-54.

Das, G. (1993). Local memoir of a global manager. *Harvard Business Review, March-April,* 38-47.

Davenport, T., & Glaser, J. (2002). Just-in-time delivery comes to knowledge management. *Harvard Business Review, 80*(7), 107-111.

Davenport, T., & Prusak, L. (1998). *Working knowledge.* Boston, MA: Harvard Business School Press.

Davenport, T., De long, D., & Beers, M. (1998). Successful knowledge management projects. *Sloan Management Review,* 443-457.

Davenport, T., Eccles, R., Prusak, L. (1992). Information politics. *Sloan Management Review, 34*(1), 53-65

Davenport, T., Jarvenpaa, S., & Beers, M. (1996). Improving knowledge work processes. *Sloan Management Review, Summer,* 53-65.

Davenport, T.H., & Prusak, L. (1998). *Working knowledge.* Boston: Harvard Business School Press.

Davenport, T.H., and Prusak, L. (2000). *Working knowledge.* Harvard Business School Press.

Davenport, T.H., DeLong, D.W., & Beers, M.C. (1998). Successful knowledge management projects. *Sloan Management Review, 39*(2), 43–57.

Davernport, T., & Prusak, L. (2000). *Working knowledge: How organizations know what they know.* Boston, MA: Harvard Business School Press.

Davidson, R.M., Martinsons, M.G., & Kock, N. (2004). Principles of canonical action research. *Information Systems Journal, 14,* 65-86.

Davis, F.D. (1989). Perceived usefulness, perceived ease of use, and user acceptance of information technology. *MIS Quarterly, 13,* 319–340.

Dawes, R., McTavish, J., & Shacklee, H. (1997). Behavior, communication and assumptions about other people's behavior in a commons dilemma situation. *Journal of Personality and Social Psychology, 35,* 1-11.

Dawson, R. (2000). Knowledge capabilities as the focus of organisational development. *Journal of Knowledge Management, 4*(4), 320-327.

Degler, D., & Battle, L. (2000). Knowledge management in pursuit of performance: The challenge of context. *Performance Improvement, ISPI, 39*(6). Retrieved October 7, 2002 from www.ipgems.com/writing/rolearticle.htm.

DeLone, W.H., & McLean, E.R. (1992). Information systems success: The quest for the dependent variable. *Information Systems Research, 3,* 60–95.

DeLone, W.H., & McLean, E.R. (2003). The DeLone and McLean model of information systems success: A ten-year update. *Journal of Management Information Systems, 19*(4), 9–30.

Denison, D., & Mishra, A. (1995). Towards a theory of organizational culture and effectiveness. *Organization Science, 6,* 204-223.

Dervin, B. (1992). From the mind's eye of the user: The sense-making qualitative quantitative methodology. In J. Glazier & R. Powell (Eds.), *Qualitative research in information management* (pp. 61-84). Englewood, CO: Libraries Unlimited.

Dervin, B., Foreman-Wernet, L., Lauterbach, E. (2003). *Sense-making methodology reader: Selected writings of Brenda Dervin.* New Jersey: Hampton Press.

Desouza, K. (2003). Facilitating tacit knowledge exchange. *Communications of the ACM, 46*(6), 85-88.

Dieng, R., Corby, O., Giboin, A., & Ribière, M. (1999). Methods and tools for corporate knowledge management. *International Journal of Human-Computer Studies, 51.* Retrieved from http://ideallibrary.com.

Dinsmore, P. C. (1999). *Winning in business with enterprise project management.* New York: AMA Publications.

Disterer, G.. (2002). Management of project knowledge and experiences. *Journal of Knowledge Management, 6*(5), 512-520.

Dixon, N. (2000). *Common knowledge.* Boston, MA: Harvard Business School Press.

Dixon, N. (2002, March/April). The neglected receiver of knowledge sharing. *Ivey Business Journal,* 35-40.

Doll, W.J., & Torkzadeh, G. (1988). The measurement of end-user computing satisfaction. *MIS Quarterly, 12,* 259–275.

Dougherty, V. (1999). Knowledge is about people, not databases. *Industrial & Commercial Training, 31*(7), 262-266.

Drucker, P. (1999). Beyond the information revolution. *The Atlantic Monthly,* Oct 1999.

Drucker, P. (1999). Knowledge-worker productivity: The biggest challenge. *California Management Review, 41*(2), 79-94.

Dunford, R. (1992). *Organisational behaviour: An organisational analysis perspective.* Sydney: Addison-Wesley.

Dwyer, J. (2005). *Communication in business: Strategies and skills,* 3rd ed. Prentice Hall.

Eales, J. (2003). Supporting informal communities of practice within organizations. In: M. Ackerman, V. Pipek, & V. Wulf (Eds.), *Sharing expertise - Beyond knowledge management* (pp. 275-297). Cambridge, MA: MIT Press.

Earl, M. (2001). Knowledge management strategies: Towards taxonomy. *Journal of Management Information Systems, 18*(1), 215-233.

Easterby-Smith, M., Crossan, M., & Nicolini, D. (2000). Organizational learning: Debates past, present and future. *Journal of Management Studies, 38*(6), 783-796.

Edvinsson, L. & Malone, M. S. (1997). *Intellectual capital.* New York: Harper Collins.

Edwards, G., Compton, P., Malor, R., Srinivasan, A. & Lazarus, L. (1993). PEIRS: A pathologist maintained expert system for the interpretation of chemical pathology reports. *Pathology, 25,* 27-34.

Edwards, J. S. & Shaw, D. (2004). Supporting knowledge management with IT. In *Proceedings of DSS 2004,* Prato, Italy.

El Sawy O. (2001). *Redesigning enterprise processes for e-business.* Boston, MA: Irwin/McGraw-Hill.

Ellingsen, G., & Monteiro, E. (2003). Mechanisms for producing a working knowledge: Enacting, orchestrating, and organizing. *Information and Organization, 13,* 203-229.

Engle-Warnick, J., & Jim, S. (2003). *Inferring repeated game strategies from actions: Evidence from trust game experiments.* Working paper.

Engle-Warnick, J., & Slonim, R. Learning to trust in indefinitely repeated games. *Games and Economic Behavior* (In press).

Eppler, M., Seifried, P., & Röpnack, A. (1999). Improving knowledge intensive processes through an rnterprise knowledge medium. In: Prasad, J. (Eds.), *Proceedings of the 1999 Conference on Managing Organizational Knowledge for Strategic Advantage: The Key Role of Information Technology and Personnel.* New Orleans.

Erickson, P. (1979). The role of secrecy in complex organizations: From norms of rationality to norms of distrust. *Cornell Journal of Social Relation, 14*(2), 121-138.

Eriksson, H., & Penker, M. (2000). *Business modeling with UML: Business patterns at work.* New York, NY: John Wiley & Sons, Inc.

Eriksson, H., Penker, M., Lyons, B., & Fado, D. (2004). *UML 2 toolkit.* Indianapolis, IN: John Wiley & Sons, Inc.

Ewusi-Mensah, K., & Przasnyski, Z. (1991). On information systems project abandonment: An exploratory study of organizational practices. *MIS Quarterly, 15*(1), 67-86.

Fairholm, G. (1993). *Organizational power politics.* Westpot, CT: Praeger.

Fehr, E., & Gächter, S. (2000). Fairness and retaliation: The economics of reciprocity. *Journal of Economic Perspectives, 14,* 159-181.

Fehr, E., & Henrich, J. (2003). Is strong reciprocity a maladaptation? On the evolutionary foundations of human altruism. In: P. Hammerstein (Ed.), *Genetic and cultural evolution of cooperation* (pp. 55-82). Cambridge, MA: MIT Press.

Fehr, E., & Schmidt, K. (1999). A theory of fairness, competition, and cooperation. *Quarterly Journal of Economics, 114,* 817-868.

Ferris, G., Fedor, D., Chachere, J., & Pondy, L. (1989). Myths and politics in organizational contexts. *Group and Organization Studies, 14*(1), 83-103.

Fine, G., & Holyfield, L. (1996). Secrecy, trust, and dangerous leisure: Generating group cohesion in voluntary organizations. *Social Psychology Quarterly, 59*(1), 22-38.

Finestone, N., & Snyman, R. (2005). Corporate South Africa: Making multicultural knowledge sharing work. *Journal of Knowledge Management, 9*(3), 128-141.

Fiol, C. M. & Lyles, M. A. (1985). Organizational learning. *Academy of Management Review, 10*(4), 803-813

Fischbacher, U., Gächter, S., & Fehr, E. (2001). Are people conditionally cooperative? Evidence from a public goods experiment. *Economics Letters, 71,* 397-404.

Fishbein, M. & Ajzen, I. (1975). *Belief, attitude, intention and behavior: An introduction to theory and research.* Addison-Wesley.

Forcadell, F., & Guadamillas, F. (2002). A case study on the implementation of a knowledge management strategy oriented to innovation. *Knowledge and Process Management, 9*(3), 162-171.

Ford, R., & Angermeier, I. (2004). Managing the knowledge environment: A case of study from healthcare. *Knowledge Management Research & Practice, 2,* 137-146.

Freire, P. (1985). *The politics of education* (Trans.). London: Macmillan.

Freire, P. (2000). *Pedagogy of the oppressed* (M. Bergman Ramos, Trans.). New York: Continuum.

Fröming, J., Gronau, N., & Schmid, S. (2006). Improvement of software engineering by modeling knowledge-intensive business process. *International Journal of Knowledge Management, 2*(4), 32-51.

Frost, P., Dutton, J., Worline, M., & Wilson, M. (2000). Narratives of compassion in organizations. In S. Fineman, (Ed.), *Emotions in Organizations* (pp. 25-45). Thousand Oaks, CA: Sage.

Gaines, B. R. & Shaw, M. L. G. (1993). Knowledge acquisition tools based on personal construct psychology. *Knowledge Engineering Review, 8*(1), 49-85.

Galbraith, J. (1977). *Organizational design.* Reading, MA: Addison Wesley.

Galliers, R. (2004). Reflections on information systems strategizing. In: Avgerou, C. Ciborra & Land (Eds.), *The social study of information and communication technology* (pp. 231-262). Oxford: Oxford University Press.

Galliers, R. D. (1992). Choosing information systems research approaches. In R. D. Galliers (Ed.), *Information systems research: Issues, methods and practical guidelines* (pp. 144-162). Oxford: Blackwell Scientific Publications.

Gallivan, M., Eynon, J., & Rai, A. (2003). The challenge of knowledge management systems—Analyzing the dynamic processes underlying performance improvement initiatives. *Information Technology and People, 16*(3), 326-352.

Gamma, E., Helm, R., Johnson R., & Vlissides, J. (1995). *Design patterns.* Addison-Wesley Pub Co.

Gargiulo, M., & Benassi, M. (2000). Trapped in your own net? Network cohesion, structural holes, and the adaptation of social capital. *Organization Science, 11*(2), 183-197.

Garud, R., & Kumaraswamy, A. (2005). Vicious and virtuous circles in the management of knowledge: The case of infosys technologies. *MIS Quarterly, 29*(1), 9-33.

Gebert, H., Geib, M., Kolbe, L., & Brenner, W. (2003). Knowledge-enabled customer relationship management: Integrating customer relationship management and knowledge management concepts. *Journal of Knowledge Management, 7*(5), 107-123.

Gefen, D., & Ridings, C. (2003). IT acceptance: Managing user - IT group boundaries. *SIGMIS Database, 34*(3), 25-40.

Geib, M., Reichold, A., Kolbe, L., & Brenner, W. (2005, March 1). Architecture for customer relationship management approaches in financial services. In *Proceedings of the 38th Hawaii International Conference on System Sciences 2005 (HICSS-38)*, Big Island, Hawaii. Los Alamitos, CA: IEEE Computer Society.

Geilhufe, D. (2005). *CRM project one pager - Confluence*. Retrieved October 29, 2005 from http://objectledge.org/confluence/display/CRM/CRM+Project+One+Pager.

Gemino, A., & Wand, Y. (2003). Evaluating modeling techniques based on models of learning. *Communications of the ACM, 46*(10), 79-84.

Ginsberg, M., & Kambil, A. (1999). Annotate: A Web-based knowledge management support system for document collections. In *Proceedings of the 32nd Hawaii International Conference on System Sciences*.

Giunipero, L., Dawley, D., & Anthony, W. (1999, Winter). The impact of tacit knowledge on purchasing decisions. *Journal of Supply Chain Management* [Electronic version].

Gloet, M., & Berrell, M. (2003). The dual paradigm nature of knowledge management: Implications for achieving quality outcomes in human resource management. *Journal of Knowledge Management, 7*(1), 78-89.

Goh, S. (2002). Managing effective knowledge transfer: An integrative framework and some practice implications. *Journal of Knowledge Management, 6*(1), 23-30.

Goldman, G. (1990). The tacit dimension of clinical judgement. *The Yale Journal of Biology and Medicine, 63*(1), 47-61.

Gordon (1990). The relationship of corporate culture to industry sector and corporate performance. In: R. Kilmann, M. Saxton, & R. Serpa (Eds.), *Gaining control of the corporate culture* (pp. 103-125). San Francisco, CA: Jossey-Bass.

Gordon, G., & DiTomaso, N. (1992). Predicting corporate performance from organizational culture. *Journal of management studies, 9*, 783-798.

Graham, A. B. & Pizzo V. G. (1996). A question of balance: Case studies in strategic knowledge management. *European Management Journal, 14*(4), 338-346. Reprinted in Klein DA (q.v.).

Grant, R. (1996). Prospering in dynamically-competitive environments: Organizational capability as knowledge integration. *Organization Science, 7*(4), 375-387.

Grant, R. (1996). Towards a knowledge-based theory of the firm. *Strategic Management Journal, 17*, 109-122.

Greenfield, J., Short, K., Cook, S., Kent, S., & Crupi, J. (2004). *Software factories: Assembling application with patterns, frameworks, and tools,* (1st ed.). Wiley.

Groff, T.R., & Jones, T.P. (2003). *Introduction to knowledge management: KM in business.* Butterworth-Heinemann.

Gronau, N., & Weber, E. (2004). Modeling of knowledge intensive business processes with the declaration language (KMDL®). In M. Khosrow-Pour (Eds.), *Innovations through information technology.* Idea Group Inc. 2004 Information Resources Management Association International Conference.

Gronau, N., & Weber, E. (2004a). Management of knowledge intensive business processes. In J. Desel, B.

Pernici, & M. Weske, (Eds.), *Business process management*. Springer: Heidelberg.

Gronau, N., Kopencny, A., & Kratzke, N. (2006). An interdisciplinary approach on operational knowledge process modeling and formal reasoning. *I-KNOW'06: Proceedings of the BPOKI'06 Conference Special Track*. Graz, Austria.

Gronau, N., Müller, C., & Korf, R. (2005). KMDL®—Capturing, analysing and improving knowledge-intensive Business Processes. *Journal of Computer Science. 4*, 452-472.

Gronau, N., Müller, C., & Uslar, M. (2004). The KMDL® knowledge management approach: Integrating knowledge conversions and business process modeling. In D. Karagiannis, & U. Reimer, (Eds.), *Practical aspects of knowledge management*. Springer-Verlag: Berlin, Heidelberg.

Gruber, T. (1992). Toward principles for the design of ontologies used for knowledge sharing. In *Proceedings of the International Workshop on Formal Ontology*. Padova, Italy.

Grudin, J. (1987). Social evaluation of the user interface: Who does the work and who gets the benefit?. In H. Bullinger & B. Shackel (Eds.), *Proceedings of INTERACT 1987* (pp. 805-811). Elsevier Science Publishers, Amsterdam.

Grudin, J. (1988). Why CSCW applications fail: Problems in the design and evaluation of oganisational interfaces. *Proceedings of CSCW 1988* (pp. 85-93). ACM Press.

Grudin, J. (1994). Groupware and social dynamics: Eight challenges for developers. *Communications of the ACM, 37*(1), 92-105.

Gupta, A., & Govindarajan, V. (2000). Knowledge management social dimension: Lessons from Nucor Steel. *Sloan Management Review, 42*(1), 71-81.

Gupta, J., & Sharma, S. (2004). *Creating knowledge-based organizations*. Hershey, PA: IDEA Group Publishing.

Hackney, R., Burn, J., & Dhillon, G. (2000). Challenging assumptions for strategic information systems planning. Theoretical perspectives. *Communications of the AIS, 3*(9).

Hahn, J., & Subramani, M. (2000). A framework of knowledge management systems: Issues and challenges for theory and practice. *Proceedings of the International Conference on Information Systems 2000* (pp. 302-312).

Hair, J., Anderson, R., Tatham, R., & Black, W. (1995). *Multivariate Data Analysis,* 4th Edition. New Jersey: Prentice-Hall.

Hall, E. (1976a). *Beyond culture*. NJ: Anchor Books.

Hall, E. (1976b). How cultures collide. *Psychology today, July,* 69.

Hall, H. (2001). Input-friendliness: Motivating knowledge sharing across intranets. *Journal of Information Science, 27*(3), 139-146.

Hall, H. (2004). The intranet as actor: The role of the intranet in knowledge sharing. In *Proceedings of the International Workshop on Understanding Sociotechnical Action* (pp. 109-111), Edinburgh.

Hamel, G., & Prahalad, C.K. (1990). The core competence of the corporation. *Harvard Business Review*.

Hampden-Turner, C., & Trompenaars, F. (2000). *Building cross-cultural competence: How to create wealth from conflicting values*. New York, NY: John Wiley & Sons.

Hannon, B., & Ruth, M. (1994). *Dynamic modeling*. New York, NY: Springer-Verlag.

Hansen M., Nohria, N., & Tierney, T. (1999). What's your strategy for managing knowledge?. *Harvard Business Review, March-April,* 106-116.

Hansen, M. (2001). Introducing t-shaped managers. *Harvard Business Review, 79*(3), 106-116.

Hansen, M. T., Nohria, N., & Tierney, T. (1999, March 1). What's your strategy for managing knowledge? *Harvard Business Review*.

Hansen, M., et al. (1999). What's your strategy for managing knowledge?. *Harvard Business Review, 77*(2), 106-116.

Harper, G. (2000). *Assessing information technology success as a function of organizational culture.* Doctoral dissertation, University of Alabama, Huntsville, AL.

Hart, D. (2002). Ownership as an issue in data and information sharing: A philosophically based view. *Australian Journal of Information Systems,* (Special Issue), 23-29.

Hart, D., & Warne, L. (1997). *Information systems defining characteristics: A stakeholder centric view of success and failure.* Technical Chapter CS0197. University College UNSW, ADFA.

Hatami, A., Galliers, R.D., & Huang, J. (2003). Exploring the impacts of knowledge (re)use and organizational memory on the effectiveness of strategic decisions: A longitudinal case study. In *Proceedings of the 36th Hawaii International Conference on System Sciences.*

Hatten, K. J. & Rosenthal, S. R. (1999). Managing the process centred enterprise. *Long Range Planning, 32*(3), 293-310.

Hatten, K. J. & Rosenthal, S. R. (2001). *Reaching for the knowledge edge.* New York: AMACOM.

Hayes, N. (2001). Boundless and bounded interactions in the knowledge work process: The role of groupware technologies. *Information and Organization, 11,* 79-101.

Hayes, N., & Walsham, G. (2001). Participation in groupware-mediated communities of practice: A socio-political analysis of knowledge working. *Information and Organization, 11,* 263-288.

Hedlund, G. (1994). A model of knowledge management and the N-form corporation. *Strategic Management Journal, 15,* 73-90.

Heisig, P. (2002). GPW-WM: Methoden und Werkzeuge zum geschäftsprozessorientierten Wissensmanagement. In A. Abecker, K. Hinkelmann, & M.Heiko, (Eds.), *Geschäftsprozessorientiertes Wissensmanagement.* Berlin. Springer.

Henderson-Seller, B. (2003). Method engineering for OO systems development. *Communications of the ACM, 46*(10), 73-78.

Hendriks, P. (2001). Many rivers to cross: From ICT to knowledge management systems. *Journal of Information Technology, 16,* 57-72.

Hendriks, P. H. J. (1999). Why share knowledge? The influence of ICT on the motivation for knowledge sharing. *Knowledge and Process Management, 6*(2), 91-100.

Hendriks, P. H. J. (2004). Assessing the role of culture in knowledge sharing. In *Proceedings of Fifth European Conference in Organization, Knowledge, Learning and Capabilities (OKLC 2004),* Innsbruk.

Hildreth, P., & Kimble, C. (2002). The duality of knowledge. *Information Research, 8*(1), (online) http://informationr.net/ir/8-1/paper142.html.

Hiltz, S., Johnson, K., & Turoff, M. (1986). Experiments in group decision-making: Communication process and outcome in face-to-face versus computerized conferences. *Human Communication Research, 13,* 225-252.

Hinds, P. J. & Pfeffer, J. (2003). Why organizations don't "know what they know": Cognitive and motivational factors affecting the transfer of expertise. In M. Ackerman, V. Pipek, & V. Wulf (Eds.), *Sharing expertise: Beyond knowledge management.* Cambridge: MIT Press.

Hinds, P., & Weisband, S. (2003). Knowledge sharing and shared understanding in virtual team. In: C. Gibson & S. Cohen (Eds.), *Virtual teams that work: Creating conditions for virtual teams effectiveness* (pp. 21-36). San Francisco, CA: Jossey-Bass.

Hinge, A. (2000). *Australian defence preparedness: Principles, problems, and prospects.* Australian Defence Studies Centre Canberra ACT.

Hislop, D. (2002). Mission impossible? Communicating and sharing knowledge via information technology. *Journal of Information Technology, 17,* 165-177.

Hoecklin, L. (2003). Culture: What it is, what it is not and how it directs organizational behavior. In G. Redding & B. Stening (Eds.), *Cross-cultural management volume*

II (pp. 75-104). Cheltenham: Edward Elgar Publishing Limited.

Hofstede, G. (2001). *Culture's consequences: Comparing values, behaviours, institutions, and organizations across nations.* CA: Sage.

Hofstede, G. (2003). Cultural constraints in management theories. In G. Redding & B. Stening (Eds.), *Cross-cultural management volume II* (pp. 61-74). Cheltenham: Edward Elgar Publishing Limited.

Hofstede, G., Neuijen, B., Ohayv, D., & Sanders, G. (1990). Measuring organizational culture: A qualitative and quantitative study across twenty cases. *Administrative science quarterly, 35,* 286-316.

Hofstede, G.H. (1980). *Culture's consequences.* Thousand Oaks, CA: Sage Publications.

Holsapple, C. (2003). Knowledge and its attributes. In: C. Holsapple (Ed.), *Handbook on knowledge management (vol. 1)* (pp. 166-188). Springer.

Holsapple, C., & Joshi, K. (1999). Description and analysis of existing knowledge management frameworks. In *Proceedings of the Thirty-second Hawaii International Conference on System Sciences,* January 3-6, Computer Society Press.

Holsapple, C., & Joshi, K. (2001). Organizational knowledge resources. *Decision Support Systems, 31*(1), 39-54.

Holsapple, C.W., & Joshi, K.D. (2000). An investigation of factors that influence the management of knowledge in organizations. *Journal of Strategic Information Systems, 9,* 235–261.

Holsapple, C.W., & Joshi, K.D. (2002). Knowledge management: A threefold framework. *Information Society, 18*(1), 47-64.

Holtshouse, D. (1998). Knowledge research issues. *California Management Review, 40*(3), 277-280.

Howells, J. (1996). Tacit knowledge, innovation and technology transfer. *Technology Analysis & Strategic Management, 8*(2), 106-116.

Huber, G., Davenport, T., & King, D. (1998). Some perspectives on organizational memory. In: F. Burstein, G. Huber, M. Mandviwalla, J. Morrison, & L. Olfman, (Eds.), *Unpublished Working Paper for the Task Force on Organizational Memory, Presented at the 31ˢᵗ Annual Hawaii International Conference on System Sciences.* Hawaii.

Hunt, K. (2005). E-mentoring: Solving the issue of mentoring across distances. *Development and Learning in Organizations, 19*(5) 7-10.

Hunter, A. (2003). *Utilisation of a corporate intranet for knowledge sharing and retention.* Unpublished honours thesis, School of Information Systems, Deakin University, Melbourne, Australia.

Huntington, S. (1996). *The clash of civilizations: Remaking of world order.* NY: Simon and Schuster.

Husted, K. & Michailova, S. (2002). Diagnosing and fighting knowledge sharing hostility. *Organizational Dynamics, 31*(1), 60-73.

Huysman, M. & de Wit, D. (2002). *Knowledge sharing in practice.* Dordrecht: Kluwer Academics Publishers.

Iakovou, E., & Douligeris, C. (2001). An information management system for the emergency management of hurricane disasters. *International Journal of Risk Assessment and Management, 2*(3-4), 243-262.

ICRISAT. (2001). Medium Term Plan 2002-2004, People First! International Crops Research Institute for Semi-Arid Tropics, Patancheru AP, India.

Iivari, J., & Linger, H. (1999). *Knowledge work as collaborative work: A situated activity theory view.* Paper presented at the 32ⁿᵈ Hawaii International Conference on System Sciences (HICSS) (pp. 1-9), Hawaii.

INDEHELA-Methods project. (1999). Retrieved March 2, 2003 from http://www.uku.fi/atkk/indehela/

Inkpen, A.C., & Dinur. A. (1998). Knowledge management processes and international joint ventures. *Organization Science, 9*(4), 454-468.

Inkpen, A.C., & Tsang, E.W. (2005). Social capital, networks, and knowledge transfer. Academy of Management Review, 30(1), 146-165.

Ithia, A. (2003). UK lawyers spend more on KM. *KM Review, 5*(6), 11.

Jafari, M., & Akhavan P. (2007). Essential changes for knowledge management establishment in a country: A macro perspective. *European Business Review, 19*(1), 89-110.

Jennex, M. (2004). *Emergency response systems: Lessons from utilities and Y2K.* Paper presented at the Americas Conference on Information Systems, New York, NY.

Jennex, M. (2005). The issue of system use in knowledge management systems. In *Proceedings of the 38th Hawaii International Conference on System Sciences, HICSS38,* IEEE Computer Society.

Jennex, M., & Olfman, L. (2005). Assessing knowledge management success. *International Journal of Knowledge Management, 1*(2), 33-49.

Jennex, M., & Olfman, L. (2006). A model of knowledge management success. *International Journal of Knowledge Management, 2*(3), 51-68.

Jennex, M.E. (2000). Using an intranet to manage knowledge for a virtual project team. In D.G. Schwartz, M. Divitini, & T. Brasethvik (Eds.), *Internet-based organizational memory and knowledge management* (pp. 241–259). Hershey, PA: Idea Group Publishing.

Jennex, M.E. (2005). What is knowledge management? *International Journal of Knowledge Management, 1*(4), i–iv.

Jennex, M.E. (2006). Classifying knowledge management systems based on context content. *Hawaii International Conference on Systems Sciences.* IEEE.

Jennex, M.E. (2006). Culture, context, and knowledge management. *International Journal of Knowledge Management, 2*(2), i–iv.

Jennex, M.E., & Croasdell, D. (2005). Knowledge management: Are we a discipline? *International Journal of Knowledge Management, 1*(1), i–v.

Jennex, M.E., & Olfman, L. (2000). Development recommendations for knowledge management/organizational memory systems. In *Proceedings of the Information Systems Development Conference.*

Jennex, M.E., & Olfman, L. (2002). Organizational memory/knowledge effects on productivity: A longitudinal study. In *Proceedings of the 35th Annual Hawaii International Conference on System Sciences.*

Jennex, M.E., Olfman, L., & Addo, T.B.A. (2003). *The need for an organizational knowledge management strategy.* In *Proceedings of the 36th Hawaii International Conference on System Sciences.*

Jennex, M.E., Olfman, L., Pituma, P., & Yong-Tae, P. (1998). An organizational memory information systems success model: An extension of DeLone and McLean's I/S success model. In *Proceedings of the 31st Annual Hawaii International Conference on System Sciences.*

Jordan, B. (1993). Ethnographic workplace studies and computer-supported cooperative work. *Interdisciplinary Workshop on Informatics and Psychology.* Scharding, Austria.

Kakabadse, A., & Parker, C. (Eds.). (1984). *Power, politics, and organizations.* New York, NY: John Wiley & Sons.

Kang, B., Compton, P., & Preston, P. (1995). Multiple classification ripple down rules: Evaluation and possibilities. In *Proceedings of the 9th AAAI-Sponsored Banff Knowledge Acquisition for Knowledge-Based Systems Workshop,* Banff, Canada, University of Calgary.

Kang, B., Yoshida, K., Motoda, H., Compton, P., & Iwayama, M. (1996). A help desk system with intelligent interface. In P. Compton, R. Mizoguchi, H. Motoda, & T. Menzies (Eds.), *PKAW'96: Pacific Rim Knowledge Acquisition Workshop* (pp. 313-332), Sydney, Dept. of Artificial Intelligence, School of Computer Science and Engineering, UNSW.

Kankanhalli, A., Tan, B., & Wei, K. (2005). Contributing knowledge to electronic knowledge repositories: An empirical investigation. *MIS Quarterly, 29,* 113-143.

Kaplan, R. S. & Norton, D. P. (1996). *The balanced scorecard.* Boston: Harvard Business School Press.

Kaplan, R. S. & Norton, D. P. (2004). *Strategy maps.* Boston: Harvard Business School Press.

Karsten H. (2000). *Weaving tapesty: Collaborative information technology and organizational change.* Doctoral dissertation, Jyvaskyla Studies in Computing, No 3.

Kautz, K. & Mahnke, V. (2003). Value creation through IT-supported knowledge management? The utilisation of a knowledge management system in a global consulting company. *Informing Science, 6,* 75-88.

Kelly, G. A. (1955). *The psychology of personal constructs.* New York: Norton.

Kendall, K., & Kendall, J. (2002). *Systems analysis and design* (p. 73). Upper Saddle River, NJ: Prentice-Hall.

Kersten, G., Mikolajuk, Z., & Yeh, A. (Eds.). (1999). *Decision support systems for sustainable development in developing countries* (pp. 293-296). Boston, MA: Kluwer Academic.

Kerzner, H. (2001a). *Strategic planning for project management using a project management maturity model.* New York: John Wiley and Sons.

Kerzner, H. (2001b). *Project management: A systems approach to planning, scheduling and controlling.* New York: John Wiley and Sons.

Kerzner, H. (2003). Strategic planning for a project office. *Project Management Journal, 34*(2), 13-25.

Kilduff, M. & Tsai, W. (2003). *Social networks and organizations.* Sage.

Kim, D. H. (1993). The link between individual and organizational learning. *MIT Sloan management Review, 35*(1).

Kim, M. (2003). *Document management and retrieval for specialised domains: An evolutionary user-based approach.* Doctoral dissertation, UNSW, Sydney.

Kim, S., Hwang, H., & Suh, E. (2003). A process-based approach to knowledge-flow analysis: A case study of a manufacturing firm. *Knowledge and Process Management, 10*(4), 260-276.

Kim, S., Lim, S., & Mitchell, R. (2004). Building a knowledge model: A decision-making approach. *Journal of Knowledge Management Practice, 5.* Retrieved from http://www.tlainc.com/articl68.htm.

King, J., Gurbaxani, V., Kraemer, K., McFarlan, F., Raman, K., & Yap, C. (1994). Institutional factors in information technology innovation. *Information Systems Research, 5*(2), 139-169.

King, W. (1999). Integrating knowledge management into IS strategy. *Information Systems Management, 16*(4), 70-72.

Kirchner, M., & Jain, P. (2004). *Pattern-oriented software architecture.* Pattern for resource management (Wiley Software Pattern Series). John Wiley & Sons.

Kitamato, A. (2005). Digital typhoon: Near real-time aggregation, recombination and delivery of typhoon-related information. In *Proceeding of the 4th International Symposium on Digital Earth.* Tokyo, Japan. Retrieved October 26, 2005 from http://www.cse.iitb.ac.in/~neela/MTP/Stage1-Report.pdf.

Klein, D. A. (Ed.). (1998). *The strategic management of intellectual capital.* Boston: Butterworth-Heinemann.

KMDL. (2006). *Knowledge modeling and description language.* Retrieved March 30, 2006: http://www.kmdl.de

Kock, N., & McQueen, R. (1998). Groupware support as a moderator of interdepartmental knowledge communication in process improvement groups: An action research study. *Information Systems Journal, 8,* 183-198.

Koeglreiter, G., Smith, R., & Torlina, L. (2005). *Identification of an emerging community of practice in a knowledge workplace.* Paper presented at the Australian

Conference for Knowledge Management and Intelligent Decision Support (pp. 197-208), Novotel, Melbourne.

Koeglreiter, G., Smith, R., & Torlina, L. (2006). The role of informal groups in organisational knowledge work: Understanding an emerging community of practice. *International Journal of Knowledge Management, 2*(1), 6-23.

Koeglreiter, G., Smith, R., & Torlina, L. (2008, forthcoming-a). *Knowledge interfaces: An informal CoP faced with formal boundaries.* Paper presented at the Australian Conference for Knowledge Management and Intelligent Decision Support, Monash University, Melbourne, Australia.

Koeglreiter, G., Smith, R., & Torlina, L. (2008, forthcoming-b). Reaching beyond the "boundaries": Communities of practice and boundaries in tertiary education. In C. Kimble & P. Hildreth (Eds.), *Communities of practice: Creating learning environments for educators.* Information Age Publishing.

Kofman, F., & Senge, P. (1993). Communities of commitment: The heart of learning organizations. *Organizational Dynamics, 22*(2), 4-23.

Kogut, B., & Zander, U. (1992). Knowledge of the firm, combative capability and the replication of technology. *Organization Science, 3,* 383-397.

Kogut, B., & Zander, U. (1996). What firms do? Coordination, identity and learning. *Organization Science, 7,* 502-518.

Koka, B.R., & Prescott, J.E. (2002). Strategic alliances as social capital: A multidimensional view. *Strategic Management Journal, 23,* 795-816.

Komorita, S., & Parks, C. (1994). *Social dilemmas.* Boulder, CO: Westview Press.

Korpela, M. (1996). Traditional culture or political economy? On the root causes of organizational obstacles of IT in developing countries. *Information Technology for Development, 7,* 29-42.

Korpela, M., Mursu, A., & Soriyan, H. (2001). Two times four integrative levels of analysis: A framework. In: N.

Russo, B. Fitzgerald, & J. DeGross (Eds.), *Realigning research and practice in information systems development. The social and organizational perspective* (pp. 367-377). Boston, MA: Kluwer Academic Publishers.

Koschmann, T. (1999). Toward a dialogic theory of learning: Bakhtin's contribution to learning in settings of collaboration. In *Proceedings of Computer Supported Collaborative Learning (CSCL '99)* (pp. 308-313). Retrieved January 21, 2005, from http://kn.cilt.org/cscl99/A38/A38.HTM

Koskinen, K.U. (2001). Tacit knowledge as a promoter of success in technology firms. In *Proceedings of the 34th Hawaii International Conference on System Sciences.*

Kostman, J. (2004). 20 rules for effective communication in a crisis. *Disaster Recovery Journal, 17*(2), 20.

Kostova, T. (1999). Transnational transfer of strategic organizational practices: A contextual perspective. *Academy of Management Review, 24,* 308-324.

Kotnour, T. (1999). A learning framework for project management. *Project Management Journal, 30*(2), 32-38.

Kram, K. (1985). *Mentoring at work: Developmental relationships in organizational life.* Glenview, IL: Scott, Foreman and Company.

Kreitner, R., & Kinicki, A. (2002). *Organizational behavior.* London: McGraw Hill.

Kridan, A., & Goulding, J. (2006). A case study on knowledge management implementation in banking sector. *VINE: The Journal of Information and Knowledge Management Systems, 36*(2), 211-222

Krippendorf, K. (1980). *Content analysis: An introduction to its methodology.* Beverly Hills, CA: Sage Publications.

Kroeber, A., & Luckhohn, C. (1952). *Culture: A critical review of concepts and definitions.* Cambridge, MA: Harvard University Press. Cited in Holden, N. (2002). *Cross-cultural management: A knowledge management perspective* (p. 26). London: Prentice Hall.

Kuofie, M. (2005). E-management: E-knowledge management for optimizing rural medical services. *International Journal of Management and Technology, 1,* September, 28-37.

Kurzban, R., & Houser, D. (2005). Experiments investigating cooperative types in humans: A complement to evolutionary theory and simulations. In *Proceedings of the National Academy of Sciences of the United States of America, 102,* 1803-1807.

Kuwada, K. (1998). Strategic learning: The continuous side of discontinuous strategic change. *Organization. Science, 2*(6), 719-736.

Kwan, M.M., & Balasubramanian, P. (2003). KnowledgeScope: Managing knowledge in context. *Decision Support Systems, 35*(4), 467-486.

Lai, H., & Chu, T. (2000). Knowledge management: A theoretical frameworks and industrial cases. In *Proceedings of the Thirty-Third Annual Hawaii International Conference on System Sciences* (CD/ROM), January 4-7, Computer Society Press.

Lal, K., Plax, J., & Yee, K. (2005). *People Finder Interchange Format 1.1.* Retrieved October 29, 2005 from from http://zesty.ca/pfif/1.1

Lane, P. J. & Lubatkin, M. (1998). Relative absorptive capacity and interorganizational learning. *Strategic Management Journal, 19,* 461-477.

Lateef, A. (1997). *A case study of Indian software industry.* International Institute for Labor Studies, New Industrial Organization Programme, DP/96/1997.

Latour B. (1993). *The pasteurisation of France.* Cambridge, MA: Harvard University Press.

Latour B. (1999b). On recalling ANT. In J. Law & J. Hassard (Eds.), *Actor network theory and after* (pp. 15-25). Oxford: Blackwell.

Latour, B. (1987). *Science in action: How to follow scientists and engineers through society.* Cambridge, MA: Harvard University Press.

Latour, B. (1999a). *Pandora's hope: Essays on the reality of science studies.* Cambridge, MA: Harvard University Press.

Lau, T., Wong, Y., Chan, K., & Law, M. (2001). Information technology and the work environment–Does IT change the way people interact at work?. *Human Systems Management, 20*(3), 267-280.

Law, J. & Hassard, J. (Eds.). (1999). *Actor network theory and after.* Oxford and Keele: Blackwell and the Sociological Review.

Lazarus, L. (2000). *Clinical decision support systems: Background and role in clinical support* (White Paper). Retrieved from http://www.pks.com.au/CDSS_White_Paper_ doc.pdf

Leavitt, H. (1965). Applied organizational change in industry: Structural, technological and humanistic approaches. In: J. March (Ed.), *Handbook of organizations* (pp. 1144-1170). Chicago, IL: Rand McNally & Co.

Lee, J., & Bui, T. (2000). *A template-based methodology for disaster management information systems.* Paper presented at the Hawaii International Conference on Systems Science, Hawaii.

Lee, S., & Hong, S. (2002). An enterprise-wide knowledge management system infrastructure. *Industrial Management + Data Systems, 102*(1-2), 17-25.

Lemken, B., Kahler, H., & Rittenbruch, M. (2000). Sustained knowledge management by organizational culture. In *Proceedings of the 33rd Hawaii International Conference on System Sciences,* p. 64.

Leonard-Barton, D. (1995). Wellsprings of knowledge. *Harvard Business Review, 71*(2), 75-84.

Leonard-Barton, D. (1995). *Wellsprings of knowledge: Building and sustaining the sources of innovation.* Cambridge, MA: Harvard Business School Press.

Lesser E., & Prusak L. (2001). Preserving knowledge in an uncertain world. *Sloan Management Review, 43*(1), 1010-1021

Lesser, E., & Storck, J. (2001). Communities of practice and organizational performance. *IBM Systems Journal, 40*(4), 831-845.

Leuf, B., & Cunningham, W. (2001). *The WIKI WAY. Quick collaboration of the Web.* Addison-Wesley.

Levina, N., & Vaast, E. (2005). The emergence of boundary spanning competence in practice: Implications for implementation and use of information systems. *MIS Quarterly, 29*(2), 335-363.

Lichtenstein, S., Hunter, A., & Mustard, J. (2004). Utilisation of intranets for knowledge sharing: A socio-technical study. In *Proceedings of Australasian Conference on Information Systems (ACIS 2004)*, Tasmania, Hobart.

Liebowitz, J., & Wilcox, L. (1997). *Knowledge management.* Ft. Lauderdale, FL: CRC Press.

Liedtka, J. (1999). Linking competitive advantage with communities of practice. *Journal of Management Inquiry, 8*(1), 5-16.

Lindgren, R., & Stenmark, D. (2002). Designing competence systems: Towards interest-activated technology. *Scandinavian Journal of Information Systems, 14,* 19-35.

Lindgren, R., Henfridsson, O., & Schultze, U. (2004). Design principles for competence management systems: A synthesis of an action research study. *MIS Quarterly, 28*(3), 435-472.

Lindgren, R., Stenmark, D., & Ljungberg, J. (2003). Rethinking competence systems for knowledge-based organizations. *European Journal of Information Systems, 12*(1), 18-29.

Loucopoulos, L., & Kavakli, E. (1995). Enterprise modeling and the teleological approach to requirement engineering. *International Journal of Intelligent and Cooperative Information Systems, 4*(1), 45-79.

Lu, L., & Leung, K. (2004). *A public goods perspective on knowledge sharing: Effects of self-interest, self-efficacy, interpersonal climate, and organizational support.* Working paper.

Lucas, L., & Ogilve D. (2006). Things are not always what they seem: How reputations, culture, and incentives influence knowledge transfer. *The Learning Organization, 13*(1), 7-24.

Lycett, M., Rassau, A., & Danson, J. (2004). Programme management: A critical review. *International Journal of Project Management, 22,* 289-299

Lyytinen, K., & Hirschheim, R. (1987). Information system failures: A survey and classification of the empirical literature. *Oxford Surveys in Information Technology,* (4), 257-309.

Lyytinen, K., Mathiassen, L., & Ropponen, J. (1998). Attention shaping and software risk - A categorical analysis of four classical risk management approaches. *Information Systems Research, 9*(3), 233-255.

Maedche, A., Motik, B., Stojanovic, L., Studer, R., &Volz, R. (2003). Ontologies for enterprise knowledge management. *IEEE Intelligence System, 18*(2), 26-33.

Maier, R. (2002). *Knowledge management systems: Information and communication technologies for knowledge management.* Berlin: Springer-Verlag.

Maier, R., & Remus, U. (2001). Toward a framework for knowledge management strategies: Process orientation as strategic starting point. In *Proceedings of the 34th Hawaii International Conference on Systems Sciences (CD/ROM)*, January 3-6, Computer Society Press.

Malhotra, A., & Majchrzak (2004). Enabling knowledge creation in far-flung teams: Best practices for IT support and knowledge sharing. *Journal of Knowledge Management, 8*(4), 75-88.

Malhotra, Y. (2005). Integrating knowledge management technologies in organizational business processes: Getting real time enterprises to deliver real business performance. *Journal of Knowledge Management, 9*(1), 7-29.

Malhotra, Y., & Galletta, D. (2003). Role of commitment and motivation as antecedents of knowledge management systems implementation. In *Proceedings of the 36th Hawaii International Conference on System Sciences.*

Mallach, E. (2000). *Decision support and data warehouse system*. Boston, MA: McGraw Hill.

Mandviwalla, M., Eulgem, S., Mould, C., & Rao, S.V. (1998). Organizational memory systems design [working paper for the Task Force on Organizational Memory]. In *Proceedings of the 31st Annual Hawaii International Conference on System Sciences*.

Manev, I., & Stevenson, W. (2001). Balancing ties: Boundary spanning and influence in the organization's extended network of communication. *Journal of Business Communication, 38*(2), 183-205.

Mansar, S. L. & Marir, F. (2003). *Case-based reasoning as a technique for knowledge management in business process redesign*. Academic Conferences Limited.

Mao, J., & Benbasat, I. (1998). Contextualized access to knowledge: Theoretical perspectives and a process-tracing study. *Information Systems Journal, 8,* 217-239.

Marakas, G. (2003). *Decision support systems in the 21st century*, (2nd ed). Upper Saddle River, NJ: Prentice Hall.

Marcoulides, G., & Heck, R. (1993). Organizational culture and performance: Proposing and testing a model. *Organization Science, 4,* 209-225.

Margolis, H. (1982). *Selfishness, altruism and rationality: A theory of social choice*. Cambridge, UK: Cambridge University Press.

Marir, F. & Watson, I. D. (1994). A categorised bibliography of case-based reasoning. *Knowledge Engineering Review, 9*(4), 355-381.

Markman, A. B. & Gentner, D. (1996). Commonalities and differences in similarity comparisons. *Memory and Cognition, 24*(2), 235-249.

Markus, L. (2001). Towards a theory of knowledge reuse: Types of knowledge reuse situations and factors in reuse success. *Journal of Management Information Systems, 18*(1), 57-93.

Markus, L., & Robey, D. (1998). Information technology and organizational change: Causal structure in theory and research. *Management Sciences, 34*(5), 583-598.

Markus, L., Majchrzak, A., & Gasser, L. (2002). A design theory for systems that support emergent knowledge processes. *MIS Quarterly, 26,* 179-212.

Markus, M. (2001). Toward a theory of knowledge reuse: Types of knowledge reuse situations and factors in reuse success. *Journal of Management Information Systems, 18*(1), 57-93.

Markus, M. L. (2001). Toward a theory of knowledge reuse: Types of knowledge reuse situations and factors in reuse success. *Journal of Management Information Systems, 18*(1), 57-93.

Markus, M.L., Majchrzak, A., & Gasser, L. (2002). A design theory for systems that support emergent knowledge processes. *MIS Quarterly, 26*(3), 179–212.

Marshall, C. & Rossman, G. B. (1995). *Designing qualitative research* (2nd ed.). London: Sage Publications.

Marshall, C., Shipman III, F., & McCall, R. (2000). Making large-scale information resources serve communities of practice. In E. Lesser, M. Fontaine, & J. Slusher (Eds.), *Knowledge and communities* (pp. 225-247). Boston, MA: Butterworth Heinemann.

Marshall, N., & Brady, T. (2001). Knowledge management and the politics of knowledge: Illustrations from complex products and systems. *European Journal of Information Systems 10,* 99-112.

Massey, A.P., Montoya-Weiss, M.M., & O'Driscoll, T.M. (2002). Knowledge management in pursuit of performance: Insights from Nortel networks. *MIS Quarterly, 26*(3), 269-289.

Mathis, J. (2006). *Teaching soldiers to think creatively*. Associated Press Newswires.

Mattison, D. (2003). Quickwiki, Swiki, Twiki, Zwiki and the Plone wars – Wiki as PIM and collaborative content tool. *Searcher: The Magazine for Database Professionals, 11*(4), 32.

Matveev, A., & Milter, R. (2004). The value of inter-cultural competence of multicultural teams. *Team Performance Management, 10*(5-6), 104-111.

McAfee, A. (2006). Enterprise 2.0: The dawn of emergent collaboration. *MIT Sloan Management Review, 47*(3), 21-28.

McDermott, R. (1999). Learning across teams: How to build communities of practice in team organizations. *Knowledge Management Review, 2*(2), 32-36.

McDermott, R., & O'Dell, C. (2001). Overcoming cultural barriers to sharing knowledge. *Journal of Knowledge Management, 5*(1), 76-85.

McElroy, M. (2003) *The new knowledge management.* Butterworth-Heinemann

McLoughlin, I. P., Alderman, N., Ivory, C. J., Thwaites, A., & Vaughan, R. (2000). Knowledge management in long term engineering projects. In *Proceedings of the Knowledge Management: Controversies and Causes Conference.* Retrieved May 19, 2003 from, http://bprc.warwick.ac.uk/km065.pdf

McLure Wasko, M., & Faraj, S. (2000). "It is what one does": Why people participate and help others in electronic communities of practice. *The Journal of Strategic Information Systems, 9*(2-3), 155-173.

Mertins, K., Heisig, P., Vorbeck, J., & Mertens, K. (Eds.) (2000). *Knowledge management: Best practices in Europe.* Springer.

Messick, D., Wilke, H., Brewer, M., Kramer, R., Zemke, P., & Lui, L. (1983). Individual adaptations and structural change as solutions to social dilemmas. *Journal of Personality and Social Psychology, 44,* 294-309.

Miles M., & Huberman, A. (1984). *Qualitative data analysis.* A sourcebook of new methods. London, England: Sage Publications.

Miles, R., & Snow, C. (1986). Organizations: New concepts for new forms. *California Management Review, 28*(62-73).

Mingers, J. (2001). Combining IS research methods: Towards a pluralist methodology. *Information Systems Research, 12*(3), 240-259.

Montequin, V., Fernandez, F., Cabal, V., & Gutierrez, R. (2006). An integrated framework for intellectual capital measurement and knowledge management implementation in small and medium-sized enterprises. *Journal of Information Science, 32*(6), 525-538.

Morales-Gomez, D., & Melesse, M. (1998). Utilizing information and communication technologies for development: The social dimensions. *Information Technology for Development, 8*(1), 3-14.

Morgan, G. (1997). *Images of organization,* new ed. Sage Publications.

Morris, P. W. G. (revised 2003). *The validity of knowledge in project management and the challenge of learning and competency development.* Retrieved May 23, 2005, from http://www.bartlett.ucl.ac.uk/research/management/Validityofknowledge.pdf

Mumford, E. (1993). *Designing human systems for healthcare: The ETHICS method.* Cheshire: Eight Associates.

Mumford, E. (2000). Socio-technical design: An unfulfilled promise or a future opportunity. In: R. Baskerville, J. Stage, & J. DeGross (Eds.), *The social and organizational perspective on research and practice in information technology.* London: Champman-Hall.

Mumford, E., & Weir, M. (1979). *Computer systems in work design—The ETHICS method: Effective technical and human implementation of computer systems.* Exeter: A. Wheaton & Co.

Munter, M. (1993). Cross-cultural communication for managers. *Business Horizons,* May-June, 72.

Myers, M., & Young, L. (1997). Hidden agendas, power and managerial assumptions in information systems development—An ethnographic study. *Information, Technology, and People, 10,* 224-240.

Nahapiet, J. & Ghosal, S. (1998) Social capital, intellectual capital, and the organizational advantage. *Academy of Management. The Academy of Management Review, 23*(2), 242-266.

Naiburg, E., & Maksimchuk, R. (2001). *UML for database design.* Boston, MA: Addison Wesley.

Nash, J. (1950). Equilibrium points in n-person games. In *Proceedings of the National Academy of Sciences, 36,* 48-49.

Nathanson, D., Kazanjian, R., & Galbraith, J. (1982). Effective strategic planning and the role of organization design. In: P. Lorange (Ed.), *Implementation of strategic planning* (pp. 91-113). Englewood Cliffs, NJ: Prentice Hall, Inc.

NCDDR. (2003). *National Center for the Dissemination of Disability Research.* Retrieved September 12, 2005 from http://www.ncddr.org/du/products/review/review6.html.

Nelson, R. R. & Winter, S. G. (1982). *An evolutionary theory of economic change.* Cambridge, MA: Belknap Press of Harvard University Press.

Neve, T. O. (2003). Right questions to capture knowledge. *Electronic Journal of Knowledge Management, 1*(1), 47-54. Retrieved February 5, 2005 from http://www.ejkm.com/volume-1/volume1-issue1/issue1-art6-neve.pdf

Nevis, E. C., DiBella, A. J., & Gould, J. M. (1995). Understanding organizations as learning systems. *MIT Sloan Management Review, 36*(2).

Nidimolu, S., Subramani, M., & Aldrich, A. (2001). Situated learning and the situated knowledge Web: Exploring the ground beneath knowledge management. *Journal of Management Information Systems, 18*(1), 115-150.

Nirenberg, J. (1995). From team building to community building. *National Productivity Review,* 51-62.

Nissen, M. (1999). Knowledge-based knowledge management in the Re-engineering domain. *Decision Support Systems, 27,* 47-65.

Nissen, M., Kamel, M., & Sengupta, K. (2000). Integrated analysis and design of knowledge systems and processes. *Information Resources Management Journal, 13*(1), 24-43.

Nissen, M.E. (2002). An extended model of knowledge-flow dynamics. *Communications of the Association for Information Systems, 8,* 251-266.

Nissen, M.E., & Levitt, R.E. (2004). Agent-based modeling of knowledge dynamics. *Knowledge Management Research & Practice, 2*(3), 169-183.

Nonaka, I. (1994). A dynamic theory of organisational knowledge creation. *Organization Science,*

Nonaka, I., & Takeuchi, H. (1995). *The knowledge creating company: How Japanese companies create the dynamics of innovation.* New York, NY: Oxford University Press.

Nonaka, I., Takeuchi, H., & Umemoto K. (1996). A theory of organisational knowledge creation. *International Journal of Technology Management, 11*(7/8), 833-845.

Nunnally, J. (1978). *Psychometric theory,* 2nd Edition. McGraw-Hill.

O'Dell, C., Elliott, S., & Hubert C. (2003). Achieving knowledge management outcomes. In: C. Holsapple (Ed.), *Handbook on knowledge management* (pp. 253-287).

O'Reilly, C., Al Chatman, J., & Caldwell, D. (1991). People and organizational culture: A profile comparison approach to assessing per-organization fit. *Academy of Management Journal, 34,* 487-516.

O'Reilly, T. (2005). *What is Web 2.0? Design patterns and business models for the next generation of software.* The O'Reilly website. Retrieved December 19, 2007, from http://oreillynet.com/pub/a/oreilly/tim/news/2005/09/30/what-is-web-20.html.

Odedra, M., Lawrie, M., Bennett, M., & Goodman, S. (1993). International perspectives: Sub-Saharan Africa: A technological desert. *Communications of the ACM, 36*(2), 25-29.

Okunoye, A., & Karsten, H. (2001). Information technology infrastructure and knowledge management in sub-Saharan Africa: Research in progress. In *Proceedings of the Second Annual Global Information Technology Management (GITM) World Conference,* June 10-12, Dallas, TX.

Okunoye, A., & Karsten, H. (2002a). Where the global needs the local: Variation in enablers in the knowledge management process. *Journal of Global Information Technology Management, 5*(3), 12-31.

Okunoye, A., & Karsten, H. (2002b). ITI as enabler of KM: Empirical perspectives from research organisations in sub-Saharan Africa. In *Proceedings of the 35th Hawaii International Conference on Systems Sciences,* January 7-10, Big Island, HI.

Okunoye, A., & Karsten, H. (2003). Global access to knowledge in research: Findings from organizations in sub-Saharan Africa. *Information Technology and People, 16*(3), 353-373.

Okunoye, A., Innola, E., & Karsten, H. (2002). Benchmarking knowledge management in developing countries: Case of research organizations in Nigeria, The Gambia, and India. In *Proceedings of the 3rd European Conference on Knowledge Management,* September 24-25, Dublin, Ireland.

Oliver, S., & Kandadi, K. (2006). How to develop knowledge culture in organizations? A multiple case study of large distributed organizations. *Journal of Knowledge Management, 10*(4), 6-24.

Orlikowski, W., & Barley, S. (2001). Technology and institutions: What can research on information technology and research on organizations learn from each other. *MIS Quarterly, 25*(2), 145-165.

Orr, J. (1990). Sharing knowledge, celebrating identity: Community memory in a service culture. In: D. Middleton & D. Edwards (Eds.), *Collective remembering* (pp. 168-189). London: Sage.

Owen, J. (2004, November). *Developing program management capabilities: A knowledge management perspec-tive.* Paper presented at the 7th Australian Conference on Knowledge Management and Intelligent Decision Support (ACKMIDS 2004).

Owen, J., Burstein, F., & Mitchell, S. (2005). Knowledge reuse and transfer in a project management environment [Special issue]. *Journal of Information Technology Cases and Applications (JITCA), 6*(4).

Owen, J., Burstein, F., Linger, H., & Mitchell, S. (2005, January). *Managing project knowledge: The contribution of lessons learned.* Paper presented at IPSI-2005, Hawaii.

Palmer, J., & Richards, I. (1999). Get knetted: Network behavior in the new economy. *Journal of Knowledge Management, 3*(3), 191-202.

Pan, S., & Scarbrough, H. (1998). A socio-technical view of knowledge—Sharing at Buckman Laboratories. *Journal of Knowledge Management, 2*(1), 55-66.

Park, H., Ribière, V., & Schulte, Jr., W. (2004). Critical attributes of organizational culture that promote knowledge management technology implementation success. *Journal of Knowledge Management, 8*(3), 106-117.

Parkin, J. (1996). Organizational decision making and the project manager. *International Journal of Project Management, 14*(5).

Parlament of Victoria. (2005). *Victorian electronic democracy —Final Report.* Retrieved October 29, 2005 from http://www.parliament.vic.gov.au/sarc/E-Democracy/Final_Report/Glossary.htm.

Patton, D., & Flin, R. (1999). Disaster stress: An emergency management perspective. *Disaster Prevention and Management, 8*(4), 261-267.

Pawlak, Z. (1991). *Rough sets: Theoretical aspects of reasoning about data.* Dordrecht: Kluwer Academic Publishers.

PeopleFinderTech. (2005). Retrieved October 29, 2005 from http://www.katrinahelp.info/wiki/index.php/PeopleFinderTech.

Pettigrew, A. (1987). Context and action in the transformation of the firm. *Journal of management studies, 24*(6), 649-670.

Pfeffer, J. & Sutton, R. (2000). *The knowing-doing gap: How smart companies turn knowledge into action.* Boston: Harvard Business School Press.

Pfeffer, J. (1981). Understanding the role of power in decision making. In: J. Shafritz & J. Ott (Eds.), *Classics of organization theory.* Brooks/Cole.

Pfeffer, J., & Sutton, R. (2000). *The knowledge-doing gap: How smart companies turn knowledge into action.* Boston, MA: Harvard Business School Press.

Polanyi, M. (1958). *Personal knowledge—Towards a post-critical philosophy.* The University of Chicago Press, Chicago.

Polanyi, M. (1966). *The tacit dimension.* Doubleday.

Porter, M., & Teisberg, E. (2004). Redefining competition in healthcare. *Harvard Business Review, 82*(6), 65-72.

Portes, A. (1998). Social capital: Its origins and applications in modern sociology. *Annual Review of Sociology, 24*, 1-24.

Poston, R., & Speier, C. (2005). Effective use of knowledge management systems: A process model of content ratings and credibility indicators. *MIS Quarterly, 29*(2), 221-244.

Powell, W. (1990). Neither market nor hierarchy: Network forms of organization. *Research in Organizational Behavior, 12*, 295–336. Retrieved from http://www.stanford.edu/~woodyp/paper_index.htm

Powell, W., & DiMaggio, P. (Eds.). (1991). *The new institutionalism in organizational analysis.* Chicago, IL: University of Chicago Press.

Powell, W.W., Koput, K.W., & Smith-Doer, L. (1996). Interorganizational collaboration and the locus of innovation: Networks of learning in biotechnology. *Administrative Science Quarterly, 41*, 116-145.

Power, D., & Kaparthi, S. (2002). Building Web-based decision support systems. *Studies in Informatics and Control, 11*(4), 291-302. Retrieved October 29, 2005 from http://www.ici.ro/ici/revista/sic2002_4/art1.pdf.

Powers, V. (2004). Improving IT wellness—Healthcare organizations adopt knowledge-enabled technology. *KM World,* 10, 11, & 26.

Prahalad, C. K. & Hamel, G. (1990). The core competence of the corporation. *Harvard Business Review, 68*(3), 79-91.

Project Management Institute. (2000). *A guide to the project management body of knowledge.* Project Management Institute USA.

Project Management Institute. (2004). *A guide to the project management body of knowledge.* Project Management Institute USA

Putnam, R.D. (1995). Bowling alone: America's declining social capital. *Journal of Democracy, 6*, 65-78.

Quinn, J. (1992). *Intelligent enterprise.* New York, NY: New York Free Press.

Quinn, P. (1998). Knowledge, power and control: Some issues in epistemology. In *Proceedings of Twentieth World Congress of Philosophy*, Boston. Retrieved January 23, 2005, from http://www.bu.edu/wcp/Papers/Poli/PoliQuin.htm

Quinn, R. (1988). *Beyond rational management: Mastering the paradoxes and competing demands of high performance.* San Francisco, CA: Jossey-Bass.

Raman, M., & Ryan.T. (2004). *Designing online discussion support systems for academic setting-"The Wiki Way".* Paper presented at the Americas Conferences on Information Systems (AMCIS). New York, NY.

Raman, M., Ryan, T., & Olfman, L. (2006). Knowledge management systems for emergency preparedness: The Claremont University Consortium Experience. *The International Journal of Knowledge Management, 2*(3), 33-50.

Rapoport, R. (1970). Three dilemmas in action research. *Human Relations, 23*(6), 499-513.

Reagans, R., & McEvily, B. (2003). Network structure and knowledge transfer: The effects of cohesion and range. *Administrative Science Quarterly, 48*(2), 240-267.

Reigle, R., & Westbrook, J. (2000). Organizational culture assessment. In *Proceedings of the National Conference of the American Society for Engineering Management,* Washington, D.C.

Remus, U. (2002). *Process oriented knowledge management, concepts and modeling.* PhD thesis. University of Regensburg. Germany. Regensburg.

Richards, D. & Busch, P. (2003, June). Acquiring and applying contextualised tacit knowledge. *Journal of Information and Knowledge Management, 2*(2), 179-190.

Ricks, T. (1997). Lessons learned: Army devises system to decide what does, and does not work. *Wall Street Journal, A1,* 10.

Robertson, M., Sørensen, C., & Swan, J. (2001). Survival of the leanest: Intensive knowledge work and groupware adaptation. *Information Technology & People, 14*(4), 334-353.

Robson, R. (1994). *Strategic management and information systems.* London: Pitman.

Rogers, E.M., & Kincaid, D.L. (1981). *Communication networks: Toward a new paradigm for research.* New York: Free Press.

Rolland, C., Nurcan, S., & Grosz, G. (1999). Enterprise knowledge development: The process view. *Information & Management, 36*(3), 121-184.

Rombach, H.D., Basil, V.R., & Selbey, R.W. (1993). *Experimental software engineering issues: Critical assessment and future directions.* International Workshop, Dagstuhl Castle. Germany. September 14   (Lecture Notes in Computer Science). Springer.

Root, F. (1994). *Entry strategies for international markets.* NY: Lexington.

Rubenstein-Montano, B., Liebowitz, J., Buchwalter, J., McCaw, D., Newman, B., Rebeck, K., & The Knowledge Management Methodology Team. (2001). A systems thinking framework for knowledge management. *Decision Support Systems, 31*(1), 5-16

Rumbaugh, J., Jacobson, I., & Booch, G. (2005). *The unified modeling language reference manual,* (2nd ed). Boston, MA: Addison Wesley.

Russell, R. (2003). *Center gathers lessons learned in Iraq.* Retrieved July 1, 2005 from http://wwwtradoc. army.mil/pao/TNSarchives/May03/CALL.htm

Sabherwal, R., Hirschheim, R., & Goles, T. (1998). The dynamics of alignment: A punctuated equilibrium model. *Organization Science, 12*(2), 17.

Sackmann, S. A. (1991). *Cultural knowledge in organizations: Exploring the collective mind.* Newbury Park, CA: Sage.

Sage, A., & Rouse, W. (1999). Information systems frontiers in knowledge management. *Information Systems Frontiers, 1*(3), 205-219.

Saint-Onge, H., & Wallace, D. (2003). *Leveraging communities of practice for strategic advantage.* Boston, MA: Butterworth Heinemann.

Sarvary, M. (1999). Knowledge management and competition in the consulting industry. *California Management Review, 41*(2), 95-107.

Sauer, C. (1993). *Why information systems fail: A case study approach.* Alfred Waller, Henley-On-Thames, Oxfordshire: Alfred Waller.

Sawyer, K. (1990). *Dealing with complex organisational problems.* PhD Consortium, International Conference on Information Systems (ICIS), Copenhagen.

Sawyer, K. (1990). Goals, purposes and the strategy tree. *Systemist, 12*(4), 76-82.

Scarbrough, H. (1999). Knowledge as work: Conflicts in the management of knowledge workers. *Technology Analysis and Strategic Management, 11*(1), 5-16.

Schäfer, G., Hirschheim, R., Harper, M., Hansjee, R., Domke, M., & Bjorn-Andersen, N. (1988). *Functional analysis of office requirements: A multi-perspective approach.* Chichester: Wiley.

Scheepers, R., Vencitachalam, K., & Gibbs, M. (2004). Knowledge strategy in organizations: Refining the model of Hansen, Nohria and Tierney. *Journal of Strategic Information Systems, 13,* 201-222.

Schein, E. (1985). *Organizational culture and leadership.* San Francisco, CA: Jossey-Bass.

Schein, E. (1999). *The corporate culture survival guide: sense and nonsense about cultural change.* San Francisco, CA: Jossey-Bass.

Schmidt, S.R., Kiemele, M.J., & Berdine, R.J. (1996). *Knowledge based management: Unleashing the power of quality improvement.* Air Academy Press.

Schneider, S., & Barsoux, J.-L. (1997). *Managing across cultures.* London: Prentice Hall.

Schreiber, A., Akkermans, J., Anjewierden, A., De Hoog, R., Shadbolt, N., Van de Velde, W., & Wielinga, B. (2000). *Knowledge engineering and management: The CommonKADS methodology.* Cambridge, MA: MIT Press.

Schreiber, G., Wielinga, B., & Breuker, J. (1993). *KADS: A principled approach to knowledge-based system development.* London, UK: Academic Press.

Schultz, R. (2003). Pathways of relevance: Exploring inflows of knowledge into subunits of multinational corporations. *Organization Science, 14*(4), 440-459.

Schultze, U. (2000). A confessional account of an ethnography about knowledge work. *MIS Quarterly, 24*(1), 3-41.

Schultze, U., & Boland, R. (2000). Knowledge management technology and the reproduction of knowledge work practices. *Journal of Strategic Information Systems, 9,* 193-212.

Schultze, U., & Leidner, D. (2002). Studying knowledge management in information systems research: Discourses and theoretical assumptions. *MIS Quarterly, 26*(3), 213-242.

Schutz, Alfred. (1967). *The phenomenology of the social world.* Evanston, IL: Northwestern University Press.

Schwartz, S. (1992). Universals in the content and structure of values: Theoretical advances and empirical tests in 20 Countries. In: M. Zanna (Ed.), *Advances in experimental social psychology, 25,* 1-65. New York, NY: Academic Press.

Scott, J. (1992). *Social network analysis.* Newbury Park, CA: Sage.

Scott, W. (1998). *Organizations: Rational, natural and open systems.* Upper Saddle River, NJ: Prentice-Hall, Inc.

Scymczak, C. & Walker, D. H. T. (2003). Boeing — A case study example of enterprise management from a learning organisation perspective. *The Learning Organization, 10*(3), 125-137.

Seibert, S.E., Kraimer, M.L., & Liden. R.C. (2001). A social capital theory of career success. *Academy of Management Journal, 44*(2), 219-237.

Sena, J., & Shani, A. (1999). Intellectual capital and knowledge creation: Towards an alternative framework. In: J. Liebowitz (Ed.), *Knowledge management handbook.* Boca Raton, FL: CRC Press.

Senge, P. (1992). *The fifth discipline: The art and practice of the learning organization.* Sydney: Random House.

Shankar, R., & Gupta, A. (2005) Towards framework for knowledge management implementation. *Knowledge and Process Management, 12*(4), 259-277.

Shanks, G., Tansley, E., & Weber, R. (2003). Using ontology to validate conceptual models. *Communications of the ACM, 46*(10), 85-89.

Shannon, C. E. & Weaver, W. (1949). *The mathematical theory of communication.* Chicago: University of Illinois.

Sharkie, R. (2003). Knowledge creation and its place in the development of sustainable competitive advantage. *Journal of Knowledge Management, 7*(1), 20-31.

Sharp, J. (1997). *Key hypotheses in supporting communities of practice.* Retrieved 14/10/04, 2003, from http://www.tfriend.com/hypothesis.html

Sharratt, M., & Usoro, A. (2003). Understanding knowledge-sharing in online communities of practice. *European Journal of Knowledge Management*. Retrieved from http://www.ejkm.com/volume-1/volume1-issue-2/issue2-art18-abstract.htm

ShelterFinder. (2005). Retrieved October 29, 2005 from http://katrinahelp.info/wiki/index.php/ShelterFinder.

Shenk, D. (1997). *Data smog: Surviving the information glut*. HarperEdge Publishing.

Shenkar, O., & Zeira, Y. (1992). Role conflict and role ambiguity of chief manager officers in international joint ventures. *Journal of Applied Communication Research, 30*(3), 231-250.

Sher, P., Sher, P., & Lee, V. (2004). Information technology as a facilitator for enhancing dynamic capabilities through knowledge management. *Information & Management, 41*(8), 933-945.

Sherif, K., & Sherif, S. (2006). Think social capital before you think knowledge transfer. *International Journal of Knowledge Management, 2*(3), 21-32.

Simon, H. (1960). *The new success of decision making*. New York, NY: Harper & Row.

Simon, H. (1993). Strategy and organizational evolution. *Strategic Management Journal, 14,* 131-142.

Simon, S. (2001). The impact of culture and gender on Web sites: An empirical study. *The DATA BASE for Advances in Information Systems, 32*(1), 18-37.

Smith, H. & McKeen, J. (2002). Instilling a knowledge sharing culture. In *Proceedings of Fifth European Conference in Organization, Knowledge, Learning and Capabilities (OKLC 2004)*, Innsbruk.

Soo, C., Devinney, T., Midgley, D., & Deering, A. (2002). KM: Philosophy, process, and pitfall. *California Management Review, 44*(4), 129-150.

Speel, P., Shadbolt, N., De Vries, W., Van Dam, P., &O'Hara, K. (1999). Knowledge mapping for industrial purposes. In *Proceedings of the Twelfth Workshop on*

Knowledge Acquisition, Modeling and Management. Banff, Alberta, Canada.

Spender, J. (1996a). Making knowledge the basis of a dynamic theory of the firm. *Strategic Management Journal, 17*(Special Issue: Knowledge and the Firm), 45-62.

Spender, J. (1996b). Organizational knowledge, learning and memory: Three concepts in search of a theory. *Journal of Organizational Change Management, 9*(1), 63-78.

Starbuck, W. (1992). Learning by knowledge intensive firms. *Journal of Management Studies, 29*(6), 713-740.

Stein, E. (2005). A qualitative study of the characteristics of a community of practice for knowledge management and its success factors. *International Journal of Knowledge Management, 1*(3), 1-24.

Stein, E., & Zwass, V. (1995). Actualizing organizational memory with information systems. *Information Systems Research, 6*(2), 85-117.

Stenmark & Lindgren (2003). Retrieved from http://w3.informatik.gu.se/~dixi/publ/dr-amcis.pdf

Stenmark, D. (1999) Using intranet agents to capture tacit knowledge. *Proceedings of WebNet'99* (pp. 1000-1005), October 20-25, Honolulu, HI: AACE press.

Stenmark, D. (2000). Turning tacit knowledge tangible. In *Proceedings of HICSS-33,* January 4-7, Maui, HI: IEEE press.

Stenmark, D. (2001). Leveraging tacit organisational knowledge. *Journal of Management Information Systems, 17*(3), 9-24.

Sternberg, R. (1995). Theory and management of tacit knowledge as a part of practical intelligence. *Zeitschrift Für Psychologie, 203*(4), 319-334.

Steven, C. (1989). *Postmodernist culture: An introduction to theories of the contemporary*. Oxford: Blackwell.

Stevenson, B., & Hamilton, M. (2001). How does complexity inform community, how does community inform complexity. *Emergence, 3*(2), 57-77.

Stewart, T. (1997). *Intellectual capital: The new wealth of organization.* New York, NY: Double Day.

Stiglitz, J. (2002). Transparency in government. In *The right to tell—The role of mass media in economic development* (pp. 27-44). Washington, DC: World Bank Institute, WBI Development Studies.

Stone, D., & Warsono, S. (2003). Does accounting account for knowledge?. In: C. Hosapple (Ed.), *Handbook on knowledge management* (vol. 1). Springer.

Straub, D. & Karahanna, E. (1998). Knowledge worker communications and recipient availability: Toward a task closure explanation of media choice. *Organization Science, 9*(2), 160-175.

Straub, D. (1994). The effect of culture on IT diffusion: E-mail and fax in Japan and the U.S. *Information Systems Research, 5*(1), 23-47.

Straub, D., Keil, M., & Brenner, W. (1997). Testing the technology acceptance model across cultures: A three country study. *Information & Management, 31*(1), 1-11.

Sugden, R. (1984). Reciprocity: The supply of public goods through voluntary contributions. *Economic Journal, 94,* 772-787.

Sugden, R. (2002). Altruistically inclined? The behavioral sciences, evolutionary theory, and the origins of reciprocity. *Journal of Economic Literature, 40,* 1242-1243.

Susman, G., & Evered, R. (1978). An assessment of the scientific merits of action research. *Administrative Science Quarterly, 23,* 583-603.

Sutton, D. (2001). What is knowledge and can it be managed?. *European Journal of Information Systems, 10*(2), 80-88.

Sveiby, K. (1996). *What is knowledge management?.* Retrieved March 4, 2000 from http://www.sveiby.com.au/KnowledgeManagement.html

Swan, J., Robertson, M. & Newell, S. (2002). Knowledge management: the human factor. In S. Barnes (Ed.), *Knowledge management systems: Theory and practice.* Thomson Learning.

Szulanski, G. (2003). *Sticky knowledge: Barriers to knowing in the firm.* Sage Publications.

Tallis, M., Kim, J., & Gil, Y. (1999). User studies of knowledge acquisition tools: Methodology and lessons learned. In *Proceedings of the Twelfth Banff Knowledge Acquisition for Knowledge-Based Systems Workshop.* Banff, Alberta, Canada.

Tanaka, B. (2005). The oddmuse wiki engine. *Linux Journal.* Retrieved October 29, 2005 from http://www.linuxjournal.com/article/7583.

Tanriverdi, H. (2005). Information technology relatedness, knowledge management capability, and performance of multi-business firms. *MIS Quarterly, 29*(2), 311-334.

Teece, D. (1998). Capturing value from knowledge assets: The new Eeonomy, markets for know-how, and intangible assets. *California Management Review, 40*(3), 55-79.

Teece, D. (1998). Research directions for knowledge management. *California Management Review, 40*(3), 289-292.

Teece, D. (2000). *Managing intellectual capital.* Oxford: Oxford University Press.

Teece, D. (2003). Knowledge and competence as strategic assets. In C. Holsapple (Ed.), *Handbook on knowledge management* (vol. 1, pp. 129-188).

Teece, D.J., Pisano, G., & Shuen, A. (1997). Dynamic capabilities and strategic management. *Strategic Management Journal, 18*(7), 509-534.

Tessler, S., & Barr, A. (1997). *Software R&D strategies of developing countries.* Stanford Computer Industry Project, Position Paper.

The World Bank Group, Data and Map. Retrieved December 27, 2004 from http://www.worldbank.org/data/countrydata/ictglance.htm

The World Bank Group. (1998-1999). *Knowledge for development*. Retrieved April 3, 2004, from http://www.worldbank.org/ks/html/pubs_pres.html

Theoretical model of knowledge transfer in organizations: Determinants of knowledge contribution and knowledge reuse. *Journal of Management Studies, 43*(2), 141-173.

Thiry, M. (2002). Combining value and project management into an effective programme management model. *International Journal of Project Management, 20*, 221-227.

Thomas, J., Sussman, S., & Henderson, J. (2001). Understanding "strategic learning": Linking organizational learning, knowledge management and sense-making. *Organizational Science, 12*(3), 331-345.

Thomas, R., Roosevelt, R., Thomas, D., Ely, R., & Meyerson D. (2002). *Harvard Business Review on Managing Diversity*. Boston, MA: Harvard Business Review Publishing.

Thompson, R.L., Higgins, C.A., & Howell, J.M. (1991). Personal computing: Toward a conceptual model of utilization. *MIS Quarterly, 15*(1), 125–143.

Thorp, J. (1998). *The information paradox, Realizing the business benefits of information technology*. Toronto: McGraw-Hill Ryeson.

Tiwana, A. (2000). *The knowledge management toolkit*. Upper Saddle River, NJ: Prentice-Hall.

Torlina, L., & Lichtenstein, S. (2004). *Integration of knowledge management in virtual groups*. Paper presented at the IRMA International Conference, New Orleans, LA.

Townsend, F. (2006). *The federal response to Hurricane Katrina, lessons learned*. Department of Homeland Security, United States of America.

Triandis, H.C. (1980). *Beliefs, attitudes, and values*. Lincoln, NE: University of Nebraska Press.

Trist, E. (1981). The socio-technical perspective. The evolution of socio-technical systems as conceptual framework and as an action research program. In: A. Van de Ven & W. Jotce (Eds.), *Perspectives on organization design and behavior* (pp. 49-75). New York, NY: John Wiley and Son.

Trompenaar, A. (2004). *Managing people across cultures*. Capstone, Ltd.

Trompenaars, F. (1993). *Riding the waves of culture*. London: The Economist Books.

Troshinsky, L. (2005). Stryker fixes in progress, Army official says. *Aerospace Daily & Defense Report, 214*(2), 4.

Tsai, M.-T., Yu, M.-C., & Lee, K.-W. (2005). Developing e-business systems based on KM process perspective—A case study of Seven-Eleven Japan. *Journal of American academy of business, 6*(1), 285-289.

Tsai, W., & Ghosal, S. (1998). Social capital and value creation: the role of inter-firm networks. *Academy of Management Journal, 41*(4), 464-476.

Tsoukas, H. & Vladimirou, E. (2001). What is organizational knowledge? *Journal of Management Studies, 38*(7), 973-993.

Tsoukas, H. (1996). The firm as a distributed knowledge system: A constructivist approach. *Strategic Management Journal, 17*, 11-25.

Tsoukas, H. (2003). Do we really understand tacit knowledge? In M. Easterby-Smith, & M. Lyles (Eds.), *The Blackwell companion to organizational learning and knowledge management*. Oxford: Basil Blackwell.

Tsui, E. (2005). The role of IT in KM: Where are we now and where are we heading. *Journal of Knowledge Management, 9*(1), 3-6.

Tuggle, F., & Shaw, N. (2000). The effect of organizational culture on the implementation of knowledge management. *Florida Artificial Intelligence Research Symposium (FLAIRS)*, Orlando, FL.

Turban, E., & Aronson, J.E. (2001). *Decision support systems and intelligent systems* (6th ed.). Upper Saddle River, NJ: Pearson/Prentice Hall.

Turner, J. R. (1999). *Handbook of project-based management: Improving the processes for achieving strategic objectives.* London: McGraw-Hill.

Turoff, M. (1972). Delphi conferencing: Computer-based conferencing with anonymity. *Journal of Technological Forecasting and Social Change, 3*(2), 159-204.

Turoff, M. (2002). Past and future emergency response information systems. *Communications of the ACM, 45*(4), 38-43.

Turoff, M., Chumer, M., Van de Walle, B., & Yao, X. (2004). The design of a dynamic emergency response management information systems (DERMIS). *Journal of Information Technology Theory and Application, 5*(4), 1-35.

Tushman, M., & Scanlan, T. (1981). Characteristics and external orientations of boundary spanning individuals. *Academy of Management Journal, 24*(1), 83-98.

Ulrich, D., & Smallwood, N. (2004). Capitalizing on capabilities. *Harvard Business Review, 82*(6), 119-128.

UNESCO Universal Declaration on Cultural Diversity. (2002). *UNESCO Universal Declaration on Cultural Diversity.* Retrieved October 2, 2005 from http://www.unesco.org/education/imld_2002/unversal_decla.shtml

Uzzi, B., & Lancaster, R. (2003). Relational embeddedness and learning: The case of bank loan managers and their clients. *Management Science, 49,* 383-399.

Vail III, E. (1999). Mapping organizational knowledge. *Knowledge Management Review, 8*(May/June), 10-15.

Van Beveren, J. (2003). Does healthcare for knowledge management?. *Journal of Knowledge Management, 7*(1), 90-95.

Van den Berge, P., & Wilderom, C. (2004). Defining, measuring, and comparing organizational cultures. *Applied Psychology: An International Review, 53*(4), 570-582.

van den Hooff, B., Elving, W., Meeuwsen, J., & Dumoulin, C. (2003). Knowledge sharing in knowledge communities. In M. Huysman, E. Wenger, & V. Wulf (Eds.), *First International Conference on Communities and Technologies.* Amsterdam, Netherlands: Kluwer Academic Publishers, Dordrecht.

Van der Aalst, W.M.P (1998). *Formalization and verification of event-driven process chains.* Computer Science Reports. Eindhoven.

Van Heijst, G., Van Der SPek, R., & Kruzinga, E. (1996). Organizing corporate memories. In *Proceedings of the Twelfth Banff Knowledge Acquisition for Knowledge-Based Systems Workshop.* Banff, Alberta, Canada.

Van Kirk, M. (2004). Collaboration in BCP skill development. *Disaster Recovery Journal, 17*(2), 40.

Van Muijen, J., Koopman, P., De Witte, K., De Cock, G., Susanj, Z., Lemoine, C., et al. (1999). Organizational culture: The focus questionnaire. *European Journal of Work and Organizational Psychology, 8,* 551-568.

Vazey, M. & Richards, D. (2005, May 15-18). Intelligent management of call centre knowledge. In M. Khosrow-Pour (Ed.), *Managing Modern Organizations with Information Technology: Proceedings of the Information Resources Management Association International Conference (IRMA'05)* (pp. 877-879), San Diego, CA. Hershey, PA: Idea Group Publishing.

Vazey, M., & Richards, D. (2006). A case-classification-conclusion 3Cs approach to knowledge acquisition: Applying a classification logic wiki to the problem-solving process. *The International Journal of Knowledge Management, 2*(1), 72-88.

Venzin, M., von Krogh, G., & Roos, J. (1998). Future research into knowledge management. In: G. Von Krogh, J. Roos, & D. Kleine (Eds.), *Knowing in firms: Understanding, managing and measuring knowledge.* Sage Publications.

von Krogh, G. (1998). Care in knowledge creation. *California Management Review, 40*(3), 133-153.

Vroom, V. (1964). *Work and motivation.* New York, NY: Wiley.

Wagner, C. (2004). WIKI: A technology for conversational knowledge management and group collaboration. *Communications of the Association for Information Systems, 13,* 265-289.

Walker, G., Kogut, B., & Shan, W. (1997). Social capital, structural holes and the formation of an industry network. *Organization Science, 8*(2), 109-125.

Walsh, J. P. & Ungson, J. R. (1991). Organizational memory. *Academy of Management Review, 16*(1), 57-91.

Walsh, N. (2003). *A technical introduction to XML.* Retrieved October 29, 2005 from http://www.dsi.unive.it/~xml/docs/introduction.pdf

Walsham, G. (1995). Interpretive case studies in IS research: Nature and method. *European Journal of Information Systems, 4,* 74-81.

Walsham, G. (2001). *Making a world of difference: IT in a global context.* New York, NY: John Wiley and Sons.

Walther, J. (1994). Anticipated ongoing interaction versus channel effects on relational communication in computer-mediated interaction. *Human Communication Research, 20,* 473-501.

Wang, S. (2002). Knowledge maps for managing Web-based business. *Industrial Management + Data Systems, 102*(7), 357-364.

Ward, A. (2000). Getting strategic value from constellations of communities. *Strategy & Leadership, 28*(2), 4.

Warne, L., Ali, I., & Pasco, C. (2003). *Social learning and knowledge management – A journey through the Australian Defence Organisation: The final report of the Enterprise Social Learning Architectures Task.* DSTO Report, DSTO-RR-0257, Defence Systems Analysis Division, Information Sciences Laboratory, Department of Defence.

Warne, L., Ali, I., Bopping, D., Hart, D., & Pascoe, C. (2004). *The network centric warrior: The human dimension of network centric warfare (U.* DSTO Report CR-0373, Defence Systems Analysis Division, ISL, Defence Science and Technology Organisation, Department of Defence, Edinburgh, S.A. (Approved for Public Release).

Warne, L., Ali, I., Pascoe C., Agostino, K. (2001). A holistic approach to knowledge management and social learning: Lessons learnt from military headquarters. *Australian Journal of Information Systems,* (Special Issue) on Knowledge Management, December: 127-142.

Warne, L., Hasan, H., & Ali, I. (2005). Transforming organizational culture to the ideal inquiring organization: Hopes and hurdles. In: J. Courtney, J. Haynes, & D. Paradice (Eds.), *Inquiring organizations: Moving from knowledge management to wisdom* (pp. 316-336). Hershey, PA: Idea Group.

Wasko, M., & Faraj, S. (2005). Why should I share? Examining social capital and knowledge contribution in electronic networks of practice. *MIS Quarterly, 29,* 35-57.

Wassenar, A., Gregor, S., & Swagerman, D. (2002). ERP implementation management in different organizational and cultural settings. In *Proceedings of the European Accounting Information Systems Conference,* Copenhagen Business School, Copenhagen, Denmark.

Webber, A. (1993). What's so new about the new economy?. *Harvard Business Review, Jan-Feb,* 24-42.

Weill, P., & Vitale, M. (2002). What IT infrastructure capabilities are needed to implement e-Business models?. *MIS Quarterly Executive, 1*(1), 17-34.

Weisinger, J., & Trauth, E. (2002). Situating culture in the global information sector. *Information Technology and People, 15*(4), 306-320.

Wellman, B., & Gulia, M. (1999). Net surfers don't ride alone: Virtual communities as communities. In: P. Kollock & M. Smith (Eds.), *Communities and cyberspace.* New York, NY: Routledge.

Wells, G. (2000). Dialogic inquiry in education: Building on the legacy of Vygotsky. In C. D. Lee & P. Smagorinsky (Eds.), *Vygotskian perspectives on literacy research* (pp. 51-85). New York: Cambridge University Press.

Wenger, E. (1998). *Communities of practice.* Cambridge, UK: Cambridge University Press.

Wenger, E. (2004). Knowledge management as a doughnut: Shaping your knowledge strategy through communities of practice. *Ivey Business Journal, 68*(3), 1-8.

Wenger, E., McDermott, R., & Snyder, W. (2002). *Cultivating communities of practice—A guide to managing knowledge.* Boston, MA: Harvard Business School Press.

Wenger, E., McDermott, R., & Snyder, W. (2002). *Cultivating communities of practice.* Boston, MA: Harvard Business School Press.

Wenger, E., McDermott, R., & Snyder, W. M. (2002). *Cultivating communities of practice.* Boston: Harvard Business School Press.

White, M. (2003). *Creating an effective intranet.* Intranet Focus Ltd. Retrieved June 24, 2005, from http://www.intranetfocus.com/information/effectiveintranets.pdf

Whitman, L., Ramachandran, K., & Ketkar, V. (2001). A taxonomy of a living model of the enterprise. In *Proceedings of the Winter Simulation Conference.* Arlington, VA.

Wickramasinghe, N., & Davison, G. (2004). Making explicit the implicit knowledge assets in healthcare: The case of multidisciplinary teams in care and cure environments. *Healthcare Management Science, 7,* 185-195.

Wickramasinghe, N., Gupta, J., & Sharma, S. (2005). *Creating knowledge-based healthcare organizations.* Hershey, PA: Ideas Group Publishing.

Wiggins, B. (2000). *Effective document management: Unlocking corporate knowledge.* Gower: Aldershot.

Wiig, K. (1994). *Knowledge management: The central management focus for intelligent-acting organizations.* Arlington, TX: Schema Press.

Wiig, K., Hoog, R., & Spek, R. (1997). Supporting knowledge management: A selection of methods and techniques. *Expert Systems with Applications, 13*(1), 15-27.

Wikipedia. (2006). *Wiki.* Retrieved March 30, 2006 from http://en.wikipedia.org/wiki/Wiki.

Wille, R. (1992). Concept lattices and conceptual knowledge. *Computers and Mathematics with Applications, 23,* 493-522.

Wilson, G., Jackson, P., & Smith, W. (2003). *Knowledge management strategies in a small and medium sized enterprise: A tale of two systems.* Paper presented at the 14th Australasian Conference on Information Systems (pp. 1-16), Perth, Western Australia.

Wilson, T. (2002). The nonsense of 'knowledge management'. *Information Research, 8*(1), (online) http://informationr.net/ir/8-1/paper144.html#sch67

Woodhouse, L. (2000). Personality and the use of intuition: Individual differences in strategy and performance on an implicit learning task. *European Journal of Personality, 4*(2), 157-169.

Yin, R. (1994). *Case study research. Design and methods,* (2nd ed). Thousands Oaks, CA: Sage Publications.

Yin, R. K. (2002). *Case study research: Design and methods* (3rd ed.). Newbury Park: Sage.

Yu, S.-H., Kim, Y.-G., & Kim, M.-Y. (2004). Linking organizational knowledge management drivers to knowledge management performance: An exploratory study. In *Proceedings of the 37th Hawaii International Conference on System Sciences.*

Yu, S-H, Kim, Y-G, & Kim, M-Y, (2004). Linking organizational knowledge management drivers to knowledge management performance: An exploratory study. In *Proceedings of the 37th Hawaii International Conference on System Sciences,* IEEE Computer Society.

Zack, H. (1999). Developing a knowledge strategy. *California Management Review, 41*(3), 125-145.

Zack, M. (1999). Managing codified knowledge. *Sloan Management Review, 40*(4), 45-58.

Zack, M. H. (1999). Developing a knowledge strategy. *Californian Management Review, 41*(3), 125-145.

Zahra, S.A., & George, G. (2002). Absorptive capacity: A review, reconceptualization, and extension. *Academy of Management Review, 27*(2), 185-203.

Zakaria, N., Amelinckx, A., & Wilemon, D. (2004). Working together apart? Building a knowledge-sharing culture for global virtual teams. *Creativity and Innovation Management, 13*(1), 15-29.

Zander, U., & Kogut, B. (1995). Knowledge and the speed of the transfer and imitation of organizational capabilities: An empirical test. *Organization Science, 6*(1), 76-92.

Zeggelink, E. (1993). *Strangers into friends. The evolution of friendship networks using an individual oriented modeling approach.* Amsterdam: Thesis Publishers.

About the Contributors

Murray E. Jennex is an associate professor at San Diego State University, editor-in-chief of the International Journal of Knowledge Management, editor-in-chief of IGI Global's *Knowledge Management book series*, and president of the Foundation for Knowledge Management (LLC). Dr. Jennex specializes in knowledge management, system analysis and design, IS security, e-commerce, and organizational effectiveness. Dr. Jennex serves as the Knowledge Management Systems Track co-chair at the Hawaii International Conference on System Sciences. He is the author of over 100 journal articles, book chapters, and conference proceedings on knowledge management, end user computing, international information systems, organizational memory systems, ecommerce, security, and software outsourcing. He holds a BA in chemistry and physics from William Jewell College, an MBA and an MS in software engineering from National University, an MS in telecommunications management and a PhD in information systems from the Claremont Graduate University. Dr. Jennex is also a registered professional mechanical engineer in the state of California and a Certified Information Systems Security Professional (CISSP).

* * * * *

Nancy Bertaux is professor of economics and human resources at Xavier University in Cincinnati, Ohio, where she teaches courses in economics and human resources, especially in the areas of workforce diversity, poverty, economic history and the history of economic thought, including honors and service learning courses. She holds a PhD in Economics from the University of Michigan and has published over 20 articles and book chapters.

Alton Y.K. Chua is assistant professor at Nanyang Technological University. He teaches in the MSc (KM) program. His research interests lie primarily in knowledge management and communities of practice. Alton has authored numerous papers in publications such as the *Journal of the American Society of Information Science and Technology*, *International Journal of Information Management*, and the *Journal of Intellectual Capital*. He has also been consulted on a number of KM-related projects. He holds a bachelor's degree in computer science, a second bachelor's degree in arts, a master's degree in education and doctorate in business administration.

Cheng-Hsui (Arthur) Chen currently is a professor of marketing at the Department of Business Administration, National Yunlin University of Science & Technology, Taiwan, R.O.C. He served as the department chairman from August 2000 to July 2003. He was a Fulbright Visiting Scholar in the Marketing Department of Marshall School of Business at the University of Southern California during

Copyright © 2008, IGI Global, distributing in print or electronic forms without written permission of IGI Global is prohibited.

the academic year of 2003-2004. He has published papers both nationally and internationally in journals in the areas of brand equity, brand extension, market orientation and knowledge management. He received his PhD in business administration (major in marketing and minor in strategy management) from National Chengchi University in Taiwan in 1996. Prior to entering the PhD program, he worked for Procter and Gamble Taiwan as a brand manager for more than four years.

Ying-Hsiou Chen is a doctoral candidate of the College of Management at National Cheng-Kung University. He received his MS degree in the Department of Business Management from the National Yunlin University of Science and Technology, Taiwan, in 2001. His research interests include knowledge management, relationship marketing, and consumer behavior.

Bonnie Cheuk has over ten years of experience facilitating knowledge sharing and managing information in both private and public organizations. She has implemented a range of Web2.0 technologies with human touch to improve enterprise performance. She currently works for Environmental Resources Management (ERM), the world's largest environmental consultancy, and heads a global knowledge sharing program which aims at promoting cross-boundary collaboration and knowledge sharing in order to deliver the best service to the clients. Prior to joining ERM, she headed up a knowledge management consultancy unit promoting knowledge sharing across the 32 Scottish local authorities and their partners. She was with the British Council (2002-2005) where she led a 14-people team and successfully created and implemented a global knowledge management strategy that is in line with the business objectives of this global organization with offices in 110 countries; and with Arthur Andersen business consulting (1999-2002) where she helped clients to establish and implement knowledge strategy in Asia Pacific region and in the United States. Two of her KM projects have been short-listed as finalists for the Information Management Award (IM2004 and IM2005). Her work has been published in international journals and she speaks frequently in conferences. She started her career as a professional librarian in Hong Kong. She received her PhD in library and information science in 1999 and since then has been applying Dervin's Sense-Making Methodology and Snowden's complexity theory to design and implement knowledge management projects and systems to deliver business benefits. She is recognized internationally for her strong interests in understanding information literacy in the workplace context.

Jane Fröming studied computer science at Berlin University of Technology, Germany. She works as a research assistant at the University of Potsdam (since July 2004). Her main research activity concentrates on the areas of process-oriented knowledge management, simulation, skill management, staffing and case-based reasoning. In the area of knowledge management, she is dealing with approaches for analyzing, modeling and simulating knowledge-intensive business activities and the development of KMDL®. Therefore, simulation methods and models need to be developed to assess management decisions, to manage knowledge and information flow and to predict knowledge propagation in companies. In the area of skill management, she is dealing with approaches for knowledge-oriented teaching concepts and combines requirement-oriented project teams through the implementation of staffing concepts. Furthermore, she researches the method of case-based reasoning.

John Gammack is professor of information systems at Griffith University, Australia. Previously, he was head of the IT School at Murdoch University, Perth, subsequently directing its research center in Electronic Commerce and Internet Studies. He has researched in areas related to knowledge-based systems for over 20 years, publishing around 180 papers. His PhD (Cambridge University, 1988) directly concerned modeling knowledge for intelligent systems where he pioneered several knowledge elicitation methods. This led to work on augmenting knowledge discovered in databases with subjective and contextual factors to build optimized decision models. This produced some innovative systems developments in the banking and insurance sector. Later work addressed the development of tools for recording collaborative design in distributed organizational environments. Recent research has examined the requirements for environments enabling end-user design of decision systems, and the uptake and adoption of e-government and e-business, both in Australia and overseas.

Norbert Gronau studied engineering and business administration at Berlin University of Technology, Germany. In summer 2000, he was deputy professor for business information systems at the University of Oldenburg. From October 2000 to March 2004, he was full professor for business information systems in Oldenburg (Lower Saxony). He holds a chair of business information systems and electronic government at the University of Potsdam. His main research activities concentrate on the areas of knowledge management and business resource management. Professor Gronau is editor of the scientific journal Industrie Management—journal for industrial business processes, and co-founder of the journal PPS Management—journal of production and logistics. He is author of more than 90 papers and author resp. editor of some books. Additionally he gives courses in Electronic Business at the French technical university "Ecole Superiore des Mines de Nancy."

Dennis Hart holds degrees in physics, wine science and philosophy as well as a PhD in information systems. He is currently a senior lecturer in the School of Accounting and Business Information Systems at the Australian National University. Dr. Hart has published his research in national and international journals and conferences and is editor and co-organizer, with Professor Shirley Gregor, of the biennial series of ANU workshops on Information Systems Foundations that began in 2002. Prior to his academic career he was, for 15 years, an instructor officer in the Royal Australian Navy, retiring in 1992 with the rank of Commander. Dr. Hart also manages the 15-acre vineyard on his and his partner's property near Canberra, and his other enthusiasms include wine appreciation, playing his baby grand piano, vintage hi-fi systems, motorcycling, and reading non-fiction, usually of a philosophical or historical bent.

Alexia Hunter is a technology specialist who is currently working in the telecommunications industry. She is a graduate of Deakin University where she completed her Bachelor of Information Technology (Hons) in 2003. She has conducted research in knowledge sharing and knowledge retention, focusing on the challenges presented in deploying intranets to enable such strategies in organisations. In Australian industry, she has worked as a web developer, UNIX programmer and technology specialist in three large multinational IT and telecommunications corporations. Alexia has published several papers in her research area and is now focusing on her career while continuing her research interests.

Wen-Jang (Kenny) Jih is currently a professor of computer information systems at the Jennings A. Jones College of Business of Middle Tennessee State University. He previously taught at Longwood University (Virginia), University of Tennessee at Chattanooga, Auburn University (Alabama), Da-Yeh University (Taiwan), and Chung-Yuan Christian University. He also served as the dean of the School of Management at Da-Yeh University from 1997 to 2001. He has consulted a number of companies in Taiwan, including a major automobile manufacturing company, on knowledge management projects. He obtained his doctorate degree in business computer information systems from the University of North Texas in 1985. His recent research interests include: e-commerce, m-commerce, knowledge management, customer relationship management, strategic impact of information technologies, network design and management, and innovative instruction methods in information systems.

Jaekyung Kim is a PhD candidate of management at the University of Nebraska-Lincoln. His research interests are knowledge management in networked organizations, electronic commerce, and business intelligence. His research articles appeared in *Decision Support Systems, Omega, International Journal of Electronic Commerce, Expert Systems with Applications,* and *International Journal of Knowledge Management.* He received his MBA from Miami University of Ohio.

Sung-kwan Kim, associate professor of management, University of Arkansas at Little Rock, received his PhD from University of Nebraska at Lincoln. He teaches database system and system development methodology. His research interests are in knowledge modeling, knowledge architecture and e-commerce. He has published in the *International Journal of Knowledge Management, Journal of Knowledge Management, Journal of Knowledge Management Practice,* and *Journal of the Society of E-Business Studies.*

Gerlinde Koeglreiter is currently undertaking doctoral studies at Deakin University (Melbourne, Australia), focusing on issues surrounding the role of Communities of Practice in organizational knowledge management. She holds a bachelor degree with honors in information systems (University of Derby, UK) and a Master of Information Technology (Swinburne, Australia). In addition to her research interests, she works as a business analyst employing group facilitation techniques for requirements engineering. Although she applies a strong technical background to her work, she focuses on bottom-up approaches to knowledge management in her research.

Matthew Henry Sam Kuofie holds a PhD in systems engineering from Oakland University, an MBA in business administration from Northern Illinois University, an MS in computer science from Old Dominion University, and a BS in statistics and mathematics from the University of Ghana. Professor Kuofie teaches business management and information technology courses. He teaches at the University of Michigan and Lawrence Technology University. Professor Kuofie has also taught, given seminars, and/or organized conferences at various universities in Europe, Asia and Africa. Professor Kuofie has broad research interests including knowledge management, business management strategies, and information technology. He has published numerous journal and conference papers. He serves as associate editor-in-chief of the *Journal of Electronic Commerce in Organizations, Journal of Global Management Research,* and *International Journal of Information System Research.* He also serves on other editorial boards including that of the *International Journal of Knowledge Management.* He has served on a number of doctoral dissertation committees around the world. He is also an internationally renowned global business management and information technology consultant to governments and businesses. Dr. Kuofie is a co-founder of Garden City University College, Ghana.

Wing Lam is associate professor at Universitas 21 Global, an online graduate business school. He teaches e-business, information technology systems for business and information systems strategy in the MBA. program. He has published over 60 journal and conference papers in the areas of systems and software engineering, IT methodology and e-business. He has collaborated with industrial research partners, including Rolls-Royce, British Telecom and Fujitsu (formerly ICL UK). Wing has significant industrial experience, having held management and consultancy positions with Logica, Fujitsu and Accenture. He was responsible for the delivery of several large-scale e-commerce solutions, including an Internet bank, B2B exchange, information services portal and B2C shopping mall. He holds a PhD from King's College, University of London.

Sang M. Lee is currently the University Eminent Scholar, Regents Distinguished University professor, and chair of the Management Department at the University of Nebraska-Lincoln. He has authored or co-authored 56 books, 242 journal articles, and has presented over 2,000 speeches. His research interests include value-networked organizations, inter-organizational information systems, and new enterprise models. He is a Fellow of Academy of Management, Decision Sciences Institute, and Pan-Pacific Business Association.

Sharman Lichtenstein is an associate professor in the School of Information Systems at Deakin University in Melbourne, Australia. She has enjoyed a thirty-year career in industry, academe and consulting in information systems and computing. Her initial research focused on information security management and the influence of the Internet in the workplace. She produced sets of guidelines for organizational Internet security policy and acceptable use that have been foundational in these areas. Her recent research has focused on exploring the socio-technical issues experienced when employing knowledge technologies for organizational knowledge sharing. Her research has been published widely at an international level and she has presented numerous seminars and papers nationally and abroad. She has supervised many research students, participated on various conference committees, and is a member of editorial boards for leading international journals.

Seong-bae Lim, assistant professor of management, State University of New York at Geneseo, received his PhD from the University of Nebraska at Lincoln. He teaches database and e-commerce. He has published in the *International Journal of Knowledge Management*, the *Journal of Knowledge Management Practices, and Service Business: An International Journal*.

Rikard Lindgren is a research manager at the Viktoria Institute in Gothenburg, Sweden. He is also associate professor of information systems at the IT University of Gothenburg. His research focuses on action research, design science, knowledge management, and ubiquitous computing. Dr. Lindgren has published his research in *MIS Quarterly, Information and Organization, European Journal of Information Systems, Information Systems Journal, Information Systems Management, Scandinavian Journal of Information Systems*, and other journals in the information systems discipline. Currently, Dr. Lindgren serves on the editorial boards of *Journal of Information & Knowledge Management and Scandinavian Journal of Information Systems*.

Robert B. Mitchell, professor of management, University of Arkansas at Little Rock, received his DBA degree from Louisiana Tech University. He teaches in the MIS field, with specialization in IT strategy, information resource management, and business applications. He is currently chairman of the Department of Management. He has published in the *Journal of Business Communication, Journal of*

Computer Information Systems, Journal of Information Systems, Journal of Knowledge Management Review, and *Journal of the Society of E-Business Studies.*

Tim Murphy is the president of Autonomechs LLC and a master's student in the Homeland Security program at San Diego State University. His professional focus is on helping federal, state, and commercial clients with situational intelligence as they work to defeat the constant problem known as the "fog of war." During Hurricane Katrina, he helped groups develop open source products that allowed families to find loved ones,.and developed a system to help responders find trapped victims. Academically, he is finishing a thesis on network centric defense and its application in disaster management. He holds a BS in computer information systems with a concentration in systems engineering.

Adekunle O. Okunoye is an assistant professor of information systems at Xavier University, USA. He holds a PhD degree in computer science/information systems from University of Turku, Finland. Dr. Okunoye is a chartered information technology practitioner and member of the British Computer Society. He is also a member of Association for Information Systems. His research focuses on knowledge management, new information and communication technologies, organizational implementation of IT and the resultant changes in organization, and IT & globalization. He has published in various journals, books and conference proceedings.

Lorne Olfman is dean of the School of Information Systems and Technology at Claremont Graduate University, Fletcher Jones chair in Technology Management, and co-director (with Terry Ryan) of the Social Learning Software Lab (SL2). His research interests are in designing effective collaboration, learning and knowledge management technologies. To this end, she and his SL2 colleagues are conducting research on a variety of topics including the design of an intelligent online discussion board, the development of an integrated set of tools to facilitate The Claremont Conversation for the 21st Century, and the design of a virtual dialogue system. He has been integrating the use of wiki technology into his research and teaching for the past couple of years.

David L. Olson is the James & H.K. Stuart professor in MIS Chancellor's professor at the University of Nebraska. He has published research in over 90 refereed journal articles, primarily on the topic of multiple objective decision making. He teaches in the management information systems, management science, and operations management areas. He has authored or co-authored 17 books, including *Decision Aids for Selection Problems, Managerial Issues of Enterprise Resource Planning Systems,* and *Introduction to Business Data Mining.* He was a faculty member at Texas A&M University for 20 years. He is a Fellow of the Decision Sciences Institute.

Jill Owen is a PhD candidate in the Knowledge Management Research Group within the School of Information Management & Systems (SIMS), Faculty of Information Technology at Monash University. She has worked at senior levels with some of Australia's major organizations in the airline, financial services, health, credit card and information technology industries, specializing in program management. Her research interests center on how knowledge management integrates with project, program and portfolio management, focusing on a bottom-up approach to knowledge management. She has published her research in both national and international journals and conferences.

Murali Raman received his PhD in management information systems from the School of IS & IT, Claremont Graduate University, USA. Dr. Murali is a Rhodes Scholar and a Fulbright Fellow. His other academic qualifications include an MBA from Imperial College of Science Technology and Medicine, London, an MSc in HRM from London School of Economics, and a bachelor's degree in economics from University Malaya (first class honors). He has prior industrial experience, working with Maybank Bhd (two years) and as a consultant for Accenture Consulting (four years). Dr. Murali is currently an academician attached to Multimedia University Malaysia, where he teaches and conducts research in the area of knowledge management systems, and management information systems. He has published more than thirty-five papers in international journals and conference proceedings. Dr. Murali can be reached at musumi_sai@yahoo.com.

Debbie Richards is a senior lecturer in the Department of Computing at Macquarie University. She is equally committed to teaching, research and service which she pursues with a strong industry focus. Her main research area is knowledge-based systems, however, in seeking to solve real problems in industry she has also been active in the areas of knowledge visualization and modeling, requirements engineering, the semantic Web, language technology, training simulations, data mining and human computer interaction.

Terry Ryan is associate professor in the School of Information Systems and Technology and Co-Director (with Lorne Olfman) of the Social Learning Software Lab (SL2) at Claremont Graduate University. His teaching and research interests are in the design, development, and evaluation of information systems to support teaching and learning, online discussions and dialogues, and preparing for and responding to emergencies. He has published articles in *Communications of the AIS, Data Base, Information & Management, International Journal of Human-Computer Studies, International Journal of Knowledge Management, Journal of Computer Information Systems, Journal of Database Management, Journal of Information Systems Education*, and other outlets.

Keith Sawyer is a director of Alpha Omega International, advising large and small organizations on strategy planning and implementation. He has pioneered new methods for aligning soft and hard activities and showing how day-to-day actions can be measured against corporate objectives. He is the inventor of the StratAchieve method and software, which aligns operational and strategic knowledge with corporate strategy. A researcher in knowledge management, Keith developed and teaches two core modules for the MSc in knowledge management at Cranfield University, UK. As a director of the UK Systems Society, he has been responsible for arranging international conferences and producing papers in knowledge management and strategy planning. He is also a part-time tutor at The Open University in the UK, teaching systems thinking and practice.

Simone Schmid studied business management at the University of Tuebingen, Germany. She works as a research assistant at the University of Potsdam (since June 2004). Her main research activity concentrates on the areas of process-oriented knowledge management, skill management and knowledge management in complex ERP systems. One goal is to provide innovative concepts to configure an ERP systems as well as methodologies to put the concepts into practice. For this purpose, she uses methodologies from knowledge management and integrates them into classical ERP reference models. In the area of knowledge management, she is dealing with approaches for analyzing and modeling knowledge-intensive business processes. In the area of skill management, she is dealing with approaches for knowledge-oriented teaching concepts and combines requirement- oriented project teams through the implementation of staffing concepts.

Karma Sherif is an assistant professor at the Rawls College of Business, Texas Tech University. She received her PhD degree in management information systems from Texas A&M University. She also holds an MS degree in MIS from Texas A&M and a BA in business administration from The American University in Cairo. Before pursuing her doctoral studies, Dr. Sherif worked as an information systems consultant at DATACOMP, a leading IT consulting firm. Dr. Sherif has articles in journals such as *MIS Quarterly, Decision Support Systems, Journal of the Association of Information Systems, Information & Management*, and *Journal of Knowledge Management*. She has taught courses on object-oriented programming, electronic commerce, systems design, knowledge management systems, and MIS research methods.

Sherif Ahmed Sherif is a senior economist at the Egyptian Ministry of Foreign Trade and Industry. He received his master's and bachelor's in economics from the American University in Cairo. He is currently working on his PhD in Public relations at Cairo University.

Dick Stenmark is an associate professor of information systems at the IT University of Gothenburg, Sweden. His teaching and research interests include knowledge and content management systems and information seeking behavior amongst non-IR-professionals. Dr. Stenmark has also more than 17 years of experience from industry where he has worked with intranet architecture and design, search engines and content management systems. His work is published in *Scandinavian Journal of Information Systems, European Journal of Information Systems, Knowledge and Process Management, Journal of Management Information Systems, International Journal of Business Environment*, and *International Journal of Technology and Human Interaction*.

Luba Torlina is a lecturer in the School of Information Systems, Faculty of Business and Law, Deakin University. She has a PhD from the Institute for System Studies, Moscow, where the area of her specialization was computer applications and mathematical methods in economics and business management. During her career, Dr. Torlina has gained considerable experience as an academic researcher and an industrial analyst. She has published a number of chapters in books, journal articles and conference papers in the areas of data modeling, decision support systems, and statistical modeling for industrial planning. Her most recent research interests and publications are in the areas of information product markets, knowledge management and organizational learning. In particular, one of the current projects focuses on the role of communities of practice (CoP) in organizational knowledge work.

Abel Usoro obtained his BSc (Hons) in management studies (banking and finance) in Nigeria, an MSc in systems analysis and design as well as a PhD in information technology in London. He currently lectures in the School of Computing, University of Paisley in Scotland, UK. His current research interests are information systems, knowledge management and e-learning for which he has widely published in refereed international conferences, journals (such as *International Journal of Information Management, International Journal of Global Information Management* and *International Journal of Knowledge Management*) and book chapters. Dr. Usoro is an international chair of the ISOneWorld conference, a full member of the prestigious Information Institute (www.information-institute.org) and British Computing Society. He is also a member of the Academic Working Group for Manufacturing Performance in Scotland; the chair for CITED2008 (Conference on Information Technology and Economic Development) and is on the organizing committee of and a program chair for International Scientific Conference on Information Technology and Quality (http://softlab.teipir.gr/synedrio/default. asp?id=1&mnu=1) and Conference on Information Technology and Economic Development (www.information-institute.org/cited/); a member of the Scientific Committee of the IADIS International conference e-Commerce 2007 (http://www.ecommerce-conf.org/); member of the Programme Committee of the Second International Conference on Knowledge Science, Knowledge Engineering, and Knowledge Management (http://www.deakin.edu.au/scitech/eit/ksem07/); and Member of the Paper Review Panel of an international Knowledge Management Conference (KMAP2006 and KMAP2007). His conference presentations have taken him across Europe, North and South America, Asia and Africa. For research and lecturing, he visits Laurea University in Finland and Anshan Normal University in China.

Megan Vazey holds a first class honours degree in electrical rngineering from the University of NSW in Sydney, Australia; a master's in business administration from the Australian Graduate School of Management; and she is completing a PhD in computing in the area of knowledge acquisition and artificial intelligence at Macquarie University, Sydney. With more than 15 years experience in research and development, she has worked with a number of prestigious companies including Alcatel, Avaya, Canon, and EMC; and across a wide span of industries including digital image processing, Internet applications, telecommunications, water management, road safety, electrical power transmission, and manufacturing. She owns and operates Freyatech Pty Ltd, a Sydney-based consulting firm specializing in Internet applications, software development, business analysis, technical writing, and patents. Her research interests include expert systems, knowledge acquisition, artificial intelligence, intelligent agents and the semantic Web.

Leoni Warne is a senior research scientist within the Defence Systems Analysis Division of the Defence Science and Technology Organisation (DSTO) in Australia. She is the Science Team leader for the research team responsible for researching and developing the human and organizational aspects of learning, knowledge mobilization and network-centricity. Dr. Warne has been with DSTO for nine years. Prior to this, she spent ten years lecturing in information systems at the University of Canberra. Dr. Warne's research work has been presented in numerous international books, journals and conferences. She is also an investigator of a current ARC (Australian Research Council) Discovery Grant on Network Centric Organisations, and a founding member of the STAR (Socio-Technical Activity Research) Group on Knowledge Management. Dr. Warne is the adjunct professor of information systems at the University of Canberra and an honorary principal research officer at the University of Wollongong. Her research in information systems has recently been recognized nationally by her elevation to the prestigious position of Fellow of the Australian Computer Society.

Index

Copyright © 2008, IGI Global, distributing in print or electronic forms without written permission of IGI Global is prohibited.